The Battles for Spotsylvania Court House and the Road to Yellow Tavern

May 7–12, 1864

Winner of the Jules and Frances Landry Award for 1997

THE BATTLES FOR SPOTSYLVANIA COURT HOUSE AND THE ROAD TO YELLOW TAVERN

MAY 7–12, 1864

Gordon C. Rhea

LOUISIANA STATE UNIVERSITY PRESS   *Baton Rouge*

06 05 04 03 02 01   5 4

Designer: Michele Myatt
Typeface: Cochin, Times Roman
Typesetter: Impressions Book and Journal Services
Printer and binder: Thomson-Shore, Inc.

LIBRARY OF CONGRESS CATALOGING-IN-PUBLICATION DATA

Rhea, Gordon C.
    The battles for Spotsylvania Court House and the road to Yellow
    Tavern, May 7–12, 1864 / Gordon C. Rhea.
        p. cm.
    Includes bibliographical references (p.   ) and index.
    ISBN 0-8071-2136-3 (cloth : alk. paper)
    1. Spotsylvania Court House, Battle of, Va., 1864. 2. Stuart,
    Jeb, 1833–1864. I. Title.
    E476.52.R46   1997
    973.7′36—dc21   96-49575
                                                              CIP

The paper in this book meets the guidelines for permanance and durability of the Committee on Production Guidelines for Book Longevity of the Council on Library Resources. ⊛

Contents

Illustrations

Acknowledgments

I COULD NOT have written this book without assistance from the outstanding staff of historians that Robert K. Krick has assembled at the Fredericksburg and Spotsylvania National Military Park. They gave willingly of their time and resources. Many thanks must go to Noel G. Harrison, Gregory A. Mertz, Francis A. O'Reilly, Donald C. Pfanz, and Mac Wyckoff. I want to thank also Robert E. L. Krick, who showed me the ground around Yellow Tavern and helped me understand Jeb Stuart's last battle.

It was my privilege to have William B. Matter review my manuscript. His *If It Takes All Summer* stands as a classic campaign study and the first modern attempt to analyze the Spotsylvania campaign. Both future scholars and I owe him a significant intellectual debt.

Gratitude is also due Bryce A. Suderow, a leading student of the 1864 Virginia campaign who generously shared his voluminous private collection, helped in the tedious business of combing through Civil War–era newspapers, and gave insightful comments on my manuscript.

For several years, Alfred C. Young had been examining records and newspapers in a Herculean effort to document strengths and losses. Although his research is not yet complete, he generously shared his findings with me. We students of the campaigns between Grant and Lee expectantly await the publication of his material, which will shed valuable light on the Civil War's final year.

This work would have been incomplete without contributions from researchers around the country who have specialized knowledge of particular Civil War units. John R. M. Bass, Keith S. Bohannon, Michael S. Cavanaugh, Chris Daw, Chris J. Hartley, John Horn, William K. McDaid, Richard F. Miller, Michael T. Russert, Marc and Beth Storch, and Zack C. Waters were especially helpful. I am also indebted to John J. Hennessy, Margery Resnick, Michael T. Snyder, and Karl E. Sundstrom for reading my manuscript and commenting on it.

Also invaluable was assistance from archivists and librarians in the institutions listed in the Bibliography. To my great advantage, Richard J. Sommers once again guided me through the massive holdings of the United States Army Military History Institute, at Carlisle, Pennsylvania, and shared insights about the contest at Spotsylvania. He has set a standard of professionalism that contributes greatly to the sense of camaraderie among modern historians of the Civil War.

I was especially honored when George F. Skoch consented to prepare maps for this volume, and when Barry L. Blose, of LSU Press, undertook to edit it. I hasten to add that my wife, Catherine, gave unwavering support and encouragement to pressing on with the story of Lee and Grant; that our son Campbell brought enthusiasm to battlefield jaunts that only a six-year-old can summon; and that our family's most recent addition—Carter Lee Rhea—remains understandably mystified by his father's fascination with old maps and diaries. Surely one day he, too, will share my interest in those battles that convulsed Virginia's countryside not so very long ago.

Abbreviations

ADAH	Alabama Department of Archives and History, Montgomery
AU	Special Collections, Auburn University Libraries
B&L	Buel, Clarence C., and Robert U. Johnson, eds. *Battles and Leaders of the Civil War.* 4 vols. New York, 1884–88.
BL	Bentley Historical Library, University of Michigan
BPL	Boston Public Library
BU	Mugar Memorial Library, Boston University
CL	William L. Clements Library, University of Michigan
CRC	Confederate Research Center, Hillsboro, Tex.
CU	John M. Olin Library, Cornell University
DU	William R. Perkins Library, Duke University
FSNMP	Fredericksburg and Spotsylvania National Military Park Library
GDAH	Georgia Department of Archives and History, Atlanta
HSP	Historical Society of Pennsylvania, Philadelphia
HU	Houghton Library, Harvard University
ISHL	Illinois State Historical Library, Springfield
IU	Lilly Library, Indiana University
LC	Manuscript Division, Library of Congress

LSU Special Collections, Louisiana State University Libraries

MC Eleanor S. Brockenbrough Library, Museum of the Confederacy, Richmond

MHS Massachusetts Historical Society, Boston

NA * National Archives, Washington, D.C.

NCDAH North Carolina Department of Archives and History, Raleigh

NYSLA New York State Library and Archives, Albany

OR *The War of the Rebellion: A Compilation of the Official Records of the Union and Confederate Armies.* 130 vols. Washington, D.C., 1880–1901. Unless otherwise stated, references are to Series I.

PMHSM *Papers of the Military Historical Society of Massachusetts.* 14 vols. Boston, 1881–1918.

RL Rundel Library, Rochester, N.Y.

SCL South Caroliniana Library, University of South Carolina

SHC Southern Historical Collection, University of North Carolina

SHSP *Southern Historical Society Papers.* 49 vols. Richmond, 1876–1944.

TSLA Tennessee State Library and Archives, Nashville

USAMHI United States Army Military History Institute, Carlisle, Pa.

UV Alderman Library, University of Virginia

VHS Virginia Historical Society, Richmond

VSL Virginia State Library, Richmond

WRHS Western Reserve Historical Society, Cleveland

The Battles for Spotsylvania Court House and the Road to Yellow Tavern

May 7–12, 1864

INTRODUCTION

THE SPRING OF 1864 opened the American Civil War's fourth year. Federal armies had scored important victories in the western theater. Blue-clad soldiers occupied Tennessee, Union gunboats steamed the Mississippi, and the only Confederate force of consequence in the west—Lieutenant General Joseph E. Johnston's Army of Tennessee—huddled defensively near Dalton, Georgia. Federal fortunes in the eastern theater were not so cheering. This was the haunt of General Robert E. Lee and his storied Army of Northern Virginia. The gray-haired Virginian's victories stood as classics of warfare, and even the Union Army of the Potomac's success at Gettysburg in July, 1863, rang hollow as Lee maneuvered the Federals to stalemate. Lee's nemesis, Major General George G. Meade, complained that Lee played a "deep game."[1]

In March, 1864, Ulysses S. Grant was placed over all Federal armies to coordinate the war effort and stiffen the Army of the Potomac's resolve. As chief architect of the western victories, Grant possessed a sound grasp of strategy. He saw that the North had to concentrate its considerable strength in sustained and coordinated offensives to prevent the enemy from reinforcing endangered areas or refitting its battered armies. Grant's strategic concept was sound. The question was whether he and his new subordinates could work together to execute his design.

Grant felt comfortable leaving the west in the capable hands of his friend Major General William T. Sherman. But the east was to be his preserve. Lee's army waited behind near-impregnable earthworks below the Rapidan River. Studying the situation, Grant decided on a three-pronged attack. Meade's Army of the Potomac, augmented by Major General Ambrose E. Burnside's 9th Corps, was to sweep around Lee's fortified line and engage him in battle. A second force—Major General Benjamin

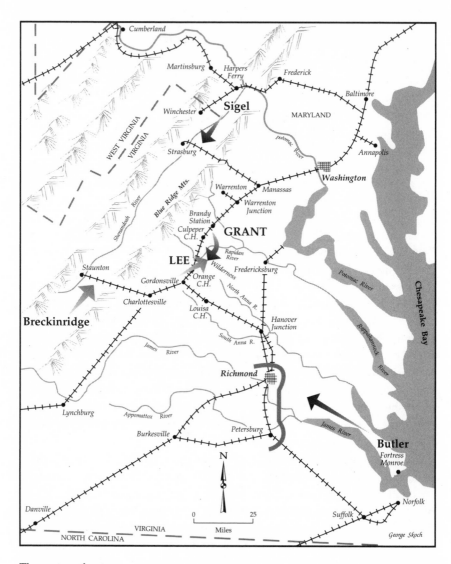

The eastern theater

Butler's Army of the James—was to advance up the James River and strike Richmond from below, severing Lee's supply line at the same time that it threatened the Confederate capital. A third army, under Major General Franz Sigel, was meanwhile to traverse the Shenandoah Valley, menacing Lee's strategic left flank and further disrupting his supplies and communications. If all went as planned, Lee's army would be shattered.

Early on May 4, the main element of Grant's blue-clad host, 120,000 soldiers strong, crossed the Rapidan east of Lee. By afternoon, it had disappeared into the Wilderness of Spotsylvania's tangled thickets. The other components of Grant's three-jawed vise moved apace. Butler's troop ships departed from Fort Monroe near midnight on May 4 and sailed without incident to City Point, where the Appomattox River flows into the James. Richmond lay a mere sixteen miles north. On the fifth, Butler's soldiers disembarked and thrust substantial parties toward the Confederate capital. Sigel was tramping south, virtually unopposed, along the Valley Pike.

Telegrams from Butler and Sigel poured into Washington apprising the War Department of their progress. But no word came from Grant. After crossing the Rapidan, he had necessarily abandoned the rail line north. Confederates swarmed between him and Washington and formed an impenetrable screen. "We get no tidings from the front," complained Navy Secretary Gideon Welles. Lincoln accepted the dearth of news with his usual homespun wisdom. "I can't tell much about it," he informed a congressman inquiring as to Grant's circumstances. "You see, Grant has gone to the Wilderness, crawled in, drawn up the ladder, and pulled in the hole after him, and I guess we'll have to wait until he comes out before we know just what he's up to."[2]

Early on May 6, reporters from the New York *Tribune* traveling with the Army of the Potomac gathered near Grant's headquarters. A volunteer was needed to carry back news of the fighting. Henry E. Wing, a twenty-four-year-old cub reporter from Connecticut, offered to try. The senior correspondent promised him a hundred dollars if he succeeded in getting through. The others looked relieved.

Before leaving, Wing sought out Grant and asked if he had any messages. "You may tell the people that things are going swimmingly down here," the Federal commander in chief responded flippantly. But as Wing turned to go, Grant stopped him. "You expect to get through to Washington?" he asked, then added without waiting for an answer, "Well, if you see the president, tell him for me that, whatever happens, there will be no turning back."[3]

Wing started north at four in the morning on May 6. Persuaded by a Union sympathizer and friend to assume a disguise, he donned a threadbare butternut suit. A band of rebel guerrillas stopped him near Richardsville, swallowed the story that he was delivering news of Lee's victory to southerners in Washington, and escorted him to Kelly's Ford, on the Rappahannock. There they discovered his deception, but he managed to escape across the river in a hail of bullets. He lost his mount soon afterward, while hiding from other guerrillas. Near sunset, he reached the Union outpost at Manassas Junction. The suspicious guard detained him, but the reporter escaped in the dark and followed the railroad tracks north. A Union picket apprehended him crossing the trestle over Bull Run and escorted him to nearby Union Mills, where he satisfied the soldiers that he was carrying news for his paper. But he soon realized that he could not reach Washington in time to get his story into the next day's edition. No trains were running, and his offer of five hundred dollars for a handcar and two men to propel it fell on deaf ears. Undaunted, he turned to a military telegraph office. When he found that the operator was under instruction not to send newspaper reports, he persuaded the man to transmit a wire to Charles A. Dana, the assistant secretary of war and an acquaintance. "I am just in from the front," read the message. "Left Grant at 4 o'clock this morning."

Knowledge of Wing's communication brought War Secretary Edwin M. Stanton to the telegraph office in Washington. "Where did you leave Grant?" Stanton demanded over the wires. Wing responded that the news belonged to the *Tribune* but went on to propose that if Stanton let him send a hundred words to the paper, he would tell the secretary all he knew. The reporter's intransigence raised Stanton's hackles, and the secretary threatened to arrest Wing as a spy unless he answered his inquiries. "This made me very anxious, but still I refused," wrote Wing. "I was disgusted that after all my enterprise my paper would not get my important news."

The telegraph at Union Mills started clattering again. Lincoln was on the line. Wing repeated his offer, with the president accepting it. The reporter dictated his dispatch—the first to reach Washington from the front—to the telegrapher.

Anxious for additional details, Lincoln sent a train for Wing, and at two o'clock on the morning of the seventh the reporter was pouring out his story to the president and a handful of cabinet officers. At the conclusion of the interview, when Wing was alone with Lincoln, he explained that he had a message from Grant. "Something from Grant to me?" replied the president. "Yes," said Wing. "He told me I was to tell you, Mr. President, that there would be no turning back." Lincoln's craggy face broke into a broad smile. He leaned over and kissed the bearer of these dramatic tidings on the cheek.[4]

Grant's simple message carried the matter-of-fact assurance that the general meant to stay the course. He was holding true to his clear vision of the road to victory. The Wilderness had sorely tested his resolve, and after two days of bitter combat he was forced to concede that Lee had maneuvered him to impasse. But he wisely recognized that the Wilderness was a tactical reverse, not the end of the campaign. Grant's strategic objective of destroying Lee's army remained unchanged. His task now was to find another way to bring the wily Virginian to battle on terms more favorable to the Federals.

The six days from May 7 through May 12 were the occasion of a contest of wits and endurance between America's premier generals. Grant boasted an overwhelming numerical advantage, but an ill-conceived chain of command isolated him from the levers of control, and his subordinates seemed incapable of concerted action. Lee was bedeviled by a deteriorating command structure and mounting deficiencies in manpower and supply. He had been caught off balance in the Wilderness, bringing Grant to stalemate as much by luck as by guile. By May 7, however, he was his former self. During the days that followed, he maneuvered his threadbare veterans with a practiced hand and orchestrated a performance that ranks as a classic of defensive warfare.

The journalist William Swinton maintained that Grant "avowedly despised maneuvering" and relied "exclusively on the application of brute masses, in rapid and remorseless blows." But there can be no doubt that Grant predicated the campaign on maneuver. He planned to flank Lee, not to attack him head on. And once battle was joined in the Wilderness, Grant strove to apply irresistible pressure against Lee's weakest point. When that failed, he shifted toward Spotsylvania to compel Lee to fight on ground more favorable to the Federals. Swinton's assertion notwithstanding, Grant eschewed frontal attacks except where he judged them to hold an appreciable likelihood of success.[5]

Lee's and Grant's intricate and bloody dance from May 7 through May 12 left a permanent imprint on the face of warfare and constituted a watershed in the accommodation of military doctrine to technology. Civil War combat had until then hewed to tactics developed in Napoleonic times, when smoothbore muskets generally had effective ranges of a hundred yards. By 1864, rifled muskets fired with considerably greater accuracy at three hundred yards and subjected attacking troops to about three times the amount of fire as smoothbores. Technology had outstripped military doctrine as battles became little more than episodes of mass slaughter between facing troops across open ground.

The Battle of the Wilderness spawned a burst of innovation, with soldiers on both sides resorting to protective barricades of earth and timber. For the outnumbered and outgunned Confederates, necessity fostered invention. During the initial fights around Spotsylvania, Lee's soldiers perfected the art of fieldworks. Frowning battlements of ingenious design soon hugged the ridges around the hamlet. Lieutenant Colonel Theodore Lyman, Meade's aide, described the remarkable evolution in a letter home. "It is a rule that, when the rebels halt, the first day gives them a good rifle-pit; the second, a regular infantry parapet with artillery in position; and the third a parapet with an abatis in front and entrenched batteries behind." The earthen mounds at Spotsylvania differed little from those at Petersburg two months later and in France during the First World War.[6]

While Lee's Confederates were learning how to defend themselves against modern weaponry, Grant's Federals were teaching themselves how to attack well-appointed earthworks. The experiments were bloody and contributed to Grant's reputation as a butcher. To a large extent, however, the bloodshed was unavoidable. Grant, like Lee, was feeling his way through the changing landscape of warfare. Not surprisingly, he stumbled often. To his credit, he kept trying.

The distinctive character of the campaign originated with the foot soldiers who fathomed the importance of earthworks and learned to fashion them with fiendish ingenuity. But the dynamic that drove events was the contest between Grant and Lee. The Virginian's task was to fend off Grant's hordes and to exact a price in blood that would lead the North to seek compromise rather than the complete destruction of Lee's army that Grant had as his goal. The stage was set for the most vicious bout of sustained combat ever to occur on the continent.

I

MAY 7, 1864

Grant and Lee Skirmish in the
Wilderness and at Todd's Tavern

"There lay both armies scowling at each other."

GENERAL ULYSSES S. GRANT was among the first in his encampment to rise. Ground fog and the smoke from two days of combat swirled through the Wilderness. Dense second growth crowded the far edge of the fields around the Lacy house, where Grant had pitched his headquarters tent. Major General George G. Meade's camp stood nearby, and across the way rose vague outlines of the two-story Lacy dwelling. The Federal commander in chief stepped from his tent and sought the comfort of a camp fire. An aide thought he looked thoroughly refreshed.[1]

Grant had much to ponder. His brand of warfare—a blend of maneuver and hard hammering—usually succeeded with flair. He had annihilated Secessionist armies at Fort Donelson and Vicksburg and had shattered another at Chattanooga. Something went awry, however, when he tried his hand against General Robert E. Lee and the Army of Northern Virginia. For two days—on May 5 and May 6—the combatants grappled in the Wilderness. The result, much to Grant's chagrin, was stalemate, with Lee holding a strong defensive position. "At present we can claim no victory over the enemy, nor have they gained a single advantage," was Grant's assessment of the affair. "There lay both armies," wrote Lieutenant Colonel Theodore Lyman, "each behind its breastworks, panting and exhausted, and scowling at each other."[2]

Putting a finger on what had gone wrong was no easy matter, but the awkward and ill-defined Union chain of command figured prominently in any plausible explanation. Grant's primary responsibility as chief of the Northern armies was to coordinate the war effort on all fronts, setting broad strategic policy and ensuring that his generals acted in concert.

Lower-level commanders were to manage tactical details. Translating the theoretical division of duties into practice, however, proved difficult, particularly with regard to the Army of the Potomac. Meade, the army's commander, had won accolades for repulsing Lee at Gettysburg in July, 1863. But after that he had faltered. Perhaps he lacked the military acumen and daring necessary to counter the Virginian's deft footwork. A skeptical President Lincoln had decided that Grant should accompany Meade, with a view to bolstering his tenacity. Grant entered the campaign expecting to accord Meade the tactical discretion he gave his other field commanders. "My instructions for that army were all through him, and were all general in their nature, leaving all the details and the execution to him," Grant explained. Once fighting started, though, Grant was drawn increasingly into the minutiae of command. The two generals, tents pitched within sight of each other, remained in constant communication. But their military styles were too divergent to provide a basis for joint action, and friction was inevitable. From Grant's perspective, the crusty, volatile Meade seemed unable to prod his army into action, and in bewilderment Grant watched his plans come to naught. As Meade saw it, Grant's penchant for attacking before preparations were complete was depriving the army of victories. The divergence between their opinions over how to fight Lee was to provoke bitter recriminations in the days ahead.[3]

The addition of Major General Ambrose E. Burnside's 9th Corps to the expeditionary force further blurred the lines of authority. Burnside cut a fine figure in his grandiose side-whiskers, and his genial wit made him a welcome companion. Still, his engaging personality did not compensate for his deficiencies as a commander. He outranked Meade and had previously commanded the Army of the Potomac. Grant's solution was for Burnside, like Meade, to report directly to him. The arrangement satisfied protocol but created a military nightmare. Grant, who had witnessed Burnside's successful defense of Knoxville in the winter of 1863, seriously overestimated him. "Rather weak and not fit for a corps commander," one headquarters aide decided about him after the Wilderness.[4]

But muddied lines of command only partially accounted for the problem. Shortly before the campaign opened, the Army of the Potomac had been reorganized into three infantry corps and one cavalry corps. Many of the generals who had been advanced to head the combat units fell sadly short of expectation in their first test. Despite distinguished service in the past, Meade's generals seemed dazed in the Wilderness. Coordination proved impossible, and they committed blunders that would have been unimaginable before.

A case in point was Major General Winfield Scott Hancock—Hancock the Superb, they called him—commander of the Union 2nd Corps. A Pennsylvanian and a close friend of Meade's, Hancock was universally admired. As fighting in the Wilderness intensified, Meade appointed him to oversee offensive operations on the army's left wing. Still suffering from a wound inflicted at Gettysburg, the general dropped his guard and committed the cardinal military sin of neglecting his flank, which permitted the Confederates to roll up his unprotected formation like a "wet blanket." Only Hancock's standing let his reputation survive the debacle. "Bully Hancock," Meade commented afterward. "He is the only one of my corps commanders who will go right in when I order him."[5]

Similar misfortune plagued Major General John Sedgwick, another army stalwart, who headed Meade's 6th Corps. "He was not an ardent, impetuous soldier like Hancock, but was steady and sure," asserted a longtime friend. "He was a very solid man; no flummery about him." The stocky, forty-eight-year-old bachelor personified solidity, and his solicitude for his men had made him immensely popular. But something about the Wilderness had clouded Sedgwick's judgment, much as it had Hancock's. He, too, had been caught napping and was driven from his earthworks by a rebel flank attack.[6]

Hancock's and Sedgwick's reverses could be chalked up to momentary lapses by otherwise capable leaders. But the misadventures of Meade's junior infantry commander—Major General Gouverneur K. Warren, leading the 5th Corps—merited genuine concern. Warren possessed a keen intellect. He had graduated second in his class at West Point, served with the prestigious topographical engineers, and taught mathematics at the academy. As the Army of the Potomac's chief engineer, he had won the nation's gratitude at Gettysburg by discerning the importance of Little Round Top and rushing troops there in time to save the day. Commanding a corps, however, taxed his abilities. Temporarily heading the 2nd Corps after Gettysburg, he had balked at attacking well-entrenched Confederate positions. His cautious streak intensified in the Wilderness and made him appear gun-shy. A New York captain who served under both Hancock and Warren opined that "compared to Hancock, [Warren] is decidedly a lightweight." He was a great card player, the captain thought, but otherwise "dull and uninteresting."[7]

Grant had entertained high hopes for the mounted arm and its new commander, Major General Philip H. Sheridan, Grant's associate from the west. Sheridan, however, had scant experience with cavalry and squabbled with Meade over the appropriate role for his horsemen. With the army heading into relatively uncharted territory, Meade understandably wanted Sheridan to screen his advance, locate the enemy, and protect the supply train. Sheridan—who was as hotheaded as Meade and, as events were soon to show, equally stubborn—insisted on using cavalry aggressively, like infantry. For all his bluster, Sheridan did poorly in the Wilderness and permitted Lee to sidle up undetected. A major confrontation was brewing between Meade and his new subordinate.

On reviewing the army's performance in the Wilderness, Grant must have harbored serious doubts about his field commanders' ability to execute his plans. He favored bold maneuver and had attempted to seize the initiative in his initial confrontation with Lee. As Grant studied the embers of his camp fire on the morning of May 7, he must have pondered the Wilderness' lessons. His strategic constructs had been generally sound, although he had underestimated Lee's aggressiveness and ability to exploit the terrain. To a large extent, Grant had stumbled because his subordinates had failed to accomplish his design. If Grant was to defeat Lee, he would have to change his style. Rather than deferring to Meade on tactical questions, he would have to become more involved in managing the army. And he needed to devise simpler plans more amenable to the eastern army's deliberate approach to warfare.

Grant's soldiers, like their commander, spent May 7 trying to understand the significance of the bitter fighting they had just endured. "I think we have not gained or lost," a man in the 1st New York Light Artillery scrawled in his diary. "As to the rebs and us, think the thing is equal." A soldier in the 124th New York put his thoughts into a letter: "We are having a pretty tough time of it, and expect to fight every day until one army or the other is vanquished." He concluded in a spirit that would have made Grant proud. "Although this is the hardest fought battle of the war, already, it is by no means finished yet."[8]

From Lee's perspective, May 7 presented a mixed military picture. Although outnumbered nearly two to one, he had stalled Grant's offensive. His troops occupied high ground and were confident they could continue to repel Grant's attacks. But much disturbed Lee about his situation. Not only did he face a powerful enemy but more Federals were harassing his lifeline to Richmond, and more still were marching into the Shenandoah Valley. Lee had foiled Grant in the short run, but tremendous casualties had gutted his capacity to wage offensive warfare. He had no choice but to curb his aggressive instincts and prepare for a defensive battle. By default, the next move was Grant's. If the Union commander played his cards right, he would try to slip between Lee and Richmond, leaving the Confederates no choice but to abandon the Rapidan sector. And if that occurred, Lee predicted to Jefferson Davis, the Confederacy's president, "great injury will befall us."[9]

The Wilderness had dramatically shortened the roster of Lee's junior officers and disrupted the leadership of his three infantry corps. Lieutenant General Richard S. Ewell, the eccentric, one-legged former dragoon in charge of Lee's 2nd Corps, was in questionable health and seemed reluctant to undertake offensive action. Lieutenant General Ambrose P. Hill, heading the Confederate 3rd Corps, was too ill to command. And Lieutenant General James Longstreet, Lee's senior general and head of his 1st Corps, lay seriously injured after his men accidentally shot him. Never— not even when Major General Thomas J. "Stonewall" Jackson was fatally wounded the previous year—had Lee faced a more serious crisis in his army's leadership. Lee's only dependable subordinate was Major General James Ewell Brown "Jeb" Stuart, commander of the Army of Northern Virginia's cavalry corps. Although outnumbered by Sheridan's riders, Stuart had in a masterly way screened Lee's maneuvers in the Wilderness.

Lee had to choose Longstreet's replacement immediately. At sunrise on the seventh, he summoned the 1st Corps' chief of staff, Lieutenant Colonel G. Moxley Sorrel, to his headquarters at Widow Tapp's farm, on Orange Plank Road. "I must speak to you, Colonel," Lee confided under a broad tree, "about the command of the First Corps." Then he outlined his thinking. Longstreet's two division heads—Major General Charles W. Field and Brigadier General Joseph B. Kershaw—had fought well in the Wilderness but lacked the experience for corps leadership. Lee had three major generals in mind for the position: Jubal A. Early, Edward "Allegheny" Johnson, and Richard H. Anderson. "You have been with the corps since it started as a brigade," Lee commented to Sorrel, "and should be able to help me."[10]

Jubal Early was an intriguing possibility. He commanded a division in Ewell's 2nd Corps and was a fine combat officer, but he was also irascible and highly opinionated. A subordinate considered him "one of the ablest and wittiest of our Generals—of quaint, dry humor, grinning like a 'possum, his voice an old woman's thin, high tenor, always joking some one, and always the butt of a joke." Often in pain from rheumatism, Early recognized that he was "never what is called a popular man." Sorrel spoke frankly to Lee. Early was talented, but his "flings and irritable disposition had left their marks," Sorrel suggested, "and there had been one or two occasions when some ugly feelings had been aroused when operating in concert."[11]

Sorrel considered Edward Johnson a more palatable choice. Also commanding a 2nd Corps division, Johnson was a tenacious fighter and had fended off an impressive multitude of Yankees in the Wilderness. He was a "splendid fellow," Sorrel acknowledged, although he felt reservations because Johnson was "quite unknown to the corps." That left Richard Anderson, a South Carolina planter and Military Academy graduate who fit Sorrel's requirement of good rapport with the troops perfectly. He had led a 1st Corps division until assigned in mid-1863 to the newly created Confederate 3rd Corps. He had stumbled badly at Second Manassas and Gettysburg and had missed most of the Wilderness combat, but there was something soothing about his style, particularly when, smoking his meerschaum pipe, he darned socks. "Gen Dick Anderson was as pleasant a commander to serve under as could be wished, and was a sturdy and reliable fighter," a Confederate artilleryman concurred. Of the choices presented by Lee, Sorrel preferred Anderson, and he said so. "We know him and shall be satisfied with him," the staffer asserted.[12]

"Thank you, Colonel," Lee replied. "I have been interested, but Early would make a fine corps commander." Lee's parting remarks convinced Sorrel that he would select Early. Later in the day, however, Lee announced that Anderson was to command the 1st Corps. Taking Anderson's place over his 3rd Corps division would be Brigadier General William Mahone, a dyspeptic Virginian who had won distinction in the Wilderness and was perceived as one of the southern army's emerging leaders.[13]

While Lee could find replacements for his ailing lieutenants, he had no way of replenishing his dwindling roster of combat veterans. The Army of Northern Virginia had marched into the Wilderness with 65,000 troops. About 11,000 had been killed, wounded, or captured, leaving Lee about 54,000 soldiers to fight Grant's 100,000. Modest reinforcements had arrived midday on May 6 in the form of Brigadier General Robert D. Johnston's North Carolina brigade, adding about 1,350 men to Lee's rolls— and a critical addition it would prove to be.

Outnumbered and outgunned, Lee's army nonetheless held a telling advantage in position and morale. Butt Hewson, reporting for the London *Morning Herald,* walked Lee's lines late on May 6 and witnessed the undaunted spirit of his men. Hewson first visited the sector above Orange Plank Road commanded by Major General Cadmus M. Wilcox. The general was conferring with Major General Martin L. Smith, Lee's chief engineer, over how best to strengthen the earthworks. Continuing northward, Hewson

saw Lee's men laboring to construct new entrenchments and gun placements, thus signaling their determination to "remain where they were."
Ewell, Early, and Johnson were engaged in animated conversation on the
Orange Turnpike. They seemed in "glowing spirits," the newsman observed, and evidenced no intention of abandoning the "great advantages
of their present position." Hewson's conclusion was emphatic: "Everything
along the front showed that Lee, judging doubtless from his knowledge of
Grant's character, looked for renewal of the attack. And far from any intention of moving from the field of his bloody triumph, [Lee] awaited its
delivery in confident preparation on the ground he then occupied."[14]

The Army of Northern Virginia was in "excellent spirits," a Confederate confirmed in a letter home. Another predicted, "Grant will recross
the river tonight." A third wrote his wife, "Our success so far has been
as decided as brilliant. Thousands of our hated foes sleep in death and
thousands are prisoners in our hands." According to camp gossip, Lee
was planning to attack the "demoralized and shattered ranks of the enemy." In truth, Lee intended to stay where he was, hoping that Grant
would renew his assaults. The next move was Grant's, and Lee resolved
to remain in the Wilderness, biding events.[15]

"Make all preparations during the day for a night march."

Grant spent the night of May 6–7 considering how to end the deadlock
in the Wilderness. Three options were available. One was to withdraw east
to Fredericksburg, where the Richmond, Fredericksburg and Potomac
Railroad would provide a steel pathway south toward the Confederate
capital. Lee would doubtless follow, moving into more open country,
where Grant could bring to bear his massive edge in troops, horses, and
artillery. A second possibility was to plow south on the direct route to
Richmond. As then constituted, Grant's line followed a north-south axis.
Some ten miles below lay the crossroads hamlet of Spotsylvania Court
House. By marching there along Brock Road and along parallel ancillary
roads, Grant would place himself squarely between Lee and Richmond.
The Confederates would have no choice but to follow, and Grant would
have the battle he wanted.[16]

The third option involved retiring across the Rapidan. It was later ru-
mored that Meade favored retreating, but no one ever suggested that Grant
entertained the idea. The political consequences were too great, and be-

sides, he intended to beat Lee, not to run from him. As Grant's aide Adam Badeau recounted, the general considered the Wilderness fight a bloody but necessary first step in bringing the Confederacy to its knees. "He would indeed have desired a more complete success, and did not assume to call this victory," Badeau reflected. But though he was painfully aware that he had not destroyed Lee, he felt that he had weakened the Confederates "materially and morally." Now was the time to strike. The question was not whether to continue fighting, but where.[17]

According to some accounts, Grant decided on the strategy of shifting to Spotsylvania during the evening of May 6. Certainly he had settled on that course by the morning of the seventh. After an early breakfast, he lit a cigar, pulled up a campstool in front of his tent, and mused about the recent combat to his aide Lieutenant Colonel Horace Porter. "We cannot call the engagement a positive victory," he remarked, "but the enemy have only twice reached our lines in their many attacks, and have not gained a single advantage. This will enable me to carry out my intention of moving to the left, and compelling the enemy to fight in a more open country and outside of their breastworks."[18]

The Federal army was arrayed in a broad arc below the Rapidan, like a bow pointed west toward the Confederates. Sedgwick held the battleground's northern sector. The upper portion of his corps was thrust across Germanna Plank Road. The remainder faced west, toward Ewell's Confederates. Warren's 5th Corps joined Sedgwick's left wing and extended the line south, confronting Ewell along the Orange Turnpike, a major east-west thoroughfare that had seen some of the war's most spirited fighting. Burnside's 9th Corps occupied the woods directly south of Warren, opposite Hill, and Hancock's 2nd Corps secured Grant's critical southern flank, across from Anderson. Most of Hancock's troops lay ensconced behind earthworks paralleling Brock Road from its junction with Orange Plank Road and running about two miles south to the Trigg farm. A strong stand of artillery closed off the Union line's lower end.

At 6:30 A.M., Grant ordered Meade to "make all preparations during the day for a night march" toward Spotsylvania. Unlike Grant's earlier directives to Meade, which suggested general strategies, this one spelled out an "advisable" way for Meade to achieve his goal. Warren's 5th Corps was to move first, passing behind Hancock's 2nd Corps and spearheading the Union advance down Brock Road. Once Warren's rear guard was safely past, Hancock was to follow. If things went according to schedule, Warren would reach Spotsylvania Court House by morning, just when

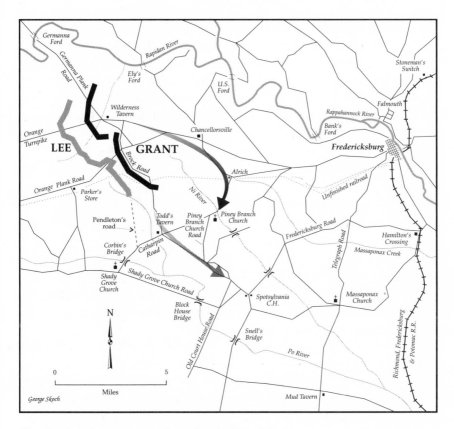

Grant's plan of maneuver to Spotsylvania Court House

Hancock's soldiers should be filing into Todd's Tavern, about three miles from their starting point.

While Warren and Hancock headed south on Brock Road, Grant's remaining infantry was to take a more easterly course through Chancellorsville, then swing southwest along Catharpin Road. Sedgwick's 6th Corps was to lead, passing on to Piney Branch Church, then south on Piney Branch Church Road. Burnside was to trundle behind. To accommodate the shift, Grant planned to abandon his tenuous supply line across Germanna Ford and establish a new base at Fredericksburg. The next step would depend on Lee's response.[19]

Grant's plan was calculated to avoid mistakes he had made during the march to the Wilderness. Then, his columns had been too widely separated to assist one another. This time, they were to move in close concert. Two corps—the 2nd and 5th—would remain near the enemy, while the 6th and 9th would advance on parallel lines a few miles east. If Lee's nimble veterans assaulted, the entire army could rally around the endangered point. It was a critical question whether Grant could slip away before Lee discovered the movement. Accordingly, Grant delayed the advance until dark. He also feared that rebel scouts might divine his purpose from the concentration of wagons and artillery and warned Meade to expect an attack during the afternoon. Sheridan was to hold "sufficient force on the approaches from the right" and to alert the corps commanders if Lee came near.[20]

Grant's plan was an audacious one, well crafted to force Lee to abandon his strong position and to fight where Grant could exploit his superiority in numbers and weaponry. The plan's drawback was its very ambition. It required the Army of the Potomac to execute a difficult night march under the enemy's watchful eye and to achieve a degree of coordination at odds with its former performance. The maneuver was vintage Grant, displaying both his talent for employing bold movements and his failure to conform his strategy to the Army of the Potomac's limitations. Until Grant learned how to wield this habitually sluggish instrument of warfare, he continued to court disappointments such as occurred in the Wilderness.

During the morning of May 7, Grant's former aide Brigadier General James H. Wilson, recently promoted to head a cavalry division, rode into Grant's camp. Grant had kept his plan secret, and rumors abounded. Wilson favored advancing rather than falling back and was anxious to voice his opinion. He dismounted, apprehension on his face. Grant spotted him and waved a cheery hello. "It's all right, Wilson," he called out, guessing the reason for Wilson's glum look. "The army is moving toward Richmond." The two men conversed briefly, with Grant stressing his commitment to fight until he achieved complete victory, "no matter how long it took." He added that he was dissatisfied with the infantry commanders' excessive caution but remained confident that he could beat Lee once he lured him out of the Wilderness. Wilson reported that he left Grant with a "lighter heart and greater confidence" than he had felt at any other time since crossing the Rapidan.[21]

Meade's veterans recognized that a march was about to begin. "There was great bustle and moving about of wagon trains," a reporter noted, "and those, along with ambulances containing wounded, droves of cattle, artillery, and everything not available for service at the front, were in motion down the Fredericksburg Pike." Meade waited until 3 P.M. to give his corps commanders details. A messenger arrived from Washington with encouraging news. Butler had moved as planned and landed his transports where the Appomattox River entered the James, at City Point. Sherman had also begun his offensive in Georgia and was expected to fight Johnston within a day. Grant became concerned that Lee might learn of the developments and retreat to Richmond or launch another attack in the Wilderness. He continued his preparations under a cloud of "anxiety in regard to the enemy's movements."[22]

"It comes like the breath of a wind."

Grant and Lee remained in doubt of each other's intentions throughout May 7. "At daylight it would be hard to say what opinion was most held in regard to the enemy," Meade's aide Lyman wrote home, "whether they would attack, or stand still; whether they were on our flanks, or trying to get in our rear, or simply in our front." A rumor made the rounds that Lee was retreating. "We doubted that," an officer from Maine remarked.[23]

At dawn on the seventh, skirmishers crept gingerly into the smoldering wasteland between the armies. Signs of carnage were everywhere. "We hold all the battle ground now and I tell you it is an awful sight," a North Carolinian wrote home. A Louisiana man quailed at the "ghastly exhibition of torn and mutilated humanity." Another Confederate observed that the woods had caught fire, "darkening the sun and filling the air with stench." A New Yorker chafed at the smell of men and horses "half roasted by the fires which had spread in the woods." One famished rebel salvaged hardtack from dead Yankees, discarding the bloody portions and eating the rest. Another southerner discerned that dead Confederates withered as their skin turned yellow and shrank against their bones, emitting little odor, but dead Yankees swelled enormously, turning dark purple, and stank. He attributed the difference to the "superior keeping of the Federal soldier, owing to the comparatively rich food upon which he lived."[24]

The day's military operations consisted of thrusts and counterthrusts to gain information about opposing lines. Confrontations flared around the Federal flanks and along two roadways—the Orange Turnpike and Orange Plank Road—that ran parallel east to west, connecting the hostile armies. The skirmishes were small, deadly to the participants but inconsequential for the larger military picture. Their importance lay in what they told Grant and Lee about each other's designs.

At precisely four o'clock in the morning, Sedgwick's artillery ushered

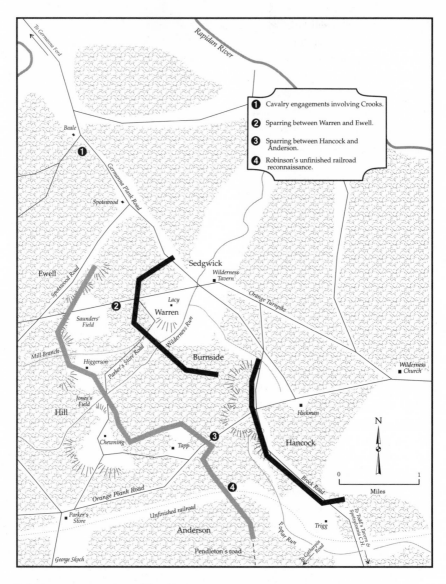

Infantry engagements on May 7

in the daylight with an "awful anthem of shot and shell." Ewell's pickets responded by stepping up their activity. Little battles flickered like heat lightning as Ewell's men probed for weak spots in Sedgwick's formation. A New Yorker recalled sitting down to boil water for coffee, when "out of the dim daylight in our front came such a yell as I never heard before, and a charge on us that brought every man to his feet with a musket in his hands." Union batteries fired into the shadows beyond the slashings. "Again and again the air was cut with canister and spherical case shell," a gunner wrote. "No longer able to withstand the terrible storm of iron which crashed in among them, they suddenly turned and made for Dixie as fast as their legs would carry them."[25]

Ewell's scouts discovered that an inviting gap of several miles separated the Federal 6th Corps from the Rapidan and exposed Grant's supply and communication line. The situation at the important Rapidan River crossing was unclear even to the Federals. Meade, who had ordered his pontoon bridges over the Rapidan removed in anticipation of installing a new supply line overland to Fredericksburg, was miffed to discover the span still intact. Glowering "fiercer than an eagle," he berated his mud-spattered chief engineer, Major James C. Duane, who rushed off to ensure that the pontoons were withdrawn.[26]

Sedgwick was exhausted. The affable bachelor, affectionately called Uncle John, had been up all night making sure that his earthworks were in order. An ordnance officer recalled a long black smudge across Sedgwick's left cheek, probably from a charred branch. Early in the morning, troops that Sedgwick had lent to Hancock returned and cheered wildly on seeing their general. "He blushed like a girl as he saluted their colors," an aide observed.[27]

Sharpshooters from Warren's 5th Corps advanced west along the Orange Turnpike toward Ewell's earthworks, defended in this sector by Brigadier General George H. "Maryland" Steuart's brigade and a brigade previously under Brigadier General John M. Jones and now commanded by Colonel William Witcher. The mist had not yet burned off, and corpses dotted the ground. About four hundred yards out, the sharpshooters encountered Steuart and Witcher's skirmish line, which refused to budge. They informed their superior, Brigadier General Joseph J. Bartlett, that infantry seemed to be gathering behind the rebel skirmishers, since they could hear commands in distinctly southern drawls. Bartlett alerted his division chief, Brigadier General Charles Griffin, that his line would give way if the Confederates launched a "rushing" attack. His men prepared for the worst behind earthworks fashioned from logs and dirt.[28]

Ewell's attack came soon enough—"spirited," a New Yorker later termed it—and the Union sharpshooters tumbled back, pursued by a ragged line in gray. "Old 'Griff' was there and he allowed them to come on until they were at close quarters," a sharpshooter recounted. "Then he ordered several batteries with double-shotted canister to open on them." Federal artillery sprang alive with hearty rounds, and musketry rippled along the pike. "They did not relish this little joke," remarked the sharpshooter. Nothing much came of the skirmish, however, for Steuart's and Witcher's men were only trying to confirm the Union line's location and withdrew once they had done that. A few rebel pickets climbed trees and fired on the Union works from hidden perches. Bartlett became so nettled that he sent his entire brigade to drive them off. "The woods were soon rid of the pests who had infested it," a Federal remarked with satisfaction.[29]

Smoke obscured the Orange Turnpike. Had Ewell left, Warren wondered, or was he massing for another, more serious, charge? As a precaution, he ordered his artillery to fire constantly down the turnpike. Around 7:00 A.M., the skittish corps commander again ordered Griffin to thrust skirmishers farther west along the road. By 7:40, even though Griffin had spotted no rebels, Warren began to suspect that Ewell was "forwarding a heavy force" toward his front. The danger could not be exaggerated, Warren admonished Meade, warning that "if the whole army lies quiet and they concentrate upon us we may be driven out." He continued, "You know how much more important our right is to our army just now than the left"—harping on the mounting concern that Lee might isolate the Army of the Potomac by exploiting the gap between Sedgwick and the river.[30]

Warren was fast earning a reputation as an alarmist, and headquarters apparently viewed his warnings skeptically. Meade sent no reinforcements Warren's way, suggesting that he gave little credence to his subordinate's fulminations. But the corps commander's agitated dispatch could not have improved tempers at the Union command center, near the Lacy house.

Things were quieter immediately below Warren, where Burnside's 9th Corps held a strongly entrenched line. Hill's Confederates tested Burnside's formation and judged it too heavily fortified to attack. And on the far Union left, Hancock's corps stood firmly behind log and earthen breastworks. During the night, Hancock's pickets had detected rebels shifting south, convincing Brigadier General Francis C. Barlow, who headed Hancock's southernmost division, that Anderson was massing opposite him, near the Trigg farm. He predicted an attack by daylight. "It is of the greatest importance that I have at my disposal troops to strengthen this point," Hancock beseeched headquarters. "The ground there is clear and the enemy have fine positions for artillery." Meade could not ignore Hancock's warnings, inasmuch as the 2nd Corps was responsible for the army's critical lower flank.[31]

Despite Hancock's ominous predictions, the woods remained eerily quiet. Only a handful of butternut scouts were spotted darting through the thickets. A lone Federal officer rode about a mile west out Orange Plank Road. Not a rebel was in sight. This raised the possibility that Anderson might have left, and speculation flared anew. Perhaps the southerners were massing below Hancock. Or perhaps, as Warren and now even Meade suspected, they intended to attack farther north and cut the Union army off from the Rapidan.[32]

Around 8:30 A.M., Meade's notorious temper got the best of him. Was Lee still entrenched, had he withdrawn, or—if events of the past two days gave any indication—was he maneuvering under cover of the forest screen to pounce on an unsuspecting portion of the Union line? Goaded perhaps by Warren's discomforting dispatches and the paucity of concrete intelligence, Meade lashed out in frustration. "I cannot understand non-receipt of intelligence from your cavalry," he fired in a note to Sedgwick. "Please send a staff officer to the cavalry and urge upon the commanding officer the importance of sending in prompt intelligence of their progress. Also feel with your pickets, and ascertain if you can anything of the position of the enemy." He was equally testy with Hancock. "It is of the utmost importance that I should know as soon as possible what force, if any, of the enemy is on your left," he wrote his 2nd Corps commander. "It is all important that I receive information at once."[33]

Sedgwick redoubled his efforts and dispatched two cavalry regiments— the 22nd New York Cavalry and the 2nd Ohio Cavalry—to patrol the strip between his corps and the river. That left him at the mercy of information from Colonel Samuel J. Crooks, of the 22nd New York Cavalry. The unit consisted of green recruits—"at least half of them were actually a little afraid of their horses," a Federal scout asserted—and its leader was prone to exaggeration. Queried by Sedgwick, Crooks reported that he had engaged enemy pickets about a mile below the Rapidan and that large clouds of dust were visible near the river, suggesting that Confederates were moving into the vulnerable strip. At about 10:15 A.M., Sedgwick reported Crooks's sightings to Meade.[34]

Meade was not disposed to mince words and berated Sedgwick for failing to keep close watch toward the Rapidan. He also instructed Sedgwick to support Crooks with infantry if Confederates were in fact moving onto Germanna Plank Road. In order to obtain reliable intelligence about this critical sector, Meade ordered experienced cavalry under Colonel John B. McIntosh, of Wilson's division, to join Crooks.[35]

Sedgwick was in no temper for Meade's barbs. "I don't know who Colonel Crooks, Twenty-Second New York cavalry, is, except that he reports himself senior officer of cavalry," he replied shortly after 11 A.M. "I sent the commanding general all the reports I received from the commanding officer of the cavalry in front. I could not judge how reliable they were." Sedgwick added that he could now identify the source of dust off to the right. "Colonel McIntosh, who has just come here, reports he has been moving from Ely's to Germanna Ford." Crooks had mistaken the plume from McIntosh's moving column for rebels.[36]

On the opposite Federal flank, Hancock scrambled to satisfy Meade's demand for information. He was "ubiquitous," an officer noted, "riding everywhere and sending staff officers in endless succession from one end to the other of the line to keep himself posted on the situation." He dispatched two companies from the 140th Pennsylvania south on Brock Road to link up with Sheridan's cavalry, thereby securing his flank against a surprise attack from the south. He was also troubled by a wagon track that angled from Catharpin Road to Brock Road below the Trigg farm. Confederate stirrings during the night suggested that Lee might use the track to attack Hancock's flank, and the fears acquired substance when a Confederate battery—probably horse artillery attached to Brigadier General Thomas L. Rosser's mounted brigade—began firing from the track at Hancock's troops. The 26th Michigan pursued the Confederates southwestward for about a mile until an aide retrieved the men giving chase.[37]

During the skirmish, the Michiganders captured a dispatch revealing that Lee intended to deploy artillery along the Trigg clearing. Was it Lee's plan simply to harass Hancock's lower flank, Grant wondered, or did Lee have a larger maneuver in mind?[38]

Hancock's flurry of activity interested Lee, who was searching for keys to Grant's thinking. A pattern seemed to be emerging. The previous afternoon, Federal cavalry had abandoned Brock Road below the Trigg place. Now they had returned and seemed bent on clearing the road to Todd's Tavern. Perhaps, thought Lee, Grant was taking precautions to protect his southern flank. Or perhaps, when considered along with the later confirmation of Grant's relinquishing his supply line back to Germanna Ford, the activity presaged a Federal shift toward Spotsylvania Court House.[39]

Lee decided to hedge his bets. Spotsylvania Court House was considerably harder for him to reach than for Grant. Whereas Grant could move directly on Brock Road, Lee had to backtrack to Parker's Store, drop south to Catharpin Road, proceed east to Shady Grove Church Road, and then sidle southeast to the courthouse town. Needing a more direct approach,

Lee ordered Brigadier General William N. Pendleton, chief of the Army of Northern Virginia's artillery, to construct a trail south from Anderson's lower flank. Pendleton's road was to strike Catharpin Road west of Todd's Tavern and afford Lee considerable strategic flexibility. Forces using it could turn right and proceed to Spotsylvania Court House by way of the Catharpin–Shady Grove Church corridor or veer left to Todd's Tavern and Brock Road.[40]

Lee also ordered two reconnaissances to determine whether Grant had abandoned his supply line across the Rapidan. The Confederate 2nd Corps' artillery chief, Brigadier General Armistead L. Long, was to take Colonel Witcher's infantry brigade and Captain William P. Carter's artillery battery and swing onto Germanna Plank Road above Sedgwick. Meanwhile, Brigadier General John R. Chambliss, a dashing young Virginian, was to lead his cavalry brigade on a second foray, exploring as far north as Grant's former camps around Culpeper Court House. The remainder of the Confederate army culled guns and ammunition from the battlefield, awaiting orders to move on. "Skirmishing was more or less brisk all day; our loss was eight or ten men wounded," a Confederate recounted. Any place seemed better than the Wilderness.[41]

Increasingly apprehensive about Lee's design, Meade ordered Hancock to muscle through the rebel 1st Corps skirmishers blocking Orange Plank Road. Major General David B. Birney, who had supervised the previous day's combat in that sector, selected Colonel John S. Crocker's brigade for the job, augmenting it with elements from Colonel Lewis A. Grant's Vermont Brigade of the 6th Corps. At 10:20 A.M., Crocker's troops fanned along Plank Road. Rows of corpses carpeted the ground where battle lines had clashed on May 5 and 6. "Here we met a sight that can hardly be described," a sharpshooter recounted. Wounded soldiers called for help with pathetic groans and pleas. As Birney and his staff jostled by, what at first appeared to be a bundle of rags stood up and fired at the general. Birney's bodyguard quickly dispatched the Confederate, who had been lying in ambush.[42]

About a mile west, Crocker reached a stand of trees draped with blankets. The blankets dropped, and a Confederate battery unleashed a storm of canister. "Such agility as we displayed hunting for the rear has few parallels in this war," a Federal admitted. Birney ordered up his "straggler brigade" of "skulkers and cowards" who had been caught running toward the rear. They tried to rush the guns, but Confederate musketry and canister created a "complete corner where death awaited all." It was, thought a participant, "useless slaughter."[43]

The 93rd New York charged along Plank Road's north side, where trees seemed thicker, but grueling Confederate musketry brought them to a halt. Then rebels began lapping around Crocker's flanks, forcing him back. Crocker left behind a contingent of sharpshooters, who traded brisk musketry with the Confederates. For amusement they fired ramrods, which "cut through the air with a hissing sound not unlike that of a bomb and were received on both sides with shouts and laughter." Crocker recorded that he lost "quite largely in this engagement having been exposed to a galling fire from the enemy's entrenched line."[44]

At noon, Birney passed along his findings to Hancock. "My reconnaissance reached the rifle-pits or barricades just beyond the extreme advance yesterday," he reported. "The line, judging by its volley, was not a very strong one. The artillery was a section of horse artillery—I thought small." The rebels, he surmised, were retreating and had left behind a small but obstinate force. In fact, they remained firmly entrenched beyond his front.[45]

While Birney probed Orange Plank Road, Warren ordered Griffin to launch a more determined reconnaissance along the Orange Turnpike. He assembled a makeshift force of three volunteer and two regular regiments under Lieutenant Colonel Charles P. Herring, of the 118th Pennsylvania, and directed him to "push the enemy back as far as possible, and ascertain his position and force." Herring advanced through undergrowth below the turnpike, flushing Confederates. "The way Johnnies did skedaddle was a caution," a soldier remarked. After skirmishing ahead about a quarter mile, Herring reached a clearing dominated by Ewell's imposing earthworks. This was Saunders' Field, the scene of severe fighting on May 5 and 6. Herring attempted to locate Ewell's flank but was repulsed by Steuart's men. "The instructions were to feel and drive the enemy," a Pennsylvanian wryly summarized the episode. "The latter part of the direction was inserted more in hopefulness than as a command. It was easy to feel, but the driving was not so readily accomplished."[46]

Warren was also curious about the strength of the Confederate line below Saunders' Field and ordered Brigadier General Samuel W. Crawford to take the 6th and 13th Pennsylvania Reserves for a look. "Tell your men we believe the enemy is retreating," Warren suggested, "and make this demonstration at once." Crawford hammered rebel pickets back to a cleared knoll called Higgerson's Field and came face to face with Ewell's main works. "Though the skirmish did not last many minutes, it was very severe," a participant reported. Unsupported, Crawford fired a few parting shots and retired.[47]

Around eleven o'clock, Meade ordered his aide Lyman to investigate the commotion on Warren's front. "I found, on the most undoubted evidence, that we were throwing solid shot and shell at the rebels, and they were throwing solid shot and shell at us," the staffer reported on returning. By noon, after digesting reports from the various probes, the Federal high command concluded that Lee did not intend to attack. "The indications now are that the enemy have retreated during the night, probably to Mine Run or other front," Lyman recorded in his journal, "leaving a rear guard which we are driving." Grant's staffer Lieutenant Colonel Cyrus B. Comstock thought it "certain [the] enemy had fallen back along [the] whole line." Grant continued to ponder the situation under a pine tree. When Lyman next saw him, he had shifted from cigars to a briarwood pipe. "Tonight Lee will be retreating south," Grant predicted. He also expressed concern to a reporter that the Confederates might be "getting back safely to such a position as would give them the start in a race toward Richmond." Preparations for the night march to Spotsylvania were to continue.[48]

Nothing during the afternoon caused Grant or Lee to revise his plans. Hard skirmishing crackled between the armies, but neither displayed aggressive designs. "We drove them back, then their line got reinforced and drove us back, then we soon drove them back, and that is the way we kept it up all day," a northerner recorded. "The enemy again assaulted us," a Confederate wrote, "but evidently from its feeble character it was only a reconnaissance to ascertain where we were."[49]

Meade's humor hit rock bottom when Lyman returned with a note from Warren. "The enemy's shells fall near my headquarters," Warren fretted. "Well, can't I see that?" bridled Meade, whose headquarters was next to Warren's. "What's that to do with it?"[50]

The efforts of Colonel Crooks and his ill-fated 22nd New York Cavalry played out to a farcical conclusion. Reaching Germanna Ford shortly after noon, McIntosh's seasoned cavalrymen found conditions there at stark variance from the scenario painted by Crooks. "Everything perfectly quiet," McIntosh informed Sedgwick. "No sign of an enemy on the left of the road." Apparently Crooks persisted in misinterpreting routine skirmishing for a rebel offensive. The unfortunate cavalryman became a lightning rod for Meade's frustration. "You will consider yourself under arrest for having sent false information in relation to the enemy," Meade exploded in a 2 P.M. message to Crooks. "You will turn your command over to the next in rank, directing that officer to report to Colonel [John] Hammond, commanding 5th New York Cavalry, for orders." Meade went on to instruct Hammond, who headed a regiment in McIntosh's brigade, to reconnoiter the Rapidan and keep him "promptly advised of any movement of the enemy." Chewing out Crooks seemed to put Meade in a better frame of mind, and he joked with Lyman about the disgraced colonel's replacement, Major Peter McClennan: "I don't believe he's a bit better."[51]

Just as Meade's reprimand reached Crooks, Armistead Long's Confederates, dispatched by Lee to probe between the Union army and the Rapidan, broke onto Germanna Plank Road above Sedgwick. Hammond's 5th New York Cavalry was near the river, Crooks's 22nd New York Cavalry was a few miles below, at the Beale farm, and the 2nd Ohio Cavalry was resting near the Spotswood house, just outside the entrenched Union line. As luck had it, Long plowed directly into Crooks's troops and gave them their first taste of combat. They "skedaddled," a Union witness fumed, and bolted south with Long in hot pursuit, throwing the Ohio men into "momentary confusion." A scout who witnessed the stampede remarked that a "green cavalry regiment is about as useless a set of men as can be got together," although the sight of riders tumbling from their mounts like "over ripe plums" provided a certain measure of humor. Cut off from the army, Hammond retired east along the Rapidan. The crisis, however, passed as quickly as it had come. The 2nd Ohio Cavalry rallied, and Crooks's successor, McClennan, steadied the 22nd New Yorkers. Realizing that the danger was less than he had thought, Hammond sheepishly returned with his regiment. The 22nd New York Cavalry was in shambles. Not even the army's crusty provost marshal, Brigadier General Marsena R. Patrick, could re-form the terror-stricken men. One soldier, Patrick observed, "was so paralyzed by fear that he did not know his own name, nor regiment." Grant, on learning of the regiment's conduct, told Meade, "Take their horses away and give them to better men, if they don't behave better."[52]

By the time the Federals regrouped, Long had withdrawn. "It was discovered that the enemy had almost entirely abandoned the ford and the road," Long reported to Lee. "It was evident that they were leaving our front."[53]

Around 3 P.M., Hancock sent the 26th Michigan, on the southern end of Grant's line, west along an abandoned railway grade. Fires set during the Wilderness fighting still crackled through the dense undergrowth. Colonel Nelson A. Miles's aide Lieutenant Robert S. Robertson and Major Lemuel Saviers mounted an embankment and spied Confederates on the far side, at ease with their guns stacked. The rebels—probably Kershaw's men, from Anderson's corps—lunged for their muskets. "We waited to see no more," Robertson acknowledged, "but thinking discretion the better part of valor, we retreated rapidly." The southerners scampered onto the embankment and fired after the Michiganders, who ran until they reached their own lines. There were no casualties, and Robertson had confirmed that Lee still evidenced no intention of disrupting Grant's movement.[54]

Robertson's mad dash along the abandoned railway grade ended the day's sorties. Sixty Federals were shot in Birney's reconnaissance, and at least that many in Griffin's Orange Turnpike offensive. Hancock's entrenched Brock Road line sustained "quite a number" of casualties, probably from rebel sniper fire. Sedgwick's corps, which lay all day under "heavy fire from skirmishers and sharpshooters," suffered comparable losses. Critics believed the cost in lives had been unnecessarily high. "If it was the intention to find out what was in front," a Federal carped, "we accomplished the purpose, paying dearly for the information."[55]

But everyone agreed on one point. "This day was very fatiguing—my heart beat strangely," a 6th Corps officer scribbled in his diary. Two days of bruising combat and another of heavy skirmishing made poor preparation for a night march to Spotsylvania Court House.[56]

Around 2 P.M., Lee's adjutant, Lieutenant Colonel Walter H. Taylor, sent the flamboyant Confederate cavalry commander Jeb Stuart a message outlining Lee's thinking. "The enemy now and then advance and feel our lines," Taylor observed. Lee, he continued, saw "nothing to indicate an intention on [Meade's] part to retire, but rather . . . an intention to move toward Spotsylvania Court House." Long's intelligence that Grant had dismantled his Germanna Ford bridge supported Lee's conclusions. With Grant's supply line severed, Lee thought the Federals had to "open some new way of communication," which would require them to move either to Spotsylvania Court House or to Fredericksburg. Chambliss' foray across the Rapidan confirmed that Grant had abandoned the countryside north of the river. His three Virginia regiments had reached Grant's campsites around Culpeper Court House to find them deserted. Stuart's job was to explore south in case Grant "continue[d] his movement toward Spotsylvania Court House, or should we desire to move on his flank in that direction." An hour later, Stuart informed Lee that a contingent of Federal cavalry was pressing west on Catharpin Road, but that he thought it represented an isolated probe. Stuart's intelligence did not change Lee's hunch that Grant might move toward Spotsylvania Court House. It merely confirmed that he had not yet begun.[57]

Later in the afternoon, Lee visited Ewell's line, probably for the first time in the campaign. "We left the breastworks and went and stood by the road as he passed," a Confederate remarked. "We pulled off our hats and yelled as loud as we could." After inspecting Ewell's dispositions, Lee threaded south along the Confederate earthworks. Hill and his staff had established headquarters on an eminence at the Chewning house. Aides had knocked out a few shingles to create a superb observation post. The Lacy fields and Wilderness Tavern were plainly visible over distant treetops. While Lee and Hill conferred on the porch, Hill's aide William H. Palmer climbed into the attic and scrutinized the Union lines through a marine telescope. A constant stream of couriers and officers convinced Palmer that he had Grant's headquarters under observation. His interest was piqued when guns rolled onto a road leading south. He scampered down and reported his sighting to Lee. "It was no doubt simply confirmatory of numerous other reports from the cavalry and other points of the line, that General Grant was moving to Spotsylvania C.H.," Palmer was to say later.[58]

Around 7 P.M., Lee ordered Anderson to prepare to march his 1st Corps south along Pendleton's road. On reaching Catharpin Road, Anderson was to turn either left toward Todd's Tavern or right toward Shady Grove Church, depending on Grant's movements. Lee directed Ewell to remain in place, since he was not fully confident of Grant's intentions. "Be prepared to follow with your command should it be discovered that the enemy is moving in that direction, or should any change in his position render it advisable," he instructed Ewell.[59]

Lee then consulted with Anderson to ensure that he understood his assignment. "As soon after dark as you can effect it, withdraw Longstreet's corps from the lines, as quietly as possible, so that the movement will not be discovered by the enemy," he told the reserved South Carolinian. "When you have done this, march the troops a little way to the rear and let them have some sleep—a guide will report to you this evening." Anderson's objective was Spotsylvania Court House. "I have reason to believe that the enemy is withdrawing his forces from our front," continued Lee, "and will strike us next at that point. I wish you to be there to meet him, and in order to do so, you must be in motion by three o'clock in the morning." Pendleton also reviewed the route again with Anderson and assigned a staff officer to guide him along the freshly cut trail.[60]

Around ten o'clock, the Confederate 1st Corps began south in search of a resting place, as Lee had instructed. It moved "as silently and rapidly as possible," but progress was slow. "Never before nor afterwards did I experience such a trying night march," a soldier complained. "On we went, with never a halt, over rough places, little streams, swamps, and through next to impenetrable thickets." The smoke and the stench of death were overpowering, so Anderson elected to continue toward Spotsylvania, as he later put it, "until I got clear of the fires." His decision ranked among the most fateful of the campaign.[61]

Hill's 3rd Corps spread into Anderson's freshly vacated trenches. The move surprised Hill's men. "We cooked our supper and prepared for a good night's sleep and a much needed rest, as we had been hard at it for over forty-eight hours," a 3rd Corps soldier recounted. "I hope I shall rest some tonight," another wrote his wife, "for I am broke down." After a tedious trek, the 3rd Corps occupied the line formerly held by the 1st. "I could see the forms of men on the ground in all directions and took for granted they were troops sleeping and did not know any better until daybreak the next morning," a Virginian related. "They were dead men we had killed on the 6th."[62]

Elements from Ewell's corps in turn filled the openings created by Hill's movement south. A 2nd Corps officer described the ordeal as "closing or extending—cannot call it marching—to the right, which continued during the entire night, the men having no time for rest or sleep." A staffer remembered horsemen and foot soldiers stumbling over stumps, running into trees, and falling into gullies. Soon the men were "about played out and mad as march hares."[63]

But Lee's veterans were relieved to be moving. Southern voices erupted spontaneously through the woods—the "sound of a charge or of good cheer, which we could not tell," a sharpshooter remembered. The eerie cry rose again as thousands of men shouted into the darkness. It rolled across Anderson's line and on to the north. "We lifted our voices as our turn came," one of Hill's soldiers recalled, "and sent the grand chorus echoing along the lines of Ewell to the distant left." Someone counted three cheers passing from one end of the Confederate formation to the other. Another thought there were ten. "I never heard so much cheering at once before in my life," remarked a Union artillerist. "I suppose one must be a soldier to feel the full charm of such cheering," a Confederate reflected. "Heard at first faintly, in the far distance, it comes like the breath of a wind, drawing nearer and nearer, till it reaches you with the blast of trumpets." The Army of Northern Virginia was marching to its next rendezvous with Grant.[64]

"Have a sufficient force on the approaches from the right."

Brock Road had to be cleared of Confederates before Grant could start south. That was the first order of business for Sheridan's cavalry. The tumbledown crossroads settlement of Todd's Tavern, about five miles below the Union flank, was particularly important. A major route—Catharpin Road—sliced in from the direction of Lee's army, brushed by the tavern, then continued east to Orange Plank Road at the Alrich place, near Chancellorsville. If Lee intended to intercept Grant on his way to Spotsylvania, he would most likely strike there. Simply put, from Lee's position, Catharpin Road was the logical place for blocking Grant's movement south.

A Confederate cavalry division under General Lee's nephew, Major General Fitzhugh Lee, had occupied Todd's Tavern and thrust units north along Brock Road. Its seven veteran Virginia regiments numbered about 3,500 men and were relatively fresh, having seen little combat in the Wilderness. Another rebel mounted division under the South Carolina aristocrat Major General Wade Hampton camped a few miles west, near Corbin's Bridge, where Catharpin Road crossed the Po River. The core of Hampton's division was Thomas Rosser's Virginia brigade, which had suffered cruel casualties in the "harvest-field of death," as one Virginian called the Wilderness. During the morning of May 7, elements from a third Confederate cavalry division—that of General Lee's son Major General William H. F. "Rooney" Lee, recently released from a northern prison—joined Hampton.[65]

Sheridan had two available routes for moving to Todd's Tavern. His first alternative was to take Furnace Road west to Brock Road, then march south. The second was to advance from the Alrich place west along Catharpin Road directly to the settlement.

Judging that he could spare only one division for the Todd's Tavern expedition, Sheridan selected Brigadier General Wesley Merritt's, which was camped along Furnace Road. At 7:30 A.M., Merritt started west. Leading was Brigadier General George A. Custer's Michigan outfit—the Wolverines. That was followed by Colonel Thomas C. Devin's mixed New York and Pennsylvania brigade. Merritt's reserve brigade under Colonel Alfred Gibbs remained behind to help protect the army's trains.[66]

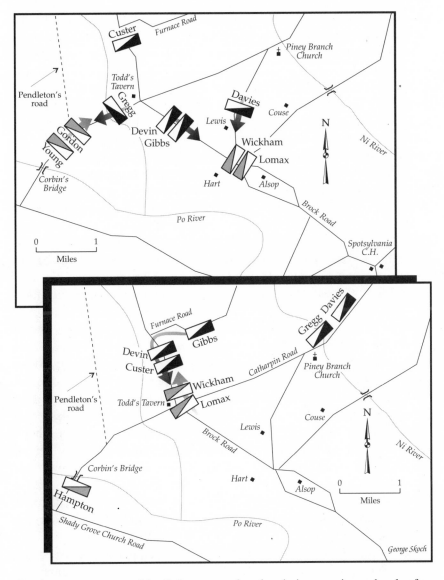

Cavalry engagements on May 7. Lower panel, action during morning and early afternoon; upper panel, action from 3 P.M. until dark.

Merritt struck Brock Road below the Trigg place, then turned south. Almost at once he encountered Fitzhugh Lee's advance patrols, who offered heated opposition. Soldiers from the 1st Michigan Cavalry dismounted and picked through the woods fringing Brock Road while Custer's main body pushed ahead on horseback. As Merritt neared Todd's Tavern, Lee's resistance stiffened. A major fight was brewing.[67]

Fitzhugh Lee's Confederates employed the novel tactic of sending their horses rearward and fighting dismounted behind makeshift log barricades. Merritt fed both Custer and Devin into the fight, and a "brisk skirmish" ensued. To break the impasse, Devin ordered the 6th New York Cavalry to charge Lee's barrier. Riding high, the Yankees made inviting targets and were repulsed with "some loss." Merritt's advance ground to a halt a mile or so north of Todd's Tavern.[68]

Events, however, were working to free up more of Sheridan's horsemen. Meade concluded from the morning's infantry probes that a major Confederate offensive was unlikely and began to breathe easier over the safety of his supply trains. Rather than continuing to tie up Sheridan, he assigned Brigadier General Edward Ferrero's 9th Corps division of black troops to guard the wagons. At 10 A.M., Sheridan received the directive that he had been anxiously expecting. He was free to detach any portion of his command for "offensive operations, cutting the enemy's communications, etc."[69]

Sheridan seized the opportunity and began piling more troopers toward Todd's Tavern. First, he ordered Gibbs to join Custer and Devin on Brock Road, which brought Merritt's division up to strength. That force was to continue battering Fitzhugh Lee's barricades. Sheridan also directed Brigadier General David McM. Gregg to move his division by two routes. One of Gregg's brigades—that of Brigadier General Henry E. Davies, Jr.—was to advance along Catharpin Road to Piney Branch Church, then hook south on Piney Branch Church Road to emerge on Brock Road behind Fitzhugh Lee. The other of Gregg's brigades—a mixed Maine, New York, and Pennsylvania outfit under Colonel J. Irvin Gregg—was meanwhile to proceed directly along Catharpin Road and strike Lee's right flank at Todd's Tavern. If all went as planned, Merritt's and Gregg's converging divisions would close around Lee and crush him.[70]

Rather than fighting Sheridan at Todd's Tavern, Fitzhugh Lee decided to shift south, where more heavily wooded terrain offered favorable defensive positions. He retired his division about a mile down Brock Road and began erecting barricades near the Hart house, which commanded the roadway. Around 3 P.M., Sheridan's pincers began closing on Todd's Tavern, and within an hour the two primary Union columns—Merritt's soldiers descending on Brock Road, and Colonel Gregg's coming along Catharpin Road—met at the crossroads. Their quarry, however, had escaped, and they now faced rebels on two fronts. To the west, out Catharpin Road, stood Hampton's division. To the south, on Brock Road, waited Fitzhugh Lee.[71]

Sheridan decided to split his force and wage battle on both fronts. He directed Colonel Gregg to attack Hampton while Merritt continued south after Lee.

Gregg pushed west along Catharpin Road to Corbin's Bridge, on the Po River. Hampton, reinforced by Rooney Lee, occupied high ground along the far bank. Rather than risking battle so far from reinforcements, Gregg retreated to Todd's Tavern. There, at a field west of the tavern, his men fashioned rail fences into earthworks and rolled two artillery sections into place.[72]

Gregg had scarcely completed his preparations when Confederates from the brigades of Brigadier Generals James B. Gordon, of Rooney Lee's division, and Pierce M. B. Young, of Hampton's division, charged the barricade. Gregg's artillery repulsed the first wave of attackers, but Gordon ordered his horsemen to dismount and charge again on foot. "Out of the woods the enemy came, yelling as only they could yell," a Federal related. "They had but fairly got into the field when cannon and carbines opened a terrific fire, and the rebel yell was turned into a whine as they quickly disappeared into the woods." Gordon's and Young's Confederates settled into earthworks on the clearing's western side and exchanged potshots with Gregg's men. To stave off boredom, soldiers hoisted their hats on sticks and invited fire. One Federal got so excited that he forgot to stay down and was shot in the rump. A Tarheel jumped onto a pine stump and flapped his arms like a chicken, crowing loudly, until a Yankee shot the stump from under him. An exchange of calls "neither euphonious nor endearing" followed.[73]

Merritt meanwhile started south with Gibbs's brigade to clear Fitzhugh Lee from Brock Road. Major James Starr's 6th Pennsylvania Cavalry found Lee deployed in two tiers about a mile below the tavern. Brigadier General Williams C. Wickham's Confederate brigade manned a first set of barricades near the Hart house, and a half mile back loomed a second pile of logs and fence rails where Brigadier General Lunsford L. Lomax' brigade waited in reserve.[74]

Confronted with a formidable rebel force, Starr sent for help. The 6th Pennsylvania Cavalry formed across Brock Road, the 1st United States Cavalry and 1st New York Dragoons on its left and the 5th United States Cavalry on its right. One regiment—the 2nd United States Cavalry—remained in reserve. Lieutenant Edward B. Williston's Union battery rumbled onto a ridge and began banging away, doing "excellent service,"

Gibbs later reported, "silencing the enemy's battery and wounding several of their men and horses."[75]

Assuming that his bombardment had weakened the Confederates, Gibbs ordered his Pennsylvania and New York regiments ahead. Wickham's line, however, extended well into the woods on both sides of Brock Road, and the charging Federals found themselves surrounded. A blast from the rebel fortification unhorsed Starr's men, who led the attack, and the contending battle lines fanned into the forest. The Pennsylvanians fought from behind trees, laying down a carpet of rapid fire with their carbines. Union losses mounted, Gibbs's horse was shot from under him, and according to a newspaper account, the "air seemed filled with leaden missiles from either side." The rest of Gibbs's troops piled in to rescue the headmost units from annihilation.[76]

Outgunned and almost out of ammunition, Gibbs called for reinforcements. At four o'clock, Devin pulled up and fanned three regiments across Gibbs's line, plugging the weak points.[77]

Then Wickham's barricade caught fire, forcing him back to Lomax' supporting line. The Confederates had fired so often that their faces were begrimed with powder. To one participant, they looked like coal heavers waiting to unload a barge. Merritt, however, was slow to press his advantage, so Lee dispatched Colonel Thomas T. Munford's 2nd Virginia Cavalry to recapture the smoldering first line of works. Several of Munford's men stopped to loot dead Yankees along the roadway. One rebel reaching for a northerner announced, "I'm going to take his boots. He'll never need them again." As he jerked off the Yankee's footgear, the supposed corpse lashed out with a vigorous kick. Just then a fresh wave of Federals appeared. "I looked and saw that our men had gotten some distance back toward our breastworks," related a Virginian who had been busy collecting spoils, "so we started back in double time."[78]

Shells and minié balls rattled through the trees while Wickham, Lomax, and Fitzhugh Lee conferred earnestly. A southerner observed "some confusion, and for the first time apprehension, as I thought, apparent in the manner of our men, some of them falling out." A West Point graduate and former Indian fighter, Lee had things firmly in hand. "Wickham, extend the line on the right; Lomax, on the left," he thundered and spurred his gray mare over the barricade and on toward the advancing enemy. Realizing that he was alone, Lee reconsidered his impetuous gesture, turned, and sped back at a full run. He vaulted the barricade and curbed his steed in a cloud of dust. "Hold your fire until the enemy reach thirty yards," he commanded. "Then take good aim and let them have it and then I want you to go over after them."[79]

The Federal assaults intensified as Davies arrived from Piney Branch Church. Fighting blazed along Lee's second line of works and into the woods on each side of Brock Road. "Enemy's cavalry in large force [made] severe assault on us," recorded Lee's aide J. D. Ferguson. "Very severe fighting." The 6th Ohio Cavalry "did prodigies of valor," a Federal affirmed. "It was a stubborn contest and a deadly one," a soldier in the 4th Virginia Cavalry confessed. "Men were struck every second and a perfect torrent of lead seemed to pour from the repeating rifles." He added, "For a half hour there was one of the hottest fights between the opposing brigades of dismounted cavalry that occurred during the war. Every tree, every sapling was marked by the flying lead, and a steady stream of wounded were going back." The 15th Virginia Cavalry on Lee's left crumpled, and disaster seemed imminent. Lee sought help from Hampton, but the South Carolinian was too occupied with Gregg on Catharpin Road to assist. Stuart, who was with Hampton, ordered a new round of assaults against Gregg in the hope of inducing Sheridan to pull troops from Lee's front. The gambit accomplished little beyond increasing the day's casualties.[80]

Lee's line held, and soon the Federals were seeking reinforcements. The 9th New York Cavalry, of Devin's brigade, "went in big on a charge dismounted" but were soon lying flat on the ground to avoid raking canister from Lee's artillery. Then the 6th New York Cavalry ventured down the road. "The head of our column was literally smashed in," a New Yorker reported. Fighting at the barricades flared so bitterly that bodies lay in heaps "literally shot to pieces."[81]

In a nearby house, Katherine Couse quailed at the din from the escalating cavalry duel. She was a Union sympathizer who had moved to Virginia from New Jersey before the war. "It is soul sickening to listen to the continual crack of small arms, then the loud resounding cannon shell, whizzing balls whistlin, soldiers yelling and howling as they rush on," she wrote. "Oh God! Human beings killing each other. This wicked war, will it never come to an end?"[82]

Darkness descended on the bloody Brock Road melee. Flaming barricades blazed like funeral pyres in the night. "The ground over which they charged was left blue with their slain," a Confederate observed. Couse scrawled in her letterbook, "I feel so weak and generally miserable I can scarcely sit up most of the time. Oh! The poor wounded dead and dying soldiers, there has been a terrible contest going on all afternoon."[83]

Nightfall saved Fitzhugh Lee. Sheridan decided against continuing the contest in the darkening forest and ordered his troopers to disengage. Gibbs and Devin retired to above the Hart house, where the afternoon's fighting had begun. Coincidentally, Wickham attacked while Sheridan was withdrawing. "We turned his left," a soldier in the 2nd Virginia Cavalry claimed, "and drove him a considerable distance." Another rebel reported that "when the enemy fell back a large number of their dead were left on the field." Colonel Gregg remained at Todd's Tavern, where Davies joined him, and Custer bivouacked at the intersection of Brock and Furnace roads. "The stench from decomposing horses, thickly strewn over the field, was almost stifling," a Michigan man complained.[84]

Sheridan's decision to withdraw was a costly mistake. He forfeited over a mile of valuable road and afforded Fitzhugh Lee an opportunity to construct new barricades for the next day's combat. Lee was rightfully proud. In what a Richmond paper termed the "most hotly contested cavalry fight of the war," he had stalled Sheridan's advance and bought valuable time for the Confederate infantry. A soldier in the 4th Virginia Cavalry aptly summarized the affair in his diary. "Off and on we drove them and they us," he wrote. "Very warm time indeed." Hampton, too, considered the day a success. He had plugged Catharpin Road and erected an impenetrable cavalry screen shielding Anderson's maneuver toward Spotsylvania Court House from the Federals.[85]

"What a curse war is," Stuart's aide Alexander Boteler wrote in his diary. "The dreadful sights I have seen this week in the Wilderness will never be banished from my memories."[86]

Sheridan was elated over his capture of Todd's Tavern and dispatched glowing reports to Meade, claiming to have driven Stuart "in confusion" toward Spotsylvania Court House. After examining the field, he waxed ebullient. Writing from Todd's Tavern at 8 P.M., he crowed that he had "handsomely repulsed" Stuart about three miles. His own troops had behaved "splendidly," he continued, and had taken prisoners from virtually every Confederate cavalry brigade. Sweetening his victory was the death of Colonel Charles R. Collins, a turncoat Pennsylvanian commanding the 15th Virginia Cavalry. What a glorious day it had been for the Union mounted arm![87]

In fact, Sheridan had failed badly. Meade's general orders contemplated that the army would begin south at 8:30 P.M., and he expected Warren to press down Brock Road to Spotsylvania Court House by morning. The pace of the advance depended on Sheridan's clearing the way. According to Meade's instructions, Sheridan was to place "sufficient force on the approaches from the right to keep the corps commanders advised in time of the appearance of the enemy." Contrary to the spirit of these orders, Sheridan had relinquished his hold on the road below Todd's Tavern and entertained no plans to begin south until daylight. Fitzhugh Lee's tenacious resistance made it impossible for Meade to meet Grant's timetable.

Sheridan clearly acted contrary to Meade's intentions. Perhaps he never saw Meade's general order and hence failed to appreciate the urgency of opening Brock Road to Spotsylvania Court House. During the early afternoon, Sheridan remained at his headquarters at the Alrich farm, near Chancellorsville. Afterward, he was busy overseeing the engagements around Todd's Tavern. He probably did not return to the Alrich place until sometime after 9 P.M. and might not have received Meade's directive setting the infantry in motion. Sheridan seemingly issued no further orders to Merritt or Gregg until 1 A.M. on the eighth, when he instructed them to begin south at 5 A.M. Plainly, Sheridan had no inkling that by then Meade intended Warren's infantry corps to have marched through Todd's Tavern and on to Spotsylvania Court House.

The cause of the slippage in communication between Meade and Sheridan is not clear. Meade resented Sheridan, whom he regarded as an upstart imposed on him by Grant, and they had clashed almost from the start. Perhaps Meade's antipathy toward Sheridan bred laxity about keeping him informed. Perhaps a wayward messenger is to blame. But whatever lay behind the misunderstanding over the army's nighttime objective, the consequences were grave. The road below Todd's Tavern remained barricaded by stubborn Confederate cavalrymen. Every hour lost afforded the Confederates opportunity to react. The Federals were squandering precious time in the race for Spotsylvania Court House.

Sheridan's troopers bedded down to distant muffled treads that were perhaps missed by their infantry counterparts, busy packing for the march. "All night long the ears of the alert cavalryman could catch the indistinct murmur of troops moving with their impediments," a Michigan horseman noted. Confederate vedettes pressed unusually close against the Union cavalry lines, as though trying to conceal what was occurring behind them. The Confederate 1st Corps was on its way to Spotsylvania, and it meant to get there first.[88]

"Never did a night's march seem harder."

At 8:30 P.M., the Army of the Potomac began threading out of the Wilderness. Warren's and Sedgwick's corps jammed the Orange Turnpike for a short distance; then Warren turned south toward Brock Road while Sedgwick continued east toward Chancellorsville. A horrible traffic jam stalled both corps until Sedgwick yielded the right of way.[89]

Heading the 5th Corps' advance was Brigadier General Lysander Cutler's division, followed by the divisions of Brigadier Generals John C. Robinson and Samuel Crawford. Charles Griffin's division closed the rear. As each unit entered the roadway, it was joined by artillery. The night was very dark, and the road seemed a narrow defile through the forest, making the march "painfully slow and wearisome." A Pennsylvanian related that the column would start, march ahead about a hundred yards, then halt. Word would come to start again. "So the exhausting march continued for hours," he recalled, "being the most cruel and aggravating kind of a night march to which tired soldiers could be subjected." A soldier in the 143rd Pennsylvania asserted that men marched fast asleep, "mechanically as it were, and were kept up at a perpendicular and under motion by their file covers." Warren's artillery chief, Colonel Charles S. Wainwright, estimated the pace at a half mile an hour. "Never before did I see such slow progress made: certainly one step at a time," he jotted in his journal.[90]

Artillery and supply trains crammed the narrow road. Warren remained behind at the Lacy house, and no officer of sufficient authority was available to untangle snarls. Grant's and Meade's entourages elbowed to the fore of the procession and became serious impediments. Provost Marshal Patrick, who had taken the ill-fated 22nd New York Cavalry under his wing after its drubbing by Armistead Long's Confederates, also unwittingly slowed the pace. The recruits were riding fresh mounts, which did not go unnoticed by veterans of the 3rd Pennsylvania Cavalry. Unable to resist temptation, the Pennsylvanians yanked the New Yorkers from their saddles and disappeared on the new horses. The New Yorkers accepted their latest reverse philosophically, as but another in the seemingly endless chain of calamities attendant on military life.[91]

Years later, an officer from Maryland described the march. "At intervals, darkness would be made visible on the right by a blazing brand dropping from some distant tree-trunk, still aglow in the depth of the Wilderness, like a signal-light of goblins," he wrote. "The low, damp air reeked with the pungent, acrid snuff of horse and human slaughter." Soldiers, he recalled, "occasionally tumbled into rocky furrows, or stumbled over carcasses."[92]

The soldiers enthusiastically received the army's new commander in chief. "When General Grant goes round the lines the cheering is deafening, the men have all confidence in him," a New Yorker reported. "The

General-in-chief wore the regulation army hat and a plain blouse, with three little stars on the shoulders," an officer recorded. "His army trousers, the same as worn by privates, were tucked in a very muddy pair of cavalry boots." Grant, he thought, "presented anything but a military appearance," busying himself with a cigar, to all appearances uninterested in the proceedings around him.[93]

Tension swelled dramatically as Grant approached Brock Road. The men were aware that what he did at the intersection would be the key to understanding his plans. If the commander in chief proceeded east, the army was likely in retreat. If he turned south, the sacrifices of May 5 and 6 would not be without purpose. The army would continue toward Richmond.[94]

Private Frank Wilkeson remembered the moment well. "The men seemed aged," he recalled. "They were very tired and very hungry. They seemed to be greatly depressed." Rumor had it that Meade had advised recrossing the Rapidan, and the soldiers believed what they were hearing. "None of the enlisted men had any confidence in Meade as a tenacious, aggressive fighter," according to Wilkeson.[95]

Grant turned south onto Brock Road. "Instantly all of us heard a sigh of relief," Wilkeson related. "Our spirits rose." Grant's aide Horace Porter considered the outpouring of emotion one of the campaign's memorable incidents. On all sides rose the cry, "On to Richmond!" Cheers resonated through the forest. Men pressed from all directions, tossing hats into the air, setting pine knots and leaves ablaze, clapping, and calling to Grant. "The night march had become a triumphal procession for the new commander," Porter observed. A soldier recorded in his journal, "I do not know that during the entire war I had such a real feeling of delight and satisfaction as in the night when we came to the road leading to Spotsylvania Court House and turned to the right."[96]

Ever practical, Grant put a damper on the celebration. "This is most unfortunate," he warned. "The sound will reach the ears of the enemy, and I fear it may reveal our movement." His staff officers urged quiet. "The enemy must have thought a night attack was intended," a Maine man surmised, "for they opened fire upon us with shells, which had the effect of silencing the cheering." But the event made a lasting impression. "Afterwards, in hours of disappointment, anxiety, and doubt, when the country seemed distrustful and success far distant, those nearest the chief were wont to recall this midnight ride in the Wilderness, and the verdict of the Army of the Potomac after its first battle under Grant."[97]

The headquarters cavalcade crossed Orange Plank Road around 11 P.M., and Meade stopped to confer with Hancock. Low entrenchments lined the road. Sentries sat on top and paced the far side while officers sauntered up and down, their greatcoats and slouch hats creating weird shapes in the dark. During the pause, Meade learned that he was delaying Warren and ordered his escort to move more quickly. The procession eased ahead a bit, then tarried for Meade, who was still talking with Hancock. Exhausted staffers sprawled in the dirt. Nearby stood Brigadier General John Gibbon, commanding one of Hancock's divisions. "A tower of strength he is," remarked Lyman, "cool as a steel knife, always, and unmoved by anything and everything."[98]

Meade arrived in a cloud of dust, and the group jolted on. Apparently the generals lost sight of the provost marshal's cavalry, which was leading. The road forked, and Grant and Meade took the branch to the right. A horseman appeared and demanded that the cavalcade stop. "Who tells me to halt?" Meade queried gruffly. "Whose headquarters are these?" Recognizing Meade, the horseman explained, "I halted you because a few steps more will bring your horses among our sleeping men, and if you go further you will be outside of our lines, and riding toward the enemy." The party backtracked to Brock Road and stationed an orderly at the fork to make sure that Warren did not repeat the mistake. Lyman summarized the ordeal in a letter home. "On again, past more sleeping men, and batteries in position, losing the road, finding it again, tearing our clothes among trees and bushes, then coming to cavalry pickets and finally to Todd's Tavern, where General Gregg had his headquarters." It was then around 1 A.M.[99]

Todd's Tavern was a ramshackle wooden structure with a dirt floor and a wooden front porch. Gregg's cavalry had occupied the decent sleeping spots. One of Meade's aides propped his head against a log for a pillow, and Grant stretched out on the hard earth. An aide spread an overcoat over the dozing commander. No one paid much notice to a nearby pigpen. All that remained of its former occupants was their odor. This mixed with the stench of bodies piled high from the afternoon's cavalry fight.[100]

Meade was infuriated to discover Gregg and Merritt still at Todd's Tavern. He had ordered Sheridan to clear the road to Spotsylvania and had predicated Warren's advance on the assumption that Sheridan had done so. Yet here were Sheridan's two lead divisions bedded down for the night. Meade's chief of staff quizzed the cavalrymen. To his dismay, they were still waiting for orders spelling out their assignment for the morning. In Meade's estimation, Sheridan had failed completely.

On learning that Sheridan was several miles away at Alrich's, Meade short-circuited the chain of command and issued peremptory orders to Sheridan's two division heads at Todd's Tavern. Gregg was to press west out Catharpin Road to Corbin's Bridge to guard against a Confederate attack from that direction. Merritt was to hurry south to Spotsylvania Court House, then disperse his three brigades to plug the western approaches to the village. "It is of the utmost importance that not the slightest delay occur in your opening the Brock Road beyond Spotsylvania Court House," Meade directed Merritt, "as an infantry corps is on its way to occupy that place."[101]

With the cavalry back in motion, Meade shot a curt note to Sheridan. "I find generals Gregg and [Merritt] without orders," he sniped. "They are in the way of the infantry and there is no time to refer to you. I have given them the enclosed orders, which you can modify today after the infantry corps are in position."[102]

It just so happened that as Meade was setting Gregg and Merritt under way, Sheridan was finally drafting orders for them. What he envisioned differed markedly from Meade's plan and was patently unworkable in light of Confederate deployments. Sheridan's scheme had Gregg advancing west along Catharpin Road at 5:00 A.M., crossing Corbin's Bridge, and halting about a mile farther on at Shady Grove Church. Merritt was to follow Gregg, swing southeast on Shady Grove Church Road, then recross the Po at Block House Bridge and advance toward Spotsylvania Court House. Wilson meanwhile was to move south through Spotsylvania Court House along Fredericksburg Road and secure Snell's Bridge below the town.[103]

Sheridan's orders assumed that Gregg could force his way across Corbin's Bridge to the west. That was a tall supposition, since Hampton held the far bank. And the orders also presumed that the Army of Northern Virginia would remain dormant in the Wilderness. But by 5 A.M.—the time Sheridan set for beginning the maneuver—the Confederate 1st Corps was pouring down Shady Grove Church Road toward Block House Bridge.

By the time Sheridan's instructions reached Todd's Tavern, Gregg and Merritt were already acting under Meade's direction. Sheridan's orders were ignored so far as they affected those two divisions. The orders to Wilson, however, were not rescinded. There is no indication that Meade even knew that they existed. This set in train events that were to culminate in a dramatic confrontation between Meade and Sheridan.

After the war, Sheridan and his supporters engaged in historical sleight of hand to justify the cavalry commander's lapse at Todd's Tavern. In his official report, drafted two years after the event, Sheridan maintained that

Meade had altered instructions Sheridan had already given to Merritt and Gregg, thereby forfeiting the opportunity to beat Lee to Spotsylvania. Grant's aide Badeau argued that if Sheridan's orders had been implemented, "every avenue to Spotsylvania would have been closed to the rebel army." Sheridan's account does not explain how Meade, arriving at Todd's Tavern, could find Gregg and Merritt with no instructions from him. Perhaps most tellingly, the orders that Sheridan finally issued did not stand a chance of being executed, since the route that Sheridan had selected for Merritt and Gregg was jammed with Confederates. As Meade's chief of staff Humphreys concluded, "The presence of Fitzhugh Lee's cavalry on the Brock Road, and Hampton's cavalry and [Anderson's] corps on the Shady Grove Road, settled the question as to who should first hold the Court House with infantry, whatever might have been the disposition of our cavalry."[104]

While Grant and Meade tried to catch a few hours' sleep, Warren continued slowly south. Hancock's men sprawled in their trenches, oblivious to the steady tramp a few yards from their heads. Wainwright noticed that not even the rumbling of artillery caissons roused them. "We wished we were in the same blissful state," a soldier in Warren's ranks recalled. The 5th Corps' advance reached Todd's Tavern around 2 A.M. and continued through the crossroads settlement. Merritt had moved ahead and started sparring with Fitzhugh Lee, who occupied the stretch of road Sheridan had abandoned the previous evening. Meade assured Warren that the cavalry would "keep out of the way" and hastened the 5th Corps toward the front.[105]

As the Army of the Potomac toiled from the Wilderness, Warren's rear guard began withdrawing. Hancock's pickets remained forward. "A dreadful quiet prevailed during that black night," a sharpshooter recalled. "Not a sound to be heard beyond our own whispers. We sat around on dead men for logs in the utter darkness, while the stench was suffocating." A Swiss volunteer admitted, "We did not feel exactly comfortable finding ourselves in those somber woods, surrounded by corpses, without any supporting party."[106]

East of Warren and Hancock, the 6th Corps pursued the Orange Turnpike toward Chancellorsville, threading through wagons and ambulances loaded with injured men. Initially, Meade had planned to send his wounded to Rappahannock Station for transport to Washington. Then, when Grant ordered the army toward Spotsylvania, Meade redirected the wagons to Fredericksburg. The procession churned up stifling dust that left Sedgwick's troops rubbing their eyes and gasping for breath. "The men were so tired that finally they could stand up no longer," a participant wrote. "One by one they dropped down, and many fell asleep the moment they touched the ground." It was slumber "as only the tired soldier can sleep." Not until dawn on May 8 did the 6th Corps reach Chancellorsville, having covered four miles in eight hours. And not until 8 A.M. on May 8 did the 9th Corps begin leaving the Wilderness.[107]

Southerners later claimed that Lee had divined Grant's probable line of march during the afternoon of May 7. Brigadier General John B. Gordon, in reminiscences published almost forty years later, reported that Lee announced, "Spotsylvania is now Grant's best strategic point. I am so sure of his next move that I have already made arrangements to march by the shortest practicable route, that we may meet him there." Gordon considered this an example of Lee's "wonderful foresight." Lee's adjutant Colonel Walter H. Taylor observed that the "faculty of General Lee, of discovering, as if by intuition, the intention and purpose of his opponent, was a very remarkable one."[108]

Gordon's and Taylor's assertions conflict with the contemporaneous record. Although Lee suspected that Grant might move to Spotsylvania, he considered Fredericksburg an equal, if not more probable, objective. Early in the afternoon, Taylor informed Stuart that Lee "thinks they may move toward Fredericksburg or Spotsylvania Court House." The next morning, on learning that Grant was in motion, Lee alerted Richmond that the Federals were "moving toward Fredericksburg." Lee's actions on the seventh underscored his uncertainty about Grant's plans. He understood that Spotsylvania figured in Grant's thinking, but he was not prepared to commit his entire army to the place. He instead detained most of his infantry in the Wilderness, waiting for Grant to reveal his hand, and dispatched a single corps to the crossroads hamlet. Lee perceived no need for haste and authorized Anderson to postpone his march until three o'clock the next morning. Neither Lee's words nor his deeds support the story that he had identified Spotsylvania Court House as Grant's destination.[109]

Extraneous conditions, however, impelled Anderson to move. Smoke and stench induced him to start five hours early and kept him going. Lee did not realize it, but Anderson was racing Grant to Spotsylvania. And fortune was affording him a chance to win.

Grant's prospects started brightly on May 7. His scheme to interpose his troops between Lee and Richmond was crafted to draw the Army of

Northern Virginia from its formidable defensive position. While disengaging from Lee presented difficulties, Grant devised a workmanlike solution to that problem as well. The cavalry was to clear the way south while the infantry withdrew in a sequence calculated to keep a stern face to the enemy.

The plan, however, failed miserably in execution. Not since the notorious "mud march" of 1863 had an advance been so badly botched. Grant was partly responsible, since his scheme required the four Union corps to march considerable distances along darkened roads with a high degree of coordination. Little thought was given to the maneuver's logistics. Ambulances and slow-moving units clogged the routes and corps vied for roads. Meade neglected to communicate urgency to his subordinates, and no staffers patrolled the byways to keep the army moving. Sheridan's failure to clear the way south—along with Meade's failure to monitor Sheridan's progress—figured large among the day's mistakes. And as the maneuver's timing went askew, the corps became dangerously separated. Warren, whose 5th Corps constituted the army's vanguard, kept pushing ahead virtually alone, far from any support. Provost Marshal Patrick aptly termed the episode "one of the most fatiguing and disgraceful rides I ever took."[110]

A soldier complained that he and his companions were "so overcome by weariness and lack of sleep that we in the ranks neither knew, nor cared much where we were." Sedgwick's aide Thomas W. Hyde recorded that three days and nights of "constant nervous strain" had left him "positively light-headed as well as ragged and dirty, hungry and thirsty." There was but one consolation. "To say we were glad to be out of the Wilderness is putting it mildly," acknowledged Hyde. "We left there and in the jolting ambulances nearly 20,000 of our best and bravest." Little did he imagine that worse was to come.[111]

II

MAY 8

The Armies Meet at Laurel Hill

"There is no force in our front but cavalry."

AT 3:30 SUNDAY MORNING, May 8, the head of Warren's 5th Corps reached Merritt's battle line across Brock Road, about a mile and a half below Todd's Tavern. It was inky black, but lively popping sounds from cavalry skirmishes confirmed that rebels were close by. Anxious to learn the state of affairs, Warren sought out Merritt. The cavalry commander had just received orders from Meade instructing him to clear the road of Confederates and had sent Gibbs's brigade south, with the 1st United States Cavalry leading. "Attacked the enemy before light without breakfast," one of Merritt's soldiers scrawled in his diary.[1]

The 5th Corps dribbled to the front over the next two hours, forming in column along Brock Road. It was an uncomfortable place to bivouac. Some soldiers dozed fitfully by the roadside while others tried to cook breakfast. Fires set during the cavalry fights had burned the woods, and ashes smeared the men's sweaty faces. "We looked more like drivers of charcoal wagons than soldiers," one warrior remarked.[2]

Merritt was making little progress. "The cavalry of Custer here got in the way, very much of the 5th Corps," Lyman observed. Warren vented his frustration to Meade, explaining that, ignorant of the "result in front," he was making the best of the delay by resting his men. He remained acutely aware of the "importance of getting on to Spotsylvania Court House as soon as may be" and had massed Robinson's division for a speedy advance. He could do nothing, however, until Merritt moved aside.[3]

Around 6 A.M., Wainwright arrived with the 5th Corps' rear guard. The prickly New Yorker called things as he saw them, and he was fuming over

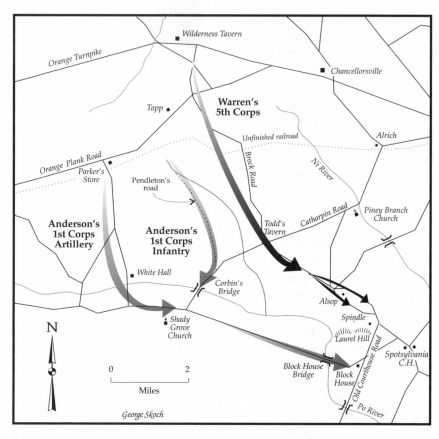

Warren's and Anderson's routes to Spotsylvania Court House

the delays, particularly when he discovered Meade and his staff asleep at Todd's Tavern. Now, riding into 5th Corps headquarters with the high command's "perfect indifference" fresh on his mind, he encountered yet another outrage. "When I reached General Warren," he confided in his journal, "I found them all quietly eating their breakfast, waiting for Merritt to open the way with his cavalry." Warren was as culpable as Meade, thought Wainwright. Neither was "pushing matters as much as [he] ought, considering how important it was to reach Spotsylvania Court House before Lee." Meade, Wainwright asserted, should have either coordinated Warren and Merritt or given Warren authority over the advance. Wainwright did not record his comments to Warren, but one can infer that he spoke freely. "The General appeared decidedly crusty this morning," the artillerist noted in his journal. "Why I do not know."[4]

Fitzhugh Lee had labored during the night to strengthen his Brock Road defenses. The 3rd Virginia Cavalry, of Wickham's brigade, manned the first barricade, but Merritt's persistent attacks drove the regiment to a second set of works, where the rest of Lee's division waited. Major James Breathed, the handsome twenty-three-year-old commander of Confederate horse artillery, posted his guns with a clear view of the approaching enemy. His mastery of the pieces, a cavalryman observed, "was a spectacle calculated to stir the most sluggish blood and make it run like quicksilver through the veins." The combination of Breathed's gunnery and musketry from Lee's dismounted horsemen firmly plugged the route south. Merritt seemed hopelessly mired in an "obstinate struggle."[5]

Fighting raged around the Hart dwelling. "Dead and wounded men and horses made the place a slaughter house," a Federal noted. Just as the 2nd United States Cavalry advanced into the yard, a cellar door creaked open and a coarsely featured woman poked out her head. Glancing first at a nearby well, then at a Union captain, she threw out an empty bucket. "Yankee, I reckon ye kin tote me a pail o' water," she shouted and promptly disappeared.[6]

The 12th Massachusetts' adjutant noticed a solitary rider directing the troopers where to deploy and demanded his identity. The figure raised his felt hat brim and answered, "Sheridan." The cavalry commander had ridden to the front to try and move things along, and he pitched into the fray, biting off each sentence. "Quick! Quick!" Progress remained slow, however, and Warren rode up, complaining that the cavalry was still obstructing his infantry. Finally Merritt conceded that he was unable to drive the rebels and asked Warren to lend a hand. Warren decided to thrust Robinson's division down Brock Road, followed closely by Griffin's. Two batteries—Captain Augustus P. Martin's and Lieutenant George Breck's—were to accompany them. Wainwright was to remain behind and dispense additional batteries as needed.[7]

Robinson's soldiers pried themselves from the ash-covered ground. "They had to be punched, kicked, and shaken up to learn that more fighting was in order, before either lodging or breakfast," an officer related. "The crack-crack of carbines, reverberating in the forest glades ahead, closed up yawning jaws and put snap into numb legs." Robinson's lead elements filed past Merritt's horsemen. "Go on boys, you'll soon find them," the troopers shouted with knowing looks. "They are just ahead." Leading was Colonel Peter Lyle's brigade, clustered left of the roadway. In immediate support and slightly to the right was a brigade of four Maryland regiments under Colonel Andrew W. Denison. Bringing up the rear was Colonel Richard Coulter's mixed Massachusetts, New York, and Pennsylvania outfit. These battle-hardened veterans were ideal shock troops for shattering Fitzhugh Lee's cavalry screen.[8]

"Fix bayonets," an officer shouted, and the "sharp click of the rattling steel ran down the line like a miniature volley of pistol shots." The infantrymen strode forward, shoulder to shoulder. A rail fence vanished under their feet. Emerging from a stand of woods, the column came under fire from Confederates posted across a clearing, where Breathed's pesky brace of cannon added to the din. "Forward, guide center!" came the command. "In grand array the blue line swept over the field with flags unfurled," a participant recounted. The southerners discharged a salvo and fled. Warren, elated at his progress, sped an optimistic note to Meade. "The opposition to us amounts to nothing as yet," he wrote at 8 A.M. "We are advancing steadily." Robinson, he added, had been instructed to "use only the bayonet, and carry every battery the enemy shows."[9]

Lee retired down Brock Road, hotly contesting every foot of ground. "Numerous barricades were encountered, and trees were felled across the road," a 5th Corps staffer reported. Robinson progressed steadily through thick timber and a little after eight o'clock emerged into the Alsop farm, three miles below Todd's Tavern. Here Brock Road forked. The eastern branch was called the new road, the western one the old road. The dirt tracks ran more or less parallel for about a mile and reunited on the northern edge of a field named after the Spindle family. These two clearings— the Alsop farm, where the road forked, and Spindle's Field, where the two branches came back together—were to become critical landmarks in the battle taking shape.[10]

Rebel artillery—Captain Philip P. Johnston's battery of Breathed's battalion—had drawn up near the Alsop house and opened on Warren's approaching column. The Confederate gunners tarried, and their battery mired in the rutted field, which had been freshly plowed for corn. Johnston's men worked frantically to drag the pieces to safety. The easy mark enticed the 13th Massachusetts, of Lyle's brigade, which redoubled its musketry.

Cavalry suddenly emerged into the clearing from adjacent woods. Assuming the riders were Federals, the Massachusetts troops stopped shooting. But when the horsemen pitched lines over the guns and began dragging them toward the far ridge, it became evident that they were rebels. Elements of the 13th Massachusetts sprinted into the field, blazing away. The rebel artillerist Captain Johnston hung on until three of his pieces had been hauled to safety. Then a bullet ripped through his shoulder. The hard-pressed rebel cannoneers limbered up the final gun, but a volley disabled the lead and swing teams of horses, and the wheel team driver fell with a shattered arm. "Surrender that gun, you rebel scoundrel," cried the Yankees. Breathed hurled himself from his horse, cut loose the injured teams, and mounted a wheel horse. A Federal recalled Breathed putting his thumb on his nose and wriggling his fingers in derision. Dodging through a hail of bullets, Breathed brought the gun into Fitzhugh Lee's lines. "Almost as by a miracle," remarked one of Stuart's aides, the plucky major emerged unscathed.[11]

Warren ordered Robinson out Brock Road's eastern fork, where his soldiers continued driving Lee's cavalrymen and their annoying horse artillery. Griffin's division came up next and was directed out the western route. His brigades under Brigadier General Romeyn B. Ayres and Colonel Jacob B. Sweitzer marched on the road while Bartlett's brigade followed a ravine through woods to the right. "The men were very much blown," a participant remembered, "and many had fallen by the way from sunstroke and fatigue." A staffer thought them "frightened from some inexplicable cause; the tendency to stampede was so great that General Warren himself had to go to the front of the leading brigade." One of Denison's colonels recalled a mood of "positive exhilaration, as the impression gained ground that Lee's army was in full retreat upon Richmond, and that we had in our immediate front only his rear guard of cavalry and horse artillery, maneuvering to cover his retreat."[12]

The dogged rebel cavalrymen fell back along Brock Road to a low ridge south of Spindle's Field known as Laurel Hill. They had been waging a bitter delaying action for five hours, a cavalry division against the Army of the Potomac. "Times were getting very serious with us," a soldier in the 4th Virginia Cavalry conceded.[13]

The situation was even more serious than Fitzhugh Lee and his troopers realized. James Wilson's Union cavalry division had occupied Spotsylvania Court House and was preparing to advance up Brock Road behind Lee.

Wilson had camped southeast of Chancellorsville during the night of May 7–8, with Colonel George H. Chapman's brigade at the Silver house, near where Catharpin and Orange Plank roads branched, and McIntosh's brigade at Tabernacle Church, closer to Spotsylvania. Early in the morning, Sheridan had instructed Wilson to advance along Fredericksburg Road to Spotsylvania Court House, then to cross the Po at Snell's Bridge. Wilson understood that Burnside's 9th Corps was to follow on the same route.[14]

Moving promptly as ordered, Wilson's column clipped south to Fredericksburg Road, McIntosh in advance. It brushed aside rebels—probably some of Wickham's men—at the Ni River, then clattered into the courthouse town around 8 A.M. Fitzhugh Lee learned of Wilson's advance from pickets but could offer no serious resistance, because he needed his entire force at Laurel Hill to fight Warren. He realized the necessity for action when word arrived that Wilson had occupied Spotsylvania Court House. Lee was now sandwiched between Warren to the north and Wilson to the south. He responded by pulling the 3rd Virginia Cavalry from Laurel Hill and sending it down Brock Road toward Spotsylvania, hoping to retard Wilson.[15]

Wilson recognized opportunity when he saw it. From Spotsylvania Court House, he was superbly situated to terminate Fitzhugh Lee's stranglehold on Brock Road. Acting decisively, he directed his brigade under McIntosh to follow Brock Road north as far as Lee's rear. Chapman's troopers meanwhile occupied the village and scouted toward Snell's Bridge.[16]

During the night of May 7–8, Anderson's Confederate infantrymen followed Pendleton's makeshift trail south. His artillery and wagons rumbled down an existing road below Parker's Store. The two columns converged at Shady Grove Church, then swept down Shady Grove Church Road toward Spotsylvania Court House. About daybreak, Anderson found a suitable bivouac where Shady Grove Church Road crossed the Po at the Block House Bridge, named after a prominent structure constructed from squared logs. A short way over the river, the route intersected Old Court House Road, which led northeast to Brock Road a little over a mile away. Old Court House Road and Brock Road converged at Laurel Hill, where Fitzhugh Lee, joined by Stuart, was deploying his cavalry.

By 7:30 A.M., Kershaw's division and most of the 1st Corps' artillery had drawn up near the Block House Bridge. Musketry from Lee's action crackled across woods and fields from a mile away. "It indicated that a great many people were bound for Spotsylvania beside ourselves," observed Anderson's artillery chief, Brigadier General Edward Porter Alexander.[17]

Like a bizarre apparition, an old Virginia gentleman—bareheaded and shoeless—arrived at the 1st Corps' bivouac in a cloud of dust. He came from Fitzhugh Lee with an urgent message. Virginia cavalrymen were holding off Grant on Brock Road, he reported, but the Yankees were forming to attack. Unless reinforcements came immediately, the Confederates would be overwhelmed. Another courier—a young man named Pegram

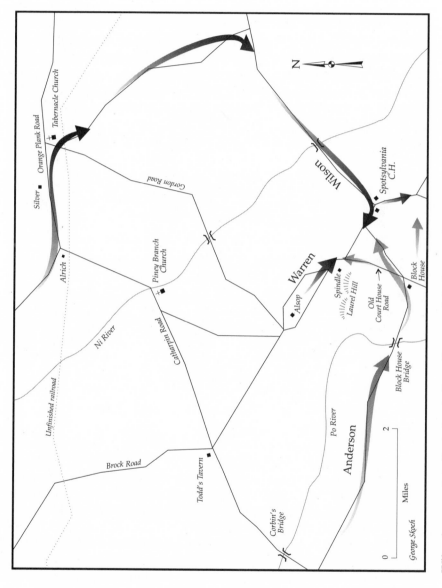

Wilson's approach to Spotsylvania Court House, and Anderson's response

George Skoch

from Baltimore—appeared on the heels of the first. Major John C. Haskell's artillery battalion was parked at the head of Anderson's column. Pegram rushed up and showed Haskell a dispatch from Stuart, addressed to General Lee and Anderson. In it, Stuart warned that he was hard pressed and needed artillery. After scribbling on the dispatch that he was hurrying to Stuart's aid, Haskell set off with two batteries "as fast as I could."[18]

Anderson summoned Kershaw and ordered the stately South Carolina planter to start for Brock Road at once with Colonel John W. Henagan's South Carolina brigade, formerly commanded by Kershaw, and with Brigadier General Benjamin G. Humphreys' Mississippians. Still another courier rushed up, and reported that Wilson's cavalry had just entered Spotsylvania Court House. Help was urgently needed there as well. Fitzhugh Lee had dispatched the 3rd Virginia Cavalry to drive Wilson back, but the single regiment was not equal to the task. Anderson again acted with decision and ordered Kershaw's remaining brigades—two Georgia units under Brigadier Generals Goode Bryan and William T. Wofford—toward the courthouse town.[19]

Henagan's and Humphreys' infantrymen, along with Haskell's gunners, made for the Spindle place with all possible speed by way of Old Court House Road. "A severe and increasing musketry fire told that the situation was growing critical," the artillerist Alexander observed. Stuart was waiting to guide the soldiers onto Laurel Hill, and Anderson offered him command of the field. "Hush, hush, boys. Be quiet. Don't say a word," Stuart cautioned, relishing the surprise he was about to administer to Warren's unsuspecting Federals. "Run for the rail piles," he ordered. "The Federal infantry will reach them first, if you don't run." Kershaw's men climbed Laurel Hill from behind—"as if by magic," a soldier said—and slipped behind the makeshift barricade. Stuart directed Haskell where to place his guns.[20]

Stuart—"cool as a piece of ice, though all the time laughing," a southerner noted—threw Henagan's brigade across Brock Road, the 3rd South Carolina east of the roadway in a copse of pine trees, the 2nd South Carolina to the west. Henagan's remaining regiments extended toward the Po. Humphreys' Mississippians shuttled next to Henagan and pushed the formation eastward. Skillfully, Stuart exploited the ridge's contours and eased some of Humphreys' elements ahead of the main line on the right, where they were superbly positioned to enfilade the Unionists when they charged. Henagan achieved similar advantage by thrusting soldiers into a finger of woods on the field's western fringe. "Hold your fire until the Federals are well within range," Stuart admonished, "and then give it to them and hold this position to the last man. Plenty of help is near at hand."[21]

One of Henagan's men looked across the Spindle farm. A "gallant column" was approaching from the north along Brock Road. It was Warren's corps, Robinson's division leading. After marching all night to get ahead of the Army of Northern Virginia, the Federals had arrived just minutes late.[22]

Warren, resplendent in a major general's uniform, pounded to the front of his column on his huge dapple gray charger. He appeared strikingly thin on the oversized horse. His hair gleamed jet black, as did his eyes, which a passing soldier thought put life into the "darkly sallow face." Warren was eager to make up time and conferred with Robinson. The heavily bearded Robinson—an officer proclaimed him the hairiest general in the Union army—warned that Lyle's brigade had pushed ahead of the rest of the division. He inquired if he could wait to charge until his other brigades caught up.[23]

Warren pondered his options. Confederates were plainly visible a few hundred yards ahead along the crest of Laurel Hill, stacking rails and pine trees as breastworks. The best approach, Warren concluded, was to attack at once, before the rebels had a chance to burrow in. "We must drive them from there, or they will get some artillery in position," he instructed Robinson.[24]

Warren returned to the Alsop house to hurry reinforcements forward. He ordered Breck's battery onto high ground next to the dwelling and thrust Martin's battery into the apex where Brock Road's two branches came together. Denison's Marylanders and Coulter's men straggled up and collapsed from "utter exhaustion." Robinson now had his entire division at the front. Griffin's division meanwhile hurried down Brock Road's western branch, with Bartlett's brigade tramping along a ravine to the right. One of Bartlett's colonels asked permission for his men to stack their knapsacks before charging. "No," Bartlett answered. "There is no force in our front but cavalry. March right up the road by fours."[25]

Warren was at his imperious best. "Never mind cannon," he shouted, gesturing crisply at the end of each sentence. "Never mind bullets. Press on and clear this road." Appealing to his troops' practical instincts, he added, "It's the only way to get your rations."[26]

By this time—it was around 8:30 A.M.—the heat had become unseasonably oppressive. "The sultriest day of the year," a correspondent called it. Fitzhugh Lee's stubborn horsemen, Warren thought, had to be near their breaking point. Coulter and the Marylanders were still forming, so Robinson ordered Lyle to charge alone along the road's east edge. Pulling up on Robinson's right came Bartlett, spoiling for a fight. The 83rd Pennsylvania and 44th New York constituted Bartlett's first line, the 1st Michigan and 18th Massachusetts his second. Two sections of Griffin's artillery drew up to cover the advance. "Hurry up, or you won't get a shot at them," Bartlett shouted, pointing across Spindle's Field.[27]

Lyle's brigade, massed in column of regiments, stepped into the Spindle clearing along the eastern edge of Brock Road. Bartlett's brigade followed suit, slightly behind Lyle and to his right. "The men were too much exhausted either to run or to yell," a Pennsylvanian observed as they shuffled into the bright spring sunlight. The remainder of Robinson's and Griffin's units pulled up behind them. Brass buttons, guns, and bayonets glistened in the sun. Banners floated in the breeze.[28]

Musketry opened from Laurel Hill. Undeterred, Lyle's troops clambered over a split-rail fence and through a stand of pines. The musketry intensified, and blue-clad forms began dropping. Lyle's sweating soldiers reached a tangle of felled pine trees the Confederates had strewn as obstacles. Just ahead, on the brow of Laurel Hill, loomed a breastwork of logs and fence rails. It should fall easily, Warren predicted, just like the other barricades. "Up to this time we thought we were fighting cavalry," Warren's aide Major Washington A. Roebling explained.[29]

At Stuart's command, a "solid and withering volley" from the 3rd South Carolina chewed into Lyle's ranks. Almost simultaneously, the 2nd South Carolina joined in. The Confederates were firing downhill, and their initial shots went high. A large portion of Lyle's brigade broke and ran for protection toward woods to the rear. Elements led by Lieutenant Colonel Charles L. Peirson continued to the foot of Laurel Hill, where they dropped to the ground and sought cover in dips and depressions. They could neither attack nor retreat, and standing was out of the question.[30]

"There appeared to have been miscalculation somewhere."

The 5th Corps rolled forward in waves. Robinson fed Denison into action in column of regiments along the west side of the roadway. Robinson and Denison rode at the head of the Maryland brigade to coordinate it with Lyle. Robinson was eccentric, but his troops had become accustomed to his ways. "He hedged himself with so much strict official dignity," a soldier observed, "that he concealed many of the good qualities he possessed." The troops respected his steadiness and called him Old Reliable.[31]

The Marylanders were too fatigued to realize they were assaulting until

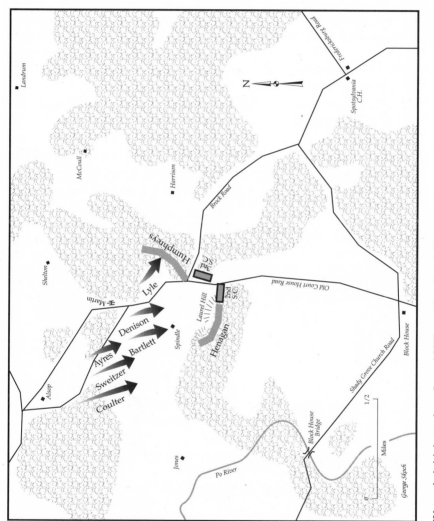

Warren's initial attack on Laurel Hill, on May 8 at 8:30 A.M.

they heard the command "Battalions forward, guide center, march." The Confederates watched Warren's approach with consternation. "In every direction I could see Federal troops deploying to my right and left," the Mississippian Humphreys recounted, but he added, "I determined to hold my position." Southern infantry blazed away while Haskell's artillery spewed projectiles into the approaching blue forms.[32]

About halfway across the clearing, Denison's Marylanders paused to shoot and reload—a costly mistake. Rebel lead seared their ranks. Robinson and Denison rode high on horseback and made inviting targets for Henagan's South Carolinians. "The place must be ours," Robinson shouted and spurred his mount. A bullet slammed into his left knee. Another projectile tore into Denison's right arm. "What remained of the movement was no longer a column, but a bunched and ragged line," a Marylander saw. "At points where the enemy's fire was most concentrated, the drone of bullets blended into a throbbing wail, like that of a sonorous telegraph wire pulsing in a strong wind, punctuated by the pert *zip* of the closer shots." Leadership devolved on Colonel Charles E. Phelps, commanding the 7th Maryland. Riding to the front of the column, he drew his saber, pointed toward the breastworks, then went down in a cloud of dust and lay pinned under his wounded horse. A captain who tried to rescue him toppled over with three balls through his body. Phelps survived but was dragged from the battlefield by rebels as his brigade fled in shambles across the clearing.[33]

Bartlett's lead elements charged on the right side of the Marylanders. The 16th Michigan, serving as skirmishers, approached Laurel Hill slightly askew and became entangled in slashings. The 44th New York and 83rd Pennsylvania, in Bartlett's first line, buckled under blistering volleys from those of Henagan's units which had been thrust forward on each side of the gently undulating field. Bartlett's second line—the 1st Michigan and 18th Massachusetts—pressed into the leaden hurricane but could make no headway. The foremost troops, bayonets fixed, became enmeshed in log and brush abatis. The 44th New York shot back at short range, and a few soldiers from the 83rd Pennsylvania mounted the rebel barricades next to the road, pitching into the South Carolinians like "infuriated tigers." Humphreys observed that "for the first and last time in my warring, I saw two hostile lines lock bayonets."[34]

The Pennsylvanians, however, were few and unsupported. Those who vaulted over Henagan's barricades were killed or captured. The rest traded stand-up musketry with Henagan's men at short range. A galling enfilading fire from Humphreys on the rebel right rendered Bartlett's position untenable, and the brigade fell back across Spindle's Field "without much regard for order." A Pennsylvanian called the charge "madness." A New Yorker agreed that there had been "miscalculation somewhere."[35]

On the Union right, where Bartlett was giving way, Griffin pumped in his remaining units under Ayres and Sweitzer. Soldiers poured down the ravine in Bartlett's footsteps, while a brass band urged them on with stirring martial airs. Colonel George Ryan, who had miraculously survived the charge across Saunders' Field three days before, called to his 140th New York, "Follow me"—which it did, still in its marching column of four abreast. Ryan tumbled from his horse riddled with bullets, and Bartlett's fugitives swamped his regiment. A few soldiers started up the slope toward the rebels but bolted "semi–panic stricken" when Haskell's batteries chimed in. The 11th United States Infantry careered into the remains of the 140th New York, which dissolved in "great confusion." A soldier remembered minié balls "flying like hailstones, while nearly every minute a shell would go over our heads." The 12th United States Infantry suffered heavily, and the 17th Regulars, which went into the fight with five hundred men, came out with only seventy-five. "They got flanked and lost their colors within a few yards of the enemy's breastworks," a diarist related. A colonel in the 155th Pennsylvania put it simply: "Charging the enemy's position, found them in too large force to push forward our column."[36]

Warren ordered Coulter's brigade toward the woods west of Spindle's Field hoping to salvage his offensive, but a leaden blast from Henagan's Confederates scored Coulter's line from left to right. A New Yorker reported that every man who could get back did so without delay.[37]

Stuart rode back and forth along Laurel Hill, seemingly invulnerable. A South Carolinian remembered him "sitting on his horse amidst a storm of bullets, laughing and joking with the men and commending them highly for their courage and for the rapidity and accuracy of their fire." On the far side of Spindle's Field, Warren sat erect on his charger, grimly watching the wreckage of Griffin's and Robinson's divisions stream back.[38]

Humphreys' Mississippians completed Warren's rout by edging around Lyle's eastern flank. Charles Peirson, of the 39th Massachusetts, ordered his color-bearer to run back, and Lyle's remnants rose and followed. The retreat, Peirson explained, "was exceedingly slow, and we lost heavily." When the color-bearer fell wounded, Peirson seized the flag and handed it to the nearest man. He too was shot, but managed to continue on. Then Peirson went down, his clothes riddled with bullet holes and a load of rebel buckshot in his elbow. An officer dragged him to the Union line.[39]

"We continued our rain of lead into their ranks," a South Carolinian remarked. "The field in our front was blue with the dead and wounded Federals." The Confederates briefly held their fire when one of Lyle's men turned back toward them, hefted a comrade onto his shoulder, then loped for the woods. "No Confederate gun was trained on that man," a rebel explained. "We all admired his pluck and imagined the picked-up body was that of his kinsman or friend."[40]

Warren, horrified at the turn of events, rode onto the field and seized a Maryland regiment's shattered flagstaff in an attempt to rally the fugitives. But nothing could hold them. The Marylanders sustained almost two hundred casualties, including their commander and several officers. Lyle's brigade was no longer a functioning unit. The 16th Maine reported nearly a hundred casualties. Captain W. C. Kinsley, of Company K, 39th Massachusetts, was heard to cry out, "Look at my company. Only seven men left out of eighty-seven!" Coulter was thoroughly routed. A brass band struck up "Hail Columbia" to inspire the men, but they "kept right on to the rear," an onlooker recounted, "helped along wonderfully by a few rebel batteries which administered an extra dose of 'Hail Columbia' as they retreated through the woods." Regrouping at the Alsop house, a Pennsylvania regiment counted fifty losses.[41]

The 5th Corps' collapse jeopardized Martin's battery, which was still parked where the two branches of Brock Road reunited at the northern edge of Spindle's Field. The gunners had maintained a steady fire of two or three shots a minute over the Union infantrymen's heads, and smoke hung so heavily in the still air that it obscured their view. Shattered 5th Corps elements rallied around the guns, but their stand was short-lived. Spying a rebel force slipping past the makeshift line, the 22nd Massachusetts' Colonel William S. Tilton ordered a retreat.[42]

Martin's gunners were exhausted. "We were doing all that mortal man could do, our tongues hanging so low out of our mouths we were liable to step on them," a Federal remembered. Things became particularly harrowing when two pieces jammed in a fence. Quick-thinking cannoneers double-shotted the guns, fired into the approaching Confederates, and "ripped them apart." The reprieve was brief as more rebels pounded up and Haskell's artillery on Laurel Hill redoubled its fire. A bullet laid open Martin's neck to the spine, and command devolved on Lieutenant Aaron F. Walcott, who evacuated the guns under a shower of shot and shell to a knoll near the Alsop house. A participant described a breathtaking race with southerners close behind. "It seemed to be every man for himself, and the devil for us all." Haskell's artillery continued to maul the battery even after it had reached the Alsop place.[43]

Robinson's and Griffin's divisions re-formed in the Alsop yard, where the rest of the 5th Corps' artillery was massing. It took a while for the disaster's magnitude to sink in. Robinson's badly mangled leg had to be amputated, and his division was so cut up that its brigades were assigned to other 5th Corps divisions. An artilleryman described the Alsop homestead as a "gruesome sight, and one calculated to make the observer feel the dangers of war very keenly." A young cavalry officer lay wounded on the porch. Captain Martin was stretched out with blood oozing from his neck, and Lieutenant Colonel Frederick T. Locke, Warren's popular assistant adjutant general, lay writhing in agony with part of his face shot away.[44]

Warren's sullen troops blamed the fiasco on their superiors. "A feeling prevailed that proper foresight had not been exercised in ordering an inadequate force to make the charge," a Pennsylvanian reported. The affair, asserted a New Yorker, was "certainly very poorly managed," and the charge had been "dissipated by dribbling into the attack regiment after regiment, each succeeding one too late to be of any service to the one which had gone before." Not surprisingly, the generals found fault with their soldiers. "The enemy's fire was not heavy enough to justify the breaking of the men," one of Warren's aides expostulated. "It was chiefly owing to their being excited, somewhat scared, and hurried entirely too much." Apparently Warren had learned nothing in the Wilderness. He pumped unsupported units into action and squandered his greatest advantage, an overwhelming edge in numbers.[45]

Grant's worst fear had materialized. Lee's infantry had won the race. The Army of Northern Virginia's vaunted 1st Corps had swung squarely across his route south. He should have beaten Lee to Spotsylvania. He had the shorter route, better roads, and a head start. Surprise was his ally. Yet he squandered his advantages. The result was an escalating confrontation involving only a portion of his force. What had gone wrong?

Responsibility lay at virtually every level of the Union command. Grant had devised too ambitious a plan. He had failed to consider the logistics of moving so many troops and to provide for inevitable delays. Meade had neglected the details, failing to ensure that Brock Road was clear and even obstructing the way with his staff and provost guard. Orange Plank Road became so congested that Sedgwick and Burnside—fully half the Union infantry—were lost to Grant. And subordinate commanders seemed oblivious of the need for haste. The artillerist Wainwright put it aptly in his journal: "The fact of our march at night was enough to tell every man that we wanted to reach some place without Lee's knowing it; and one would think that a desire for their own safety would spur them all up to do it, so as to avoid a fight." The picture is that of an army without a firm sense of purpose and the will to see its plans through. Grant had fumbled in the Wilderness. As he groped toward Spotsylvania, there was no sign that he had learned from his mistakes.[46]

Not only were the Federals doing almost everything wrong, but the Confederates seemed to be doing everything right. Although Lee had failed to grasp that Grant was heading to Spotsylvania with his entire army, Anderson had acted with decision. Unpleasant conditions in the Wilderness induced him to start early, and the absence of acceptable resting places led him to push steadily on, outdistancing Grant in the process. Unknown to Anderson, the bivouac that he selected placed him where he would be needed most. And on receiving Fitzhugh Lee's summons for help, he had responded without delay. Anderson's performance on May 8 ranked as the most significant contribution of his military career.

Stuart's and Fitzhugh Lee's dogged delaying action had been magnificent. This had been one of the Confederate mounted arm's finest days. A soldier remarked that the cavalry had finally shown itself "signally possessed of the quality that the infantry and artillery naturally admired most in others—obstinacy in fighting." After the war, Lee's aide Lieutenant Colonel Charles S. Venable related that the "conduct and skill of Stuart in this fight on the 8th, on which so much depended, always met the warm approval of the Commanding General, and he spoke of it, with grateful remembrance, in the days of March, 1865, when disasters began to crowd upon us."[47]

At 10:15 A.M., Warren informed Meade that Robinson and Griffin had been repulsed "in much confusion." With luck, he thought, their troops could "perhaps be assembled again today." But Warren was not about to quit. He had been criticized in the Wilderness for delaying until every unit was in place. Today, with his corps at the army's front, he saw an opportunity to redeem his reputation. The remaining 5th Corps divisions—Cutler's and Crawford's—were advancing in "fine style," he assured Meade, and could be expected to reverse the morning's ill fortunes. As fresh troops came pouring through the Alsop clearing, Warren waved them toward the little ridge below the Spindle house.[48]

But time was against Warren. While Cutler and Crawford girded to dash across the Spindle farm, sorely needed reinforcements were filling Anderson's earthworks. At about 8 A.M., Charles Field's soldiers—finishing what one of them described as a "most fatiguing night march"— reached the 1st Corps' bivouac by the Po and consumed a hasty breakfast of cold rations, accompanied by musketry from the Spindle place and Spotsylvania Court House. Anderson dispatched Brigadier General Evander M. Law's brigade, now under Colonel William F. Perry, to join Humphreys and Henagan at Laurel Hill. Some of the newcomers resented hav-

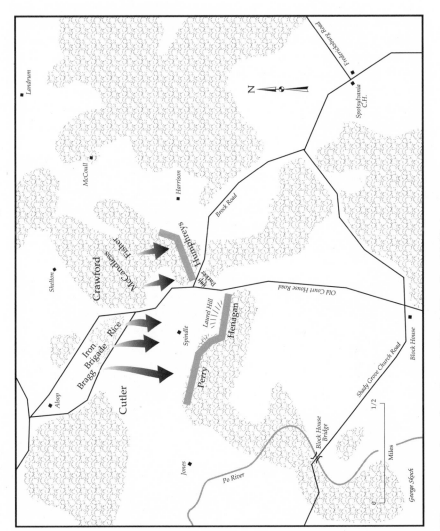

Warren's second attack on Laurel Hill, on May 8 at 10:30 A.M.

ing to rescue Stuart's cavalrymen and told them "to get down off their horses and go and fight them; that they hadn't tried to keep them back; and that they were not going to help them until they got rested." Field's remaining brigades started toward the village to fight Wilson.[49]

Stuart greeted Perry's Alabamians as they puffed up the back slope of Laurel Hill. He ordered the 15th and 48th Alabama, under Colonel William C. Oates, to Henagan's left and directed the rest of the brigade to fill in where they were needed. More artillery rumbled up. Lieutenant Colonel Frank Huger's battalion, twenty-five guns in all, went to Haskell's right, and Colonel Henry C. Cabell's outfit buttressed the far Confederate left, providing a firm anchor near the Po. If Warren wanted to resume his ill-considered charges, Stuart was prepared for him.

In preparation for renewed battle, the Confederates destroyed the Spindle homestead, which occupied a small rise between the emerging battle lines. It was a simple wooden farmhouse of two and a half stories, with an orchard and outbuildings nearby. At the outbreak of war, Sarah Spindle lived there with five children and eighteen slaves. At least one son was fighting in Lee's army. His mother was inside eating breakfast on May 8 when the battle swirled into her yard. Federal sharpshooters occupied the dwelling and its outbuilding and began picking off South Carolinians across the way. To end the nuisance, the Confederates hurled incendiary shells into the house. "And then I saw a sight I never wanted to see again," a southerner reminisced. Sarah Spindle, her hair streaming behind her, darted from the flaming building and crossed the field between the armies toward the Po to seek shelter.[50]

Warren's plan for regaining the initiative had engaging simplicity. Elements from Griffin's division had established a line that began near the junction of the two branches of Brock Road on the northern fringe of Spindle's Field. This was to become the Union formation's nucleus. Cutler was to march onto Griffin's right flank and secure it. Crawford was to press into the void on Griffin's left created by Robinson's repulse.[51]

The Wilderness had dealt harshly with Cutler's division, which had started the campaign under Brigadier General James S. Wadsworth, a fifty-six-year-old New Yorker of considerable wealth. Wadsworth had been mortally wounded leading a foolhardy charge on May 6, and the division had taken serious casualties. Cutler, who had led the fabled Iron Brigade, assumed command. Now he marched his division through a ravine, formed it on Griffin's right, and dutifully moved out under Anderson's guns. "He advanced in fine style," a staffer reported, "all his bands playing." The hopeful beginning, however, deteriorated rapidly into a familiar nightmare.[52]

A Pennsylvania brigade under Colonel Edward S. Bragg formed Cutler's right wing. Bragg came under "very rapid" fire from rebel cannon, veered into a finger of woods, and ran headlong into Oates's Alabamians. A soldier in the 143rd Pennsylvania commented that his regiment had "struck a bees nest and sent them a buzzing." The brigade's right wing recoiled from the woods, which enabled the rebels to concentrate against the remaining Pennsylvanians, who dropped to the ground or sought shelter behind stumps. A soldier pinned by the deadly Confederate cross fire observed that it "didn't take long to discover that a stump would only cover from one direction."[53]

The Iron Brigade dashed to Bragg's support. Heavy musketry sounded along Cutler's front as his men knelt in the woods, firing as quickly as they could into the dense foliage that obscured the portion of Laurel Hill before them. Hoping to deter a flank attack, the 2nd Wisconsin formed at right angles to the 7th Wisconsin. Their fears were borne out as Oates's Alabamians marched up a ravine that funneled onto their right end. "Outflanked both ways and pressed by the enemy on both sides, the line broke in disorder," Colonel Rufus R. Dawes, of the 6th Wisconsin, reported. Cutler's officers finally rallied the Iron Brigade and Bragg's troops. Advancing from tree to tree in a brutal round of combat, they drove Oates back to Laurel Hill. "Here we received and returned a very brisk fire for half an hour," Oates was to recall, "when they retired beyond range."[54]

Then Brigadier General James C. Rice's mixed New York and Pennsylvania outfit pushed onto the Spindle farm. Henagan's skirmishers barred the way, and soon Rice and the South Carolinians were fighting "like tigers." Unable to hold, Rice retired to the clearing's far side, and Cutler ordered the rest of his division back. A stand of "hateful" Confederate colors waved from Laurel Hill and so irked Bragg's Pennsylvanians that they busied themselves trying to shoot it down. They thoroughly riddled the banner, but the staff remained upright. "We soon had good breastworks built and made us some coffee, and got our rations," a soldier in the 143rd Pennsylvania wrote, "but the flag in the fence was an eye sore to us all."[55]

While Cutler assaulted without success west of Brock Road, Crawford attempted to advance east of the roadway. Misfortune dogged him from the start. A Confederate artillery shell knocked a tree onto him, stunning him. Colonel William M. McCandless assumed command and ordered a charge but sustained a severe hand injury. The Pennsylvania Reserves became "somewhat mixed up" and floundered knee-deep in a swamp while Porter Alexander's artillery raked them with shrapnel. In an officer's words, the charge did not "come off." Crawford withdrew and slipped onto Griffin's left wing to extend Warren's line eastward.[56]

Taking a cue from Anderson's Confederates, Warren's troops began constructing defensive works north of Spindle's Field. It was a spontaneous act of self-preservation. Across the way, Anderson's rebels used the respite to refine their defenses by running poles along the top of their works, braced with short sticks underneath to form openings for shooting. "The pole saved many a head," a Confederate recounted. To enable an increased rate of fire, the rebels spread cartridges on the ground and jammed their ramrods under the head logs. "It is astonishing how fast troops that are practiced can load and fire," a Confederate boasted. "The old trained veterans decided that the only way to succeed was to be quick and deliberate, fire with precision, so as to kill as many as possible; but after a slaughter of thousands in a few days they seemed to multiply like flies that had been poisoned."[57]

Troops had taken advantage of man-made structures before. The unfinished railway bed at Manassas, the stone wall at Gettysburg, and the sunken roads at Sharpsburg and Fredericksburg all lent themselves to military use. Western armies felled logs for protection at Chickamauga, the Army of the Potomac fashioned breastworks on Culp's Hill, at Gettysburg, and in November, 1863, the Army of Northern Virginia erected formidable barriers above Mine Run. The art of constructing log barricades and scooping out trenches with bayonets and cooking gear progressed by leaps and bounds in the Wilderness. Then Fitzhugh Lee advanced the craft on May 7 and 8 by demonstrating that dismounted cavalry behind well-placed fence rails could delay an army. Now Anderson's men were adding refinements as they came to recognize that only ingenuity could compensate for their sparse numbers.

The initiative had slipped through Warren's fingers. Headquarters, however, did not realize how completely the fighting spirit had been beaten out of him. "Attack vigorously," Meade urged in a noon dispatch. "Let the men know it is our interest to prevent a concentration to stop our march, and that they should drive them." Warren responded with a rambling epistle that reflected his humiliation at the sharp reverse. "I have done my best," he insisted, "but with the force I now have I cannot attack again unless I see very great weakness on the enemy's left flank. I incline to think, that if I let the enemy alone he will me." The 5th Corps had suffered heavily, he added, going on to complain, "My staff is all tired out, and I have lost the old white horse"—his mount. "I cannot gain Spotsylvania Court House with what force I have," he emphasized, and he closed with a dismal postscript: "I dare not fall back, for then I shall disclose my feeling of weakness."[58]

Warren had badly managed the Laurel Hill assault. Brigades went into action piecemeal, reinforcements failed to arrive when needed, and artillery support was negligible. There was no maneuvering. Troops simply marched across open ground into the teeth of concentrated Confederate firepower. Ironically, Warren took pride in being a "scientific soldier." Meticulous preparation was his strong point, and blind assaults were anathema to him. Yet his conduct on the morning of May 8 illustrated only the futile blood-letting he professed to abhor.

Warren must have experienced an unsettling feeling as his bloodied ranks dug trenches along the Spindle clearing's northern edge. Three days earlier, the 5th Corps had met Lee in the Wilderness. On that occasion, Warren had bided his time, waiting for his troops to form and for Sedgwick's supporting corps to arrive. Meade, however, had refused to delay until Warren's dispositions were complete and had ordered the 5th Corps ahead. The result had been a bloody repulse for which Warren was severely criticized.

No doubt still smarting from Meade's reproaches, Warren had not dallied at Laurel Hill. As quickly as troops pulled up, he had hurled them at the rebels. Predictably, the results were the same as in the Wilderness. A few Confederate brigades, well entrenched, had repulsed Warren's entire corps. Laurel Hill further lengthened the shadow over the young New Yorker's fortunes.

"He had worked himself into a towering passion."

While Warren battered in vain against Laurel Hill, McIntosh's brigade of Wilson's cavalry, the 1st Connecticut leading, circled through Spotsylvania Court House and swept north, endangering Anderson's vulnerable rear. The 3rd Virginia, which Stuart had dispatched to detain Wilson, retired north up Brock Road, fighting a vigorous but futile action.[59]

Anderson, however, had rallied to the danger posed by Wilson's surprise visit by sending two of Kershaw's brigades to Spotsylvania with orders to loop below the town and hit Wilson from behind. If possible, Kershaw was to "capture the entire party." Soon after those two brigades started out, Field's division arrived, and Anderson directed three of his brigades to move directly on the courthouse town. If all went as intended, Wilson would be caught in a vise formed by Field and Kershaw, isolated behind the Confederate lines and outnumbered.[60]

Before Anderson could spring his trap, McIntosh reached the rear of Laurel Hill. A Yankee shell almost killed Porter Alexander, who frantically swung his artillery around to confront the new threat. But just as

McIntosh began pressing his attack, Wilson received alarming news. Kershaw was approaching. "It was evident," Wilson reported, "that, unless promptly supported by Burnside or other infantry from the rear, I should have to give up the advantageous position I had so easily gained." Concerned for his division's safety, Wilson canceled McIntosh's attack and ordered him back to Spotsylvania. It had been a close call. As the horsemen began withdrawing, Field's Confederates appeared and began tightening the Confederate encirclement around the Yankee interlopers.[61]

A courier from Sheridan spurred up and alerted Wilson that he risked being cut off. Burnside had not followed as Sheridan had expected, and reinforcements were unavailable. Wilson needed no further information. Three days before, on his first independent mission, he had become separated from the army and had almost been captured with his entire division. He quickly withdrew up Fredericksburg Road, retracing his earlier movement. Just as his rear guard left Spotsylvania Court House, Kershaw stormed in. Bullets ricocheted through the little town.[62]

Wilson later boasted that his division was the only part of Grant's army to occupy Spotsylvania Court House. He maintained that if Burnside had pushed promptly through the Wilderness, he might have arrived in time to secure the position for the Federals. In Wilson's estimation, "With such a union of cavalry and infantry in Lee's right rear, there would have been nothing left for him but to fall back to a new position beyond the next river, or suffer an overwhelming defeat." Deploring the "great opportunity lost," Wilson claimed that had he been reinforced, "the bloody battle which took place for the capture and defense of Spotsylvania Court House would have been avoided and many thousand lives would have been spared to continue operations under much more favorable circumstances."[63]

Wilson's hypothetical suppositions were flawed. Burnside could not have assisted him. When Wilson set out from the Alrich place, near Chancellorsville, the 9th Corps had not yet left the Wilderness. Burnside did not start his march until almost 8 A.M. on the eighth, and his most forward element—Brigadier General Orlando B. Willcox' division—did not reach Chancellorsville until around noon. By then, Wilson had been to Spotsylvania, fought his skirmish, and returned. Even if Burnside had found a way to catch up with him at Spotsylvania, his troops might not have contributed much. Not only would they have been exhausted but they would have faced the same formidable opponents who two days before had repelled a Federal force several times their size. There is no reason for confidence that Burnside's inexperienced troops could have defeated the Confederates arrayed against them.[64]

What gave Wilson the notion that the 9th Corps was going to support him at Spotsylvania remains a mystery. Grant's plan of May 7 envisioned Burnside tagging behind Sedgwick and advancing through Chancellorsville as far as Piney Branch Church on Catharpin Road. Meade's orders noted only that "General Burnside's command will follow the Sixth Corps." At 8 A.M. on the eighth, Grant directed Burnside to stop at the Alrich farm to protect the army's supply trains. No mention was made of his supporting Wilson. Indeed, Grant and Meade apparently had no idea that Wilson was moving to Spotsylvania Court House, and there is no indication that Sheridan told them about the young cavalryman's mission until after Wilson had returned. It is possible that Wilson's misunderstanding concerning Burnside originated with Sheridan, whose grasp of Meade's plan was muddled. As Sedgwick's infantry collected around the Alrich place, Sheridan undoubtedly learned that Burnside was also on the way. Perhaps he misconceived Burnside's route, and from that error grew the further misunderstanding that Burnside would arrive in time to support Wilson. The strained relationship between Meade and Sheridan was hampering the army, and Grant was neglecting his responsibility to coordinate Meade and Burnside.

The day had been a fiasco for Meade. First had come Merritt's failure to punch through Fitzhugh Lee's barricades, then Warren's disaster at the Spindle farm. As headquarters perceived it, Warren's played-out troops lacked "nerve for a vigorous attack," and Robinson's division had "behaved badly." It was hot and dusty, and nothing was going right.[65]

Grant took the reverses with equanimity. Awaking at sunrise, he removed his coat and shook it vigorously to get rid of the dust. Oblivious to the nearby pigpen, he shared soldier's rations with his staff, then sat on the ground for a smoke. As the morning wore on, he decided to move down Brock Road to its junction with Piney Branch Church Road. That was more evenly between the two advancing columns, of Warren and Hancock on Brock Road, Sedgwick and Burnside rolling through Chancellorsville. It was also a more open spot and inspired lighter spirits. A drum corps caught sight of Grant and struck up a popular Negro air. "What's the fun?" asked Grant, who was tone-deaf. "Why, they are playing, 'Ain't I glad to get out ob de wilderness,'" a staffer answered. Grant laughed. "Well, with me a musical joke always requires explanation. I know only two tunes. One is 'Yankee Doodle,' and the other isn't."[66]

The feud between Meade and Sheridan escalated sometime around noon. Meade considered the botched advance to be Sheridan's fault. In his view, if Sheridan had cleared Brock Road as ordered, the army would have been at Spotsylvania rather than digging trenches along the northern fringe of Sarah Spindle's farm. Meade meant to give him a piece of his mind. Sheridan was boiling too. As far as he was concerned, Meade had made a perfect mess of his cavalry dispositions and had unnecessarily endangered Wilson. It was purely through luck that the division had managed to extricate itself from Spotsylvania Court House before the rebels closed in.

Sheridan strode into Meade's tent, and things went downhill from there. Several witnesses observed the fireworks and wrote about them later. Sheridan immediately sensed that Meade's "peppery temper had got the better of his good judgment, he showing a disposition to be unjust, laying blame here and there for the blunders that had been committed." As the aide Porter recalled it, "Meade was possessed of an excitable temper which under irritating circumstances became almost ungovernable." These were such circumstances. "He had worked himself into a towering passion regarding the delays encountered in the forward movement," related Porter, "and when Sheridan appeared went at him hammer and tongs, accusing him of blunders, and charging him with not making a proper disposition of his troops, and letting the cavalry block the advance of the infantry." Sheridan was not about to suffer Meade's abuse in silence. He responded that if his cavalry had been in the way, it was because Meade had changed their orders without his knowledge. "I also told him," Sheridan recounted, "that he had broken up my combinations, exposed Wilson's division to disaster, and kept Gregg unnecessarily idle, and further, repelled his insinuations by saying that such disjointed operations as he had been requiring of the cavalry for the last four days would render the corps inefficient and useless before long."[67]

Meade was very irritated, Sheridan recalled, "and I was none the less so." A witness described Sheridan's language as "highly spiced and conspicuously italicized with expletives." Meade composed himself at one point and apologized, but the gesture fell on deaf ears. "Sheridan was plainly full of suppressed anger," Lyman recalled, "and Meade too was in ill temper." Sheridan also got in a swipe against Warren. He had seen nothing that explained the 5th Corps' failure to advance, he sneered. The infantry's behavior was "disgraceful." The exchange climaxed with Sheridan proclaiming that he could whip Stuart if Meade would only let him. Since Meade insisted on giving directions without consulting him, Sheridan declared, Meade could assume command of the cavalry corps and he would not issue another order. Meade placed his hand on Sheridan's shoulder and said, "No, I don't mean that." The cavalry commander impatiently pulled away and stomped out.[68]

Meade stalked over to Grant's tent and narrated the conversation. When he got to Sheridan's remarks about whipping Stuart if Meade would only let him, Grant perked up. "Did Sheridan say that?" the rumpled general asked, his calmness in stark contrast with Meade's excitement. "Well, he generally knows what he is talking about. Let him start right out and do it."[69]

At 1 P.M., Meade's chief of staff Humphreys issued orders granting Sheridan his request. "The major-general commanding directs you to immediately concentrate your available mounted force, and with your ammunition trains and such supply trains as are filled proceed against the enemy's cavalry." Sheridan was free to test his mettle against Jeb Stuart, but the Army of the Potomac was to pay dearly. It was losing its cavalry at a time when the mounted arm's reconnaissance was sorely needed.[70]

"It nearly melted the marrow in our bones."

With Wilson's threat gone, Anderson turned his full attention to Warren. He recalled his infantry units that had been diverted to Spotsylvania Court House, forming Field on Kershaw's left to create an unbroken line of infantry that stretched from the Po across Brock Road and about a half mile to the right. Stuart directed the rest of Anderson's artillery into place. "With bright, pleasant, smiling face, he returned our hearty salute with a touch of his hat," a Confederate noted. Mud-splattered troopers from the 3rd Virginia lounged on the ground, recuperating from their fight against McIntosh.[71]

Private William M. Dame, of the Richmond Howitzers, peered over Laurel Hill. He could see Warren's corps several hundred yards away, filling the clearing from the Alsop place to the Spindle farm. "There were lines of infantry, batteries, wagons, ambulances, ordnance trains massed all across the open ground," he observed. The spectacle "looked very blue," he conceded, "and I dare say, we looked a shade 'blue' ourselves." Rebel gunners hauled their pieces just behind Laurel Hill's crest, where a slight rise masked them. Only the muzzles were visible to the Unionists. Stuart rode along the artillery placements. "Boys, I want you to knock them all to pieces," he called, gesturing toward the Federals. "So go to work."[72]

"Fourth detachment commence firing, fire," Captain Edward S. McCarthy, of the Howitzers, shouted. Private Dame jerked the lanyard. "A lurid spout of flame about ten feet long shot from the mouth of the old 'Napoleon,'" Dame noted, "then, in the dead silence, a ringing, crashing roar, that sounded like the heavens were falling, and rolled a wrathful thunder far over the fields and echoing woods." The entire 1st Corps' artillery, more than fifty guns, let loose. A cloud of snow white smoke puffed open. "We gave a yell of delight," Dame recounted. "Our shell had gone right into the midst of the Federals, and burst beautifully." More puffs appeared, and shrapnel scoured the northern line. Dame could see men running wildly about and teamsters furiously lashing their horses. "All was in confusion, worse confounded," he gleefully observed. "We saw one wagon, flying like the wind, strike a stump, and thrown, team and all, a perfect wreck, on top of a low rail fence, crushing it down, and rolling over it."[73]

Warren's response was not long in coming. By about 11:30 A.M., Colonel Wainwright had arrived with the rest of the 5th Corps' ordnance. He stationed Breck's, Captain Charles E. Mink's, and Captain George B. Winslow's batteries near the Alsop place, from where they commanded the shallow valley that funneled into the Spindle farm. Walcott's and Lieutenant James Stewart's batteries jangled forward to the wooded triangle where Brock Road's two branches joined. Rebel sharpshooters kept the gunners under "very ugly fire" from a finger of woods east of the road.

Alexander's cannonade exploded over Wainwright's two frontline batteries. Wainwright ordered Stewart to straddle the road with his lead section and to extend his remaining guns to the right, with Walcott's next to them. "Walcott's men did not behave well, nor did he push them forward as well as he might," Wainwright later observed. Stewart remained steady, but some of his men wasted valuable time dodging. "All this obliged me to keep in the open ground among the guns myself, until I could get them quieted down and firing to please me," explained Wainwright. Rebel sharpshooters made Wainwright a special target, and their shots kicked up dust around his feet. The colonel ordered his staff away and tried to keep his horse between himself and the "rascals."[74]

Martin's pieces, under Walcott's temporary command, rolled up to the northern edge of Spindle's Field. The gunners, swinging their caps and cheering, immediately began firing. "It seemed we had struck a hornets nest by the yell they gave us," recalled George Bucknam, of the 3rd Massachusetts, Battery C.[75]

Wainwright estimated that he faced Confederate guns equal in number to his. His pieces, however, were exposed, whereas Laurel Hill protected the rebels. "We could only see the puffs of smoke from their explosions,"

Wainwright observed. Fortunately for the Federals, the Confederates were firing high. Wainwright directed his gunners to explode their shells on top of the ridge line. The tactic, he could record, proved effective.[76]

To Dame, the air seemed filled with projectiles: "bursting shells, jagged fragments, balls out of case shot, it sounded like a thousand devils, shrieking in the air all about us." It was, he concluded, the "hottest place I ever saw, or hope I shall ever see, in this world, or in the world to come. It nearly melted the marrow in our bones." Wainwright called the affair "one of the prettiest little duels I have seen" and declared it an even match. "Had they run their guns up to the top of the knoll so as to get a good sight of us," he confided in his journal, "the chances are that we should have got the worst of it, for their skirmishers hurt us badly."[77]

A Union gunner, Augustus Buell, left a vivid account of the exchange. "We always considered the work of the battery the first day of Spotsylvania as the finest piece of purely artillery practice under difficulties of position and ground that it had ever made," he observed. Hitting rebel pieces while dodging ricocheting shot and exploding case required precise marksmanship. "On the whole," Buell concluded, "it is always easier for a battery to face infantry at close quarters, with all the attendant excitement and enthusiasm of such a fight, than to stand up under a cold-blooded and methodical cannonade such as that of Spotsylvania." The artillery duel petered out sometime around 1 P.M. Aside from making life miserable for the participants and soldiers huddled nearby, it accomplished no military purpose. Neither side could drive the other with artillery alone.[78]

If artillery could not budge the rebels, infantry had to handle the job. The tenor of Warren's dispatches made it clear that the 5th Corps could not accomplish the task alone. Reinforcements, however, were close at hand. Hancock's 2nd Corps was massed three miles north, at Todd's Tavern, and Sedgwick's 6th Corps was advancing from Chancellorsville along Catharpin Road, headed Warren's way. At 1:30 P.M., Meade issued instructions calculated to bring on a grand assault. "Sedgwick's whole corps is sent to join you in the attack," he informed Warren. "It is of the utmost importance the attack of yourself and Sedgwick should be made with vigor and without delay." Meade decided to leave Hancock at Todd's Tavern in case Lee tried to spring a surprise assault from that quarter. The push toward Spotsylvania would be made by two corps rather than three.[79]

Despite Meade's urgent orders, five hours were to pass before Sedgwick and Warren were prepared to mount a joint offensive. By then, Anderson's two Confederate divisions had been augmented by three more divisions under Ewell, destroying any chance of a Union breakthrough. Why did Sedgwick take so long to move into place? And by detaining Hancock at Todd's Tavern, did Meade unnecessarily restrict his ability to attack Laurel Hill?

Sedgwick exhibited a lackadaisical mind-set typical of the Federal leaders on May 8. His aide Hyde summarized the situation perfectly: "The dim impression of that afternoon is of things going wrong, and of the general exposing himself uselessly and keeping us back, of Grant's coming up and taking a look, of much bloodshed and futility."[80]

The 6th Corps had been delayed by ambulances carting wounded soldiers from the Wilderness. It passed through Chancellorsville around dawn and halted for breakfast at 9 A.M. After a half hour to boil coffee and wolf down rations, the procession started off again, with Major General Horatio G. Wright's division hurrying toward the sound of Warren's battle. The troops turned abruptly right onto Catharpin Road and made for Todd's Tavern. "The day had been the most sultry of the season," a surgeon recalled, "and many of the men, overcome by the intensity of the heat, and exhausted by the constant fighting and marching since the morning of the 4th, had fallen by the wayside." An officer termed the march distressing. Undergrowth shut out a feeble breeze and men shuffled along in dust to their ankles. Before noon, they stumbled into the hamlet of Piney Branch Church in a state of near collapse.[81]

At 1:30 P.M., Meade directed Sedgwick to advance to Spotsylvania Court House and join Warren in a "prompt and vigorous attack on the enemy now concentrating there." He was to make "every exertion to move with the utmost dispatch." Sedgwick's haggard soldiers pried themselves from the ground and trudged down Piney Branch Church Road—the same route that Davies' cavalry brigade had used the previous day. An hour later they reached the Alsop place and formed on Warren's left. "We saw the usual signs of battle in mangled men brought to the rear on stretchers," a Massachusetts man recounted. "Found woods afire and bodies of Reb and our men just killed and scorching," scribbled an aide. "The sight made the heart sick." A gunner in Battery B of the 1st New York Light Artillery expressed a common sentiment. "I think of home and those who are at church," he scrawled. "Such a Sabbath it is."[82]

As Sedgwick's lead elements arrived, Warren demanded excitedly, "What brigade is this? Where is the commanding officer? I want to move this brigade forward at once. I must have this brigade." The soldiers belonged to the 6th Corps' New Jersey brigade, "very much exhausted by the hot march." They dutifully shuffled onto the wooded slope above the Spindle farm. By then, active fighting had sputtered out. "The forces opposed to us," a New Jersey man noted, "were fully occupied in entrenching and strengthening the line they held."[83]

Under Meade's direction, Sedgwick extended the Union line eastward, opposite Kershaw. Thorny questions arose concerning who would direct the proposed assault. Warren knew the ground, but Sedgwick was senior. In light of Warren's sagging spirit, Meade preferred Sedgwick, but he was hesitant to declare his preference. Warren had provided valuable service at Gettysburg and was close to Meade. Reluctant to humiliate his former staffer, Meade chose a middle course that satisfied nobody. He rode out to inspect the lines, grumbling in disgust about the earthworks that seemed to be sprouting everywhere. The advance had ground to a standstill. "Warren, I want you to cooperate with Sedgwick and see what can be done," he directed. "General Meade," Warren retorted, "I'll be damned if I'll cooperate with Sedgwick or anybody else. You are the commander of this army and can give your orders and I will obey them; or you can put Sedgwick in command and he can give the orders and I will obey them; or you can put me in command and I will give the orders and Sedgwick will obey them; but I'll be God damned if I'll cooperate with General Sedgwick or anybody else." The strain was clearly affecting him.[84]

Around 3:30, Lyman joined Meade, Sedgwick, Warren, and Wright. He was struck by the generals' "worn and troubled aspect, more especially in Sedgwick, who showed its effect more from contrast with his usual calmness." In Lyman's opinion, "Never were officers and men more jaded and prostrated." Hard marching, sleepless nights, and protracted fighting had "produced a powerful effect on the nervous system of the whole army." Sedgwick seemed distraught by the absence of his favorite unit. "Where is the Vermont Brigade?" he fretted. "Not up yet. Just when I wanted it. Everything unlucky."[85]

An hour later, Meade and Grant reconnoitered with their staffs. Sedgwick had formed on high ground on Warren's left. Skirmishing rippled along the front. Grant went exploring where the musketry seemed most intense. "We could not see a thing except our own men lying down," Lyman later informed his wife. "But there we sat on horseback while the bullets here and there came clicking among trunks and branches and an occasional shell added its discordant tone." Neither Warren nor Sedgwick could predict when they would be ready to assault. It seemed to Lyman that Grant was angry that things were not moving faster "and so thought he would go and sit in an uncomfortable place" where the firing was thickest. Meade outdid Grant, lingering under fire longer. Lyman breathed a sigh of relief when he was directed to show Grant the way back to headquarters.[86]

Brigadier General William H. Morris, heading one of Sedgwick's brigades, later described the chaos riddling the Federal command. His outfit and another under Colonel Benjamin F. Smith constituted the infantry component of Brigadier General James B. Ricketts' division. Shortly after 3 P.M., Morris reported to Warren, who pointed out where he was to form and ordered him to coordinate his actions with Wright. Then Sedgwick's chief aide rode up with instructions from Meade for Morris to move to the left. There was no time to communicate with Ricketts, the aide explained, but he assured Morris that he would inform Ricketts of what had occurred. No sooner was the movement under way than the aide reappeared and instructed Morris to halt and await further orders. Shortly afterward, one of Meade's staffers directed Morris to move farther left. After complying with these latest orders, Morris sought out Meade and inquired if his line was where Meade wished. "He seemed satisfied," recounted Morris. Soon, however, Roebling, of Warren's staff, appeared and told Morris to shift to the right so as better to face the enemy. Then Warren cantered by and remarked that Morris should advance his left. "All this I communicated to General Ricketts," the befuddled general reported.[87]

Finally, around 6:30, Meade had patched together a unified line above the Spindle farm. Meade was there to direct Warren and Sedgwick. Dust-caked soldiers in blue squinted ahead, wondering what new discomfort awaited them. The answer lay just across the clearing, where a line of slouch hats peered back over Laurel Hill. Perhaps Lyman evaluated the situation best. "I think there was more nervous prostration today among officers and men than on any day before or since," the aide concluded, "the result of extreme fatigue and excitement." General Patrick remarked on Meade's "circling and swooping as usual." Grant's aide Comstock shared the pessimistic mood. "Time wasted until dark when it was too late to produce any result," he wrote in his diary.[88]

"The great battle of Todd's Tavern was never fought."

The paralysis gripping the 5th and 6th Corps seemed to have infected the normally energetic 2nd Corps. Hancock was still drawn up at Todd's Tavern, where Meade had positioned him to guard the Union army's rear. "I do not remember ever to have known Hancock appear so anxious regarding the discharge of any duty as he did this day," an aide recalled. Barlow occupied the field west of Todd's Tavern that Colonel Gregg's cavalry had fortified the previous evening. Gibbon extended Barlow's left wing in a sweeping arc back to Brock Road. Brigadier General Gershom Mott's division did the same on Barlow's right, and Birney bivouacked in reserve at the tavern.[89]

Gregg's horsemen meanwhile reconnoitered west on Catharpin Road to Corbin's Bridge, over the Po River. At their approach, Hampton's Jeff Davis Legion launched a brutal charge that ended abruptly when Confederate reinforcements failed to materialize. Hampton retired to the Po's far bank, but dust clouds boiling up behind him deterred Gregg from pursuing. From the look of things, rebel infantry were massing to attack.[90]

Around 11 A.M., Nelson Miles dispatched his brigade, Gregg's horsemen, and an artillery battery to the Po. Hampton's ordnance opened from above Corbin's Bridge, so Miles extended his infantry along both sides of Catharpin Road and replied with his guns. In the distance, well behind Hampton, Miles could see a "seemingly interminable column" of Confederates moving southeast along Shady Grove Church Road. Hampton later boasted about his successful bluff. "Placing artillery in position," he wrote, "their advance was soon checked, their skirmish line lying down under our fire." Meade reacted in ill humor to the standoff. "Why didn't [Hancock] reinforce it?" he snapped, referring to Miles's brigade. "I would as soon fight there as anywhere."[91]

Anticipating that Lee might attack along Catharpin Road, Meade decided to keep Hancock at Todd's Tavern. Warren, however, asked Hancock for a "good division" without first clearing the request with Meade. Assuming that Warren had secured Meade's approval, Hancock ordered Gibbon toward the Alsop place and extended Barlow and Birney to fill the gap. When Meade learned what had happened, he ordered Gibbon to halt short of the Alsop house. "I believe I did right in sending [Warren] a division," Hancock sheepishly explained to Meade. To his inquiry what he should do if Warren renewed the request, Meade answered that Sedgwick's arrival rendered Hancock's assistance unnecessary.[92]

Signs multiplied of an impending rebel attack against Hancock. Around 3 P.M., more dust and smoke billowed up behind Hampton, prompting Meade's chief topographical engineer, Nathaniel Michler, to investigate. Michler confirmed that Confederates were tramping south behind Corbin's Bridge in considerable numbers. Which units they belonged to and where they were going he could not say, but Hampton clearly had several guns in position and was not shy about using them.[93]

Two of Miles's regiments under Lieutenant Robertson—the 81st Pennsylvania and the 26th Michigan—remained stationed north of Catharpin Road near the Po. The rest of Miles's brigade—the 61st New York, the 183rd Pennsylvania, and the 140th Pennsylvania—deployed about a half mile back. In midafternoon, Gregg left to join Sheridan at the Alrich place, which required Miles to extend his pickets northward to plug the vacancy created by the mounted arm's departure. Robertson was scouting out a track above Catharpin Road when he heard Confederate voices shouting, "Come on in, you damned Yankee, we'll take good care of you." He spurred his horse over a fence and sped back into Miles's line "with my saddle under my horse, instead of under me." Gray-clad soldiers from the Confederate 3rd Corps came swarming behind him.[94]

The harried Federal commanders would have been delighted to learn that Lee was having difficulties as well. For the second time in two days, he faced the agonizing task of selecting a corps head. Hill had been plagued with ill health and by the morning of May 8 was too sick to command. A reporter thought that Hill's impatience over his incapacity was hindering his recovery. Having already puzzled through the selection of Longstreet's replacement, Lee quickly reached a decision. "General Hill has reported to me that he is so much indisposed that he fears he must relinquish the command of his corps," he wrote Ewell. "In that case, I shall be obliged to put General Early in command of it."[95]

Assigning Early to command the Confederate 3rd Corps afforded Lee the opportunity to make other changes. John Gordon had impressed Lee in the Wilderness as a talented commander with an eye for offensive warfare. Lee placed him in charge of the 2nd Corps division Early had headed. That necessitated transferring the Louisiana brigade that had been under Brigadier General Harry T. Hays, who outranked Gordon, to another division. Lee solved the problem by consolidating Hays's brigade with the Louisiana brigade that had been under Brigadier General Leroy A. Stafford, who was mortally wounded in the Wilderness, and assigning the enlarged outfit to Edward Johnson's division. To equalize the size of the reconstituted 2nd Corps divisions, Lee shifted Johnston's brigade from Rodes's division to Gordon. With accustomed tact, Lee had juggled his command structure to make room for his most promising generals.[96]

Lee remained uncertain about Grant's objective. At dawn on May 8, he sent patrols forward to determine whether Grant's entire force had left the

Wilderness. Climbing over the recently abandoned earthworks, they discovered a "rich field of spoils." Order evaporated as the Confederates became a "wild and reckless mob, rushing hither and thither in search of plunder." A detachment from the 11th Alabama stumbled onto a field of horses, equipped with bridles and saddles, that had been deserted by the Federals. The delighted Alabamians raced around the clearing on their new mounts. One soldier had a particularly difficult time controlling his steed but finally reigned up and announced, "Captain, he tried to nullify, but damn him, I hilt him to it!"[97]

Positive intelligence that Grant had left the Wilderness, combined with insistent reports from Stuart that Federals packed Brock Road leading south, confirmed for Lee that Grant meant either to pass through Spotsylvania Court House on his way toward Richmond or to occupy it to protect his lower flank while he retired toward Fredericksburg. In either event, Lee perceived Spotsylvania as an ideal spot to mount his defense, and he decided to move his entire army there. Circumstances dictated the route. The 3rd Corps, which occupied the trenches south of Orange Plank Road formerly held by the 1st Corps, would remain in place. The 2nd Corps would slip behind the 3rd and join the 1st at Laurel Hill. Then the 3rd would close up the rear. "I desire you to move on with your corps as rapidly as you can, without injuring the men," Lee directed Ewell. "I will proceed to Shady Grove Church, and wish you to follow me on to that point." Then he informed Richmond of his decision. "The enemy has abandoned his position and is moving toward Fredericksburg," Lee telegraphed the Confederate war secretary. "This army is in motion on his right flank, and our advance is now at Spotsylvania Court House."[98]

Around 10 A.M., Ewell started south along Hill's former earthworks to the Chewning farm and thence to Parker's Store. "Moved very slowly at first," a Virginian remarked, "but as soon as we got strung out, we went like race horses." The route traversed the previous days' battlefield and was "very oppressive," a soldier in the Stonewall Brigade noted, "owing to the fact that the brush on both sides of the narrow road had been set on fire; and the men were almost suffocated by the dense clouds of smoke rising from the decaying leaves and numberless blankets." Ewell's column hit Catharpin Road near White Hall and jogged left toward Shady Grove Church, sharing the route with women and children dressed in their Sunday finest. Ewell's cartographer paused to savor the sights and smells of spring. "The trees are just getting fully out," he jotted in his diary. "The apples and peaches in full bloom."[99]

Around 3 P.M., Early started the 3rd Corps south in Anderson's wake along Pendleton's makeshift forest road. Mahone's division led, followed by Major General Henry Heth's, then Wilcox'. Lee had instructed Early that when he reached Catharpin Road, he was to proceed east to Todd's Tavern, then press south along Brock Road to Spotsylvania Court House. Little did Lee realize that Hancock was firmly entrenched at Todd's Tavern, awaiting precisely the move that he was contemplating.[100]

Early decided to send his most forward division—William Mahone's— on a reconnaissance in force before committing his corps to Lee's proposed route. Mahone's assignment was to follow Pendleton's road south to Catharpin Road, then to scout east to determine if Federals occupied Todd's Tavern and, if so, in what strength. Hampton in the meantime reported to Early that Miles's Federal brigade held portions of Catharpin Road and offered to assist Mahone. As the plan developed, Mahone was to send Colonel David Weisiger's Virginians, supported by two brigades, south along Pendleton's trail to Catharpin Road. At the same time, one of Hampton's brigades under Pierce Young was to attack eastward along Catharpin Road. His other brigade, under Rosser, was to charge Miles's flank and rear.[101]

With evening descending, Hancock thought a Confederate attack unlikely and started to breathe easier. Then Mahone's rebels came screaming down from the north. It was this force that surprised Lieutenant Robertson. Hampton simultaneously attacked from the west. "Both movements were executed handsomely and vigorously," Hampton reported.[102]

Miles hastily reoriented his line facing north toward Mahone, throwing three regiments above Catharpin Road and two below, their left flanks bent back to prevent Hampton's cavalry from punching through. In the confusion, a Union wagon jammed against a tree, forcing the panicked driver to abandon a considerable supply of hardtack. Then a herd of hamstrung cattle sent to feed Miles's men stampeded. For a short while it was difficult to tell whether cattle or Confederates posed the greater threat.[103]

Hampton's troopers slammed into Miles's leftmost elements. A Michigander related that when the southerners reached the provisions—"hundreds of boxes of hardtack, barrels of beef and pork and sugar, the like of which they had not seen for a long time"—they halted and started gathering booty. Miles opened fire, but the hungry rebel troopers were not about to abandon the rations. Then Hampton's horse artillery chimed in with a "terrible shelling." According to Hampton, Miles retreated "rapidly and [left] us in possession of his camp, with the rations that had just been issued to him." One of Rosser's officers called to the Federals to come back and get what belonged to them. "You Johnny Rebs have noth-

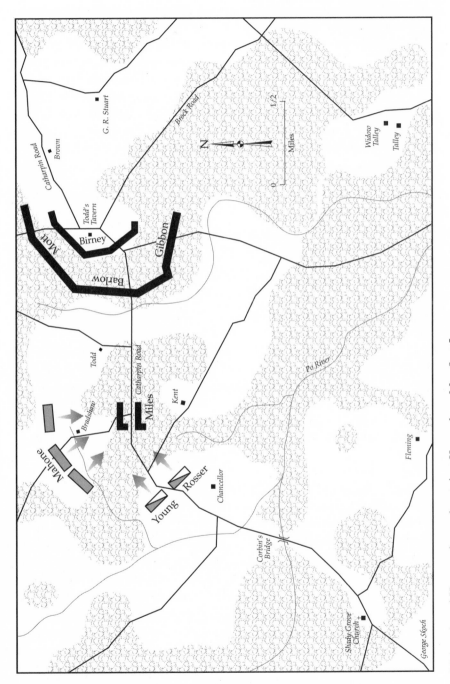

Mahone's and Hampton's attacks against Hancock on May 8 at 5 P.M.

ing but corn bread to eat, and we want you to have a good square meal," Miles's men shouted in reply.[104]

Mahone also performed "hot work" on Miles's right, flanking the 61st New York and overwhelming the 140th Pennsylvania with "superior numbers." Then the 183rd Pennsylvania folded, which imperiled Miles's entire line. Performing a feat that won him a medal of honor, Robertson seized the colors and rallied the 183rd Pennsylvania. "The line was saved," Robertson wrote, "and our little brigade was proud." But the Pennsylvanians remained skittish. "The 183rd tried to run again," Robertson added, "but we got them stopped by cutting some of them down with our swords."[105]

Combat raged fiercely around the Bradshaw house, north of Catharpin Road. A 12th Virginia contingent rushed the dwelling but was repelled by galling fire. "How the balls did whiz through those old buildings," a Confederate remarked. The place changed hands several times before the southerners finally overran it.[106]

Hancock ordered Colonel Thomas A. Smyth's Irish Brigade into the fray to extricate Miles. The 116th Pennsylvania was holding a prayer meeting, which closed with a solemn Amen as the soldiers ran toward the sound of musketry. Mahone's Confederates fought obstinately, leaving Hancock no choice but to bring Miles and Smyth back to Todd's Tavern. There they resumed the positions they had held in Barlow's entrenched line, facing west across Catharpin Road. The 116th Pennsylvania was cut off in Smyth's withdrawal but returned at nightfall to demonstrations of "gladness and joy."[107]

Just when the fighting seemed over, Hampton's troopers attacked dismounted, punching in Hancock's pickets and charging his works. Hancock easily broke the assault from behind his entrenchments. Early toyed with sending Heth's division into the fight but decided against it. Renowned for his stubbornness, this time Early wisely elected to call off the contest. "This affair developed the fact that the enemy was in possession of Todd's Tavern and the Brock Road," he reported, "and a continuation of my march would have led through his entire army." He recalled Mahone and bivouacked his corps near Shady Grove Church. Horsemen from Cobb's Legion, of Young's cavalry brigade, deployed in the fringe of woods facing the Federals and kept up a skirmish fire until nine or ten that night.[108]

The fracas left Hancock on edge. "Expectation of battle was now at its height," the adjutant Francis A. Walker recounted, "as it was not doubted that the Confederates were attempting to 'counter' upon General Meade, answering his advance upon Spotsylvania by a movement into his right and rear." More Union artillery rumbled to Todd's Tavern, and Gibbon rejoined the corps. Reports arrived that rebels were descending Brock Road, but reconnaissances as far north as the Trigg farm found nothing. "And so the Second Corps stood to arms," Walker observed, "all the afternoon and into the early evening, believing that another of its great days of battle had come." But Hancock's apprehension was for naught. As Walker put it, "Darkness came on, and the great battle of Todd's Tavern was never fought." By dint of reputation and good fortune, Lee had immobilized the Army of the Potomac's premier corps.[109]

Meade was later criticized for failing to bolster his Laurel Hill line with Hancock. The reporter William Swinton deemed Meade's decision to detain the 2nd Corps at Todd's Tavern "very unfortunate," the consequence of "rather timid generalship." In Swinton's opinion, "The army, having been cut loose from the Wilderness, should have been pushed to Spotsylvania with the utmost vigor." He hypothesized that a modest force at Todd's Tavern, such as Miles's brigade, would have sufficed to protect the Federal rear. With the rest of Hancock's troops joining Warren and Sedgwick at Laurel Hill, the Confederate line—held by only two divisions—would certainly have collapsed. According to Swinton's critique, Meade's caution had once again forfeited an excellent opportunity.[110]

Swinton's criticism drew on hindsight. A single Federal division behind earthworks might indeed have sufficed to hold Todd's Tavern against Early. But Meade was unsure of the whereabouts of several Confederate units, and Hancock's reports suggested considerable enemy activity on Catharpin Road. He reasonably assumed that Lee might attack along Catharpin Road, and perhaps down Brock Road as well. Although Meade's decision reflected his obsession with safeguarding his flanks and rear rather than thinking offensively, his positioning of Hancock made sense in light of what he knew at the time.

"I cannot tell you the half or tenth part of the terrors of that horrid night."

While Early and Hancock sparred, Ewell pushed south along Shady Grove Church Road. Around six in the evening, his lead element—Rodes's division—reached Block House Bridge. Anderson's Laurel Hill line lay just ahead. The marchers suffered "unmistakable signs of extreme fatigue, and began to fall out at every shade." Night was fast approaching, but musketry signaled that Ewell's work had not ended. Brigadier General Stephen D. Ramseur hurried along Ewell's column with a message from Anderson. Everything would be all right, the 1st Corps commander assured Ewell, if the 2nd Corps could arrive in time to block Meade's anticipated evening

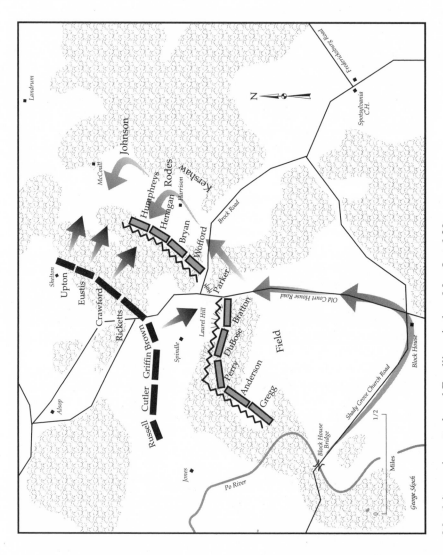

Meade's evening attack and Ewell's arrival on May 8 at 6:30 P.M.

offensive. "Some of the men were so tired and worn out they could hardly halloo," a North Carolinian noted.[111]

Meade was determined to clear the road to Spotsylvania before dark. Anderson's two divisions held Laurel Hill, but Warren's and Sedgwick's six divisions extended well past the Confederate line's eastern end. Meade's plan was to pin Anderson in place with a frontal attack by Colonel Henry W. Brown's New Jersey brigade and Ricketts' division while Crawford's Pennsylvania Reserves, buttressed by units from the 6th Corps, circled around his eastern flank.

The New Jersey brigade, a seasoned combat outfit, occupied trenches immediately west of Brock Road. Dead Zouaves sprinkled the Spindle farm in front of them, their blue jackets and red trousers imposing colorful patterns on the newly plowed field. At 6:20, Meade initiated his attack by directing the 3rd and 15th New Jersey to "develop the enemy's strength and position." The 3rd regiment stretched out into a skirmish line. The 15th followed, more tightly massed. When the Federals came within fifty yards of Laurel Hill, Anderson's Confederates "poured in a deadly shower of bullets, with hideous yells," reported a Yankee. A few Federals reached the rebel works only to be killed or captured. The 10th New Jersey came to their assistance but withered under a "most galling fire" and was swiftly repulsed. The ill-advised affair lasted only a few minutes and cost the Union brigade 150 casualties. "It was a terrible thing to lay some of our best and bravest men in a long row on the blankets," a chaplain lamented. "All this dash, so costly to us, accomplished nothing."[112]

Ricketts' division, which straddled Brock Road, was to advance in tandem with Brown's men. Sedgwick canceled the charge, however, when he discovered that Parker's Confederate battery would enfilade Ricketts' advancing line. On Ricketts' left, Crawford's 5th Corps division and Brigadier General Henry L. Eustis' 6th Corps brigade moved out alone to turn Anderson's right flank. An onlooker noted that "deafening musketry and a dense volume of smoke rolled up from the place."[113]

The Pennsylvania Reserves marched in two lines, Colonel William C. Talley's brigade in front and Colonel Silas M. Baily's behind. Elements from Griffin's division formed in support. Eustis' brigade, temporarily commanded by Colonel Oliver Edwards, of the 37th Massachusetts, charged on Crawford's left. It was growing dark, forms could scarcely be identified in the pine woods, and the Federals became intermingled as they advanced. Then a "wild, savage yell" rent the forest.[114]

In a breathtaking appearance seemingly orchestrated by fate itself, Ewell's corps swung past Anderson's exposed right flank and plunged toward the approaching Unionists. Rodes's division led the attack. Brigadier General Cullen A. Battle's Alabamians, joined by elements from Colonel John Bratton's South Carolinians of Anderson's corps, hit Crawford head on. "Our brigade was thrown in front of a lot of Pennsylvanians, who seemed to think no one had the right to stop them from going right on to Richmond," a Carolinian reminisced. "But it did not take us more than a couple of hours that evening to convince them this was not the day or time to go undisputed." An Alabamian boasted that Battle's charge "made the saucy Yankees 'about face' and hunt a more comfortable position a short distance further back." Talley was captured, Crawford's second line crumbled, and in the darkening twilight, the confusion became "indescribable."[115]

Battle repulsed Crawford to the Union earthworks and vaulted over the ramparts shouting, "Forward!" Bayonets fixed, the 6th, 12th, and 61st Alabama overran the Pennsylvanians at considerable loss to themselves. A soldier in the 6th Alabama recalled "firing in the direction of the enemy from almost every tree and those who moved to the front were in more real danger from our own men than the Yankees."[116]

Ramseur's Confederates joined the fray. Eustis' leftmost elements— the 10th Massachusetts and 2nd Rhode Island—lost their bearings in a thicket-filled swamp and abandoned the rightmost regiments to fight Ramseur. Reports of rebels slipping through the woods threw Colonel Emory Upton's 6th Corps brigade, which had been slated to assist Crawford and Eustis, into confusion. The 95th and 96th Pennsylvania warily probed the thickets but halted as bullets "zipped past us thick and fast." Upton found himself too busy extricating his men to assist Eustis.[117]

Ramseur plowed into Eustis' and Upton's jumbled elements and drove them back. Then Rodes advanced Brigadier General Junius Daniel's North Carolinians and Brigadier General George Doles's Georgians. Edward Johnson's division pulled up next, and Brigadier General James A. Walker's Stonewall Brigade charged "amid the bursting of the enemy's shell and the hurtling of the deadly Minnie balls." As Ewell's forces became mixed, Battle seized the 3rd Alabama's colors and, with Ramseur's help, tried to restore order. The 3rd Alabama moved up "with a quick step," Battle reported, "but the result did not correspond with my high hopes and confident expectations." They were simply too exhausted to sustain their momentum. A bullet mangled Battle's foot, and Rodes ordered the men back. "Slowly the firing ceased, the litter-bearers came in along the line and bore away the wounded," a Confederate recounted. "The dead, for the time, and in many instances perhaps for all time, were left undisturbed where they fell."[118]

The Union assault had failed. Lyman concluded that the "only result

of Warren's grand plan of attack [was] an advance of the Pennsylvania
Reserves, who came back in a hurry." A soldier in Eustis' brigade thought
that "the thing was so poorly executed that it does not amount to much."
Meade's chief engineer, James Duane, who had helped organize the assault, expected a tongue-lashing from Meade, but the general kept his
composure. "I suppose you did all you could," he consoled Duane.[119]

Pockets of fighting continued well into the night. "It was almost dark
and we knew not which way to go," one of Eustis' men explained, "so
we concluded to make the best of it and stay where we were all night."
The decision raised eyebrows when the men found themselves in a cross
fire between the opposing lines. "I cannot tell you the half or tenth part
of the terrors of that horrid night," a soldier told his family.[120]

A detachment from Griffin's division under Lieutenant Colonel Herring
remained between the armies. "We were alone," a soldier from Maine recalled. "The other regiments had all fallen back; our men were in just the
right mood to fight, —weary, hungry, discouraged, mad." A desperate
struggle ensued, with Confederates seemingly pressing from all sides. "The
air was filled with a medley of sounds," as a survivor put it, "shouts, cheers,
commands, oaths, the sharp report of rifles, the hissing shot, dull, heavy
thuds of clubbed muskets, the swish of swords and sabers, groans and
prayers, all combining to send a thrill of excitement and inspiration to every
heart." Herring's detachment captured a haul of prisoners and the 6th Alabama's flag but lost about 150 of its own men. The Union soldiers remained
wedged between the contending lines until about 3 A.M., when they slipped
back to their earthworks. After the war, Warren commented to Herring that
his "successful engagement" helped compensate for the "many gloomy
repulses so trying to us all."[121]

May 8 was thus a Sabbath of dashed hopes for the Federals. Grant began
the day assuming that he would soon occupy Spotsylvania. At 11:30 in
the morning, he informed Washington that "the best of feeling prevails in
this army, and I feel at present no apprehension for the result." He intended
to join Butler "as early as possible." A little over an hour later—though
Warren lay stymied and Wainwright's artillery barrage was getting nowhere—Grant remained optimistic. He planned for Warren and Hancock
to move by way of the Block House to Dabney Mills the next day, for
Sedgwick to proceed through Spotsylvania to Davenport's Ford, on the
North Anna, and for Burnside to continue on to Chilesburg. By evening
on May 9 he expected the army to be united well below Spotsylvania.
Orders to proceed were issued at 4:10 P.M. Then the evening offensive

failed. "The army will remain quiet tomorrow, 9th instant, to give the men rest and to distribute ammunition and rations," Meade informed his subordinates in a missive that reflected headquarters' change of heart. No more mention was made of offensive operations. Instead, Meade directed the corps commanders to "strengthen their positions by intrenchments." The Army of the Potomac had been foiled, and there was no point denying it.[122]

That night, Meade unburdened himself to Lyman. Burnside, he fumed, had been too late in the Wilderness to "do any good." Sedgwick had been "constitutionally slow," and Warren a bitter disappointment. "I told Warren today that he lost his nerve," Meade blurted, "at which he professed to be very indignant." At a meeting of his corps commanders after dinner, Meade let Sedgwick have it. "I desire you to take command of your own corps," he informed his 6th Corps head, sarcastically referring to Sedgwick's tendency to defer to Warren. After the conference, Warren invited Sedgwick to spend the night at his headquarters, but Sedgwick declined. Feelings were running high, and he wanted to be alone. Accompanied by a few aides, Sedgwick dispensed with tents and blankets and curled up next to a haystack. Even Warren's stamina had failed. "I am so sleepy I can hardly write intelligently," he confessed in a rambling note to Meade.[123]

The Army of the Potomac seemed incapable of executing its commander's will. Anderson defeated Warren's disjointed attacks piecemeal, and by the time Sedgwick arrived, the rebels were up in strength. Meade had been unable to renew the offensive until nearly dark, which gave the Confederate 2nd Corps opportunity to pitch in. And even though Sedgwick and Warren adjoined each other, coordinated action had failed. Warren's aide Roebling later expressed his firm conviction that "had the attack been made in stronger force as was originally intended, it would under the circumstances have doubtless been successful." By Warren's official count, his loss for the day was 1,448 officers and men.[124]

What had gone wrong? Warren was to put his thoughts on paper. "I fought yesterday with all the rapidity possible," he scrawled in a note to Humphreys, "and I know I could have kept going on if supports had been nearby." He added, "If we yesterday had moved according to the programme of the General Order for the day, General Sedgwick would have been so close to me that we should have undoubtedly whipped [Anderson], and all of Ewell that came to his support." Sedgwick, Warren complained, had moved too slowly, and Meade had remained in the rear, depriving the army of a strong guiding hand when it was most needed. Four years later, an officer wrote Warren that "there is a great deal of force in your statements . . . that after Meade's delaying your advance, you had nothing left but to push on the head of column as rapidly as possible in hopes to gain Spotsylvania first."[125]

The shortcomings in Union leadership that stood in the way of victory in the Wilderness were creating even worse nightmares at Spotsylvania. Grant's plans were too complicated, and Meade failed to ensure that his subordinates understood their assignments and worked together. Most important, neither Grant nor Meade provided energetic direction at the front. Meade was incapable of controlling Sheridan and equally baffled coordinating Warren and Sedgwick. He was absent from the front during the crucial morning engagements and equivocated over important decisions later in the day. And Grant appears to have taken no active role in directing the day's warring aside from impulsively backing Sheridan's ill-considered request to ride off with the army's cavalry.

For Lee, May 8 had been a lucky day. At 2:30 P.M., he proudly reported to Richmond that "General R. H. Anderson with the advance of the army repulsed the enemy with heavy slaughter and took possession of the Court House." At 9:00 P.M., following Meade's evening offensive, he sent another terse message. "After the repulse of the enemy from Spotsylvania Court House this morning, receiving reinforcements, he renewed the attack on our position, but was again handsomely driven back." With Ewell filing onto Anderson's right, Lee's position seemed secure. Early was expected the next day with the 3rd Corps, which would unite the Army of Northern Virginia across a formidable front. Lee had won a victory at little cost to himself. Henagan and Humphreys, who had borne the brunt of the fighting, lost fewer than three hundred men. Because of Confederate casualties in the Wilderness and the formidable size of Grant's army, Lee did not believe that he could launch an offensive. He held a strong defensive position, however, and his army's fighting edge remained sharp. Anderson had staved off Meade with only two divisions, and Stuart's cavalry had executed its rearguard action faultlessly, rivaling John Buford's performance at Gettysburg. Despite the Wilderness' toll of Confederate leaders, the army was doing everything Lee asked of it.[126]

During the night, Johnson's division extended Ewell's line to the right. Captain William W. Old, Johnson's aide-de-camp, worked without guides or lights. Keeping to high ground, Johnson's troops filed along the brow of a ridge until they saw camp fires ahead—probably Union pickets near the Landrum House. Then Old deflected the formation south, placing

Steuart's brigade on the extreme right Confederate flank. Ewell, who supervised the deployment, became conspicuously cranky as the night wore on. First, he ordered Captain McHenry Howard, of Steuart's staff, to advance Colonel Witcher's brigade as quickly as possible; then, a few minutes later, when asked about it by Johnson, he denied having issued the order. Not until Johnson began berating Howard did Ewell recollect his earlier order. "Stop, stop, General Johnson," he intervened. "I did give Captain Howard the order—it was an emergency." Later, he got into a "sharp altercation" with Walker over the placement of the Stonewall Brigade.[127]

Lee, Ewell, and Anderson bivouacked at the Block House, behind the 1st Corps' left flank. Unlike the Federals bickering across the way, Lee's corps commanders enjoyed harmonious relations. Ewell relaxed a bit with Colonel Talley, who had been captured leading his Pennsylvania Reserves. As they chatted, Ewell discovered to his delight that the son of an acquaintance from Carlisle, Pennsylvania, was a captain in the Reserves. Ewell offered to parole Talley on the spot, but the colonel politely declined.[128]

"Our generals seem in fine spirits and the men also," a cavalryman assigned to Lee's headquarters wrote home. "Mr. Grant fights with determined obstinacy, but so far with no success."[129]

III

MAY 9

Grant and Lee Shift for Position
and Sheridan Starts South

"The worst was yet to come."

NEITHER ARMY RESTED during the night of May 8–9. Exhausted rebel infantrymen dug trenches with bayonets and tin cups, stacked timber and fence rails in front, and then tossed dirt against the face of the completed works. They laid logs on top to create loopholes for firing and crafted emplacements for artillery, with shallow ditches to protect the cannoneers. Every fifteen to twenty yards they threw back short breastworks—called traverses—at right angles to block flanking fire and to contain the enemy if they tried to punch through. Finally, they cleared fields of fire and erected obstacles fashioned from intertwined branches, called abatis. Near dawn, hungry and sleepy, the tired Confederates sank down "where each one happened to find himself," a rebel acknowledged.[1]

A southern reporter noted that the approaches to Lee's works lay "partly through forest, partly through field, but presented at many points excellent positions for artillery, while those open to the enemy for that purpose were generally much inferior." Anderson's 1st Corps held the formation's left wing, Field's division occupying the mile-long stretch from the Po to the Spindle place, and Kershaw's continuing the line from Brock Road east another half mile toward the Harrison house. Alexander's artillery, fifty-four pieces in all, was arrayed along Laurel Hill, with a formidable concentration at Brock Road. The terrain's natural contours swung north on Anderson's right. There stood rough fortifications erected during the night by Ewell's 2nd Corps. Lee's chief engineer, Martin Smith, examined the position and agreed that the high ground it encompassed had to be kept out of Union hands. The result was a salient, a huge bulge in the Confederate earthworks, later dubbed the Mule Shoe. Rodes's division held the salient's

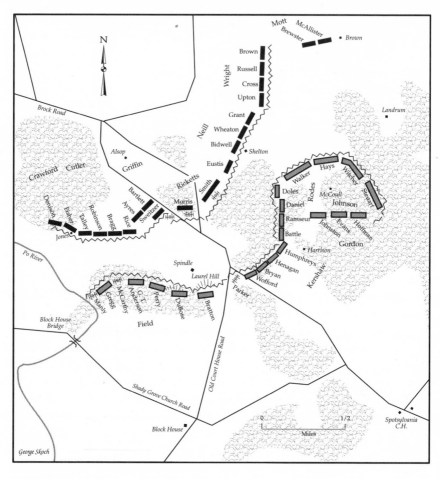

The situation on the morning of May 9

left leg, which extended northeast for about a mile in an uneven curve. Near the apex stood Johnson's division, forming the Mule Shoe's top and then knifing a short distance southward. Gordon's division dug supporting trenches between the Harrison and McCoull houses, near the salient's center. The rest of the projected Confederate line—from the unprotected right end of Johnson's division across Fredericksburg Road and on below Spotsylvania Court House—was to be occupied by Early's 3rd Corps when it arrived from Shady Grove Church later in the day.

Ewell's Confederates felt uneasy about the Mule Shoe. "Our men did not like it all," a Louisianian stated. "It was so liable to be enfiladed by artillery and would be a dangerous trap to be caught in should the line be broken on the right or left." Another southerner called it an "unfortunate work." Lee expressed reservations when he examined the Mule Shoe during the morning but decided to leave things as they were, on Ewell's assurances that he could defend the position.[2]

Grant also labored to strengthen his lines. Warren's 5th Corps manned the earthworks west of Brock Road, facing Anderson. Sedgwick's 6th Corps continued the formation eastward, arching back to follow the contours of Ewell's salient. Hancock's 2nd Corps remained in the rear at Todd's Tavern, and Burnside's 9th Corps camped at Alrich's, on the army's eastern flank.[3]

A no-man's-land, in places only a few hundred yards wide and crackling with musketry, separated the combatants. Artillery shells howled through the darkness, and sharpshooters searched for the glow of camp fires. Death came silently on the wings of a sniper's bullet, devoid of pageantry. Soldiers dug for their lives, pitching up earthworks against the incessant rain of lead. "If any one got any sleep," a Pennsylvanian affirmed, "it was in very short naps in line on the ground with their guns by their sides, or in their grasp, ready to meet threatened attacks which came almost hourly." Just as the troops began to doze, rattling musketry would inevitably jar them awake. "Thus passed the night of the 8th of May," a Federal observed. "The indications were quite promising that the worst was yet to come."[4]

The price for failing to breach Lee's line on May 8 was proving high. Two rebel divisions had then fought behind improvised barricades, but sturdy earthen fortifications now loomed where there had been fence-rail contrivances. Meade's chief of staff Humphreys remarked, "With such entrenchments as these, having artillery throughout, with flank fire along their lines wherever practicable, and with the rifled muskets then in use, which were as effective at three hundred yards as the smooth-bore muskets at sixty yards, the strength of an army sustaining attack was more than quadrupled, provided they had force to man the entrenchments well." Humphreys' prognosis was glum. Lee's works were so well constructed that there was "scarcely any measure by which to gauge the increased strength thereby gained." A newsman with the Boston *Evening Transcript* described the situation succinctly: "The lines were in a form of a horse-shoe. It was Gettysburg reversed—Lee having the inner circle."[5]

"Wonder what General Grant thinks of Master Bob today," a Confederate in the Stonewall Brigade recorded in his diary. "Here he is right in his way to Richmond."[6]

During the morning of May 9, Lee rested his men and gave Early a chance to deploy across Fredericksburg Road east of Spotsylvania Court House. "I don't remember anything about the early morning," a southerner acknowledged. "We were dreadfully tired, and I suppose we slept late, and then lounged about, with nothing to do, in a listless, stupid state." Another Confederate spent his time recovering from the fatiguing thirty-six-hour march and greeting stragglers as they arrived.[7]

Incessant warfare—the armies had been marching and fighting for six days without letup—had left its mark on Grant's soldiers. An officer thought that the men's "nerves and strength" showed the strain. "Peal after peal of thousands of muskets would startle the whole army from a deep and greatly needed sleep," a soldier asserted. "For six days not fifteen minutes had elapsed that we did not hear the rattle, and see the effects of these infernal engines of war." A squad of pickets staggered into a 6th Corps camp "crazy from want of sleep." The aide Hyde offered them food and a spot by his camp fire, but their vacant expressions were so "mournfully pathetic" that he was glad when they left. The lull in the action offered the Federals their first chance to bury their dead, which increased the depression settling over the army. Soldiers lowered corpses into shallow graves and scribbled the names of the fallen on makeshift gravestones. Circumstances afforded little time for reflection. "While we were digging [a] grave and the chaplain was addressing those around it," a Pennsylvanian wrote his family, "a missile from a rebel gun fell in such close proximity, that the number of auditors was perceptibly diminished."[8]

The artillerist Alexander retained vivid memories of wounded Federals strewn across Spindle's Field: "They could be heard to call out for water and seen to move and throw up their hands, and one in particular would sometimes sit up." Neither side called for a truce, and the field remained a killing zone. "So there was nothing left for those men but to die there," Alexander observed. When a segment of woods in front of Anderson's works caught fire, Henagan's South Carolinians tried to rescue the wounded men before they burned alive. Federal sharpshooters opened on the southerners, who retaliated by shooting any northerners who tried to save the invalids. "Such sometimes is war, but it is terrible," a Confederate concluded.[9]

Sedgwick and his staff awoke hungry and disheveled by their haystack near Warren's headquarters. Orders arrived at 6:30 A.M. ending any ambiguity over who was in charge at the front. "In any combined operation on the left by both the Fifth and Sixth Corps," read Meade's instructions to Sedgwick, "the major-general commanding directs that you will, in his absence, assume command of both, besides continuing to command your own corps." Warren's stumbling on the eighth had cost him Meade's confidence. In hope of salvaging some measure of harmony, Sedgwick visited Warren's camp. "Tell General Warren to go on and command his own corps as usual," Sedgwick instructed Warren's aide Roebling. "I have perfect confidence that he will do what is right, and knows what to do with his corps as well as I do."[10]

The head of the 6th Corps soon confronted a crisis within his own command. Brigadier General Thomas H. Neill broke under the strain and started withdrawing his division from the front. Sedgwick rode over with his staff officer Charles A. Whittier and discovered that Neill had "entirely lost his nerve." Whittier thought him a "wreck from no fault of his, simply tension too great for him to bear."[11]

Sedgwick visited the angle formed where Brock Road's two branches joined on the northern border of the Spindle farm. Battery H of the 1st New York Artillery was stationed there, and the place had gained notoriety as a favorite target of Confederate sharpshooters. General Morris had been shot from his horse while overseeing his brigade that morning, and the 15th New Jersey's color sergeant had been shot through the breast. A rebel sharpshooter posted in a tree appeared to be inflicting most of the damage. "He seemed to kill at almost every shot," a soldier lamented, "and was said to have taken twenty lives."[12]

"General, do you see that section of artillery?" Sedgwick's chief of staff, Martin T. McMahon, asked in a jesting tone. "Well, you are not to go near it today." Sedgwick answered good-naturedly, "McMahon, I would like to know who commands this corps, you or I?" Playfully, the aide responded, "Well, General, sometimes I am in doubt myself." He continued in a sterner vein: "Seriously, General, I beg of you not to go to that angle; every officer who has shown himself there has been hit, both yesterday and today." Sedgwick answered, "Well, I don't know there is any reason for my going there."[13]

Sedgwick established temporary headquarters behind the earthworks. "It is intended to remain in position today to distribute ammunition and rations, to bring up stragglers, and to afford the men rest," McMahon informed the division commanders. "Please send in to these headquarters for tools, and strengthen your position by entrenching."[14]

In an effort to repel the pesky sharpshooters, Sedgwick ordered his aide Hyde to advance his pickets closer to the rebel line. Hyde rode toward the picket outposts in a zigzag fashion. "Little spurts of smoke kept bursting from the distant woods," he noticed, "and the unpleasant whistle of rifle bullets was very apparent." After delivering his instructions, Hyde returned and sat on the ground next to the general, who was perched on a cracker box. Sedgwick affectionately pulled his aide's ears and chided him about his hair-raising ride. During this playful interlude, the New York artillery withdrew and was replaced by a section of Captain William H. McCartney's battery.[15]

Around 8 A.M., Grant visited Sedgwick. The commander in chief was riding a black pony named Jeff Davis and was accompanied by his staff. Sedgwick seemed "particularly cheerful and hopeful," Grant's aide Porter recalled, and "looked the picture of buoyant life and vigorous health." Grant and Sedgwick chatted about recent hardships. Sedgwick discounted the difficulties and expressed confidence in his troops. Satisfied that Sedgwick had things well in hand, Grant and his entourage rode off.[16]

Sedgwick had noticed during his earlier reconnaissance that the terrain sloped toward the rebels and unduly exposed Colonel Brown's New Jersey brigade. He ordered new pits constructed, and when they were completed, directed the New Jersey troops to occupy them. Once the shift was under way, Sedgwick complimented his aides on their work. "I at once suspected that he had some joke on the staff which he was leading up to," related McMahon, for the general was an "inveterate tease."[17]

Sedgwick was disturbed to discover that soldiers had moved in front of the guns, obstructing their fire. "That is wrong," he muttered and sauntered over with McMahon to correct the alignment. McMahon ordered the troops to move, which aroused the rebel sharpshooters. Bullets began spattering. Some of the men dodged, making Sedgwick laugh: "What! What! Men dodging this way for single bullets! What will you do when they open fire along the whole line? I am ashamed of you. They couldn't hit an elephant at this distance." A bullet whined, and a sergeant standing next to Sedgwick "got down to the bosom of Mother Earth as nearly as possible, without actually crawling on his hands and knees." The general prodded him with his boot. "What are you dodging at?" he scolded. "They can't hit an elephant at that distance." The sergeant jumped up and saluted. "General, I dodged a shell once," he explained, "and if I hadn't, it would have taken my head off. I believe in dodging." Sedgwick laughed. "All right, my man. Go to your place." There was another shrill whistle, followed by a dull thud. Sedgwick rotated slowly in McMahon's direction. Blood spurted from a small hole just below the general's left eye, and he fell heavily onto McMahon. The two men tumbled to the ground as aides came running. Sedgwick's lips were curled in a smile, perhaps frozen on his face after his banter. A doctor poured water from a canteen onto the wound. Blood continued to pulsate like a little fountain. General Ricketts joined the stricken group. He was next in command after Sedgwick, but he informed McMahon that he preferred not to head the corps, since Sedgwick had wanted Wright to succeed him.[18]

Aides carried Sedgwick's body to the rear and attempted to keep the sad news from spreading, but word traveled quickly. "What is the matter?" Lyman asked McMahon, who was visibly distraught. "They have hit General Sedgwick just here under the eye, and, my God, I am afraid he is killed," he replied. "The dismay of General Sedgwick's staff was a personal feeling," Lyman wrote home. "He was like a kind father to them, and they loved him really like sons." Grant was flabbergasted. "Is he really dead?" he asked Porter. "Is he really dead?" Sedgwick's loss, declared Grant, was greater than that of a whole division. A newspaper correspondent thought the general's death "cast a gloom over the entire army." Many Confederates were also saddened. Stuart's aide Boteler mentioned in his diary that Stuart said he would "most gladly have shared his blanket and last crust with him, as he was one of the best friends he had in the old army." The rebel cavalryman reminisced about a discussion he had had with Sedgwick concerning his decision to join the Confederacy. "Stuart, you are wrong in the step you are taking," Sedgwick had warned, "but I cannot blame you for going to the defense of your native state. I am a northerner and will go to the defense of my section."[19]

"From the commander to the lowest private, he had no enemy," Lyman proclaimed. The observation was not entirely accurate. At 9:30 A.M.— almost precisely when Sedgwick was killed—Warren was writing privately to Meade. The letter reflected the 5th Corps commander's pique at Meade's obvious distrust of his ability. The failure on the 8th, Warren protested, was not his fault. If Sedgwick had arrived earlier, Anderson would have been defeated. Meade should never have permitted Sedgwick to deviate from the original timetable, and he should have more actively coordinated the two corps when Sedgwick finally appeared. "I don't think our other two corps commanders are capable," Warren stressed. "General Sedgwick does nothing of himself. I have lost confidence in General Hancock's capability." Word of Sedgwick's death apparently reached Warren as he was finishing his diatribe. For once, he exercised sound discretion, folding the letter and placing it in his papers. It did not see the light of day for over a hundred years.[20]

Bent on revenge, a 6th Vermont detail crept into the field from which Sedgwick had been shot. Sergeant Sanford Grey and D. R. Sanborn waited behind a stack of fence rails, their rifles trained on the far woods. "There he is, Grey," Sanborn whispered as he pointed to a red shirt visible through the greenery. "Don't fire," warned Grey. "Don't you see he has a red cloth upon a stick, with his hat placed upon the top? He is waiting for our men in his front to expose themselves." Grey caught sight of movement, exclaimed, "There he is now!" and squeezed off a shot. The man jerked erect and tumbled into a rifle pit. Toward nightfall, Sanborn examined the area and found the rebel sitting up, still holding his rifle and quite dead. "I have always thought that this man killed General Sedgwick," Sanborn claimed, "and that his own life, forfeited within the hour, was all the revenge we could get." Several surviving rebels, however, claimed the honor. The top contender was Ben Powell, of the 12th South Carolina. "A few days before the battle of Gettysburg," Powell wrote in a postwar letter, "I was presented with a long range Whitworth rifle with telescope and globe sights and with a roving companion as an Independent sharpshooter and scout. This rifle killed General Sedgwick at Spotsylvania Court House." Others maintained that Thomas Burgess, of the 15th South Carolina, who had fired a single shot from the picket line, deserved credit for killing the head of the 6th Corps.[21]

The Federal 5th and 6th corps lay most of the day under "ceaseless and deadly fire" from rebel sharpshooters. Forays launched periodically to dislodge the Confederate marksmen proved ineffective. Native Americans from the 7th Wisconsin donned pine boughs and ran across the no-man's-land shouting war cries to flush out snipers while the rest of the regiment fired at the handful of rebels who fell for the ruse. Around two in the afternoon, elements from Cutler's brigade rushed a patch of sniper-infested woods, but the sortie ended when the Confederates ignited the woods and withdrew. "The assault was fruitless," a Pennsylvanian complained, "and many of the dying were left to perish in the flames." Near nightfall, elements from Griffin's division managed to secure the shallow ridge around the Spindle ruins to eliminate a stronghold for rebel marksmen. The position, however, was too far from the main Union works to defend, and at midnight the Federals retired.[22]

Meade respected Sedgwick's wish and named Wright to head the 6th Corps. He "brought high qualifications to the command of the corps," thought a Vermonter. Brigadier General David A. Russell assumed charge of Wright's division, and Eustis stepped to the head of Russell's brigade. It had been a costly morning for the Army of the Potomac.[23]

"One of the most daring raids on record."

While Meade's foot soldiers dodged sniper fire and sweltered behind earthworks, Sheridan was initiating an ambitious cavalry expedition. The foray was a direct result of his heated lunchtime exchange with Meade on May 8. By early afternoon on May 8, Sheridan had received permission to attack Stuart with his "available mounted force," which he took to mean his entire command. He summoned his division heads—Wilson, Merritt, and Gregg—to the Alrich place, read them Meade's communication, and underscored the mission's importance. More was at stake than simply defeating the enemy. Sheridan's reputation was on the line—and a shaky reputation it was, given his poor showing in the Wilderness and his even worse performance in clearing Brock Road. "We are going out to fight Stuart's cavalry in consequence of a suggestion from me," he explained. "We will give him a fair, square fight. We are strong, and I know we can beat him, and in view of my recent representations to General Meade I shall expect nothing but success."[24]

Sheridan reviewed the proposed line of march. Meade's instructions authorized him to proceed against the enemy's cavalry, and he planned to do that by heading for Richmond, convinced that Stuart would elect to follow. When his supplies gave out, he expected to obtain more from Butler on the James, then to return. Previous Federal raids, Sheridan was aware, had been hurried strikes aimed at destroying rebel supplies while avoiding pitched battle. He had a different objective in mind. He meant to conduct his operations openly and deliberately, leaving Stuart no option but to attack. The resulting battle, he believed, would wreck the rebel mounted arm and materially accelerate Lee's demise. He planned to keep his force compact and to move in a single column, four horsemen abreast. "At first the proposition seemed to surprise the division commanders somewhat," Sheridan recognized. But once they understood the raid's purpose they wholeheartedly endorsed the project. "A challenge to Stuart for a cavalry duel behind Lee's lines, in his own country," is how Sheridan explained it to them.[25]

Practical considerations determined the route. From the Alrich place, it was reasonable to head east around Lee's army and pick up Telegraph Road, which ran to the North Anna River, twenty-five miles south, then on to Richmond. With only a half day's fodder on hand, fresh sustenance was of paramount concern. Food was plentiful in the North Anna region, which had seen little fighting. The Virginia Central Railroad ran directly below the river, and destroying the line was considered a worthwhile ancillary goal. Sheridan was also confident that if he failed—unimaginable as that might be—he could escape by swinging west toward Gordonsville and Orange Court House.[26]

The evening of May 8 hummed with preparations. Each soldier was given fifty rounds of ammunition and eighteen pistol rounds. Three days'

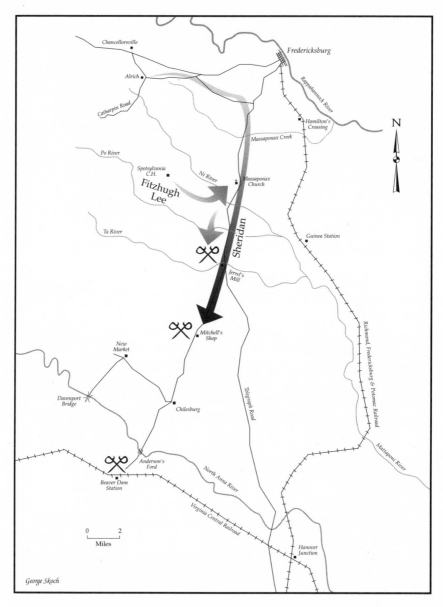

Sheridan's route to Beaver Dam on May 9

rations of coffee, sugar, and hard bread were issued, one day's of salt beef, and five of salt. Wagons were kept to a minimum and carried only ammunition. If the troops needed more food, they would have to forage. To a growing sense of excitement, riders poured into the Alrich place from scattered outposts. This was the first time that Sheridan's corps had assembled since crossing the Rapidan. "You fellows had better turn in and get what sleep you can tonight," a sergeant admonished, "for it will probably be the last chance you'll get for several days." A soldier in the horse artillery wrote home that he was "grim and black with smoke and dust and guess you would hardly know me." Some men stole a few hours rest with their boots on. A wagon train of wounded soldiers, accompanied by Ferrero's black division, rumbled slowly by. Their cries pierced the night.[27]

At the beginning of the campaign, Custer's Michigan brigade and the 2nd and 5th New York Cavalry regiments had been armed with seven-shot Spencer carbines. Now Spencers were issued to the 1st Connecticut, of Wilson's division. These troops had performed exemplary service above Spotsylvania Court House, and Wilson informed them that they had "earned the right" to carry the new weapons.[28]

Reveille sounded before daylight on May 9. A tired cavalryman noticed that the rising sun looked like a "ball of fire through the smokey atmosphere." Staff officers darted everywhere, urging men onto their mounts. Alrich's Field presented an inspiring sight. Ten thousand horsemen blanketed the plain, "their tattered and torn battle flags hanging lazily from the staffs in the quiet morning air." Regiments gathered in solid masses, and eyes strained toward a knot of officers near Plank Road. It was Sheridan and his staff. Speculation ranged over where the martial host were headed. Some thought that they were retiring north to protect Grant's communications. None guessed that they were about to begin "one of the most daring raids on record." A newspaperman noted that "utmost enthusiasm prevailed."[29]

"By fours, march!" came the command, and the mounted horde set out. First came a brief bottleneck while the troopers and some of Burnside's infantry vied for a stretch of road. Then Sheridan's column overtook the ambulance train. It was a sobering sight. Soldiers missing right legs were packed together on their left sides like spoons in a drawer, while those without left legs lay in the opposite direction. Those missing arms walked. "It was a sad and sorrowful procession," commented a cavalryman. "The groans of the wounded could be heard, and occasionally a wagon would be halted long enough to take out the body of some poor fellow who had died on the way." Hardened troopers could not resist the cries for water and gave freely from their canteens. The cavalrymen picked their way beside the invalids until they reached a road that forked south.

There Sheridan turned off, Merritt leading, Wilson and Gregg closing the rear. Ten thousand horsemen four abreast and six batteries of horse artillery stretched nearly thirteen miles. According to a witness, the column took four hours to pass.[30]

Exuberance swept the procession. Sheridan moved at a walk as though daring Stuart to attack. The steadiness of pace, a veteran remarked, "calmed the nerves, strengthened self-reliance, and inspired confidence." It was also a grueling business. "The clouds of dust, sent up by the thousands of hoof-beats, fill eyes, nose, and air passages, give external surfaces a uniform, dirty gray color, and form such an impenetrable veil, that, for many minutes together, you cannot see even your hand before you," another soldier recorded. Sweat, dust, and horsehair stuck to the men and made them feel as though "covered by a creeping mass of insects." Many troopers discarded their overcoats after slashing them into pieces to render them useless to the enemy. "For some distance the road was strewn with the fragments," noted a soldier from Ohio. Heat and dust led a Michigan man to pronounce the ordeal "one of the worst marches I ever experienced." The main topic was Sheridan: "It was the unanimous opinion that he had, at least, demonstrated one thing—that he knew how to march a cavalry force without exhausting it."[31]

The column swung around Lee and pressed south on Telegraph Road. No significant opposition appeared. Gray-clad riders flitted and buzzed around the flanks but were easily driven away. Sheridan's chief concern was that Stuart might attempt to interdict him at one of the four small streams that lay across his path—the Ni, the Po, the Ta, and the Mat, from north to south in that order—but his fear proved groundless. After putting the last of the creeks behind him, Sheridan found that "all anxiety as to our passing around Lee's army was removed."[32]

"We found few houses with any pretensions to elegant architecture," Wilson remarked, "and none to prosperity." White men of military age were in Lee's army, and everyone else fled when the column appeared. "Even the Negroes and the farmstock hid in the woods till we passed," Wilson wrote. "It was a glorious sight," thought an artilleryman who stopped to watch the mounted column. "The long even lines of cavalry obliquely descending the slope showed boldly against the summer green. Over all hotly shone the sun. My eye could not tire with gazing."[33]

"Their skirmish lines are deployed as though they meant to fight."

Grant occupied the morning of May 9 trying to make out the shape of Lee's formation from fragmentary intelligence. According to the aide Badeau, Grant was disappointed in the Army of the Potomac's leadership. Mistakes, inattentiveness, and slippage in communication had thwarted excellent chances to beat Lee in the Wilderness, and the march to Spotsylvania had been a fiasco, leaving Lee ensconced behind nearly impregnable earthworks. "But though disappointed," Badeau added, "Grant was not discouraged." He only became more resolute. "No syllable of censure escaped him," the aide reported. "He lost no time in criticizing or complaining, but at once attempted to repair the situation."[34]

Repairing the situation held no promise of being simple. Combat along Laurel Hill had reached a stalemate after Sedgwick's death. Musketry sputtered incessantly as sharpshooters plied their deadly trade and skirmishers dueled for footholds between contending lines. Neither side was willing to resume full-scale combat. "The same intolerable heat which we have had ever since this movement commenced still continues," a New Yorker complained. "It is, however, one compensation for the best that it keeps the roads in excellent travelling condition, saving and excepting the dust, which is here of the most malignant type."[35]

If Grant wanted to renew the offensive, he would have to do so on his flanks. In Sheridan's absence, however, he had no ready means of reconnoitering past the ends of Lee's line. Accordingly, he initiated two major infantry probes. Hancock was to explore toward the Po on the battlefield's western perimeter, and Burnside was to advance along Fredericksburg Road east of Lee's burgeoning earthworks, tracing the route Wilson had taken to Spotsylvania Court House the previous morning.

Hancock's reconnaissance got off to a clumsy start. The Federal 2nd Corps faced west in a protective arc near Todd's Tavern, and conflicting intelligence kept Hancock on edge all morning. Shortly after daylight, Union scouts filed gingerly out Catharpin Road but could find no rebels. A second surveillance also failed to turn up graycoats, which led Hancock to inform headquarters at six o'clock that the Confederates had left his front. But events quickly shattered his optimism. Reports began filtering in that rebel cavalrymen—the Jeff Davis and Hampton legions of Wade Hampton's division—were probing Catharpin Road toward Todd's Tavern. Union sharpshooters pushed west to test Hampton's resolve, but the southerner declined battle and retired to the far side of the Po. Evidence concerning his intentions remained equivocal. Smoldering camp fires suggested that the main body of Confederates had moved on, but wagons clanking behind Hampton's cavalry screen implied considerable activity. Perhaps Early was massing to repeat his previous evening's attack along

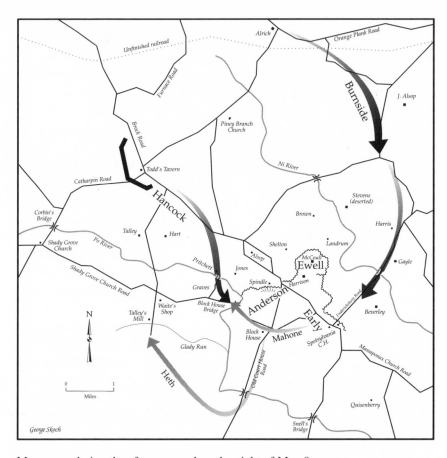

Maneuvers during the afternoon and on the night of May 9

Catharpin Road. Hancock's sharpshooters hunkered down along the eastern bank of the Po, two miles in advance of Todd's Tavern.[36]

After digesting this latest information, Hancock put the worst face on it and dramatically reversed his earlier opinion. "There is no doubt, I believe," he wrote headquarters at seven, "that the enemy are moving infantry and artillery in my front in order to take the junction of the Spotsylvania and Catharpin roads, now in my possession." In order to prepare for a major fight—the Confederate assault on Todd's Tavern that he had been expecting all night—Hancock mobilized for action. A calming response came from Meade's chief of staff, Humphreys, who concluded that since Anderson and Ewell were in front of Warren and Sedgwick, Hancock had no reason to fear a "heavy attack." The worst possibility was an assault by Early's 3rd Corps, which had occupied Shady Grove Church during the night. Since Hancock was protected by earthworks, presumably he could fend off Early. But Humphreys was unwilling to throw caution to the winds. He directed Gibbon, who had been held below Todd's Tavern in support of Warren, to shift closer to Hancock.[37]

On Grant's other flank, Burnside missed a superb opportunity. Reconstituted primarily from green recruits, the 9th Corps had rolled onto the Alrich land on May 8 too late to contribute to Warren's and Sedgwick's offensive. For May 9, Grant proposed sending the corps through Spotsylvania Court House and on to Chilesburg. Warren's and Sedgwick's abortive evening offensive, however, forced the Federal commander to modify his plan. Instead, Burnside was to advance two divisions to a point marked "gate" on the Federal war maps. This would put his forward elements on Fredericksburg Road well above Spotsylvania. He was expected to be in place by 6 A.M. His next move would depend on developments on the rest of the field.[38]

"The bugle called us at the earliest blush of day," noted an officer in Orlando Willcox' 9th Corps division. It was about 4 A.M. "Coffee was soon made, and breakfast eaten," he added. "A very simple breakfast it was—and before sunrise we were in line and ready for the word to move." No sooner had the soldiers stepped out, however, than they encountered Sheridan's horsemen, who had started at the same time on their excursion toward Richmond. No one had bothered to coordinate Sheridan and the 9th Corps, and Willcox finally yielded. For over an hour, his men stood idle while Sheridan's rode past. A Michigan rider thought the 9th Corps soldiers a "motley aggregation" drawn from the "odds and ends of the service." Willcox started again around six—the time, ironically, that Grant had projected for him to reach his destination—and wound along country byways to Fredericksburg Road, where he turned right.[39]

At 7:15, Willcox approached the Gayle house, which occupied high ground a short distance above the Ni, a mile and a half northeast of Spotsylvania Court House. He assumed that the Gayle house's driveway was the "gate" depicted on the Union war maps. Fitzhugh Lee had posted Wickham's brigade to guard this approach to Spotsylvania Court House until Early's 3rd Corps could arrive from Shady Grove Church. Willcox' lead unit—the 60th Ohio—met some of Wickham's advance pickets as it entered the Gayle house yard and drove the Confederates back across the Ni.[40]

The Union high command remained confused over Willcox' location.

In fact, the Gayle house had nothing to do with the war map's "gate," which was an obscure track that entered Fredericksburg Road farther north. Willcox projected dangerously in front of the Union army, but no one, including Willcox, realized the mistake.[41]

Willcox looked things over with Colonel Benjamin C. Christ, who commanded one of his brigades. Christ's troops were deploying on the crest near the Gayle place, at right angles to Fredericksburg Road. From there, the road descended sharply to the Ni, then rose in a "gentle swell." Rebel cavalry occupied the far rise. Willcox fired a round into them with a three-inch gun, and when the southerners scattered, directed Lieutenant Colonel Byron M. Cutcheon, of the 20th Michigan, to seize the far heights. Once Cutcheon secured the ridge, Christ was to cross with the rest of his brigade. Willcox informed headquarters that the "enemy show considerable force of cavalry and, I think, infantry, but it is hazy, and I am not sure." He added, "Their skirmish lines are deployed as though they meant to fight."[42]

Cutcheon advanced two companies "briskly" across the stream while the rest of his regiment trailed in column along the road. About halfway up the hill, Cutcheon reached a lane that ran to the Beverly house, on the left. The track had been worn three feet into the ground and made a good defensive position. Cutcheon formed his regiment there, while the 60th Ohio continued to the crest. The 1st Michigan Sharpshooters filed onto Cutcheon's left wing toward the Beverly house, and the 79th New York occupied the Beverly grounds. The 50th Pennsylvania connected with Cutcheon's right wing on Fredericksburg Road and extended the line west. Captain Jacob Roemer's 34th New York Light Battery and Captain Adelbert B. Twitchell's 7th Maine Battery provided support from high ground north of the river.[43]

Hunched over maps, Grant and Meade remained preoccupied with developments on Hancock's front, where fighting seemed imminent. They did not expect Burnside to encounter trouble, because nothing indicated that rebel infantry had reached Fredericksburg Road. Sometime after 9 A.M., Grant learned of Willcox' engagement at the Gayle house. It caused no immediate alarm, because Grant could account for Lee's three infantry corps. Early was posturing before Hancock, he thought, and Anderson and Ewell were in front of Warren and Sedgwick. That meant Willcox faced nothing more substantial than Confederate scouts. As the morning progressed, however, Hancock's reports began to suggest that Early had moved on. Perhaps, Grant rightly surmised, he was circling through Spotsylvania Court House and pressing toward Fredericksburg Road. The prospects were alarming. A concerted rebel push there stood to annihilate Willcox and sever the Army of the Potomac from its base at Fredericksburg. Concern that Lee might be working east dominated Grant's thinking for the rest of the day.

Grant was unable to monitor Lee's movements, since his mounted arm was gone. Without cavalry, he was perplexed over how best to position the 9th Corps. He wanted Burnside to support Willcox, but he also did not want Burnside's remaining units too far from Meade. His compromise was to leave Willcox in place and to alert Burnside—who was still at the Alrich place—to prepare his other divisions to shift where needed. Brigadier General Thomas G. Stevenson, posted near Piney Branch Church, was to identify routes toward both Meade and Willcox. "When the division receives orders to move," Grant directed, "it must be conducted by one of those staff officers who have familiarized themselves with the roads on which it is to move, that there may be no delay." Grant also instructed Meade to extend pickets toward Willcox to determine if rebels occupied the ground between the Army of the Potomac and the 9th Corps. If so, Meade was to "recall the trains and push the enemy's left flank vigorously." Headquarters also began to suspect that the maps were in error. "The position occupied by General Willcox is at Mr. Gayle's house," Burnside informed Grant around 10:30, "there being no such place as 'Gate' in this section." That placed Willcox considerably farther past the Alrich place than the map suggested and made it impossible for him to connect with Meade. "I mention this so that you may see whether or not the position is not too much isolated," Burnside cautioned.[44]

Not long after headquarters recognized Willcox' precarious situation, serious fighting erupted on his front. Robert Johnston's brigade of Gordon's division occupied the reserve line behind Ewell. During the morning, Johnston accompanied about four hundred of his soldiers in a reconnaissance toward Fredericksburg Road, where they joined Wickham and his horse artillery. Together they aggressively tested Willcox' advanced formation on the Beverly property's lane. Their goal was to impede Willcox until Early could bring up his infantry.[45]

Wickham's and Johnston's Confederates instinctively probed for weak points and found one in the 60th Ohio, which projected a few hundred yards in front of Christ's line along the Beverly lane. The Ohio regiment had been recruited less than three weeks before and had never faced fire. This was the first day that many of its troops carried rifles.[46]

Confederates burst from the woods fringing the Beverly fields, scattered the Ohioans "in some confusion," then continued onto high ground near the Beverly house. There they opened a deadly enfilading fire on the 1st Michigan Sharpshooters. Some of Wickham's troopers attacked the 79th New York's skirmish line, which was manned by Native Americans. "We watched their movements with a good deal of interest," a New Yorker related. "At first the advance regiment stood firm, returning the enemy's fire, but when the rebels, with a yell, jumped over the rail fence, crossed the brook and prepared to charge, the skirmish line broke, turned, and ran into their own regiment, throwing it into disorder, and causing a stampede." Union batteries above the Ni misdirected their shots among the New Yorkers. Flanked by Confederates and bombarded by Federal guns, Christ's left wing began a "rapid and disorderly" retreat. The Michigan and New York troops broke and fled, which placed the neighboring Pennsylvanians in an untenable position. "This action of our batteries was inexcusable," a northern soldier complained, "as they were within plain sight and must have seen, if they had tried to see at all, that they were firing upon us."[47]

Then Captain Samuel K. Schwenk, of the 50th Pennsylvania, ordered a bayonet charge. Emboldened by Schwenk, the 20th Michigan and 79th New York rallied. Federals and rebels alike sprinted toward a high rail fence. "It was a close race," Cutcheon recounted, but the Michiganders caught up with the Pennsylvanians, shifted left into a battle line, "and without an instant's pause, hurled themselves forward to the fence on the crest, just in time to save it." Cutcheon boasted that his regiment "moved like a machine." Hand-to-hand fighting bloodied the field. "We lost a good many men—some killed," a southerner conceded. Outnumbered, Johnston and Wickham retired, leaving Christ holding the Ni's southern bank.[48]

Willcox felt uneasy, however, about leaving Christ on the rebel side of the stream and ordered his second brigade, under Colonel John F. Hartranft, to reinforce him. The 8th and 17th Michigan splashed over the Ni and formed on the road behind the 60th Ohio, while the 51st Pennsylvania pulled up on the 1st Michigan's right and extended the line west. Then Willcox' two brigades advanced. The Confederates, a Michigander explained, "fell back pell mell to the woods, while our men poured their volleys of minnies into them, cutting their lines severely." Apprehensive of being surrounded, Johnston withdrew closer to Spotsylvania Court House.[49]

Willcox consolidated his hold on the summit south of the Ni and began throwing up earthworks, while Christ ordered his forward units to hold the crest "at all hazards." Willcox continued to overestimate the enemy's strength. "The contest extremely doubtful," he wrote Burnside at 11:45 A.M. "I am heavily engaged against superior numbers. Where is Stevenson?"[50]

No sooner had Willcox' runner left with that latest plea than Stevenson's exhausted troops appeared. They had started from the Alrich place at four that morning, moved toward Piney Branch Church, and then, as an officer explained, "had [the] usual luck of being obliged to wait for a couple of hours or more." They had doubled back and lost their way "owing to the neglect of higher authorities to provide us with a guide or map." Finally, at noon, they reached the Gayle house. Willcox' little battle had sputtered to a close.[51]

At 12:30, Willcox reported Stevenson's arrival. From the roof of the Gayle house, Willcox could see gray-clad troops marching across his front. He surmised that the object of the rebel attacks had been to conceal a flanking movement. "I am confirmed in my opinion that their trains are moving off to the left," he reiterated in a dispatch marked 1:15 P.M., and continued, "We have taken prisoners from Longstreet's, Ewell's, and Hill's corps." All of rebeldom seemed to be coming his way. "They massed heavily in my front," he emphasized, "but, thank God, we have repulsed them so far."[52]

In fact, Willcox had badly misinterpreted the troop movements in front of him. The activity he found so ominous involved only Hill's corps, now under Early, deploying across Fredericksburg Road to protect Spotsylvania Court House.

Serious fighting had concluded in Burnside's sector by early afternoon. The engagement came to be called the Battle of the Ni, although given the relatively few soldiers involved, it scarcely warranted the name. Cutcheon's 20th Michigan, which was the first regiment across the river and probably the heaviest engaged, reported "small losses." Willcox' tally stood at 167 killed and wounded, 21 missing. Burnside tabulated his total losses at 215. Among the disabled was Christ. The official version declared him "sunstruck," but Cutcheon blamed his condition on drinking. "The colonel was a man who indulged freely in the use of liquor, and," Cutcheon ventured, "I have an impression that his liability to prostration was increased in that way." Willcox reorganized his division. Cutcheon came to command the 51st Pennsylvania as well as his own regiment, and Hartranft absorbed the remainder of Christ's brigade into his own.[53]

The 9th Corps settled comfortably into the prevailing defensive spirit. Willcox and Stevenson occupied the ridge south of the Ni, and a "slow sharp-shooting fire" rattled all day between Federal skirmishers and Ear-

ly's advance patrols. Burnside remained at the Alrich place until late afternoon, stubbornly resisting Grant's prodding to assume active command at
the front. A key to Burnside's disinclination appears in a New York cavalryman's diary. "General Burnside's corps was passing our train," he
wrote, "and the General himself came to our quarters where he stayed for
near two hours refreshing himself with some of my brandy, etc., and amusing ourselves in conversation about the tide of battle." Later, Burnside
moved to the J. Alsop house, still nearly three miles behind the front.
Potter's division lumbered up and camped nearby.[54]

The Confederates were surprised at Burnside's failure to press ahead
into Spotsylvania Court House. "It occurred to many of us at the time,"
Stuart's aide Theodore S. Garnett reminisced, "that the enemy here lost
the best opportunity they had during the whole campaign, to fall upon our
flank and destroy our army." Garnett recounted that Stuart directed him
during the fight to find Ewell's right flank, which Stuart presumed to be
near Fredericksburg Road. "I hunted in vain at least a half hour," Garnett
explained, "in which I must have ridden quite a mile in a straight line
from the said Road, without finding a vidette or picket, or any human
being who could tell me where our troops were." To Garnett, the danger
was clear. "If General Grant could have known, and it seems to me that
nothing could have been easier to ascertain, that his line overlapped ours
for such an immense distance, it would have been the work of a very few
minutes to move against our right flank, throw it into confusion and seize
the very ground on which we held him at bay for more than a week."[55]

In Sheridan's absence, Grant lacked reliable means of assessing the
situation in front of Burnside. He should have visited Fredericksburg Road
himself or sent a staff officer. By doing neither, he permitted a rare opportunity to pass.

While Willcox and Stevenson contemplated the dust clouds from Early's
wagons, Hancock was still trying to fathom whether the Confederates at
Shady Grove Church entertained aggressive designs. Reports seemed to
verify that Early had moved on, which left only Hampton's cavalry. At 11:45
A.M., Hancock revised his earlier dire predictions and assured Meade that
he was "satisfied that the enemy have left my right and front." This time,
he was correct. Early had abandoned Shady Grove Church at daylight and
was marching through Spotsylvania to concentrate east of town.[56]

Hancock's latest report fueled headquarters' conviction that Lee was
shifting his entire army toward Burnside. "All information here leads to

the belief that [the rebels] are passing to our left and you will be needed here," Meade alerted Hancock at noon. At 12:45, Grant reconfirmed to Meade that Burnside's and Hancock's reports "indicate the enemy to be moving toward Gate." Should the intelligence be accurate, Grant added, "we must follow and attack vigorously." At one o'clock, Grant spelled out his thoughts to Major General Henry W. Halleck, his chief of staff in Washington. "The enemy are now moving from our immediate front either to interpose between us and Fredericksburg or to get the inside road to Richmond," he reported. He went on, "My movements are terribly embarrassed by our immense wagon train."[57]

Meade and Grant reacted differently as they became confident that Lee was shifting eastward. Meade was in his usual defensive frame of mind, and his instinct was to prepare to support Burnside by advancing Hancock from Todd's Tavern. At 1:30, he directed Humphreys to ascertain "whether there are any roads from our left up to the Gate, as we may have to reinforce Burnside."[58]

Grant, however, responded aggressively and displayed his penchant for turning unfavorable developments his way. He realized that Lee, by shifting east, stood to menace the Union army's supply line to Fredericksburg. But he also saw that Lee's maneuver would expose the Confederates to a thrust against their western flank. Grant's response was to direct Burnside to hold firm while Hancock maneuvered against the western end of Lee's line. As Grant explained to Meade, if Lee was moving, "we must follow and attack vigorously." Burnside was to be the anvil and Hancock the hammer, while Warren and Sedgwick remained poised to attack frontally. If all went as planned, Lee would be dealt a severe blow.[59]

Grant set the stage for his new offensive by alerting Burnside that Lee was heading his way. "Direct Willcox to entrench and hold his position strongly," he ordered the 9th Corps commander, "only falling back at the last extremity, expecting the enemy, if they have gone in force toward him, to be attacked from here." Then he rode toward Hancock's sector of the field to see what could be done there. His thinking was summarized by the assistant secretary of war Charles Dana, who had visited the front to keep Washington apprised of developments: "If, as now appears to be the case, Lee has left anything open in front of our right by massing on our left, [Grant] may attack at this weakened point of their lines, with a view of passing toward Richmond on that side." Grant was going to try to beat Lee at his own game.[60]

To initiate the concentration against Lee's left flank, Grant ordered Hancock onto high ground southwest of Todd's Tavern overlooking the Po.

One division—Gershom Mott's two-brigade outfit, which had performed badly in the Wilderness—was to remain at Todd's Tavern to guard the army's rear. Hancock's sharpshooters fanned southwest onto the plateau above the Po. The banks were steep and the approaches clear, affording the rebels on the far side an unobstructed view of Hancock's activities. Hancock's sharpshooters began firing at Confederate signal stations across the river. Their Sharps rifles, however, were sighted for a thousand yards, and the southerners were fifteen hundred yards away. An enterprising Yankee elevated his gunsights with a stick. The shot went high, so he whittled the stick and tried again. Rebels began dodging, which indicated that he had found the range. The rest of his detail fitted their sights with sticks of the same length and sent the Confederates scurrying. Hancock, who watched the exercise with interest, seemed pleased.[61]

Hancock's infantry, without Mott's division, moved into position between noon and two o'clock. Barlow's division marched down Brock Road about a mile and shifted west into fields around the Tally house. Birney formed on Barlow's right and Gibbon on his left. Shady Grove Church Road was partially visible across the river.[62]

Hancock, Meade, and Grant met near the Tally house while the 2nd Corps maneuvered into place. Grant was interested in Hancock's progress because the 2nd Corps was to be the lead element in his plan to strike Lee's western flank. The generals peered across the Po and spotted a Confederate wagon train—the tail of Early's column, on the way from Shady Grove Church to Spotsylvania Court House—wending along Shady Grove Church Road. An aide suggested shelling the wagons, but Meade shot an exasperated look and scoffed, "Yes! And what good would you do? Scare a few niggers and old mules?" Others urged that firing on the train had merit and recommended sending troops across the river. Meade relented, and several units—including the 1st New Hampshire and 1st Rhode Island batteries—opened on the rebels. "The first few shots," a Rhode Island gunner reported, "created a wild stampede among the nonbelligerents, and sent the wagons flying along the road toward the cover of the woods." An onlooker thought that the drivers' frantic efforts to get out of the way were "most laughable."[63]

The barrage elicited an immediate response from the Confederates. Captain T. Frederick Brown had advanced his Rhode Island battery to within six hundred yards of the river. Thomson's Confederate battery of horse artillery posted along the Po focused on the Union battery and killed two gunners. Brown, backed by the rest of the corps' available guns, responded in kind and drove Thomson's pieces out of range. Under cover of his artillery, Meade dispatched troops across the stream. The 148th Pennsylvania crossed first, some men using a fallen log and others splashing over. The soldiers—along with reinforcements from the 145th Pennsylvania—clawed up a steep and heavily wooded bank and secured a lodgment on the far side. A pontoon bridge was soon in place, and Barlow's entire division began shuffling across. Colonel John R. Brooke's brigade went first, then Colonel Paul Frank's, then Miles's and Smyth's.[64]

Thomson was surprised by Barlow's Pennsylvanians debouching from the river and fled "in a double-quick style amid a storm of Yankee bullets and shell." A rebel gunner struck by a shell fragment rolled off his horse looking white as a sheet. "I knew that he already felt the pangs of his terrible wound," a companion remarked, "but when he looked for blood and was searching for the gaping flesh he found nothing but a half-pound fragment of warm casting in his trousers pocket, which had lodged there from the exploding shell." Sharp fighting continued for about an hour. Brigadier General Ambrose R. Wright's brigade, which was accompanying the wagons, came to Thomson's assistance. With the help of Lieutenant Colonel Matthew R. Hall's 48th Georgia and 2nd Georgia Battalion, Hampton was able to detain Barlow's Federals until the wagon train had passed.[65]

The wagons had escaped, but the Po had been breached and Hancock's men kept swarming across. "Now something besides the wagon train was pressing upon the mind of the commander in chief," Walker recounted. "He thought he saw an opportunity of getting, in this way, upon the flank of the Confederate force at Spotsylvania." Grant decided to send the entire 2nd Corps over. Birney crossed on an old mill race at Tinder's Mill, slightly upstream from Barlow, and Gibbon went over downstream near the Pritchett house. Thomson's horse artillery unleashed a hail of lead from nearby woods. "I do not remember ever having heard guns fire with greater rapidity," a New Yorker averred. "The thunder of discharge and explosion, added to the rattle of small arms, now gave the affair the semblance of a battle of considerable magnitude." Another Federal observed that "the rebs were as thick and as bloody as mosquitoes, and seemed determined we shouldn't cross." But once Birney's lead elements had splashed over—the water was only a foot deep at the race—the rebel guns limbered up and disappeared farther into the woods. Around six o'clock, Barlow reported that he was securely athwart Shady Grove Church Road. Federal casualties were few, but precious time had been lost.[66]

By 7 P.M., Hancock's three divisions had united south of the Po and were marching toward the Block House Bridge and the flank of Anderson's Laurel Hill defenses. Hampton bitterly opposed the advance. Hancock, apprehensive that Confederate infantry might be waiting close by, moved cautiously. Hancock's only significant casualty was Lieutenant Colonel Richard McMichael, of the 53rd Pennsylvania. Well fortified with drink, he skinned his nose on a tree, complained loudly about being the only man wounded in his regiment, then unsteadily led the way several hundred yards ahead of his troops. Somehow he survived until darkness, when he attracted a crowd by beating his horse to punish it for sniffing conscripts. "Such was the drama of our officers who freely indulged in that dark beverage of hell," a witness declared.[67]

Barlow reached the Block House Bridge at nightfall, but the river was too deep to ford, and he was reluctant to cross in the dark. Hancock's chief of staff, Charles H. Morgan, halted the column and sent to Hancock for instructions. The 2nd Corps commander was wary. It was dark, and Anderson was on the other side of the tiny river. If the 2nd Corps started across, it risked being defeated piecemeal. Union engineers erected temporary pontoon bridges at the three Po crossings to the north so that Hancock could escape quickly if something went wrong.[68]

Meade meanwhile directed Warren to mount a diversion against Laurel Hill to prevent Lee from shuttling reinforcements toward the Po. Crawford's Pennsylvanians charged and after a brief but spirited engagement tumbled back to their earthworks. There could be no question that Confederates held Laurel Hill in strength. Whether they had detached soldiers to oppose Hancock remained anyone's guess.[69]

Since early morning, General Lee had been seeking an opportunity to go on the offensive. According to the 1st Corps aide Sorrel, "In the afternoon an attack by [Edward Johnson] was projected to be assisted by the advance of our skirmishers." Hancock's operations near the Po, however, caused Lee to wait. He recognized that reinforcements were necessary to buttress Anderson's vulnerable left flank. He was uncertain, however, whether Hancock's venture presaged a major Union thrust or was only a diversion to mask Grant's plan to attack elsewhere. That made him reluctant to pull Anderson's or Ewell's troops from their earthworks to counter Hancock. Doing so would weaken his defenses and risked playing into Grant's hands.[70]

Early's 3rd Corps had the uncommitted troops that Lee needed. One of Old Jube's divisions—Wilcox'—was firmly entrenched across Fredericksburg Road and seemed perfectly capable of holding off Burnside. Early's remaining divisions—Heth's and Mahone's—were at Spotsylvania

Court House awaiting instructions. Since Burnside posed no active threat, Lee decided to withdraw Mahone from Spotsylvania Court House and dispatch him to the Block House Bridge, where he could buttress Anderson's flank against Hancock. As Lee reflected on the situation, he came to realize that he could accomplish more than simply repelling the Union 2nd Corps. What if he sent Heth across the Po below Hancock, then advanced him north into Hancock's exposed underbelly? If Mahone attacked from the east at the same time that Heth attacked from the south, the Union 2nd Corps would be caught between two Confederate divisions. That was precisely the type of surprise Lee delighted in administering, and he began issuing orders to make sure it would happen.

Lee's first step in setting his trap to snag Hancock was to send Mahone to the Po. Brigadier Generals Nathaniel H. Harris' and Abner Perrin's brigades of Mahone's division reached the Block House Bridge around seven that evening, at about the same time that Hancock's lead elements arrived on the other side of the Po. Mahone extended his pickets along the river's eastern bank, started digging a fortified line paralleling it on high ground a few hundred yards back, and ordered more of his troops to join him from Spotsylvania Court House. Soon Brigadier General Edward A. Perry's Floridians and Wright's Georgians had added their strength to his line, deploying at right angles to Anderson's flank and facing Hancock. "Mahone had just made his dispositions when masses of men were heard moving down to the opposite bank of the Po," a rebel stated. "A thundering cheer from the midnight darkness which reigned around revealed that the Confederates on this side of the river lay in the presence of a host of armed men." When they first arrived, the Federals seemed determined to force their way across the river. But concerned about Mahone's strength, Hancock postponed the attack.[71]

At ten o'clock, Hancock sought Meade's guidance. He was at the Block House Bridge, he reported, and the situation was hazardous. "The river is so deep that the flankers and skirmishers could not cross without swimming," he wrote, "and the darkness and thick woods near the stream caused great confusion and risk of firing into our men." Hancock wanted Meade to tell him what to do. "Knowing that General Grant's intention was for the column to move on," Hancock gently reminded his friend and fellow Pennsylvanian, "I can still give the order, but do not think it wise, and await your instruction." He concluded by placing responsibility unequivocally on Meade, writing, "You can judge the propriety of the measure."[72]

Meade's response did not reach Hancock until after midnight. He was to stay put until morning. Instead of aggressively pursuing Grant's plan, the Army of the Potomac would wait until daylight.[73]

The 2nd Corps, isolated from the Union army, dangled like a tantalizing morsel below the Po. And unlike Meade, Lee did not waver when he saw opportunity. Under cover of the dark May night, he was laying a trap calculated to bag Hancock's entire corps. Shortly after midnight, Heth's division, augmented by Colonel David Weisiger's brigade from Mahone's division, slipped quickly and silently from Spotsylvania Court House. Early rode with Heth. His assignment was to cross the Po below Hancock, then turn north and explode into Hancock's unsuspecting flank. "We soon saw that there was 'something out,' " one of Heth's men scrawled in his diary. "It was a great, an immense piece of luck for us," Porter Alexander reminisced. "Hancock had made his move across the Po late in the afternoon, giving us the night to make preparation to meet him." If Lee had his way, morning would find the Federal flankers flanked in turn. The hunter was about to become prey in a twist of fortune much to Lee's liking.[74]

"Determination mixed with sadness was there."

Stuart's tireless scouts discovered Sheridan's movement south shortly after it began. At eight in the morning, Stuart informed General Lee of a "demonstration of the enemy's cavalry on the Fredericksburg Road about one mile and a half from Spotsylvania Court House." Wickham's patrols monitored the dusty column as it snaked past the rebel right flank, but there was little he could do. Hampton was busy with Hancock on the Po, and Fitzhugh Lee was occupied holding Burnside in check on Fredericksburg Road. By midday, however, Early's 3rd Corps had begun entrenching across Fredericksburg Road northeast of Spotsylvania Court House, which freed Lee's cavalrymen to strike out after Sheridan. Confederate scouts placed Sheridan on Telegraph Road somewhere around Massaponax Church, east of Spotsylvania. Wickham started off "at a gallop." Pulling into the hamlet, he learned that Sheridan had just passed through. If he moved quickly, he could catch his rear guard crossing the Mat at Jerrell's Mill.[75]

Sheridan, meanwhile, had decided to alter his route. The bridge where Telegraph Road crossed the North Anna was reputedly well defended. But an alternate route held promise. A road slanted southwest at Jerrell's Mill, passing through Mitchell's Shop, Chilesburg, and then across the North Anna at Anderson's Ford. Since Anderson's Ford presented no obstacle,

Sheridan decided to leave Telegraph Road and follow the route through Chilesburg. He would avoid fighting until the next day, after his troops and their mounts had rested and eaten.

Sheridan's rear ranks were in the able hands of Henry Davies—"polished, genial, gallant," a fellow cavalry officer described him. No sooner had Davies crossed at Jerrell's Mill than a flurry of shots announced Wickham's arrival. It was between two and three in the afternoon. "The rebels are closing in on us," warned a breathless courier. "The advance guard of their cavalry opened on us back there in the woods. We gave them a volley and closed up to keep them from cutting us off, as they are deployed well out on both sides of the road."[76]

Davies selected a defensive line a quarter mile below the stream and arrayed the 1st Massachusetts Cavalry across the road, facing the rebels. The 1st New Jersey Cavalry formed on the left, and a squadron of the 6th Ohio Cavalry rode toward the Confederates to cushion the expected attack. "The enemy's advance came down on us in a furious charge which drove us back on our supports," an Ohio trooper reported. Panic ensued, pack mules scattered in all directions, and Davies hurried back to straighten out the confusion. The 1st Massachusetts Cavalry saved the day. "The rebels were checked just in time," a Federal asserted. "It was a most disgraceful affair, but resulting from surprise." Contrary to expectation, a full-scale battle failed to develop.[77]

After a half hour of sparring, Davies moved on. For the next several hours, he and Wickham waged a running fight, Davies trailing the Federal column while Wickham probed for weak points. "We had the satisfaction of harassing the enemy to our heart's content," a rebel in the 2nd Virginia Cavalry wrote, "hanging upon his flank, watching an opportunity to strike, and then hurrying off to another point, occasionally getting a chance at him with our little piece of artillery." A Federal complained that the Confederates "seemed to be familiar with the country round about, for they 'cut cross lots' and came in on our flanks at different points." Davies' troopers did their work well. Sheridan later commended them for exercising "tact and good judgment, following the main column steadily as it progressed to the south, and never once permitting Fitzhugh Lee's advance to encroach far enough to compel a halt of my main body."[78]

Things came to a head at the little settlement of Mitchell's Shop, where the road crossed a creek and wound around the base of a small hill. Confederate attacks had become increasingly bold, which convinced Davies that it was time to teach Wickham a lesson. He formed the 1st Massachusetts Cavalry in woods on the road's right side facing the bridge. The 1st Pennsylvania Cavalry hid in woods on the left. A detachment from the

6th Ohio Cavalry waited in the roadway to bait the trap. Watches read five o'clock.[79]

The Confederate column came into view. Wickham rode at its head, next to Captain George Mathews, of the Cumberland Troop of the 3rd Virginia Cavalry. The sight of the isolated Ohio squad was irresistible, and Wickham ordered Mathews to charge immediately. "I remember the look on our captain's face," a Cumberland man wrote. "Determination mingled with sadness was there." Mathews waved his saber overhead and shouted, "Come on, boys."

As the Cumberland Troop thundered along in a cloud of dust, the Ohioans—Davies' bait—retreated between the two hidden lines of dismounted cavalry. The Virginians pressed ahead. An Ohio trooper recalled glancing over his shoulder as rebels "charged down the narrow road in column of fours, and with a yell they were on us." Flames erupted from both sides. "I remember the cross fire in the lane that cut our squadron in two," recounted Confederate James J. Robinson, who survived by throwing himself low against his horse's neck until the volley passed. Mathews—Fitzhugh Lee described him as "one of my most promising officers"—jerked his horse to a halt and was shot dead by a Yankee behind a bush. "There was nothing for the rebels to do but to get out of that hornets nest as expeditiously as possible," a Massachusetts soldier recognized.[80]

Several Cumberlanders concluded that it was safer to proceed than to retreat. "The dust was thick enough to cut," Robinson observed. "We mixed in with a squadron of Yankees and they with pistols and we with sabres had it, while the Yankees nearby fired into both parties." A Federal recounted that the "ring of sabre, the sharp crack of carbines and revolvers, the shouts of the men, and the horse commands of the officers filled the air with an infernal din." Robinson hefted his heavy English saber until his horse fell with a bullet through its head. Jumping to his feet, he attempted to draw his pistol, only to find a half dozen carbines leveled at his face. "I surrender," he announced, but a Federal sang out, "Shoot the damned rascal. I have just seen him kill one of our men." Hammers were clicking back when a Union sergeant rode up. "I have surrendered and demand to be treated as a prisoner," Robinson called to him. He was led away under guard.[81]

Determined to break through, Wickham ordered a detachment to circle around Davies while the 3rd Virginia Cavalry charged once more down the roadway. Working cross-country, the flanking party came upon Davies' horses, which had been put in the rear out of harm's way. Portions of the

Union line dissolved as Federals bolted from the lane to return to their mounts, which were being tended by a light force of horse holders. Attacking again from the front, soldiers from the 3rd Virginia Cavalry managed to fight down the road to the Union guns. A brazen rebel reached a cannon and screamed, "That gun is mine!" Nonplussed, the chief gunner shouted, "Not by a damned sight," and flogged the southerner into submission with a rawhide whip. Another Confederate broke past the foremost guns and started after a piece that had limbered up and was rolling rearward. Discovering that he was alone and surrounded by Yankees, he turned and began hacking his way out. Fighting dissolved into a confused fracas in which dust disguised friend from foe. A high fence lined the lane and hampered maneuver. "In consequence, our loss was severe in the hand to hand struggle in the narrow road," an Ohio man reported.[82]

Wickham's advance had isolated Captain Walter R. Robbins' 1st New Jersey Cavalry squadron that had been scouting along a nearby farm road. Alerted by the sound of musketry that something was amiss, Robbins entered the main road behind Wickham, then charged into the rear of the unsuspecting rebels. Strengthened by Robbins' reinforcements, Davies braced for another Confederate assault. Wickham, however, decided against attacking and ordered artillery to fire at the Federals, who sought protection in a sunken section of the roadbed. Captain Joseph W. Martin's Union battery rolled forward and began dueling the Confederate guns. A Jersey trooper summed up the fighting at Mitchell's Shop: "A man or two killed, a few men wounded, an equal number of prisoners from each side, and considerable temporary confusion were all the results from an affair which threatened at first to be disastrous." The rearguard action had cost Davies seventy-six men.[83]

While Davies held Wickham at bay, the rest of Sheridan's column continued south, spearheaded by the 6th Michigan Cavalry, of Custer's brigade. According to the regiment's commander, Colonel James H. Kidd, "Things were kept moving, and it was very enjoyable, as service with the advance of a marching column always is." An uneasy moment occurred at a fork in the road, where a local guide selected the eastern prong. An officer, however, suspected treachery and slipped a noose around the guide's neck. The man's memory was miraculously refreshed and he recommended the other branch, which turned out to be the correct one. He was sent back in chains.[84]

Late in the afternoon, Sheridan reached Chilesburg, and before dark he was at Anderson's Ford, on the North Anna. Gregg and Wilson bivouacked on the north bank while Custer took his brigade and elements of Devin's troopers over the river and on toward Beaver Dam Station on the Virginia Central Railroad. Around 8 P.M., a thunderstorm broke. A New Yorker recalled the "rain falling in torrents, and the thunder and lightening exceeding anything of the kind I had ever witnessed." Ahead, through a lashing downpour, Custer's scouts could see vague outlines of soldiers. These turned out to be Union prisoners under escort to the station at Beaver Dam. Major Melvin Brewer's 1st Michigan battalion scooped up most of the guards and liberated the captives. They were predominantly from the 5th Corps and had been captured during the abortive attacks against Laurel Hill on May 8. Among their number was Colonel Phelps, of the 7th Maryland, and Colonel Talley, of the 1st Pennsylvania Reserves. In all, 278 Union soldiers were freed.[85]

Whistles tooted impatiently at Beaver Dam Station, where two trains were waiting to unload provisions and to take on the prisoners. Brewer, followed by the 1st and 6th Michigan Cavalry, pounded up to the siding, and the engineers found themselves staring into carbines. Two locomotives and their cars fell into Union hands. The Federals also captured supplies that Sheridan estimated at two hundred thousand pounds of bacon, a million and a half rations, and nearly all of Lee's medical stores. Custer's soldiers stuffed their haversacks with booty, then stacked and burned the rest. They set the station buildings on fire, derailed the trains, and ripped up track in each direction. Before morning, eight to ten miles of railway and telegraph lines lay in ruin. "With the blazing buildings in front of us, the drenching rain falling, the thunder peeling overhead, and the blinding flashes of lightning, the situation can be better imagined than described," a witness decided.[86]

Custer's soldiers bivouacked near the pyre. The only annoyance came from the 1st Maryland Cavalry battalion, a small Confederate unit under Colonel Ridgely Brown that had been camped ten miles away, at Hanover Junction. While the Federals were busy wrecking tracks, Brown and some of his troopers crept close. "He found the enemy in great glee," a soldier recounted, "laughing and shouting at the top of their voices, whilst at the same time they were busily engaging in burning railroad ties, and generally seemed to feel the existence of an enemy to be an absurdity." Brown quietly returned to his command and gathered 150 men. They silently approached the railroad, deployed in line, then charged, firing and shouting at the top of their lungs. Brown had second thoughts when he learned from prisoners that his little band had taken on the lead elements of Sheridan's entire corps. "There was something of sublime audacity in this attack of not more than 150 men upon a body who numbered not less than 8000 of as finely-equipped and organized cavalry as had ever been brought together on this continent," a Marylander concluded. "Colonel Brown was obliged to decline such odds, and we withdrew," another southerner explained.[87]

During the night, a few Confederates ventured to the edge of the woods and took potshots at the intruders, but they were easily driven away. The erstwhile prisoners paraded back to Sheridan's camp on the North Anna. "How glad the boys were to be again under the stars and stripes," a soldier remarked, "and to realize that the horrors of prison pens were not to be theirs, for the present at least." Celebrations continued into the night. Farther north, Davies' troopers, still at Sheridan's rear, constructed barricades to deter Wickham. The 6th Ohio, which had sustained eighty-seven casualties serving as the rear guard, was relieved by the 1st Maine. "We unsaddled and made coffee, fed our horses and prepared for a little sleep, which was not of long duration," an Ohioan reminisced. Skirmish fire crackled, but the rebels did not renew their assaults.[88]

Around three o'clock in the afternoon on May 9, Stuart left his temporary headquarters in an old church near Spotsylvania Court House and rode south to join Fitzhugh Lee. Playful as usual, the general turned to his aide Boteler with a "rough laugh" and joked, "Don't let any of those fellows get my share of the coffee, Colonel," referring to a trick he had earlier played on his staff. Then he disappeared in a cloud of dust singing "Take your time Miss Lucy and pour your coffee out."[89]

Near nightfall, Stuart overtook Fitzhugh Lee near Mitchell's Shop. Threading through the dismounted cavalrymen, he reined in his horse to avoid hitting a soldier. The man recognized Stuart by his distinctive hat and feather and shouted, "Hurrah, boys! Here's old Jeb!" Hoping to quell demonstrations so near to the enemy, Stuart cautioned, "Don't holler, boys, until you get out of the woods."[90]

Fitzhugh Lee recollected that Stuart seemed in "good spirits, always incident to a prospect for a fight." He remembered Stuart's "singing his usual refrains, laughing, joking, dressed too as common—top boots, spurs, grey pants, vest and jacket, the latter lapped back and buttoned— hat and long black feather." To others, Stuart appeared unusually silent. "General, I believe you are happy in a fight," a bugler interjected in an attempt to lighten Stuart's mood. "You're mistaken," the cavalry commander answered. "I don't love bullets any better than you do. It is my duty to go where they are sometimes, but I don't expect to survive this war."[91]

Lomax soon arrived from Spotsylvania, bringing Lee's division to full strength. More reinforcements were expected, since Stuart, before leaving Spotsylvania, had ordered Hampton to send James Gordon's brigade. Gordon's men—the 1st, 2nd, and 5th North Carolina Cavalry—had bivouacked at Locust Grove, several miles northwest of Spotsylvania on the Orange Turnpike. It was uncertain how long they would take to arrive.[92]

Stuart dispatched his aide Garnett to find Gordon and hurry him along. Garnett backtracked and located the brigadier at Mud Tavern, on Telegraph Road, just below the Po. His soldiers were thoroughly winded from the day's ride. On learning that Stuart wanted him to press ahead, Gordon—doubtless frayed by the day's exertions—lost his temper. "By God, my men shall not move one foot until they are fed up," he expostulated, pointing out that his troopers had covered forty miles without food or water. After regaining his composure, Gordon invited Garnett to rest on his headquarters' porch. Both men fell immediately asleep, but before long Gordon was up and riding to join Stuart at Chilesburg. "Devastation and waste characterized the section through which the raiders had passed," a Tarheel noted, "and no vestige of a Yankee, save their dead, was seen."[93]

Stuart had meanwhile framed a plan to catch Sheridan. Although severely outnumbered—Stuart's three brigades faced Sheridan's three divisions—the rebel cavalry commander hoped to use the North Anna to his advantage. If he could strike while Sheridan was crossing, the Federal force would be divided and could be fought piecemeal. With such a strategy in mind, Stuart split his force. Fitzhugh Lee was to remain to Sheridan's rear, with Wickham's brigade, to delay the Federals who were camped north of the river. Stuart meanwhile would circle west with Lomax and Gordon, cross the North Anna upstream at the Davenport Bridge, and loop back to strike the portion of Sheridan's command below the river. Under cover of darkness, Stuart started out with Lomax' and Gordon's exhausted troopers.[94]

Sheridan must have felt no small satisfaction over his accomplishments. He had reached his objective, freed an impressive batch of prisoners, and materially damaged Lee's commissary. Most important, his quarry—Stuart's cavalry—was near at hand and away from the protective umbrella of the Confederate infantry. But in the rush of events surrounding Sheridan's whirlwind departure, an important consideration had been overlooked. Cavalry constituted the Army of the Potomac's eyes and ears, and Sheridan had taken all but three of Meade's mounted regiments. Stuart, mindful of the importance of cavalry to Lee's infantry, had left behind fully fifteen regiments. Without horsemen, how was Grant to gauge Lee's whereabouts and intentions? Sheridan, in his avidity to win a point against Meade, had severely handicapped Grant in fighting Lee at Spotsylvania.

For Grant, May 9 had yielded mixed results. Sedgwick's death cast a pall over the morning. During the afternoon, however, Grant tried to revive the stalled offensive. Willcox' Fredericksburg Road operation suggested that Lee was shifting east, and Early's disappearance from Hancock's front supported the inference. Grant responded by directing Burnside to hold firm while Hancock maneuvered against the western end of Lee's line in hope of striking the Confederate army while it was moving. But Grant's scheme was defective. First, Lee was not shifting east as Grant presumed. Instead, he was consolidating his army around Spotsylvania Court House. Willcox had overestimated the force opposing him and had misinterpreted Early's appearance as heralding a rebel offensive. Without Sheridan's cavalry, Grant had no reliable means of evaluating Willcox' observations. He also had no way of determining where Early's Confederates were going after they disappeared from Shady Grove Church. Lacking trustworthy intelligence, Grant resorted to educated guesses, but he guessed wrong.

Grant's second problem involved Meade's failure to wield the Army of the Potomac consistently with his larger design. Perhaps Grant neglected to explain his intentions adequately to Meade or to force the issue. But rather than preparing for the "vigorous attack" envisioned by Grant, Meade instead conducted timid operations at odds with the spirit of Grant's aggressive plan. "There were two officers commanding the same army," Humphreys later remarked. "Such a mixed command was not calculated to produce the best results that either singly was capable of bringing about." Each commander's sphere was ill defined, which "took away from the positiveness, fullness, and earnestness of an intended operation or tactical movement that, had there been one commander, would have had the most earnest attention and corresponding action." Lincoln had hoped that Grant would stiffen Meade's resolve. Any gains, however, had been offset by the blurred division of responsibility between the two men.[95]

In addition, Grant's decision to send Hancock thundering into Lee's flank lacked adequate preparation. Grant had ordered no reconnaissances. He had no idea how many Confederates Hancock would encounter or where they were positioned. And he had no plans for supporting Hancock or for extricating him if the Confederates countered in strength. Grant was devoted to sustaining the initiative, which required moving rapidly. This time, however, he reacted precipitately without first determining the practicality of his plans or arranging to follow through with them. The Po River expedition contained an impulsive element that exemplified a disturbing trend in Grant's generalship.

To confound matters, Grant and Meade issued orders during the night starkly at variance with the aggressive spirit in which Hancock's expedition had been launched. Caution became the watchword. At 11:15, Meade instructed his corps commanders to hold their troops "in readiness to advance against the enemy." Hancock was to "endeavor to ascertain the position and force of the enemy in his front," and Wright to "feel for" Lee's other flank. Mott, who had shifted from Todd's Tavern toward the gap between Wright and Burnside, was to remain "ready to move to the assistance of Major General Burnside on hearing heavy firing in that direction." Grant directed Burnside to "hold your position at Gayle's," but added, "If you ascertain that you cannot hold it quietly withdraw to the head of the column near Alsop's." In sum, Grant would continue to probe Lee's position and send his corps forward if developments warranted. Six days below the Rapidan had taught him respect for the Army of Northern Virginia and its leader.[96]

May 9 had also been trying for Lee. During the morning, he had worried about his flanks. On the Confederate left, Early risked being isolated near Shady Grove Church, and on the right, Wickham's cavalry had to counter Burnside with little infantry support. By noon, however, both problems had been resolved. Early had gotten away safely at daybreak and was tramping into Spotsylvania Court House. While Wilcox' division entrenched, rebel scouts crept to Burnside's burgeoning works near the Beverly house and kept them under close surveillance.[97]

By afternoon, Lee's flanks were relatively secure, but his line still included two troublesome features. One was the salient toward Grant. The other was a gap of about a mile between Ewell's right wing and Early's left, which was only lightly guarded. Until Early could close the space, it invited attack.

From Lee's perspective, Hancock's appearance on the Confederate left side was the day's exciting development. By nightfall, Mahone had tossed up a rugged barricade of earthworks that stretched above and below the Block House Bridge, at right angles to Anderson's flank and across from Hancock's skirmishers. Heth was marching below Hancock, planning to slice into the Union corps' lower flank at first light. Here was Lee's chance to wrest the initiative from his opponent, and he intended to make the most of it.

IV

MAY 10

Grant Feels for Openings
at the Po and Laurel Hill

"As hot as any fire they were ever in."

EARLY ON THE morning of May 10, Hancock was to resume his previous day's turning maneuver, cross the Po at the Block House Bridge, and plow into the western end of Anderson's entrenched line. As Anderson's line crumpled, Warren and Wright were to charge Laurel Hill, and Burnside was to renew his advance down Fredericksburg Road into Spotsylvania. It was a complex plan that required coordination beyond anything that the Federals had achieved thus far in the campaign.

Lee's plan also involved Hancock. During the night, Mahone had constructed strong defenses along the Po's eastern bank. While Mahone pinned Hancock in place, Heth, guided by Early, was to cross the Po a few miles south, then swing north into Hancock's lower flank. Lee's plan, like Grant's, required coordination, but it was precisely the type of flanking maneuver that his generals had learned to deliver with flair.

An unusual quirk in topography complicated Hancock's assignment and aided Lee. Near the Block House Bridge, the Po turned sharply from southeast to southwest, enclosing a finger of land with the Block House Bridge at its tip. Hancock's objective—Anderson's flank—lay directly across the bridge. "It was an ugly stream to cross under fire, unless the movement was made along both banks simultaneously," a 5th Corps aide remarked. Hancock's difficulty was that Lee had one bank firmly in hand. If the attack failed, Hancock would have to cross the Po twice—once at the Block House Bridge, then again to the north—before reaching safety. A determined rebel counterattack might inflict considerable damage before he could escape. This, it turned out, was exactly what Lee had in mind.[1]

Union probes on the morning of May 10

George Skoch

The night of May 9–10 proved tense for Hancock. His engineers worked feverishly to span the upper Po crossings with two canvas pontoon bridges and a stronger wooden structure. Barlow's division remained nervously alert on Shady Grove Church Road west of the Block House Bridge, facing Harris' Mississippians on the stream's far side. Brisk musketry punctuated the blackness. At daylight, rebel guns opened from across the river. Shrieking shells, a Union man observed, were "less musical than fife and drum, but more certain to wake one, quickly and thoroughly." Hancock's pieces above the Pritchett house, north of the river, began replying around six o'clock, and soon both sides were pounding away in a lively manner. The artillery practice was uncomfortably close for Hancock's soldiers wedged into the finger formed by the Po. One shell descended with noise like the "tearing of five hundred pieces of canvas" onto a group eating breakfast. A soldier dodged, missed his footing, and splattered sizzling bacon grease onto his messmates. "It is easier to imagine the swearing that followed than it is to describe it," a witness concluded.[2]

The rising sun illuminated a situation that augured poorly for Hancock's turning movement. Hancock's three divisions lined Shady Grove Church Road, with Barlow next to the river at the Block House Bridge, Gibbon behind, and Birney farther back at the tiny settlement of Waite's Shop. From the Block House Bridge, Barlow could see freshly dug earthworks a few hundred yards east of the river, skillfully sited on a ridge and extending at right angles to the roadway in both directions. Mahone's Confederates, backed by Lieutenant Colonel David G. McIntosh's eleven guns, commanded the bridge and the adjacent stretch of river. Parading the 2nd Corps four men abreast over the narrow span in the teeth of Mahone's firepower struck Hancock as a bad idea, but he sent his aide Morgan to take a closer look and report on the prospects. The rebels confidently permitted Morgan to reconnoiter unmolested, almost daring him to bring the troops across. Hancock did not miss the point. "After a careful survey had been made," he explained, "I concluded not to attempt to carry the bridge."[3]

Hancock dispatched several reconnaissances in an effort to find a passable ford. Then he informed headquarters of his quandary. "I am anxious to meet your views," he assured Meade, "but I desire to make an explanation as to the causes of the delay." Although rebels commanded the bridge, he would cross if headquarters insisted, and his men would fight "as well as any." He preferred, however, to have his entire corps on the eastern bank before fighting, and he could do nothing until he heard back from his scouting parties. The planned offensive was assuming a decidedly defensive character.[4]

Major James C. Briscoe, of Birney's staff, started south from Waite's Shop with the 4th and 17th Maine on a reconnaissance in force. Hampton's troopers, who had been hovering around Hancock all night, began nipping at the expedition. About a mile south, Briscoe reached Glady Run, a small stream that flowed east into the Po, and spotted gray forms on the ground across the creek. Suspecting an ambush, he crossed the 4th Maine on a dam and deployed the 17th Maine in line of battle. The precaution, however, was for naught. The suspicious shapes were stumps, not Confederates, and Briscoe had wasted precious time evading an ambuscade that existed only in his imagination.

Briscoe united his command below Glady Run and began following a trail that swung gradually eastward toward the Po. Hampton's riders fell back before the Federals, harassing them with skirmish fire. A woman found herself between the contending lines and in her "fright and flight tumbled off a high fence astride of a rail and slid to the ground seemingly careless which end struck first," according to a soldier. Hampton was hard pressed, but Confederate reinforcements were close at hand. Heth's flanking column, it developed, was marching from the opposite direction along the same trail. Briscoe's first hint of Heth's approach came when he encountered skirmishers from the Lamar Rifles, of the 11th Mississippi. Briscoe and his staff were flabbergasted. This was their first inkling that Confederates had come onto their side of the Po. "We were out on open ground and far in advance of any of our army," a Federal explained, "our right flank in the air and our left the devil knew where."[5]

Briscoe ordered a charge, but his two regiments declined to take on a Confederate division. "You must all now look out for yourselves," Briscoe reportedly exclaimed as he bolted rearward "with surprising agility and brilliancy of execution." Heth pursued Briscoe to Talley's Mill, on Glady Run, where the Federals crossed and deployed along the northern bank. The Mississippi riflemen leading Heth's advance formed on a small rise at the head of the pond at Talley's Mill and fired into the Federals as they scrambled to escape. Many of Briscoe's men ran over the dam, while others jumped into the creek and swam across under musketry from the southern bank. "This scrabble," a Maine man noted, "caused us to indulge in sundry unscriptural remarks concerning the rebels in general and Briscoe in particular." Most of Briscoe's men made it over the run, and Birney, who had been alerted to Briscoe's predicament, hurried two regiments to his rescue. Throughout the morning, they heatedly contested Heth's advance along the wagon road toward Waite's Shop.[6]

Collecting near Talley's Mill, Heth's road-worn troops discovered a well-provisioned residence that had been abandoned when the fighting started. The icehouse was particularly welcome, and the Confederates enjoyed a cold drink of water before moving on.[7]

Lieutenant Robertson, of Miles's staff, conducted a second reconnaissance with the 61st New York, marching southeast from Shady Grove Church Road to reach the Po about a mile below the Block House Bridge. He tried crossing on a fallen log, but Mahone's well-placed pickets drove him back. Then Robertson learned—from the "unwilling lips" of a local farmer—about a ford where Glady Run entered the Po. He was heading south toward the run when he noticed dust boiling up nearby. Rebels—the tail of Heth's column that was mauling Briscoe—were swinging below Hancock. Robertson dispatched a courier to the 2nd Corps commander. "A large column is marching toward our rear," he warned, "and is likely to do for us what we are trying to do for them—flank and destroy us in the bend of the river."[8]

Major Morgan, of Hancock's staff, meanwhile took Brooke's brigade on a third mission, marching south from the Block House Bridge along the Po's western bank. About a half mile below the bridge, Morgan found a shallow spot in the river and sent Lieutenant Colonel John S. Hammell over with the 66th New York. On the far bank stood freshly dug earthworks. Mahone had extended his line south, and Wright's brigade of Georgians occupied this sector of his entrenchments. The 66th New York crossed the river with cheers under heavy fire, drove back Wright's pickets, and began forming a battle line on the Confederate side of the river. Morgan sent word of Hammell's lodgment to Hancock, who optimistically viewed it as his best opportunity thus far for crossing the Po. He began preparations to send Brooke's brigade over, and to follow it with the rest of the corps.[9]

While Hancock probed for openings across the Po, Warren's ordnance opened a blistering barrage against Laurel Hill. Warren's divisions—extending west from Brock Road under Griffin, Cutler, and Crawford, in that order—waited behind their entrenchments for orders to charge. "The ball opens this morning along the entire line with artillery and musketry and it bids fair to be a day of great struggle," a Union aide jotted in his diary.[10]

Warren was unusually aggressive this sticky May morning, hoping to impress his superiors after his slipshod performance on May 8. He was at the front early, natty in his dress uniform. His assignment was to feel for weak spots in Anderson's defenses and to attack if he discovered an opening. The earthworks, however, seemed as formidable as ever. The line that Jeb Stuart had extemporized from the Po to Brock Road remained in the able hands of Charles Field's division of Anderson's corps. And with two days to fine-tune his dispositions, Porter Alexander had crafted Laurel Hill into an artillerist's dream. It bristled with gun pits commanding the approaches. Cabell's battalion anchored the rebel left wing near the Po, Haskell's battalion held the center, and on the right, covering the critical stretch of open fields immediately west of Brock Road, stood Huger's battalion. Parker's battery, supported by the Bedford Light Artillery, occupied prime high ground near the apex of the Old Court House and Brock roads. Parker's four rifled guns faced nearly west to enfilade any force that attempted to cross Spindle's Field.[11]

At first light, skirmishers from the 4th Michigan and 22nd Massachusetts ventured down Brock Road. Parker's artillery greeted them from the far rise. Shot and shell whistled overhead, but the Federals pressed on. Then Field's riflemen, assisted by Kershaw's soldiers east of Brock Road, chimed in with "terrible effect," observed a rebel. The Union skirmishers tumbled back in disorder. "We were well protected behind good breastworks of logs," a Confederate in Bratton's brigade recalled. "The way we did give it to those Yankees would have done your heart good to see." Sergeant Moses A. Luce, of the 4th Michigan, fell prostrate in a ditch "listening to the whiz of the balls over my head and the cries of the wounded and the yells of the enemy." Fearing capture more than Confederate bullets, Luce stood and ran. A bullet split his rifle's stock, another cut the skin above his eye. "With all the speed I had I ran down the hillside and across the valley, under the fire of the enemy, and succeeded in reaching the first rifle pit of our pickets and leaped into it," he recounted. But on learning that a fellow officer lay wounded between the lines, he crawled back toward the frowning works. His friend's leg had been shattered and it was impossible to lift him, so Luce knelt while the invalid climbed onto his back. "Then rising and in a stooping position," as Luce described it, "I carried him rapidly to the rear of our line." The sergeant received a medal of honor for the courageous rescue.[12]

One of Alexander's batteries—the 1st Richmond Howitzers—was pleasantly surprised around 5 A.M. when some of Crawford's Pennsylvania Reserves marched across its front. "It was a beautiful mark," a Confederate gunner reflected as rebel ordnance decimated the brazen northerners. Warren's artillery responded. A lucky shot bowled over four or five rebels and went on to shatter Private Sam Bailey's head, spattering brains and punching Bailey's rifle through a nearby soldier. "I was knocked down by the dirt driven through the breastwork before the shell came through or I would have been killed," reflected a Texan who had just loaded Bailey's gun and was handing it to him when the projectile hit.[13]

Satisfied that the southern guns had been silenced, Warren ordered fresh soldiers from Crawford's division to advance toward Laurel Hill. "Then we began to plow up the columns with shrapnel," a rebel gunner reported. The Pennsylvanians broke and made "good time back to their woods." Again Warren's artillery raked Field's Confederates with little effect. "We quietly sat behind our works," a southerner put it, "and interchanged our individual observations on what had just taken place, and waited for further developments."[14]

Under instruction from Warren to find a chink in Laurel Hill, Crawford continued easing patrols into the no-man's-land between the armies. "My line is steadily advancing as you desire," he assured Warren at 8:30 A.M. An hour later, he informed the corps commander that his right wing was "within grasp" of the enemy's works, and that his left was pushing through the woods, driving back Confederate skirmishers. Contact with Field's entrenchments seemed imminent. "As soon as my line is connected and well up," Crawford went on, "I shall feel strongly for the enemy."[15]

Around 10:30, Cutler's division, positioned on Crawford's left, advanced close to Laurel Hill and waited within musket range of the Confederates while 5th Corps pieces shelled the far woods. Alerted by the renewed cannonading that another Federal attack was coming, Alexander's guns opened. "We could hear their shells screeching over our heads on into this enemy's column," noted a Confederate hunkered in the trenches. Some of the rebel shells were poorly balanced: "Instead of going quietly, point foremost, like decent shells, where they were aimed, they would get to tumbling, that is, going end over end, or 'swappin' ends,' as the Tar Heels used to describe it, and then, there was no telling where they would go, except that they would certainly go wrong." Each errant projectile emitted a "wild, venomous, fiendish scream that makes every fellow, in half a mile of it, feel that it is looking for him particularly."[16]

Warren remained determined to find a weak point in Field's line. Rather than continuing his piecemeal attacks, he decided to send his entire corps ahead in unison. The attack was more ambitious than the probe that Grant had ordered, but Warren believed that an assault by all his troops would uncover a chink in Field's defenses. "Push the enemy back to his breastworks," he directed Crawford. "Form your line close to it, but don't assault until we get the others up."[17]

Crawford and Cutler charged at Warren's signal. Field's gunners and riflemen quickly routed them. "Canister went through us with the shriek of a thousand demons, tearing the brush around us and dropping limbs of the trees upon us," a soldier in the 143rd Pennsylvania recounted. Fire rippled along Perrin's works. The Alabamians "cheered to the echo and begged the Yankees to come on, but they recoiled and disappeared from our front," according to one of Field's men. Some troops from Bragg's brigade of Cutler's division made it to the Confederate abatis, where they groped through burning pine needles. "I began at once to brush the blaze from my pants legs and kick the fire from me to keep me from burning," a Yankee wrote. "No man could stay there under the enemy's fire at short range and fire under his feet, and the line at once broke in utter rout." A few Federals ran toward the Po, where Confederates scooped them up. And on Warren's left, Griffin again sent the 22nd Massachusetts and 4th Michigan forward, in a mission as foolhardy as any Crawford or Cutler had attempted. Commanded by Major Mason W. Burt, of the 22nd Massachusetts, the two regiments overran the advanced Confederate rifle pits near the Spindle house's charred remains. "Our loss was about eighty men in a brief moment of time," a Federal wrote home. After a short breathing spell, Burt continued toward the main Confederate works, where he was greeted by a "sweeping fire of canister and shrapnel" from Parker's guns. Some survivors ran back to the Spindle ruins. Others huddled in depressions in the field. Many lay quietly, baking all day under the hot sun.[18]

Late in the morning, Warren called off his attacks. They had cost his corps an estimated four hundred casualties and had achieved nothing. Laurel Hill fell silent. "So we piled some more canister in front of our guns," a southerner remarked, "and watched to see what they would do next."[19]

The day was not progressing as Grant had hoped. Hancock was still trying to find a way across the Po, and Warren was sacrificing his corps bit by bit in isolated attacks against Laurel Hill. Confederates had massed in substantial force near the Block House Bridge, and Lee was showing no signs of continuing his easterly shift. The time had come, Grant concluded, to abandon his morning's plan. At 9:30, he wrote his chief of staff Halleck in Washington that the "enemy hold our front in very strong force and evince a strong determination to interpose between us and Richmond to the last." Stressing his resolve to "take no backward steps," he requested additional forage, provisions, and ammunition. He also urged Halleck to send "all the infantry you can rake and scrape." Grant remained confident, but the strident tone of his earlier dispatches was absent. "We can maintain ourselves at least," he assured Halleck, "and in the end beat Lee's army, I believe."[20]

As Grant contemplated his next move, he received a report from Wright with serious implications. The 6th Corps lay entrenched on Warren's left, in front of the rebel salient, and Wright believed that Confederates were migrating from there toward Hancock. That raised the possibility that the Union 2nd Corps might be seriously imperiled. Hancock already faced the prospect of a two-front fight, against Heth and Mahone. Now, according to Wright, more rebels seemed heading his way. Hancock's flankers appeared to have fallen into a trap that was about to snap shut.[21]

But Grant, ever alert for opportunity, discerned possibilities in this otherwise darkening picture. If rebels were swarming toward Hancock, Lee had to be pulling troops from some other part of his line. It appeared from Wright's report that Lee was borrowing soldiers from the salient and perhaps from Laurel Hill, opposite Wright and Warren. If so, the low ridge ought now to be Lee's weak spot. The way to regain the initiative, Grant concluded, was to extricate Hancock from the horseshoe bend in the Po, reunite him with Warren and Wright, and then hurl the entire Army of the Potomac against Laurel Hill.

Grant recognized that this new plan—abandoning the Po River operation and launching an armywide assault across Lee's entire front—would take time to implement. He also realized the importance of misleading Lee into believing that Hancock still planned to attack from the Block House Bridge. As soon as Lee perceived that Hancock was retiring, the Confederate commander would doubtless restore to their former positions the troops he had withdrawn to protect his flank. To fool Lee into believing that Hancock continued to pose a threat, Grant decided to leave a token 2nd Corps force of one division below the Po, dangling like bait from a line. This entailed risk, but Grant deemed it critical for his plan's success that Lee continued to anticipate an attack from the Po.

Orders went out at ten o'clock designed to effect a powerful frontal assault across Lee's entire formation involving all of Grant's corps. Grant scheduled the attack for 5 P.M. to give Hancock time to pull two of his divisions from the Po and shift them next to Warren. One division was to remain below the river "so as to keep up your present threatening attitude on the enemy's left, but so that it can be withdrawn promptly to your support, if necessary." Hancock, "by virtue of seniority," was to command the 2nd and 5th Corps in a combined assault against Laurel Hill, and Wright was to "attack on your front promptly at 5 P.M., using General Mott's [2nd Corps] division for this purpose." Grant ordered Burnside to "reconnoiter the enemy's position in the mean time, and if you have any possible chance of attacking their right do it with vigor and with all the force you can bring to bear." Mindful of Burnside's uninspired performance thus far in the campaign, Grant added, "Do not neglect to make all the show you can as the best co-operative effort."[22]

Wright had been toying with the idea of sending one of his most aggressive officers, Upton, against Lee's works, and Grant and Meade decided to incorporate Upton's foray into the general assault. Scouts began exploring for a suitable place to mount the charge.

Paradoxically, Grant's new scheme rested on assumptions as faulty as those behind the abandonment of Hancock's flanking maneuver. It was true that Lee had mobilized to confront Hancock, but he had not taken troops from Laurel Hill as Grant presumed. The two rebel divisions threatening Hancock had come from Lee's far right wing, opposite Burnside. Little did Grant suspect that his proposed five o'clock attack would run directly into the Confederate 1st and 2nd Corps' massed firepower. And he certainly had no inkling that the weak point in Lee's defenses lay in front of Burnside. Without cavalry to reconnoiter, Grant resorted once again to guesses. And once again, he guessed wrong.

The new scheme also raised practical difficulties. With Heth circling below the Po, how was Hancock supposed to withdraw? Whom was he to leave behind to maintain his "present threatening attitude," as Meade put it in his directive? And what was to become of the troops serving as bait when Lee's trap snapped shut?

"The combat now became close and bloody."

Hancock acted immediately upon Meade's instructions to evacuate his corps from the loop in the Po, which was starting to take on a frightening resemblance to a noose. He could not, however, remain to supervise the withdrawal. After directing Birney and Gibbon to begin pulling out, he rode over to Warren's headquarters to inspect the location proposed for the evening attack against Laurel Hill.

Before leaving, Hancock selected Francis Barlow's division to serve as the decoy. The thirty-year-old patrician, still recovering from a wound he received at Gettysburg, was fast earning a reputation as a strict disciplinarian. He was also a casual dresser and on May 10 sported a flannel checkered shirt, threadbare blue trousers, and an oversized saber for prodding slackers into action. Clean-shaven and "almost boyish," the gangly

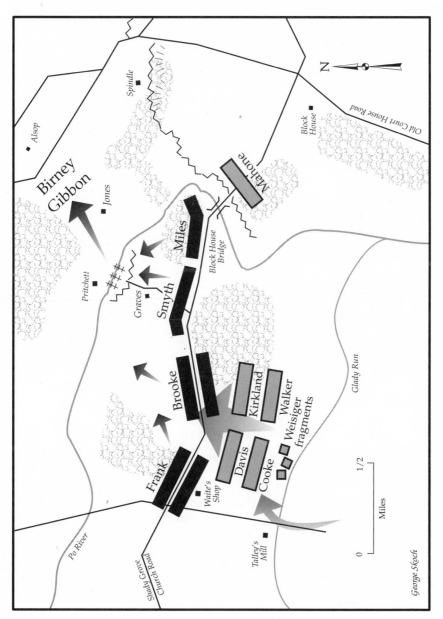

Heth's attack against Barlow below the Po River during the afternoon of May 10

general was one of the Union army's ablest field commanders, and he was served by an impressive set of brigade heads, all of whom were colonels. Nelson Miles, who oversaw a mixed New York, Michigan, and Pennsylvania outfit, was "fine looking, courageous, [and] a natural born soldier [who] always proved more than equal to the emergency." Thomas Smyth commanded the Irish Brigade, a rough-and-tumble band that excelled where combat was hottest. And John Brooke, heading a brigade drawn from New York, Pennsylvania, and Delaware, was, in the words of a soldier, "equaled by few officers in the army and should have been a brigadier-general long ago." The division's weak link was Paul Frank. Lyman, echoing the prevailing sentiment, proclaimed him a man "who tried to make up for want of nerve with strong drink."[23]

Around eleven that morning, Gibbon and Birney left Waite's Shop and fell back to the pontoon bridges. Rebel gunners posted on Laurel Hill began firing diagonally across the fields at the blue specks moving in orderly lines up the embankment. "As we came over the Po we received a murderous charge of canister and spherical case, which rattled over and around us like pebbles in a bladder," one of Birney's men recounted. "A fellow in front of me had the flesh torn from his back—as one would strip a salt fish." Colonel Samuel S. Carroll's brigade, bringing up Gibbon's rear, suffered cruelly. "It seemed as if all Rebeldom concentrated here," a Federal observed, "with the sole purpose of crushing us."[24]

While Gibbon and Birney crossed to the Union side of the Po, Barlow constructed defenses along Shady Grove Church Road, facing south toward Heth's approaching Confederates. Miles's brigade anchored Barlow's left wing on a crest north of Shady Grove Church Road, near the Block House Bridge. Smyth's Irish Brigade stood entrenched on Miles's right and extended Barlow's line westward. A broad pasture interspersed with clumps of trees spread a half mile or so north behind Miles and Smyth to the pontoon bridges and safety. Barlow's remaining two brigades lay ensconced on Smyth's right, behind makeshift works immediately south of Shady Grove Church Road, and extended the Federal line west toward Waite's Shop. Brooke's brigade was posted on Smyth's right, and Frank's near Waite's Shop. Behind them was a dense forest, which threatened to hinder their escape if Heth pressed his attack. At Barlow's rear, on the river's north side, loomed the 2nd Corps' artillery, minus two batteries that remained with Barlow.[25]

Hancock was sensitive to Barlow's precarious position. "Don't push your reconnaissances too far nor with large parties," he warned his subordinate. "No attack is to be made or crossing without orders." Most important, Barlow was to remain in readiness to recross the river.[26]

Hancock had scarcely left to inspect Laurel Hill when Heth's rebels began probing Barlow. The first sign of the impending storm appeared about noon when Briscoe's jaded men, mud-spattered and dragging their wounded, came pounding back along the wagon trail from Talley's Mill. Heth's division clattered behind in hot pursuit. Barlow's skirmishers managed to stave off the first wave of pursuing rebels until the Maine regiments had passed safely through to Shady Grove Church Road. The Confederates retired slightly to form a screen protecting Heth's infantrymen pouring across the fields behind them.

Heth moved to the attack, accompanied by Early, who was no doubt cursing and impatiently waving the winded soldiers into place. A courier from Lee arrived while Early was busily deploying the troops. "He led the sharpshooters and the minnieballs rattled around us like hail," the messenger remarked. Early instructed the artilleryman McIntosh where to place his guns in a "low whining voice" that McIntosh found incomprehensible. He asked Early to repeat his instructions, but the general's words still eluded him. When McIntosh again requested instructions, Early lost his temper. "Well, God damn it, if you don't understand, go put them where you damned please!"[27]

Hancock was reconnoitering Laurel Hill with Meade when a dusty messenger spurred up to them with news from Barlow. At least a division of Confederates had deployed to attack below Shady Grove Church Road, Barlow reported. More rebels—Mahone's outfit—were nearby, just across the Block House Bridge and considerably nearer to Barlow than the closest Union reinforcements. Birney and Gibbon had crossed to the northern bank and were unable to assist him. The bait that Hancock had left below the Po—one of the Army of the Potomac's best combat divisions—was about to be devoured by Heth and Mahone. Meade became "extremely anxious" and instructed Hancock to return to the Po immediately and save Barlow.[28]

Hancock hurried back and discovered that the situation was, in Walker's words, "already critical." Rebel artillery stationed near the Block House Bridge was enfilading Barlow, and Heth's skirmishers were aggressively probing for weak points, like wolves closing for the kill. As Walker summarized the predicament, "A defeat to our troops in such a situation, far from the rest of the army and with the river between them, would have meant something very like destruction." Hancock's only recourse was to extricate Barlow. "This was, however, by no means an easy matter," Walker observed.[29]

Hancock wisely declined Early's invitation to battle. "I immediately joined General Barlow," he reported, "and instructed him to prepare his command to recross the river on the bridges we had laid in the morning." The withdrawal was to proceed in stages. First Brooke's and Frank's brigades, which made up Barlow's right wing, were to shift above Shady Grove Church Road and re-form on the right of Miles and Smyth, presenting a unified line along Shady Grove Church Road facing Heth. Then Miles and Smyth were to retire north across the open field to a new line in front of the pontoon bridges and throw up breastworks of rails and fallen trees. Once the bridgehead was secure, Brooke and Frank were to slip east along Shady Grove Church Road, then escape up the field to the bridges. Barlow's guns—except for Arnold's A, 1st Rhode Island—were to join the rest of the 2nd Corps' artillery on the ridge across the river. When Barlow reached the bridges, he would be under the Union ordnance's protective umbrella.[30]

At 2:30, Barlow began the first stages of his withdrawal. Brooke and Frank abandoned their trenches below Shady Grove Church Road and scampered into new entrenchments above the roadway. At the same time, Smyth retired to the pontoon bridges and began throwing up earthworks to protect the river crossing. Early assumed that the northerners were retreating and hurried his preparations to attack, deploying Heth's division below Shady Grove Church Road from Waite's Shop and into the fields immediately east of the settlement. Brigadier Generals Joseph R. Davis' and William W. Kirkland's brigades formed Heth's first line, John R. Cooke's and Henry H. "Mud" Walker's brigades his second line. After "some little delay," Early ordered them to charge.[31]

Heth's battle line covered Frank's and Brooke's fronts. "The rebels advanced in skirmishing order and opened fire," a captain in Frank's brigade commented. "As soon as they came within range, we gave them a warm reception and expected to easily dispose of them, but the skirmish line was quickly followed by a line of battle, and it soon became clear we were in for a pitched fight." Screaming Confederates clambered over the recently abandoned entrenchments below Shady Grove Church Road and charged into a "heavy and destructive fire" from Frank's and Brooke's men behind their new works. Captain William A. Arnold's guns, still stationed near Waite's Shop, enfiladed Davis' soldiers, who staggered momentarily, then re-formed and charged again. Brooke asserted that he repulsed three assaults. The colonel of the 55th North Carolina, of Davis' brigade, confirmed that his colors were shot down three times. Finally the southerners vaulted over Brooke's entrenchments, swinging their muskets like clubs. "The combat now became close and bloody," Hancock reported. Union artillery on the north bank opened, Confederate batteries replied, and shells arched over the confused mass of struggling infantry-men. The blue and the gray were no longer battling at long range from distant earthworks. They were intermingled and piled on top of each other, and they fought ferociously, as though the anger accumulated during the past days of maneuver had finally burst forth. "The rebs came up yelling as if they'd got a special license to thrash us," a Federal affirmed.[32]

Barlow's situation deteriorated as McIntosh's artillery enfiladed Bar-low's left from across the Block House Bridge and Heth's ordnance opened from directly ahead. The bombardment ignited the woods where Brooke and Frank had entrenched. "The surroundings were appalling," a Pennsylvanian testified. "The men knew that everyone was getting to the rear, that soon the bridges would be cut away and their only chance of escape gone." Barlow's instructions kept going astray, and several units fought without direction. "Our men were falling like game before hunt-ers," a Union soldier lamented, "and still no relief and no orders."[33]

Frank's brigade, on Barlow's right, received the brunt of Heth's attack. An officer in the 126th New York watched as rebels "came rushing, with wild cries, through the woods." A segment of Frank's formation broke, and fugitives streamed into Smyth's works near the bridges with tales of disaster. Barlow, who rode anxiously to and fro behind his line, was ap-proached by Frank's officers, who complained that the colonel had become too intoxicated to command. Barlow undoubtedly knew of Frank's repu-tation for drunkenness and of his abysmal combat record. He concluded, however, that it would be dangerous to switch commanders while under fire and deferred his decision until after the engagement.[34]

Arnold's guns were posted near the front and made attractive targets. A column of rebels rushed the pieces, but the gunners worked their can-nons vigorously and managed to keep the attackers at bay. Barlow ap-peared in the swirling smoke. "Why don't you get out of here?" he de-manded of Arnold, who answered that he had received no orders to retreat. "I have sent three men to you, to tell you to get out," the general ex-claimed. Arnold immediately dispatched the pieces along a narrow path through the woods toward the Po. "The guns were hurriedly limbered to the rear," a witness reported, "flying before the exulting, cheering mass behind." Then the lead piece wedged between two trees. The wheel team driver jumped down, grabbed an ax from the limber chest, and chopped the gun free. No sooner had the column started than the other gun jammed between some trees. Again men frantically chopped to free the piece, but it remained securely lodged. Pressed by surging lines of Confederates, the gunners cut the traces, spiked the piece, and abandoned it. Hancock listed the ordnance as the first artillery lost by the 2nd Corps. It was afterward said that Captain Arnold "wept at the loss of his gun, as you might for the loss of a dear friend."[35]

With rebels closing in and flames licking all around, Brooke's and Frank's fought-out men faced disaster. Early sensed that the Federals were spread thin. "Well, men, we must charge them once more, and then we'll be through," he declared to Davis' troops. "General, we are all out of ammunition," a soldier pointed out. "Damn it, holler them across!" he bellowed, and the Confederates renewed the assault. Barlow shifted units to fend off Heth's attacks, but smoke and confusion made it difficult for his regiments to maintain contact. Hancock rode grandly in the thick of the fighting. Concluding that further resistance was futile, Barlow directed Brooke and Frank to sidestep east to the clearing that funneled back to the bridges.[36]

"We unstrapped our blankets from our knapsacks, and spread them over our heads and shoulders to protect us from the flames," a soldier in the 52nd New York, of Frank's brigade, remembered. "It took fully ten minutes or more of blindly groping and butting against trees to reach the clearing, and then only to be fired upon by the Confederates, who in the meantime had taken advantage of our confusion to advance their lines."[37]

Barlow's instructions to retreat failed to reach the 148th Pennsylvania and 64th New York, posted on Brooke's right, which fought on unaware that they had been left behind. Heth's rebels poured "murderous fire" into the 148th Pennsylvania's exposed line. The last straw came when the Pennsylvanians discovered musketry emanating from their right, where Frank was supposed to be, and dispatched a scout to determine what had happened. "He had scarcely gone beyond our flank," an officer explained, "when he returned on a full run, with eyes blazing, and in emphatic language said, 'Colonel, the rebels are in there!' " Frank had bolted—whether he was under orders to do so remains unclear—leaving Brooke to fend for himself.[38]

Brooke's brigade shifted into the plain and retreated in sections through a deadly gauntlet. One of Mahone's Confederates gloated that "for 15 or 20 minutes we pumped the lead into them as fast as we could fire and load." Brooke penned a graphic account. "In retiring to the Po my command crossed a wide plain, swept by the enemy's artillery and infantry from the front and left flank, but notwithstanding the enemy and the burning forest, we retired with a scarcely perceptible break in our lines. Many of the gallant wounded perished in the flames." Hancock commended the troops for "such order and steadiness as to merit the highest praise." He added, "Their right and rear enveloped in the burning wood, their front assailed by overwhelming numbers of the enemy, the withdrawal of the troops was attended with extreme difficulty and peril." Brooke took severe casualties. "It seemed, indeed, that these gallant soldiers were devoted to destruction," Hancock marveled.[39]

Colonel James A. Beaver's 148th Pennsylvania formed a rear guard and backed toward the river while its forward elements maintained a "continuous fusillade." They reached the Po well above the pontoon bridges and slogged across a marsh, dragging wounded comrades to safety. Beaver carried an injured officer over the stream, then fell exhausted. An artilleryman handed the grateful colonel a flask of whiskey. "I drank it down, and, although strangled, was immediately revived," he owned. "It was the only drink of whiskey I took during the War." The 148th Pennsylvania's adjutant reported 167 men killed, wounded, and missing. The 64th New York escaped by the skin of its teeth. With the regiment facing destruction, the 64th's colonel dispersed his troops, instructing that each man was to "take care of himself and get out the best we could." Most of the soldiers ended up behind Smyth's line near the bridgehead.[40]

By 3:30, Brooke's men had crossed on a pontoon bridge while Frank's— who had worked north through the woods firing from tree to tree—had splashed over upriver. The 116th Pennsylvania, of Smyth's brigade, fought a determined rearguard action. "At last, when all others were gone, the welcome order came to fall back and try to save the regiment," a Pennsylvanian recounted. Dodging through burning trees—"flames were crackling and roaring"—the survivors reached the bridges. One soldier reckoned that he had been "saved almost by a miracle" and sorrowfully contemplated the thirty members of the regiment who were "still among the blazing trees dead or helplessly wounded, a prey to the pitiless fire."[41]

Only Miles remained below the Po. Three of his regiments occupied entrenchments in front of the bridges, and two—the 26th Michigan and 81st Pennsylvania—waited near the Block House Bridge to keep Mahone at bay. Once Barlow's three other brigades were safely over, Miles's frontmost units bolted for the bridgehead. The prospect of trapping the isolated regiments was more than Early could resist, and Heth's men charged in a "splendid line, with colors flying and an alignment as if on parade." Miles's last troops reached the bridgehead just ahead of the southerners. "All is still for a moment," a Federal wrote, "then the order to fire rings out on the air, and our muskets answer with a volley which seems fired from one great gun." Blistered by musketry from the bridgehead and by devastating plunging fire from the hillside beyond, Early wavered. Miles seized the opportunity and ordered a dash to safety. The 81st Pennsylvania was the last regiment to thunder across the pontoons. Then Federal engineers freed the remaining bridge and watched it drift to the southern shore. The river once again stood between them and the rebels.[42]

A fierce artillery duel accompanied Barlow's dramatic escape. Colonel John C. Tidball, commanding the Federal 2nd Corps' ordnance, had massed his guns above the crossing and scored Early's approaching Confederates. But to Tidball's dismay, his guns also started firing into each other. Birney, without consulting Tidball, had decided to rearrange the artillery, inappropriately placing some batteries in front of others. Tidball angrily corrected the dispositions, but Birney intervened and again ordered the guns positioned according to his design. Brigadier General Henry J. Hunt, chief of the Army of the Potomac's artillery, excoriated Birney for "thus sacrificing the fire of four batteries except one section to his crude notion of advantage of position."[43]

Heth's artillery—Lieutenant Colonel Charles Richardson's artillery battalion and a section of Thomas Ellett's battery—took on Tidball's guns from straight ahead. Cabell's Confederate battalion, sited on an elevation near Anderson's left, chimed in and peppered Tidball's flank. Some of McIntosh's guns rumbled across the Block House Bridge as Heth's soldiers uncovered the route. The rebels served their pieces to good effect and disabled one of Brown's guns on the Federal left. Shell fragments swept through the 10th Massachusetts battery, taking down several horses and gunners and severing a sergeant's leg. "He did not lose consciousness, but looked with melancholy interest at his severed limb, which lay nearby," a soldier remarked. "I was so sorry for him. I understood afterwards he died from the shock." Rebel sharpshooters considered the Union gunners special targets. "Never in their terms of service did they suffer such an hour of soul-harrowing agony as that spent on the eminence overlooking the Po, back of Pritchett's house," a Federal cannoneer declared.[44]

Early retired to the earthworks along Shady Grove Church Road formerly occupied by Barlow. "We were under the heaviest cannonading I ever saw or expect to see," a southerner judged. Another agreed that the shelling was as "brisk as I ever heard and did as good execution as is general."[45]

The engagement sputtered to a close around 5 P.M. Heth and Mahone entrenched along Shady Grove Church Road west of the river. Wright's Georgians anchored the line on the Po; Perrin's Alabamians extended the formation to the left, with Perry's Floridians, Harris' Mississippians, and Weisiger's Virginians reaching over to Heth. Approximately a mile north, across smoldering woods and fields, waited Hancock's Federals. The opposing forces, a reporter with the London *Herald* observed, "continued to look at each other during what remained of the day, without demonstration or attack save only to the extent of occasional shelling."[46]

Early exulted that Heth's men had behaved "handsomely." A soldier in Davis' brigade wrote that "although subjected during this charge to a fire from both artillery and small arms, the loss was not very great; we were charging up hill and the fire of the enemy went over our heads." Among the casualties were two of Heth's brigade commanders. Cooke, who had led his North Carolinians with spirit, was slightly injured. More seriously wounded was Walker, whose badly shattered foot had to be amputated. The Confederates rightfully considered the action a success. "The enemy soon gave way and broke," a Mississippian reported, "hastily leaving the breastworks and rushing pell-mell in the direction of General Grant's main body of troops." The artillerist Alexander noted that "after Barlow got across, Hancock's guns, as if specially mad with us for what we had done, duelled with us sharply for quite a while." Lee was so pleased with the results—the threat to his left flank had been removed once and for all, and the sector was now well fortified—that he directed Heth to issue an order congratulating the troops. Early later emphasized that his success "relieved us from a very threatening danger, as the position the enemy had attained would have enabled him to completely enfilade Field's position and get possession of the line of our communications to the rear."[47]

The Federals disputed the Confederate boasts. "The simple fact was that the withdrawal took place in consequence of General Meade's explicit and peremptory order," Walker somewhat disingenuously insisted. "Not a regiment gave way for a moment in the critical movement; the Confederates did not hasten the pace by anything they did; our troops retired just when and as they were directed." Hancock crowed that Heth had been repulsed several times with great loss. "This is not my recollection of what occurred," Heth protested when he learned of Hancock's version. "My division was not driven back at any time that I am aware of during this fight."[48]

Everyone agreed, however, that poor Federal planning had doomed Hancock's turning movement. Humphreys lamented that initiating the maneuver late on May 9 forewarned Lee and gave him time to respond. If Hancock had started at daylight on the 10th, he believed, "the Confederate left would have been turned and taken in rear while the Fifth Corps attacked in front." And rather than abandoning the venture, Humphreys suggested, Grant should have continued, reinforcing Hancock with a division from Warren. But Humphreys seems not to have realized that by the morning of May 10, Mahone's strong entrenchments had rendered the flanking movement impracticable.[49]

At the time, however, no one agonized over missed opportunities. Attention was shifting to Laurel Hill, the scene of Grant's next attempt to break the rebel stranglehold on Spotsylvania Court House.

"I tell you this is sheer madness."

Barlow's adventure had been breathtaking, but it was a mere sideshow. The day's main event was the attack slated for five o'clock. Grant gave his subordinates seven hours to prepare. But once again, a push intended to be unified fragmented into uncoordinated assaults. The chain of events that undermined this offensive revealed much about the shortcomings in the Federal leadership.

Under Grant's new plan, while Barlow was fixing Lee's attention on his western flank, Birney and Gibbon were to join the 5th Corps in attacking Laurel Hill. The 6th Corps, augmented by Mott's division, was to pound the Confederate salient's tip and western face, and Burnside was to assault Lee's eastern flank on Fredericksburg Road. Subjected to Grant's full weight, Lee's formation was expected to buckle somewhere and give Grant the opening he sought. But the plan had shortcomings. Its timing, for instance, was awkward, since an attack so near day's end would leave Grant insufficient time to exploit a breakthrough. And it relied on the faulty premise that Lee had weakened his Laurel Hill defenses by sending troops to attack Barlow.

Once again, incomplete and misleading intelligence had led Grant to dangerously erroneous conclusions. Warren's probes had established that Anderson still held Laurel Hill, and Early's troops were engaged on both Confederate flanks. Nothing, however, had been heard from Ewell. At 1:30 P.M., a Boston newsman wrote, "It seems to be currently credited at [Grant's] headquarters that but two corps of the rebel army lie in our front, and that Lee with one corps"—presumably Ewell's—"has gone to Richmond." He added that the "departure of that portion of the rebel army alluded to has no doubt been induced by the near approach to Richmond of troops under Generals Butler and Smith, thereby threatening the rebel capital during the absence of its almost entire army." In fact, Ewell still occupied the salient in force. But in Sheridan's absence, Grant lacked the cavalry necessary to investigate.[50]

The first slippage in Grant's plan occurred in Warren's sector. Although the attack against Laurel Hill was primarily a 5th Corps affair, Meade had selected Hancock to lead it. Warren's reflections concerning Meade's pointed snub have not survived, but the slight must have stung him. His star was not ascending as he had hoped.

Around two, when Hancock left to oversee Barlow's withdrawal, the dynamics at headquarters changed. Warren now commanded the forces across from Laurel Hill, and he was anxious to redeem his sinking reputation. Soon after Hancock departed, he went to Meade. No doubt motivated by Grant's and Meade's barbs to try demonstrating that he could successfully attack Lee's works, Warren petitioned Meade to permit him to assault right away rather than waiting until five o'clock. Meade agreed, and Grant, who was headquartered next to Meade, in all likelihood concurred. "The opportunity for attack immediately is reported to be so favorable by General Warren that he is ordered to attack at once," Meade informed Hancock at 3:30, adding, "Gibbon is directed to cooperate with him." Thousands of soldiers were to pay the price for Warren's ambition.[51]

Several observers remarked on Warren's zeal to attack, which served to cloud his judgment. "Burning with conviction," one soldier said of him. "Conspicuously prominent," remarked another, "encouraging his soldiers by his presence and stimulating them by his example to unusual activity." Determined to prove himself once and for all, Warren refused to recognize that Laurel Hill was impossible to attack. The point, however, was not lost on his troops. "Every man in the ranks saw the folly in the attempt," one soldier maintained. "I observed the countenances of the officers, from colonels down, and I must say that there were the longest faces upon this occasion of any previous one; and the experience they had had upon this same field two days before, was not calculated to light them up with a smile." On learning of the proposed assault, one of Warren's soldiers expressed "gloomy forebodings of disaster and death." His concern was well founded. Across the clearing, Field's men were stacking fresh supplies of ammunition. "The wooden boxes with rope handles were brought up from the ammunition wagons, two men to a box, each box containing eight hundred cartridges," a Confederate in the 4th Alabama reported. "The boxes were distributed at regular intervals behind the regiment, opened; the thick paper wrapping was taken out, spread upon the ground, and the cartridges placed on it. The officers assisted in loading."[52]

Warren directed Gibbon to deploy on the 5th Corps' right flank, next to the Maryland brigade. Gibbon was unfamiliar with the ground and undertook a quick reconnaissance. Like Warren's soldiers, he did not like what he saw. A patch of dead cedars lay straight ahead. Their stiff branches projected like bayonets and were certain to disrupt the advancing troops. Somewhere beyond lurked Field's Confederates and their infernal earthworks. Gibbon, who was accustomed to speaking his mind, told Warren that "no line of battle could move through such obstacles to produce any effect." The 5th Corps commander, however, "seemed bent upon the attack with some idea that the occasion was a crisis in the battle of which advantage must be taken." When Gibbon failed to persuade Warren to postpone the assault, he and Warren went to army headquarters to confer with Meade.[53]

To Gibbon's chagrin, Meade supported Warren and approved sending the 5th Corps and a single 2nd Corps division against Laurel Hill according to Warren's accelerated timetable. Altering the hour of Warren's attack was to throw Grant's plan horribly off.

Confederate artillery shells rained on Warren's assembling troops. The 3rd Maine's Colonel Moses Lakeman was using a stump as a chair and leaning against a tree when a shot shredded the timber above his head. "See what the careless cusses have done to my chair back," he mumbled as he poked out the slivers. "Colonel, haven't you better move before they hit you?" a soldier asked. "Oh no," he replied. "They have not got the bullet molded yet to kill old Mose." Bark flew as another shell slammed into the tree several inches closer to the colonel's head. "If you want that chair you can have it," he quipped as he stood and moved away. "I am not going to sit there any longer."[54]

As Warren prepared to charge, he found that his complement of troops was diminishing. Hancock recalled Birney to the north bank of the Po to cover Barlow's retreat. Gibbon remained with Warren, but since it appeared that Hancock might need more reinforcements at the Po, Warren chose to use only two of Gibbons' three brigades—those of Samuel Carroll and Brigadier General Alexander S. Webb. And at the last minute, Warren inexplicably placed one of his three 5th Corps divisions—Griffin's—on hold. Webb's and Carroll's brigades from Gibbon's division formed the western end of Warren's battle line as it was finally constituted. Immediately to their left stood Crawford's Pennsylvania Reserves, augmented by an orphan brigade created when Robinson's division was dissolved after its disastrous attack against these same works on May 8. Cutler's division stood ready to charge on Crawford's left.[55]

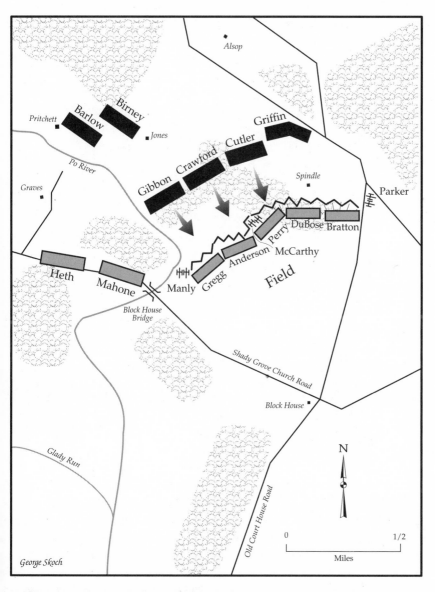

Warren's attack against Field on May 10 at 4 P.M.

"Boys, we have a hard job before us," Carroll warned his men. They needed no reminder. Veterans of fighting Lee, they knew the hazards of charging the fresh dirt line cresting the far ridge. In small groups, the soldiers crept forward to get a better look at the rebel position. The Confederates had cleared the ground in front of their works, dragging trees and bushes up the hillside and stacking them so that the sharpened branches pointed downward, toward the Federals. "As each group returned to the line it was plainly written on each face that they considered it an almost hopeless job," one of Carroll's soldiers was to recall. Four o'clock approached, and the men pitched their knapsacks into a pile. Officers peeled off their coats and threw them into the heap. Guns were inspected and loaded. The same soldier remembered, "Comrades gave messages to comrades for the loved ones at home; no jest or gay banter now; every face wears a serious but determined look; that strange hush which precedes a battle was over all."[56]

Crawford's troops were instructed to cheer when they stepped out as a signal to Webb and Carroll to move with them. Things looked grim from the start. Rebel artillery forced the Federals to "hug the ground pretty closely until the order was given to charge." At the cue, a "mournful cheer" sounded above the gunfire, and the soldiers began weaving toward the patch of prickly cedars that so concerned Gibbon. An Ohioan noticed that sandy soil under the trees appeared to be moving. As he drew closer, he saw why: "It was the bullets which whipped the sand like a switch."[57]

On the right of Warren's attacking line, Webb made a grudging advance that he later conceded "could hardly be termed a charge." Brigadier General John Gregg's mixed Texas and Arkansas brigade, supported by the Richmond Howitzers, held the segment of Confederate works in front of Webb. Their musketry tore bloody gaps in Webb's line, forcing the Federals to lie on the ground. Then the pine needles ignited, and Webb's soldiers beat out flames with their caps as they crawled on their bellies to escape Gregg's bullets. "We advanced about the same distance as Crawford's division did, which was not very far," a soldier in the 19th Maine stated. Carroll's troops on Webb's left elbowed through the smoldering cedars—"the sharp prongs of which scratched and tore the men as they crept through them"—only to mire in a freshly plowed field. Sharpened abatis pinned them under a "concentrated and murderous fire," to use Carroll's description. A few soldiers reached the rebel works and were never seen again. "Not enough human beings could pass through that deadly storm of musket balls and canister to reach the crest of the hill or do anything but surrender when they got there," a participant affirmed. Survivors retreated to the smoking cedar thicket. "How we got through it all I don't know," a Connecticut man confided in his memoirs. A New Jersey soldier recollected, "We remained over two hours fighting the enemy and the fire, the heat and smoke almost suffocating." Gibbon later summed up how things went: "At a given signal the men moved forward, made a feasible effort to get through the woods and stem the storm of bullets hurled against them, then gave it up."[58]

On Carroll's left, "well directed" Confederate fire—probably from Brigadier General George T. "Tige" Anderson's Georgians—slammed Crawford's Pennsylvania Reserves as soon as they began charging. Some Federals pushed to within a hundred yards of the works, but none went farther. "We were using double shot of canister nearly every time, on masses of men at short range," a rebel cannoneer recounted. "Rapid and deadly" fire decimated the Reserves. The 88th Pennsylvania lost one in four of those who went into action. As the fragmented Pennsylvania units staggered back, Texans swarmed behind them, scooping up abandoned rifles and cartridge boxes. "We piled up more canister, and waited again," related Private Dame, of the Richmond Howitzers.[59]

Cutler's division, situated on the left wing of Warren's assaulting line, started with parade-ground order, dipped into a brush-filled ravine, lost its alignment, then floundered toward the rebel works with little semblance of organization. Leading was a predominantly New York brigade under Brigadier General Rice, who cut a fine figure on his plunging charger. Within minutes he came back in a blanket, his leg shattered. The limb was amputated at a field hospital. Asked by a Union surgeon which direction he preferred to face, Rice allegedly insisted, "Turn me over towards the enemy. Let me die with my face to the foe." He died shortly afterward.[60]

With Rice's troops in disarray, Colonel Bragg's brigade moved to the front. The men were still smarting from their morning bout in the burning pine needles, and they wondered this time whether they were to be "boiled, fried, fricasseed, or roasted," recollected a Federal. They went in grudgingly a short distance to the right of where they had attacked that morning and came under riddling flanking fire from Parker's guns. "Our firing was probably never so destructive as on that day," one of Parker's men boasted. "Dead are falling," a participant observed, "and wounded go streaming to the rear in every direction." Then Colonel Robinson's Iron Brigade crossed the field and started up the far brow only to be slammed by "terrific and continuous fire." A soldier in the 2nd Wisconsin proclaimed it "sure death to stand up there and a waste of powder to fire." Most of Robinson's men hugged the hillside for protection. Some made it as far as the abatis, and a few reached the rebel parapets, but they lacked the momentum to continue over the works.[61]

Colonel Dawes was laboring to rally the 6th Wisconsin when he saw Warren and Carroll, sheltered by a dip in the ground. To Dawes's horror,

Warren ran ahead for a better look. "To have exposed himself above the hill was certain death," Dawes recounted. "I seized his yellow sash and pulled him back." Grant also paid a visit and displayed his usual disdain for safety. A shell fragment ripped away part of a nearby horse's head, and the mount began to plunge wildly. "During it all the general remained as unconcerned as if nothing had happened, not even removing the glasses from his eyes," a soldier noted. After persuading his superiors to retire, Dawes resumed the difficult task of extricating his troops. One resourceful soldier strung suspenders together, lassoed exposed men, and pulled them to safety. Another rolled a body in front of him for protection. One of Lyle's regiments ended up "flat upon the ground, under the enfilading fire of artillery from the left and the direct fire of musketry to the front." An artillery shell severely wounded Lieutenant Colonel Peirson, of the 39th Massachusetts, and tore his liquor flask in half. The bottom portion, still containing brandy, landed in front of a private, who drained it and declared in wonderment, "They are throwing good brandy at us."[62]

Flames crackled along Laurel Hill, spewing acrid, resinous fumes north, into the Federal's faces. Union soldiers stumbled about, "stifled and blinded by the heat and smoke." Searing volleys of overlapping rebel musketry and artillery churned the stubbled Virginia farmland. "Some portions of the corps advanced to the abatis, others halted part way and discharged a few volleys, but speedily the whole line fell back with terrible loss," according to a witness. The charge never had a chance. A correspondent reported that the "devouring element" consumed many of the wounded men.[63]

Robinson's Iron Brigade slowly fell back, the 6th Wisconsin remaining at the bottom of a small hill, about one hundred yards from the Confederate entrenchments. The soldiers watched in horror as flames spread along the hill. "Three dead bodies within forty feet of my position were now enveloped in the red mantle of flames, the smoke of which came drifting madly into my face," a Wisconsin soldier recounted. Crawling behind a log, he managed to pull a few men to safety.[64]

Over the next hour, soldiers dribbled back to the Union line. "My loss was quite heavy," Cutler noted in a report typical of those filed for that day. A witness pronounced Spindle's Field a "dreadful scene," where any movement provoked angry bursts of Confederate musketry. "It was only necessary to hoist a hat on a stick and the bullets at once begin to fly about it," a New Yorker observed. A Massachusetts man recalled lying "right in range of a heavy fire of solid shot and shell killing and wounding a great many, cutting down great trees over our heads." The attack had been a disaster for the Federals. "Our troops stood to their breastworks and mowed down the enemy," a Confederate recalled. A newsman from Philadelphia wrote that "such an incessant rattle of musketry as was kept up the whole afternoon is rarely witnessed."[65]

Cool heads at Union headquarters recognized the futility of continuing to batter against Laurel Hill. "This preliminary attack showed that the enemy was all set for us," Warren's aide Roebling commented, "and that the subsequent attack would have but little chance." Unfortunately for the Union cause, men with Roebling's acumen were not in charge on May 10.[66]

Five o'clock arrived—the time Grant had set for his grand offensive. Corpses in blue uniforms covered the area of Warren's ill-conceived attack. Soldiers still straggled in from the bloodstained field, some singly, some dragging wounded. The cost in lives had been high, and morale had been shattered. It was questionable whether the 5th Corps could continue fighting. "For once the rebs acted honorably and let the rescuing party save those wounded and dead comrades from the devouring flames without firing on them," a Pennsylvanian conceded. Resentment against the officers who had ordered the charges ran high. "Let the fault lie where it will," a soldier penned years later. "There is a just God that knows, and the shrieks and groans of the traitor's victims should follow him to his grave, and a common hell would be too good for him."[67]

At 5:50, Hancock returned to the Laurel Hill front. Barlow's evacuation had been completed and the last of Warren's men were dribbling back. "Here, as in the Wilderness, the woods prevented me from observing the conduct of the troops, although close to the point of attack," Hancock explained. "But it was soon evident we had failed." Grant, however, was determined to keep trying. A force of 6th Corps soldiers under Colonel Upton stood poised near Warren's left. For Upton to succeed, Meade had to keep the rebels on Laurel Hill busy. So he ordered Hancock to organize the 2nd and 5th corps and send them forward at 6:30. This time, suggested Meade, more of the 2nd Corps should participate. Birney had returned and deployed on Gibbon's right. Barlow sat ensconced above the pontoon bridges.[68]

At 6:25—five minutes before Hancock was slated to attack—a courier pounded up. Rebels, it seemed, had been sighted above Barlow's right, presumably intending to turn his flank. In light of this threat—a mirror image of Hancock's earlier attempt to flank Lee—Hancock was directed to return Birney to the Po, and the charge was postponed. "Mules hitched up, tents rolled," a correspondent noted. Meade had scarcely finished instructing Hancock to concentrate westward, however, when new intelligence arrived. The first report had been false. Hancock countermanded his order to Birney and directed him back into line for the Laurel Hill assault. The time lost shuffling Birney, however, entailed more delay. The attack was rescheduled for 7:00 P.M., two hours behind Grant's initial timetable.[69]

Union army cheering as Grant turns south on Brock Road on May 7
Drawing by Edwin Forbes, in Library of Congress

Warren trying to rally the Marylanders at the Spindle farm on May 8
Drawing by Alfred R. Waud, in Library of Congress

Spindle's Field as seen from the Confederate position, near the intersection of Brock and Old Court House roads, about a year and a half after the battle. *MOLLUS Collection, USAMHI*

Spotsylvania Court House
MOLLUS Collection, USAMHI

View from near the Alsop house, looking toward the Confederate lines, drawn by Edwin Forbes on May 9. Forbes's key designates the numbered landmarks: (1) Confederates, Anderson's corps, (2) Sedgwick's and Warren's Union troops behind breastworks facing the Confederates, (3) the Alsop house, (4) Brock Road, (5) Sedgwick's corps, (6) the point where Sedgwick was shot, (7) Spotsylvania Court House, hidden behind trees, (8) Warren's corps, (9) Hancock's corps, (10) reserve batteries, (11) Grant and staff, (12) fence-rail breastworks, (13) Coehorn mortar battery, (14) the road where Sedgwick's body was brought from the field.
Library of Congress

Confederate prisoners captured in Upton's charge streaming past the Shelton house.
Drawing by Alfred R. Waud, in Library of Congress

Confederate earthworks near the Bloody Angle
Library of Congress

Confederate earthworks on Laurel Hill, with abatis
Library of Congress

The McCoull house after the war
Library of Congress

Brooke's and Miles's 2nd Corps brigades attacking the salient near the east angle.
MOLLUS Collection, USAMHI

Hancock and Wright studying the salient from near the Landrum House at 6 A.M. on May 12.
Drawing by Alfred R. Waud, in Library of Congress

Union troops seeking cover in the swales and hollows near the salient on May 12.

Drawing by Alfred R. Waud, in Library of Congress

V

MAY 10

Grant Attacks Across Lee's Line

"By gross neglect somewhere, that beautiful attack was unsupported."

THE CENTERPIECE OF Grant's strategy for the evening of May 10 was a grand charge against Lee's entire entrenched line. On the Federal right, Hancock was to hurl the 2nd and 5th Corps against Laurel Hill, held by Field's Confederates. In the Union center, Colonel Upton was to attack with an elite 6th Corps unit against a point halfway up the Confederate salient's left leg, occupied by Rodes's division of Ewell's corps. Once Upton breached the Confederate works, Mott's division was to charge from the left and exploit the breakthrough. And on the far Union left, Burnside was to advance along Fredericksburg Road in an attempt to penetrate Early's defenses and continue into Spotsylvania Court House.

Grant's scheme suffered from the shortcomings that had marred his turning movement across the Po. It contemplated a blind assault, launched with insufficient understanding of Lee's strength and dispositions, and it required an unprecedented degree of coordination among the Union corps commanders. Hasty planning, uninspired leadership, and a chain of mishaps resulted in a bloody evening of missed opportunities for the Federals.

The campaign was only a week old, but already earthworks and rifled firearms had changed the face of warfare. Parade-ground tactics favored during the war's earlier years no longer worked. The corpses moldering in front of Laurel Hill gave mute testimony to the impotence of traditional charges against entrenchments supported by artillery. Grant needed a different approach to punch through Lee's line.

No one knew what that different approach should be, but Emory Upton, who commanded a brigade in David Russell's 6th Corps division, held some strong opinions. His success in capturing seemingly invulnerable

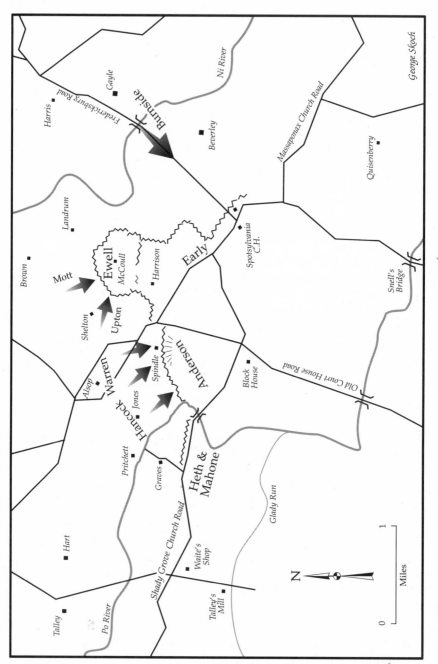

Grant's plan of attack for May 10 at 5 P.M.

positions gave his ideas a ring of authority. In early November, 1863, he had stormed a formidable Confederate bridgehead at Rappahannock Station and had carried it. Upton's unexpected triumph had made him one of the army's minor heros. Fame, however, had not brought popularity. A fervent abolitionist from upstate New York, he was arrogant, self-important, and intensely serious about soldiering. An assignment to Upton's command guaranteed combat.

Upton believed that he could break the campaign's pattern of unsuccessful attacks. The way to overrun Lee's works, he argued, was to reach them quickly. The nonsense of firing and reloading while charging had to end. Lightning forays held the secret to breaching Lee's entrenchments, and once the attackers had secured a lodgment, they should focus on widening the cleft to enable supporting troops to jump in.

Grant decided to give Upton's plan a try. The idea evolved during a conference between Grant, Meade, and Wright. Meade asked Wright to handpick a dozen regiments to charge the rebel line at a point Meade's engineers were to designate. Wright selected Russell to oversee the assault, and Russell selected Upton to lead it. The aide Thomas Hyde later claimed that when his former regiment—the 7th Maine—was suggested for the assignment, he coaxed Wright's chief of staff Martin McMahon into substituting another. Hyde considered Upton "ambitious to gain his star" and feared that the venture would involve "bloody work."[1]

McMahon summoned Upton to his tent and handed him a list of twelve regiments. "Upton, what do you think of that for a command?" he asked. Running his eyes over the list, Upton responded, "Mack, that is a splendid command. They are the best men in the army." Then McMahon explained the mission. "Upton, you are to lead those men upon the enemy's works this afternoon, and if you do not carry them, you are not expected to come back, but if you carry them I am authorized to say that you will get your stars." Upton's reply was predictable. "Mack, I will carry these works. If I don't, I will not come back." As he rode off, Upton exclaimed, "Mack, I'll carry those works. They cannot repulse those regiments."[2]

Upton's force represented the cream of the 6th Corps. Three regiments from Upton's brigade—the 5th Maine, the 121st New York, and the 96th Pennsylvania—formed its nucleus. From Russell's former brigade, now commanded by the mercurial Henry Eustis, came the 6th Maine, the 49th Pennsylvania, the 119th Pennsylvania, and the 5th Wisconsin. Colonel Daniel D. Bidwell's brigade contributed the 43rd and 77th New York. And from Lewis Grant's brigade came three combat hardened regiments, the

2nd, 5th, and 6th Vermont. In all, the force included approximately five thousand soldiers.[3]

Captain Ranald S. Mackenzie, of the United States Corps of Engineers, determined the site for Upton's projected assault. In his opinion, the most promising location lay halfway up the salient's western face. A protuberance—later dubbed Doles's Salient after George Doles's brigade, which was entrenched there—constituted a weak point in the formation. A relatively flat field sloped from a stand of thick woods two hundred yards gently uphill to the works. If Upton drove away the rebel pickets, he could mass his command undetected in the woods, then pounce across the clearing onto the unsuspecting Confederates.

The hazards were formidable. The Federals would have to traverse the open field, chop through tangled abatis, then scale an earthen wall surmounted with logs, all the while subjected to Confederate musketry. To the right of the proposed point of attack stood a Confederate battery, and about a hundred yards behind the first set of works loomed more entrenchments.[4]

Russell and Upton reconnoitered Mackenzie's position and concurred with the engineer's assessment. A farm road led from the Shelton house behind the Federal lines through the woods and across the field to the rebel earthworks. Upton decided to use the path as a conduit for his troops and began assembling them at the Shelton place. Then he led his regimental commanders to an observation point and carefully explained the plan to them. No room was left for misunderstanding.[5]

Upton's soldiers quietly shunted out the road and deployed in four battle lines near the edge of the woods. Orders came to stack knapsacks and haversacks. "We know what is coming," a soldier scrawled in his diary. "Another one of those desperate bloody charges on the enemy's strong earthworks." Skirmishers from the 65th New York drove Doles's pickets back to their works to preserve the mission's secrecy, and officers gave commands with hand signals. Soldiers in the first line loaded their muskets and affixed their percussion caps. Their mission was to charge across the clearing without pausing. Only after reaching the works were they to fire, and they were to use their bayonets freely. After breaching the ramparts, the lead troops were to expand the gap, the 121st New York and the 96th Pennsylvania turning right and silencing the nearby battery, the 5th Maine swinging left to enfilade northward up the entrenchments. The second line was to halt at the works and fire to the front if necessary. The third line was to follow the second, and the Vermont volunteers were to remain in the woods and await developments. Upton cautioned Colonel Thomas O.

Seaver, commanding the Green Mountain men, to be prepared to hurry to the 5th Maine's assistance.[6]

One point was stressed. "All the officers were instructed to repeat the command 'Forward' constantly, from the commencement of the charge till the works were carried," Upton explained. "No man was to stop and succor or assist a wounded comrade." A soldier distinctly remembered Upton's injunction "not to fire a shot, cheer or yell, until we struck their works."[7]

Early on May 10, after Grant had become satisfied that Lee's entire army was in front of Spotsylvania, he shifted Gershom Mott's 2nd Corps division to the 6th Corps' left flank, near the Brown house. Grant and Meade initially intended for Mott to bridge the gap between Wright's left flank and Burnside's right. As they honed their plans for the evening assault, however, they concluded that Mott was handsomely situated to assist Upton. The Brown house was about four-fifths of a mile north of the rebel salient. By charging south, they assumed—erroneously, it developed— that Mott could plow into the Confederates on Upton's left. Upton elaborated in a postwar letter that "the object of my assault was to break the enemy's line; that Mott would then move through the opening; and, forming at right angles to the works, would charge, continuing to roll up the enemy's flank." To ensure coordination between Upton and Mott, Meade placed Mott under Wright's direct command.[8]

Meade, however, seemed unable to decide whether it was more important for Mott to extend across the distance between Wright and Burnside or to mass his division to assist Upton more effectively. At 8:15 A.M., Meade had directed him to "establish connection with Burnside and Wright." Two hours later, Meade instructed Wright to charge at 5:00 P.M. in conjunction with Hancock and Warren and to "use General Mott's division for this purpose." Wright duly notified Mott to examine the terrain in front of him, and at 11:00 A.M., Wright's aide Oliver Wendell Holmes, Jr., visited Mott "to make him press the enemy more vigorously in a [southward] direction toward our right." Holmes thought Mott "somewhat stupid and flurried." Later, a story circulated that Mott had been drunk. One soldier bragged of slipping behind the intoxicated general and surreptitiously cutting a blanket roll from his saddle.[9]

Holmes instructed Mott to probe toward the salient with three regiments to determine how strongly it was defended. The answer was unambiguous. "They found an earthwork and grape across an open field," the aide jotted in his diary. A Confederate in Hays's Louisiana brigade observed that

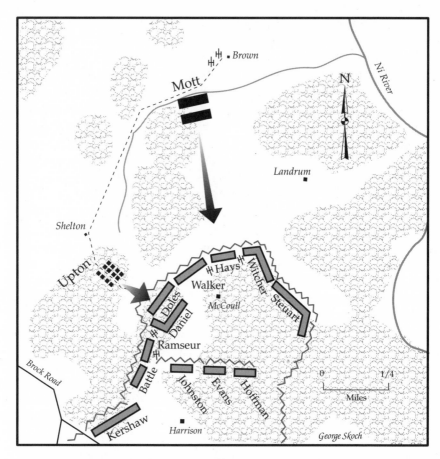

Upton's and Mott's attacks against Ewell on the evening of May 10

Mott's men "felt the strength of our line and were so well satisfied that they did not attempt to gain any further information on the subject." Mott returned with disturbing facts bearing on the wisdom of attacking Ewell's entrenchments.[10]

Mott faced the impossible task of patrolling a two-mile front at the same time that he had to prepare to assault strongly defended works. At 2 P.M., two more communications arrived at the Brown house to compound his troubles. The first, from Meade, directed him to "attack vigorously where you are" if Burnside came under assault. It said nothing about supporting Upton. The second, from Wright, directed him to charge at 5 P.M., "promptly and vigorously." Mott was thoroughly confused. How could he both connect with Burnside and prepare to assault? And was he to charge only if Burnside came under fire, as Meade suggested, or was he to attack peremptorily at five o'clock in accordance with Wright's directive?[11]

Mott sought guidance. "I was ordered to connect with Burnside, on my left," he informed Wright. "My line of pickets is so extended that my troops for assault will not be more than 1,200 to 1,500 men, so that I am very weak." If Wright wanted him to attack, he could recall his pickets, he said, but he doubted that they could return in time. Wright's reply was not reassuring. "I regret that your skirmish line is so extended," the 6th Corps' commander responded, "but if you cannot withdraw a part of the left in full time, you will not attempt to do so, but advance the whole at 5:00 P.M., as previously ordered, following it at the proper moment by your columns of attack, made as strong as your numbers will permit." Mott must have been dumbfounded. What did Wright imagine a skirmish line could achieve against Ewell's fortifications? And what "columns of attack" did Wright suppose could be forged from fifteen hundred men? Wright's closing sentence—"I rely much on the effect of your attack"— underscored the order's absurdity.[12]

Mott did his best in impossible circumstances, deploying his available units. Colonel Robert McAllister's brigade formed the first line, and Colonel William R. Brewster's Excelsior Brigade—temporarily commanded by Colonel William Blaisdell, of the 11th Massachusetts—the second. The 6th New Jersey fanned out in front as skirmishers. Sources do not say whether Mott drew in his pickets, but assuming that he did not, his assaulting force numbered at most fifteen hundred men. To reach the location of Upton's attack, they had to charge along the salient's face, fully exposed to Ewell's muskets and artillery.

Then, through a series of mishaps at the command level, the timing of Mott's attack became thoroughly muddled. Wright had initially instructed Mott to charge at 5:00 P.M. At 3:45, new orders emanated from army headquarters. Grant and Meade had permitted Warren to attack Laurel Hill ahead of schedule, and apparently at the last minute decided to accelerate Wright's and Mott's timetable as well. The order, however, never reached Wright or Mott. Then, after Warren's repulse, headquarters delayed the main attack until six o'clock. Word was delivered to the 6th Corps, and Upton received instructions to wait. But no one told Mott. So at five, true to Wright's initial instructions, Mott's truncated column, augmented by the 1st and 15th New Jersey, stepped into the sights of Ewell's gunners. They were to run the gauntlet of Ewell's artillery, and if they survived, to charge into a breach in the rebel lines made by Upton. Mott's errand was impossible. Upton had not yet attacked, and there was no breach for him to exploit.[13]

Mott's troops started through a stretch of woods, slogged waist-deep through a bog, dislodged a covey of rebel skirmishers, and emerged into a clearing across from the salient's tip. "On reaching the open field, the enemy opened his batteries, enfilading our lines and causing our men to fall back in confusion," McAllister reported. The 11th New Jersey reeled as canister swept the ridge. "Artillery and musketry was terrific," a diarist recorded. "Unit all ran," observed another. Then the 7th New Jersey broke, persuading Mott that "there was nothing left but to fall back"—which he did. "The troops whose term of service is just coming to a close do not fight well," McAllister informed his family the next day. "I am sorry to say that in our division we have too many of this kind."[14]

Mott pulled his division back to the Brown house. Headquarters had severely miscalculated. There was no possibility that he could assist Upton. No one, however, informed Upton of Mott's repulse. So far as he knew, the plan as explained to him by Wright was still on.

"They came on us with a yell and never made any halt."

Upton's charge had been set for five o'clock, then rescheduled for six, owing to Warren's abortive attack against Laurel Hill and the concern about a suspected Confederate envelopment of Hancock's right flank. At ten minutes to six, Wright's aide Henry R. Dalton instructed Upton to attack as soon as his column had formed. Five minutes later, three Federal batteries—Captain William McCartney's, Captain Andrew Cowan's, and Captain William B. Rhodes's—opened on the stretch of works across from Upton. "Batteries firing hell bent," the aide Holmes noted in his diary.[15]

Then word came that Hancock needed more time to organize his Laurel Hill assault. The 6th Corps' artillery continued firing to buy time, but Meade grew increasingly concerned that the Confederates would figure out that an attack was imminent. Ewell was indeed becoming suspicious and ordered Doles to restore his picket line "at any cost." The Federal skirmishers seemed "particularly active and spiteful," and "muffled sounds" could be heard from the far woods, increasing Ewell's feeling that something was brewing. The severe Union artillery barrage—it seemed to one rebel that the Yankees "dealt the death missiles with an unsparing hand"—only served to heighten Ewell's apprehension.[16]

Meade decided he could not afford to wait and ordered Upton to begin. A Union officer waved a handkerchief overhead. The batteries fell silent, and Upton rode to the front of his column. Holmes's watch read 6:35. It was nearly sundown. The air seemed damp, and battle smoke gave the scene a dreamlike quality. An officer galloped along the right side of the waiting troops. Word was whispered down the line: "Fall in. Forward!"[17]

Doles's soldiers stared over their earthworks toward the woods where Upton's men were stirring. "For a moment, a death-like stillness [hung] over the lines," a southerner noted. "Make ready, boys—they are charging!" someone shouted.[18]

"I felt my gorge rise, and my stomach and intestines shrink together in a knot, and a thousand things rushed through my mind," a Federal recounted. He pulled his cap over his eyes and stepped forward. "Like one man, that immense mass of thousands of men rose up, and instantly were met by a severe and staggering fire." Faster ran the mass of soldiers, oblivious to the volley. They broke from the woods into the field and began to yell, unmindful of orders. Puffs of smoke dotted the earthworks ahead. Tufts of dirt spit skyward, and men began falling. The front wave surged on without pausing to shoot. A slow minute ticked by, and they were across the field. Abatis broke their formation, but they clawed through them, only to be mauled by a second volley from the entrenchments. A Union officer vaulted onto the top log of the frowning earthworks and screamed, "Come on, men!" then fell riddled with bullets. Another mounted the works, followed by swarms of blue-clad soldiers. "Many a poor fellow fell pierced with rebel bullets before we reached the rifle pits," a soldier in the 96th Pennsylvania wrote. "When those who were left reached the pits we let them have it." The rebels fought back viciously, lunging with bayonets and swinging muskets like clubs. But the second Union line poured over the works, screaming and shooting. "Forward," cried Upton, who had accompanied his men. Over the top they went, swooping left and right to clear the trench behind the works. A breach yawned in Lee's line.[19]

Upton had struck Doles's portion of the salient, which had three supporting lines of entrenchments. Daniel's North Carolinians and Battle's Alabamians occupied the works on Doles's left, and Walker's Stonewall Brigade stood on Doles's right. Ramseur's North Carolina brigade continued the rebel line southward. Lieutenant Robert A. Hardaway's artillery battalion supported this segment of the Confederate formation. The 3rd

Richmond Howitzers, under Captain Benjamin H. Smith, commanded the junction of Daniel's and Doles's brigades. A hundred yards to the south, in Ramseur's position, stood the 2nd Richmond Howitzers, under Captain Lorraine F. Jones.[20]

The northerners "came on us with a yell and never made any halt," a Georgian exclaimed. Twenty-one-year-old Thomas J. Dingler, of Spaulding County, waved the 44th Georgia's flag overhead defiantly. Soldiers in Upton's first line, bayonets flashing, stabbed him fourteen times. He fell still tightly clutching the banner. Another Confederate writhed in agony, bayoneted through the eyes. Lieutenant John D. Howell, of the 49th Pennsylvania, split open a Confederate's head with his cavalry saber while fending off another rebel with his left hand. He was saved by his friend Miles Wakefield, who stabbed a third Confederate, who was in the act of thrusting a bayonet toward the lieutenant's stomach.[21]

Smith's battery fired a few canister rounds, then received orders to stop. Rebels were leaping from the works and streaming into the field toward the woods. The Confederate gunners assumed that Doles was countercharging and hopped onto the breastworks and cheered. Quickly they realized their misinterpretation of the scene. Doles had been captured, and his men were surrendering wholesale. The gunners could not shoot into the Federals for fear of slaughtering their own men.[22]

Like clockwork, the 121st New York and 96th Pennsylvania headed for Smith's guns. To a Confederate artilleryman, Yankees seemed to be "pouring in upon us in a perfect avalanche," creating the "direst confusion." Federals overran the battery and scooped up most of the gunners, including a young boy who defiantly straddled one of the pieces. A Yankee decided not to shoot him, "because of his grit." Smith, the battery's commander, had lost part of a foot the previous year. He tried to hobble to safety, but a Federal grabbed him around the waist, tossed him onto his shoulder, and carried him back to the Union lines. A few northerners dismantled the gun carriages and blocked the vent holes with twigs in an attempt to render the pieces unserviceable in case the rebels returned. "We captured, killed, or wounded the big majority of the first pit," a soldier in the 96th Pennsylvania recorded. "We sent the prisoners to the rear and went for the second pit about 75 yards away."[23]

Upton claimed that the struggle lasted but a few minutes. "Numbers prevailed, and, like a resistless wave, the column poured over the works, putting hors de combat those who resisted, and sending to the rear those who surrendered." He had accomplished his mission. He had broken Ewell's line and made an opening for Mott to exploit.[24]

Upton, however, had not reckoned with the Confederate 2nd Corps' resilience. Ramseur began to charge by the right flank, and Hardaway, who was with Jones's battery, corralled Smith's remaining gunners and set them to helping Jones's men work their pieces. Anxious to repair the breach, Ewell rode toward the commotion, heedless of his own safety. Lee, who was near the Harrison house, mounted his horse Traveller. His aides were concerned. Four days before, a Union assault had broken Lee's line, and the general had tried to lead a countercharge. His men had refused to advance until he had retired to safety. Fearful that the Confederate commander might repeat his earlier performance, the aides demanded that he stay near the Harrison house. "Then you must see to it that the ground is recovered," Lee insisted. The staffers scattered through a "pandemonium of excitement and confusion" to bring up reinforcements.[25]

Ewell seemed to be everywhere. He rode up in a spray of dust to Daniel's brigade, which adjoined Doles's lower flank. In his excitement, he had outdistanced his staff. Halting behind the 45th North Carolina, he shouted, "Don't run, boys. I will have enough men here in five minutes to eat up every damned one of them!" Daniel retired the right portion of his brigade and formed it across the trench, so as to intercept Upton's men dashing down behind the works. Daniel's 2nd North Carolina Battalion— "my little mob," he had affectionately christened the outfit—bore the brunt of the attack. According to a North Carolinian, they "fought almost hand-to-hand with the enemy until nearly annihilated."[26]

Ewell quickly deployed Battle and Ramseur along Daniel's refused line. The three brigades then began pressing the 121st New York and 96th Pennsylvania north toward the captured guns. Upton's second and third lines meanwhile poured through the rupture and made a stand at the disabled pieces. An officer from the 6th Maine, saber drawn, encouraged his men to fight on until a bullet ripped through his neck. "The Yankees fought with unusual desperation," a Confederate confirmed, "and where the artillery was, contended as stubbornly for it as though it was their own." The sun was setting, and an Alabamian noted that the "immense volumes of smoke which rose from the musketry so darkened its rays as to give the appearance of a bright moon-shining night."[27]

Robert Johnston's brigade of Gordon's division had been positioned on Ramseur's left, behind Kershaw, with instructions to support Ewell's line wherever threatened. Riding toward the breach, Johnston met Ewell. The corps commander appeared very excited, pulling nervously on his moustache and demanding that Johnston hurry up his brigade. "Charge 'em, General," he shouted. "Damn 'em, charge 'em." Lee sat mounted nearby.

In contrast to Ewell, the army commander remained "very calm and quiet," in one observer's view, even though bullets whizzed by uncomfortably close. A shell plowed a furrow fifteen feet from Lee, and a minié ball ricocheted off the general's saddle. "I looked for him to fall every minute," a southerner remarked. Lee's aide Taylor had his horse wounded under him twice, and the bullets were described as flying "thick as hail."[28]

Johnston's Tarheels double-quicked in column by the right flank and formed near Lee. The general rose high in his saddle and pointed toward the rupture in the earthworks. Something about his demeanor told the warriors that he meant to accompany them. They shouted promises to retake the line if he went back. Lee nodded and turned his horse to the rear. True to their word, the Carolinians charged into the thick of the fighting. Johnston's aide Joseph F. Johnston and the 20th North Carolina's Major John F. Brooks raced toward a Federal flag planted on the embankment. Seizing the banner, Brooks triumphantly carried it back to General Lee as proof that the brigade had kept its promise to him.[29]

The 5th Maine and 5th Wisconsin meanwhile pressed northward along the works, routing the Stonewall Brigade's 2nd and 33rd Virginia on Doles's right. Walker rallied the rest of his brigade toward the intruders. In an impetuous charge, the 25th Virginia, led by Colonel John C. Higgenbotham, directed "oblique fire" into the Federals filling the trench. Higgenbotham died in the assault, and General Walker sent an aide, Randolph Barton, to seek help. Barton found Edward Johnson on the salient's eastern side, where Maryland Steuart's brigade was entrenched. "He asked me when I delivered my message what troops he could send," Barton recounted, "and knowing that Steuart's brigade held the right of the division, which was 'refused' at that point, I suggested that if Steuart's brigade was faced about and marched back of the rest of the division on a line of battle at right angles with it, it would come face to face with the enemy." Johnson protested that if Steuart left, the Federals might attack his vacant trenches. Barton answered in a voice he made sound authoritative, "No they won't," and to his surprise, Johnson adopted his suggestion.[30]

Steuart's brigade sprinted across the salient's interior. It arrived next to Walker "exhausted and strung out," as a Marylander put it. Sheets of musketry—"perhaps some of it coming from our own friends on the other side of the gap," the Marylander surmised—greeted the brigade. Some of Upton's troops worked into a stand of woods behind Steuart's soldiers. To a Confederate in the 10th Virginia, the Federals seemed "as thick in the woods behind me as bees." Realizing that they risked being cut off, some of Steuart's men dropped back. One southerner told how when a "cloud of Yanks crossed our line of works, demanding surrender," he pitched his musket and ran "in extra-triple-quick time, with holes in my clothes and a bruise on my shoulder that turned black and was as large as the palm of my hand." Casualties were severe, particularly in the 3rd North Carolina, which deployed across the trench to block Upton's northward progress. Steuart exhorted his men to hold steady. "A more disagreeable half hour, with a bullet striking a man lying on the ground every now and then, could not well have been spent," a staff officer maintained.[31]

Ewell's counterattacks—by Daniel, Battle, Ramseur, and Johnston from the south, and by Walker and Steuart from the north and east—sealed each end of the rift. The Georgia brigade, formerly commanded by Gordon and now in the able hands of Colonel Clement A. Evans, piled in next. Taylor met the Georgians near the McCoull house. "Come on, boys. Come on," he urged, then spun his horse toward the firing. Evans' men came running behind. Ahead were Upton's Federals, grappling with Johnston. Ewell was conspicuously at the breach, and he directed Evans' troops into the fight, including a twelve-year-old soldier riding a pony. "I may live to a hundred years of age, but I will never forget that little boy—his pony rearing up and pawing in the direction of the enemy, and the gallant little soldier firing his tiny pocket pistol as earnestly as Murat heading a charge," a Confederate declared.[32]

Upton's attack, so promising at first, had faltered. As Ewell concentrated his brigades toward the rift, Upton's troops climbed back over the entrenchments and sought cover against the outer face. Daniel's rebels wrested back the guns, and Smith's surviving artillerymen wheeled the pieces around, cleared the vents of obstructions, and blasted the retreating Federals with canister. "We then saw why it was that we had not been fired upon by our own guns," a southerner remarked. The Richmond Howitzer's quick-thinking cannoneers had taken the rammers when they fled, rendering the guns useless to Upton. Hardaway pitched in to help work the guns, only to discover corpses heaped so thickly on one of the Napoleons that his men could not fire it. Major David Watson, standing next to Hardaway, was mortally wounded by a shot through his bowels, and Hardaway's clothes were pierced with nine bullet holes. Droves of Confederate prisoners not yet sent back were freed, including Doles, who had saved himself by falling to the ground when Ewell counterattacked. To maintain pressure against Upton, Ewell asked Ramseur to drive the Federals back across the field. According to a Confederate gunner, Ramseur's men "behaved badly" and refused to go after the fleeing Unionists. Sword in hand, Ramseur jumped onto the works and ordered his troops to follow him, but he was unable to organize an effective pursuit.[33]

Upton called for the Vermont regiments, thinking they were still in reserve, only to discover that they had already advanced to the contested works. "The boys could not be restrained in their wild excitement," a soldier reported, "and without waiting for orders (for I certainly heard no order but 'halt,' and I know of no one that did) they rushed in." Upton had no more reserves, and, as he stated in a postwar letter, "the twelve regiments had become mixed up so that there was not a single unit under my control."[34]

Upton's venture had been predicated on immediate support. But Mott had been repulsed, and Wright was at a loss concerning what to do next. He rode to headquarters and asked Grant for guidance. "Pile in the men and hold it!" the commander in chief advised. Wright returned to a disturbing situation. It was nearly dark, and Upton was embroiled in an unequal fight three-quarters of a mile from the Union line. His position was untenable. Wright directed a regiment on Upton's right—the 65th New York, from Colonel Nelson Cross's brigade—to advance, but he was reluctant to risk any more troops. Then Upton showed up at the forest's edge and asked for permission to withdraw. Russell granted it immediately.[35]

Upton instructed his troops to fall back, but the Vermonters kept fighting. Only after repeated requests from staff officers and an order from General Wright—"coming too positive to be trifled with," reported a man from Vermont—did they retreat. "This I assure you was galling to the pride of brave men," Lieutenant Colonel Samuel E. Pingree, of the 2nd Vermont, explained. "When I got by myself where I would not be ashamed of it I cried like a whipped spaniel—I saw many soldiers cry like girls, and many who took things less to heart, gave vent to their mortification at having lost all they had gained so nobly—by the fault of others, by letting of unnumbered salvos of profanity."[36]

Upton's offensive was over by 7:30. It was almost dark, and flashes from rebel muskets seemed to spark from all directions. "The wounded between us and the Rebs were in terrible plight," a New Yorker observed, "and must have been shot to pieces by the fire from both sides." Retreating across the open field presented additional horrors. Forms sprawled everywhere. Exhausted men dragged wounded comrades, instinctively bending low to avoid bullets. Many injured soldiers had to be abandoned. "The woods were full of these unfortunate creatures, and sounded all night with their cries and groans," a Union officer remembered. "I sat down in the woods," admitted another, "and as I thought of the desolation and misery about me, my feelings overcame me and I cried like a little child."[37]

Upton estimated his loss at a thousand soldiers. Some regiments were more than halved. The 49th Pennsylvania, for example, lost 246 of the 474 men engaged. "Bitter were the reproaches to which both Russell and Upton gave utterance when upon Upton's return he gained the shelter of the woods," an aide recalled. A staffer described Upton as depressed. Upton's friend Colonel Clinton Beckwith procured a pair of brigadier general's shoulder straps and reminded Wright of his promise to promote Upton if he took the works. Beckwith asked Meade if he would act on the promise, and the general replied, "Certainly." The next morning, Beckwith laid the stars in front of his friend. Upton fixed him with an inquiring stare, then the two men cut off Upton's eagles and sewed the stars on his shoulder. "He remarked how proud and glad his men would be to know that their efforts had been so distinguished, and his pale face lighted up with animation," Beckwith related.[38]

Upton proclaimed his assault a "complete success," as his men had overrun "two lines of formidable entrenchments and made a break at least half a mile long." He asserted that if "fresh troops, in good order, [had] been at hand, the enemy must have been badly beaten." His soldiers agreed. "When we charged, if we had been supported, it would have been a great success," an infantryman insisted. A diarist in the 96th Pennsylvania criticized the "supporting regiments [for] not attending to their duty."[39]

Mott's superiors blamed Mott. Dana asserted that the army had been "disgraced," incorrectly alleging that Mott's men had retreated "without loss, and apparently without any considerable force to oppose them." They had run "like cowards," he complained. Holmes confided that "a brilliant magnificent charge [was] made useless except locally by entire failure of promised cooperation—Burnside didn't attack, nobody did anything to speak of except 6th Corps." Reflecting on the campaign three months later, Lyman concluded, "At Spotsylvania the whole army would have been stronger without Mott's division." And Grant, penning his memoirs on his deathbed, declared that Mott's "feeble action" had forfeited Upton's advantage. "Mott was ordered to his assistance but failed utterly," the old warrior wrote.[40]

Others, however, realized more correctly that Mott's superiors had bungled the operation. A diarist fumed that "all the generals and field offices drank considerable whiskey. I think General Wright is the man to blame for the disaster and no other man." An officer reported that "more than once I heard the exclamation that night, 'this would not have happened if old 'Uncle John' had not been killed.'" Anger ran especially deep among Upton's men. "I still believe that the only true way to save us was to send a column to take the enfilading work on our left," a Vermonter wrote home a few weeks after the assault. "It might have cost 500 men that night. I do not think it would have cost a man more. The next day it cost us over ten times that number."[41]

History has judged Mott unfairly. Grant and Meade asked him to perform an impossible task, gave him far too few men to accomplish it, and sent him forward at the wrong time. His repulse was no more reprehensible than that experienced by every other Union commander that day. Most important, Mott's superiors had positioned him at the wrong place. To exploit Upton's success, they should have deployed him nearer to Upton, perhaps immediately to his rear. And it was Grant, Meade, and Wright who had changed the time for the assault without ensuring that the field commanders had been notified. As Lyman remarked in a postwar letter, "By gross neglect *somewhere* that beautiful attack was unsupported. If it had been, the whole salient would have been captured."[42]

Ewell had restored his line, but his casualties were severe. "We lost several killed, great many wounded, most of them thrust with bayonets and nearly all prisoners," a soldier in Doles's brigade wrote home. "We left camp last Wednesday with 1567 men (3 regiments), this morning we number 550," he added. "In the company from Morgan County, the captain and one man only are left." Daniel's brigade also suffered heavily. A soldier in the 32nd North Carolina claimed that 225 men and 6 officers from his regiment were captured. The historian of Doles's brigade estimated total rebel loss at 650 men, 350 of them as prisoners. Lee's aide Taylor also placed the loss at 650. Meade's provost marshal, however, recorded that Upton captured 913 men and 37 officers. A more recent count based on a thorough examination of Confederate records indicates that Daniel lost over 400 soldiers, Doles at least 600, Smith's battery about 40, and the supporting brigades between 200 and 300. Ewell's losses exceeded Upton's by two or three hundred.[43]

"The situation was a sad one," a soldier in the 44th Georgia commented. The regiment was virtually obliterated and lost its colonel, William H. Peebles. A Confederate band solemnly assembled near the works and played "Nearer My God to Thee." A Yankee band replied with the "Dead March," and the Confederates answered with "The Bonnie Blue Flag," followed by full-throated rebel yells. Then "The Star Spangled

Banner" wafted from the northern lines, accompanied by cheers, and the southerners replied with "Home Sweet Home." What happened next remained vivid to a Georgian almost forty years later. "A united yell went up in concert from the men on both sides," he reminisced, "such a one as was never heard among the hills of Spotsylvania county before or since."[44]

"This is sheer madness."

By 7 P.M.—after Upton had charged, broken through Doles's fortifications, and fought desperately on, waiting in vain for reinforcements—Hancock at long last felt prepared to attack Laurel Hill. Still apprehensive about his right flank, he kept Barlow near the Po, supported by Colonel Crocker's brigade of Birney's division. That left only Gibbon and Birney's other brigade—Brigadier General J. H. Hobart Ward's outfit—to participate with the 5th Corps in the Laurel Hill assault. The troops who had failed a few hours earlier under Warren, augmented now by Ward, were to charge again, and they had little stomach for it. "The men regarded the effort as hopeless from the start, and the officers failed to secure any enthusiasm in their troops," a chaplain recorded. Crawford paced the battle line, wringing his hands and muttering in an anguished voice, "This is sheer madness. I tell you this is sheer madness, and can only end in wanton slaughter and certain repulse." Timber still smoldered from fires set during the earlier combat. Farther on, behind Laurel Hill's frowning works, Charles Field's Confederates cleaned their muskets and stashed their ammunition close at hand.[45]

"No officer of higher rank than a brigade commander had examined the approaches to the enemy's works on our front," a Union staffer noted. Men exchanged knowing looks when a courier arrived with orders to charge. "The moment the order was given," a soldier observed, "the messenger put spurs to his horse and rode off, lest by some misunderstanding the assault should begin before he was safe out of the range of the enemy's responsive fire." To Sergeant Charles A. Frey, of the 150th Pennsylvania, the order seemed a death sentence. He contemplated the black smear of fresh earth that marked Field's works, scarcely visible in the waning evening light. "I could not picture myself going beyond that line," Frey affirmed. "I could not imagine the possibility of ever getting back. Then the thought suddenly occurred to me: this is death."[46]

Lincoln's emissary Dana witnessed the assault from Warren's front. "It was executed," he informed the president the next morning, "with the caution and absence of comprehensive *ensemble* which seem to characterize [Warren]." Griffin's division, positioned on Warren's left near Brock Road, never left its entrenchments. A soldier quipped that May 10 would be remembered as the day "they got ready to make a charge and didn't." A man in Cutler's division recollected a "deafening Hurrah, and musketry as hard as I ever heard it, all along the line." Cutler's troops rose, advanced a short distance, then received orders to march back to their breastworks, "the storming being abandoned." A staff officer passed near Sergeant Frey and announced, "The charge will not be made this evening. General Warren says the loss of life would be too great to risk it." Blanched faces resumed their normal color, and formerly silent men began chattering. But the terror of that afternoon remained palpable to Frey twenty years later. "I do not know how many bullets passed within a few inches of my body," he reminisced, "or how many hundreds passed within a few feet of me; but this much I do know—I can never go nearer the jaws of death and come out unscathed than I did on the 10th day of May, 1864, at Laurel Hill, Virginia."[47]

Warren's rightmost division, Crawford's Pennsylvania Reserves, sallied forth but soon came "tumbling and scrambling back in the greatest confusion, a wild panic taking possession of the men and causing them to break to the rear without ceremony." Warren rode into the field and attempted to rally the fugitives by waving a flag. He looked "gallant enough," the artillerist Wainwright thought, "mounted on a great tall white horse, in full uniform, sash and all, and with the flag in his hand, he must have made a prominent mark." Despite Warren's prodding, the Reserves "acted abominably, breaking all to pieces," asserted Wainwright. Looking somewhat dazed, Warren disappeared behind the lines, still clutching the flagstaff, which had been shot in half. "Made an assault towards dark," he later wrote. "Not very vigorously made and no result."[48]

From the 5th Corps, only Lyle's brigade braved the leaden hurricane to reach the Confederate line. Perry's men opened deadly musketry. "As fast as a gun was fired it was thrown back to the rear to be reloaded," an Alabamian observed. "Often the officers would only take time in their haste to bite cartridges, insert in the muzzle, and with a quick sharp blow of the butt of the piece on the ground send the cartridge home." An officer in the 16th Maine stumbled down a ravine, thrashed through brush, and emerged in front of Field's entrenchments. "The works flamed and roared with a sudden outburst of fire," he recounted. "Cursing and stumbling, and helping our wounded as best we could, we made our way back to our starting place." The 39th Massachusetts charged to within about ten feet of the breastworks only to be repulsed by "heavy fire of musketry right in the face."[49]

Gibbon's soldiers, on the assaulting force's right wing, grumbled at being obliged to assault and refused to budge. They had weighed the risks and decided that the attempt was hopeless. Some ventured a token advance, then scurried to safety. "Fruitless as the first," a soldier from Carroll's brigade concluded. Owen's brigade broke under Confederate artillery fire, and Webb's retired "in some disorder." Webb could find only three of his nine regiments. Staff officers located the rest, gathered around their flags, brewing coffee and discussing their recent ordeal. "Our men were demoralized by fruitless work," Webb reported.[50]

Ward's brigade—the only fresh outfit to participate in the charge—constituted the attacking line's right flank. Serious questions surrounded Ward's fitness to command, since the general had been cited in the Wilderness for abandoning his troops. Shortly before the Laurel Hill attack was slated to begin, a shell fragment sliced his right temple. Colonel Thomas W. Egan, of the 40th New York, helped Ward clean the wound and wrapped a handkerchief around his head.[51]

Ward's troops started forward tightly massed, with the 86th New York leading, officers beside their commands. They marched double quick toward the works, holding their fire. Just ahead, Gregg's mixed Texas and Arkansas brigade and Tige Anderson's Georgians were busy preparing supper. They jumped for their guns at the sight of Ward's approaching northerners. The scene was forever etched in Private Dame's memory: "Pouring out of the woods, yelling like mad men, came the Federal infantry, fast as they could run, straight upon our lines. The whole field was blue with them!"[52]

Gregg's brigade anchored the rebel line near the Po, and its works projected forward slightly to form a semicircular fort. A North Carolina battery, commanded by Captain Basil C. Manly and including several colorful Irishmen, was attached to the brigade and had arranged its guns to sweep the approaches. Gregg's troops smashed open fresh boxes of ammunition at the sight of Ward's approach. "Then we were ready," a Texan remarked. Ward unwittingly funneled his troops into a deathtrap.[53]

Rebel gunners fired canister while Gregg's riflemen blazed away at the approaching Federals. The Confederate line presented a deadly spectacle. "Rapidly and regularly it threw up cloud after cloud of smoke," a northerner commented, "and the flashes of its fire burst along its front in thread-like lines." A New Yorker remembered a "horrid crash and roar, to right and left." To a soldier in the 3rd Maine, the air seemed as "full of bullets as honey bees at swarming time." Undeterred, Ward's three lead regiments—the 86th New York, the 3rd Maine, and the 124th New York—plunged through the abatis and toward the ramparts. The 1st Texas folded as Ward's men jumped into their trench and swept toward the guns. "Squawk, damn you, I like to hear you squawk," a Yankee screamed as he drove his bayonet deep into a southerner. Come upon by surprise at his cooking fire, Colonel Robert S. Taylor, of the 3rd Arkansas, showered the intruders with grease. A bullet slammed into his side, and his messmates ran for their lives. Two Yankees lunged at Lieutenant Durk Ardry, who caught a bayonet in each hand, parted the blades, and darted away. Ward, like Upton over a mile to the east, had ruptured the Confederate line.[54]

Two Napoleons from the 1st Richmond Howitzers swung around and fired down the trench with double canister. Rebel gunners rammed home fresh loads as quickly as they could serve the pieces. "It was fast and furious work," a Confederate noted. "The bullets sounded like bees buzzing above our heads." General Field watched from a nearby hill. His line appeared hopelessly broken, and he had no reserves.[55]

Although the fracture seemed serious, the attackers never stood a chance. Most of Ward's men streamed back from the abatis under "continuous fire of shot and shell which made fearful havoc among them." The 124th New York hugged the earth "as closely as possible" for a short while, then broke and ran. A Texan recalled Yankees in a "crowded mass quite close to our breastworks and our men were firing into their midst." The 86th New York and 3rd Maine were left to the mercy of the Texans and Georgians, who rallied and charged, "leaping like tigers," according to a rebel. An enraged Texan, remarked another man from the state, wielded a frying pan "at once as sword and banner." Anderson's Georgians also fought bravely. Colonel Brown, of the 9th Georgia, seemed to a nearby soldier like a demon of war with his shirt sleeves rolled up, pants bloodied, and a look "grim and defiant as Astrides." It seemed to one Confederate that "every man in our thin gray line was standing loading and firing with that cool steady aim of the tried veteran."[56]

The 86th New York and 3rd Maine joined the "flying mob," as a Federal termed the retreating soldiers. Ward was powerless to rally his brigade, which continued back over its works and disappeared in the woods behind. Hancock's and Birney's staffers finally steadied them. Casualties were "considerable," according to Union reports.[57]

"Men, it was perfectly magnificent," Field commended his troops in relief. "If the line had been broken here I don't know what we should have done." The Texans were so vexed that they charged after the fleeing Unionists. "They are running, boys," someone shouted. "Shoot them as fast as you can." A Texan blustered, "We mowed them down in piles as they attempted to escape." The charge involved the "heaviest fighting I was ever in—artillery and musketry combined," a Pennsylvanian conceded. An Indiana man described the fighting simply as "terrific."[58]

Ward's and Upton's charges bore striking similarities. Each had overrun the rebel entrenchments by attacking without pausing to fire. And each had failed because Grant and Meade had neglected to provide proper support. Reflecting on Ward's attack, a soldier from the 86th New York criticized the other units for failing to render assistance. "Some of the support said they went until the place they reached was hotter than any place known to sacred or profane history," he observed. "Be that as it may, it was still hotter where the 86th were, for when the 86th scaled their works they were greatly outnumbered by the enemy." Ward's men had performed as gallantly as Upton's and were as deserving of praise. Upton's attack, however, received accolades, while Ward's was quickly forgotten. Developments during the remainder of the war were responsible. Ward was to be drummed out of the army for drunkenness on May 12, while Upton emerged from the war a hero.[59]

"It was a profound mystery to the men in the ranks."

Of all the missed opportunities on May 10, Grant's failure to bring the 9th Corps into play was perhaps the most tragic. Grant was unaware that Lee had weakened his defenses in front of Burnside by dispatching Heth and Mahone to the Po River. A single Confederate division under Cadmus Wilcox barred Fredericksburg Road. Here was Lee's vulnerable point. Yet as Meade's soldiers shed their lifeblood at Laurel Hill and the salient, the 9th Corps engaged in halfhearted maneuvers off Lee's eastern flank, never seriously engaging the enemy or exploiting its own considerable numerical advantage.

At daybreak, Burnside's headquarters lay at the J. Alsop house, along a byway leading from the Alrich place to Fredericksburg Road. Potter's division camped nearby. Willcox' and Stevenson's divisions stood entrenched north of the Ni at the Gayle house, almost four miles by road from that of J. Alsop. Stevenson's lead elements occupied high ground south of the stream, where rebel snipers maintained an incessant tattoo.

Colonel Zenas R. Bliss—one of Potter's brigade commanders—woke to a disturbing sight. The field around him was strewn with dead men, not sleeping soldiers as he had assumed the previous night when he had spread his blanket. "Their appearance was horrible," Bliss remembered. "Their faces were terribly drawn up as though they had died in great agony, and their hands were full of grass which they had torn up in their dying agonies."[60]

Burnside spent the morning trying to cement his link with the Army of the Potomac. Hartranft's brigade extended a picket line northwest along the Ni, reaching to connect with Mott on the Army of the Potomac's left flank. Pickets from the 2nd Michigan loosely achieved the junction. As the morning warmed, Burnside's troops sought relief in the woods. They lay there for "long and tedious hours," listening to the sounds of battle on their right, under orders to be "ready to move at a moment's notice," a soldier related.[61]

Stevenson was arguably Burnside's ablest division commander. A Bostonian, he had recruited the 24th Massachusetts in 1861 and had served under Burnside during much of the war. A dirt bank sheltered Stevenson's camp from Confederate artillery and musket fire. As the morning progressed, Stevenson and his staff moved a short distance back and lounged under a shade tree, smoking. Bliss and Christ rode by, and Christ jokingly proposed to Stevenson that they trade places. He would rather be sitting under a tree eating lunch, he remarked, than reconnoitering in the heat. Suddenly a bullet drilled through Stevenson's skull from the back and exploded out his temple. He died without regaining consciousness. "His loss is irreparable," the aide Charles Mills lamented. "He was the most gallant, brave, and thorough soldier, the most kindhearted, considerate, generous-spirited man, and one of the most agreeable companions I ever knew." Colonel Daniel Leasure, next in rank to Stevenson, assumed temporary command of the division.[62]

Stevenson's death forced Burnside to reconsider his troop dispositions. Leasure had performed well in the Wilderness, but Burnside lacked confidence in him. Fighting appeared imminent, and scouts reported that rebels had begun probing Burnside's fragile junction with Mott. A Confederate attack there threatened to isolate the 9th Corps, and Burnside feared that Leasure and Willcox might not be able to hold their advanced position at the Ni. "I am pained beyond measure to hear of the death of General Stevenson," Burnside wrote Willcox at 9:45. "Unless you are pretty certain of connecting and maintaining your connection with [Mott], you had better fall quietly back."[63]

Shortly, however, Grant informed Burnside of the attack planned for 5:00 P.M. and urged him to assault along Fredericksburg Road "with vigor and all the force you can bring to bear." Burnside assigned Willcox to lead the attack. Then he temporarily broke up Leasure's division, dispatching some regiments toward Mott and others to Willcox. He was undecided, however, about what to do with his remaining division, under Potter. Should he use Potter to support Mott or to reinforce Willcox? Grant's aide Porter strenuously urged Burnside to assemble all three available 9th Corps divisions for a determined assault, but Burnside wavered and at 2:15 P.M. sought Grant's advice. "By concentrating the three divisions of the corps at Gayle's I can make a very heavy attack upon the right flank of the enemy, or I can have the two divisions at Gayle's make a demonstration, and put the other division in rear of Mott's division," Burnside suggested. Grant's answer arrived an hour later. "It will now be too late to bring up your third division," he replied, leaving Burnside to choose whether to attack with his "two divisions as they are, or whether one of them should be sent to Mott." Grant expressed confidence that Burnside would be able to fend off any attack the Confederates might mount, whichever choice he made. But above all, Grant emphasized, the 9th corps had to do something. "I want the attack promptly made in one or the other of the modes proposed," he insisted.[64]

Contrary to Grant's injunction, Burnside decided to advance Potter to the Gayle house above the Ni's north bank, which delayed his attack. Potter did not reach the front until six. By then, Willcox had formed at right angles to Fredericksburg Road south of the Ni. Hartranft's line extended to the right of the roadway and Christ's to the left. Colonel Simon G. Griffin's brigade from Potter's division moved up to support Hartranft, and Bliss's mixed Pennsylvania, New York, Massachusetts, and Rhode Island brigade deployed behind Christ. Leasure's elements scattered about as needed. The formation pointed south along the road and trailed back on either side. A battery stood on a nearby ridge.[65]

Shortly after 6 P.M., Burnside's cannon roared into action. Orders to advance rang through the muggy spring air. Cutcheon's 20th Michigan headed south "in splendid style" along Fredericksburg Road. Cadmus Wilcox' Confederates still held the roadway in force, and the Union alignments quickly unraveled. Hartranft, who commanded Willcox' right wing, received orders to halt and swing more to the right. He did, only to learn that the left wing was continuing on without him. "I was ordered to fill in and lengthen my line in order to keep up the connection until I had much less than a line of battle," he reported. Then Cutcheon raised his right arm to signal a general right wheel. A rebel shell burst close by and sent fragments tearing into his uplifted arm. Cutcheon stared at his mangled limb, mumbled, "Good-bye, right arm," and left the field.[66]

Willcox re-formed in columns by regiments and pressed on, the 79th New York leading. Wilcox' Confederates fought from behind barricades of felled timber, forcing the Federals to break ranks and batter their way through as best they could. "A portion of our line reached within a few rods of the enemy," a New Yorker realized, "for we could hear the voices of the rebels as they awaited our coming." Darkness was setting in, and Willcox found the country "so bewildering, and the enemy so completely concealed from view, that it was impossible at the time to know the exact relative positions of the contending forces."[67]

From woods to the west sounded distant musketry that "surpassed anything I have ever heard," one of Burnside's officers wrote. Upton had started his attack.[68]

Confronted by Wilcox' formidable barriers across Fredericksburg Road, Willcox' advance ground to a standstill. Some accounts placed him a quarter mile from Spotsylvania Court House. Willcox, to secure his position, began erecting his own earthworks, and some of his men occupied abandoned Confederate rifle pits. "All quiet," the brigadier general informed Burnside at 7:15. "Well intrenched. Feel perfectly safe." Burnside, however, was concerned that Willcox had advanced too far in front of Potter's supporting elements. "I think I can hold the position and am willing to take proper risks," Willcox assured Burnside, also pointing out that withdrawing raised difficulties of its own: the Confederates might pursue and "mass everything here suddenly on Meade's left."[69]

As fighting sputtered to a close along Laurel Hill and the salient, Grant came to share Burnside's concern that Willcox might be too isolated. Now that Lee was no longer being pressed on his other fronts, he might counterattack along Fredericksburg Road. Accordingly, Grant decided to relinquish the 9th Corps' forward position and at 11 P.M. directed Burnside to "get up at once so as to connect on your right with Wright's command." Willcox was to retire and help secure the connection.

Grant came to regret his decision to withdraw Burnside's lead elements. "This brought [Willcox] back about a mile," he admitted, "and lost to us an important advantage. I attach no blame to Burnside for this," he added, "but I do to myself for not having had a staff officer with him to report to me his position." In fact, Grant's aide Porter had been with Burnside, but his dispatches did not reach Grant. Willcox' men were perplexed on receiving orders to retire. "It was a profound mystery to the men in the ranks, at the time, why such a movement should have been made," a soldier remarked. "We failed to comprehend why, after having struggled so near to the Court House that we could plainly discern the Stars and Bars flying above the principal building of the little hamlet, we should then be faced to the rear and withdrawn, without having accomplished, or even attempted to accomplish, anything whatever."[70]

Lincoln's emissary Dana reported that Burnside lost only six men during his halfhearted advance. Other sources suggest a considerably higher toll, although nothing like the slaughter at Laurel Hill and the salient. A visitor to the field hospital at the Harris house saw wounded men spilling from outbuildings onto the neatly manicured garden. "One by one the poor groaning fellows would be laid upon a table," he reported, "chloroform would be administered, a surgeon would wield his glinting knife and saw, and, in a few moments, a severed and ghastly limb white as snow but spattered with blood would drop upon the floor, one more added to the terrible pile." Corpses lay at right angles to the driveway with papers pinned to their breasts identifying them for burial.[71]

A 9th Corps staffer thought that the rebels were learning to respect Burnside. "They have always talked about the 'little Ninth,'" he explained, "but they call us now the 'bully Ninth.'" In truth, Burnside's halting performance had done nothing to enhance his standing with anyone. The Confederates were puzzled by his behavior. Lee, by shifting Heth and Mahone to the Po, had left a single division guarding the eastern approach to Spotsylvania Court House, but Burnside neglected to exploit his advantage. After pressing almost to the village, he stopped, forfeiting an excellent opportunity to crack open the back door to Lee's defensive line. As darkness fell and Early began returning Heth's brigade from the Po to Fredericksburg Road, Burnside's brief opportunity slammed shut forever.[72]

May 10 had been Grant's bloodiest day since leaving the Wilderness. A Union telegrapher considered it the "fiercest battle of the campaign up to date." Casualty returns, however, put Grant's losses at less than originally thought. Humphreys calculated the killed and wounded at approximately 4,100 men, the 2nd Corps accounting for about half the casualties, the 5th and 6th Corps almost evenly for the rest. By comparison, Union losses at the Wilderness had averaged close to 9,000 casualties a day. Nonetheless, Grant's attacks on May 10 came to epitomize in the popular mind his penchant for ill-conceived charges. A Confederate informed his hometown newspaper that "Grant's tactic is to form his line of battle, fortify, arrange his artillery, supported in those fortifications by a reserved corps, and then hurl his whole force in heavy columns on the weakest part of our line. So you may imagine the carnage that follows his advance and repulse. I never saw as many dead and wounded men, as lay piled in front of every place he has yet assaulted."[73]

For the most part, Grant had kept Lee on the defensive. But forcing Lee to dance to Grant's tune required the Union army to maintain an exhausting pace. It had flanked Lee from his Rapidan entrenchments on May 4, fought bitterly in the Wilderness on May 5 and 6, maneuvered Lee toward Spotsylvania on May 7, sparred on May 8, maneuvered on the 9th, and fought again on May 10. Grant initiated major operations on the spur of the moment, undeterred by uncertainties about Lee's dispositions and strength. The Po River expedition exemplified the difficulties that Grant's style of warfare incurred, at least for the Army of the Potomac. Turning Lee's left flank was an excellent idea and could have severely damaged the rebels, but Grant afforded Meade no time for preparation and initiated no reconnaissance. He thrust Hancock over the river too late on May 9 for the 2nd Corps to complete its maneuver, and with no idea of what stood in its path. When night fell, Hancock felt compelled to stop at the Block House Bridge, thereby revealing his hand and enabling Lee to counter. Humphreys later expressed regret that Hancock had not been "directed to cross the Po at daylight of the 10th, instead of being ordered to cross later in the afternoon of the 9th." Had that been done, Humphreys argued, "the Confederate left would have been turned and taken in rear, while the Fifth Corps attacked it in front." Patience, however, did not figure in Grant's plans. Haste cost him excellent opportunities.[74]

As with the Po River operation, Grant initiated his attacks against Laurel Hill with no firm understanding of Lee's troop dispositions. "Whether Lee's entire army is here, or whether any part has been detached to Richmond, is a question concerning which we have no positive evidence," Dana recorded shortly before the assaults. Grant correctly surmised that Lee had weakened his defensive line to gather troops to attack Hancock, but he could only guess which portion of the formation Lee had drawn upon. It just so happened that Lee had thinned his defenses along Fredericksburg Road, but Grant did not know that. Consequently, he sacrificed thousands of men in futile charges against well-defended positions but ventured no meaningful assault along Fredericksburg Road, where success was likely.[75]

Grant's idea of attacking across Lee's entire formation was seriously flawed. Colonel Wainwright conceded that "there may have some plan in it, but in my ignorance I cannot help thinking that one big, sustained attack at one point would have been much more likely to succeed." Hancock's aide Walker complained that the "characteristic fault of the campaign then opened was attacking at too many points." In his view, Grant's responsibility as commander in chief was to "discover that weak point; to make careful and serious preparation for the attack, and to mass behind the assaulting column a force that shall be irresistible, if only once the line be pierced." Instead, went Walker's argument, Grant's attacks had been "weak affairs in almost every case, unsupported; and mere shoving forward of a brigade or two now here now there, like a chess player shoving out his pieces and then drawing them right back." One soldier denounced the charges as "demoralizing." Another proclaimed them "not very cheering to us."[76]

Upton's charge, however, provided food for thought. It showed that the Federals could break Lee's line if they moved fast enough. And gains could be consolidated if sufficient reserves were available. What if the attacking force were larger? What if an entire corps, just before daylight, muscled against the tip of the salient and hence the weakest point of Lee's line? And what if the reserve consisted not of Mott's discredited division but of the expeditionary force's remaining three infantry corps? Perhaps Upton's charge held the key to victory. The prospect was enough to set a general like Grant to thinking.

Lee had fought a splendid defensive battle. He had countered Hancock in a masterly way by shifting Heth and Mahone from the far side of his line. The maneuver necessarily weakened Lee's right flank, but it was a risk that he felt comfortable taking. The only threat in that quarter came from Burnside, Grant's least able commander, a point Lee doubtless considered in leaving a single division to protect Spotsylvania's eastern approaches. His judgment proved flawless as he adroitly repelled Grant's assaults and sealed the one serious rupture on Doles's front. Lee managed his defensive line on May 10 with the skill that he had exhibited at Antietam, in a textbook example of a smaller army deflecting a larger one.

After the dust settled, Ewell and his subordinates gathered at the McCoull house. Lee sat with them on the porch, doubtless reviewing their conduct. Anderson and Early had performed well, and Ewell had responded vigorously after Upton attacked. But why had he and Rodes not anticipated the charge and better prepared to receive it? Lee hinted at this concern by leaning across the porch toward Rodes and inquiring, "General, what shall we do with General Doles for allowing those people to break over his lines?" Rodes replied, "We shall have to let Doles off this time, as he has suffered quite severely for it already." Lee said nothing more about the subject, perhaps concluding that his subordinates had learned from the mistake and would be better prepared next time. He was soon to be disappointed.[77]

Shortly after 8 P.M., Lee instructed Ewell to strengthen his line, cautioning that Grant might venture a night attack, "as it was a favorite amusement of his at Vicksburg." And he urged everyone to prepare for renewed fighting in the morning. Before retiring, he wrote the Confederate war secretary that despite a "most obstinate" assault, the men had rallied and regained their line. "Thanks to a merciful Providence," Lee observed, "our casualties have been small."[78]

Under cover of darkness, Lee shifted Heth back to Spotsylvania Court House, leaving only Mahone west of the Po to protect the Army of Northern Virginia's left flank. "The flashes of the exploding cartridge boxes on the dead and wounded could be seen as the long sweep of flame went over them, and the cries of the wounded for help, which could not come, was something heart rending," a Mississippian wrote. "Night closed upon the two armies in repose that was unbroken, outside the lines, save by the venomous whirring of bullets from the sleepless sharpshooters." The Army of Northern Virginia remained "in fine spirits, and eager for the enemy to come."[79]

VI

May 11

A Cavalryman Dies
and Grant Prepares to Attack Again

"I never saw such a distressed looking body of men."

SHERIDAN'S TROOPERS WERE having the adventure of their lives. Their squat, bowlegged leader with an oddly bullet-shaped head and fiery temper was fast winning their respect. The foray south had the earmarks of a triumphal march to Richmond.

The first night's bivouac—May 9–10—proved uneventful. Wilson's and Gregg's divisions camped above the North Anna while Merritt's continued its destructive work around Beaver Dam Station. Flames from burning crossties reddened the sky. Occasional musketry signaled that rebels were skulking about, but the Federals felt secure in their numbers.

Sheridan busily plotted the next day's maneuver. At first light, he intended to advance Gregg and Wilson across the North Anna and consolidate his corps at Beaver Dam. From there, his route ran through the tiny settlement of Negro Foot, then on to Mountain Road, which crossed the South Anna and continued to Telegraph Road six miles above Richmond. "The possession of Beaver Dam gave us an important point, as it opened a way toward Richmond on the Negro-foot road," Sheridan observed. "It also enabled us to obtain forage for our well-nigh famished animals, and to prepare for fighting the enemy, who, I felt sure, would endeavor to interpose between my column and Richmond."[1]

Around midnight, Sheridan met with Merritt and Captain Abraham K. Arnold, of the 5th United States Cavalry, Gibbs's brigade. Although Sheridan felt confident that he could hold off the rebel cavalry gathering behind him, he worried that Stuart might cross the North Anna upriver and harass his flank. Studying a map by candlelight, Sheridan identified the Davenport Bridge as the most likely place for the rebels to cross. To secure his

Cavalry maneuvers on the morning of May 10

flank, he directed Arnold to take his regiment and the 1st New York Dragoons to the bridge and hold it at all hazards, until he was relieved.[2]

Stuart meanwhile concentrated his troopers to confront Sheridan at morning's first light. Wickham wrapped close around the rear of the Federal column while Stuart accompanied Lomax and Gordon as they circled west to Davenport. Stuart's plan was just as Sheridan had feared. He meant to catch Sheridan in a pincer, with Wickham closing from behind while Lomax and Gordon attacked from the flank. Stuart also had a personal motive for his hard ride. His wife and children were visiting the home of Colonel Edmund Fontaine, near Beaver Dam Station.[3]

Wilson and Gregg were stirring by 4 A.M. on the tenth. "The reveille," a Maine trooper reminisced, "was the sounds of shells flying thick and fast from a rebel battery posted on the hills in rear of the column." A Pennsylvanian thought the Confederate guns "in such close proximity that to say their early morning salute was exciting and dangerous, would be putting it mildly." Gregg sent a force to quiet the interlopers so his men could eat breakfast before they set off. Soon after daylight, Sheridan's two rear divisions started over the river, Gregg's leading.[4]

More Confederate horse artillery jangled up and began lobbing shells in an attempt to catch the northerners astride the stream. "Very hot it was for an hour or so," one of Gregg's riders admitted. Wilson pitched in and sent a regiment to drive off the Confederate ordnance. In short order, it had cleared the rebels from the north bank and formed a barrier protecting the ford. Spirited fighting echoed along the river as Wickham nipped at Gregg's rear guard, but the two Union divisions were soon across and pounding toward Beaver Dam Station to join Merritt. A trooper summarized the affair: "We succeeded in getting over the river without great loss, as [Wilson] covered our crossing, and our flying artillery did splendid work in silencing the rebel battery that gave us the most trouble, and then sending cannon balls among the Johnnies who were peppering us at close range."[5]

Before daybreak, Captain Arnold had started upriver along the North Anna's southern bank; then, a little after sunrise, he turned north to Davenport. Confederate engineers were busy repairing the bridge, which a Union raiding party had destroyed during the winter. Arnold's men routed the workers and wrecked their new beam framework. An elderly black man living nearby showed Arnold a wagon road below the bridge that the Confederates had been using. Satisfied that he had found the ford, Arnold hid and waited to see what would happen.

He did not remain in suspense for long. Soon rebel cavalry emerged at the span's far end, then disappeared west into a stand of trees. The Confederates—Gordon's and Lomax' brigades, maneuvering to flank Sheridan—seemed to be heading upriver, so Arnold detached a platoon under Lieutenant Wilson to search for another crossing farther upstream. Scouting above the bridge, Wilson found a ford and crossed. Presently he met the approaching Confederate column and hurried back to sound the alarm. Rebels would arrive on the south bank any minute.[6]

For a short time, battle seemed imminent. A detachment from the 5th North Carolina, of Gordon's brigade, dismounted and drove Arnold's sharpshooters back from the bank. Another 5th North Carolina squadron splashed across the ford, sabers drawn, and charged screaming into Arnold's formation. A courier from Sheridan spurred up and ordered Arnold to rejoin the main column. Greatly relieved, he retired to Beaver Dam Station only to find that Sheridan had moved on. When he started south in search of Sheridan, Confederates blocked the way. Gordon and Lomax were close behind, and in front were elements from Wickham's brigade, pursuing Sheridan. First Arnold tried cutting through Wickham, but that only stirred up the 2nd and 3rd Virginia Cavalry. "There was a general melee, sabres and pistols being used freely," Arnold recounted. The Confederates claimed that they executed a "quick and decisive" charge with drawn sabers that scattered Arnold's men "to the winds."[7]

Arnold was in a tight place. He managed, however, to slip a skirmish line past Wickham's flank and kept the route open with sharp carbine fire. He reached Little River, the next stream south, ahead of the Confederates. The rear of Sheridan's column had just crossed, and Union engineers were severing the bridge's last span. Arnold rumbled over while the engineers held his pursuers at bay. "Our command suffered severely," Arnold's superior, Gibbs, admitted. The captain counted his losses at two officers— one of whom was Lieutenant Wilson—and sixty-eight enlisted men. "An enterprising enemy should have annihilated the command," was his candid appraisal of the escapade.[8]

While Arnold was scouting toward Davenport, Sheridan had assembled the rest of his corps near the Virginia Central Railroad's smoldering ruins. "Custer had knocked the bottom out of everything," a trooper recorded, "and our boys were particular that the destruction should be complete." By eight o'clock, Sheridan had started south. As he vacated Beaver Dam Station, elements from Wickham's 4th Virginia Cavalry closed in and captured a handful of northerners. Among the prisoners were unfortunates who had been caught three days before at Laurel Hill by the Confederates and then liberated by Custer on the 9th.[9]

Stuart united Wickham, Lomax, and Gordon below Beaver Dam. Fitz-

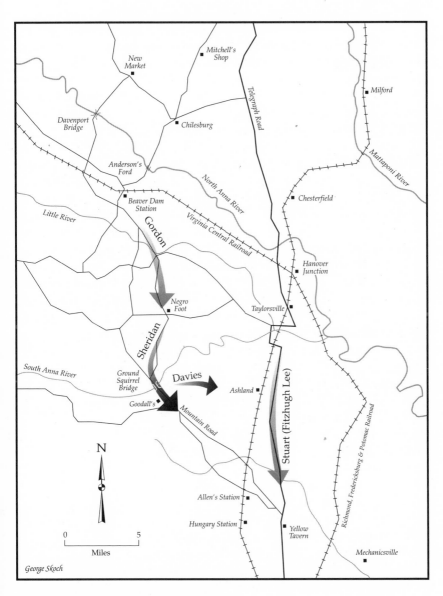

Cavalry operations on May 10 and May 11

hugh Lee had thrust some of Wickham's men after Sheridan, but the Federals had taken a page from Lee's own book and littered the road behind
them with barricades, forcing the pursuers to struggle in vexation behind.
They had failed to snag Sheridan, who was well on his way toward Negro
Foot. Stuart judged that his three brigades stood little chance against Sheri-

dan's three divisions on open ground. His solution was to try to ambush the Federals near Richmond, where Confederate infantry guarding the capital could assist. With such a plan in mind, he divided his already outnumbered force. Gordon was to follow Sheridan and harass him to delay his progress while Lee hurried east to Hanover Junction, then descended Telegraph Road to interdict him at the Mountain Road junction. As Lee later summarized the scheme, "Discovering Richmond to be the object of the enemy, and knowing the entire absence of troops in the works guarding its western side, General Stuart determined to move upon the chord of the arc the enemy were advancing upon, and by outmarching them interpose our little force in the enemy's front at some point contiguous to the city."[10]

Stuart's plan was risky. His tired Confederates would have to ride nearly all day and night to beat Sheridan to the intersection. And the expected fight's outcome was in question, since Sheridan outnumbered Stuart by better than three to one. But Stuart thought that the opportunity for victory justified the risk, particularly if infantry from Richmond could reinforce him. After satisfying himself that his family was safe at the Fontaine place, the rebel cavalry commander made for Hanover Junction at the head of Lee's winded riders.[11]

Sheridan pressed steadily south, the 1st Maine Cavalry, of Gregg's division, leading. A single trooper rode in front, trailed by two men a few yards back, then by a sergeant and four more soldiers. Behind came a squad of eight soldiers, then a company, then a regiment, and then a seemingly endless line of horsemen, four abreast. Flankers hovered several hundred yards off the column's sides. A colonel in the 6th Michigan Cavalry later explained the formation's purpose. If Confederates attacked, "it was only necessary to wheel by fours in that direction to be in line of battle with a very strong line of skirmishers well out in front." Sheridan's plan was simple. He was on a "slow and steady march, straight toward the Confederate capital, all the time in position to accept battle should Stuart offer it."[12]

Stuart was not yet ready to offer battle, but while Fitzhugh Lee raced toward Hanover Junction, Gordon pecked insistently at Sheridan's column. His 1st North Carolina Cavalry had perfected the art of ambush in the Wilderness, where it had delayed the 6th Corps several critical hours. This time the Tarheels gave Sheridan no quarter. All day, rebel horsemen emerged from the woods, fired, then evaporated into shadows. A trooper complained of "bushwhackers on our flanks and fences on fire both sides of the road."[13]

Skirmishing intensified a few miles below Beaver Dam. Twenty butternut soldiers—from the intrepid Colonel Brown's 1st Maryland Cavalry,
which was under orders from Stuart to annoy the head of the Union
march—had drawn up on a hill. "Charge," a Federal shouted, and a contingent from the 1st Maine Cavalry galloped for the rise, scattering
Brown's Confederates. When the northerners crested the brow, they ran
into a "hornet's nest," as a participant called the spirited action that followed. More rebels hid in a ravine and fired at the Federals, starkly sil-
houetted against the clear spring sky. The northerners fell prone and exchanged "lively fire." Again the rebels retired, leaving the approach
spotted with dead and wounded Yankees. While Sheridan continued on,
a detachment lingered to bury the dead. They confiscated a meal chest
from a neighboring house, kicked out the partitions, and deposited the
corpses into the makeshift coffin. "The burial was one that will never be
forgotten by any one of the half dozen who were present," an onlooker
predicted. The owner protested against burying Yankees in his chest but
desisted after a Federal drew a revolver and threatened to stuff him into
the box with the cadavers.[14]

"The day was very hot," Merritt recorded, "and the march, a long one,
was made with but little water or rest for our animals." The farms seemed
well cultivated compared with the war-ravaged country around Spotsylvania. Sheridan's flankers, although operating under stern orders to "commit no depredations," secured numerous delicacies from the surrounding
plantations. "It is astonishing what a wide latitude the needs of human
subsistence extend over," an officer remarked on surveying the bounty. A
trooper from Massachusetts exclaimed, "What a picnic we enjoyed!" A
Vermonter admitted that the men had been enjoined to take only what they
required but noted that their requirements "extended to hams, butter,
chickens, flour, meal, [and] anything of an edible nature they could lay
their hands on; and by long experience in this kind of purveying they
knew just where to look for such articles when they struck a rich old
planter's premises."[15]

Invading armies had spared this part of Dixie, but signs of war lay
everywhere. "We saw no whites, excepting old men, women, and children," a Federal noted. "They were intensely 'Secesh,' and the chaffing
between them and our boys was amusing." At one homestead, a spade
with C.S.A. on its handle served as a headstone, and three ladies, eyes red
with grief, peered from darkened windows. An old man sporting shoulder-
length white hair and a beet-red nose angrily waited at another dwelling.
"Sir, we are enemies," he hissed. "If I were able to bear arms I should

be in Lee's army today, fighting the vandal horde that has invaded the sacred soil." After stripping the planter of his corn and hams, the Federals rode on, leaving the enraged patriarch glaring with undisguised hatred as he strode back and forth on his porch. A woman at another house spoke her mind. "You Yankees mistake the character of the people you are trying to subjugate," she warned. "The gown I now wear was made by my own hands from the raw material; that's the way we ladies of the South will aid in the defense of our homes by working while the men are fighting." One of Sheridan's horsemen had a reply: "If the war has been the means of teaching your people to work and to take pride in it, as you appear to do, it has been productive of some good."[16]

Not all Federals encountered hostility. James D. Rowe, of the 1st Michigan Cavalry, felt sick and stopped at a farmhouse for food. "I am kind to both sides on the sick," said the woman who answered the door. "I can't give you a square meal, but I reckon I can give you a snack and some blackberry vinegar." Rowe reported that the repast did him "lots of good," and he continued on his way refreshed.[17]

Around 4:15 in the afternoon, Sheridan reached the Ground Squirrel Bridge, on the South Anna eighteen miles below Beaver Dam. He took his men across, then ordered the bridge burned. The 1st Maine Cavalry picketed the southern bank while the rest of the Federals cooked supper, groomed their horses, and as a soldier in the 10th New York put it, "enjoyed a good night's rest."[18]

Sheridan made his headquarters at a nearby plantation. "The owner, an old man, had his slaves concealed down by the smoke house, and was vainly endeavoring to keep them together," a soldier related, "but in spite of his efforts, some of them went with us the next morning." He added, "I saw General Sheridan at this place playing with some small children on the front porch, which act was somewhat antagonistic in those days to my idea what a great general really was."[19]

While the northerners reposed, Stuart pushed Fitzhugh Lee's men to their limit. Around 9 P.M., they reached Hanover Junction, near where Telegraph Road crossed the Virginia Central Railroad, then continued on another mile and a half to Taylorsville. Stuart learned from scouts that Sheridan was at the Ground Squirrel Bridge. He fired off a dispatch alerting Richmond to the danger and inquired whether any of Sheridan's men had reached the capital. "Please answer tonight, if practicable," Stuart pleaded, "as I am very anxious to give my command a night's rest, if compatible with duty."[20]

The Confederates were "thoroughly worn out," and Lee persuaded

Stuart to remain at Taylorsville for a few hours. To ensure that they started promptly, Stuart directed his aide McClellan to stay with Lee and, as McClellan later remembered it, "not to close my eyes until I saw his command mounted and on the march at the appointed hour."[21]

Scouts arrived while the Confederates were dozing. Sheridan, they reported, was planning to move at midnight. With luck, Stuart calculated, he could win the race to where Mountain and Telegraph roads joined. To help neutralize Sheridan's numerical superiority, he sought and received permission to take along Captain W. Hunter Griffin's Baltimore Light Artillery. This battery, along with Captain Johnston's 1st Stuart Horse Artillery and Captain James F. Hart's section of the Washington South Carolina Battery already attached to Stuart, gave him ten guns in all.[22]

At 3 A.M., as his troopers set out under a starry sky, Stuart sent another dispatch to Richmond. "I am moving to Ashland," he wrote, referring to a station ten miles south on the Richmond, Fredericksburg and Potomac Railroad. "If I reach that point before the enemy, I will move down the Telegraph Road." He expressed his determination to intercept Sheridan even if doing so cost every horse in his command. McClellan drifted into slumber to the sound of Stuart's voice. "Leave a courier with him," the general whispered, "and tell him to come on when his nap is out."[23]

Sheridan decided to divide his command for the drive toward Richmond. While Colonel Gregg's brigade remained by the river as a rear guard, Merritt's and Wilson's divisions were to continue along Mountain Road, cross the Richmond, Fredericksburg and Potomac Railroad at Allen's Station, then proceed to Telegraph Road, a march totaling about twelve miles. Meanwhile Davies was to undertake an independent mission and advance along country roads to Ashland Station—about five miles above Allen's Station—destroying tracks and inflicting mischief as he saw fit. Afterward, he was to rejoin the main column.

Sheridan rode off shortly after sunrise on May 11, leaving Gregg to picket the South Anna. The colonel felt secure because the Ground Squirrel Bridge had been burned the night before and everyone assumed the river was unfordable. "This, however, proved not to be so, as the regiment found to its sorrow the next morning," a Federal noted. What was supposed to be a simple holding action quickly escalated into a major engagement.[24]

Gregg's first intimation that something was amiss came as pickets along the river's southern bank called for support. The 1st Maine Cavalry dispatched a handful of men to investigate while the rest of the regiment began packing. Flurries of musketry rippled through the woods, and dismounted men came tumbling back. "There was a scramble for their horses," a Maine soldier recalled, "and the men had scarcely got mounted before the enemy appeared in three columns, mounted, but a few yards away, in the road and on each side, charging down upon them like so many demons."[25]

James Gordon's three North Carolina regiments were responsible for the ruckus. Early in the morning, Gordon had located an old ford whose fifteen-foot-high banks appeared impassable. The general galloped to the ford at the head of the 5th North Carolina Cavalry. He cut a stirring figure—"tall and commanding," a witness described him, "stately set and splendidly muscled, a massive chest and athletic limbs," the epitome of an "educated soldier." Pointing to the ford, Gordon shouted, "Forward!" then plunged over. His brigade followed and was soon across the river and tangling with Gregg's pickets.[26]

The main body of Gregg's horsemen was camped around Goodall's Tavern, a rambling country hotel with several outbuildings, barns, and stables on the old stage road from Gordonsville to Richmond. As Gordon's men emerged from the low ground near the river, Federal sharpshooters began firing at them from the tavern. The building stood in an open field, and Gordon, who had no artillery, was brought up short. Taking temporary command of the 1st North Carolina Cavalry, he directed the regiment's colonel, William H. Cheek, to flank the structure with a squadron from the 5th North Carolina Cavalry. The ruse was successful, and Gregg's men retired from around the tavern into the open road. Gordon then thrust the 1st and 5th North Carolina Cavalry ahead, dismounted in column of fours on the road. The 2nd North Carolina Cavalry meantime pitched into Gregg's flank. The Maine troops careered in "some confusion" into the 10th New York behind them, a Federal conceded, and the "torrent of wild horsemen" reduced the New York regiment to a "bewildered mass." A southerner boasted that "the rout was complete." A New Yorker confessed that "none of the boys appear to have retained a very clear recollection of just how things had occurred or where the regiment was 'when last seen'; but all agreed that the regiment as a unit did not remain there long." Another Union participant admitted that "for a few moments it was every man for himself and the rebels take the hindermost." The 1st North Carolina Cavalry's bugler added insult to injury by wresting a horn from the 1st Maine's bugler and spurring the Confederates on with stirring tunes.[27]

Colonel Cheek later described the little battle as the "most desperate hand-to-hand conflict I ever witnessed." The 1st North Carolina Cavalry and 1st Maine Cavalry were considered by many to be the best cavalry regiments from each side, and they fought as though their reputations were at stake. Combatants tangled viciously at close range with sabers and pistols. The 1st North Carolina's color sergeant resorted to wielding his flagstaff to fend off cutlass blows. Colonel Gregg's tall form was conspicuous as he tried unsuccessfully to stem the rout. "The entire regiment went to pieces for the first time in its career," a soldier in the 1st Maine Cavalry conceded, "and every man took the road for himself." Just as all seemed lost, a Federal battery rolled up, fired a blank cartridge to clear the road, then blasted away with canister. Gregg formed a second line under the protective umbrella of shot and shell. The Union formation extended a hundred yards or so into woods on both sides of the roadway near Ground Squirrel Church. There the Federals returned fire with "all the lead we could from our carbines and revolvers." Hoping to dislodge Gregg and perhaps capture a cannon, Gordon sent Cheek on another flanking maneuver, this time with a squadron from the colonel's own regiment. Working through the woods in column of fours, Cheek's men fell on Gregg's extreme right. Close-quarters fighting resumed as the Federals fell back once again. Cheek was exuberantly chasing a Union trooper at saber point when the man's companion shot him in the shoulder at close range. For the next several hours, Gregg waged a heated rearguard action against Gordon. Several times his men dismounted and formed a skirmish line to repel a threatened attack. Then they mounted, retired a short distance, and stopped to fight on foot again.[28]

Gordon's Confederates were encouraged by their victory over Gregg at Ground Squirrel Bridge. They had attacked with "great vigor and success," a Carolinian preened, "sweeping [the Union] columns in a mounted charge, in the most handsome style, routing and driving them in the greatest precipitation for several miles; killing and capturing a good number." But aside from generating exciting tales for future veterans, Gordon's exhilarating charge accomplished little. Gregg's battered soldiers continued to shield Sheridan's rear, and the Union column advanced inexorably toward Richmond.[29]

Several miles away, Davies was also having his fill of combat. His mixed Massachusetts, New Jersey, Ohio, and Pennsylvania command broke camp around 2 A.M. and hastened by side roads to Ashland Station. When it arrived, Stuart's lead element—Lomax' brigade—had already passed through, but a substantial contingent of Wickham's rebels was approaching. Munford's 2nd Virginia Cavalry dismounted and initiated a "lively fight." Davies drove Munford from the hamlet, then set fire to the depot, an engine and some railroad cars. The raiders also seized the contents of a post office and, according to a 10th New York account, ransacked a local girls' school and amused themselves by reading the correspondence they found there. When more rebels arrived, Davies tried to drive them away but was ambushed by Confederates hiding in houses. A murderous volley seared Davies' ranks and killed the 1st Massachusetts Cavalry's popular Lieutenant Edward P. Hopkins. Davies considered shelling the town in retaliation but was reluctant to risk a pitched battle so far from the main Union column. During a lull he disengaged and pursued a tangle of "narrow and tortuous woodland roads" south to rejoin Sheridan at Allen's Station. The rebels got their revenge by threatening to throw the Union captives into the smoldering train cars. "The prisoners evidently didn't relish the joke," a Confederate observed. "Their looks bespoke very decidedly fear that they would not stand the test quite as well as Shadrach, Meshac, and Abednego."[30]

At 6:30 A.M., Stuart informed Richmond that the enemy had reached Ashland but had been "promptly whipped out after a sharp fight by Fitz Lee's advance, killing and capturing quite a number." By continuing south, Stuart observed, he would "intersect the road the enemy is marching on at Yellow Tavern, the head of the turnpike, six miles from Richmond." That was his goal. "My men and horses are tired, hungry, and jaded, but all right," he added.[31]

While General Gregg's two brigades engaged in spirited encounters at Ground Squirrel Bridge and Ashland, Merritt and Wilson maintained their measured advance along Mountain Road. Davies, fresh from his destructive foray, joined them at Allen's Station, and together they laid waste to that place as well. A contingent lingered to tear up tracks south toward Hungary Station, and the powerful column tramped on, Merritt leading, Wilson following, and Gregg in the rear. Gibbs's Reserve Brigade scouted ahead of the column, and the 6th Pennsylvania Cavalry deployed in a skirmish line that spread "well into the country, and moved straight ahead, despite of fences, barn-yards, woods, or anything else." A Pennsylvania youth spied a rebel hiding in a tree and ordered him down from his "undignified and unwarlike position," his regiment's historian reported. It developed that the Confederate had been visiting his family when the Federals appeared and had climbed the tree to avoid detection. "A more sullen, uncommunicative rebel was never gobbled," a Pennsylvanian remarked.[32]

"It was a lovely day," an officer in the 7th Michigan reminisced. "The

air was mild, the country charming, and we thought it was a holiday-time
we were having as we rode easily along."[33]

Several miles ahead, at the junction of Mountain and Telegraph roads,
Lomax was drawing up in battle array. The roads formed a Y, with Mountain Road constituting the western branch, Telegraph Road the eastern,
and the Brook Turnpike dropping south. A short distance down the Brook
Turnpike, on the roadway's eastern side, stood the remains of an abandoned hostelry, the Yellow Tavern, that Stuart had mentioned in his communication to Richmond. Six miles farther on was Richmond. Lomax held
the eastern fork while Sheridan approached on the western. It was about
8 A.M., and the Confederates were anything but rested. They had beaten
Sheridan to the crossroads, but at considerable cost, having covered much
of the distance from Taylorsville at a gallop. Weary and road-worn, they
were in a questionable condition to fight.[34]

Fitzhugh Lee arrived shortly after Lomax and supervised the brigade's
dispositions. The 6th Virginia Cavalry formed near the intersection of
Telegraph and Mountain roads, with the 5th and 15th Virginia Cavalry
stretching north along Telegraph Road. In front of the Confederates—that
is, west of Telegraph Road—spread fields fringed with dense woods. Lomax, after positioning his men, rode to an observation post on a high ridge
that ran at right angles across his brigade's northern flank, leaving Colonel
Henry Clay Pate, of the 5th Virginia Cavalry, in immediate command of
the line. Pate scouted toward Sheridan's expected approach and discovered
a gully bordering the open land and woods, parallel to Telegraph Road.
He posted lookouts before the gully and skirmishers behind it. Sharpshooters waited on the rebel line's left to rake any Federals who tried to
slip around from the south.[35]

Stuart reached Lomax' command post and reviewed his options. Sheridan's column was approaching on Mountain Road. The choices were to
form across Sheridan's path on the leg of the Y, or to mass above the
intersection along Telegraph Road—the position Lomax had taken—and
slam Sheridan's flank as he passed. There was the third possibility of
retiring to the outer earthworks defending Richmond, but Stuart did not
take that choice seriously. It was not in character for him to consider
anything that smacked of retreat.

Stuart decided to leave Lomax along Telegraph Road. Wickham was
not yet up, having been delayed by the engagement at Ashland. When he
arrived, Stuart planned to place him on Lomax' right, along the hills at
right angles to Telegraph Road. Stuart would hold a strong defensive po-

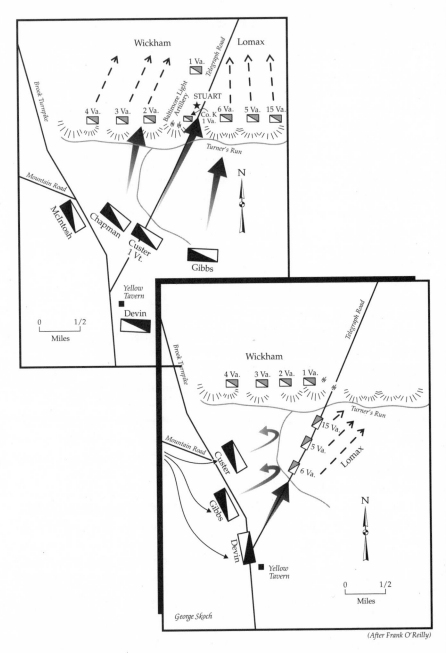

Sheridan's attack against Stuart at Yellow Tavern on May 11. Lower panel, morning action; upper panel, afternoon action.

sition, and if Sheridan tried to pass onto the Brook Turnpike, the Confederates could attack his flank and rear. Stuart was anxious for reinforcements and directed McClellan to ride to the capital and ascertain whether troops were available. If Sheridan could be caught between Stuart on Telegraph Road and another body of Confederates marching up the Brook Turnpike, he would have no means of escape.[36]

"We thought we had him penned and would surely capture his whole command," a Confederate explained. "With this expectation we closed in on him."[37]

Around nine o'clock, Sheridan approached along a relatively flat, open stretch of Mountain Road. "A nice level country, corn three inches high," a cavalryman observed. "Trees in full bloom, nature looks too beautiful to be devastated by war." The 6th Pennsylvania Cavalry, leading the Union advance, encountered the 6th Virginia's skirmishers as it neared the road junction. Gibbs deployed skirmishers and ordered his men into battle formation. Devin's brigade came immediately behind and passed onto Gibbs's right. Then Custer pulled up and formed on Gibbs's left. Merritt's entire division was in battle array facing Lomax, and Merritt assumed responsibility for the developing front. Custer massed his regiments in column in the field and thrust skirmishers toward the commanding ridge that was beginning to fill with Wickham's Confederates. "Merritt was in charge and the battle was on," a Union participant recounted.[38]

Musketry crackled through the spring air as Sheridan began probing Stuart's formation. With only one division up, he decided against risking a full-scale attack. Custer was especially concerned about Confederate artillery posted on the ridge to the north, which had him in "perfect range," and he tried to gain breathing room by driving Lomax' pickets from an adjacent stand of woods. The 5th and 6th Michigan Cavalry dismounted while the 1st and 7th Michigan Cavalry remained in reserve on horseback. At Custer's command, the dismounted troops clambered over a fence and ran, yelling and firing, at the Confederate pickets, driving them back. Confederates from the 5th and 15th Virginia opened devastating fire and brought Custer to a halt.[39]

Stuart, as usual, was everywhere. His aide Theodore Garnett saw him among the skirmishers, "directing their fire, and making his dispositions for the coming battle." On the field's far side, Custer was also spitting out orders with his accustomed energy. He darted into the fray and shifted the 6th Michigan Cavalry to the left of the 5th, which gave him the weight he needed. In bloody hand-to-hand fighting, he pushed Lomax' pickets toward Telegraph Road. "As soon as our line appeared in the open—indeed, before it left the woods the Confederate artillery opened with shell and shrapnel," Colonel Kidd, of the 6th Michigan, related. "The carbineers and sharpshooters joined with zest in the fray and the man who thinks they did not succeed in making that part of the neighborhood around Yellow Tavern an uncomfortably hot place, was not there at the time." For the time being, Custer's advance was stymied.[40]

The Federals on Custer's right had somewhat better success. Gibbs hammered ahead, as did Devin on the lower flank. Punching past Yellow Tavern, Devin's 17th Pennsylvania Cavalry interposed between Stuart and Richmond. Then the 6th New York Cavalry wedged into the opening and occupied the road south. Lomax, flanked on his left, began withdrawing the 6th Virginia north along Telegraph Road. In response, Merritt increased the pressure across his front, forcing the 15th and 5th Virginia Cavalry regiments to scurry for a place to rally.[41]

About a half mile above the intersection, Telegraph Road had been worn below the level of the surrounding fields. Stuart selected that spot for Lomax to make his stand, and Colonel Pate began piling the 5th Virginia Cavalry into the road cut. A short way north, the road crossed a little creek and climbed the ridge to where Wickham was deploying. Stuart placed the Baltimore Light Artillery battery that he had acquired at Taylorsville on Telegraph Road near the ridge line. The 1st Virginia Cavalry anchored Wickham's left at the battery, with the 2nd, 3rd, and 4th Virginia Cavalry stringing west along the heights.[42]

"Go and tell Colonel Pate to hold the position at all hazards," Stuart directed his aide Garnett. The staffer rode into the cut and found Pate, who was dismounted, sword in hand, rallying his men. "I delivered the order in the very words I had received it," Garnett explained, "and I can see Colonel Pate now as he stood, looking me square in the eye, with his cold grey eyes and pallid face." Thinking Pate had not heard him, Garnett repeated his message. "Still no reply came from his lips," Garnett recounted. "But I saw he had heard and understood my orders in their full significance, as a veritable 'death sentence.'"[43]

Gibbs's Federals poured into the cut from west and south and slammed into Pate. Devin's 9th New York Cavalry fought conspicuously on Gibbs's right. The sunken road furnished Pate some protection, but the Yankees kept coming. Pate shouted, "One more round, boys, and then we'll get to the hill," just before a bullet bored through his forehead and killed him. According to one of Gibbs's men, the "boys broke into a yell, and began pumping the lead from their deadly seven-shooter carbines into that line of gray at such a terrible rate that they broke and ran like a flock of sheep." Some Confederates jumped a fence and fled across the fields. Others crept to safety through a culvert. As many as two hundred stood their ground and were captured. "Fearfully cut up," a rebel said of the brigade. Lomax' battered Confederates retired north on Telegraph Road to the ridge occupied by Wickam and re-formed on his left.[44]

Wickham's troopers opened on the northerners below, and Stuart's artillery quickened its pace. Lacking sufficient support and caught in Wickham's flanking fire, Custer retired toward Mountain Road. His withdrawal left Gibbs and the 9th New York fighting alone. Concerned that they might become isolated, they, too, disengaged.[45]

Stuart was heartened. Although severely outnumbered, his men had stopped Sheridan's. Wickham's were now arrayed west of Telegraph Road along high ground, facing south. Lomax had deployed on Wickham's left, extending the Confederate line eastward. The rebel position was exceptionally strong, and Stuart believed he could hold it, particularly if reinforced. Sheridan, it appeared to Stuart, had been stunned by his repulse and was staying quiet.

In fact, Sheridan was doing a great deal. As he had suspected, a single division could not dislodge Stuart. Since Stuart was showing no signs of leaving, Sheridan decided to wait for Wilson, then try again. He was troubled, however, by reports that the Confederate General Pierre G. T. Beauregard might reinforce Stuart from Richmond. So while Custer and Gibbs regrouped, Sheridan directed Devin to reconnoiter toward the Confederate capital with two regiments—the 17th Pennsylvania Cavalry and the 6th New York Cavalry—and a section of Edward Williston's battery of horse artillery. Devin advanced two miles south across the Brook Bridge to Richmond's outer defenses, breached the lightly held entrenchments, then pressed on to the city's inner defensive line. "The bells could be heard ringing, locomotives whistling, and general alarm and bustling seemed to prevail in Richmond," Devin reported. That must have encouraged Sheridan. Stuart was not being reinforced, and the way to Richmond lay open.[46]

As dust settled over the Yellow Tavern battlefield, a courier arrived at Stuart's headquarters. Garnett took the message and delivered it to the general. It was from Gordon, reporting his victory over Sheridan's rear guard at the Ground Squirrel Bridge. Stuart read the missive, slapped his thigh, and exclaimed, "Bully for Gordon!" Then he lowered his voice to a stage whisper. "I wish he was here!"[47]

Around 2 P.M., McClellan returned. Bragg had ample men to hold Richmond and was sending reinforcements. Stuart was optimistic and expressed his intention of "retaining his position on Sheridan's flank, and the hope that, aided by a strong attack by the infantry in Richmond, he might be able to inflict serious disaster on the enemy's cavalry."[48]

The sun moved slowly across the spring sky. Still Sheridan waited. Around three o'clock, Stuart wrote to Bragg that he felt "confident of success." He recommended that Bragg dispatch Brigadier General Eppa Hunton's brigade from Richmond and ventured that "if we make a combined attack on them with Hunton's brigade I cannot see how they can escape." He predicted that Gordon would join him soon, which would give him sufficient strength to "try them again," and he closed on an enthusiastic note: "The enemy fights entirely as infantry today—though yesterday we got in with sabres with good execution. I am glad to report enemy's killed large in proportion."[49]

During the lull, Wilson arrived and formed on Merritt's left, facing the range of hills. The opposing battle lines now ran roughly east to west, with Stuart's two brigades along the crest of the ridge and Sheridan's two divisions—Merritt's and Wilson's—facing them from less than a half mile away. It would be hours before reinforcements could arrive from Richmond or before Gordon could circle around Sheridan and join Stuart. The cavalier's time had run out. He would have to wage his battle alone.

Sheridan decided to renew the assault with a mounted charge, followed by soldiers on foot. Custer was to spearhead the attack by charging the Baltimore Light Artillery that commanded Telegraph Road. Reconnoitering the surrounding country, Custer concluded that the battery could be taken by a rapid assault and invited Colonel Addison W. Preston, of the 1st Vermont Cavalry, to join him. Preston agreed, but his brigade commander, Colonel Chapman, objected. Custer appealed to Sheridan, who told him that he could take any regiment that was willing to go. Making the best of an awkward situation, Chapman decided to ride with the 1st Vermont.[50]

Custer cut a striking figure as he rode to the front of his Wolverines. He was in "fighting trim," a correspondent wrote. "He has a sharp, blue eye, a very slight impediment in his speech, and dresses somewhat in the old cavalier style—black velvet jacket, with a blue shirt collar turned over the same, his brigadier's star being worn in each corner. He wears a slouched hat with a star in the front, and a red scarf cravat around his neck. Whenever he orders a charge he always leads in person and bursts upon the enemy with a yell equal to that of any of the Rocky Mountain aborigines."[51]

Custer's plan was straightforward. The 5th and 6th Michigan Cavalry were to march dismounted across the field toward the heights held by Wickham. The 1st Michigan Cavalry, supported by the 7th Michigan Cavalry and the 1st Vermont Cavalry, was to charge up Telegraph Road toward the Baltimore Light Artillery. Wilson would meanwhile attack on Custer's left, hitting Wickham, while Gibbs pounded Lomax on Custer's right. A soldier in the 5th Michigan Cavalry recalled Custer's terse orders. "Colonel Alger, take your [5th] regiment and the 6th, and engage the enemy on foot. Colonel Stagg, form your [1st Michigan] regiment for the charge. Major Walker, support the 1st Michigan with the 7th. Colonel Preston, form the 1st Vermont by squadrons, and at the rear of the 1st Michigan, and be ready to fill any break in their line." The 5th and 6th Michigan Cavalry deployed facing Wickham while the three regiments assigned to charge up Telegraph Road sought cover in woods near the roadway.[52]

At four o'clock, bugles sounded and Lieutenant Edward Heaton's battery began firing. "Now boys," Colonel Russell A. Alger cautioned, "keep a good line, for General Sheridan is watching us." It was an "enlivening spectacle to behold," a spectator thought. "In all directions over the field, regiments, or brigades, upon the trot or gallop, in columns of fours, companies, squadrons, or battalions, with batteries galloping into position, and here and there reserves drawn up in line as straight and motionless as stone walls." Stuart's guns raked Sheridan's formation. Then nature joined in, as a thunderstorm burst over the countryside. "The lightening and cannonading were so terrific, that sometimes we couldn't tell the flash of one from the other," a Virginian remarked. "The rain was just pouring and often the ammunition would get so wet, as we were loading our guns, that they wouldn't fire."[53]

Stuart was reckless, as usual. He sat mounted near Telegraph Road, not far from the Baltimore Light Artillery, holding binoculars to his eyes with both hands. His attention was fixed on the far woods, where Custer was deploying. "Sergeant, they are preparing yonder to charge this battery," he told a courier, William B. Poindexter. "If I don't have a regiment mounted to meet them, they will capture it." Pointing along the Confederate line, Stuart directed Poindexter to bring up the 1st Virginia, a part of which he had stationed in the rear as a mounted reserve. As Poindexter rode off, he glanced back at the plumed figure. Stuart had draped his right arm through his bridle rein to help steady his binoculars.[54]

Custer attacked the ridge in a seemingly irresistible advance. "Forest and field for miles rang with the din of galloping squadrons, rattle of carbines, crashing of sabers, and screaming of shells," a Federal observed. The 1st Michigan Cavalry, which had formed in columns of squadrons under cover of the woods, sprinted uphill toward the Baltimore Light Artillery. In support came the 1st Vermont Cavalry and the 7th Michigan Cavalry, under Major Henry W. Granger. Gibbs attacked simultaneously on Custer's right, and Wilson attacked on Custer's left. "Almost continuous discharges blazed out from the enemy's carbines, smoke and dust enveloped all in a cloud, and horses and riders were blended," a Confederate officer commented. Whipped into a frenzy, blue-clad horsemen vaulted over a barricade, splashed through a small stream—Turner's Run—and pounded up the ridge. Elements from the 6th Virginia Cavalry launched a suicidal countercharge back down Telegraph Road that repulsed the 1st Michigan Cavalry to the creek, and the hillside convulsed in hand-to-hand fighting. "The dull sound of sabres descending upon hapless heads could be heard amid the rattle of carbines and the cracking of pistols," a participant related.[55]

Under Wilson's supervision, the 3rd Indiana and 8th New York Cavalry, of Chapman's brigade, advanced dismounted on Custer's left into thick pine woods and came under intense artillery fire. Although "warmly engaged," in a participant's description, they managed to crest the ridge and overpowered a portion of Wickham's line. Sheridan meanwhile rode among the 5th Michigan Cavalry, which was advancing under blistering fire from the hillside. "Lie down, men, lie down," he shouted. "We'll fix them. I have sent two regiments around on the flank." He was referring to Wilson's men. As Wilson pushed Wickham back, Colonel Alger screamed, "Forward," and Custer's full brigade lunged ahead. The 5th Michigan Cavalry climbed over a fence and a hedgerow, dislodged Confederate pickets, and began up the ridge. "To our right a quarter of a mile could be seen the 1st Michigan in full charging squadrons across fields, over fences—'five of them,' over a small bridge, with the 7th and 1st Vermont in close support," a soldier recalled.[56]

Stuart rushed to the Baltimore Light Artillery, where seventy troops from Company K stood massed under the guidance of Captain Gus W. Dorsey. These Marylanders had joined the 1st Virginia Cavalry in 1861, when Stuart was the regiment's colonel. "Bully for old K! Give it to them, boys!" Stuart shouted. Steadied by the general's presence, the company held its ground while northerners streamed past on both sides. Suddenly the blue tide began flowing in reverse. The 1st Virginia, summoned by Poindexter, was driving them back. Stuart was in his element, gleefully firing at Yankees as they sped past.[57]

Private John A. Huff, of the 5th Michigan, was a crack shot. He had served in Berdan's Sharpshooters and held a prize as the regiment's best marksman. The forty-eight-year-old soldier was running back when he spied a rebel cavalier sitting proudly erect, plume jauntily waving in the breeze. Huff turned and fired his pistol. A slug of lead bore into Stuart's abdomen. "Dorsey, save your men," the general shouted as he struggled to remain mounted. "Are you wounded badly?" a trooper inquired. "I am afraid I am," Stuart replied. "But don't worry, boys. Fitz will do as well for you as I have." Tom Walters, of Baltimore, began leading the general, who was still mounted, to the rear.[58]

Fitzhugh Lee rode up among the 1st Virginia troopers. Stuart was sitting in his saddle, erect as ever, but clutching the pommel of his saddle with both hands. A soldier walked on either side supporting him, and an orderly led his horse. The line was in shambles, and Lee had no time to tarry. "As I went rapidly by our eyes met," he wrote. "He recognized me, his whole face was illumined in an instant, the old battle smile came back, and his voice rang out as clear and sonorous as I had ever heard it." Stuart gave his last order. "Go ahead, Fitz old fellow," he cried. "I know you'll do what's right." And he managed to exhort the retreating Confederates, "Go back! Go back! I had rather die than be whipped."[59]

Although the 1st Virginia Cavalry had cleared the northerners from around the guns, Fitzhugh Lee's position had become untenable. The 7th Michigan came tearing up Telegraph Road, along with the 1st Vermont. Major Granger fell riddled with bullets, but his men fought on, and under the combined weight of Sheridan's flashing sabers, Stuart's formation folded. Most of the shattered rebel units fled north across the Chickahominy River, others headed toward Ashland, and a few looped around to the south seeking safety within the Richmond defenses. Wilson later summarized the action: "We captured his guns, crumpled up his dismounted line, and broke it into hopeless fragments." Sheridan, who had made good his boast of destroying Stuart, later lauded the charge as "brilliantly executed."[60]

Gordon, who was still harassing Sheridan's rear lines, received a mauling almost as demoralizing as that meted out to Lomax and Wickham. While battle raged above Yellow Tavern, Colonel Gregg's rear guard had been tearing up railroad tracks around Allen Station. Gordon formed to attack, and Gregg retired to a ridge below the railbed. Gordon's men came screaming through the pounding rain, but Gregg's carbines and Captain Alanson M. Randol's battery shredded them before they could reach the Union line. Darkness closed on a dismal scene. "Along the ridge the boys lay with their rubber blankets drawn about them," a Massachusetts soldier recalled, "banging away at the enemy as the lightning's flash would reveal their position."[61]

For the aide Garnett, the afternoon had been a nightmare. First he met Lomax, who told him that Pate was dead. "I did not feel that I was losing any time or neglecting my duty by stopping a moment to view Colonel Pate's body and note the fatal wound—full in the forehead—which had caused instant death at the very moment I rode away from him as the enemy closed in on him." Riding toward the Baltimore Light Artillery, Garnett witnessed Custer's charge and joined Fitzhugh Lee's futile attempt to repair his broken ranks. He fled north to the Chickahominy, where he found McClellan, who informed him that Stuart had been wounded. Hearing a rumor that Stuart had fallen into enemy hands, the two aides began organizing a rescue party. Then they learned that Stuart had been brought off the field and went in search of his ambulance.[62]

"I never saw such a distressed looking body of men," the courier Poindexter wrote, "many of them shedding tears when they heard our gallant General had been shot." Stuart was carried to the ambulance, insisting that he be taken to his wife.[63]

Through thunder, lightning, and driving rain, Stuart's sad procession crossed the Chickahominy, then turned toward Richmond. It stopped under a large tree near Atlee's Station on the Virginia Central Railroad, where the staffers urged the ailing general to sip whiskey from a canteen. He resisted, having once solemnly promised his mother that he would never imbibe alcohol. The doctor insisted, and Stuart relented. "This was the first and only drop of whiskey that passed Stuart's lips in all his life," Garnett held.[64]

Stuart was transported to a relative's house on Grace Street, in Richmond, where he suffered excruciating pain and drifted between delirium and lucidity. Around noon the next day, President Davis visited his bedside. Toward evening, the general's delirium increased. He spoke in broken sentences of his battles, then of his wife and children, then again of his battles. By nightfall, he was racked with agony, which he tried to relieve by applying ice to the wound. Knowing that his wife had been summoned, he asked the attending doctor if he would survive the night. Death, the physician answered, was fast approaching. At 7:30, it became evident that the end was near, and Stuart was asked if he had any last messages. Lillie Lee, of Shepherdstown, was to have his golden spurs, he directed, and his staff officers his horses. "You had better take the larger horse," he suggested to a heavyset aide. "He will carry you better." His young son was to have his sword. Then he asked a clergyman to sing "Rock of Ages." After a brief prayer, he announced, "I am going fast now. I am resigned. God's will be done." With those words, the Army of Northern Virginia's cavalry chief breathed his last.[65]

Yellow Tavern had been a crushing defeat for the Confederates. Their cavalry had been decisively beaten, and Stuart, whose pluck and dash epitomized the rebellion's resilient spirit, lay dead. Fitzhugh Lee later asserted that Stuart's death "was more valuable to the Union cause than anything that could have happened, and his loss to Lee irreparable." Stuart, he maintained, was "the army's eyes and ears—vigilant always, bold to a fault; of great vigor and ceaseless activity, he was the best type of a *beau sabre*." The campaign had also exacted a severe toll in Confederate horsemen. Wickham lost about a hundred troopers on May 11, Lomax nearly two hundred. Since crossing the Rapidan, Wickham's casualties amounted to some 20 percent of his brigade, and Lomax' over 30 percent. Many riders were without mounts. The blow to southern fortunes was in proportion to the growing optimism in Federal ranks. Wilson later described Yellow Tavern as the "turning point in the history of the two cavalry forces operating in Virginia." Thereafter, he contended, the rebels were "wary of meeting the Federal cavalry in an open field." To Davies, the important point was that Union troopers were now "confident in their leader, and fully satisfied of their own ability to meet and conquer their opponents in the field and to move at will through the enemy's country." Sheridan echoed their sentiments. Yellow Tavern, he thought, punctured the myth of the southern mounted arm's invincibility. "The discomfiture of Stuart at Yellow Tavern," the aging warrior wrote in his memoirs, "inflicted a blow from which entire recovery was impossible."[66]

Stuart's death unquestionably damaged southern morale. But in retrospect, it is clear that it did little to advance Union fortunes. Wade Hampton, a South Carolina planter who had learned the business of war in the saddle rather than in the schoolroom, would soon fill Stuart's position. While Hampton lacked Stuart's flamboyance, he brought the Army of Northern Virginia's cavalry corps discipline and notions of warfare more appropriate to the times. In destroying Stuart, Sheridan had paradoxically set in motion forces that were soon to confront him with a more formidable foe.

After the war, Union participants quarreled over who deserved the greatest credit for the victory at Yellow Tavern. Custer received favorable publicity for his charge along Telegraph Road. The 1st New York Dragoons' historian countered that "Custer was a brave fighter, as were also his splendid Michigan brigade; but it is nevertheless fact that his ambition to rise led him, on more than one occasion, to claim for himself the lion's share of honors. That he bore the brunt of the fighting, and drove the enemy from the field, is an unwarranted stretching of the truth." Wilson touted his own division's accomplishments, arguing in his memoirs, "From the accounts of this brilliant affair, which soon found their way into the newspapers, it might have been supposed that Custer's brigade did all the fighting and was entitled to all the credit, while as a matter of fact my whole division was present, and it was well understood by all who saw it that the modest Chapman did fully half the fighting and was entitled to fully half the credit." Union casualty returns, however, supported Custer's boast. His four regiments sustained 113 casualties, as opposed to Gibbs's 19 and Wilson's 11.[67]

In the larger picture, Sheridan's raid proved to be a costly mistake. Chasing Stuart was another sideshow for the campaign, which would be decided by what the armies did at Spotsylvania. By abandoning the main theater of conflict to pursue his whimsical raid south, Sheridan deprived Grant of an important resource. His victory at Yellow Tavern offered scant solace to the blue-clad soldiers hunkering in trenches above the courthouse town. Sheridan's absence hurt Grant at Spotsylvania in much the same way that Stuart's absence from Gettysburg had handicapped Lee.

"It was an exquisitely ludicrous scene."

Grant rose early on Wednesday, May 11, and sat down to a cup of coffee and a morsel of beef charred black. He was a particular eater and abhorred blood—a peculiar trait, it was remarked, for a man whose profession involved killing. He was joined by Elihu B. Washburne, a congressman and friend who had accompanied him during the campaign's initial battles. Washburne was returning to Washington and suggested that Grant draft a note to the president. "We are certainly making fair progress, and all the fighting has been in our favor," Grant answered. "But the campaign promises to be a long one, and I am particularly anxious not to say anything just now that might hold out false hopes to the people."[68]

Grant entered his tent and began writing to Halleck, expecting him to pass the missive on to Lincoln. "We have now ended the sixth day of very heavy fighting," Grant began, a cigar firmly clenched between his teeth. "The result to this time is much in our favor, but our losses have been heavy as well as those of the enemy." By Grant's estimate, he had sustained twenty thousand casualties, the Confederates even more. His resolve remained unshaken, and he renewed his request for troops, emphasizing that reinforcements would be "very encouraging to the men, and I hope they will be sent as fast as possible, and in as great numbers." He closed on a strong note. "I propose to fight it out on this line if it takes all summer," he promised in a sentence soon to be blazoned across northern newspapers. He added, "The enemy are very shaky, and are only kept up to the mark by the greatest exertions on the part of their officers, and by keeping them entrenched in every position they take. Up to this time there is no indication of any portion of Lee's army being detached for the defense of Richmond." Folding the communication, Grant gave it to Washburne and watched him ride away.[69]

Early in the afternoon, Grant made an appearance on horseback to inspect his lines. He and his staff paused on a rise next to the 5th Wisconsin, near where Sedgwick had been shot two days before. Warren's skirmishers were busy feeling Anderson's advance rifle pits. "As the crackle of the skirmishers rose to the roar of a volley, I would see him lean forward on his horse and listen intently, evidently to learn whether the sound were receding or coming toward him," a Wisconsin man observed. From time to time, couriers dashed up with dispatches. Grant read them carefully, handed them to staffers, then resumed his thoughtful pose. The Wisconsin soldiers watched with interest the "silent man," as they called Grant, "with the ever present cigar in his mouth."[70]

Neither side ventured major infantry movements during the day, and the exhausted soldiers were thankful for the lull. Seven days of battle had blurred into a nightmare of fighting and digging. "The sharpshooters of the enemy commanded completely the position of our line of battle," a Federal complained. In an attempt to keep the rebel marksmen at arm's length, rifle pits were dug as far in front of the Union entrenchments as possible. One of Upton's aides learned just how dangerous the interface between the opposing armies had become when he approached the front line. First he had to cross a clearing through the "zip, zip, and hiss of minnies." Then a Confederate battery opened on him as he dismounted, sending a twelve-pound shot through his stirrup and disemboweling his horse. "It was a rough place at best," a northerner recollected. Others found it "conducive to longevity to spread ourselves on the ground as thin as the butter on a slice of boarding-house bread."[71]

Just when it seemed that things could not get worse, they did. Rain—the same deluge that accompanied Custer's fateful charge near Yellow Tavern—came in torrents from a black sky. "The wind was raw and sharp," a Yankee noted, "our clothing wet, and we were just about as disconsolate and miserable a set of men as ever were seen." Acrid smoke sputtering from wet kindling left one Federal wondering whether the little warmth obtained was worth the unpleasantness. The rain and wet wood made cooking impossible. The soldiers, "cheerless and disconsolate," a Pennsylvanian related, "sank to sleep in the falling rain, wet to the skin, with their soaked feet to the smouldering embers."[72]

Much of the conversation dwelt on developments on other fronts. Dispatches read to the troops carried word that Butler had taken Petersburg and that Sherman had been successful against Johnston. "This tended to give our boys encouragement to fight on—hoping to defeat their ablest general and largest army here," a Pennsylvanian wrote home. The dispatches, however, were in error. Butler had been thwarted, and Sherman was snarled in a patchwork of maneuvers trying to bring Johnston to bay.[73]

George M. Barnard, a soldier in the 18th Massachusetts, caught the prevailing sentiment in a letter home. "This is the seventh day and we have been fighting constantly," he wrote his father. "It exceeds anything we have been through yet but we must have whaled the enemy too." He stated his firm belief: "We are bound to fight the thing out and so are the rebs. Both sides are pretty well played out but are the best armies and ready to cut one another up. Still I think we have a little the advantage of them." William Fowler, of the 146th New York, was not so optimistic. "We are completely used up, officers and men being overpowered by fatigue and excitement," he informed his family. "All of us have grown a year older during this week."[74]

During the morning, Grant concluded that the Brown house—the starting point for Mott's abortive charge on May 10—was ideally situated for staging a massive attack against Lee. Broad fields afforded ample room for deploying large numbers of troops. And by this time, Union scouts had mapped the salient's general contours. According to conventional military wisdom, the Confederate formation's broad, blunt tip rendered the position exceedingly vulnerable by preventing troops on one leg from merging their fire with those on the other leg. Neither leg could support the tip. A corridor of cleared land bordered by thick woods extended like a welcome mat three-quarters of a mile from the Brown house to the salient. Grant understood that surprise was important and decided to mass a corps near the Brown house under cover of night, then send it forward before dawn on May 12, quietly and without warning. Drawing on Upton's example, he commanded that not a shot be fired until the troops breached the works. He could take satisfaction that even the storm making life miserable for his soldiers would work to his advantage by masking the movement from Lee.

Humphreys later described Grant's prospective assault as a "repetition of Mott's attack on the 10th, on a much larger scale in every way." In fact, though Grant intended to attack from Mott's former position, he modeled the charge's essential mechanics on Upton's assault. This time, however, rather than assaulting with only twelve regiments, Grant planned to throw in Hancock's entire 2nd Corps, which numbered slightly under twenty thousand troops. The remainder of the army was to lend support, with Burnside charging the salient's eastern leg while Warren pinned the Confederates on Laurel Hill and Wright pitched in wherever he was needed. The hammer pounding Lee's weak point would be Meade's largest and best corps, with everyone else actively assisting.[75]

Hancock would have to shift from the Union right to the Brown house, which would inevitably weaken the Federal flank nearest the Po. Grant, having to know whether Lee entertained aggressive designs on that sector of his forces, assigned Nelson Miles to reconnoiter the approaches to the Union right wing. Miles sent out two parties. One—consisting of the 26th Michigan and the 183rd Pennsylvania—waded across the Po near the former site of the pontoon bridges, drove off a small body of rebels, and continued toward the Block House Bridge, where it stirred up Mahone's Confederates. "It was a sharp fight while it lasted," a Michigan man remembered. "Bullets whizzed around us like bees in swarming time, and with heavy loss to our company." The Federals retraced their route, satisfied that Mahone was well entrenched and had no intention of attacking. Miles's other party—the 61st New York, the 81st Pennsylvania, and the 140th Pennsylvania—followed Brock Road north to Todd's Tavern, where those queried confirmed that no rebels had passed through since Sunday. Then the northerners pressed west along Catharpin Road to Corbin's Bridge, pausing along the way to bury comrades killed on May 8. Not a single gray-clad soldier was in evidence. Miles had established to Grant's satisfaction that the Union right flank was safe from attack.[76]

Grant also initiated a set of reconnaissances to explore the site of Hancock's projected attack. During the morning of May 11, the aide Comstock walked the picket line between Mott and Burnside. On the basis of what he saw, he concurred that the Brown house would be a suitable staging area but suggested that the Landrum house would suit Grant's purposes even better, because it stood nearer Lee's line. Although rebel pickets occupied the Landrum site, Comstock believed it could be carried "with-

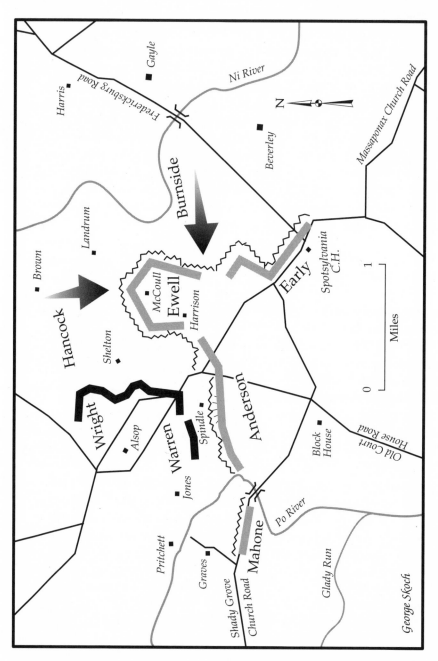

Grant's plan of attack for May 12

George Skoch

out a heavy fight." At the aide's suggestion, elements from the Excelsior Brigade seized the ground. The very feature that made the spot attractive to Comstock—its proximity to the salient—also made it, however, an impossible place for massing troops. Confederate pickets swarmed out from Ewell's nearby entrenchments, sparking lively little fire fights around the dwelling all day. Around five in the evening, Mott gave up trying to secure the Landrum area and retired to the Brown place.[77]

Concluding that the Landrum place could not be held, Comstock returned to headquarters for another assignment. Because Grant had heard precious little from the 9th Corps all day, he sent his industrious staffer off again, this time to Burnside's headquarters to help ensure both that the general understood his role in the assault and that he prepared appropriately. Another of Grant's aides, Orville E. Babcock, accompanied Comstock, as did some of Hancock's staffers. According to Hancock's aide-de-camp William G. Mitchell, the aides of the 2nd Corps were under orders to "examine the ground in front of Spotsylvania as close to the enemy's lines as practicable between the Sixth and Ninth Corps of our army, where it was intended to make an assault with the Second Corps [the next] morning at daybreak."[78]

The staffers started off under heavy rain and followed the picket line to Burnside's headquarters. Comstock and Babcock went inside, while Hancock's aides circled back to the Brown house to acquaint themselves with the terrain. It was nearly dark, but they made as careful a survey as possible before night set in, creeping close to the rebel pickets and trying to memorize the main features of the ground.[79]

Talking things over with Burnside made Comstock realize that the 9th Corps was badly deployed. Burnside's most forward elements, which were under Willcox, had retired from their advanced position in front of Spotsylvania Court House the previous night, as Grant had ordered. But Burnside had concluded that Willcox' new line, stretching along the heights south of the Ni, was still too exposed. Between two and three in the afternoon, he directed Willcox to withdraw north of the river. As the movement commenced, it began to rain enough to help conceal the operation from the rebels. The retrograde maneuver—"Some movement we can only call strategy," a wag commented—was completed by six. Willcox' division at that time extended from the Gayle house northwest across Fredericksburg Road. Leasure's rested on Willcox' right, and Potter's continued the 9th Corps' line northward, toward Mott.[80]

Comstock was dumbfounded. Burnside occupied the "worst line," he scrawled in his diary. He moved to correct the situation with his usual bluntness and ordered Burnside back to his previous position below the river. The bewhiskered general did as Comstock directed "at once without difficulty, but with some grumbling at the change." At dusk, the 9th Corps lumbered over the Ni to the southern bank. "It is all blind work, this Virginia fighting," a New Hampshire man complained. "The shower settled into a steady rain," a soldier recorded, "and the night was cold and cheerless." Another Federal wished he did not have to lie on the ground "without blankets to protect me from the storm overhead and the mud beneath." And an officer was grateful for a rain-soaked barn. "The place was filthy and disagreeable," he conceded, "but any shelter was welcome on such a night."[81]

The 9th Corps' movement cost it another field commander. The storm had swollen the Ni, and Colonel Bliss, heading one of Potter's brigades, could not make his horse jump across. Exasperated, he asked his orderly to strike the animal with his scabbard. The horse jumped suddenly, Bliss slipped in the mud, and the horse fell heavily onto the colonel's ankle, which became "very painful and soon very much swollen." A doctor found no broken bones but confined Bliss to his bed, where he lay in excruciating pain.[82]

During the night, Burnside made important changes in his corps' leadership. He removed Leasure, who had not impressed him, and appointed Major General Thomas L. Crittenden to head the division. The change did not bode well. A Kentuckian, Crittenden was new to the eastern theater, unfamiliar with the 9th Corps, and reputedly a "political" general. The ever-quotable Lyman thought him the "queerest-looking party you ever saw, with a thin, staring face, and hair hanging to his coat collar—a very wild appearing major-general, but quite a kindly man in conversation, despite his terrible looks." There was as well the question of what to do about Bliss. Burnside apparently decided to let the injured colonel sleep and appointed Colonel John I. Curtin, of the 45th Pennsylvania, in his place. Bliss was informed neither of the substitution nor of the plans for the next morning's operation. In a few hours, he was to be sorely missed.[83]

Around ten that night, Burnside's water-logged soldiers received word that they were to participate in a general advance at 4 A.M. They were not optimistic. Adverting to the mood in the camp, a Federal remarked, "So we knew that within six hours we were to file out over our own fortifications in the dark, and, not knowing anything at all of our way twenty yards ahead, were to go down into swamps, thick woods, and underbrush, in the face of a vigilant and deadly foe." A soldier listened to the call of "whippoorwill! whippoorwill!" all night long. "Captain, I wish those pesky birds would stop their crying; I don't like to hear them," he remarked. "I like to hear them," a veteran quipped. "They keep saying, 'Whip-you-will,' which means we shall whip the 'Johnnies' tomorrow sure."[84]

For the Confederates, May 11 opened with "confident expectations of a renewal of the attack by the enemy." Lee spent the morning rectifying his lines, resting his men, and trying to anticipate Grant's next move. One Confederate recalled the day as involving "bitter sharpshooting and angry artillery practice." Another remembered eating a muskrat and casting an interested eye toward his adjutant's plump hound. Dead Yankees covered the ground in front of Doles's Salient, and Ewell dispatched ambulances to retrieve the wounded soldiers. Union skirmishers, however, put a bloody end to the rescue efforts. "So the poor fellows were left to die in agony," a southerner mourned. Across the Po, Mahone's men woke to a "most sickening scene of dead human beings with their clothes burned off."[85]

The rebels redoubled their efforts at strengthening their entrenchments, which had proved extremely effective in repelling Grant's charges. The salient continued to cause concern. "It was a bad piece of engineering and certain to invite an attack as soon as the enemy understood it," a Confederate remarked. Lee's engineers had approved the configuration to encompass high ground for strong artillery positions, and two 2nd Corps battalions—thirty guns in all—were arrayed across the salient's broad face, ready to rake the adjacent field. The trade-off lay at the corner angles, where firepower from the southern guns necessarily diverged. Alexander, the 1st Corps artillery chief, later passed informed judgment on the position. "By all the rules of military science we must pronounce these lines a great mistake although they were consented to, if they were not adopted by General Lee's chief engineer."[86]

Allegheny Johnson's division occupied the vulnerable bulge. Maryland Steuart's brigade constituted Johnson's right wing, after which came Witcher's brigade, then the brigade of Louisianians who had served under Brigadier General Stafford before he was killed in the Wilderness. The Stonewall Brigade continued Johnson's line around a gentle bend to the salient's western leg, where other Louisianians, who had fought under Brigadier General Hays—wounded on May 10 and out of service—were stationed. Johnson's left wing connected to Rodes, but his right dangled unsupported, with a gap of over a hundred yards separating Steuart's troops from Early's closest brigade, under Brigadier General James H. Lane.[87]

Johnson's division was in bad shape. Its ten Louisiana regiments had been consolidated under Colonel William Monaghan, who lacked experience beyond the regimental level. Jones's Virginia brigade had been decimated in the Wilderness, Jones had been killed, and his replacement, Colonel Witcher, was energetic but unseasoned. The brigade felt a "good deal disheartened by its losses and for want of such a commander as Jones had been." Only Walker's Stonewall Brigade and Steuart's mixed North Carolina and Virginia brigade retained experienced leadership. In all, the division numbered about 4,500 soldiers.[88]

Lee scrutinized Grant's movements on May 11 for clues to the Union commander's intentions. In particular, Miles's probes toward the Po piqued Lee's interest. Was Grant preparing to move around the Confederate left end, or was he simply making sure that Lee had no aggressive designs that would spoil a general withdrawal toward Fredericksburg? Mahone was well placed to defend the Confederate left wing, but cautiously Lee instructed Early to shift additional units to the Po. Two of Wilcox' brigades—those under Brigadier Generals Alfred M. Scales and Edward L. Thomas—marched from Spotsylvania to join Mahone.[89]

Late in the day, Ewell's map maker, Jedediah Hotchkiss, scouted Burnside's formation and found it vulnerable. Rooney Lee reported that Burnside's wagons and infantry were retiring, as did Wilcox. This intelligence tipped the balance in Lee's mind. Grant, he concluded, intended to withdraw toward Fredericksburg. Never before had Lee so completely misread his opponent. Grant had no intention of withdrawing. He was instead deploying his army to launch its most powerful attack thus far in the campaign.[90]

Lee met with Ewell, Rodes, and the 2nd Corps artillery chief, Armistead Long, at the Harrison house. The generals sifted through the conflicting intelligence they had received during the day. Lee discerned a pattern. "Gradually, the conviction spread that they were retiring towards Fredericksburg," Ewell's aide Campbell Brown noted. Miles's excursion, the generals decided, had been a feint to distract the Confederates from the significance of Burnside's withdrawal. Lee directed preparations to begin for a forced march to counter Grant's probable shift up Fredericksburg Road. He was not yet ready to abandon Spotsylvania, but the army's slower-moving elements had to prepare to evacuate to pursue Grant. His aide Taylor related that orders were given to "withdraw the artillery from the salient occupied by Johnson's division to have it available for a countermove to the right." In issuing one of the most fateful directives of his career, Lee had no suspicion that he was weakening the very portion of his line Grant had targeted for attack.[91]

At 3 P.M., Grant dictated his plan of attack in a message to Meade. The communication detailed each corps' role and left no room for misunderstanding. "Move three divisions of the Second Corps by the rear of the Fifth and Sixth Corps under cover of night, so as to join the Ninth Corps in a vigorous assault on the enemy at four o'clock A.M. tomorrow," he instructed. "Warren and Wright should hold their corps as close to the enemy as possible to take advantage of any diversion caused by this attack and to break in if the opportunity presents itself." Grant assured Meade that he would impress on Burnside the "importance of a prompt and vigorous attack." He concluded by emphasizing, "There is but little doubt in my mind that the assault last evening would have proved entirely successful if it had commenced an hour earlier, and had been heartily entered into by Mott's division and the Ninth Corps."[92]

Meade spent the remainder of the rainy afternoon making sure his corps commanders knew their roles. He resented Grant's intrusion in the Army of the Potomac's affairs and was "cross as a bear," according to Provost Marshal Patrick, who appended, "at which I do not wonder, with such a man as Grant over him." At 4:00 P.M., Meade ordered Hancock to withdraw Birney and Barlow from the western Union flank and to reposition them between Burnside and Wright. Gibbon's division, intermingled with 5th Corps units, was to remain near Laurel Hill until after dark so as not to give notice to the Confederates. Then it was to join Hancock's column. At 6:30, Warren received his orders. As Hancock withdrew, the 5th Corps was to extend and occupy the vacancy, shortening its line if necessary. As for Wright's 6th Corps, Ricketts was to occupy the forward rifle pits while Russell and Neill retired to the Alsop house in a position to support Warren or Hancock as needed.[93]

Grant sent Burnside his orders at four. The 9th Corps and Hancock would be attacking together, and Comstock and Babcock would coordinate them. Grant was adamant about one point: "You will move against the enemy with your entire force promptly and with all possible vigor at 4 o'clock tomorrow morning."[94]

Near sundown, Meade reviewed the maneuver with his corps commanders. Hancock was to march to the Brown house after dark, Warren was to hold his position and that vacated by Hancock, and Wright was to shift two divisions to the Alsop place to make up the army's reserve. Warren and Wright were to hold their troops "in readiness at [4 A.M.] for the combined attack of Burnside and Hancock, when, it was understood, they might be required, according to the developments of the day, either to attack in their fronts, or move elsewhere and attack." Wright volunteered that he knew a shortcut to the Brown house and suggested that an engineer, Captain George H. Mendell, show Hancock the way.[95]

As Meade's generals talked, it became evident that they knew little about the terrain on which they would be fighting. Rebel pickets had prevented the 2nd Corps aides from conducting thorough surveillances. Although they had quizzed Mott, he could tell them little. Humphreys later wrote that "details of the enemy's works were not known, but it was known that open ground, four hundred yards wide at its narrowest part, led from Brown's fields nearly due south to the apex of the salient, and that a line from Brown's house to McCoull's house, which was just inside the enemy's entrenchments, ran along the middle of this open ground."[96]

After the meeting adjourned—about seven o'clock in the evening— Hancock met with Barlow, Birney, and Gibbon at corps headquarters. Barlow was told to report with his division at ten, so that Mendell could lead him to the Brown house. Barlow later maintained that "no information whatever, so far as I can remember, was given us as to the position or strength of the enemy, or as to the troops to be engaged in the movement (except that the 2nd Corps was to take part in it), or as to the plan of the attack, or why any attack was to be made at that time or place." He learned only that the movement was of "more than usual importance," and that the 2nd Corps would assault at daylight.[97]

Word passed through Hancock's camps to prepare to move with the "utmost quiet" and close together. The men secured their tin cups to prevent rattling, and officers spoke in whispers. The pioneers, who used mules to carry some of their tools, had a man march with a club so that when the mules started to bray, "as all the boys knew they would do in the early morning, [he could] hit them a whack and stop it." The destination was a mystery, but the soldiers generally agreed that anywhere would be better than their sodden bivouac. Some supposed that they were shifting rearward to wash their clothes and rest. Others surmised that they were retreating to Fredericksburg.[98]

At nine o'clock, the 2nd Corps prepared to march. "It did not take long to obey the order," a Federal remembered. "Each one had only to rise from the earth, shake himself in vain to get rid of the chills that were ever coursing up and down the spine on nights like this, wring the water out of his shoes, lift the cold, heavy musket from the stack, and all was ready."

By ten, Barlow was under way. Gibbon and Birney shuffled into line behind.[99]

Mendell's route to the Brown house covered about three miles, but judging from descriptions afterward, these were the longest three miles of the war. "Oh, what a dreary, tedious movement it was!" was one officer's summation. Another agreed that "a more dismal night march of two hours was never known." The line wound east behind the 5th and 6th Corps, through fields and forests and over streams and swamps. The night, a participant swore, was "dark as Erebus," and sheets of rain scoured the column. "Mud à la Virginia," another expostulated, "and just as dark as Egypt." Each man sloshed behind his file leader, keeping contact, a soldier maintained, "not by sight or touch, but by hearing him growl and swear, as he slipped, splashed, and tried to pull his 'pontoons' out of the mud." Troops dozed whenever the column paused. "I have never before suffered such acute agony from any cause," an officer insisted after the war. "My eyes would close, do what I would to prevent it; and, in order to escape a fall from my horse, I would lean forward and wind my arms about his neck, but the poor brute's head would invariably sink lower and lower, until I would find myself sliding head foremost toward the earth." A pack mule strapped with cooking utensils rampaged and set some of Gibbon's regiments in flight "as though his Satanic Majesty was after them."[100]

Barlow, Miles, and Brooke rode near the column's head. The engineers who accompanied them were indignant at having to conduct an important movement without information about the enemy's position or strength. Hancock's staff was in an equally foul mood and openly cursed the conduct of the war. Brooke denounced the "madness of the undertaking," and Miles became so outspoken that Barlow ordered him to keep quiet. After a while, however, even the stoic division commander fell under the prevailing spell. "As we staggered and stumbled along in the mud and the intense darkness," Barlow recalled, "and I vainly sought for information, the absurdity of our position—that we were proceeding to attack the enemy when no one even knew his direction, and we could hardly keep on our own legs—appealed to me very strongly." Soon he was snickering with the rest. "It was an exquisitely ludicrous scene," Barlow recounted, "and I could hardly sit on my horse for laughter." He ended up pleading with the staffer Charles Morgan, "For heaven's sake, at least face us in the right direction so that we shall not march away from the enemy and have to go round the world and come up in their rear."[101]

Around 12:30, Barlow's mud-spattered troops began collecting in the spongy fields around the Brown house. "I have since laughed with Colonel Morgan as to his utter ignorance of the whole situation," Barlow wrote. The ground where the attack was to start seemed a "mass of darkness, mud, and rain," and Morgan and Mendell could indicate only the general direction of the Confederate works. Barlow sarcastically asked whether there might be a thousand-foot ravine between himself and his objective. "When he could not be assured even on this point," Morgan related, "he seemed to think that he was called upon to lead a forlorn hope, and placed his valuables in the hands of a friend."[102]

Birney arrived at the Brown house around two o'clock. An aide— Major William Houghton, of the 14th Indiana—entered the dwelling to see Hancock reclining on a couch, Gibbon staring into the fire, and Barlow sound asleep on the floor. Hancock spoke briefly with Birney, then settled in for a nap, asking to be awakened at 3:30. Gibbon and Birney sat together by the fire, talking through the middle of the night.[103]

On rising, Hancock consulted his division heads. He, too, had never seen the ground where his corps was to attack. Lieutenant Colonel Waldo Merriam, of the 16th Massachusetts, who had served as Mott's field officer of the day and knew the terrain as well as anyone, sketched the rebel position on the wall of the Brown house. Hancock used the drawing to orient his corps.[104]

Barlow, still without any information concerning the Confederate position, announced that he was going to mass his division in a compact body. To the objection that this would make him vulnerable to rebel artillery, Barlow retorted, "If I am to lead this assault, I propose to have men enough when I reach the objective point to charge through hell itself and capture all the artillery they can mass on my front." Heated debate followed, but Barlow remained obdurate. "I never remember seeing General Barlow so depressed as he was on leaving Hancock's headquarters that night," a witness recalled. "He acted as if indeed it was a forlorn hope he was to lead." A staffer heard him say, "Make your peace with God and mount, gentlemen. I have a hot place picked out for some of you today."[105]

An adjutant described the scene of Barlow briefing his brigade commanders in a small clearing: "The flickering light of a lantern shed its dim, uncertain rays over the dreary woods, and on a little group huddled together in the dismal storm to map out the plan of the morrow's desperate business." Barlow traced the projected assault in the dirt. "It was a rude map," the onlooker explained, "but the brigadiers followed each outline with eagerness, and when the Druid Council was over, each understood the part he was to play."[106]

The 2nd Corps formed behind Mott's pickets, oriented along a compass line drawn from the Brown house to the McCoull place, which was known to lie within the salient. Barlow's division occupied two lines, with Brooke's and Miles's brigades in front, Brown's and Smyth's behind. The division was tightly massed, as Barlow intended—five paces between regiments, and ten between brigades—and was to charge straight along the cleared strip from the Brown house to the field near the Landrum place, then on to the rebel works. Birney's division extended west in two lines from Barlow's right, behind a marshy patch of low pines. Gibbon deployed behind Barlow, and Mott behind Birney. "We thus formed a huge sledge-hammer," one of Barlow's officers commented, "of which our division was the head and Birney's the handle." Hancock's aide-de-camp Mitchell described the corps as a "solid rectangular mass of nearly 20,000 men to hurl upon the enemy's works as soon as it should be sufficiently light for our purpose."[107]

Late in the afternoon, Lee directed Pendleton, his artillery chief, to remove from the front any guns that would be difficult to withdraw during the night, "so that everything might be ready to march at any hour." A little before sundown, Pendleton instructed his subordinates to prepare their artillery for a "swift and silent movement during the night, should one prove necessary." Alexander feared that removing his 1st Corps guns would unnecessarily weaken Laurel Hill. He left his pieces in place but mounted his ammunition chests, readied his carriages, and cleared paths to the main roadway. His intent was to accomplish the order's purpose without strictly following its terms. His was a soldierly exercise of discretion that was to serve the Confederate cause well.[108]

Armistead Long, commanding the 2nd Corps' artillery, faced a different situation. His instructions also were to have his guns "in readiness to move during the night," but a narrow and difficult path was the only route available for evacuating Lieutenant Colonel William Nelson's and Major Richard C. M. Page's battalions from Johnson's portion of the salient. Long was concerned that unless he withdrew these pieces before dark, they would be stranded until the next morning and might impede Lee in an attempt to pursue Grant. Accordingly, he ordered Nelson and Page to Spotsylvania Court House, stripping the salient's tip and eastern edge of ordnance. He left in place Hardaway's battalion, which supported Rodes's division on the salient's western edge. That was where Upton had attacked on May 10. If Grant renewed his assaults, Long reasoned, he would most likely strike there. And since Hardaway had access to decent roads, Long felt justified in leaving his battalion where it was.[109]

Long began withdrawing Nelson and Page shortly before dark. No one informed Johnson, who on his evening inspection was astonished by the spectacle of his supporting artillery rolling rearward. He protested to Colonel Thomas H. Carter, one of Long's subordinates. "I told him we greatly preferred to remain," Carter related. "The breastworks were built, we would be in place and, supported by infantry, absolutely impregnable against successful assault, but must, of course, obey orders." The brigade commander Steuart and his staff discussed the situation with "some uneasiness" but convinced themselves that headquarters was intending to replace the guns with others.[110]

Lee's infantrymen settled into their trenches for a miserable night. "Rain—MUD," a Confederate wrote in his diary. A Mississippian sought comfort by nibbling soggy corn pone and raw bacon, then wrapped himself in a soaking blanket and stretched out on the water-logged ground "with about as much comfort as a wet starving deer."[111]

That evening, Lee met with his 3rd Corps staff. Hill, although sick, was in attendance. Many were critical of Grant for throwing men at the Confederate works to be slaughtered, but Lee voiced some admiration. "Gentlemen," he remarked, "I think that General Grant has managed his affairs remarkably well up to the present time." Addressing Heth, whose troops had been shifted from the Po to Early's earthworks across Fredericksburg Road, Lee continued, "My opinion is the enemy are preparing to retreat tonight to Fredericksburg. I wish you to have everything in readiness to pull out at a moment's notice, but do not disturb your artillery until you commence moving. We must attack these people if they retreat."[112]

As the night deepened, Ewell's pickets heard rumblings in the direction of Grant's lines. A Confederate staffer discerned a "subdued roar or noise, plainly audible in the still, heavy night air, like distant falling water or machinery." Reports filtered back of troops marching and of bushes being chopped away as though the Federals were preparing to charge. A Louisiana officer alerted Johnson that Yankees were massing in front of the salient, and Colonel William Terry, of the 4th Virginia, on the Stonewall Brigade's picket line, reported that he could hear northern voices. Steuart also sent an urgent warning to Johnson: "The enemy is moving and probably massing in our front and we expect to be attacked at daylight. The artillery along our front has been withdrawn, by whose orders I know not and I beg that it be sent back immediately."[113]

Around midnight, Johnson dispatched his adjutant general, Major Robert W. Hunter, to Ewell to tell him that Grant was preparing to attack and that the salient would be indefensible without artillery. Ewell answered that the artillery had been withdrawn because Lee had "positive information" that Grant was moving to the right. Johnson found it dispiriting that Ewell would not understand the situation's gravity. "I will go at once," he declared, riding off to Ewell's headquarters. Ewell, "apparently very uneasy," reiterated his reasoning but finally yielded to Johnson's entreaties. The artillery would return at once, he assured a relieved Johnson, who, from his headquarters at the McCoull house, was soon distributing a circular to his brigade heads warning that an assault was expected at daylight and enjoining them to employ "utmost diligence" in preparing to repel the enemy. He and his staff then stretched out on the floor, fully clothed and "ready to leap to horse at a moment's notice."[114]

Ewell's headquarters forwarded to Lee a dispatch from Johnson about his need for artillery support. The missive puzzled its recipient. "See, gentlemen, how difficult it is to have certain information or how to determine what to do," he remarked to his staff. "Here is a dispatch from General Johnson stating that the enemy are massing in his front, and at the same time I am informed by General Early that they are moving around our left. Which am I to believe?" Impelled by the urgent air of Johnson's communication, however, Lee ordered the artillery returned to the salient by daylight.[115]

Lee's and Ewell's orders took inordinately long to reach the artillery officers. Nelson's and Page's guns had parked near Spotsylvania Court House, and the artillerists had unhitched their horses and erected tents against the chilling rain. At 3:30 A.M.—more than three hours after Johnson had begun pressing for the return of his supporting ordnance—a courier entered Long's tent with a note from Johnson, endorsed by Ewell, directing him to send the artillery back immediately. Carter, who was sleeping nearby, was awakened and told to be in position by daybreak. "Striking a light," Carter later recalled, "I indorsed on the order that it was then twenty minutes to daybreak, and the men all asleep, but the artillery would be in place as soon as possible."[116]

Rebel gunners sloshed through rain and mud to their horses. Carter hurriedly conversed with Page and saw that the battery his brother, Captain William P. Carter, commanded was best situated to occupy the salient's tip. He was to be followed by Captain Charles R. Montgomery, who would take position on his left, then by Lieutenant William A. Deas, of Captain Charles W. Fry's Virginia battery, who, with two rifled guns, would take position on his right, and finally by William J. Reese's Alabama battery, which was to slip onto Deas's right. In all, fourteen pieces from Page's battalion began north through the misty blackness. Nelson's battalion remained in camp.[117]

Couriers from the Stonewall Brigade roused Johnson at the McCoull house. The Federals were stirring, they warned. Johnson and his staffers rode to the works and placed their men on alert. Mist carpeted the field in front, but there could be no doubt that something was brewing. Occasional shots sounded from the haze, and gray-clad pickets came scurrying back. "The fog was so dense we could not see in any direction," the aide Hunter recalled, "but soon we could hear the commands of officers to the men, and the buzz and hum of moving troops."[118]

It was fortunate that Grant had dispatched Comstock to oversee the 9th Corps' dispositions. Burnside at first misinterpreted Grant's orders as requiring him to attack southwest along Fredericksburg Road, which would have taken him away from Hancock. But Comstock set him straight. "Upon consultation with the staff officers from the headquarters of the lieutenant-general commanding," Burnside reported, "it was decided to assault farther to the right at points nearer to the salient of the enemy's works, with a view to establishing and keeping up, if possible, a connection with the Second Corps." Burnside selected Potter to lead the attack and cement the important junction with Hancock's left flank. Stevenson's division—now commanded by Crittenden—was to advance on Potter's left, and Willcox was to deploy next to Crittenden on the corps' southern flank. Colonel Elisha G. Marshall's Provisional Brigade was positioned to deflect Jubal Early's Confederates if they sauntered out from Spotsylvania Court House along Fredericksburg Road. After Comstock had reoriented the 9th Corps, it faced generally west, at right angles to the Army of the Potomac and conforming to the salient's eastern edge. By advancing straight ahead, Burnside's right flank would link up with Hancock's left. A quarter mile or so east through the forest stood part of Early's corps— Heth's division and two brigades of Wilcox'—manning works that extended from Johnson's right flank south across Fredericksburg Road. "A curtain of gray mist enshrouded the earth as with a pall," a 9th Corps soldier who had experienced the interminable wait in the early-morning darkness remembered. "The hours dragged drearily. The men were under arms, and the pickets, though almost exhausted, were alert and vigilant." Thoughts turned to home and "our dear ones there."[119]

The morning held little encouragement for Hancock's exhausted soldiers gathering around the Brown house. For some units, the trek had taken seven grueling hours. "Great events have a power of self-proclamation," a participant observed, "and although nothing had been communicated to the troops as to what was expected of them, the feeling ran through the ranks that they were near to momentous happenings." Skirmishers stood at one-pace intervals, under instructions to advance with their arms at right shoulder. Firing was strictly forbidden. The corps was to rush silently forward, engulf Ewell's outposts, then overrun the main Confederate works. Surprise was the watchword, and everything depended upon it.[120]

Four o'clock arrived, and Hancock sought Barlow's advice. The subordinate looked out the window and concluded, "It's too dark. I think it would be better to wait half an hour." Hancock agreed. "Twenty thousand men were standing still in a compact formation, silently awaiting the word to advance," a soldier recounted. "Surrounded by the silence of night, by darkness and by fog, they stood, listening to the raindrops as they fell from leaf to leaf." Some dozed in the mud. Most stood in ranks, swaying restlessly, lifting their feet from the ooze and putting them down again, fretting, complaining, wiping rain from their eyes, and above all, straining to hear the order to advance. Colonel Miles gathered his regimental commanders. They were to carry the works at all hazards. "We then shook hands and bid each other good-bye," an aide remembered. "Gentlemen, today may be for some of us the last on earth," an officer interjected. "Whilst we are waiting here would it not be well to say a prayer?"[121]

Four-thirty came. The sun struggled to peek through a swirling, clinging mist. Hancock paced the floor of the Brown house, frequently peering out a window. "Anyone who knew him could see that he was thinking intently, with every faculty alert," an aide noted.[122]

Colonel Charles H. Weygant, of the 124th New York, in Ward's brigade, unstrapped a rubber coat from his saddle and wrapped it around his overcoat to ward off the chill. He was biting his tongue to stay awake when he felt a hand on his shoulder. It was General Ward. "Colonel, you have been assigned a post of honor," he confided. "I expect you to take your regiment over the works this time or die in the attempt. Give your orders in a whisper, preserve strict silence in your ranks, and do not fire a shot this side of the enemy's works." Like a great many Federals that morning, Ward did not believe the charge would succeed. With a gloomy look back, he passed on, repeating the message to his other regimental commanders.[123]

Grant was up early, listening intently for sounds that the assault had begun. His headquarters stood near the angle formed by Brock and Piney

Branch Church roads. Warren's 5th Corps occupied works to the south and west, facing Laurel Hill. Wright's 6th Corps was massed nearby at the Alsop place. A mile or so to the left stood the Brown house, and still farther to the left and south was Burnside's 9th Corps, slated to charge in tandem with Hancock. The salient was well over a mile away, and Burnside more than two miles off. To help Grant communicate with his far-flung elements, engineers had strung telegraph wires to the various corps. Hancock's aide Morgan first used the lines to confer with Burnside about his deployments. "Here the telegraph came forcibly into play, showing to what great benefit it could be used," an operator observed.[124]

Grant's aide Porter had spent the night monitoring the troop movements and returned shortly before daylight. The general-in-chief sat wrapped in an overcoat next to a sputtering camp fire. He was in playful spirits. "We have just had our coffee, and you will find some left for you," he told his staffer, who was soaked to the bone. Then he added with a smile, "Perhaps you are not hungry." Porter downed a cup of steaming coffee "with the relish of a shipwrecked mariner" and presented to his boss the details of Hancock's difficult march. Shortly before sunrise, Meade and his aides joined them. The two generals chatted while their staffers gathered nearby, anxiously awaiting news.[125]

Lee, too, had awakened around three in the morning. He breakfasted by candlelight in his tent near the Harrison house, then mounted Traveller and ventured forth to inspect his lines. Foremost in his mind were Grant's intentions. Did the sounds of troops moving during the night mean that Grant was retiring to Fredericksburg, as he had predicted? Or was Grant massing for an attack against the salient, as Johnson had warned in his communications?[126]

At 4:35, the suspense was over. "To your commands," Hancock quietly ordered his division chiefs. An aide noticed how the order was taken up by the various regimental and company commanders, "and I heard the word repeated down the line until it was lost in the distance." The mass of soldiers—a collection larger by thousands than the one Pickett had mustered in his famed charge at Gettysburg ten months before—started forward.[127]

Hancock's right wing—Birney in front, Mott behind—charged through tangled underbrush and a swamp with water waist-deep. The troops emerged on a ridge traversed by the Landrum lane. Mistaking for Lee's main line the rifle pits along the lane that pickets from the Stonewall Brigade occupied, they yelled and rushed on. "The enemy's pickets must have been sleeping," Weygant remarked afterward, "for notwithstanding the noise made by the snapping of dry twigs as we passed over them, and the rattle of brush as we were forcing our way through it, they evidently had not the slightest intimation of our approach until we were close upon them, when they hurriedly discharged their pieces, and fled to give warning to the troops of the main body." The field ahead sloped down to a shallow ravine, then slanted up again. Through the gray mist ran an ugly scar of fresh dirt. To reach the Confederate works, Birney's Federals had to charge across the field, up the other side, and through an imposing tangle of abatis. Once the rebels were alerted, the situation had the makings of another Laurel Hill.[128]

Barlow meanwhile advanced on Birney's left along the cleared strip beside the Landrum place. "Not a sound disturbed the moving line," an officer reported. "Instinctively every man knew the importance of covering as much ground as possible before being discovered." Barlow's skirmishers—Colonel Hammell's 66th New York, the same outfit that had crossed the Po below the Block House Bridge two days before—quickly encountered pickets from Witcher's 21st, 42nd, and 48th Virginia. "Double-quick," came the whispered command, and Hammell's skirmishers, like Birney's on their right, overran the outpost. "With a mad rush our boys were upon them and a dull thud here and there, as the butt of a musket compelled a more speedy surrender, told how well the order had been obeyed," a Federal remarked. Witcher was with the 21st Virginia, posted by him to the east to help cover the gap between Steuart's right flank and Lane's left. Warned by the rattle of musketry that the Federals were attacking, Witcher sent a soldier, John H. Worsham, to reconnoiter. "Running to the field, I saw that the far end of it was perfectly blue with Yankees," Worsham was to remember.[129]

Barlow pushed on, his right wing touching Birney, his left passing the Landrum house. Order evaporated and the division, in Barlow's words, "became confused into one mass." Scattered shots peppered the 2nd Delaware and killed the popular lieutenant colonel David L. Stryker. The northerners continued without pausing to return fire, peeling off a regiment to disperse a body of Witcher's pickets shooting at them from the Landrum house. After traversing a thin stretch of woods, Barlow's soldiers emerged onto a ridge. The sight was daunting: "The red earth of a well defined line of works loomed up through the mists on the crest of another ridge, distant about two hundred yards with a shallow ravine between," observed a Federal. The Union 2nd Corps' objective lay straight ahead.[130]

VII

MAY 12

Grant Captures the Salient

"The morning light broke upon a scene of blood and death."

GRANT AND MEADE stopped talking and tilted their heads to the sound of a distant rumble. It was not thunder but the growl of artillery—probably Burnside's guns posted near the Ni. "It was a strange sight, in that early morning," an aide reminisced. "The general in chief, with a few officers, standing beside a fire that was almost quenched by the driving rain; within sound of the musketry, receiving reports, issuing orders, directing the battle, but unable to perceive any of its movements—shut in entirely by the trees." The woods and the rain's muffling effect left Grant to guess what was happening.[1]

Hancock's 2nd Corps paused at the ridge across from the Confederate salient's broad face. Barlow's division had emerged at the rebel formation's eastern wing, held by Witcher and Steuart. Birney's division, sweeping along on Barlow's right, was opposed by Monaghan's Louisiana troops and the Stonewall Brigade on the salient's western sector. Gibbon's and Mott's divisions were pressing urgently from behind to add their weight to the onslaught.

At the salient, Johnson's men for the most part stood ready, muskets poised over the earthworks. A southerner noticed a sound like the roaring of a tempestuous sea. The Confederates cocked their muskets and studied the far ridge, barely visible in the haze. Suddenly, eerily illuminated in the early glow of dawn, a wave of blue uniforms crested the rise. "Never have I seen such an exciting spectacle as then met my gaze," a Louisianian asserted. "As far as the eye could reach, the field was covered with the serried ranks of the enemy, marching in close columns to the attack."[2]

A rebel artillery shell winged over the approaching Federals. "It did

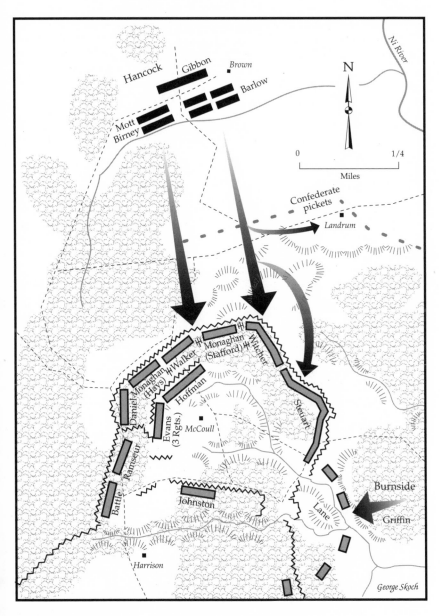

Hancock's and Burnside's attacks on May 12 at 4:30 A.M.

not require anyone to tell us what to do," a northerner commented. "Everyone seemed to catch the inspiration that his safety depended on getting to those works." As though by instinct, Hancock's thousands broke

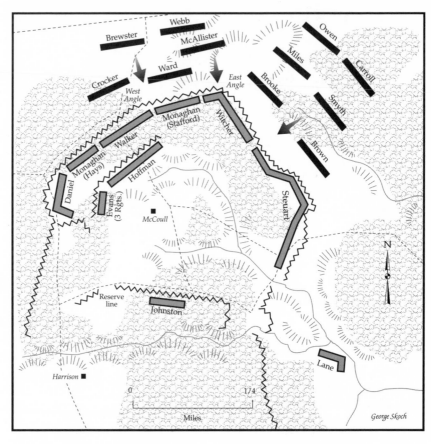

Hancock's attack against the Mule Shoe, by brigade, on May 12, 4:30 A.M.–5:00 A.M.

into a run toward the breastworks. "Enthusiasm c[ould] no longer be controlled," an officer in Miles's brigade wrote. "The arms had been carried at a 'right shoulder shift.' Now, they [we]re brought to a 'charge,' and the charging column, with cheers which might almost wake the dead, and were omens of victory, [broke] into a double quick." Down the slope the Federals ran, across the swale, then up the far side. Abatis fashioned from interlacing trees with sharpened branches barred the way. Hancock's men, in the high pitch of their enthusiasm, clawed the branches aside. Some crawled through, and some tumbled over the man-made obstacles. Then came a ditch. Close beyond loomed Ewell's earthworks, lined with Confederates.[3]

Johnson was with the two Virginia regiments at Witcher's segment of the works when the storm hit. His aide Hunter ran looking for Steuart, failed to find him, then began ordering Steuart's soldiers to close tightly against Witcher on their left. From behind sounded pounding hooves and screeching wagon wheels. Carter's guns were lumbering into place. Farther to the left, Walker's Stonewall Brigade aimed at Birney's men emerging from the fog-enshrouded woods and squeezed the triggers on their muskets. "Instead of the leaping line of fire and the sharp crack of the muskets came the pop! pop! pop! of exploding caps," Walker complained. The powder was damp, and most of the guns misfired. The Confederates jammed on fresh caps, but still the powder refused to ignite. Encountering no serious opposition, Birney's soldiers began dismantling the abatis. "I saw Federal officers ride up to the lines and step from their stirrups onto our breastworks without harm to themselves or their horses," Walker fumed.[4]

Barlow's soldiers had covered the final stretch as a compact mass, instinctively swaying slightly to the left to hit the salient head on. They slammed into the eastern part of the salient's nose and lapped around the point—later dubbed the east angle—where the works turned sharply south. Brooke's brigade, constituting Barlow's right wing, struck first and tore into Witcher's entrenched regiments. Brown's brigade and Brooke's leftmost elements slipped past the salient's eastern edge and swung west, toward Steuart. "It was a brilliant charge with the bayonet, hardly a gun being fired," a soldier from the 64th New York took pride. Smyth's Irish Brigade, which had become jumbled with Brooke's outfit while struggling through the abatis, came crowding close behind.[5]

"All line and formation was now lost," a Pennsylvanian stated, "and the great mass of men, with a rush like a cyclone, sprang upon the entrenchments and swarmed over." A New Jersey man remembered troops leaping over the earthworks, "yelling and firing like a pack of demons, with our guns right in their faces."[6]

Men shouted and muskets roared. "The storm had burst upon us," Hunter recounted. General Johnson strode on the ramparts, a hulking figure swinging a walking stick at Yankees and warding off bayonets. Hunter, inconspicuous in a black raincoat scavenged from the battlefield, ran through the cresting tide of Unionists, jumped on an artillery horse, sunk his spurs into the mount's sides, and galloped for the rear, bullets whizzing around him. One thought was foremost. Reinforcements had to be brought up immediately. Otherwise, Lee's line was likely to disappear in a wave of blue uniforms.[7]

"A fierce and bloody fight ensued with bayonets and clubbed muskets," a Federal who had witnessed the breakthrough at Witcher's entrenchments related. "Veteran campaigners had never looked upon such a sight as they beheld when the enemy had been driven out. Dead and dying were heaped in piles." Sergeant Albert Marsh, of the 64th New York, killed the 44th Virginia's color-bearer and waved the Confederate banner triumphantly overhead. A lieutenant in the 116th Pennsylvania impaled another Confederate color-bearer with his sword. Nearby, a rebel shot a Federal at point-blank range, then threw down his musket and announced, "I surrender." Dan Crawford, of Company K, was so enraged that he shot the Confederate, while his messmates Billy Hager and Henry Bell scooped up prisoners. "Throw down your arms, quick now, or I'll stick my bayonet into you," they threatened as they herded the captives rearward. A soldier in the 25th Virginia realized that resistance was hopeless as Yankees teemed over the works shouting, "Boys, surrender." He and most of his compatriots threw down their muskets, and an unarmed artilleryman implored the Federals, "Don't kill me." A hulking Virginian, Woodsides by name, shot one of the Federals, but in the confusion, the act went unnoticed. The artilleryman clung to Woodsides' arm in terror, "like a child." John Keener, of the 25th Virginia, refused to submit and was shot through the breast. The bullet deflected off a picture of his daughter that he kept in his breast pocket, saving his life. "Men became insane with the excitement of victory," a northerner was to remark in reflecting on those moments.[8]

In the confusion, Colonel Robert W. Withers, of the 42nd Virginia, managed to slip away. "My escape was a miracle," he exclaimed. "I walked out through them and did not receive a scratch. My whole regiment that were in the works were captured, except myself and two men that were in the ambulance corps."[9]

Miles's fine brigade compressed into a column forty men deep and crowded forward in lockstep on the right of Smyth. Buffeted by a "fearful storm of bullets," the 140th Pennsylvania had the good fortune to strike where the slashings were thin and led Miles's men over the works. "You could hear the sputtering sound, like the fall of hail, as the thud of their bullets fell on the head or shoulders of the men of our ranks," Miles wrote. "As those in front fell, the ranks in rear stepped, or jumped, over their bodies; and with one bold determined rush, and a loyal shout that made the forest ring, the Union lines quickly tore away the strong chevaux-de-frise, and brushed aside the rebel bayonets that were bristling over their works." A Pennsylvanian testified that the Confederates fought "hand to hand after we reached this vantage ground." The 26th Michigan's Major

Lemuel Saviers fell, shot through the breast, but his regiment, "maddened with the battle fury," scrapped on in a savage hand-to-hand conflict.[10]

Brown's brigade and elements from Brooke's meanwhile continued to swing around the angle's point and struck Steuart from the east. "No pen can adequately portray what happened then and there," a Confederate held. Steuart's leftmost regiments—the 1st and 3rd North Carolina, next to Witcher—surrendered with scarcely a fight. "Some of the rebels were yet rubbing their eyes at awaking from sleep when they were made prisoners," a New Yorker recounted. Another Federal confirmed that the rebels "fired only a very few shots, and were mostly asleep when we rushed into their works." A Union officer considered the charge a "complete success."[11]

A rolling mob of Yankees and Witcher's terror-stricken fugitives inundated Steuart's remaining regiments. A Confederate reported that the "rattle of musketry made such a din in that early morning as I have rarely heard." It was a scene of "blood and death, an indescribable pandemonium."[12]

The Confederate aide McHenry Howard was standing in Steuart's trenches when the cloud of blue uniforms emerged from where Witcher had folded. Howard directed some of Witcher's runaways behind traverses, hoping to rally them, but the earthworks became traps. Suddenly Federals surrounded Howard and his charges. "I retained my sword in my hand, after some hesitation whether or not to throw it away or stick it in the ground," Howard recalled. "One man took it out of my hand and another came up while he was doing so and drawing a large clasp knife from his pocket and opening it (I wondered if he was going to stab me), he cut the scabbard from my leather belt, and they went their several ways with their trophies."[13]

The 52nd New York's Sergeant William Westerhold seized the 23rd Virginia's flag as Brown's brigade joined the fray. A Yankee and Herman Seay, of the 23rd Virginia, popularly known as Hickory-hat, locked bayonets, struggled to impasse, then tried to brain each other with their gun butts. "Damn your soul," Seay cried, "put down that gun and I'll be damned if I can't throw you down!" Pitching their weapons aside, the men began wrestling. Seay, renowned in Louisa County, Virginia, for his prowess at the sport, jammed his thumbs into the Federal's eyes. "I surrender," his antagonist screamed, but Seay's victory was short-lived. Yankees marched Hickory-hat and the remainder of his command away at gunpoint, with everyone laughing heartily over the incident.[14]

Colonel Beaver, of the 148th Pennsylvania, was corralling prisoners when he spotted a distinguished-looking Confederate. "I would like to surrender to an officer of rank," the southerner explained. "I am General Steuart." A surprised Beaver exclaimed, "What! Are you Jeb Stuart?" The man replied, "No, I am George H. Steuart," to which Beaver responded, "I will accept your surrender. Where is your sword, sir?" Steuart answered sarcastically: "Well, sir, you all waked us up so early this morning that I didn't have time to get it on." Beaver turned Steuart over to an officer from the Irish Brigade, who passed him on to Hancock's adjutant Mitchell with the remark, "Here is a rebel general." Mitchell instructed a captain in the 53rd Pennsylvania to take Steuart to Hancock.[15]

General Johnson meanwhile labored to rally his Confederates in the hope of detaining Hancock until his artillery could return. He limped atop the breastworks, clothes torn, angrily brandishing his walking stick. A rebel saw him standing alone with a musket in his hand, "contesting the ground single-handed with the multitudinous foe." Captain Carter's battery pulled up, too late to help. A single piece managed to unlimber and fire before Barlow's men overran the battery. "Stop firing that gun," a northerner hollered, and Carter found himself staring at a line of muskets leveled at his chest. "Don't shoot my men," Carter pleaded as he surrendered. Quick-thinking troops from the 1st North Carolina shot the horses to prevent the Federals from hauling away the guns.[16]

Johnson, like Steuart, was captured, and Dick McClean, in Company K, of the 116th Pennsylvania, in Smyth's brigade, led him to Hancock. "This is damned bad luck," Johnson exclaimed on meeting his former friend, "yet I would rather have had this good fortune fall to you than to any other man living." Steuart, however, was in a wrathful mood and refused to treat his captors with civility. Hancock had known Steuart before the war and offered his hand. "How are you, Steuart?" he asked. The southerner replied, "Under the circumstances, I decline to take your hand." Hancock snapped back, "And under any other circumstances I should not have offered it."[17]

Birney's division extended west from Barlow in two lines, Ward's brigade on the left, touching Barlow, and Crocker's on the right. Birney's first line struck the salient near the east angle, then lapped progressively westward. A Federal thought that the sight "all the way across the field was most superb, elbow touched elbow from flank to flank—not a break or a waver in it." While Barlow pulverized Witcher and Steuart, Birney tore into Monaghan and Walker.[18]

Monaghan's Louisiana troops were stretched thin. During the night, as signs of a Federal attack multiplied, elements from Hoffman's brigade, in Gordon's division, had occupied a backup line a short distance behind Monaghan. "What's the matter here?" a tired Virginian grumbled, openly miffed at having been roused from his camp. "You've had us waked up before day and brought out of our shelter into the rain." A Louisianian drawled in reply, "We will have the Yankees over here directly to take breakfast with us."[19]

As Birney pressed to the salient, the center of Ward's brigade outran its edges, creating a horseshoe-shaped battle line that jumbled the lead units. A volley buffeted Ward's men, but they never faltered, and with a "cheer and a bound" cleared the embankment. Monaghan's officers were frantically pulling on their boots. "Then ensued one of those hand-to-hand encounters with clubbed rifles, bayonets, swords, and pistols which defies description," Colonel Weygant, of the 124th New York, wrote. One Federal splintered his rifle butt over a southerner's head, and another pinned a Confederate to a tree by firing a ramrod through him. A New Yorker stabbed his flag into the captured works, and Confederates from the 17th Louisiana defiantly planted their regiment's flag not three feet away. "But it did not float there more than a minute," a witness boasted, "when Archibald Freeman of [Company E, 124th New York] sprang on the works and as quick as a flash jerked up the traitor rag and was back in his place without getting a scratch." Rebels tried to duplicate Freeman's feat by charging the Union flag only to be "completely riddled with bullets every time they came near it."[20]

Witcher's collapse had uncovered Monaghan's right flank. "Look out, boys! We will have blood for supper!" a Louisianian screamed as Yankees streamed down the trenches "yelling like devils." A Louisianian leapt onto the parapet and began firing. The men of his company kept loading their guns and passing them to him until he was shot. Some of Monaghan's men retired to Hoffman's supporting line and joined the Virginians in trying to stem the blue-clad tide. A "volley from the rebs checked us," a Federal acknowledged. The Unionists regrouped, tried again, and were again repulsed by "steady and murderous fire." A Louisianian observed, "I have as you know been in a good many hard fights but I never saw anything like the contest of the 12th." A Federal from the 20th Indiana agreed. "Great slaughter on both sides," he scratched in his diary.[21]

Ewell's aide Colonel A. S. "Sandie" Pendleton shouted to one of Hoffman's officers, "Captain, stay here at all hazards until I return." Spinning his horse around, he galloped for Ewell's headquarters to seek reinforcements.[22]

The Stonewall Brigade was positioned along an obtuse angle where the salient's tip bent west and south. This segment of the earthworks—known to the men who fought there as the west angle—was hit next. "I had peculiar opportunities for witnessing this assault," General Walker recounted, "because the enemy . . . attacked immediately on [the Stonewall Brigade's] right, directly in front of [Witcher's] Virginia and [Monaghan's] Louisiana brigades, and with perfect safety and without a shot coming in any direction, I stood upon the breastworks in front of the right regiment of my brigade and witnessed it all." What he saw was daunting. Masses of Federals—Ward's brigade—shredded the Louisiana troops adjoining Walker and then tore into Colonel Terry's 4th Virginia on the Stonewall Brigade's right. Terry formed at right angles to the works to intercept Ward's men as they circled behind the entrenchments. "Fire," he commanded, but rain had soaked his men's powder, and there was only a pathetic round of clicks. Walker ventured that a "muzzle-loading musket with damp powder behind the ball is as useless to a soldier in an emergency like that as a walking cane."[23]

Then Birney's rightmost brigade—Crocker's—slammed into the Stonewall Brigade. "For a time, every soldier was a fiend," a man in the 17th Maine recollected. "The attack was fierce—the resistance fanatical." It was one officer's conviction that the scene "beggar[ed] description." Another recalled that "for a time it was difficult to say which was the larger column, the Union troops pressing to the front, or the rebel prisoners going to the rear." Exuberant Federals seized additional Confederate guns, swung them around, and fired at the fleeing southerners. "It was impossible to aim since almost nothing could be seen through the clouds of smoke and fume," a northerner conceded, but there was no mistaking that Hancock had won a spectacular victory. The stars and stripes fluttered from the rebel parapet as Federals rallied around their regimental colors. "Our men were seized with veritable raptures of joy," a Union sharpshooter remembered.[24]

An officer in the 33rd Virginia turned toward a blast of musketry from the right and rear. Louisianians streamed past, hollering that Federals were capturing everyone in the salient. "All that escaped had to 'run for it' some distance," according to a Virginian. "The figures of the men seen dimly through the smoke and fog seemed almost gigantic, while the woods were lighted by the flashing of the guns and the sparkling of the musketry. Men in crowds with bleeding limbs, and pale, pain-stricken faces, were hurrying to the rear."[25]

Mott followed closely behind Birney. McAllister's brigade wedged into a gap between Birney and Barlow, then scaled the parapet and plunged among the Confederates. McAllister captured a Confederate battery and ordered it hauled back to the Union line while the rest of his soldiers pressed ahead. On McAllister's right, Brewster assisted Crocker in enveloping the Stonewall Brigade.[26]

The Confederates had constructed traverses along the earthworks at frequent intervals. "The battle was raging from traverse to traverse, our men standing boldly to our duty," one of Walker's men recorded. "Heaps of the enemy's dead told how stubborn had been the resistance to this fierce attack." A bullet tore into Walker's left elbow, then Terry fell wounded, but the Stonewall Brigade fought on. "It was terrific beyond any description," in a Confederate's opinion. "Every twig seemed cut down. We continued desperately not dreaming of capture until we were completely surrounded by their overwhelming numbers." The 5th Virginia's color-bearer tore his regiment's flag from the staff and stuffed it inside his shirt for safekeeping.[27]

After rolling up the Stonewall Brigade, Crocker continued toward where Upton had made his breakthrough two days before. Ewell had filled this segment of his line with Louisianians previously under Hays. Daniel's North Carolinians stood south of the Louisianians. Behind them, in supporting works, waited three of Colonel Clement Evans' Georgia regiments.

Federals erupted from the fog close enough for a soldier in the 61st Georgia to recognize the corps badges on their caps. They called on the Confederates in language "more expressive than chaste" to throw down their arms and surrender. Daniel hollered, "About face," pivoted the 45th North Carolina in a right wheel, and halted the regiment astride the works where it could enfilade Crocker's troops approaching down the trenches. The rest of Daniel's brigade followed suit, and Confederate artillery at Daniel's rear—Jones's and Captain Archibald Graham's batteries of Hardaway's battalion—rained canister and shrapnel onto the northerners. "We dropped upon our knees and opened fire upon the enemy," Major Cyrus B. Watson, of the 45th North Carolina, recounted, "every man loading and firing as rapidly as possible." It seemed to Watson that Yankees "in unbroken lines reaching back as far as we could see came sweeping on in our front, but this combined fire of infantry and artillery was more than human flesh could stand and it was impossible for them to reach our lines."[28]

Around 5:15, a courier ran to Grant's command center with a dispatch from Hancock, time-stamped 5:00. "Our men have the works, with some hundred prisoners," the wire read. "Impossible to say how many; whole line moving up." A telegraph clerk had added a postscript: "General Hancock's troops are in second line of works."[29]

News arrived at a quickening pace. "Prisoners come in rapidly; probably over 2,000," Hancock reported. Another message from Hancock arrived: "I have captured Major General E. Johnson and another General Johnston . . . I have captured General Steuart." The scene at headquarters was "exciting in the extreme," with everyone smiling broadly. "Aides galloped up one after the other in quick succession with stirring bulletins, all bearing the glad tidings of overwhelming success," Porter wrote. "The group of staff-officers standing about the camp fire interrupted their active work of receiving, receipting for, and answering dispatches by shouts and cheers which made the forest ring." Lyman mentioned that Grant's staffers were "absurdly confident and were sure Lee was entirely beaten." Brigadier General John A. Rawlins seemed beside himself. "By God! They are done! Hancock will just drive them to hell!" he bellowed. Lyman was not so certain. "My experience taught me a little more skepticism," he said in a letter to his family. Grant remained seated stoically on his camp-stool, every now and then blinking from camp-fire smoke or stopping midsentence as wind whipped his greatcoat over his face. Porter recalled the general's animation when reports arrived of the large numbers of prisoners. "That's the kind of news I like to hear," he said. "Hancock is doing well."[30]

Hancock had torn open the end of the salient, wresting from Confederate control a stretch over a half mile wide, but his charge was losing momentum. "The troops which had made the assault were in the most complete confusion," Barlow observed, "and this remark applies as well to Birney's division as to my own." Union field commanders were powerless to restore order. "Not only were they broken up by the rush of the attack," Barlow continued, "but the men huddled together in the comparatively small space occupied by the Angle and the enemy's guns in search of flags, prisoners, etc." A Federal confirmed that the "turmoil and excitement in capturing the prisoners and getting them out of the works scattered and jumbled up our men so that I don't believe there were ten men out of any one company together." The time had come for Hancock's field commanders to regroup their forces.[31]

Still, Federals kept crowding into the narrow battle front. "Finding that Barlow had undoubtedly carried the entrenchments and that fighting was still going on," Gibbon explained, "I rode rapidly back to bring up my troops." After conferring with Hancock, Gibbon sent Carroll's and Owen's brigades into the works occupied by Barlow to eliminate remaining pockets of Confederates. Gibbon's other brigade, under Webb, meanwhile elbowed between Barlow and Birney, then swung to the right to help Birney scour Monaghan from his backup line.[32]

Fiery Samuel Carroll—described as "a fine looking officer, a bold rider, a skillful tactician, and one of the bravest and most brilliant brigade commanders in the army"—sprinted past the salient's eastern angle and nosed toward the lower end of Steuart's position. "Double-quick!" he shouted as he led his troops through the fog, over the works, and into combat against the remnants of Steuart's brigade. The resulting fight has been called "hand-to-hand and bloodthirsty in the extreme." Reese's Alabama battery spewed "deadly compliments of canister and grape, double shotted, mowing a swath right through our ranks at every discharge, and cutting down small trees and bushes," one of Carroll's men reported. But the northerners overran the guns, and a man from the 1st Delaware jumped on top of one of the artillery pieces and cheered. Conspicuous through the mist and gunsmoke was Lieutenant Colonel Thomas H. Davis, of the 12th New Jersey, his long beard streaming and his sword flashing overhead until a rebel bullet cut him down. According to Colonel Franklin Sawyer, of the 8th Ohio, nearly all Carroll's regimental commanders were killed or wounded.[33]

Owen charged on Carroll's right into heavy fire from pockets of Witcher's Virginians. The rebels were quickly silenced, and the brigade captured prisoners, guns, and colors. An Irishman zestfully swung a captured cannon around and tried to discharge it into the retreating Confederates. When an officer suggested lowering the muzzle, which was pointing into the air, he responded, "Niver fare. It's bound to come down on somebody's head." The 152nd New York re-formed and continued into the salient. "Charge! Forward! To the interior line!" Owen's men shouted. Gibbon's remaining brigade, under Webb, found itself in a grueling contest with troops from the Stonewall Brigade. An officer pronounced it the "fiercest hand-to-hand fighting of the war." After capturing the 33rd Virginia's flag, Webb's soldiers continued toward the McCoull house. Urging his men on at the head of his brigade, Webb sustained a serious head wound.[34]

Birney was trying to bring order into his division when he saw General Ward running rearward, excited and mumbling excuses about retrieving his horse. Birney gave Ward an aide's mount, ordered him back to the front, and informed Hancock of the incident. "I noticed General Ward was laboring under great excitement [and] was disposed to do some things which I thought foolish," the corps commander later said of the matter. "He was being reckless and insisted upon making a charge upon the enemy's works along the parapet." Hancock admonished Ward to be careful, but the subordinate was manifestly out of control. "His appearance and actions indicated that he had been drinking more than proper," Hancock concluded, and he passed that assessment on to Birney. "I immediately rode to the rifle pits, where Ward was, to satisfy myself as to the correctness of Major General Hancock's opinion," Birney wrote in his official report of the affair. "Watching his movements, I felt it my duty to order him to the rear under arrest. I believed him to be grossly intoxicated."[35]

Hancock's success had been dramatic. He had destroyed Johnson's division and breached Lee's line. "I never shall forget what I there saw," a southerner averred. "The woods and fields were thick with refugees, confused and panic stricken." A Federal enlarged on the treatment the horde received: "We followed up the enemy driving them before us through the woods and brush." Birney and Mott had cleared the salient's western sector as far south as Daniel's brigade and were pounding the backup line manned by Evans, Hoffman, and Monaghan's shattered refugees. Barlow and Gibbon had overrun the salient's eastern tip and several hundred yards of the eastern leg. "The country immediately in the rear of the Angle was nearly open," Barlow wrote. "It could be plainly seen that there was no force of enemy there." Hancock's success, however, contained the seeds of its undoing. Nearly twenty thousand men had shoehorned into a space about a half mile wide. All semblance of organization was lost. "The enthusiasm of a broken line resulting from a victory is only a little more efficient than the despondency of one broken by defeat," a Federal perceived. "The officers commanding the divisions were capable men and knew what the situation demanded, but they were almost powerless."[36]

Hancock rode along the captured works. "Forward! Double-quick!" he insisted. One of his trouser legs was almost torn off, exposing his leg from his hip to his boot top.[37]

Southeast of Hancock, Burnside was displaying unaccustomed vigor. Robert Potter's rightmost brigade—Simon Griffin's New Englanders, drawn from Maine, New Hampshire, and Vermont—had been assigned to lead the 9th Corps' assault. As soon as musketry signaled that Hancock had begun attacking, Griffin sent his regiments forward "obliquely to the right and front, directly toward the point whence came the roar of the fight." They groped through heavy ground fog, crested a knoll, then descended into a swamp. "Shall we ever forget that advance?" a soldier asked rhetorically. "On through the dense woods, under the dripping trees, now stumbling over the interlacing vines and undergrowth, now ankle deep in a marshy swamp, scarce seeing through the mist, with which the smoke of battle was beginning to mingle."[38]

Griffin broke into a clearing and straightened his line. "I thought that the enemy had retreated," an officer commented, "and that we were following him, and had no idea that we were going right into a fight." Then Early's sharpshooters fired into Griffin's ranks. "This is the hardest place in which men can be put," a Federal reflected. "I saw the falling men and listened to the buzz of the minnies."[39]

Pressing ahead, Griffin struck immediately south of Steuart to assault Lane's brigade of Early's corps. The 28th North Carolina had entrenched below Steuart's lower flank, its right end anchored on a bog. The 18th North Carolina occupied high ground south of the 28th regiment and, along with the 33rd and 7th North Carolina, projected east along the southern bank of a stream. The 37th North Carolina terminated Lane's line and bent back around to the south to connect with the rest of Early's formation.[40]

Steuart's collapse had exposed the 28th North Carolina's left flank, and Griffin, along with some of Hancock's units, charged the vulnerable spot, overrunning the 28th North Carolina and the adjacent 18th North Carolina. Bluecoats streamed through the breach, scooping up prisoners and two guns. A Tarheel proclaimed it a "subject of wonder" that any of his companions escaped capture. A Federal bragged that "after a hard fight we cut a brigade of them all to pieces." Griffin could see Hancock's jubilant soldiers on his right, cheering, waving flags, and tossing hats into the air. But the picture was not entirely encouraging. Hancock was "almost wholly broken up," Griffin thought, "the inevitable consequence of an assault such as they had just made."[41]

Lane struggled to rally the 18th and 28th North Carolina's remnants. "You must hold your ground," he shouted. "The honor and the safety of the army demand it." The rest of his brigade remained on high ground below the little stream and enfiladed Griffin with fire that in Lane's opinion was "so deadly that no troops, however brave, could withstand it." Lane later described his firm stand. "In the best of spirits the brigade welcomed the furious assault, which soon followed, with prolonged cheers and death dealing volleys—the unerring rifles of the 37th and part of the 7th thinning the ranks of the enemy in front, while the rest did good execution in rear."[42]

By 5:30 A.M., an hour after Hancock's soldiers had started south from the Brown house, the battle had reached a crisis for the Confederates. Hancock had driven in the salient's blunt tip and wrecked Johnson's division, almost cutting the Army of Northern Virginia in half. Daniel and Evans blocked Hancock's advance halfway down the Confederate formation's left leg, but unless reinforcements arrived quickly, they risked being overwhelmed. And on the salient's right leg, Lane faced an impossible task. Griffin's 9th Corps brigade hammered him from the east while Barlow's troops, then occupying Steuart's works, pressed from the north. The rest of Burnside's corps appeared ready to join the attack.

Only John Gordon's thin reserve line near the Harrison house connected the two wings of Lee's army. If Hancock regrouped and punched through Gordon, Lee faced the prospect of being defeated through multiple Federal action, with Burnside crushing Early, Warren attacking Anderson, and Wright lending a hand wherever needed. Grant's challenge was to coordinate his units before Lee could respond. The Confederates had to seal the fissure before Grant could exploit his opportunity. The contest of wills that had begun with Grant's passage of the Rapidan nine days before was building to a climax of heroic proportions.

"We'll not fail him."

The Army of Northern Virginia's fate rested in the able hands of Gordon, whose division made up the Confederate 2nd Corps' reserve. No southerner was better suited for the bloody work ahead. The lanky thirty-two-year-old Georgian lacked formal military training, but he was a fighting general in every respect and ranked among Lee's most aggressive subordinates. He had an intuitive grasp of military matters and a temperament suited to audacious maneuvers. Above all, he knew how to inspire men to bold action. The moment was Gordon's, and he seized it with verve.

On the afternoon of May 11, Ewell had directed Gordon to arrange his division so that it could support either Johnson or Rodes as circumstances required. Gordon had placed his largest brigade—his former Georgia command, now under Colonel Evans—in front of the McCoull house. His other two brigades—Hoffman's Virginians and Johnston's North Carolinians—had bivouacked a half mile farther back near the Harrison place. During the night, as rumors of a Federal assault mounted, Ewell had ordered Gordon to reinforce Johnson. He had done so by advancing Hoffman's Virginians to the second line of works behind Monaghan and

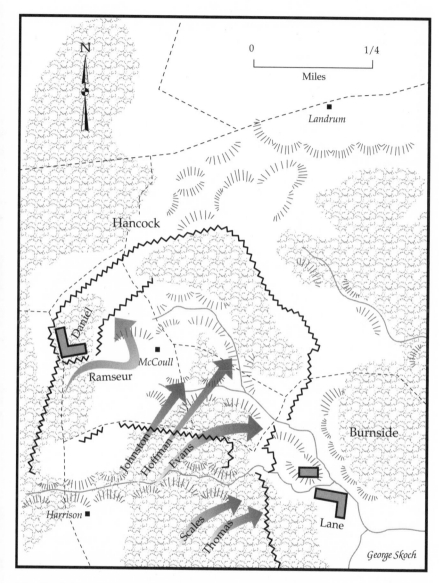

The Confederate response, by brigade, on May 12, 5 A.M.–6 A.M.

Walker and by sending three of Evans' regiments to the backup line behind Daniel.[43]

Gordon rose early on May 12. Around 4:30, a vedette dashed in from the front. "General," he warned, "I think there's something wrong down in the woods near where General Edward Johnson's men are." Reports arrived of a Union breakthrough, but Gordon and his staffers could hear no significant fighting and dismissed the reports.[44]

Gordon was with his brigadier Johnston when confirmation of the breach arrived. He immediately ordered Johnston to march his brigade diagonally to the right, across the interior of the salient toward Steuart. "The mist and fog were so heavy that it was impossible to see farther than a few rods," Gordon recalled of the ride. A few hundred yards short of the earthworks, they stumbled into Barlow's and Gibbon's lead elements. "In front of us was a line of battle, and not twenty steps from my line," remembered Johnston. "In rear of them I could see other lines—I saw at once that we were confronting a division, the lines of battle were so close together that we could hear the commands of their officers." A "sudden and unexpected blaze" brought Johnston up short. Major Brooks, who had so boldly captured one of Upton's flags two days before and brought it to Lee, was shot while leading the 20th North Carolina into what another Confederate termed the "hottest conflict we ever engaged in." The Federals twice called on Johnston to surrender. "Our answer in both instances was a volley," a soldier in the 23rd North Carolina boasted. Then Johnston, who was riding next to Gordon, was shot in the head. The wound was not fatal, but it disabled him. Colonel Thomas M. Garrett, of the 5th North Carolina, assumed command of the brigade, only to be killed. Command passed to Colonel Thomas F. Toon, of the 20th North Carolina, who was racked by a debilitating illness. "It was still not light and the woods were dense and the morning rainy," Gordon recounted. "You could not see a line of troops a hundred yards off."[45]

Gordon drew Johnston's brigade back slightly, then deployed it across Barlow's advancing front. He hoped that the "sheer audacity of the movement would confuse and check the Union advance long enough for me to change front and form line of battle with the other brigades." The plan was typical of Gordon's unorthodox military style and of the "splendid audacity which characterized him," Lee's aide Venable observed.[46]

Johnston's brigade, concealed by the dense fog, extended into a single line facing the interior of Steuart's and Witcher's ruptured works. Seizing the initiative, Gordon sent them screaming into Barlow's and Gibbon's startled Unionists, who lacked the cohesion to resist. In fighting accurately described by a 12th North Carolina soldier as "one of the bloodiest scenes of the war," Gordon endeavored to thwart Hancock's advance in the salient's eastern sector.[47]

Portions of Barlow's division—predominantly from Brown's brigade—slipped below Gordon, however, pressed to the Confederate reserve line, and captured the eastern portion of it. The peril to Lee's army was extreme. Lee's and Ewell's headquarters at the Harrison house stood less than a quarter mile away. Grant's ploy to split the Confederate army in half was close to success.

Gordon spun his horse around and hurried back to rally Evans and Hoffman. A bullet pierced his coat near his waist. "General, didn't that ball hit you?" inquired the aide Thomas G. Jones. "No," the general replied, with a glance at Jones, who was hunched over his horse. "But suppose my back had been in a bow like yours? Don't you see that the bullet would have gone straight through my spine? Sit up or you'll be killed."[48]

On the way back, Gordon met Ewell, who asked to borrow a staff officer. The man Gordon gave Ewell as an aide was perplexed by Ewell's rapid and excited manner of speaking and began to repeat the orders to make sure that he understood them. Ewell threw up his hands and emitted a loud "whoo-oo-oot!" to punctuate his exasperation. Gordon and the rest of his aides, familiar with the eccentric Ewell's agitated demeanor on the battlefield, enjoyed a hearty laugh.[49]

Gordon began assembling his remaining units near the Harrison house. Hoffman was heavily engaged behind the works Monaghan had occupied, but he managed to withdraw under scathing fire. Evans could not disengage the portion of his brigade fighting alongside Daniel. His three regiments near the McCoull house, however, were available, and Captain Old, previously of Johnson's staff, directed Evans to send Gordon whatever men he could muster.[50]

Johnson's aide Hunter was among the Confederates fleeing to the rear. He came upon Lee a few hundred yards behind the works, waving his hat and imploring the men to rally. Hunter, sensing that Lee did not fully comprehend the disaster, shouted, "General, the line is broken at the angle of General Johnson's front!" Lee's face grew grave. "Ride with me to General Gordon," he instructed Hunter, and they turned back toward the Harrison place.[51]

Hunter and Lee met Gordon forming his battle line. Bullets spattered nearby as the rebel commander in chief paused to survey Evans' and Hoffman's troops. "Not a word did he say," a witness noted of Lee, "but simply took off his hat, and as he sat on his charger I never saw a man look so noble, or a spectacle so impressive." A soldier in the 52nd Virginia recalled the scene years later. "The picture he made, as the grand old man sat there on his horse, with his noble head bare, and looked from right to left, as if to meet each eye that flashed along the line, can never be forgotten by a man that stood there."[52]

Lee rode in front of Gordon's line at the point where Hoffman and Evans joined and turned Traveller toward the Federals. It was evident that he intended to lead a charge. Gordon spurred in front and seized the horse's bridle. An officer heard him say, "You must not expose yourself. Your life is too valuable to the army and to the Confederacy for you to risk it so wantonly. We are Georgians, we are Virginians, we need no such encouragement." By way of emphasis, Gordon repeated, "They will not fail you here." To underscore his point, he called out, "Will you, boys?" A chorus responded, "No, we'll not fail him."[53]

Gordon's voice rose. "You must go to the rear," he importuned Lee. Gordon recalled that his soldiers crowded around Lee and "turned his horse in the opposite direction, some clutching his bridle, some his stirrups, while others pressed close to Old Traveller's hips, ready to shove him by main force to the rear." Men shouted, "Come back, General Lee. We cannot fight while you are in our front." Gordon led Lee back, and one of Hoffman's officers—reportedly Sergeant William A. Compton, of the 49th Virginia—took Traveller's bridle. "Lee, Lee, Lee to the rear. Lee to the rear," the soldiers chanted.[54]

Colonel J. Catlett Gibson, of the 49th Virginia, met Lee as he passed between Hoffman's and Evans' brigades. Federals could be seen dimly through the distant haze, perhaps no more than sixty yards away. "Shall we give them the bayonet, General?" Gibson asked. "Yes," Lee answered. Just then the enemy fired a scattered volley. "No time for fixing bayonets," Gibson cried as he turned to his men. "Charge!" he shouted. Gordon rose grandly in his stirrups and roared out in his finest martial voice, "Forward, guide right."[55]

"There was no shout, no rebel yell," an officer recalled. "But, as I looked down the line, I saw the stern faces and set teeth of men who have undertaken to do a desperate deed, and do not intend to fail."[56]

Gordon's two brigades advanced double quick into what has been called a "swirling vortex of battle." Gordon's right wing comprised Evans' three regiments, with the 61st Georgia on the extreme right flank. Hoffman's brigade, along with elements of Johnston's fought-out Carolinians, now under Toon, advanced on the left. Lee's aide Venable watched as Gordon, carrying the colors, led the "headlong, resistless charge."[57]

Gordon almost immediately encountered Barlow's men, who were occupying portions of the Confederate reserve line. "A stream of bullets were coming out of these pines and rattling against the sides of some old farm building behind us," a Confederate related. A soldier in the 49th Virginia remembered Federals "packed thick as blackbirds" in the reserve works between the McCoull and Harrison houses. Rebel yells drowned out the clatter of Yankee musketry. "It makes my blood jump quicker as I recall the scene," a southerner reminisced. "Never pausing a second, our boys mounted the works. In a moment the blue and the gray were mixed in a dense struggling mass." Gordon's impetus carried him over Barlow's startled Unionists. Colonel Brown, commanding one of Barlow's brigades, was caught up in the swirling mass of Confederates and captured. "We could not afford to send men back from the charging line with prisoners," a southerner explained. Gordon's men swept past, calling to the Yankees, "Throw down your guns and go to the rear." Hoffman bent low to the ground. "Are you hit?" Colonel Gibson inquired. Hoffman answered that he had lost his spectacles and was looking for them. Gibson detailed a soldier to help him search and hurried his troops on.[58]

Gordon rode exultantly in front. "Every officer on horseback in my division, the brigade, and regimental commanders, and my own superb staff, were riding among the troops, shouting in unison, 'Forward, men, forward!'" he reported. The result was electrifying. "Onward they swept," Gordon continued, "pouring their rapid volleys into Hancock's confused ranks, and swelling the deafening din of battle with their piercing shouts." A Federal confirmed that Gordon's troops "fought like demons."[59]

But ground fog and forest disrupted Gordon's men, much as they had disordered Hancock's. Gibson noticed Confederates on his right and inquired who was in command. A sergeant replied that they belonged to Evans' brigade but that he had no inkling where Evans was. "I told him that I would take command of his little squad," Gibson recounted, "that the only command I had to give was to keep in general alignment with my right flank; and not to waste his ammunition on the pine thickets." Gibson returned to discover his own regiment under fire. He first suspected that the nearby 13th Virginia had mistaken his men for Yankees but soon learned that pockets of Federals left in the rear were to blame.[60]

Gordon clawed toward the salient in a free-for-all involving pistols, muskets, bayonets, and swords. The blue and the gray became, in the words of a soldier, a "dense, surging mass." A lieutenant in the 52nd Virginia grabbed a Yankee and ordered him to surrender, but the northerner jerked free and skewered the rebel on his bayonet. M. S. Stringfellow, of the 49th Virginia, emptied his revolver into Federals standing so close that the discharges ignited their clothes.[61]

Hoffman's men slogged through a knee-deep marsh, then up a rise to dislodge Brown's and Brooke's Federals from the outer works. A portion of the salient's eastern face was theirs. His troops badly scattered, Hoffman nonetheless continued into the adjacent field until Union guns positioned near the Landrum place brought him to a halt. "I ordered the men back to the little ditch and to gather the cartridge boxes of the dead and wounded as they went," one of his colonels elaborated. Hoffman tried to extend his brigade north along the works but encountered fierce opposition from Smyth and Miles, firing from behind traverses. Concerned that his line had become too attenuated, Hoffman retracted it southward, which created a gap between him and the Federals holding the east angle. "That was the hardest fight we had fought since the war," a soldier in the 52nd Virginia wrote in his diary.[62]

On Gordon's southern flank, near Lane, Francis Marion McDow, the color-bearer of the 61st Georgia, planted the Confederate battle flag on the works. Evans' rebels rallied around the banner, swinging their muskets like clubs. McDow, the flag, and a good portion of the 61st Georgia were captured. "Evans' brigade was cut to pieces," according to a participant, and the brigade's remnants streamed back to the interior line. "We were badly confused and mortified," a Georgian confessed. With Evans' outfit crumbling, Hoffman risked becoming isolated in the outer works, and Lane's northmost flank was placed in jeopardy.[63]

Just as Gordon began to question whether he could hold the works that he had recaptured, a courier dashed up with hopeful news. "General Ewell says that if you will hold this line for fifteen minutes that he will have four brigades to help you," the courier disclosed.[64]

Below Gordon, Lane's adroit juggling had brought the Union 9th Corps to a standstill. Colonel Griffin, whose brigade constituted Burnside's right wing, had looked to Hancock for support, but what he saw was hardly propitious. "Across an open field to the south and west," he recounted, "I saw large masses of the enemy pouring out of the woods beyond and coming down on Hancock's men in a countercharge." This was Gordon's attack. Griffin responded by shifting his brigade at right angles to Hancock and enfilading Gordon's lower flank. But as Hancock retired before Gordon's counteroffensive, Griffin's right flank became dangerously exposed. Soon Griffin was battling Gordon to the north and Lane to the south. "They turned upon us," Griffin remarked of the Confederates, "and we had one of the most furious fights we were ever engaged in during the whole war."[65]

Zenas Bliss, the commander of Potter's other brigade, had injured his ankle the previous evening. The din of battle and exploding artillery shells awakened him well after the attack was under way. He later wrote that he was "very angry," but his aides assured him that they had let him sleep because he was too badly injured to participate in the battle. Bliss painfully mounted a horse and rode off to find his brigade, his injured foot dangling outside the stirrup. After stopping to help position some of the 9th Corps' artillery, he found Burnside, who told him he should not be riding in his condition. Bliss visited the 9th Corps' field hospital, where a doctor replaced his bandages. "I was in such pain by that time, from the exercise, that I was very willing to remain in the field hospital," Bliss acknowledged.[66]

He was sorely missed. In order to quell the mounting Confederate counteroffensive, Potter tried to form Bliss's brigade, now under Colonel John I. Curtin, on Griffin's left. In Bliss's absence, orders seemed to go astray, and a combination of rough terrain and persistent Confederate musketry slowed the maneuver to an excruciating crawl. Then Crittenden, who was supposed to support Potter, failed to arrive, and Early's rebels ventured from their works below Lane to edge around the lower end of Potter's line. "It seemed to us that the dire experience of the Wilderness was about to be repeated," a northerner observed. "The lurid flash of musketry lighted up the dim woods, and the din of battle resounded on every side." Weld's mixed Massachusetts and Regular brigade appeared in the nick of time and formed at right angles to Bliss's, only to discover that its ammunition was wet. "The storm of war burst again upon us," a Federal commented. "It seemed as though instead of being human we were turned into fiends and brutes, seeking to kill all in our way."[67]

Lane was in serious need of reinforcements and petitioned his division commander, Wilcox, for assistance. Fortune was indeed smiling on the Confederates. The previous evening, Wilcox had sent Thomas' and Scales's brigades to the Confederate left to fortify Mahone on the Po. In the nick of time, the two brigades returned to Spotsylvania Court House, and Wilcox immediately ordered them to Lane's aid. They deployed behind Lane and slightly to his left, bridging the gap northward to Gordon. Elements from Doles's brigade pitched in as well. Now firmly supported, Lane expelled Griffin's Federals from his works, then charged. A Federal reported that "perhaps for fifteen minutes, perhaps for not more than ten,

[Griffin] held the enemy at bay, and then its shattered remnant gave way before [Lane's] repeated onsets."[68]

Lane, Scales, Thomas, and scattered units from Evans pressed Potter slowly back, which relieved some of the pressure against the lower end of Gordon's line. Private Leonard Cranford—"cool as if he was squirrel hunting," one of his companions remarked—led the 34th North Carolina, of Scales's brigade, in an attack. Once they had the Federals on the run, Scales's troops retired to occupy Lane's former line. Thomas' brigade continued ahead, battering Potter. After clambering down a steep bluff and traversing a ditch, the 14th Georgia, of Thomas' brigade, came under a "terrible fire of grape canister shells and minnie balls." The 45th Georgia flailed through heavy pine thickets and joined the fight. Griffin, however, had taken up a strong position on the far side of a field and refused to budge. A southerner told how intense Union musketry "mowed down my comrades by scores in every direction." The two captured rebel guns— Captain Asher W. Garber's pieces, of the Staunton Battery—lay stranded in a section of works between the hostile forces. Garber, accompanied by Major Wilfred E. Cutshaw and a handful of Confederate gunners, rushed to the pieces, turned them on the Federals, and dragged them to safety after a brutal duel.[69]

Burnside's offensive ground to a halt as Potter's division began erecting defensive works. The opposing forces, in some places mere yards apart, fired steadily into each other. "If there ever was a hell on earth it was then," a Federal noted. "It is impossible to tell how any man lived through that hour." The 36th Massachusetts, on Potter's left, was especially hard pressed. One of its number hit upon an unusual ploy and ventured toward the southerners shouting, "Come in, Johnnies! We won't hurt you. Come in!" Lane answered with a "murderous volley which will never be forgotten by any who survived it." Men stretched on the ground, frantically loading and firing. Then the 21st Massachusetts joined the 36th, and both regiments charged into an inferno of Confederate artillery fire. "They poured into our ranks a storm of lead and iron killing and wounding many," a Bay Stater reported. "It was here we piled dead bodies one on top the other to lie behind for protection."[70]

Once again, Burnside had failed. Grant had intended for him to smash through the salient's eastern leg, but Early's strong defense and Burnside's inability to bring the full weight of his three available divisions into play had doomed the assault. Although Griffin had achieved brief success, he was unsupported and had to retire. Griffin later inflated the importance of his attack by claiming that he had saved the 2nd Corps. "Had not the 9th Corps arrived on the ground at that critical moment, and in the right position, Hancock's troops must have been swept away, and the results of the battle might have been very different from what they were," he wrote. In recognition of Griffin's achievement, Burnside recommended his promotion to the rank of brigadier general.[71]

Gordon and Lane had redeemed Lee's fortunes on the salient's eastern leg. Gordon boasted that his three brigades had "charged with the greatest spirit, driving the enemy with heavy loss from nearly the whole of the captured works from the left of Wilcox's division to the salient on General Johnson's line, and fully one-fourth of a mile beyond." Lee's aide Venable agreed that Hancock's left wing had been "hurled back by this splendid charge." And Lane's defense of the works below Steuart had been equally important. If Lane and his reinforcements had faltered, Burnside might well have sliced through the salient's eastern edge and opened the way for a decisive Union victory.[72]

"Thro hissing shot and screaming shell."

The situation along the salient's western leg remained critical for the Confederates. Birney and Mott had overrun Monaghan and Walker and captured portions of the backup line, where Daniel's Confederates, buttressed by three of Evans' regiments and a stand of artillery, were waging a desperate defense to stem the Federal tide. "I shall never forget the scene of confusion," a Carolinian stated. "The scattered fugitives, the mingled shouts of inquiry and of apprehension, the multitudinous voices of command and entreaty, the faces of anxiety and dismay, the cries of the wounded and the perpetual fusillades of musketry." Beleaguered Confederates hunkered low "to keep from being hit in the back owing to the crooked works."[73]

Ewell's aide and stepson Campbell Brown went in search of reinforcements. Stephen Ramseur's North Carolinians and Cullen Battle's Alabamians were positioned below Daniel, but Brown was reluctant to pull them from the line without first consulting their division commander, Rodes. He found some of Doles's soldiers, ordered them to the endangered spot, then spurred over to Kershaw, whose 1st Corps division adjoined Battle. Kershaw explained that he had no troops to spare but promised that if Battle or Ramseur were shunted to the threatened sector, he would extend his division to cover the resulting gap. Brown decided to bolster Daniel with Battle's troops and went in search of Ewell to secure his approval.[74]

Ewell was laboring to rally Johnson's broken fugitives. He was a "tower of passion," according to a witness, hurling a "terrible volley of oaths" at stragglers and calling them cowards. "Yes, goddamn you, run," he shouted in his most sarcastic voice. "The Yankees will catch you. That's right, go as fast as you can!" Lee was also there, "calm, collected, and dignified," appealing to duty and manhood. Several soldiers remarked on the contrast. "All that General Lee addressed at once halted and returned to the assistance of their comrades," a Louisianian commented. "All that General Ewell so angrily reproached continued their flight to the rear." When Ewell began beating fleeing soldiers over their backs with his sword, Lee ordered him to restrain himself. "How can you expect to control these men when you have lost control of yourself?" Lee asked. "If you cannot repress your excitement, you had better retire."[75]

Still suffering acutely from the wound he had received on the eighth, Battle led his brigade into the "thickest of the fight" and drove the Federals from the southernmost portion of Daniel's and Evans' backup line. "The brigade was a solid wedge driven into the very heart of the enemy," Battle asserted.[76]

In the meantime, Rodes went on the offensive. "Check the enemy's advance," he commanded Ramseur, "and drive them back." Ramseur shifted into the clearing west of the McCoull house. A Confederate described the repositioning: "We were out in the open field, with no breastworks in front, save those held by the Federals. Thro the lifting fog the stars and stripes were seen waving over the captured works." To a soldier in the 14th North Carolina, it looked as if "everything was in confusion." Many Confederates lay behind their knapsacks and pitched dirt in front with their bayonets. "The enemy had captured the main line of rifle pits, and about 200 yards in rear of them was a temporary line of work," one of Ramseur's men noted. "Both these lines were soon held by the enemy, and the space between the lines presented a living mass of Yankees, in full view of us, so we could readily see the work before us." Remarked another southerner, "We were one line of men, with two ranks front and rear, and in front of us were two lines of breastworks, filled with men and artillery placed at convenient points." A rebel judged the prospect a "gloomy one for the boys in gray."[77]

Ramseur ordered his troops to advance slowly without firing. At his signal, they were to charge, screaming at the top of their lungs. No matter what happened, no one was to pause "until both lines of works were ours." Mott's and Birney's soldiers held the captured Confederate works in front of Ramseur. Their ranks had become "unavoidably mixed," which worked to Ramseur's advantage. Smoke enshrouded the field and hung heavily in the thick mist.[78]

"Charge," Ramseur shouted, and his Confederates stepped ahead and somewhat to the left "into the very jaws of death," in the phrase of a participant. The general rode in front like an "angel of war," in the words of another. A southern correspondent marveled at the audacity of Ramseur's attack: "So close was the fighting there, for a time, that the fire of friend and foe rose up rattling in one common roar. Ramseur's North Carolinians dropped in the ranks thick and fast, but still he continued, with glorious constancy, to gain ground, foot by foot."[79]

A bullet hit Ramseur in the right arm, but he kept on, blood spurting from a gaping wound below his elbow. His troops rushed up a gentle rise to the backup trenches without firing a shot and overran a portion of the line. With Ramseur incapacitated, Colonel Bryan Grimes, of the 4th North Carolina, assumed command of the brigade. Fifty yards ahead stood the main works, filled with Birney's and Mott's men, who were pouring galling fire into the North Carolinians. "Being no one to apply to," Grimes wrote after the dust had settled, "I saw the necessity for speedy action and ordered a second charge, myself leading them." At Grimes's command, the brigade bolted toward the outer works. Tisdale Stepp, of the 14th North Carolina—reportedly "as fine a specimen of physical manhood as there was in the brigade"—struck up "The Bonnie Blue Flag" and stepped grandly ahead, loading, firing, and singing at the same time. A Confederate accidentally fired into the back of Stepp's head, killing him. In a remarkable feat of bravery, Ramseur's men ran through a veritable blizzard of musketry and piled into a segment of the main line, just below the Stonewall Brigade's former position.[80]

Grimes's men had jumped from the frying pan into the fire. They now stood wedged into a short segment of the salient's earthworks. Large numbers of Federals had found refuge against the outer face of the same works, and more Yankees occupied the trenches to their right. Union soldiers on Grimes's right opened killing fire, and the opponents pitched into each other in a brutal, face-to-face brawl. Federals pulled the 30th North Carolina's adjutant over the works by his hair and ripped another regiment's flag from its color-bearer's hands. More Yankees flanked the 30th North Carolina and captured a third of the regiment. The 14th North Carolina saved the day for Grimes by butting northward through several traverses and driving the Federals back with, in the words of a rebel, "great slaughter." An elderly conscript from Edgecomb County, bent over with rheumatism, led the attack, wielding a ramrod and shouting to his comrades, "Strike home!" A witness remarked, "For cool and unflinching courage, I never saw it surpassed."[81]

Terrain played an important part in what happened next. The McCoull house stood on a slight elevation. Around the structure, the ground fell away fairly sharply to the north, east, and west. Then it rose again to form the curving ridge crested by the main Confederate works. Ramseur's men had recovered a short segment of the entrenchments there. On Ramseur's right, however, the line dipped gently downhill, then rose pronouncedly toward the west angle, earlier held by Walker's Stonewall Brigade. Mott's and Birney's men were able to fire from behind the traverses of their elevated position at the west angle into Ramseur's troops below. The traverses that Ramseur's brigade occupied afforded little protection from such plunging fire.

Grimes correctly concluded that his brigade's survival required capturing the works to his right. "Yankees held a position on our right, upon a hill, which enabled them to keep up an incessant enfilading fire upon us; two thirds of the men which we lost were done that way," a Confederate complained. "Men were killed while squatting just as low and as close to the breastworks as it was possible for them to get." Grimes continued battling north toward the salient's west angle, recapturing one traverse at a time. "It was here for the first time I ever knew the enemy to run upon our bayonets," a Confederate noted, "but they came down with such fury that we pitched many of them with the bayonet right over into the ditch." Whizzing minié balls reminded another southerner of a musical instrument. "Some sounded like wounded men crying; some like humming of bees; some like cats in the depth of the night, while others cut through the air with only a 'Zip' like noise." A Tarheel proudly remarked that "North Carolina boys were in the place where Virginians had failed."[82]

The North Carolinians pressed toward the west angle, reaching to where a farm road from the McCoull house crossed the works. Mott and Birney called for reinforcements. "Encouraged by their success so far," a Federal wrote of Ramseur's men, "and with traverses in their recaptured works behind which their sharpshooters could take deadly aim and be protected, our position was critical."[83]

Hancock became increasingly worried. "If no one else attacks I may be turned and forced back," he warned in a dispatch to Meade. "Still, I trust not," he added more optimistically. At 5:55, as Gordon's and Ramseur's counterattacks began to register, Hancock made an urgent plea. "It is necessary that General Wright should attack at once," he urged. "All of my troops are engaged." At the same time, Hancock telegraphed Burnside. "I am in the inside of second line of enemy's works," he wrote. "Hurry forward, or I may be driven back."[84]

By six o'clock, Grant's offensive had stalled. On the eastern side of the salient, Burnside lay pinned under a brutal Confederate artillery barrage and Hancock was occupied fighting Gordon. On the salient's western leg, Battle and Ramseur had started the bloody business of recapturing the occupied works. Hancock's grip had shrunk to a few hundred yards of earthworks between the east and west angles. Ewell later praised Ramseur's "unsurpassed gallantry" in waging a "most desperate" fight. Venable termed Ramseur's feat "wonderful," adding that "without unjust discrimination, we may say Gordon, Rodes and Ramseur were the heroes of this bloody day." Lee also expressed his gratitude. "We deserved the thanks of the country; we had saved his army," Grimes wrote in describing the general's words of commendation.[85]

"All the hosts of hell in assault upon us."

While Lee had blunted Grant's momentum, the Federals still held two important cards. The 5th and 6th Corps—half the Union infantry force— stood poised to enter the fray. It seemed to Grant that Lee had to be near his breaking point. One more hard push, and the Confederate defenses would surely crumble.

Grant responded immediately to Hancock's appeal. "Your good news is most welcome," Meade telegraphed his 2nd Corps head at six o'clock. "Burnside attacked at the appointed hour. Wright is ordered in at once on your right. Hold all you get and press on." Meade also instructed Warren to "keep up as threatening an attitude as possible to keep the enemy in your front. Wright must attack and you may have to. Be ready and do the best you can." Also at six, Grant's aide Rawlins shot a directive to Burnside. "General Hancock is pushing forward vigorously," the message read. "He has captured 3 generals. Push on with all possible vigor."[86]

While Meade was ordering Wright into battle—Lyman recorded the time as 6:30—a prisoner rode on horseback into the command center. It was Johnson, crestfallen but unhurt. The southerner was "most horribly mortified" at having been captured and kept coughing to hide his embarrassment. Grant and Meade shook hands cordially with the distinguished captive, a fellow veteran of the Mexican War, and the three generals struck up an animated conversation. Grant offered the prisoner a cigar and a seat by the fire and did his best to set him at ease. They spoke only about the past, although Johnson managed to interject some face-saving bravado. "Doubtless you have gained an advantage," he conceded to Grant's aide

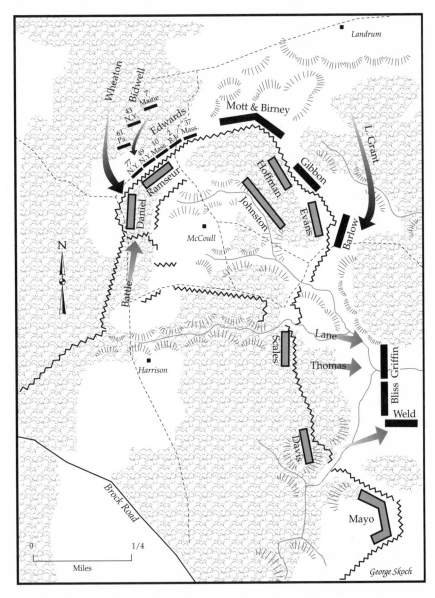

Neill's division of Wright's corps joining the fray on May 12, 6:30 A.M.–7:30 A.M.

Seth Williams, "but you are much mistaken if you think we are beaten yet!" Porter noticed that Johnson was covered with mud and that a tuft of hair protruded through a hole in his felt hat, giving him the appearance of a Sioux chief. Arrangements were made to have him transported to prison in an ambulance. Steuart, however, had become sharply vituperative. Lyman thought him a "little creature . . . who insulted everybody who came near him, and was rewarded by being sent on foot to Fredericksburg, where there was plenty of mud and one stream up to his waist." Meade's aide Colonel James C. Biddle wrote his wife that Steuart was a man of "little mind, without character."[87]

As the generals conversed, another message arrived from Hancock. "I have finished up Johnson," it said, "and am now going into Early." Out of consideration for Johnson's feelings, Grant handed the dispatch around rather than reading it aloud.[88]

Wright's 6th Corps constituted Grant's second wave. Two of Wright's three divisions—Ricketts' and Russell's—had bivouacked near the Alsop house, from where they could support either Hancock at the salient or Warren near Laurel Hill. Wright's third division, under Neill, waited near the Brown house, well situated to assist Hancock. Of Neill's brigades, the closest to Hancock was that of Oliver Edwards, one of Neill's most tenacious scrapers. On May 12, Edwards commanded three regiments—the 10th and 37th Massachusetts, and the 2nd Rhode Island, numbering about nine hundred men.[89]

At Neill's direction, Edwards' New Englanders—followed by Brigadier General Frank Wheaton's Pennsylvania and New York brigade—filed toward the west angle. Lyman caught up with Edwards and told him the good news: Hancock had captured three thousand Confederates, two generals, and twenty cannon. A northern soldier overheard the conversation and interjected, "How many did they take from us?"[90]

Edwards continued to a stand of woods in front of the salient's west angle. Shells howled into the brigade and convinced Lyman that the enemy could "probably see some indication of the movement." It made no sense to remain where they were, so Edwards ordered his men across the clearing toward the rebel works.[91]

The scene was chaotic. Mott's and Birney's troops had become completely scrambled. Soldiers stood plastered against the outer face of the ramparts and huddled behind traverses near the west angle, battling Ramseur's Confederates, who were clawing their way north. Ewell had massed his remaining artillery pieces near the Harrison house, from where they bombarded the west angle. "Our position became very critical," a Federal appreciated. "It was a life or death contest." A New Yorker regretted that a "piercing Southern squeal, instead of Northern shout, now rent the air, carrying joy to the wounded Confederate, but bringing bitter disappointment to the expiring Unionist who had hoped to die shouting victory on a field his valor had helped to win."[92]

Edwards' brigade charged by the left flank into the fight. The 10th Massachusetts advanced to the west angle's right face, the 2nd Rhode Island wrapped around the angle's tip, and the 37th Massachusetts hugged the works to the left. Edwards' right flank connected with elements from Mott's Excelsior Brigade, and pockets of Birney's and Mott's troops occupied the traverses on Edwards' left. A dip paralleled the works on Ramseur's side, from which rebels emerged as though "suddenly springing from the bosom of the earth." The Federals sought shelter behind stumps, trees, and anything that offered safety. "We went up to hold the enemy's rifle pits and redoubts and had not been there long before the enemy charged them," a soldier in the 10th Massachusetts noted. "The Rebels came into the same rifle pit with us and commenced an enfilading fire before we knew they were there and we had any quantity of men killed and wounded in much less time than it takes to tell of it." The 10th Massachusetts' historian reported that "sometimes the fighting was so close that the muskets of the enemy were knocked aside, and in some instances wrenched from their hands."[93]

Two more of Neill's brigades arrived in quick succession. First, Colonel Bidwell's mixed Maine, New York, and Pennsylvania outfit pulled up behind Edwards. One officer felt that "spurts of dirt were as constant as the pattering drops of a summer shower. Overhead the swish and hum of the passing bullets was like a swarm of bees." Part of the brigade formed in trees behind Edwards, while two regiments, the 49th and 77th New York, worked onto Edwards' right.[94]

Wheaton meanwhile circled behind Bidwell and reached south on Bidwell's right, defining the far right edge of the 6th Corps' lodgment. It was a "hot place." A soldier in the 139th Pennsylvania saw that the "task now blocked out for us was an entirely different one from the one Hancock had," for at this juncture, the rebels were "waiting for the attack, and in full force in the works." Wheaton dashed toward the entrenchments only to be slammed by Battle's and Ramseur's musketry. Concluding that the venture was "doomed to be a failure," Wheaton retired his brigade a short distance to a rail-and-debris barricade that the rebels had constructed the previous day. There, Wheaton discovered that his men "were exposed to a terrible musketry fire, losing heavily, including many valuable officers."[95]

Hoping to restore order, Wright made his way to a depression near the west angle. Shortly after he arrived, a shell fragment knocked him several feet and bruised his thigh. Onlookers feared that he was about to share Sedgwick's fate, but the wound, though painful, was not disabling. Lyman found Wright and his staff sitting on the ground, sheltered from direct fire by the ravine's natural contours. "Just by us lay a dead infantryman on his back with his knees drawn up," the aide noticed. Then Birney, who had also been bruised by a shell fragment a few days before, joined the assemblage. Rain and musketry blended into an uninterrupted roar. Bullets, to Lyman's consternation, "came dropping into our hollow, killing one horse and wounding another."[96]

Grant also tried to renew the offensive on the salient's eastern leg, but was unsuccessful. Barlow maintained a tenuous hold on the outer edge of Steuart's former works, where Gordon's musketry and Early's artillery combined to make life miserable. The Federal units were "mixed up to a great extent," a soldier in the 116th Pennsylvania remarked. Many regiments fought in squads, wherever an officer could be found to command them. All that remained of the Irish Brigade were scattered parties hunkering low under "infernal" fire.[97]

With Burnside unable to advance, Barlow became concerned about his lower flank's safety and sent his aide John D. Black for reinforcements. On his way to the Landrum house, Black spied an officer waving to him. "Before he could speak," Black recounted, "a shell took off that part of the head above the lower jaw, as smooth as if it had been cut with a knife, and as I passed he fell backward and in looking down at him the tongue was moving in its socket as if in the act of speaking—a horrible sight I can never forget."[98]

Black located Hancock. "Give my compliments to General Barlow," the general requested, "and say to him he has done splendidly, to hold what he has captured at all hazards, protect his flank as best he can, and I will send him reinforcements as soon as I can get them from the 6th Corps." He went on, "Also direct him to give my compliments to Miles and Brooke and assure them that they may consider themselves brigadier generals from today."[99]

Black carried the good news to Barlow, who directed him to ask Burnside to "establish connections with the left of our command, with his skirmish line, if he could not with his line of battle." Barlow cautioned Black that he would probably be captured. "If you are," he said, "remember it is by my order." Black's tentmate clasped the aide's hand. "Look out for yourself, my boy," he recommended. Referring by nickname to the notorious Confederate prison, he added, "That order will be cold comfort for you in Old Libby." A hair-raising ride took Black to Burnside, who had him convey instructions to Potter to connect with Barlow. Black then followed the 9th Corps' skirmish line toward the 2nd

Corps but stumbled into a squad of Lane's Confederates. He whirled his horse and jammed his spurs into the mount's sides. A volley brought the horse down. "I struck the ground running," he asserted, "and am positive a shell from a thirty-two pounder would not have dented my coat tails for the next two hundred yards."[100]

Hancock sent a telegram to Burnside that underscored Barlow's need for assistance. "I hope you will connect your right with my left," he urged. "It is the only weak point I have, and that is very weak until you closely connect." At seven o'clock, Grant reminded Burnside, "Push your troops so as to keep up the connection with Hancock. Wright is now attacking and Warren is in readiness to push in also." Burnside was touchy. He would command his own divisions, he snapped at Comstock, who he suspected was sending uncomplimentary reports to Grant. But he soon calmed down and apologized. Comstock smugly wrote in his journal that after making amends, Burnside "asked my advice again."[101]

Meade found more substantial help for Barlow in the form of Neill's only uncommitted brigade—Lewis Grant's Vermonters. These soldiers, who numbered among the Union army's most tenacious combat veterans, had been slated to follow Edwards, Bidwell, and Wheaton to the west angle. At Hancock's request, Meade directed them instead to reinforce Barlow. Marching parallel to the salient's eastern leg under "brisk fire of musketry and artillery," they swept behind Barlow's line, then charged to the outer face where Barlow was holding on.

Far from bringing relief, though, the Vermont Brigade's unexpected appearance added to Barlow's difficulties. Barlow had been attempting to re-form his division—"there was no organized line in our front," Grant was to say in his report—and the arrival of extra soldiers contributed to greater confusion. Deeply upset, Barlow rode back to the Landrum house and beseeched Hancock, "For God's sake, do not send any more troops in here!" After the war, Colonel Grant maintained that his timely arrival had saved Barlow from destruction. In fact, Grant had deployed his brigade ineffectually, through no fault of his own. Rather than piling into Barlow's entrenchments, he would have done better by shifting his men into the space between Barlow and Burnside. Hancock, however, had not communicated to Grant the importance of bridging the 2nd and 9th Corps, and consequently the Vermonters had no discernible impact on Federal fortunes below the east angle. Through the remainder of the day, Gordon's Confederates maintained their grip on the entrenchments. Combat in this sector—the stretch of works formerly occupied by Steuart—settled into a ragged sputter of musketry.[102]

The Brown family had been at home on May 10 when the Federals took over their house. Mr. Brown, a Confederate soldier, had been ill and was taken prisoner. Around eight in the morning of May 12, shells began raining around the house, and Hancock ordered the family into the cellar. Mrs. Brown tarried to secure a pillow and blanket for her sick husband. Just as she started down the stairs, a shell passed by where she had been standing, crashed through a wall, exploded a barrel of flour, and embedded in yet another wall. Her granddaughter reminisced that the projectile "went far enough in for my uncle, a boy of twelve years, to pull it out from the other side."[103]

Hancock decided that his headquarters was no place for women and children and delegated a guard to take Mrs. Brown and her family—except for her husband, who remained in the cellar—to the 2nd Corps hospital, which was at the Couse place. "So in the midst of one of the greatest battles ever fought," recalled Mrs. Brown's granddaughter, "grandmother, her three small children and the cook with her three little children went out into the rain and mud, and a constant thunder of shot and shell, and went down the hill and away from the house where her sick husband was a prisoner, and the only baggage she thought to take was the family silver around her waist and the family Bible under her arm. When my uncle would see a shell coming very close he would order them to fall down, and down the whole crowd would go, in the mud and water which was over their shoes when standing."[104]

Katherine Couse welcomed her neighbors. One of Grant's staffers dropped by for breakfast, and later she played host to the battlefield artist Edwin Forbes, Provost Marshal Patrick, and other Union notables. "It sounded as if the very earth was breaking up from the direction of Captain Brown's old place in one continuous line to Miss Pritchetts," Couse remarked in a letter. "The earth shakes. Great God, how more than awful. Shells whizzing oh so fearfully. My very soul almost dies within me." To her distress, her house was "perfectly muddy and hoggish, tracked all up, with refugees, children, dogs, and soldiers."[105]

At Lee's headquarters, near the Harrison house, a Confederate cavalryman reacted very like Couse. "The roar of thunder and the roar of artillery and musketry intermingled, made an uproar of elements hardly conceivable," he wrote his wife. "I never had such awful feelings in my life. Could only pray silently for deliverance."[106]

VIII

MAY 12

The Armies Reach Stalemate at the Bloody Angle

"All the hosts of hell in assault upon us."

BY 7 A.M.—two and a half hours after Hancock's and Burnside's soldiers had stepped blindly into the foggy morning glow—the battle had achieved a deadly equilibrium. On the salient's eastern leg, Gordon and Wilcox had fought Barlow, Gibbon, and Potter to stalemate. Attention had focused on the earthworks near the west angle that had been occupied by Monaghan's Louisianians and the Stonewall Brigade. Birney and Mott had pushed on to the second line of works, only to be repelled to the outer ramparts by Ramseur's North Carolinians. The impetuous rebel counteroffensive had recovered the fortifications almost to the west angle. In an attempt to regain the initiative, Grant had ordered the 6th Corps into the fray. Three brigades from Neill's division—Edwards', Bidwell's, and Wheaton's— had added their weight in an attempt to crush the rebel defenders near the disputed western bend in the line.[1]

Lee correctly perceived Grant's objective and shunted more Confederates to the threatened area. Elements from William Wofford's Georgians, of Kershaw's division, hurried east from Old Courthouse Road, behind the 1st Corps line. Two regiments piled into the salient near where Daniel and Battle had secured a lodgment. A Georgian reported that they drove the Federals "beyond our rifle pits." Rodes, a handsome figure grandly riding a black, froth-flecked horse, oversaw the deployments. "Rodes' eyes were everywhere," a Confederate noticed, "and every now and then he would stop to attend to some detail of the arrangement of his line or his troops, and then ride on again, humming to himself and catching the ends of his long, tawny mustache between his lips."[2]

More Confederates were desperately needed in the salient. Lee peti-

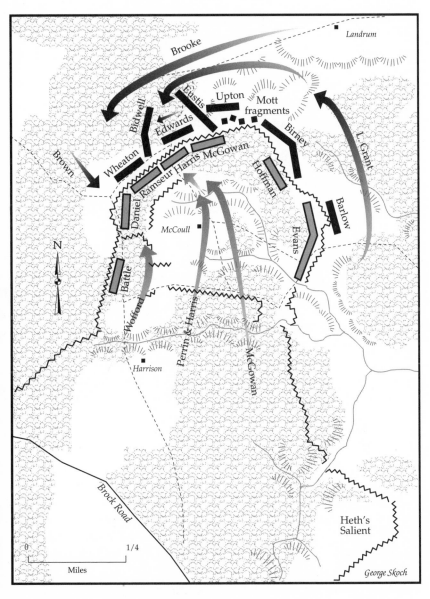

Grant and Lee reinforcing the Bloody Angle on May 12, 7:30 A.M.–10:00 A.M.

tioned Mahone, whose men were west of the Po, to send reinforcements. The sound of a courier's mount sloshing through the mud interrupted Harris' Mississippians, of Mahone's division, from their morning reveries. "Where is General Harris?" the horseman shouted. A bundle of filthy rags stood and replied, "Here. I am General Harris." The courier handed the general a dispatch. "Attention, brigade. Fall in," Harris called. "March by the right flank and follow the courier!" Perrin's Alabamians, camped nearby, led the procession across the Po and on toward the salient. Harris' men snatched the cans of mush they had started cooking, picked up their muskets, and followed next in line. Wright's Georgians remained west of the river to guard the Confederate left flank. "We floundered along in the mud at a double-quick," a Mississippian remembered, "every man in his place and as silent as a tomb."[3]

A four-mile march brought the soldiers to the clearing around the Harrison house shortly after seven. Neill's Federals had massed against the west angle. Walker had been wounded, Daniel had been mortally shot through the abdomen, and Ramseur fought on with a lame arm dangling at his side. "Appalling," an Alabamian deemed the scene. "The field was covered with fugitives, some of the artillery was rushing headlong to the rear, and it looked as if some dreadful catastrophe had happened or was about to happen to the army." Another southerner gauged the fight to be a "fierce one, and one could hear the remark through the ranks that it was Missionary Ridge repeated." Perrin quipped that he expected to become a live major general or a dead brigadier.[4]

Lee, Ewell, Rodes, and Gordon were conferring as Perrin rode up. Reluctant to interrupt, Perrin bade his troops lie down until he received instructions. "Things looked desperate and there was a considerable show of excitement," a soldier reminisced. "Gordon was talking rapidly and literally foaming at the mouth." Ewell noticed the troops and exclaimed, "Oh, for God's sake boys, don't lie down. It don't look well for a soldier to lie down in the presence of the enemy." An Alabamian stood and exculpated the men's behavior: "We were ordered to lie down, General." Ewell piped back, "Oh well, if you were to lie down, lie down. That's all right." The man responded, "No, General, I don't want to do anything that looks badly in a soldier," and remained standing. In his excitement, Ewell could not let the matter rest. "That's all right," he repeated. "Lie down, lie down, if that was the order."[5]

Gordon intervened. "I will take the responsibility and order you to charge," he told Perrin. "Attention!" The soldiers jumped to their feet. The idea was for Perrin to help Ramseur consolidate his hold on the salient and capture the works on Ramseur's right.[6]

The Alabamians charged through the McCoull yard and on toward the works. "As I passed under a heavy cherry tree near the front gate I distinctly remember the shower of the bits of leaves floating to the ground in the still sultry air," a southerner was to mention in his memoir. "They were falling in a constant steady shower from the whole tree, and as I passed through them, I remember that the sight at the moment suggested to my mind a constant fall of snow floating to the ground."[7]

Perrin rode along the brigade's exposed left flank and was shot early in the action while vaulting his horse over the inner works, thus becoming the dead brigadier general of his jest. The 9th Alabama's color-bearer was shot just before reaching the McCoull house. His replacement fell as he swept past the homestead, and a third bearer was hit while between the house and the nearby spring. The Confederates were fortunate in that the Federals tended to shoot high. "If the bullets had been sweeping closer to the ground as thick as they were through the trees," one of Perrin's men concluded, "I don't see how many of us could have gotten through."[8]

In the confusion following Perrin's death, the Alabama brigade drifted in half. On the left, Colonel J. Horace King, of the 9th Alabama, ordered his regiment and Captain William H. Mordecai's 8th Alabama to lie down while he reorganized the command and determined where to attack. Under King's direction, the two regiments charged a fifty-yard stretch of the second line still in Ward's hands, wrested the position back under cover of battle smoke, then continued on to the main works, "without regard to organization, but every man for himself," according to one account. The rightmost regiments swept forward under Colonel John C. C. Saunders, of the 11th Alabama, and managed—"in the face of a storm of grape, canister, and bullets, and finally, at the point of the bayonet"—to join Ramseur. As Federals pressed from the far side of the works, a lieutenant in the 14th Alabama instructed his men, "Now you stand here, and as you see them come I will run the bayonet through them and pitch them over to you and you catch them."[9]

The Alabamians had narrowed the rupture, but reinforcements were essential. The musketry, a witness declared, "exceeded anything I ever heard in its rapidity and volume." Another likened the bullets to a "very river of death." Blistering cross fire raked the traverses, which in places stood too low to afford adequate protection.[10]

Harris' brigade followed closely behind Perrin's and drew up next to Lee and his staff. Lee, it was later said, seemed "very much absorbed with the view he was taking through his glass." A shell exploded nearby, killing two horses, and the general's mount reared just in time for a round shot to pass under his stirrup. Private Burton Conerly, of the 16th Mississippi, was trading shoes with Archie Robertson, another private in his regiment, and had bent over to tie the new footgear "for the benefit of my blistered feet" when the errant ball bounced over his head. He looked up. Lee continued riding to the right of the brigade as though nothing had happened.[11]

"Whose brigade is this?" Lee asked. "Harris' brigade," the men answered proudly. Lee surveyed the powder-stained faces, but did not see Harris. "Where is the general?" he inquired. "I want to see him. But never mind. I'll command this brigade myself. Left face, forward, march." With Lee at its head, the column moved toward the firing. Then, in a dramatic repeat of Gordon's intervention a short time before, Harris rode up, saluted Lee, and insisted that he go back. Lee assented, but on condition that the Mississippians charge and plug the gap between Perrin and Gordon. His face was flushed and his eyes "sparkled with anxiety" as he said, "If you will promise me to drive those people from our works, I will go back." The soldiers replied, "We will! We will, General Lee."[12]

As the Mississippians started toward the Federals, an aide dashed up from Rodes. Ramseur could hold but a few minutes more. Harris had to form immediately on Ramseur's right. "The morning was dark and rain was falling slowly from lowering clouds," a Mississippian noticed. "An almost impenetrable fog hovered near the surface of the ground, which with the smoke of battle, rendered it difficult to see beyond a short distance."[13]

The brigade crossed the creek to the left of the McCoull house in column, pursuing the route Perrin had taken along the McCoull wagon road. Soldiers from the Stonewall Brigade lay sprawled on the ground. One of them shouted, "Boys, you are going to catch hell today!" Harris planned to advance evenly ahead but instead careered endways into pockets of Federals who had remained in the second line of works after Perrin had passed through. Musketry raked the brigade's flanks and killed Colonel Samuel F. Baker, of the 16th Mississippi. "In the emergency," Harris later wrote, "I brought the brigade into line as promptly as possible under a withering musketry fire, by filing the two right regiments to the right, and bringing the two left regiments 'forward into line,' and giving the command to charge." The men ran ahead "at the double," piling into the segment of works already occupied by Ramseur and Perrin, and capturing a stretch farther to the right. Federals blazed back from adjacent traverses and from the salient's far side. "Never did a brigade go into fiercer battle under greater trials," Venable later contended. "Never did a brigade do its duty more nobly."[14]

Rodes's guide unaccountably disappeared, and fog and battle smoke obscured the field, so Harris mounted the earthworks for a better view.

The left extremity of his brigade overlapped Ramseur in the vicinity of the McCoull road. A glance showed that he needed to shift farther right. Harris shouted his command above the din, and the 16th Mississippi's color-bearer, Sergeant Alexander Mixon—"brave and impetuous," in the view of a fellow soldier—sprang over the works with the regiment's flag. "Apprehending the desperate and bloody character of the prospective charge, the men at first hesitated," according to a Mississippian. "But seeing their colors moving forward, borne by the gallant Alexander Mixon, whose clarion-like voice resounded along the line, urging the men to follow, they hesitated no longer." More of Harris' commanders fell, including Colonel Thomas J. Hardin, of the 19th Mississippi, but Mixon was irrepressible. He again climbed the works, fell wounded, then picked up the flag and started forward once more. A bullet ripped through his head and killed him instantly.[15]

Under Harris' direction, the rightmost Mississippi regiments—the 12th and 16th—began fighting their way up the traverses toward the high ground at the west angle. "The movement was executed by the brigade in an admirable manner," one Confederate judged. But the brigade lacked sufficient strength to recapture the entire stretch of earthworks. Neill's Federals continued to press from the entrenchment's far side and to fire into Harris' right flank from adjacent traverses. "To this was added the repeated and determined charges made by the enemy in front," reported a Mississippian. "But for some traverses in the works the position would have been untenable." In places, the combatants pressed so close that their flagstaffs crossed. "The fighting was horrible," a Mississippian recalled. "The breastworks were slippery with blood and rain, dead bodies lying underneath half trampled out of sight." The 16th Mississippi's flag stood at the salient's apex, like a challenge to the Federals. Wave after wave of Union assaults battered the point. Between charges, the Confederates cleared corpses from the trenches and loaded and stacked their rifles in preparation for the next onslaught. "The powder smoke settled on us while the rain trickled down our faces from the rims of our caps like buttermilk on the inside of a tumbler," penned a Mississippian who had stood not ten feet from the flagstaff. "We could hardly tell one another apart. No Mardi Gras Carnival ever devised such a diabolical looking set of devils as we were. It was no imitation affair of red paint and burnt cork, but genuine human gore and gun powder smoke that came from guns belching death at close range."[16]

To Colonel Edwards, whose 6th Corps brigade huddled against the outer face of the salient's tip, Perrin's and Harris' Confederates seemed to attack in waves. He ordered his regiments to hold their fire until the rebels came within fifteen yards. "Five times the enemy charged desperately in three lines in close column, and five times they went down before that wall of fire," Edwards later wrote. "The ground seemed covered with dead, dying, and wounded." Then southern skirmishers charged in open order, attempting to mass sufficient soldiers to overwhelm the works. "We then began file-firing, each man loading and firing as fast as was practicable," Edwards continued. During the remainder of the day, his brigade expended an average of four hundred rounds per man.[17]

Ewell later assured Harris that the "manner in which your brigade charged over the hills to recapture our works was witnessed by me with intense admiration for men who could advance so calmly to what seemed and proved almost certain death." He claimed never to have seen troops under hotter fire. Little did the Mississippians imagine that their ordeal was to continue virtually uninterrupted for twenty hours more. The bend in the salient close by their right flank would henceforth be known as the Bloody Angle.[18]

Hancock was alarmed by Perrin's and Harris' "repeated and desperate" attacks. It seemed to his aide Mitchell that the Confederates had concentrated in "great force, pressing most heavily toward the salient angle of the works." Edwards remained plastered against the angle's face, with the Excelsior Brigade, Bidwell, and Wheaton reaching around to the right. Elements of Mott's division lay interspersed among the 6th Corps units, with most of McAllister's brigade on Edwards' left. Birney connected to McAllister's left wing; then Gibbon and Barlow continued the line around the salient's eastern leg.[19]

At eight o'clock, as Harris pressed his counterattack, Neill called for reinforcements. Wright, still ensconced in his hollow, had already ordered Russell's 6th Corps division to the front, but it would take those troops time to arrive. Wright relayed Neill's plea to Hancock, who began shuttling more men toward the west angle. First he resorted to Brooke's brigade, which had retired to the Landrum house to replenish its ammunition. It was instructed to support Neill but to become engaged only if absolutely necessary. Brooke circled above the Landrum field and emerged a short distance past the west angle, where Wheaton asked him to relieve his fought-out brigade. Brooke explained that he was not to become engaged. Wheaton, however, insisted that Brooke attack "peremptorily," and Brooke acquiesced. Around 9 A.M., he pitched in alongside Wheaton.[20]

Next Hancock directed Lewis Grant to withdraw from Barlow's front and join Neill. The colonel led a portion of his brigade around the salient's face to where Wheaton and Brooke were fighting. The 4th Vermont managed to cross the fire-swept clearing, and soon the rest of Grant's brigade—minus the 6th Vermont, which remained in reserve—had piled into what the colonel described as the "key-point to both armies." Fighting was of a "most desperate and determined character" as soldiers reached over the breastworks and discharged their muskets in their enemies' faces. Men swung muskets and fence rails like clubs, and the air pulsated from an "incessant stream" of rifle balls and exploding shells. "It was a literal saturnalia of blood," a Pennsylvanian remarked as blue and gray battled from opposite sides of the earthworks. "It was grim visaged war in full panoply of horror." To a Mississippian, "the enemy seemed to have concentrated their whole engine of war at this point. Shell of every kind and shape from field pieces raked the approaches of reinforcements, while a forest of muskets played with awful fury over the ground itself."[21]

Lee also considered the west angle a key point and cast about for more troops to tip the deadly balance his way. He found what he needed in Brigadier General Samuel McGowan's 3rd Corps brigade. Less than a week before, Hancock's Federals had overrun these South Carolinians. "This disaster to their prestige was mortifying in the extreme to our brave soldiers and their minds were well prepared to retrieve it at the next opportunity," a southern officer understood. Besides, he continued, the men had become so familiar with danger that they seemed "lost to all sense of fear."[22]

McGowan marched from his bivouac on the far right of Early's line toward the sound of musketry escalating in front of Ewell. "A feeling of unrest among officers of high rank indicated disaster," a colonel recalled of those moments. Then word came to shift to the left. Shells tore up the soggy earth around McGowan's advancing soldiers, "bespattering us with dirt, crashing down the limbs about us and the minnie balls whistled around us at a terrific rate." General Rodes emerged from the haze and demanded the identity of the mud-smeared troops. "McGowan's South Carolina brigade," they replied, to which the general responded, "There are no better soldiers in the world than these." The brigade halted near the McCoull house, the 12th South Carolina on the right, and the 1st, 13th, Orr's Rifles, and 14th Regiments extending to the left. Musketry peppered the formation obliquely from the right. Cheering loudly, the Carolinians charged along the McCoull road and over the inner works, the 12th South Carolina leading. It seemed to one southerner that "Grant had all the hosts of hell in assault upon us."[23]

A minié ball shattered McGowan's arm. Then the brigade's senior officer, Colonel Benjamin T. Brockman, fell wounded. Command devolved on Colonel Joseph N. Brown, of the 14th South Carolina. Tightening the formation, Brown ordered his men to charge. "We did so," a Confederate related, "with a cheer and at the double-quick, plunging through mud knee-deep." A rattling fire decimated their flanks, wounding Colonel Comillus W. McCreary, of the 1st South Carolina, Colonel George McD. Miller, of Orr's Rifles, and several line officers. The 12th South Carolina was wrecked. "They entered the point of greatest danger," a southerner explained, "and received a concentrated fire of artillery that crashed through the works, and the fusillade of infantry from the front and across the traverses on the right flank." Some of McGowan's men accidentally fired into Harris' soldiers, and the two brigades became thoroughly mixed. They stood packed into the little pens between the traverses five or six men deep, "closing constantly to the right, and thus losing all distinct organization," according to one account. A survivor declared it "certain death" for a man to put his head above the works.[24]

Brown recognized that his brigade's survival depended on capturing the angle's eastern face, where Federals were firing into the right flank and rear of his troops. He gave the assignment to Lieutenant Colonel Washington P. Shooter, of the 1st South Carolina, and Colonel Isaac F. Hunt, of the 13th. Shooter waved his sword overhead and fell riddled with bullets. Emboldened by Shooter's example, his men clawed to the salient's tip, some of them running on top of the works. They became jumbled with Harris' Mississippians and occupied the angle's apex and a short stretch of embankment to the right.[25]

The situation, a southerner thought, was "not calculated to encourage us." Dense masses of Federals maintained an incessant fire from traverses to their right. In the Confederate pens, dead men lay on the ground and floated in pools of water, crimsoned with blood. The wounded sprawled in every attitude of pain. A soldier in the 1st South Carolina recollected that "in stooping or squatting to load, the mud, blood, and brains mingled, would reach up to my waist, and my head and face were covered or spotted with the horrid paint." Yankees kept charging the entrenchments, thrusting their guns over, and firing. It was, a Confederate wrote, "plainly a question of bravery and endurance now."[26]

Jammed between traverses, the Confederates lost their regimental organization, nudging ever to the right to fill vacancies created as soldiers nearest the enemy were killed. McGowan held the west angle's tip and part of its right face, Harris its left face, and Ramseur and Perrin the works on Harris' left. In places, the Confederates fought nearly back to back. Communication among units was impossible.[27]

McGowan's onslaught drove the Excelsior Brigade from the salient and back into a deep ravine. That dangerously uncovered Edwards to its left. "The reverse at this point exposed the 10th Massachusetts to a heavy flank fire, and threw them into confusion," Edwards reported, "but with the aid of my staff I soon reformed the line, with the right of the 10th somewhat refused." From the outer face of the angle's tip and eastern leg, the 2nd Rhode Island and 37th Massachusetts poured "well directed oblique fire" into Harris and McGowan. Edwards thought the constant musketry "prevented the enemy from getting up any support to those under cover of the 'Angle,' and materially lessen[ed] the advantage gained." His brigade, however, paid a terrible price. A bullet tore through the scalp of Lieutenant Colonel Samuel B. M. Read, of the 2nd Rhode Island. Major Parker, of the 10th Massachusetts, was killed, and Major Moody, of the 37th Massachusetts, was seriously wounded.[28]

The gap in the Union formation created by the Excelsior Brigade's withdrawal did not last long. Around 9:30, yet another wave of Federals— Russell's 6th Corps division—approached the Bloody Angle.[29]

Early in the morning, David Russell's four brigades—those of Upton, Brown, Eustis, and Cross—had marched to the Shelton house, where Upton had initiated his attack on May 10. Colonel Beckwith, of the 121st New York, suspected something was brewing when an officer started reading from yellow tissue paper. A rebel division and twenty cannon had been captured, the officer announced, and he ordered Upton's brigade to start marching again. "Damn those yellow paper orders," a soldier exclaimed. "That means more fight."[30]

Upton set off toward the Brown place, then turned south toward the west angle. "All the troops further to the right had given way, and here a line had to be formed," he later elaborated, referring to the space created by the Excelsior Brigade's withdrawal. Russell's inspector general, Lieutenant Colonel James N. Duffy, rode up, obviously distressed. "We are going to lose the day," he warned Upton. "The battery you captured on the tenth is now firing to the right, and instead of attacking them the corps is moving off to the left."[31]

Duffy's concern was well founded. Hardaway's Confederate artillery, posted along the salient's western leg, ruthlessly pounded the Federals gathering around the Bloody Angle. Upton was acquainted with the terrain from his attack on May 10 and realized the importance of silencing the pieces. His orders, however, were to relieve Mott. So against his better judgment, he headed straight toward the point of the west angle.[32]

Upton's lead elements slipped into a hollow about a hundred yards from the Confederate works, just west of the Bloody Angle and across from Harris. No general familiar with the situation was available to direct him where to deploy. Wright, who should have been managing his corps' units as they arrived, remained huddled behind a dip in the ground, sheltered from the rebel musketry. Grant and Meade were more than a mile away, completely out of touch with the situation on the field. Union brigades were jamming into a narrow stretch of ground pell-mell, with no sense of purpose and completely uncoordinated.

Soldiers from Colonel Joseph B. Parsons' 10th Massachusetts had already fallen back to the swale for shelter. "This is no position for this regiment," Upton snapped at Parsons. "Swing this regiment over this slope and up against the works." Parsons, having just extricated his men from the deathtrap at the angle, declined to budge. Confused by the total absence of leadership at the front, Upton stamped off muttering about a court-martial, then returned and demanded to speak with Parsons' superior, Edwards. Pulled into the controversy, Edwards directed Parsons to obey Upton, who outranked them both. Parsons again objected and urged Edwards not to follow Upton's orders. In a huff, Upton commanded his regiments to charge the works. It was a foolhardy act, rendered in a spirit very unlike that which had animated him on May 10. The 5th Maine sprinted forward and "received a tremendous fire as they came up out of the ravine, on the front and flank," Parsons observed. "No troops could stand such a fire and they were driven back in confusion, leaving the ground strewn with their dead and wounded." A man from Maine described the charge as "one of the most stubborn fights ever witnessed." Undeterred, Upton ordered the 95th Pennsylvania to attack. The men received a "heavy volley at close range," then lay down "somewhat in disorder," according to a participant. Then the 49th Pennsylvania tried its hand. "Before we had time to shoot we received a terrible volley of musketry, which thinned our ranks fearfully," a participant recorded. Upton, persuaded that he had misjudged the rebel position's strength, conceded to Edwards that "troops cannot live over that slope. I have ordered the [11th New Jersey, which had just arrived] to report to you and I advise that the line be extended from your right around the knoll." Edwards summarized the incident in his unpublished memoirs by saying that Upton "put his brigade in the breastworks which had been occupied by the 10th Massachusetts and Excelsior Brigade, but he quickly found the enfilading fire was so severe that he vacated the works, retiring to the bottom of the slope in his rear."[33]

Eustis' brigade—which had been Russell's—arrived next. "The wounded were streaming to the rear in a steady flow, and the dead from Hancock's charge strewed the field thickly," a soldier in the 5th Wisconsin remembered. "Shot and shell tore the limbs from the trees overhead, or burst above us, while the steady, continuous rattle and crash of the musketry gave indications of the deadly work going on in front." Eustis' men slipped past Upton's right wing and formed on the exposed shelf of land in front of the west angle. The 5th Wisconsin's left wing rested on the rebel works, while the rest of the troops extended at a forty-five-degree angle into the clearing. The Confederates refused to budge. The opposing lines, a Wisconsin soldier explained, "stood at distances varying from half a dozen rods to half a dozen feet, and shot and stabbed each other until the rebel breastworks were filled with dead in gray, and outside, on the glacis in front, the corpses in blue were piled on each other in heaps."[34]

The Bloody Angle had become a killing ground. Upton's lead regiments, joined shortly by the rest of his brigade, hunkered in the ravine and traded fire with the Alabamians, Mississippians, and Carolinians in the works. Union soldiers dug rifle pits along the edge of the depression facing the angle. "We received a continual shower of lead over the pits," a Pennsylvanian wrote. "The rain fairly poured down this forenoon, but we kept up the fire and we were covered with mud from head to foot." Bidwell shifted to support Upton, and the two brigades became so intertwined that they melded into a mass of men firing up the slope. Eustis elbowed behind Bidwell, and Edwards packed close on Upton's left, Wheaton on Upton's right. Grant's Vermont Brigade also wedged into the sector, as did Brooke's 2nd Corps brigade and most of Mott's division. At least six Union brigades and a handful of stray regiments focused their firepower into the west angle, held by Ramseur's, Harris', Perrin's, and McGowan's Confederates.[35]

Battery C of the 5th United States Artillery, commanded by Lieutenant James Gilliss, rolled up in support of Upton and began firing into the works. Then orders arrived for the ordnance to advance nearer to the angle. Lieutenant Richard Metcalf pushed his section within feet of the Confederate entrenchments, on a relatively flat shelf of land, where it began spitting iron at point-blank range. The guns' wheels crushed the dead and wounded into the mud. A soldier in the 95th Pennsylvania believed this the "only instance in the history of the war of a battery charging on breastworks." One gun fired nine rounds, another fourteen. "The effect of our canister upon the Confederates was terrible," a gunner recognized. "You can imagine the execution at that distance." A contingent from the 95th Pennsylvania stuck to the works "like leeches," it was said, firing at any Confederate who looked over the top. Captain John D. Fish, of Upton's staff, rode between the caissons and guns to ensure an uninterrupted flow of ammunition until he was shot from his mount.[36]

Captain Lewis S. Wisner, of the 124th New York, received instructions to reduce the height of a section of breastworks near the angle by eighteen inches so that Union artillery could fire to better effect. Whoever wrote the order was ignorant of conditions at the salient, but Wisner did his best to comply. A heavy log capped the earthworks. Wisner directed soldiers to each end of the beam to lift it off, but it was wired securely and would not budge. Screaming, "I'll do it myself," he grabbed an ax, leaped onto the log, and with two swift strokes severed each end. He sprinted back unhurt, although his clothes were riddled with bullet holes. The battery commander, however, asked him to replace the log, since its removal had made the works too low and exposed the gunners. Wisner ran back, heaved the log into place, and returned unscathed. "You have accomplished the most heroic act I ever witnessed," an officer remarked as he shook Wisner's hand.[37]

Then Mississippians charged the section. Metcalf opened with double canister, and assisted by the 121st New York, drove them back. "I then kept up a fire of spherical case and shell with 1 second fuse until I had lost 11 men wounded," he reported. In a short while every artillery horse had been killed and all but two of Metcalf's men lay dead or injured. Soldiers from the 5th Wisconsin began working the guns, firing two limbers' worth of ammunition that wreaked terrible havoc among McGowan's 1st South Carolina. A Federal estimated the distance to the Confederate works at ten rods. "Solid shot went through their breastworks every time," he remarked, "scattering the rails and logs over the top of it, and giving the lines in the rear a taste of what was going on." When the limbers were empty, more horses were brought up to haul off the guns, but they too were killed. Soon the pieces lay silent, their muzzles still projecting over the works and their wheels buried to the hubs in mud.[38]

Meade concentrated more cannon fire on the salient. The 2nd Corps' artillery chief, Colonel John C. Tidball, deployed Lieutenant John W. Roder's 4th United States battery to relieve Gilliss. Roder advanced a section under Sergeant Thomas Cusack to within four hundred yards of the works, where it did "good execution," according to Roder, "firing solid shot, shell, and spherical case." Tidball also moved Captain Brown's and Captain Albert N. Ames's batteries to the Landrum place, from where they began spewing iron across the field into the works. Captain Arnold was positioned nearby in support, and Captain Edwin B. Dow and Captain R. Bruce Ricketts unlimbered behind the Landrum house, from where they participated in the heavy cannonade toward the salient. Ames dispatched horses and caissons to the rebel works, according to a letter home, and carried off nine Confederate guns captured during the initial charge in "double quick time." A southerner commented that although the artillery fire was not as brisk as at Gettysburg, "at some places along the lines the cannons boomed rapidly and fiercely and the screaming shells filled the trembling air with whizzing fragments and pinging slugs." Federals near Warren's headquarters dodged "tons of railroad iron" tumbling end over end and "screaming like the very devil," recollected a New Yorker.[39]

Wright's aide Hyde brought up more guns—probably Captain James McKnight's section of Battery M of the 5th Regulars—and ordered them over a crest to "assist our musketry with canister." According to Colonel Grant, half of the artillerymen and all of the horses were killed outright. The remaining men tried to unlimber the guns by hand but, unable to manage the pieces in the soft ground, had to abandon them. A subsequent attempt to bring additional guns to the angle also failed. A soldier in the 122nd New York—a small 6th Corps outfit that had become separated from its brigade during the morning's marching and had attached itself to Mott's units at the angle—mentioned that two guns and a caisson dashed to a clear spot less than thirty rods from the angle. The artillerists and their horses were killed instantly. So intense was the Confederate musketry that "no soldier could live there a moment," the New Yorker realized.[40]

"The battle was now at white heat," a Federal observed. "There was one steady stream of iron and lead. It seemed impossible that troops could withstand so severe a fire." Northerners huddled in ranks eight to ten men deep, mire up to their ankles. Rebel artillery cut bloody swaths in the Union formation, which closed as more men jockeyed into position. "Already there were heaps of our dead lying about and impeding our operations," one of Upton's officers recorded. "Our troops got gunpowder crazy, and standing up in the most exposed position, would fire with deliberate aim."[41]

Some Confederates broke under the pounding. A rebel captain vaulted over the works and dashed into Upton's swale screaming, "The devil couldn't stand it in there." The toll in Confederate officers ran so high that rebel foot soldiers fought by reflex, instinctively drawing on the trait—cohesion between their combat units—that made them such formidable adversaries. Colonel Brown, of McGowan's brigade, remarked that the Confederates "had not an officer with them nor did they seem to need them for all along the lines they had special orders to move rapidly to any point of greatest danger."[42]

When the Confederates ran short of ammunition, volunteers tried running back across the McCoull clearing for more powder and balls but could not make it without being shot. Holden Pearson, of the 16th Mississippi, came up with the idea of working to the left, hugging the traverses until he reached a depression that extended to the rear. Crouching low, he made it back and informed Ewell of the situation. Soon a line of Confederates occupied the depression, passing along cartridges bundled in tent cloth. Some hung cartridge boxes on fence rails and hauled them with a man at each end of the load. Prisoners posed a difficult problem. One of Ramseur's men captured five Federals and was directed to take them to the rear. The captives protested that he might as well shoot them, since exposure to the "fusillade of shot and shell then flying over [their] heads" would be "certain death." The Confederate started back with the prisoners, and all five were shot within seconds. "Such was war," the Confederate later reflected. "I never regretted any incident of the war more than this one."[43]

Russell's last uncommitted unit—Brown's New Jersey brigade—slogged from the Shelton place to the edge of the clearing below the Bloody Angle. Couriers told the soldiers that Hancock had captured ten thousand Confederates and twenty-eight guns. "The cheers were interrupted by rebel shells which showed they were still in position," a skeptic gibed in his diary.[44]

At ten o'clock, under driving rain, Brown's men moved partway down the salient's western face to a point just below the battle's storm center, toward where Upton had attacked on May 10. Grant thought that Lee had weakened this sector to reinforce the angle, but it turned out that the works were fully manned and Brown's Federals made inviting targets. They formed in two lines, the 12th, 2nd, and 3rd New Jersey in front, the 4th, 10th, and 15th New Jersey behind. Colonel William H. Penrose, riding at the head of the 15th New Jersey, enjoined his troops from firing until they could see the Confederates behind their entrenchments. "Men were falling everywhere as the brigade emerged into the open field," the brigade's historian reported. The first line broke in confusion, but the second line stood firm while the remainder of the brigade regrouped behind it. The entire formation shifted about a hundred yards to the south, then charged again. Flanking fire nearly obliterated the leading line's right end, where the 15th New Jersey was stationed, but the left continued on. Abatis lay ahead, and beyond loomed dirt embankments topped by logs. "As soon as we appeared, charging over the open plain, they poured upon us their deadly, concentrated fire," a Federal was to write.[45]

Portions of the first line continued through the abatis and over the works but were powerless to exploit the breakthrough. "The tenure of our part of the captured works was brief," a New Jersey man explained. "We were engaged a single half hour," an officer confirmed, "but there are occasions when minutes exceed, in their awful bearing, the weeks and years of ordinary existence."[46]

No sooner had Brown's survivors retreated to the safety of the far woods than a German in the 15th New Jersey turned back toward the works. The Confederates assumed that he was deserting and cheered. But on reaching the ramparts, he grabbed a rebel flag and ran back across the field, dodging bullets all the way. He arrived with a hole through his hat and three holes through his shirt. Amazingly, he was unhurt, and he proudly presented the flag to an officer. "I had a conversation with the soldier a few minutes after his arrival," a member of the regiment affirmed, "and he was fittingly looked upon at the time as the hero of the regiment."[47]

Brown and his adjutant were wounded. The New Jersey brigade's historian reported the unit's loss as very heavy, "the regiments at line up showing mere skeletons." The 15th New Jersey counted 151 casualties, more than half the number of troops who had reported that morning. Only four out of fourteen line officers remained. "The gallant 15th Regiment is no more a regiment and it brings tears to one's eyes as he looks upon the little band which now gather around our colors," a soldier wrote home. "The whole Jersey Brigade, comprising six regiments, will not make more than one good-sized regiment when it is consolidated." It played no further part in the battle.[48]

Wright continued passively to monitor his corps' progress—or its lack of progress—from his sheltered hollow near the west angle. The spot, Lyman recorded, remained "very hot," with artillery shells screeching overhead from both directions. General Russell dropped by for a chat, "calm and natural as a May morn." After exchanging pleasantries with Wright, Russell announced that he intended to "go up and see how they are getting along." Upton left with Russell, and almost at once his horse was shot from under him.[49]

By 10:30, the Confederates had fought the Union 2nd and 6th Corps to an impasse. Victory, which had seemed so certain a few short hours before, had eluded General Grant. Again he cast about for opportunities to regain the initiative. He could ram more troops toward the west angle, but the morning's experience suggested that piling on more men was not the answer. It was time, he concluded, to apply pressure against Lee's flanks, which he assumed the Confederate commander in chief had weakened to bolster his center. So once more, in a pattern that was becoming all too familiar, a courier set off with orders to Warren to attack Laurel Hill.

"Meade has assumed the responsibility and will take the consequences."

Warren's assignment for May 12 was to occupy the entrenchments west of Brock Road—which included his own works and those vacated by Hancock during the evening of the 11th—and to exploit opportunities as they arose. Griffin's division anchored Warren's left flank on Brock Road, then Cutler and Crawford continued the line westward. During the early morning, Warren extended his line still farther by shifting Bartlett's brigade to the right, easing the Maryland brigade west of Bartlett, and then buttressing his far right flank with Colonel J. Howard Kitching's Heavy Artillery brigade, recently sent over by Meade. By sunrise on the twelfth, the 5th Corps was strongly posted to defend Meade's right wing while the rest of the army attacked the salient.[50]

Opposing Warren was Field's division of the Confederate 1st Corps, which still filled the strong entrenchments along Laurel Hill. Bratton's South Carolina brigade faced Griffin's division across the Spindle farm. Dudley M. DuBose's Georgians, Perry's Alabamians, Anderson's Georgians, and Gregg's Texas and Arkansas outfit continued Field's line west to the Po.

Around 5 A.M., Warren received word that Hancock had carried the salient. "Have your command in readiness to advance," he instructed Crawford, "and press forward your skirmishers where it is possible." At six o'clock, as Hancock faltered and Lee counterattacked, Meade alerted Warren to "keep up as threatening an attitude as possible to keep the enemy in your front." He added that Wright "must attack and you may have to," and instructed Warren to "be ready and do the best you can." Warren in turn advised his division heads to expect orders to advance at any moment. They were to lead off with a strong skirmish line to draw the enemy's fire.[51]

As Wright's offensive stalled, Grant and Meade concluded that the time had come to throw the 5th Corps into the fray. "Wright says his right is attacked strongly and wants support," Meade informed Warren at 7:30 A.M. "Your attack will in a measure relieve him, but you must also support him with some of your troops or you will be turned." Warren responded by intensifying his artillery bombardment and by directing most of Bartlett's brigade and all of Kitching's to shift left and help Wright. He felt uncomfortable, however, ordering his corps to charge. Despite headquarters' growing conviction that Lee had to be drawing troops from his flanks to reinforce the salient, Warren saw no signs that the Confederates were abandoning Laurel Hill.[52]

At eight o'clock—Perrin and Harris had charged into the west angle, and Meade had countered with Brooke, Lewis Grant, and Upton—Meade instructed Warren to "attack immediately with all the force you can, and be prepared to follow up any success with the rest of your force." The order struck Warren as ludicrous. The previous four days had convincingly established that Laurel Hill could not be taken by direct assault. He protested that he had "no time to attack the key points first." In particular, he expressed reservations about attacking the strong Confederate works in front of Crawford and further agonized that the Confederates fighting Wright might flank him if he advanced. Nevertheless, Warren assured Meade, "Your orders have been issued and reiterated."[53]

After signing the missive, Warren felt compelled to remind Meade that Laurel Hill was so strong that a few Confederates could hold it. Meade, however, was under intense pressure from Grant to send Warren forward. It was against his own better judgment, too, that he had directed the 5th Corps to attack. "Push on, for now is our time," Meade concurrently telegraphed Hancock. "Warren is going in to do all he can and keep troops from you."[54]

At 8:15, bowing to Meade's unequivocal order, Warren sent part of his corps forward to probe Laurel Hill. "It was the fourth or fifth unsuccessful assault made by our men, and it is not a matter of surprise that they had lost all spirit for that kind of work," Roebling was to report. "Many of them positively refused to go forward as their previous experience had taught them that to do so was certain death on *that* front."[55]

Portions of Sweitzer's brigade—the 62nd Pennsylvania, the 9th Massachusetts, and the 32nd Massachusetts, commanded by Colonel George L. Prescott—charged as far as the ashen ruins of the Spindle house. "I knew what the result would be when I started," Prescott lamented. Parker's Confederate gunners jerked their lanyards, and the clearing exploded in a blaze of fire. Bratton's South Carolinians waited until

Prescott was about fifty yards away, then, according to Bratton's report, "by a deliberate and well-directed volley, . . . strewed the field with dead and wounded from their scattered and flying hordes." Prescott retired in disorder with heavy losses. The 32nd Massachusetts, which sent 190 men forward, suffered 103 casualties.[56]

The rest of the 5th Corps refused to budge. Crawford's division stayed behind its earthworks, and Cutler's moved up until it stood even with Crawford but declined to advance farther. Confederate gunners unleashed another hefty round, then stopped firing to conserve ammunition. "As I remember it, the quiet was almost unbearable," a Federal reflected. "Our men, yet weary from continuous marching and fighting and digging, lay at full length on the cool, fresh earth; silent, too tired even to grumble."[57]

Warren canceled the attack. "My left cannot advance without a most destructive enfilade fire until the Sixth Corps had cleared its front," he reported. "My right is close up to the enemy's works, and ordered to assault." He continued that the Confederate line was "strongly held," then capped his objections by suggesting that the position was Lee's "point-d'appui if he throws back his right."[58]

Meade lost his temper. He was under intense pressure from Grant to keep attacking, the 2nd and 6th Corps were locked in a death struggle, and Warren was busy explaining why he could not help. And he was making excuses in French! Meade directed Warren that his order was "peremptory that you attack at once at all hazards with your whole force, if necessary." An aide related that Grant and Meade were "greatly chagrined at this delay, for it was losing all the advantages that Hancock's brilliant achievement had obtained." A 6th Corps staffer suspected that Warren "represented himself harder pressed than he was." In fact, Warren had realistically appraised the situation. Laurel Hill was impregnable. Grant, however, remained bent on pressing Lee across his entire formation, regardless of the cost. His fighting blood was up and he sought to bring every Federal corps into play, even if the chance for success at any particular location was negligible. This style of warfare—a repeat of Grant's disastrous tactics of May 10—was antithetical to Meade's, but the Army of the Potomac's commander saw no practical choice but to acquiesce. Warren was taking the brunt of that acquiescence.[59]

Humphreys had been assigned to monitor the 5th Corps. He was Warren's longtime friend and professional associate, having supervised Warren on his first assignment with the Topographical Engineers, in 1850, and he did his best to persuade Warren to order the charge that Grant and Meade were demanding. Warren's future in the army depended on it.

"Don't hesitate to attack with the bayonet," Humphreys counseled, then appended another consideration bearing on Warren's career. "Meade has assumed the responsibility and will take the consequences," he promised, signing the note, "Your friend." In a companion dispatch, Humphreys reminded Warren that Hancock and Wright were hard pressed, which meant that the Confederates could not be very strong in front of him.[60]

The pressure was too much for Warren. He gave in, although he distanced himself from the decision. "General Meade repeats in most peremptory manner the orders to attack at once with your whole force," he informed Griffin. "Do it," he directed, then paraphrased Humphreys' advice. "Don't mind consequences." He sent similar messages to Cutler and Crawford.[61]

A hushed silence prevailed as the 5th Corps troops lay sprawled in mud. "We were stiff with cold," a Federal had not forgotten years later. "The ground was soft and we could hardly move." A colonel took out his watch and pointed glumly toward Laurel Hill. "Attention! Forward, double-quick!" he shouted, and the 5th Corps started ahead with a yell.[62]

Griffin's soldiers again stepped into Spindle's Field. A leaden blizzard slammed them back. Bratton boasted that he "routed and put the whole mass to flight, most precipitate and headlong." He gloated, "In their haste and panic a multitude of them ran across a portion of open field and gave our battery and my line on the right a shot at them, the skirmishers too." Union casualties were severe. A Yankee, running back, heard the "dull peculiar thud sound of a ball as it entered some poor fellow." Another Federal called the field a "slaughter pen." A third deemed the venture an "utter failure."[63]

Advancing on Griffin's right, Cutler immediately ran into trouble. Edward Bragg commanded Cutler's first line, which consisted of his own brigade of Pennsylvanians and William Robinson's Iron Brigade. A second line comprising Peter Lyle's and Colonel Edward B. Fowler's brigades followed close behind. Griffin's collapse had uncovered Cutler's left flank, and Crawford was slow in starting on Cutler's right, which meant that the division charged alone with both flanks exposed.

Cutler's first line descended into a ravine near the works occupied by DuBose's Georgians. There Colonel Rufus Dawes, whose 6th Wisconsin was leading, halted to give the second line time to pull up. Ahead rose a cleared stretch of ground, then sharpened abatis, and finally frowning Confederate earthworks. "It was plain that no body of troops could pick its way through such a formidable obstruction as long as the works were

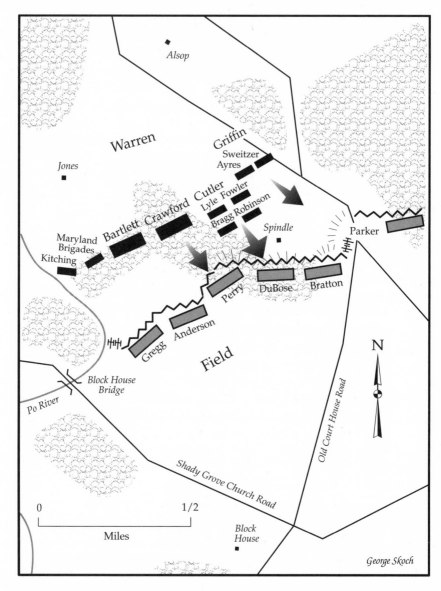

Warren's attack against Field on May 12 at 10 A.M.

properly manned," a Federal concluded as he dodged under a shower of musketry and canister. Cutler's first line lay pinned in place. "In less than fifteen minutes after we became engaged the ravine lay full of dead men, while hundreds of wounded were on their way to the hospital," a Pennsylvanian noted in horror.[64]

Lyle and Fowler joined the front line in the ravine. "Down from the rebel right thundered shot and shell, making great gaps in our ranks, while on swept the brigade, until suddenly loomed up in our front, three lines of works—literally a tier, one above the other—bristling with rifles, ready aimed for our reception," a northerner related. "Again and again did our brigade charge, and as often came those terrible sheets of flame in our faces, while solid shot and shell enfiladed our lines." Men were literally swept away, "even as the coming wind would sweep the leaves from the laurel overhead." The Iron Brigade's 7th Indiana endured what one soldier termed the "most thrilling, frightful experience of its entire three year service." Pushing ahead to explore an apparent gap in the Confederate works, the regiment found itself enfiladed from both sides. "To advance, was certain death or capture; to remain here, no better; to get away, its only chance for safety, and that was what it did," a participant reported. The color-bearer fell back to a dilapidated farm house, climbed onto the roof, and unfurled the regiment's banner, shouting, "Rally round the flag, boys! Rally once again!" His brave action halted the stampede to the rear, but the regiment was out of the fight.[65]

Lyle directed the 16th Maine's major, Abner Small, to secure either more ammunition or permission to withdraw. Small found Cutler nervously watching shells tear through the branches around him. "Don't know that I can get a round of ammunition to your brigade," Cutler responded. "Tell Colonel Lyle to hold his position until relieved." No sooner had Small returned to the ravine than an exploding projectile whirled the 16th Maine's adjutant around like a top. "The ranks were fast disappearing," a Pennsylvanian objected, "and to hold men to such an unequal contest was only a useless sacrifice of life." A soldier in the Iron Brigade considered the movement "almost a farce for we scarcely got but a few paces beyond our lines."[66]

Colonel Dawes scrambled out of the ravine and confirmed to Cutler the dire picture that Major Small had drawn. It was impossible to advance. Cutler informed Warren of the situation, but the corps commander was concerned that withdrawing the division would bring Grant's and Meade's wrath down on him. He refused to let Cutler retire unless the general put the request in writing. Cutler dutifully scribbled that he was "losing badly" and could not get his men to charge.[67]

Meanwhile Crawford's Pennsylvania Reserves charged toward the works held by Perry. "Things are never so bad but that they might be worse," a Pennsylvanian remarked, "and this was proved when the brigade was again ordered to assault the works." Perry opened fire with "all the vigor characteristic of our ubiquitous Southern friends," a Federal observed. Another expressed dismay that he had "scarcely reached the crest of the hill until the same staggering fire that told so fearfully upon our ranks on the morning of the 10th, was again experienced." Crawford withdrew. A soldier observed in disgust that the charge had accomplished nothing "except to add more names to the long list of disabled." An officer in the 11th Pennsylvania grieved that his regiment left "on that fatal hill, as an additional sacrifice to its evil genius, seventy-five men."[68]

Field reported that the Federals "made a determined effort to break through, but they were repulsed with great slaughter." Pendleton, commanding Lee's artillery, added that the "column of the enemy as it came up to assault was shivered by the tremendous destructiveness of missiles hurled upon them at close range from our guns." A Confederate cannoneer claimed, "We have given them the worst whipping they ever got on the 12th." Major Campbell, of the 47th Alabama, was shot through the head to become Field's only significant casualty.[69]

The 5th Corps' attack against Laurel Hill ended in slaughter, just as Warren had predicted. Protected by earthworks, a single Confederate division had fended off a Union army corps. Grant had hoped that Warren's assault would either overrun Laurel Hill or force Lee to divert troops from the salient. It did neither. Colonel Dawes later proclaimed May 12 the "most terrible twenty-four hours of our service in the war," and many of Warren's soldiers agreed. A man in the Iron Brigade wrote home, "Gettysburg is a skirmish compared to this fight."[70]

Humphreys, who was with Warren when news of the 5th Corps' repulse filtered back from the front, agreed with Warren's assessment. Satisfied that the assaults could not succeed, he ordered them to stop. Meade, however, was extremely irritated. "Warren seems reluctant to assault," he complained to Grant shortly after 10 A.M. "I have ordered him at all hazards to do so, and if his attack should be repulsed to draw in the right and send his troops as fast as possible to Wright and Hancock." Grant was in no mood to humor Warren. "If Warren fails to attack promptly, send Humphreys to command his corps, and relieve him," he commanded Meade, noting also that he had ordered Burnside to push "vigorously" and to send a division to Hancock.[71]

As it became clear that Warren was stymied, Grant and Meade reconsidered how best to employ the 5th Corps. Warren could defend his line with relatively few troops, and Hancock and Wright were calling for reinforcements. So they decided to leave Warren a division to hold his earthworks and to send his remaining two divisions to Hancock and Wright, where they might do some good. When Humphreys wired that the 5th Corps' pickets needed more time to withdraw, Meade snapped, "Do not wait for the pickets, but move on. I wish at least two divisions of the Fifth Corps, one for Wright (Cutler's) and one for Hancock (Griffin's)." He added, "Make the best disposition of the balance and your artillery, and let even the balance be ready to come this way." Thus Meade stripped Warren of all but Crawford's division and left him to police the line across from Laurel Hill with his diminished force. He would have no further involvement in the day's contest.[72]

Warren's reputation was in shambles. On May 3, Warren had assured his wife that the campaign offered great opportunity for advancement. Now Grant was considering relieving him of his command. "I feel sorry to be obliged to send such an order in regard to Warren," the commander in chief told his staff. "He is an officer for whom I had conceived a very high regard. His quickness of perception, personal gallantry, and soldierly bearing please me, and a few days ago I should have been inclined to place him in command of the Army of the Potomac in case Meade had been killed. But I began to feel, after his want of vigor in assaulting on the eighth, that he was not as efficient as I had believed, and his delay in attacking and the feeble character of his assaults today confirm me in my apprehensions."[73]

Grant's appraisal was unfair. It was patent to Warren, his subordinates, and Humphreys, who was with them at the front, that Laurel Hill could not be taken. But Grant and Meade continued issuing orders from their distant headquarters with no appreciation of the situation that Warren faced. As he had on May 10, Grant persisted in demanding assaults on the basis of his blind faith that attacking across Lee's line was bound to find a weak point somewhere. Unfortunately for the 5th Corps, the weak point was not in front of them.

Humphreys assumed responsibility for terminating the Laurel Hill offensive, thereby saving Warren from dismissal. Meade found himself in an uncomfortable situation. His warrior instincts agreed with Warren, but his survival as the army's commander required him to preserve his uneasy alliance with Grant, and Grant was extremely annoyed with Warren. A few weeks later, Meade penned a carefully hedged letter to Grant's aide Rawlins that managed to praise Warren at the same time that it criticized him. "On the morning of May 12 when Hancock was so severely pressed, under the instructions of the Lieutenant General commanding, I sent a clear and positive order to General Warren directing him to attack immediately," Meade began. Meade contended that Warren had misled him into believing that a vigorous attack would be made, when in fact it was not. Meade accepted Warren's right to protest against assaulting Laurel Hill, since "so far as such matters could be judged in advance, his opportunities were much better than mine." What rankled Meade was that Warren had "no right to delay executing his orders under any circumstances, and that if he did not think himself justified in [attacking] he should have advised me promptly of what his views were, saying 'such is my opinion, but I shall proceed to attack unless otherwise ordered.'" Meade added, "Such is my opinion of General Warren's judgment that in nine cases out of ten, I would have yielded my judgment—possibly in this case, where the attack was intended as much for a threat and to occupy the enemy, as for other objects—[or] I might still have reiterated my order, for there are occasions where doubtful attacks are rendered of the highest importance for their bearing and influence at other points."[74]

In truth, Warren had acted responsibly. He had been directed to execute a charge whose futility was apparent to everyone at the battlefront, including Humphreys. And after doing his best to avoid sacrificing his corps, he had obeyed Meade's order. But in questioning the wisdom of attacking, he had run afoul of Grant, planting the seeds of his own ruin in Laurel Hill's blood-soaked soil. Within a year, they would bear bitter fruit.

"A scene indescribable in its terrible horror."

By late morning, Lee had decided against trying to hold the salient any longer than necessary. The remnants of Johnson's shattered division labored to construct new entrenchments along a ridge immediately behind the Harrison house. By eliminating the salient, Lee planned to array Anderson and Ewell along a relatively straight line from the Po, on the west, to a point below Steuart's former position, on the east. He needed time, however, to prepare the earthworks. Until then, the frontline troops would have to hold the salient. The Army of Northern Virginia's survival depended on it.

Grant considered the Bloody Angle Lee's weak point and continued to concentrate troops there, seemingly haphazardly and with no one at the front exercising overall control. Around 10:30, the first of the 5th Corps' detached units—Kitching's brigade of Artillery Heavies—piled into a sheltered dip near Upton's right flank. Lyman caught a glimpse of Kitching in a tall felt hat, its brim turned down against the rain, riding about in a "cheery manner." Kitching's first assignment was to try to man some pieces—probably Metcalf's—that stood abandoned near the earthworks.[75]

Only one 6th Corps division, Ricketts', remained unengaged. At eleven o'clock, that unit was ordered forward. The troops reached the front around noon and advanced in a stoop. Wright, mindful of the division's poor reputation, asked Ricketts if the men would fight. Ricketts answered, "I think they will," and reiterated, "I have been talking to the officers; and I think they will." Wright responded, "Very well, then, move in by the left flank and attack."[76]

Ricketts held most of Benjamin Smith's brigade in reserve and advanced his other brigade—commanded by the 87th Pennsylvania's Colonel John W. Schall after General Morris was wounded on May 9—so that its position was close to the fighting. Schall's men became engaged at once and suffered severely. The 126th Ohio, of Smith's brigade, pressed to within a hundred yards of the west angle, next to Wheaton. "Having no protection but a few small pines six or eight inches in diameter, the men lay down," a soldier explained. "They loaded lying; then rising to their knees, took deliberate aim at the heads of the rebels above the parapet and fired." The Ohioans fell at a "fearful rate" and soon exhausted their ammunition. Some resorted to scrounging cartridges from the dead. The 126th regiment lost about seventy men, including its commander, who was wounded in the head.[77]

During the morning, Company F of the 2nd Battalion of the 15th New York Heavy Artillery brought out eight 24-pound brass Coehorn mortars. These weapons heaved shells some 1,200 yards in high, curving arcs and were ideal for bombarding entrenched positions. Soon the air groaned with all the "hideous deviltry of warfare," as a regimental history called it. New Jersey troops near the mortars passed their time making macabre wagers whether an arm, foot, or head would next be blown into the air. According to a Mississippian, most of the mortar shells landed harmlessly in the rear, and a few fell short and detonated among the Yankees. One round, however, exploded near the 16th Mississippi's flag, blowing a Confederate to pieces and decapitating another. The headless body remained erect, blood spurting out in a slowly descending fountain. "Clear the ditch!" shouted an officer, and the Confederates pitched the corpses out. Federals who later examined where the projectiles had fallen proclaimed the sight one "from which the hardest heart recoiled."[78]

The Civil War had seen its share of horrors. The Bloody Lane at Antietam, the stone wall at Fredericksburg, and the Wheatfield at Gettysburg were synonymous with carnage. They paled, however, when measured against the slaughter along the short stretch of earthworks where the salient's western tip bent south. "It was the concentration of each party in one of the grandest struggles of the war," a New Jersey officer asserted. "At every assault and every repulse new bodies fell on the heaps of the slain, and over the filled ditches the living fought on the corpses of the fallen. The wounded were covered by the killed, and expired under piles of their comrades' bodies."[79]

Terrain made the Bloody Angle the focal point of the day's fighting. On the Union side of the works, two ravines—one running roughly east to west, the other roughly north to south, off the eastern face of the west angle—served both to funnel attacking forces toward the Bloody Angle and to afford them relatively safe places to regroup, sheltered from Confederate musketry. Along the nose of the salient, between the west and east angles, the approaches from the Federal side were exposed for a considerable distance. Hence few assaults came from that direction. A relatively flat wedge of land, however, extended from the front of the west angle toward the ravines. Union troops formed in the nearby swales, then charged across the table in front of the angle in the attempt to overrun the earthworks. Ceaseless musketry swept this sector, which was soon carpeted with blue-clad corpses mutilated beyond recognition.

Hancock's aide Walker concluded that "never before, since the discovery of gunpowder, had such a mass of lead been hurled into a space so narrow as that which now embraced the scene of combat." A gauge of the firepower concentrated against the Bloody Angle lay in the damage inflicted on foliage. "Large standing trees were literally cut off and brought to the ground by infantry fire alone, their great limbs whipped into basketstuff that could be woven by the hands of a girl," according to a soldier. Converging Union musketry chewed through a twenty-inch oak. The tree tumbled into a traverse manned by the 1st South Carolina. Virtually every Federal unit stationed near the salient claimed credit for the feat.[80]

"Here was nothing of glamor, but unmitigated slaughter, a golgotha without a vestige of the ordinary pomp and circumstances of glorious war," Meade's biographer later wrote. For the aide Hyde, the day blurred into scenes of "bloodshed surpassing all former experiences, a desperation in the struggle never before witnessed, of mad rushes, and of as sudden repulses, of guns raised in the air with the butts up and fired over log walls, of our flags in shreds." Colonel Grant, of the Vermont Brigade, described how "nothing but the piled up logs or breastworks separated the combatants. Our men would reach over the logs and fire in the faces of the enemy, would stab over with their bayonets. Men were shot and stabbed through crevices and holes between the logs. Men mounted the works with muskets rapidly handed them, kept up a continuous fire until they were shot down, when others would take their places and continue the deadly work."[81]

The slaughter raged so intensely for so long and involved such close and sustained contact that several otherwise articulate chroniclers fumbled for words to convey its enormity. "Nothing can describe the confusion, the savage blood-curdling yells, the murderous faces, the awful curses, and the grisly horror of the melee," a veteran remarked. "Of all the battles I took part in, Bloody Angle at Spotsylvania exceeded all the rest in stubbornness, ferocity, and in carnage." Another referred to the fight as a "seething, bubbling, roaring hell of hate and murder." One of Miles's officers termed the salient a "hissing cauldron of death," and a man in McAllister's brigade thought it the "death-grapple of the war." A Massachusetts soldier said simply that "it was so bloody, and had such an aspect of savagery about it, that it is well to leave the details to be filled in by the imagination of those who wish for the completed picture." A participant scrawled in his diary, "I have seen so much that I can't nor will put it in this book. I will seal this in my memory by myself."[82]

Incidents impressed themselves indelibly on the participants. "I never over four years of active service witnessed so many individual acts of daring and foolhardiness on the part of soldiers as on this day," a Federal affirmed. He was particularly struck by a drunken artillery officer who rode a spirited horse, swinging his hat and calling on the men to charge. The officer escaped unharmed while the men around him were killed or wounded. Several Union soldiers later commented on the carnage around a twelve-pounder that the rebels had abandoned during Hancock's initial charge. Mott's soldiers tried to drag the piece into their lines, but Ewell's sharpshooters picked them off. By the end of the day, bodies lay heaped around the gun. A soldier retained vivid memories of his companions, soaked with rain, "their faces so begrimed with powder as to be almost unrecognizable; some standing ankle deep in red mud, firing, while the edge of the ditch was lined with others sitting and loading as fast as possible and munching hard bread, the crumbs of which were scattered around their smutty mouths and besprinkled their beards." A Mississippian remembered a fellow soldier who had been shot in the head, blood and brains oozing from the wound. The injured man reached into his pocket, took out a piece of tobacco, and rolled over dead while attempting to take a chew. It was, marveled the Mississippian, the "most singular thing I ever saw in my life." Overall, concluded a man who fought there, the Bloody Angle was "ghastlier than anything ever seen before in this land."[83]

Perhaps Hyde best summarized the contest there. "I never expect to be fully believed when I tell what I saw of the horrors of Spotsylvania," he wrote after the war, "because I should be loath to believe it myself, were the case reversed."[84]

"The hottest place I have been in since Manassas."

By two o'clock in the afternoon, the struggle at the Bloody Angle had reached an impasse. Grant and Lee, each seeking to break the deadlock, searched for opportunities elsewhere. In a remarkable coincidence of vision, each selected the salient's eastern leg, where Early faced Burnside, as offering the most promise. Grant decided to attack what he presumed to be a thinly defended segment of the Confederate works. And Lee saw an opportunity to attack Burnside's vulnerable left flank and force Grant to divert troops from the salient. If Lee's luck held, he might roll up the Federal line, much as Longstreet had done in the Wilderness. By chance, Lee and Grant selected the same moment and place to launch their attacks. The result was a confused and bloody muddle completely in keeping with the rest of the day's fighting.

Grant had tried various ploys all morning to induce Burnside to put the 9th Corps into play. First he asked Burnside to link firmly with Hancock on his right. When nothing happened, he sent Burnside increasingly pointed missives. "Push the enemy with all your might," he insisted. "That is the way to connect. We must not fail." Around nine o'clock, Burnside reported that he had advanced his northernmost division under Potter onto Hancock's left flank. He gave no indication, however, that he intended to go on the offensive.[85]

As fighting escalated around the Bloody Angle, Burnside's inaction increasingly distressed Grant. At ten o'clock—Russell was by then piling into the west angle to join Mott, Neill, Getty, and Brooke, and Warren was attacking Laurel Hill—Grant instructed Comstock to tell Burnside to "push hard with everything he can bring into the fight." Still nothing happened, so Grant issued a peremptory order. "Move one division of your troops to the right to the assistance of Hancock, and push the attack with the balance as vigorously as possible," he commanded. Perhaps hoping to shame Burnside into activity, he added, "Warren and Wright have been attacking vigorously all day." He concluded with a barb: "See that your orders are executed."[86]

Grant's acerbic dispatches incensed Burnside, who vented his anger on Comstock, accusing the aide of complaining to Grant about his conduct. Comstock denied that he criticized Burnside behind his back, but the general was not mollified. "General Burnside," the staffer responded to a repetition of the accusation, "I told you, sir, that I had only telegraphed what you were actually doing—that Grant's telegram contained no reference to anything I have telegraphed." Burnside mumbled something about Warren's and Wright's failures, fumed that Hancock was too disorganized to renew his attack, and terminated the conversation in a huff.[87]

Around noon, Grant and Comstock succeeded in finally prodding Burnside into action. Early's artillery had pinned down Burnside's two northern divisions, under Potter and Crittenden. But Willcox' division—posted on Burnside's left, along with the 9th Corps' artillery—was unengaged and available for use elsewhere. Burnside pulled Colonel Hartranft's brigade from its trenches and directed it to join Hancock. But before Hartranft could complete his movement, Grant changed his mind about what he wanted Burnside to do and instructed Burnside to renew his attack against the salient's eastern leg rather than send 9th Corps elements to support the 2nd Corps. The tactical objective was to compel Lee to pull troops that faced Hancock. Orders went out to Hartranft to return to his former position, and to Willcox to prepare his entire division for mounting an assault. Hartranft turned his brigade around and marched it back to its trenches.[88]

Across from Burnside, Early's earthworks traced a ragged line from the right flank of the entrenchments formerly occupied by Steuart to below Fredericksburg Road. During the morning, Early had reshuffled his brigades to satisfy Lee's call for troops, sending McGowan to the west angle and filling the vacancy with Lane's soldiers, exhausted from their earlier fight against Potter. Scales and Thomas were holding the northern end of Early's line. On their right stood Joseph Davis' Mississippians. Below Davis, a huge bulge—dubbed Heth's Salient—jutted west toward the lower portion of Burnside's line. Colonel Robert M. Mayo's Virginians— which had been under Mud Walker until he was wounded, on May 10— and a Tennessee brigade temporarily assigned to Mayo occupied the bulge. Lane filled the works along the underside of Heth's Salient, his left flank oriented toward Burnside. Weisiger's Virginians formed in reserve behind a low ridge, near Lane.[89]

Burnside's ordnance, massed on high ground about a quarter mile east of Heth's Salient, severely enfiladed Lane and Weisiger. Lieutenant Colonel Everard M. Feild, of the 12th Virginia, demanded that his men quit dodging under the "severe shelling," then ducked as a round shot bored into the ground next to him. "Stop that dodging," his men hollered in jest. Some of Weisiger's officers hesitated to seek cover in the mud, "but when the shells shrieked over us, they got closer and closer to the mud, to the amusement of the men," one of the troops recalled. Heth ordered the Crenshaw Battery, of Lieutenant Colonel William J. Pegram's battalion, to shift closer to the Union guns and silence them. The Federal fire, however, proved uncannily accurate. One shell exploded an ammunition caisson and ignited another. Private Chew Coleman, of Spotsylvania, was driving the wheel team of the flaming caisson. His jacket on fire, Coleman subdued the plunging horses and brought them back to the Confederate lines. As Coleman tumbled from his seat, cannoneers unlimbered the burning ammunition chest. Within seconds, it exploded with a roar. A witness considered Coleman's conduct the "bravest exploit that came under my observation in the four years of the war."[90]

Lee visited Heth's Salient near 2 P.M. and selected it as an ideal location for launching an attack against Burnside's left flank. From Mayo's earthworks, he could see Burnside's artillery positioned on a far rise. He could not, however, ascertain the strength of Burnside's infantry protecting the guns, and it was also unclear to him whether the pieces occupied the extreme Union flank, or whether Burnside's line extended farther south. To gather that valuable information, Lee asked Captain W. T. Nicholson, of the 37th North Carolina, to reconnoiter toward the guns.[91]

Nicholson ran several hundred yards in front of the salient to the rebel picket line. Soldiers there warned that even raising a hand risked drawing fire. Undeterred, Nicholson crept ahead to a rise for a better view. Federal sharpshooters wounded a companion who had accompanied Nicholson, but not before the captain had acquired the information Lee needed. He pitched the incapacitated man over his shoulder and started back through a storm of shells. A fragment killed his friend, but Nicholson returned unhurt to tell Lee that no soldiers guarded Burnside's flank.[92]

Lee quickly assembled a force for the assault. Two brigades, Lane's and Weisiger's, were to advance to a patch of woods southeast of Heth's Salient, then attack Burnside's flank, capturing the guns and routing the 9th Corps. The overall strategy, as Lee explained it to Lane, was to create such havoc that Grant would have to withdraw troops from the Bloody Angle, thereby diminishing the pressure against Ewell. Lane initiated the maneuver by sending the 7th and 33rd North Carolina, under Lieutenant

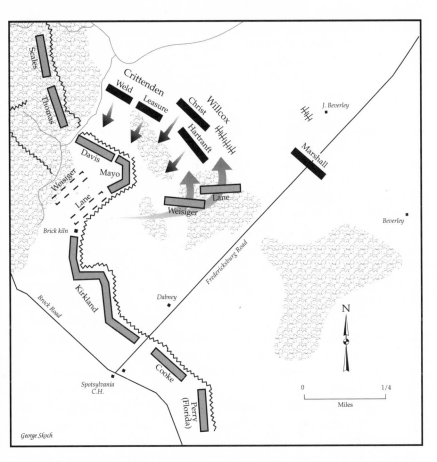

Fighting near Heth's Salient on May 12, 2 P.M.–3 P.M.

Colonel Robert V. Cowan, to the stand of oak trees that was to serve as the attack's staging area. Captain Thomas G. Williamson, of the 7th North Carolina, cleared Burnside's skirmishers from the woods and advanced within striking distance of the artillery. Then Lane arrived with the rest of his brigade, which he arrayed generally north to south, conforming to Burnside's line, its left in the oak woods. The 7th North Carolina was bent back, or refused, to protect Lane's right flank. Weisiger formed in support about a hundred yards behind Lane.[93]

Early directed his two brigades to advance "at once and rapidly." Lane's men charged into the clearing and continued toward the nearest Union battery, which was posted on a small ridge identified in postwar maps as Bald Hill. Weisiger charged more to the north, angling toward Hartranft's brigade immediately above the guns.[94]

Lieutenant Charles T. Haigh, of the 37th North Carolina, led Lane's attack, hat in one hand and sword in the other, shouting, "Charge, boys, charge! The battery is ours!" A soldier observed, "We read often of such things, but they seldom happen. [Officers] generally remain in rear of their men to keep from being shot by them." Inspired by Haigh's example, Lane's troops sprinted "very handsomely" toward Burnside's guns. Canister and round shot crashed through the trees and plowed the ground around them. Haigh fell mortally wounded, and his regiment was severely cut up. "It was terrible, terrible, yet exciting," a survivor of the charge wrote home.[95]

Lane's momentum carried him to the Union guns. Fighting raged fiercely around the 19th New York Battery, which fired a continual stream of canister into the attacking rebels. Captain Edward W. Rogers enlisted his drivers to replace the battery's fallen gunners, and Joseph W. B. Wright's battery and two sections of Adelbert Twitchell's battery, stationed nearby, merged their fire with Rogers'. Willcox' artillery chief, Lieutenant Samuel N. Benjamin, received a horrible neck wound but refused to stop fighting, holding the ragged pieces of flesh together with his hand. Colonel William Humphrey, whose Michiganders defended Rogers' pieces, asserted that nearly every man in Rogers' battery was killed or wounded but that the 2nd Michigan checked the Confederates. Lane maintained that he captured the battery but could not haul it off because he had neither horses nor an adequate road.[96]

Almost simultaneously with Lane's attack, Willcox began his assault toward Heth's Salient. And at the same moment, Weisiger sprang toward the lower edge of Hartranft's brigade, on Willcox' southern flank. Colonel Constant Luce, of the 17th Michigan, learned of the Virginians' attack when a private shouted that Confederates were approaching from the left. A shell killed the soldier, pitching him into Luce and knocking the colonel face down as rebels swarmed over him. "We got in it very heavy," a Virginian succinctly allowed of the close-quarters brawl. "The hottest place I have been in since Manassas," asserted another. Ben May, the 12th Virginia's color-bearer who had won distinction in the Wilderness, was shot by a Federal less than ten feet away. Some of Lane's men apparently shifted north and joined the fray. In the confusion, Luce and several of his soldiers escaped, bringing with them as a prisoner the 37th North Carolina's Colonel William M. Barbour.[97]

On Hartranft's right, Christ's brigade, of Willcox' division, pushed ahead toward Heth's Salient. Early's gunners opened on Christ as he approached, and Weisiger's troops continued their wild advance north across Hartranft and into Christ's lower flank. Bayonets flashing, the Virginians sliced into the 50th Pennsylvania, captured about a hundred Yankees, then continued into the 20th Michigan. "No words of mine can describe the scene that ensued," a Union man wrote. "It literally rained shot and shell all around us and our comrades were falling on every side by scores." Major George C. Barnes faced the 20th Michigan toward Weisiger and "attacked boldly and cut his way out," according to a Union report filed after the battle. He was later commended for his "most reckless bravery, exposing himself where it seemed impossible for a man to live, encouraging and steadying his men regardless of danger."[98]

On Christ's northern flank, the 1st Michigan Sharpshooters advanced under "destructive fire" of musketry and canister to within fifty yards of Heth's Salient. Concluding that it was safer to continue on than to retreat, Colonel Charles V. DeLand led his own 1st Michigan Sharpshooters and the 27th Michigan over the works that Mayo's Virginians occupied. But he was unable to hold his position and fell back across the field, leaving a carpet of bodies behind.[99]

Crittenden's division, positioned on Willcox' right, also joined the attack upon Heth's Salient. Crittenden's leftmost brigade, under Leasure—consisting of the 21st Massachusetts and the 100th Pennsylvania, the 3rd Maryland having shifted northward to assist Potter—marched through the woods toward the northern face of the salient, its left wing reaching toward Christ's right. Mayo's soldiers, well fortified behind their works, pinned Leasure's men to the ground with deadly fire, and Lieutenant Colonel Pegram's artillery battalion unleashed a ferocious volley of shot. Leasure was bending over to hold a wounded soldier when a twelve-pound solid shot crashed through a nearby tree. A branch struck the brigade commander on the head, badly stunning him. After suffering "devastatingly brutal" casualties, as a Federal put it, his soldiers retired about fifty yards to a shallow ravine. There they shot back at the rebel works in an effort to prevent the Confederate defenders from aiming over the ramparts. Some of Pegram's gunners jumped onto the earthworks and dared the Yankees to charge again, shouting, "Come on!" Leasure, who had been in ill health since Vicksburg, a year before, was unable to regain his equilibrium and turned command of his brigade over to Lieutenant Colonel George P. Hawkes, of the 21st Massachusetts. Lieutenant Colonel Stephen M. Weld, Jr.'s brigade pitched in on Leasure's right but failed to reach the Confederate works. Lacking effective artillery backing or infantry support on his flanks, Crittenden was stymied.[100]

After a half hour of fighting, Burnside and Early called off their respective assaults. Flanked by Weisiger and Lane and buffeted in front by Early's artillery, Willcox' column was thoroughly routed "with a slaughter so sickening that the heart heaves at the details," in the words of a Confederate. A Tennessean who had helped defend Heth's Salient contended that, "had there been no Bloody Angle on our left, the Angle held by [Mayo] would have been so regarded." Lane and Weisiger also retired under a rain of Union and Confederate shells. Lane found that "the infantry fire in our rear was for a short time more severe than that in front, as [Weisiger's] Brigade poured such a fire into us that Lieutenant-Colonel Cowan and Lieutenant-Colonel McGill had to rush back and ask them not to fire into friends." He requested Weisiger to form on his right "that we might sweep around to the left and up to our works," but coordination proved impossible. The Confederate attackers retreated "in some confusion," Lane reported, "as the lines had been broken in capturing prisoners, and the woods through which they withdrew rendered it almost impossible to preserve anything like a line of battle."[101]

Lane calculated his losses at 470, although recent research indicates a higher toll. Lane was almost shot during the retreat but was saved by Private P. A. Parker, Company D of the 37th North Carolina, who, Lane wrote, "killed the Yankee that had levelled his gun and was in the act of firing upon me—the Yankee was not more than ten paces from us at the time." Lane and Lieutenant O. A. Wiggins captured a Federal color-bearer and the 51st Pennsylvania's flag on their way back, then rejoined the brigade at Spotsylvania Court House to resounding cheers. In all, Lane claimed a flag from the 17th Michigan and 51st Pennsylvania, Rogers' guidon, and about 410 Federal prisoners. Weisiger's brigade claimed another flag from the 51st Pennsylvania, the same 17th Michigan flag that Lane claimed, and four hundred Federal prisoners. "We captured a number of prisoners greater than we had men in line," one Virginian bragged in a letter home. But they paid severely for the boast. The 12th Virginia alone counted some seventy-four men killed, wounded, and captured, and the brigade's loss approximated 250.[102]

Mahone, who had previously commanded Weisiger's brigade, saw Lane's men pouring back and erroneously concluded that they had abandoned the Virginians. "Where in the hell are you taking these men to?" he demanded of Lieutenant Colonel John W. McGill, of the 18th North Carolina, who was helping an injured companion. McGill started to explain, but Mahone interrupted and ordered him back into the fray with the comment that the "damned North Carolinians were deserting his brave Virginians." McGill retorted that quite the opposite had happened, but this only provoked another vituperative outburst from Mahone. McGill terminated the conversation with the parry that Mahone "might 'go to hell' or anywhere else, but as for me I would form with my command."[103]

Colonel Cowan also experienced Mahone's brusqueness. First the general imperiously questioned why Cowan was "cowardly deserting his 'brave Virginians' to continue the fight without support." Then he crowed that Private Thomas W. Savage, of Company I of the 41st Virginia, had captured the 17th Michigan's flag. It just so happened that Lieutenant James M. Grimsley, of the 37th North Carolina, was standing nearby clutching the disputed banner. According to a later account, Grimsley "became justly indignant, and displaying his flag, exclaimed in the hearing of quite a number of his comrades, and also in the presence of several general officers, 'I captured this flag with my own hands and I can whip the man who says I did not!'" Lane was to report receiving complaints that Mahone had been "riding around on horseback in the edge of the woods, near the Fredericksburg Road, abusing my brigade generally, and claiming for his own most, if not all, of the prisoners that were brought to the rear, when really his brigade was leaving the woods guided by my Adjutant General, unconscious at the time that they were all to be made heroes of by their General for having unnecessarily taken charge of the captives of another command."[104]

Lane and Weisiger failed to roll up the 9th Corps' flank as Lee had hoped. The two Confederate brigades were simply too small a force to overrun Burnside's three divisions, particularly in this confusing terrain. But the foray reaped some advantages for the Confederates. Fortuitously, Lee had struck at precisely the moment that Burnside had initiated his own attack. Lane and Weisiger had caused the flank of Burnside's moving column to collapse, disrupting his charge. Perhaps the Confederate assault was most significant not in what it accomplished but rather in what it demonstrated about Lee's generalship. Hard pressed by Grant's relentless pounding around the Bloody Angle, Lee had lashed back at the first opportunity. He remained as aggressive—and as dangerous—as ever, alert for openings to strike his own blows.

As soon as Lane and Weisiger returned, Lee began exploring the feasibility of assaulting northeast along Fredericksburg Road in another ploy to turn Grant's flank and divert his attention from the salient. Lee again had Nicholson reconnoiter with his sharpshooters. As Nicholson's men started along the roadway, they marched past Lee, removing their hats and cheering. Lee lifted his hat in acknowledgment.[105]

The news Nicholson brought back was discouraging. Burnside's Federals were entrenched in two lines above Fredericksburg Road, waiting to enfilade the Confederates if they marched past. Deciding to test Willcox' resolve, Early ordered Weisiger's and Cooke's brigades to probe the entrenchments, despite the protests of Weisiger and Mahone. One North Carolinian was so incensed that he could only imagine that Early had been drunk.[106]

The two Confederate brigades advanced to where Nicholson's sharpshooters had deployed. Burnside's Provisional Brigade, under Elisha Marshall, comprising green artillery Heavies and dismounted cavalrymen, was waiting in force. The Confederates overran two sets of Marshall's works but were stopped by a third, where massed 9th Corps artillery and Marshall's musketry raked Weisiger's brigade, killing Lieutenant Colonel William F. Niemeyer, of the 61st Virginia, and seriously wounding Colonel Feild, of the 12th Virginia. Even Early was forced to concede that the fortifications posed an "almost insuperable obstacle to the proposed flank movement," and he directed Weisiger and Cooke to retire. The soldiers held the two lines of captured works until dark, when they returned by marching around the extreme right of the Confederate line. According to a rebel, they were "very much fatigued by the day's operations."[107]

"The warmest fight we have yet been called upon to enter."

Grant's attempt to breathe life into his offensive by attacking Lee's flanks had failed. "[Burnside] is a damned Humbug—Warren who is a ditto did about the same," a 6th Corps staffer seethed. Ever hopeful, Grant decided to redouble his efforts against the Bloody Angle. To Meade's inquiry whether Wright could carry the salient if the 5th Corps joined in, Wright responded that he could. Concerned that Grant might ask him to attack alone, Wright quickly added that he could succeed only if reinforced.[108]

It was Grant's decision to augment Wright's corps with two of Warren's divisions, then to try another assault against the salient's tip. At three o'clock, Meade assured Grant that Cutler and Griffin were moving to the 6th Corps' support. "I trust [Wright] will break through the enemy's line," Meade added, promising that "Hancock will press forward at the same time, and I trust Burnside will do the same." Grant put Burnside on alert.

"The Fifth Corps is now moving up to the Sixth and will together form a heavy column of assault," Grant telegraphed his 9th Corps commander. He appended a warning to remain "on the lookout to take advantage of any weakening on your front to meet it."[109]

Shortly after three, Cutler reached the salient. Wright, however, deployed the division contrary to Grant's instructions. Rather than preparing Cutler to assist the 6th Corps in the assault, as Grant had envisioned, Wright dispersed Cutler's units to bolster portions of the 6th Corps' line. Lyle's brigade went to the 6th Corps' right, Bragg's to the left, and Robinson's and Fowler's to the west angle. Wright then notified Meade that he had "put Cutler's division to relieve a part of my troops," but assured the army commander that "with the rest of the Fifth Corps and a part of mine, a column of assault can be formed, which I am confident can carry the enemy's line at the angle." He explained that he had moved Cutler to the front "to relieve exhausted troops who have been firing all day, and can't be used for [the intended assault]." Cutler's scattered elements soon lay pinned under sheets of lead flying from both directions. It was the "warmest fight we have yet been called upon to enter," a Federal held. Lyle's soldiers huddled in rifle pits while the Iron Brigade fired at the salient to keep the Confederates from shooting over their works.[110]

Several Federals remonstrated that the rebels hoisted white rags in token of surrender, "and when we slackened in fire would take advantage of it and shoot at us." In one such episode, Colonel Grant's men took a white handkerchief they spied waving from a musket for a flag of truce, only to be blasted when they looked over the works. Private William W. Noyes, of the 2nd Vermont, was "infuriated beyond control by such treachery." He jumped onto the breastworks, killed the nearest rebel, and called on his comrades to hand him their rifles. Shooting as fast as they could pass him their muskets, he fired until a bullet knocked off his hat. According to Noyes, who subsequently received the congressional Medal of Honor, "fifteen guns had been emptied during this brief and peculiar assault."[111]

In another encounter typical of that afternoon's confused combat, a contingent from the 26th Michigan, under Major Nathan Church, crawled close along the outside of the works from the east angle to a point near the Bloody Angle, then vaulted into McGowan's men, "crossing guns and bayonets." Church noticed several Confederates waving white handkerchiefs and ordered his men to stop firing. In the bizarre conference that followed, Colonel Brown, commanding McGowan's brigade, called on the Federals to surrender. A witness recalled that "the two lines stood, bawling, gesticulating, arguing, and what not." Then a gun discharged, and the killing frenzy resumed. Church visited the spot the next morning. "The dead were literally piled in heaps," he wrote, "and it is a wonder how any one could have lived through those long hours of murderous conflict in which trees were cut down and the breastworks themselves torn up by musket balls."[112]

Near five o'clock, Ayres's and Sweitzer's brigades, of Griffin's division, arrived, thoroughly exhausted after marching through the rain and mud. Wright began thinking of reasons why he could not attack. Cutler, he decided, had become embroiled in the fighting around the salient and could not be massed effectively. And Ricketts' right flank rested on a morass and was not as defensible as he had hoped. Should he not use Griffin's reinforcements to strengthen Ricketts, Wright asked Meade. Then Wright voiced concern that Griffin's reinforcements were fewer than he had expected—Bartlett's brigade had gone on assignment elsewhere— and that he could spare only a thousand men himself. "I doubt whether that is enough to ensure success," he worried, adding that he would "make all preparations and assault, or not, according to my discretion and that of General Hancock, unless positively ordered." He confessed, "What I fear most is a counter assault if ours fails."[113]

At 5:10, Wright abandoned any pretense that he was preparing to attack. It was not, he assured Meade, that he feared failure. Rather, he was concerned about the "disaster which would possibly follow a failure; also the want of a sufficient available and suitable force to insure a reasonable prospect of success." He mentioned that Hancock concurred with him.[114]

Wright's communication spelled the end of the day's offensives. Shortly after six o'clock, Grant instructed Burnside to "strengthen your position so as to hold it against any attack of the enemy, and give your men as much rest as you can consistent with your work in fortifying your position." The 9th Corps was to be under arms by 3:30 the following morning, "for it is not unlikely the enemy will take the initiative; and, if so, your position he will most probably attack." Meade also directed his corps commanders to rest "as far as practicable." The 2nd and 6th Corps were to strengthen their lines and return Warren's troops, and Warren was to shorten his line "so as to afford the greatest number of men available to meet an attack tomorrow, should one be made." Wright protested that he still needed Cutler's and Griffin's divisions, but Humphreys was unmoved. "They were sent to you not to relieve your troops nor to hold your line, but to form a column of attack, which has been abandoned," he reminded

Wright. "Can you not shorten your line?" Wright, fatigued by the day's exertions and perhaps having yielded to his notorious fondness for drink, sullenly insisted, "I can't shorten my line a single foot."[115]

Grant's decision to cancel the evening offensive afforded little relief for the soldiers jammed around the Bloody Angle. Since morning, the same four Confederate brigades—Ramseur's, Perrin's, Harris', and McGowan's—had been fighting there, some without interruption for over twelve hours. A half mile back, near the Harrison house, Johnson's men were still working to complete new entrenchments. Until they were finished, the front line would have to keep fighting. Warren had been quiescent since midmorning, and Lee felt comfortable ordering Anderson to send two brigades to support the forces holding the angle. Bratton and Humphreys shifted into the former reserve line between the McCoull and Harrison places.[116]

Near sundown, the Confederates at the angle slackened their fire. Edwards, sensing an opportunity to rest his men, withdrew three regiments, but his division commander, Neill, ordered him back with instructions to remain "in command of the angle all night." When Edwards protested that his brigade was "too exhausted to stand, load, and fire much longer," Neill explained that Wright had authorized Upton and Bidwell to withdraw at dark and that he wanted Edwards to hold not only his own ground but also the entrenchments the other two brigades had occupied. That struck Edwards as unfair, for he had fought at the angle longer than the others and had sustained heavier losses. "I left him feeling that the load imposed upon my brigade was heavier than they should have been expected to carry," Edwards recounted. Russell rode to the front, commiserated with Edwards, and promised to send help.[117]

The promised reinforcements—the 10th New Jersey—soon arrived and moved into position in front of Upton. Shortly afterward, Bidwell, Upton, and Grant received permission to retire. Some soldiers were so eager to leave that they ran through a gauntlet of bullets to the woods behind them. Colonel Beckwith, of the 121st New York, remained in the trenches until dark, then joined his regiment in the rear. "We were all covered with mud and powder and smoke and grime," he recalled. "We presented a very tough appearance, but being very near exhaustion it was possible for us to huddle about the smokey pine fire with our rubber blankets over us and get some sleep, even though bullets and shells flew in close proximity to us, at frequent intervals during the night." Another Federal claimed to have fired 160 rounds at the angle. He wrote home that his right arm was "useless tonight from the re-bound of my rifle." He admitted, "I am completely fagged out."[118]

After dark, a jumble of 2nd, 5th, and 6th Corps units—primarily from Edwards' and Robinson's 6th Corps brigades, with elements from Mott's 2nd Corps division—remained in the pits across from the Bloody Angle. Edwards was responsible for holding the commands together. Communication proved difficult, because the regiments were mixed and the men and officers were exhausted. When a regiment on Edwards' left retired without permission, the colonel shifted elements from the 37th Massachusetts into the gap. Then the commander of a supporting 2nd Corps brigade threatened to withdraw, complaining that his men were out of ammunition and had not eaten all day. Pointing a gun, Edwards persuaded him to leave his troops in place.[119]

Darkness brought some respite from the killing. Grant's Vermont brigade, its ammunition spent, slipped back to the woods. The Iron Brigade's 7th Indiana and 7th Wisconsin continued fighting, plastered against the outside of the Confederate works and firing at musket flashes less than fifty yards away. The Federals kept "firing so fast that [the Confederates] did not dare stick up their heads," an Indiana man remembered. "We did not dare to stop or the rebs would have given us a volley." The 24th Michigan and 6th Wisconsin relieved them at ten o'clock. A Wisconsin man had the ineradicable memory of standing in mud "half way to our knees, with dead bodies lying all around." The 24th Michigan's historian reported that the regiment's muskets became so foul that details were formed to clean the rifles while the rest of the men continued shooting. Soldiers collapsed in mud and slept soundly "amid the thunders of battle, despite all efforts to arouse them."[120]

There was no moon visible, and a cold drizzle enshrouded the landscape. The blackness, a Confederate observed, was broken only by the "flashing of the guns to light up the horrid scene." Midnight came. Still the firing continued. One of McGowan's men corroborated that among the Confederates, too, "numbers of the troops sank, overpowered, into the muddy trenches and slept soundly." Several hundred yards to the rear, Confederates worked feverishly to complete their new defensive line. Weary men chopped trees in the darkness and stacked them to form breastworks. Others, using picks, shovels, bayonets, and tin cups, heaped dirt on the logs. Bullets hummed around the laboring troops. Ewell and Lee rode among them, reminding them that "the fate of the army depended on having that line done by daylight."[121]

Around three in the morning, the Confederates received orders to retire from the salient. A courier crept into the angle and announced that a new line had been completed. The soldiers were to exercise extreme care in falling back. "The night was dark," an Alabamian reminisced, "but we finally groped our way by pairs or threes until we came to the [new] line." The withdrawal was virtually unopposed. When Edwards discovered that the Confederates had left, he sent skirmishers in pursuit, capturing a captain and sixty men.[122]

One of Harris' men stopped for a final look at the entrenchments. A dead Yankee lay close by, his feet stuck in the mud of the breastworks and his head in the ditch. Debris and bodies filled the pens. Wounded men were cursing, calling for water, and pleading to be pulled out from under the corpses. "I don't expect to go to hell," the soldier reflected, "but if I do, I am sure that Hell can't beat that terrible scene."[123]

"Everyone looks as if he had passed through a hard spell of sickness, black and muddy as hogs," a Tarheel observed when he and the rest of his company had re-formed behind the new line. "Exhausted, hungry and worn out for want of sleep, we were a sorry looking crowd," a South Carolinian conceded. A Mississippian contemplated the haggard men and recorded his impressions in his diary: "With blackened faces and crisped hand, from laying in the water so long; our clothing stained with red mud and blood, we marched out of this place where more than one-third of our men lay dead to sleep forever. We stopped in a grove of trees where General Harris told us to build fires and dry our clothes. Our men stood around in groups, inquiring of each other about our missing comrades— some men in tears at the loss of a brother or near relative."[124]

The Battle of the Bloody Angle was over.

Epilogue

"I had no enmity towards those men."

MAY 13 DAWNED to an eerie silence. Colonel Dawes, of the 6th Wisconsin, crept to the Bloody Angle and peered over. Bodies crammed the traverses. A rebel lay sprawled against an embankment, his head gone and the flesh burned from his neck and shoulders by a Coehorn mortar shell. Charles Brewster, of the 10th Massachusetts, gaped in disbelief at the slaughter. "I cannot begin to tell you the horrors I have seen," he jotted later that day. "The pit is filled with them piled up dead and wounded together." He saw one man "completely trodden in the mud so as to look like part of it and yet he was breathing and gasping." Brewster thought it "bad enough on our side of the breast work but on theirs it was awful." Wounded Confederates were writhing under several layers of dead men. Federal corpses—"many nothing but a lump of meat or clot of gore where countless bullets from both armies had torn them"—carpeted the ground in front of the entrenchments.[1]

A section of Union guns faced the Bloody Angle from less than a hundred yards away. Its horses were hitched, dead in the mud, and the drivers sat in their saddles, dead as well. The gunners—also dead—were propped erect, back to back on ammunition boxes. They looked so natural that an officer had to touch them to persuade himself that they were not alive. "The one exclamation of every man who looks on the spectacle is, 'God forbid that I should ever gaze upon such a sight again,'" a Federal observed. A New Yorker considered the angle "one of the most ghastly sights one could wish to look upon, and the horrors of war will go with me to my grave." A Pennsylvanian thought it "no exaggeration to say the dead lay as thick as pumpkins in a corn field in autumn." Even so hardened

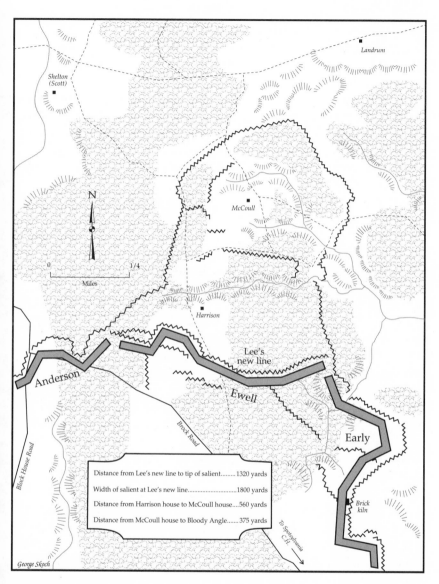

Lee's new line on May 13

a soldier as Lewis Grant declared the angle "terrible and sickening." The field at Antietam, which he had also experienced, was strewn with bodies, "but they were not piled up several deep, and their flesh was not so torn and mangled as at the Angle."[2]

At 5:30 A.M. on May 13, Wright informed Meade that he had occupied the Bloody Angle. No Confederates remained, at least none capable of fighting. General Grant spent the morning trying to determine where Lee had gone. If Lee was falling back to Richmond, Grant wanted to pursue without delay. But with Sheridan off on his own, reliable intelligence was scarce. "The first news which passed through the ranks the morning after the battle of Spotsylvania was that Lee had abandoned his position during the night," Charles Dana, Lincoln's emissary, reported. "Though our army was greatly fatigued from the enormous efforts of the day before, the news of Lee's departure inspired the men with fresh energy, and everybody was eager to be in pursuit."[3]

Hancock's skirmishers advanced past the McCoull house before they found Lee's picket screen. By six o'clock, Grant had concluded that Anderson still held Laurel Hill and that Early's corps still stretched roughly north-to-south across Fredericksburg Road. The change was in Lee's center. He had pulled Ewell from the salient and apparently deployed him in a new line a short distance back.[4]

Around 7:30, Samuel Carroll led a force to probe from the east angle diagonally across the salient's interior. Riding in front in his "usual intrepid manner," as Humphreys put it, Carroll was shot in the arm early in the advance and had to be carried from the field. His soldiers continued until they located Ewell's new line, then retired. By 10:30, Hancock was satisfied that Ewell had assumed a relatively straight line from Anderson's right to Early's left. His position was exceptionally strong, since it ran along the crest of a ridge and could be approached only across several hundred yards of cleared ground.[5]

After skirmishers had confirmed Ewell's withdrawal, Dana and Grant's chief of staff, Rawlins, visited the Bloody Angle. Only low moans broke the silence. "I remembered that as I stood there I was almost startled to hear a bird twittering in a tree," Dana was to write. The foliage appeared burned, and the ground seemed trampled into a mush "like thin hasty pudding." Filling the trenches was a "great pool of mud, its surface as smooth as that of a pond." A mud-smeared leg emerged from the puddle to interrupt Dana's reveries. "It was so unexpected, so horrible, that for a moment we were stunned," he recollected. A soldier tugged the leg and found a wounded rebel attached. Carried to a hospital, the Confederate miraculously survived.[6]

Grant's aide Porter also visited the salient and left a chilling description. "Our own killed were scattered over a large space near the 'angle,'" he recorded. "In front of the captured breastworks the enemy's dead, vastly more numerous than our own, were piled upon each other in some places four layers deep, exhibiting every ghastly phase of mutilation. Below the mass of fast-decaying corpses, the convulsive twitch of limbs and the writhing of bodies showed that there were wounded men still alive and struggling to extricate themselves from the horrid entombment. Every relief possible was afforded, but in too many cases came too late. The place was well named the 'Bloody Angle.'" [7]

A detachment of Union volunteers assembled to bury the dead. The men ventured into the angle under a leaden sky. Occasional sniper bullets whizzed overhead. In many places, the corpses had been "chopped into hash by the bullets, and appear[ed] more like piles of jelly than the distinguishable forms of human life," a soldier thought. Fred Sanborn, an officer on Upton's staff, searched through the corpses and found his friend's body, riddled with bullets, lying near the angle. "There was not four inches of space about his person that had not been struck by bullets," Sanborn could see. "I noted eleven bullet marks through one of the soles of his shoe." The troops cut the name, company, and regiment of each of the Federal dead onto discarded ammunition boxes, to serve as headstones. They left the Confederates heaped in the trenches, simply shoveling the earthworks over the bodies to make common graves. [8]

Uberto Burnham, of the 76th New York, stared into the muddy traverses, contemplating the carnage. "My feelings while looking at the bodies of our dead enemies were not of joy alone," he wrote his family. "I thought how many hopes were bound up in the lives of those men whose broken bloody bodies were lying helpless on that muddy field. I had no enmity towards those men, not even any for their living companions who from the woods beyond were even then occasionally sending a whistling bullet after us. They are brave and believe in the cause they fight for." [9]

The butchery of May 12 rivaled that of either day in the Wilderness. On the Federal side, Humphreys estimated 2nd Corps casualties at 2,043, 5th Corps casualties at 970, 6th Corps casualties at 840, and 9th Corps casualties at slightly over 1,500. Including about 800 soldiers who were captured or missing, Humphreys tallied 6,820 Union losses for the day. Surviving unpublished returns indicate that the numbers were considerably higher than Humphreys' estimate. The 2nd Corps' official recapitulation, for example, showed 2,537 losses for May 12, Burnside's tabular statement claimed 2,534, and Wright's actual losses must have exceeded 1,000. Overall, May 12 reduced Grant's force by some 9,000 soldiers. As for the Confederates, Meade's provost marshal reported 3,000 rebel prisoners, and Humphreys estimated Lee's killed and wounded at between 4,000 and 5,000. Modern estimates place Lee's total loss for May 12 in the range of 8,000 soldiers. The day's harvest in killed, wounded, and captured from both armies approached 17,000 men.[10]

Aside from a few miles of churned Virginia farmland and thousands of dead and maimed soldiers, Grant had little to show for his efforts. The campaign had come full circle. After eight days of brutal combat, the armies stood in much the same relative posture as when they had started. Lee again held an exceptionally strong position and confidently waited behind earthworks for Grant to attack. Grant's onslaught on May 12 capped a week of futile maneuvers and charges. The Bloody Angle served as a dramatic punctuation mark closing this phase of Grant's program to destroy Lee. In the next phase of his campaign, he would rely increasingly on maneuver and resort only sparingly to frontal assaults. His attempt to renew his bludgeoning tactics at Cold Harbor in early June provided an emphatic reminder of the folly of attacking Lee's army when it held an entrenched position.

Grant's handling of his army from May 7 to May 12 brought mixed reviews. The new Union commander had floundered as he tried to establish a working relationship with an army whose style of warfare was considerably more timid than his own. And he confronted for the first time a foe whose guile and aggressiveness matched, or perhaps even exceeded, his own. To Grant's credit, throughout this difficult period, he remained true to his strategic objective of destroying Lee's army, ever shifting and probing for weaknesses. That was his strongest point. Never had a Union general in the east waged war so relentlessly. Unlike his predecessors, Grant refused to admit defeat, even when his tactical combinations failed. A year before, Major General Joseph Hooker had retreated when he sustained heavy losses after crossing the Rapidan. Grant lost more men in the Wilderness than Hooker had lost, yet he persisted, moving forward toward Richmond rather than backward. The very pace of Grant's warring worked to his advantage. Lee's stock-in-trade was surprise, but Grant left the rebel leader no opportunity to perform his tricks. In this contest of wills, Grant held the initiative and remained determined to keep it. None of his ploys succeeded, but each exacted a toll on Lee, bringing victory closer, by attrition if nothing else. Lincoln finally had a general who shared his resolution to batter the Army of Northern Virginia steadfastly until it collapsed. "The great thing about Grant is his perfect coolness and persistency of purpose," Lincoln is reported to have remarked. "He has the grit of a bulldog! Once let him get his 'teeth' in, and nothing can shake him off."[11]

Although Grant demonstrated commendable strategic vision, his tactics, both in concept and execution, left much to be desired. Grant had twice as many men as Lee and superior weaponry, yet he was unable to achieve victory. Why were his offensives unsuccessful? Who was to blame?

Ranking officers in the Army of the Potomac placed the onus on Grant. "I look upon General Grant as responsible for the disasters of the campaign to a great extent," asserted an officer. "The trouble was more in the orders given than in the execution." Twenty years after the war, the prominent military historian John C. Ropes viewed Grant's campaign as offering "but few lessons, except by way of avoidance." Grant's failing, thought Ropes, was his "burning, persistent desire to fight, to attack, in season and out of season, against intrenchments, natural obstacles, what not." Occasional, well-prepared charges could produce great results, Ropes conceded. But Grant's daily regimen of combat only sapped the army's fighting spirit.[12]

While Ropes's criticism was perhaps overdrawn, it contained an irrefutable kernel of truth. Grant's impulsiveness often constituted questionable generalship. The general habitually announced plans on the spur of the moment, paying little attention to the mechanics of implementing them and frequently in ignorance of Lee's dispositions. A case in point was the night march to Spotsylvania. It was an excellent strategic gambit but failed miserably in execution, partly because Grant imposed an unrealistic timetable, and partly because Meade neglected to supervise Sheridan and his own infantry corps. Comparable criticism could be leveled against Grant's turning movement across the Po and his armywide assault on May 10. He conceived the operations without understanding Lee's troop deployments, initiated them too late in the day to succeed, and thoroughly botched the critically important coordination of his attacking elements. Meade was also remiss, but ultimate responsibility lay with Grant.

The attack against the salient on May 12 underscored the shortcomings of Grant's style of fighting, at least when he tried to wage it with the Army of the Potomac. Grant correctly recognized the salient as a weak point in Lee's line, but in his rush to attack he gave insufficient heed to preparation. The generals assigned to lead the massive 2nd Corps assault had virtually no information about the location, configuration, or strength of the rebel works they were to charge. Most of them viewed the venture as suicide. Blind luck—Lee had removed his artillery, and the powder in his men's muskets was damp—accounted for the initial Union success. Writing of the attack years later, Barlow attributed his breach of the rebel earthworks to fate rather than to Grant. "It was an accident that we struck this angle, always a weak point in a line; an accident that the morning was misty to an unusual degree; an accident that we found a space for our rush so free from obstacles; an accident that we so escaped the observation of the enemy's outposts and pickets that we were upon them before they could make any substantial resistance," Barlow had concluded. "That we were in that solid formation which was practically irresistible was of course designed, but that such a formation was practicable was because at the last minute it was found that the nature of the ground permitted it."[13]

It might be added that Grant's haphazard planning contributed to the attack's ultimate failure. Sending the entire 2nd Corps forward at once provided the mass necessary to overwhelm Lee's works, but it spawned a command nightmare. What was Hancock's tightly packed mob to do once it broke the rebel line? Where were fresh troops to be stationed to exploit the breakthrough? And who at the front was to wield authority to coordinate the various corps as they entered the fray? Surprisingly, Grant neglected to address any of these crucial questions with sufficient care.

Grant's failure to position fresh troops to exploit the breakthrough proved fatal to his plan. He had placed the 6th Corps more than a mile from the salient, where it was powerless to assist Hancock. He had given Burnside, posted on the Union left end to turn Lee's flank, no support at all. And he had delegated to no ranking officer at the front the authority to coordinate the various corps. Instead, he and Meade communicated with their subordinates through couriers and telegrams. They were dependent on others for interpretations of the battle's progress. Messages were frequently delayed at pivotal junctures, and sometimes—as with those to Warren—they demanded attacks that were manifestly impossible and stood no realistic chance of advancing the designs behind them. Hancock later remarked that the "great obstruction lay in the fact that there was no corps commander [at the front] who was invested with the general command. Had General Meade come up, or had there been another Commander in Chief at the Angle or vicinity, a great deal more might have been done." The dribbling of brigades to the Bloody Angle throughout the morning underscored Grant's failure to lay his plans with care and to exercise effective field leadership.[14]

Perhaps Grant's greatest misjudgment of the campaign was permitting his friend Sheridan to leave with the Army of the Potomac's cavalry. In a single, impulsive stroke, he deprived the Federal force of its eyes and ears. There can only be speculation about why Grant acceded to Sheridan's entreaty. He had little experience with the mounted arm and fought most of his western battles without cavalry. Before one of his earlier victories, he had dispatched his horsemen on a raid to create havoc at the rear of his opponent, and the gambit had succeeded brilliantly. In light of that experience, Sheridan's proposition may have seemed reasonable. And coming at a time when Grant was especially exasperated by Meade's inability to produce tangible results, Sheridan's show of aggressiveness must have been refreshing. But whatever the underlying motive, Grant sorely missed the cavalry's service on May 9, 10, and 12, when reliable intelligence about Lee's troop dispositions might have led him to act differently. By contrast, Stuart rode in pursuit of Sheridan with only three brigades, prudently leaving behind three brigades of experienced cavalry to assist Lee.

Some of Grant's associates defended his performance at Spotsylvania and blamed subordinate generals for the debacle. Grant's plans were fundamentally sound, they argued, but the incompetents serving under him had fumbled their assignments. To Grant's apologists, it seemed as if his predicament resembled that of a skilled surgeon trying to perform a delicate operation with dull knives. James Wilson contended that the Army of the Potomac was "bad throughout," and he referred to a conversation he had had with Grant a few weeks after Spotsylvania. "Wilson, what is the matter with this army?" Grant reportedly asked his former staffer. "General, there is a great deal the matter with it, but I can tell you much more easily how to cure it," Wilson replied. "Send for [Colonel Ely S.] Parker, the Indian chief, and, after giving him a tomahawk, a scalping knife, and a gallon of the worst whiskey the Commissary Department can supply, send him out with orders to bring in the scalps of major generals." Grant found the suggestion intriguing and inquired with a smile, "Whose?" Wilson had a ready answer: "Oh, the first he comes to, and so on in succession till he gets at least a dozen." Grant's interest was sufficiently piqued for him to probe further. "But where shall we get generals to fill their places?" he wanted to know. "Oh, that's easy!" Wilson retorted. "To use a favorite phrase of yours, every brigadier in this army will 'step up and take sugar in his'n.'"[15]

The conduct of the army's major generals lent a measure of support to Wilson's arguments. Wright was manifestly a poor substitute for Sedgwick. He neglected to coordinate Mott and Upton on May 10 and handled his troops lethargically on May 12, doing little to influence the battle's outcome. Instead of preparing an assault column as Meade had instructed, Wright used fresh troops to relieve his frontline units. His behavior revealed a general paralyzed at the prospect of taking risks. The aide Whittier considered Wright a "well-mannered, temperate man—not at all deficient in physical courage, but when responsibilities came on him he took to drink." The record is silent concerning whether Wright indulged his weakness on May 12. But whatever the cause, his actions betokened a general promoted beyond his ability.[16]

Hancock had also faltered. He was excessively cautious on May 8 at Todd's Tavern and also on May 9 at the Block House Bridge. He demonstrated his accustomed energy when he rescued Barlow from Heth on May 10 and supervised his corps' charge against the salient on May 12. But he became disturbingly lethargic after the breakthrough. Half of Hancock's corps—Barlow and Gibbon—did no significant fighting after 7 A.M. on the twelfth, even though they might have won the battle for Grant by attacking the salient's thinly defended eastern leg. Hancock, doubtless exhausted and pained by his Gettysburg wound, let opportunity pass. While Hancock's readiness to attack when requested kept him in Grant's good graces, his record at Spotsylvania did nothing to advance his reputation.

Warren was particularly troubling. He displayed stirring valor on May 8 but failed signally in deploying troops for a concerted attack. His assaults on May 10 were disjointed, and his hesitancy on May 12 led a frustrated Meade temporarily to reassign most of his corps. His erratic performance almost cost him his job. "An excess of caution, a delay in assuming the offensive, even when ordered, an indisposition to take tactical risks, an unwillingness to trust that his superiors would protect, or perhaps knew how to protect his advance, or his equals support it, destroyed the effect of otherwise brilliant talents, and marred his reputation as a soldier," is how Badeau put the case against Warren. Wilson proclaimed Warren "captious and impatient of control," and Meade saw his fatal flaw as a penchant for exercising discretion "where no discretion is left him by his orders." Meade considered Warren a "serious embarrassment" but kept the young commander on, hoping, as he wrote, to "overcome the difficulty."[17]

But disparagements of Warren can be too pat. His growing resistance to fighting Grant's kind of battle stemmed from his heartfelt conviction that impulsive attacks against earthworks were wrong. Warren preferred carefully planned initiatives, and the bloodshed that attended Grant's rash aggression only served to confirm that preference. Warren's restraint might have worked well under a commander such as Meade, who was governed by similar instincts. Warren's predicament lay in being forced to carry out the program of a commander in chief whose apparent disregard for lives revolted him. His attempt to reconcile the abhorrence he felt at Grant's generalship with his robust personal ambition goes far toward explaining his erratic behavior during the difficult days at Spotsylvania.

As for Burnside, his failings were so flagrant that the army talked about them openly. He stumbled badly in the Wilderness and worse still at Spotsylvania. His advance along Fredericksburg Road on May 9 was tardy in the extreme, he missed the Union army's best opportunity of the campaign on May 10 by failing to attack Lee's thin defenses east of Spotsylvania Court House, and his poorly coordinated assaults on May 12 never achieved their objectives. Since Burnside reported directly to Grant, the general-in-chief must share responsibility for his mistakes. Certainly Burnside's shortcomings were painfully obvious to Grant. Burnside's seniority and political ties, however, complicated Grant's ability to control him effectively or to remove him from command.

Grant and Meade's unsettled relationship also augmented the army's difficulties. At the campaign's outset, Grant had intended to let Meade run his own battles. The two men, however, had very different ideas about how to fight. Meade was a cautious soldier, cast somewhat in Warren's mold, and given to painstaking preparation. From his appointment to head the Army of the Potomac in June, 1863, through Grant's arrival ten months later, he never ventured a major attack. Grant's agenda of bold maneuvers and assaults came as a profound shock to him. The battles in front of Spotsylvania were Grant's show, not Meade's, and the eight days of combat from the Wilderness to the Bloody Angle saw a frustrated Grant increasingly dictating how the Army of the Potomac would wage combat. Complicating the situation was Grant's responsibility of coordinating Burnside's independent force. "This was distinctly a bad arrangement," the Confederate Alexander suggested a few years later. "There are few axioms of war better established than those which condemn divided commands and in this case experience again pronounced against it."[18]

By May 12, Meade had been reduced to little more than the staff officer responsible for ensuring the Army of the Potomac's compliance with Grant's orders. Grant's regular aides considered Meade a hindrance and complained that he was uncommitted to the spirit of Grant's programs. Grant allowed that he was painfully aware of Meade's "embarrassments" but felt that the general served useful purposes. "I am commanding all the armies, and I cannot neglect others by giving my time exclusively to the Army of the Potomac, which would involve performing all the detailed duties of an army commander, directing its administration, enforcing discipline, reviewing its court-martial proceedings, etc.," Grant explained. "Besides, Meade has served a long time with the Army of the Potomac, knows its subordinate officers thoroughly, and led it to a memorable victory at Gettysburg. I have just come from the west, and if I removed a deserving eastern man from the position of army commander, my motives might be misunderstood, and the effect be bad upon the spirits of the troops." In sum, Grant considered Meade "capable and perfectly subordinate," and he insisted, "By tending to the details he relieves me of much unnecessary work, and gives me more time to think and to mature my general plans."[19]

On May 13, Grant displayed his mastery of army politics by recommending Meade for promotion as one of the "fittest officers for large commands I have come in contact with." And in his campaign report, he praised Meade as the "right man in the right place." But official proclamations hid the real story. Meade complained to his wife that Grant had "taken control," and a staff officer professed to be "sickened" at the way Meade was ignored. "If there was any honorable way of retiring from my present false position I should undoubtedly adopt it," Meade wrote to his wife, "but there is none and all I can do is patiently submit and bear with resignation the humiliation." Perhaps out of frustration with his predicament, Meade suffered "terribly" during May 12 from "nervous dyspepsia" and delegated many of his responsibilities to Humphreys.[20]

Grant and Meade's military partnership had failed. Humphreys accurately perceived that the divided command "was not calculated to produce the best results that either [general] singly was capable of bringing about." Badeau thought that "the result of [Grant's] having a middleman was to make the whole organization wooden. Meade severed the nerve between the general-in-chief and the army. He was a non-conductor." Grant's decision regarding Sheridan was a stark reminder of how badly relations had deteriorated between the two generals. By overruling Meade and backing Sheridan, Grant severely damaged Meade's prestige and authority. Although Meade did not dwell on the cause of his "humiliation" to his wife, the incident with Sheridan must have figured prominently.[21]

Wilson later contended that Grant should have consolidated the four infantry corps into a single army and run it himself. It is worth asking whether either general might have been more successful without the other. Certainly Meade would have waged a more cautious campaign. The bloodbaths of May 10 and May 12 would never have happened, and the Union cavalry would have remained close by. But by the same token, Meade might never have dared advance past the Wilderness, or might have retreated, as Hooker had done under similar circumstances. Eighteen sixty-four might have looked much like 1863, and the war might have reached a very different conclusion.

Reasonable men could differ over the relative merits of Grant's and Meade's generalship, but agreement was universal on one point. Grant's fondness for attacking well-defended earthworks was a deadly business. From May 5 through May 12, the Army of the Potomac's official returns reported 29,410 soldiers killed, wounded, and captured. Burnside had lost about 4,000 more, which put Grant's total combat losses after crossing the Rapidan at over 33,000, or 28 percent of his combat force.[22]

Some units were hit especially hard. Hancock's 2nd Corps had started the campaign with approximately 27,000 officers and men. It was the strongest and most reliable of the army's corps, and Grant had used it to spearhead most of his offensive operations. On May 13, it could muster no more than 16,000 effectives. The Wilderness, the Po, and the salient had reduced its rolls by 40 percent. Expired terms of enlistment and casualties had so depleted Mott's division that Hancock incorporated it into Birney's. In the Wilderness, the 2nd Corps had lost a brigade commander and numerous field officers. After that, five more of its brigade commanders and approximately eighty-five field officers were disabled from combat. The outfit would never recover from the blow.[23]

Warren's 5th Corps, which started the campaign with slightly more than 24,000 soldiers, had lost 37 percent of its strength. The Wilderness had claimed a division head and two brigade commanders; Spotsylvania had taken another division head and five more brigade commanders. The 6th Corps suffered losses comparable to those of the 5th, and its commander, Sedgwick, was killed. The three 9th Corps divisions available for combat—Ferrero's black soldiers were still relegated to guarding wagon trains—sustained 1,640 casualties in the Wilderness and another 2,500 at Spotsylvania, totaling about 25 percent of their numbers. Attrition, it seemed, was a double-edged sword. If the trend continued, Grant risked compromising his army's ability to wage combat.[24]

"Grant is beating his head against a wall."

Lee's adjutant Taylor declared May 12 an "unfortunate day for us—we recovered most of the ground lost but could not regain our guns. This hurts our pride—we are determined to make our next success all the greater to make amends for this disaster." He thought the Army of Northern Virginia "in good heart and condition—our confidence, certainly mine, unimpaired. Grant is beating his head against a wall." Heth's briga-dier Scales penned that "Grant with a much larger army has been badly whipped in every fight and driven back." And Lee's artillery chief, Pendle-ton, observed that the Confederates had been "quite successful against General Ulysses," except for the "accident" of the twelfth, which he feared might "partially encourage" Grant. "No army in the world was ever in finer condition," he assured his wife.[25]

Some Confederates, however, saw ominous signs in Grant's persistence. "Grant has shown no remarkable generalship—only a bull-dog tenacity and determination in a fight, regardless of the consequences or the loss," a Virginian wrote home. "If it required the loss of twenty-five thousand to rob us of six thousand he was doing a wise thing for we yield our loss from an irreplaceable penury, he from super abundance. Ultimately, such bloody policy must win." A North Carolinian predicted that Grant was "twice as badly whipped now as was Burnside or Hooker but he is so determined he will not acknowledge it, but I think before he gets through with Lee he will have to own up." He cautioned, however, that the Union general was a "sly fellow and has to be watched closely."[26]

Lee viewed the loss of the salient as unfortunate but of no lasting con-sequence. His chief concern involved reinforcements. To Jefferson Davis, he wrote, "If General [Robert F.] Hoke with fresh troops can be spared from Richmond it would be of great assistance. We are outnumbered and constant labor is impairing the efficiency of the men."[27]

Lee had waged an impressive defense. Wherever Grant turned, he was there. He had deadlocked Grant in the Wilderness and drawn a strongly fortified line across his path at Spotsylvania, deftly deflecting the Federal's powerful blows. He had managed his troops with a practiced hand, shifting two divisions from his right flank to block Grant's thrust against his left on the Po, then drawing on nearby brigades to seal the breach in Doles's portion of the line. On May 12, he had judiciously shunted brigades from all three infantry corps to recover and buttress endangered points. Even while Grant hammered, Lee sought to counterattack, thrusting Lane and Weisiger against Burnside's exposed flank. He had orchestrated a perfor-mance as stirring as any he had delivered in the past.

Lee's style of leadership differed radically from Grant's. Lee remained in close communication with his army and personally supervised its de-ployments. As a Tarheel put it admiringly in a letter, "General Lee is present wherever the hardest fighting is." On May 10, he was at the site of Upton's penetration. And on May 12, Gordon's, Ramseur's, Perrin's, Harris', and McGowan's foot soldiers sealed the rift in the salient under

Lee's personal direction. The Confederate counterattack—Lane and Weisiger's operation against Burnside—was the work of Lee's hand. He placed himself personally at risk, to the esteem and consternation of his troops. During the morning of May 12, a shell burst so close to Lee that the general and his staff disappeared in a cloud of black smoke. The explosion blew the legs off two horses, but Lee emerged unscathed. "I have often thought what might have been the result had General Lee been killed then," a witnesses later remarked. "The expression on his face as he rode out of that smoke has always remained firmly vised in my memory." Never was Lee's imposing battlefield presence more important than at Spotsylvania, and never did a general use the force of his personality to greater effect.[28]

Lee's formidable military instincts, however, failed him at two critical junctures, almost disastrously. He miscalculated on May 7 by failing to grasp the full importance of Spotsylvania Court House. If Anderson had left the Wilderness at 3 A.M. on the eighth, as Lee instructed, he would not have reached the Po until noon. By then, Warren would have crushed Fitzhugh Lee and occupied Spotsylvania Court House, with Hancock following close behind. Anderson's fortuitous decision to start early saved Lee's army.

Lee's instincts let him down a second time, on May 11, when he misread Grant's intentions and withdrew Nelson's and Page's artillery from the salient. Lee understood the salient's inherent weakness but believed that Ewell could defend it if backed by artillery. By withdrawing the supporting guns, Lee willingly left the formation indefensible. He later conceded that his "fatal mistake was in removing the artillery on our line." A Confederate asserted that he "never saw an occasion where artillery would have done such execution," and Ewell's chief gunner Long agreed that "had the artillery been in position the result might have been different, or had the weather been favorable, the disaster might have been avoided." Porter Alexander, whose expertise was unimpeachable, insisted that if Ewell's ordnance had been in place, "it is quite certain that the charge would not have been successful." He observed that "nowhere else, in the whole history of the war, was such a target, so large, so dense, so vulnerable, ever presented to so large a force of artillery." In his view, "there would have been no escape but flight, with phenomenal loss for the time exposed to fire."[29]

Why did Lee take chances with his defensive line's integrity? The answer lies in his firm determination to seize the initiative. Grant had almost stolen a march on him on May 7. On May 11, Grant seemed to be retiring toward Fredericksburg, and Lee wanted his army ready to attack as the enemy withdrew. Removing the salient's artillery entailed risk, but in Lee's mind, the importance of exploiting Grant's apparent retreat justified it. By temperament, Lee inclined toward offensive warfare, and he was loath to let an opportunity pass. He ordered the artillery withdrawn with complete awareness of the possible consequences. It was a responsibility that he accepted in full.

Unanswered questions linger concerning why Long's artillery did not return expeditiously. By midnight, Johnson had learned that Federals were massing across from the salient, and he petitioned Ewell to bring the pieces back. Ewell approved Johnson's request with Lee's knowledge and concurrence. The message took over three hours to reach the sleeping gunners, in a delay that has never been explained. Whatever the reason, Lee and Ewell were remiss in failing to monitor a matter of such importance.[30]

Unlike Grant, Lee had reason to be satisfied with the performance of his chief subordinates. His two new appointments—Anderson, who had replaced Longstreet over the 1st Corps, and Early, substituting for Hill over the 3rd Corps—had fought exceptionally well. Only his senior corps head—Ewell, of the 2nd Corps—continued to fall short of expectations.

Judging from Anderson's performance at Spotsylvania, Lee's initial concern about the South Carolinian's reputed indolence seemed unwarranted. Anderson's march to Spotsylvania had saved the Confederate army. Skeptics may quibble that the dearth of campsites rather than military perspicacity spurred Anderson on, but no one can quarrel with his results. And no one can deny that Anderson exercised commendable discretion once he reached the Block House Bridge, directing troops to Laurel Hill and Spotsylvania to deal with emerging threats. On perceiving that Stuart had a sound grasp of the Laurel Hill front, Anderson appropriately gave him a free hand in deploying the 1st Corps' troops. Thereafter, Anderson defended Laurel Hill with unflinching steadiness. Longstreet himself could not have done better.

Early, too, deserved praise, for his handling of the 3rd Corps during Hill's incapacity. Lee employed the 3rd Corps as his maneuverable element, and Early executed the assignment to perfection. On May 8, he protected the army's rear and tested Hancock's defenses at Todd's Tavern. On May 9 and 10, he maneuvered two of his divisions against Hancock on the Confederate left flank, while his third division detained Burnside on the opposite flank. And on May 12, Early assigned Harris, Perrin, and McGowan to defend the west angle, Ambrose Wright to keep watch across the Po, and the rest of his corps to defend the salient's eastern leg. When Lee sought to renew the offensive, he again turned to Early, who sent Lane and Weisiger thundering into Burnside's flank. But while Early handled his corps with skill, he was not severely tested. His withdrawal from the Wilderness went unchallenged, Hancock offered but feeble opposition at Todd's Tavern, Burnside never pressed his advantage at Spotsylvania, Barlow was preparing to retreat when Early attacked at the Po, Burnside's attacks on May 12 were feeble and inept, and Lee oversaw Lane's and Weisiger's assault. No one, however, could dispute that Early possessed an aptitude for offensive operations. The point was not lost on Lee.

It was Ewell who raised eyebrows. On May 8, he had energetically blocked Meade's turning movement against Anderson's flank and efficiently extended his corps into a defensive formation. And on May 10, he had personally orchestrated the response to Upton's attack. But he did not always exercise vigilance. On May 10, the Federals drove in Doles's pickets and opened with their artillery, but not until Upton swarmed over his works did Ewell respond. And during the night of May 11–12, after Johnson pointedly warned Ewell that an attack was imminent, he failed to position his guns with appropriate dispatch. Ewell manifested energy in deploying troops to seal the breach, but his agitation seemed to impair his leadership. It was Lee's steady presence that got the job done. It has been said that in a postwar conversation, Lee complained that he "found Ewell perfectly prostrated by the misfortune of the morning [of May 12], and too much overwhelmed to be efficient." That was a serious indictment by the army's commander, if accurately reported.[31]

The Army of Northern Virginia continued to boast remarkable strength at the division, brigade, and regimental level. Anderson's division chiefs, Kershaw and Field, had waged a magnificent defense against daunting odds on May 8, and his brigade commanders Henagan and Humphreys were the toast of the army. In Early's corps, Wilcox, Heth, and Mahone had each executed their assigned tasks with energy and precision. And in Ewell's corps, Gordon, on May 10 and May 12 had twice rescued the army from impending disaster. Many southerners faulted Johnson for neglect on May 12. "There was no surprise," Johnson replied to his critics. "My men were up and in the trenches prepared for the assault before the enemy made their appearance." A Virginian conceded, however, that Johnson's pickets had been caught "somewhat by surprise." Although some Federals met strong resistance, others rousted Johnson's men out of their sleep, which suggests that his preparations were not as thorough as he claimed. Witcher's brigade, which was the first of Johnson's units to collapse, elicited strong censure. One soldier blamed Witcher's "coward-

ice." Another complained that Witcher's troops, "seeing the overwhelming force advancing against them, became panic stricken and ingloriously
fled the field without firing scarcely a shot." And another argued that if
Witcher had "held for fifteen minutes longer, two other brigades would
have reinforced them, and the artillery would have been in position, and
the repulse of the Yankees certain; but they broke." Such accusations
against Witcher were unfair. Fully half of his brigade were deployed as
pickets and received the full weight of Hancock's offensive. As Colonel
Withers, of the 42nd Virginia, recognized, "it was not their fault—being
simply overpowered."[32]

Overall, Lee's foot soldiers remained confident. They were the genuine
southern heroes of the battles for Spotsylvania. The valor of the men of
North and South Carolina, Mississippi, and Alabama who recaptured the
Bloody Angle and held it for twenty long hours against Grant's concentrated might still inspires admiration. Because Lee's army possessed men
such as these, the general continued to consider success a possibility.

From May 7 through May 12, Lee had lost about 12,000 soldiers, bringing his casualties after crossing the Rapidan to about 23,000 men. That
amounted to a third of his combat force, a level of attrition slightly more
than Grant's. The losses came disproportionately from Ewell's 2nd Corps,
which began the campaign with 17,000 men and could muster only 6,000
a few weeks later. Three of Rodes's brigade commanders and one of Gordon's were killed or injured on May 12. But the toll was heaviest on
Johnson's division, which had started the campaign with about 6,000 men
and a full complement of officers. Two of Johnson's four brigade commanders, half of his field officers, and a third of his soldiers became
casualties in the Wilderness. Upton and Hancock completed the division's
destruction. Johnson and Steuart were now captives, and Hays, Witcher,
and Walker lay wounded. Only about 1,500 of Johnson's soldiers survived
the Bloody Angle. "The capture of Johnson's division was a terrible blow
to the army," a Virginian wrote of the calamity. "This was [Stonewall]
Jackson's old division, and those were the men who had done so much
fighting and who had made those wonderful marches for him. . . . It is
true that, for a division, their numbers were small, but they were such
trained soldiers that they counted as many in a fight."[33]

Lee was perhaps fortunate in the way his losses were concentrated in one
corps, leaving his other two corps strong if not intact. Anderson fought behind earthworks and sustained minimal casualties. Most of Early's losses
occurred when he took the offensive, but only three of his commanders

at brigade level or above—Mud Walker, Cooke, and McGowan—were wounded, and only one, Perrin, was killed.[34]

On May 13, Lee received news of another grievous casualty when a courier handed him a telegram. "Gentlemen," he announced sadly after reading it, "We have very bad news. General Stuart had been mortally wounded." The cavalry still had effective leaders in Fitzhugh Lee and Wade Hampton, but Stuart held a special place in the commanding general's heart. Lee paused, then went on, his voice choked with emotion, "He never brought me a piece of false information." When the aide Boteler informed the staff of the sad tidings, he was struck by how "those brave men bowed their heads and wept like children."[35]

Grant and his staff ate breakfast at the Armstrong place, halfway between Piney Branch Church and Spotsylvania Court House. The lady of the house dispensed bread, butter, and honey, apologizing that she had nothing more elegant to serve.[36]

Grant remained optimistic despite his failure to defeat Lee at Spotsylvania. Lee, he thought, was obstinate but had "found the last ditch." Grant informed his wife, Julia, that the Confederates were "really whipped yesterday but their situation is desperate beyond anything heretofore known. To lose this battle they lose their cause. And bad as it is they have fought for it with a gallantry worthy of a better." He remained "full of hope" and predicted victory.[37]

Meade, although stunned by the mounting casualties, shared Grant's optimism and wrote home of a "decided victory" over the Confederates. Losses had been "frightful," but the army had the "prestige of success," which assured victory. He also congratulated his troops. "Your heroic deeds and noble endurance of fatigue and privations will ever be memorable," he assured them in a circular, emphasizing the importance of pressing ahead. "Let us determine then to continue vigorously the work so well begun, and, under God's blessing, in a short time the object of our labors will be accomplished."[38]

The Union soldiers gave voice to their profound weariness. "This is the severest battle of the war, and none in history can come up to it," the aide James Biddle told his wife. "We have fought the most terrible series of battles ever fought by hostile armies in the same time in modern history," Samuel Pingree wrote his parents. A soldier in the 125th Pennsylvania thought that the "privations endured have been great, but the hope that this campaign will be the means of obtaining the grand end sought for, will lead us to endure even greater hardships." George M. Barnard apprised his father that the army had "never suffered as much as it has in this campaign, not only in casualties but in hardship, and I have never seen such a horrible time before." He had witnessed men in the ranks "so utterly wretched that they threw themselves in the middle of the road wallowing in the mud under the horses feet, howling and crying like mad men." He concluded, "General Meade's order congratulating the troops is, I fear, a little premature especially as to [the Confederates'] having abandoned their last entrenched position." Another Federal mused, "I guess Grant thinks that he has got a harder nut to crack than he had out west."[39]

The battles around Spotsylvania had no clear victor. Once again, Lee had blocked Grant's southward progress, but at an awful price. He had been forced to abandon the critical Rapidan line and to accept a battlefront fifteen miles closer to Richmond. In absolute numbers, his losses had been exceeded by Grant's, but the percentage of troops lost was higher for him than for the Federals. The Confederates were technically correct in considering May 10 and 12 as victories. After all, they had foiled Grant's assaults on each occasion. But a few more such victories would leave Lee's army in shambles. Eight days of fighting Grant had gutted the Army of Northern Virginia's capacity to go on the offensive. For the future, Lee had little choice but to continue his defensive tactics, hoping to thwart Grant's thrusts and to buy time for a political solution to the war.

As for Grant, he had failed in his primary objective of defeating Lee. In his eyes, however, the reverses at Spotsylvania were mere tactical setbacks. To the extent that attrition weakened the Confederates' ability to resist, some good had come from the exercises. In the short run, the battles at Spotsylvania were Union defeats. But Grant took the longer view. He remained committed to his strategic vision of destroying Lee's army. Laurel Hill, the Po, and the salient were unfortunate, but perhaps necessary, steps along the road to achieving that goal.

Men packed the roads north and south from Spotsylvania. Wounded Federals and Confederate prisoners poured into Fredericksburg, then on to nearby Belle Plain. From there, ships transported the injured to Washington. The captives were temporarily detained in a set of hilly depressions called the Punch Bowl, then taken to Point Lookout, Maryland. A procession of wounded Confederates and captured Yankees threaded south to the Virginia Central Railroad, then on to Richmond.

Fresh earthen mounds served as tangible reminders of the terrible contest raging near Spotsylvania Court House. Sedgwick lay in state at Meade's headquarters on May 9, then his aide Whittier and two staffers began the slow journey with the general's body back to Connecticut. The body was displayed in Washington for a day, then the staff officers took him to New York for more ceremonies. There the governor of Connecticut joined the entourage and accompanied it home. On May 15, the Reverend Charles Wetherby uttered a few words over the corpse and Sedgwick finally came to rest in a cemetery near Cornwall Hollow.[40]

On May 13, at 5 P.M., while Sedgwick reposed in New York, another group of mourners assembled at St. James' Church in Richmond. The Reverend Charles Minnigerode read the service while President Davis looked on. Pallbearers lowered Jeb Stuart's remains to the sound of cannon growling in the distance. Stuart's men were still fighting Sheridan on the city's outskirts. "It was a dull, dark gloomy day and rainy," noted Stuart's aide Garnett, who attended the service. "The interment took place in Hollywood Cemetery, and all that was mortal of the best soldier I ever knew rests there."[41]

Near nightfall on May 13, another procession started south. Having determined that Lee was still in front of Spotsylvania, Grant had decided, once again, to try to maneuver him from his works. He first considered turning Lee's left flank but abandoned the idea out of concern that it would tax the Union supply line and give Lee an opportunity to flee south—perhaps to gain an even stronger position behind the North Anna River. Maneuvering around Lee's right, however, appeared promising. Perhaps, thought Grant, he could steal a march on Lee by withdrawing his westernmost units—the 5th and 6th Corps—and swinging them behind the 2nd and 9th Corps to re-form below Burnside. From there, they could assault Lee's right flank and rear, all the while covering the Union supply route to Fredericksburg.[42]

Once again, Warren's troops started through the Virginia darkness on a march designed to pry Lee from his fortifications. They had led the army south across the Rapidan on May 4, and again on May 7 toward Spotsylvania Court House. "The mud was deep over a large part of the route," an officer remarked. "The darkness [was] intense, so that literally you could not see your hand held before your face." The situation was chillingly reminiscent of Hancock's night march on May 11 preceding his grand assault upon Lee's fortified works. Heads bowed against the rain, Warren's men could not help wondering what the morning had in store for them.[43]

Twenty-five miles south, toward Richmond, the North Anna beckoned.

Appendix
The Order of Battle

ARMY OF THE POTOMAC
Major General George G. Meade

PROVOST GUARD
Brigadier General Marsena R. Patrick
1st Massachusetts Cavalry, Companies C and D
80th New York
3rd Pennsylvania Cavalry
68th Pennsylvania
114th Pennsylvania

ARTILLERY
Brigadier General Henry J. Hunt

RESERVE ARTILLERY
Colonel Henry S. Burton

1st Brigade
Colonel J. Howard Kitching
6th New York Heavy Artillery
15th New York Heavy Artillery

2nd Brigade
Major John A. Tompkins
5th Maine, Battery E
1st New Jersey, Battery A
1st New Jersey, Battery B
5th New York Battery
12th New York Battery
1st New York, Battery B

3rd Brigade
Major Robert H. Fitzhugh
9th Massachusetts Battery

1st Brigade Horse Artillery
Captain James M. Robertson
6th New York Battery
2nd U.S., Batteries B and L
2nd U.S., Battery D
2nd U.S., Battery M
4th U.S., Battery A
4th U.S., Batteries C and E

2nd Brigade Horse Artillery
Captain Dunbar R. Ransom
1st U.S., Batteries E and G
1st U.S., Batteries H and I
1st U.S., Battery K
2nd U.S., Battery A

15th New York Battery
1st New York, Battery C
11th New York Battery
1st Ohio, Battery H
5th U.S., Battery E

2nd U.S., Battery G
3rd U.S., Batteries C, F, and K

VOLUNTEER ENGINEER BRIGADE
Brigadier General Henry W. Benham

50TH NEW YORK ENGINEERS
Lieutenant Colonel Ira Spaulding

BATTALION U.S. ENGINEERS
Captain George H. Mendell

2ND ARMY CORPS

Major General Winfield S. Hancock
1st Vermont Cavalry, Company M

1ST DIVISION

Brigadier General Francis C. Barlow

1st Brigade
Colonel Nelson A. Miles

26th Michigan
61st New York
81st Pennsylvania
140th Pennsylvania
183rd Pennsylvania

2nd Brigade
Colonel Thomas A. Smyth

28th Massachusetts
63rd New York
69th New York
88th New York
116th Pennsylvania

3rd Brigade
Colonel Paul Frank [a]

39th New York
52nd New York
57th New York
111th New York
125th New York
126th New York

2ND DIVISION

Brigadier General John Gibbon
2nd Company Minnesota
Sharpshooters

1st Brigade
Brigadier General Alexander S. Webb [b]

19th Maine
1st Company Sharpshooters
15th Massachusetts
19th Massachusetts
20th Massachusetts
7th Michigan
42nd New York
59th New York
82nd New York (2nd Militia)

2nd Brigade
Brigadier General Joshua T. Owen

152nd New York
69th Pennsylvania
71st Pennsylvania
72nd Pennsylvania
106th Pennsylvania

3RD DIVISION

Major General David B. Birney

1st Brigade
Brigadier General J. H. Hobart Ward [d]

20th Indiana
3rd Maine
40th New York
86th New York
124th New York
99th Pennsylvania
110th Pennsylvania
141st Pennsylvania
2nd U.S. Sharpshooters

2nd Brigade
Colonel John S. Crocker

4th Maine
17th Maine
3rd Michigan
5th Michigan
93rd New York
57th Pennsylvania
63rd Pennsylvania
105th Pennsylvania
1st U.S. Sharpshooters

4TH DIVISION

Brigadier General Gershom Mott [e]

1st Brigade
Colonel Robert McAllister

1st Massachusetts
16th Massachusetts
5th New Jersey
6th New Jersey
7th New Jersey
8th New Jersey
11th New Jersey
26th Pennsylvania
115th Pennsylvania

2nd Brigade
Colonel William R. Brewster

11th Massachusetts
70th New York
71st New York
72nd New York
73rd New York
74th New York
120th New York
84th Pennsylvania

4th Brigade
Colonel John R. Brooke

2nd Delaware
64th New York
66th New York
53rd Pennsylvania
145th Pennsylvania
148th Pennsylvania

3rd Brigade
Colonel Samuel S. Carroll[c]

14th Connecticut
1st Delaware
14th Indiana
12th New Jersey
10th New York battalion
108th New York
4th Ohio
8th Ohio
7th West Virginia

Artillery Brigade
Colonel John C. Tidball

6th Maine, Battery F
10th Massachusetts Battery
1st New Hampshire Battery
1st New York, Battery G
4th New York Heavy, 3rd battalion
1st Pennsylvania, Battery F
1st Rhode Island, Battery A
1st Rhode Island, Battery B
4th U.S., Battery K
5th U.S., Batteries C and I

[a] Relieved for drunkenness on May 10 and replaced by Colonel Hiram R. Brown, who was captured on May 12.

[b] Wounded on May 12.

[c] Wounded on May 13.

[d] Relieved for drunkenness on May 12.

[e] Division incorporated into Birney's division on May 13.

5TH ARMY CORPS
Major General Gouverneur K. Warren
12th New York battalion

1ST DIVISION
Brigadier General Charles Griffin

1st Brigade
Brigadier General Romeyn B. Ayres
140th New York
146th New York
91st Pennsylvania
155th Pennsylvania
2nd U.S., Companies B, C, F, H, I, and K
11th U.S., Companies B, C, D, E, F, and G, 1st battalion
12th U.S., Companies A, B, C, D, and G, 1st battalion
12th U.S., Companies A, C, D, F, and H, 2nd battalion
14th U.S., 1st battalion
17th U.S., Companies A, C, D, G, and H, 1st battalion
17th U.S., Companies A, B, and C, 2nd battalion

2nd Brigade
Colonel Jacob B. Sweitzer
9th Massachusetts
22nd Massachusetts
32nd Massachusetts
4th Michigan
62nd Pennsylvania

2ND DIVISION
Brigadier General John C. Robinson [a]

1st Brigade
Colonel Peter Lyle
16th Maine
13th Massachusetts
39th Massachusetts
104th New York
90th Pennsylvania

2nd Brigade
Colonel Richard Coulter
12th Massachusetts
83rd New York
97th New York
11th Pennsylvania
88th Pennsylvania

3rd Brigade
Colonel Andrew W. Denison [b]
1st Maryland
4th Maryland
7th Maryland
8th Maryland

3RD DIVISION
Brigadier General Samuel W. Crawford

1st Brigade
Colonel William McCandless [c]
1st Pennsylvania Reserves
2nd Pennsylvania Reserves
6th Pennsylvania Reserves
7th Pennsylvania Reserves
11th Pennsylvania Reserves
13th Pennsylvania Reserves

3rd Brigade
Colonel Joseph W. Fisher
5th Pennsylvania Reserves
8th Pennsylvania Reserves
10th Pennsylvania Reserves
12th Pennsylvania Reserves

4TH DIVISION
Brigadier General Lysander Cutler

1st Brigade
Colonel William W. Robinson [c]
7th Indiana
19th Indiana
24th Michigan
1st New York Battalion Sharpshooters
2nd Wisconsin
6th Wisconsin
7th Wisconsin

2nd Brigade
Brigadier General James C. Rice [d]
76th New York
84th New York
95th New York
147th New York
56th Pennsylvania

3rd Brigade
Colonel Edward S. Bragg
121st Pennsylvania
142nd Pennsylvania
143rd Pennsylvania
149th Pennsylvania
150th Pennsylvania

3rd Brigade
Brigadier General Joseph J. Bartlett
20th Maine
18th Massachusetts
1st Michigan
16th Michigan
44th New York
83rd Pennsylvania
118th Pennsylvania

Artillery Brigade
Colonel Charles S. Wainwright
3rd Massachusetts, Light Battery C
5th Massachusetts, Light Battery E
1st New York, Battery D
1st New York, Batteries E and L
1st New York, Battery H
4th New York Heavy, 2nd battalion
1st Pennsylvania, Battery B
4th U.S., Battery B
5th U.S., Battery D

[a] Wounded on May 8; division disbanded on May 9. Lyle's brigade was assigned to Cutler's division and Coulter's brigade was assigned to Crawford's division. Denison's brigade reported directly to Warren.

[b] Wounded on May 8. Denison was succeeded by Colonel Charles E. Phelps, who was captured on May 8 and was succeeded in turn by Colonel Richard N. Bowerman.

[c] Wounded on May 8 and succeeded by Colonel William C. Talley, who was captured on May 8 and replaced by Colonel Wellington H. Ent.

[d] Killed on May 10 and succeeded by Colonel Edward B. Fowler.

6TH ARMY CORPS
Major General John Sedgwick[a]
8th Pennsylvania Cavalry, Company A

1ST DIVISION
Brigadier General Horatio G. Wright[b]

1st Brigade
Colonel Henry W. Brown

1st New Jersey
2nd New Jersey
3rd New Jersey
4th New Jersey
10th New Jersey
15th New Jersey

2nd Brigade
Colonel Emory Upton

5th Maine
121st New York
95th Pennsylvania
96th Pennsylvania

3rd Brigade
Brigadier General David A. Russell[c]

6th Maine
49th Pennsylvania
119th Pennsylvania
5th Wisconsin

2ND DIVISION
Brigadier General Thomas H. Neill

1st Brigade
Brigadier General Frank Wheaton

62nd New York
93rd Pennsylvania
98th Pennsylvania
102nd Pennsylvania
139th Pennsylvania

2nd Brigade
Colonel Lewis A. Grant

2nd Vermont
3rd Vermont
4th Vermont
5th Vermont
6th Vermont

3rd Brigade
Colonel Daniel D. Bidwell

7th Maine
43rd New York
49th New York
77th New York
61st Pennsylvania

3RD DIVISION
Brigadier General James B. Ricketts

1st Brigade
Brigadier General William H. Morris[e]

14th New Jersey
106th New York
151st New York
87th Pennsylvania
10th Vermont

2nd Brigade
Colonel Benjamin F. Smith

6th Maryland
110th Ohio
122nd Ohio
126th Ohio
67th Pennsylvania
138th Pennsylvania

Artillery Brigade
Colonel Charles H. Tompkins

4th Maine, Battery D
1st Massachusetts, Battery A
1st New York, Independent Battery
3rd New York, Independent Battery
4th New York Heavy, 1st battalion
1st Rhode Island, Battery C
1st Rhode Island, Battery E
1st Rhode Island, Battery G
5th U.S., Battery M

4th Brigade
Colonel Nelson Cross
65th New York
67th New York
122nd New York
82nd Pennsylvania

4th Brigade
Brigadier General Henry L. Eustis [d]
7th Massachusetts
10th Massachusetts
37th Massachusetts
2nd Rhode Island

---

[a] Killed on May 9 and succeeded by Brigadier General Horatio G. Wright.

[b] Promoted to head the 6th Corps on May 9. Brigadier General David A. Russell assumed command of the division.

[c] Promoted to command the division on May 9 and succeeded by Brigadier General Henry L. Eustis.

[d] Shifted to head Russell's brigade on May 9 and replaced by Colonel Oliver Edwards.

[e] Wounded on May 9 and succeeded by Colonel John W. Schall.

CAVALRY CORPS
Major General Philip H. Sheridan
6th U.S.

1ST DIVISION
Brigadier General Wesley Merritt

1st Brigade
Brigadier General George A. Custer

1st Michigan
5th Michigan
6th Michigan
7th Michigan

2nd Brigade
Colonel Thomas C. Devin

4th New York
6th New York
9th New York
17th Pennsylvania

Reserve Brigade
Colonel Alfred Gibbs

19th New York
6th Pennsylvania
1st U.S.
2nd U.S.
5th U.S.

2ND DIVISION
Brigadier General David McM. Gregg

1st Brigade
Brigadier General Henry E. Davies, Jr.

1st Massachusetts
1st New Jersey
6th Ohio
1st Pennsylvania

2nd Brigade
Colonel J. Irvin Gregg

1st Maine
10th New York
2nd Pennsylvania
4th Pennsylvania
8th Pennsylvania
16th Pennsylvania

3RD DIVISION
Brigadier General James H. Wilson

1st Brigade
Colonel John B. McIntosh

1st Connecticut
2nd New York
5th New York
18th Pennsylvania

2nd Brigade
Colonel George H. Chapman

3rd Indiana
8th New York
1st Vermont

Major General Ambrose E. Burnside
8th U.S.

1st Division
Brigadier General Thomas G. Stevenson[a]

1st Brigade
Lt. Col. Stephen M. Weld, Jr.

35th Massachusetts
56th Massachusetts
57th Massachusetts
59th Massachusetts
4th U.S.
10th U.S.

2nd Brigade
Colonel Daniel Leasure

3rd Maryland
21st Massachusetts
100th Pennsylvania

Artillery
2nd Maine Battery (B)
14th Massachusetts Battery

2nd Division
Brigadier General Robert B. Potter

1st Brigade
Colonel Zenas R. Bliss[b]

36th Massachusetts
58th Massachusetts
51st New York
45th Pennsylvania
48th Pennsylvania
7th Rhode Island

2nd Brigade
Colonel Simon G. Griffin

31st Maine
32nd Maine
6th New Hampshire
9th New Hampshire
11th New Hampshire
17th Vermont

Artillery
11th Massachusetts Battery
19th New York Battery

3rd Division
Brigadier General Orlando B. Willcox

1st Brigade
Colonel John F. Hartranft

2nd Michigan
8th Michigan
17th Michigan
27th Michigan
109th New York
51st Pennsylvania

2nd Brigade
Colonel Benjamin C. Christ[c]

1st Michigan Sharpshooters
20th Michigan
79th New York
60th Ohio
50th Pennsylvania

Artillery
7th Maine, Battery G
34th New York Battery

4th Division
Brigadier General Edward Ferrero

1st Brigade
Colonel Joshua K. Sigfried

27th U.S. Colored Troops
30th U.S. Colored Troops
39th U.S. Colored Troops
43rd U.S. Colored Troops

2nd Brigade
Colonel Henry G. Thomas

30th Connecticut (Colored)
19th U.S. Colored Troops
23rd U.S. Colored Troops

Artillery
Pennsylvania Independent Battery D
3rd Vermont Battery

Cavalry
3rd New Jersey
22nd New York
2nd Ohio
13th Pennsylvania

Artillery Reserve
Captain John Edwards, Jr.

27th New York Battery
1st Rhode Island, Battery D
1st Rhode Island, Battery H
2nd U.S., Battery E
3rd U.S., Battery G
3rd U.S., Batteries L and M

Provisional Brigade
Colonel Elisha G. Marshall

14th New York Heavy Artillery
24th New York Cavalry (Dismounted)
2nd Pennsylvania Provisional Heavy Artillery

[a] Killed on May 10 and succeeded by Colonel Daniel Leasure, who was replaced by Brigadier General Thomas L. Crittenden on May 11.
[b] Injured on May 11 and replaced by Colonel John I. Curtin.
[c] Disabled from command on May 11 and replaced by Colonel William Humphrey on May 12.

ARMY OF NORTHERN VIRGINIA
General Robert E. Lee

1ST ARMY CORPS
Major General Richard H. Anderson

FIELD'S DIVISION
Major General Charles W. Field

Jenkins' Brigade
Colonel John Bratton

1st South Carolina
2nd South Carolina (Rifles)
5th South Carolina
6th South Carolina
Palmetto Sharpshooters

Gregg's Brigade
Brigadier General John Gregg

3rd Arkansas
1st Texas
4th Texas
5th Texas

Law's Brigade
Colonel William F. Perry

4th Alabama
15th Alabama
44th Alabama
47th Alabama
48th Alabama

KERSHAW'S DIVISION
Brigadier General Joseph B. Kershaw

Kershaw's Brigade
Colonel John W. Henagan

2nd South Carolina
3rd South Carolina
7th South Carolina
8th South Carolina
15th South Carolina
3rd South Carolina battalion

Humphreys' Brigade
Brigadier General Benjamin G. Humphreys

13th Mississippi
17th Mississippi
18th Mississippi
21st Mississippi

Wofford's Brigade
Brigadier General William T. Wofford

16th Georgia
18th Georgia
24th Georgia
Cobb's (Georgia) Legion
Phillip's (Georgia) Legion
3rd Georgia Battalion Sharpshooters

ARTILLERY
Brigadier General E. Porter Alexander

Haskell's Battalion
Major John C. Haskell

Flanner's (North Carolina) Battery
Garden's (South Carolina) Battery
Lamkin's (Virginia) Battery
Ramsay's (North Carolina) Battery

Huger's Battalion
Lieutenant Colonel Frank Huger

Fickling's (South Carolina) Battery
Moody's (Louisiana) Battery
Parker's (Virginia) Battery
Smith's (Virginia) Battery
Taylor's (Virginia) Battery
Woolfolk's (Virginia) Battery

Cabell's Battalion
Colonel Henry C. Cabell

Callaway's (Georgia) Battery
Carlton's (Georgia) Battery
McCarthy's (Virginia) Battery
Manly's (North Carolina) Battery

Bryan's Brigade
Brigadier General Goode Bryan
10th Georgia
50th Georgia
51st Georgia
53rd Georgia

Anderson's Brigade
Brigadier General George T. Anderson
7th Georgia
8th Georgia
9th Georgia
11th Georgia
59th Georgia

Benning's Brigade
Colonel Dudley M. DuBose
2nd Georgia
15th Georgia
17th Georgia
20th Georgia

2ND ARMY CORPS
Lieutenant General Richard S. Ewell

EARLY'S DIVISION
Major General Jubal A. Early [a]

Pegram's Brigade
Colonel John S. Hoffman

13th Virginia
31st Virginia
49th Virginia
52nd Virginia
58th Virginia

Johnston's Brigade
Brigadier General Robert D. Johnston [b]

5th North Carolina
12th North Carolina
20th North Carolina
23rd North Carolina

Gordon's Brigade
Brigadier General John B. Gordon [c]

13th Georgia
26th Georgia
31st Georgia
38th Georgia
60th Georgia
61st Georgia

JOHNSON'S DIVISION
Major General Edward Johnson [e]

Stonewall Brigade
Brigadier General James A. Walker [f]

2nd Virginia
4th Virginia
5th Virginia
27th Virginia
33rd Virginia

Jones's Brigade
Colonel William Witcher [g]

21st Virginia
25th Virginia
42nd Virginia
44th Virginia
48th Virginia
50th Virginia

Steuart's Brigade
Brigadier General George H. Steuart [h]

1st North Carolina
3rd North Carolina
10th Virginia
23rd Virginia
37th Virginia

RODES'S DIVISION
Major General Robert E. Rodes

Daniel's Brigade
Brigadier General Junius Daniel [i]

32nd North Carolina
43rd North Carolina
45th North Carolina
53rd North Carolina
2nd North Carolina battalion

Ramseur's Brigade
Brigadier General Stephen D. Ramseur [k]

2nd North Carolina
4th North Carolina
14th North Carolina
30th North Carolina

Battle's Brigade
Brigadier General Cullen A. Battle [l]

3rd Alabama
5th Alabama
6th Alabama
12th Alabama
26th Alabama
61st Alabama

ARTILLERY
Brigadier General Armistead L. Long

Braxton's Battalion
Lieutenant Colonel Carter M. Braxton

Carpenter's (Virginia) Battery
Cooper's (Virginia) Battery
Hardwicke's (Virginia) Battery

Nelson's Battalion
Lieutenant Colonel William Nelson

Kirkpatrick's (Virginia) Battery
Massie's (Virginia) Battery
Milledge's (Georgia) Battery

Page's Battalion
Major Richard C. M. Page

W. P. Carter's (Virginia) Battery
Fry's (Virginia) Battery
Page's (Virginia) Battery
Reese's (Alabama) Battery

Cutshaw's Battalion
Major Wilfred E. Cutshaw

Carrington's (Virginia) Battery
A. W. Garber's (Virginia) Battery
Tanner's (Virginia) Battery

Hays's Brigade
Brigadier General Harry T. Hays [d]

5th Louisiana
6th Louisiana
7th Louisiana
8th Louisiana
9th Louisiana

Stafford's Brigade
Colonel Zebulon York [i]

1st Louisiana
2nd Louisiana
10th Louisiana
14th Louisiana
15th Louisiana

Doles's Brigade
Brigadier General George Doles

4th Georgia
12th Georgia
44th Georgia

Hardaway's Battalion
Lieutenant Colonel Robert A. Hardaway

Dance's (Virginia) Battery
Graham's (Virginia) Battery
C. B. Griffin's (Virginia) Battery
Jones's (Virginia) Battery
B. H. Smith's (Virginia) Battery

[a] Placed in temporary command of the 3rd Corps on May 8. Brigadier General John B. Gordon assumed command of the division. His reconstituted division consisted of the brigades of Hoffman, Johnston, and Evans.

[b] Wounded on May 12.

[c] Elevated to division command on May 8 and succeeded by Colonel Clement A. Evans.

[d] Brigade consolidated on May 8 with Stafford's brigade, also from Louisiana. The resulting brigade, with Hays commanding, was in Johnson's division. Hays was wounded on May 10 and succeeded by Colonel William Monaghan. On May 12, Colonel Zebulon York commanded the portion of the brigade formerly under Stafford.

[e] Captured on May 12.

[f] Wounded on May 12.

[g] Wounded on May 12.

[h] Captured on May 12.

[i] Consolidated with Hays's brigade on May 8.

[j] Mortally wounded on May 12.

[k] Wounded on May 12.

[l] Wounded on May 10.

3RD ARMY CORPS
Lieutenant General Ambrose P. Hill [a]

HETH'S DIVISION
Major General Henry Heth

WILCOX' DIVISION
Major General Cadmus M. Wilcox

ARTILLERY
Colonel R. Lindsay Walker

ANDERSON'S DIVISION
Brigadier General William Mahone [b]

Perrin's Brigade
Brigadier General Abner Perrin [c]

8th Alabama
9th Alabama
10th Alabama
11th Alabama
14th Alabama

Mahone's Brigade
Colonel David A. Weisiger [d]

6th Virginia
12th Virginia
16th Virginia
41st Virginia
61st Virginia

Harris' Brigade
Brigadier General Nathaniel H. Harris

12th Mississippi
16th Mississippi
19th Mississippi
48th Mississippi

Davis' Brigade
Brigadier General Joseph R. Davis

2nd Mississippi
11th Mississippi
26th Mississippi
42nd Mississippi
55th North Carolina

Cooke's Brigade
Brigadier General John R. Cooke [e]

15th North Carolina
27th North Carolina
46th North Carolina
48th North Carolina

Walker's Brigade
Brigadier General Henry H. Walker [f]

40th Virginia
47th Virginia
55th Virginia
22nd Virginia battalion
13th Alabama
1st Tennessee (Provisional)
7th Tennessee
14th Tennessee

Lane's Brigade
Brigadier General James H. Lane

7th North Carolina
18th North Carolina
28th North Carolina
33rd North Carolina
37th North Carolina

McGowan's Brigade
Brigadier General Samuel McGowan [g]

1st South Carolina (Provisional)
12th South Carolina
13th South Carolina
14th South Carolina
1st South Carolina (Orr's Rifles)

Scales's Brigade
Brigadier General Alfred M. Scales

13th North Carolina
16th North Carolina
22nd North Carolina
34th North Carolina
38th North Carolina

Poague's Battalion
Lieutenant Colonel William T. Poague

Richard's (Mississippi) Battery
Utterback's (Virginia) Battery
Williams' (North Carolina) Battery
Wyatt's (Virginia) Battery

Pegram's Battalion
Lieutenant Colonel William J. Pegram

Brander's (Virginia) Battery
Cayce's (Virginia) Battery
Ellett's (Virginia) Battery
Marye's (Virginia) Battery
Zimmerman's (South Carolina) Battery

McIntosh's Battalion
Lieutenant Colonel David G. McIntosh

Clutter's (Virginia) Battery
Donald's (Virginia) Battery
Hurt's (Alabama) Battery
Price's (Virginia) Battery

Perry's Brigade
Brigadier General Edward A. Perry

2nd Florida
5th Florida
8th Florida

Wright's Brigade
Brigadier General Ambrose R. Wright

3rd Georgia
22nd Georgia
48th Georgia
2nd Georgia battalion
10th Georgia battalion

Kirkland's Brigade
Brigadier General William W. Kirkland

11th North Carolina
26th North Carolina
44th North Carolina
47th North Carolina
52nd North Carolina

Thomas' Brigade
Brigadier General Edward L. Thomas

14th Georgia
35th Georgia
45th Georgia
49th Georgia

Richardson's Battalion
Lieutenant Colonel Charles Richardson

Grandy's (Virginia) Battery
Landry's (Louisiana) Battery
Moore's (Virginia) Battery
Penick's (Virginia) Battery

Cutts's Battalion
Colonel Allen S. Cutts

Patterson's (Georgia) Battery
Ross's (Georgia) Battery
Wingfield's (Georgia) Battery

[a] Temporarily replaced by Major General Jubal A. Early on May 8, while too ill to command.

[b] Succeeded Richard H. Anderson on May 8.

[c] Killed on May 12.

[d] Replaced William Mahone on May 8.

[e] Wounded on May 10.

[f] Wounded on May 10 and succeeded by Colonel Robert M. Mayo.

[g] Wounded on May 12 and succeeded by Colonel Joseph N. Brown.

CAVALRY CORPS
Major General James E. B. Stuart[a]

HAMPTON'S DIVISION
Major General Wade Hampton

Young's Brigade
Brigadier General Pierce M. B. Young

7th Georgia
Cobb's (Georgia) Legion
Phillips' (Georgia) Legion
20th Georgia battalion
Jeff Davis (Mississippi) Legion

Rosser's Brigade
Brigadier General Thomas L. Rosser

7th Virginia
11th Virginia
12th Virginia
35th Virginia battalion

FITZHUGH LEE'S DIVISION
Major General Fitzhugh Lee

Lomax' Brigade
Brigadier General Lunsford L. Lomax

5th Virginia
6th Virginia
15th Virginia

Wickham's Brigade
Brigadier General Williams C. Wickham

1st Virginia
2nd Virginia
3rd Virginia
4th Virginia

WILLIAM H. F. LEE'S DIVISION
Major General William H. F. Lee

Chambliss' Brigade
Brigadier General John R. Chambliss

9th Virginia
10th Virginia
13th Virginia

Gordon's Brigade
Brigadier General James B. Gordon

1st North Carolina
2nd North Carolina
5th North Carolina

HORSE ARTILLERY
Major R. Preston Chew

Breathed's Battalion
Major James Breathed

Hart's (South Carolina) Battery
Johnston's (Virginia) Battery
McGregor's (Virginia) Battery
Shoemaker's (Virginia) Battery
Thomson's (Virginia) Battery

---

[a] Mortally wounded on May 11.

Notes

Introduction

1. George Meade, ed., *The Life and Letters of George Gordon Meade, Major General, United States Army* (2 vols.; New York, 1913), II, 154.
2. Horace Porter, *Campaigning with Grant* (New York, 1897), 98.
3. Louis M. Starr, *Reporting the Civil War: The Bohemian Brigade in Action, 1861–65* (New York, 1962), 246.
4. Starr proffers details of Wing's escape in *Reporting the Civil War,* 246–49. See also Henry E. Wing, *When Lincoln Kissed Me: A Story of the Wilderness Campaign* (New York, 1913), and Ida Tarbell, *A Reporter for Lincoln* (New York, 1927).
5. William Swinton, *Campaigns of the Army of the Potomac* (New York, 1866), 440n.
6. Theodore Lyman to family, May 18, 1864, in *Meade's Headquarters, 1863–1865: Letters of Colonel Theodore Lyman from the Wilderness to Appomattox*, ed. George R. Agassiz (Boston, 1922), 100.

I   MAY 7, 1864 *Grant and Lee Skirmish in the Wilderness and at Todd's Tavern*

1. Horace Porter, *Campaigning with Grant,* 74.
2. Ulysses S. Grant to Henry W. Halleck, May 7, 1864, in *OR,* Vol. XXXVI, Pt. 2, p. 480; Theodore Lyman to family, May 18, 1864, in *Meade's Headquarters,* ed. Agassiz, 101–102.
3. Ulysses S. Grant's report, in *OR,* Vol. XXXVI, Pt. 1, p. 18.
4. Cyrus B. Comstock Diary, May 12, 1864, in Cyrus B. Comstock Collection, LC.
5. Theodore Lyman Journal, May 6, 1864, in Theodore Lyman Collection, MHS.
6. Charles A. Dana, *Recollections of the Civil War* (New York, 1899), 190–91.
7. Josiah M. Favill, *The Diary of a Young Officer Serving with the Armies of the United States During the War of the Rebellion* (Chicago, 1909), 274.
8. Elbert Corbin Diary, May 7, 1864, in Civil War Miscellaneous Collection, USAMHI; J. Finnegan to friend, May 8, 1864, *This Regiment of Heroes: A Compilation of Primary*

Materials Pertaining to the 124th New York State Volunteers in the American Civil War, comp. Charles J. LaRocca (N.p., 1991), 208–209.

9. Robert E. Lee to Jefferson Davis, April 15, 1864, in *OR,* XXXIII, 1282–83.

10. G. Moxley Sorrel, *Recollections of a Confederate Staff Officer* (New York, 1917), 249.

11. David French Boyd, *Reminiscences of the War in Virginia,* ed. T. Michael Parrish (Austin, Tex., 1989), 24–25; Jubal A. Early, *Autobiographical Sketch and Narrative of the War Between the States* (Bloomington, Ind., 1960), xlvi–xlvii; Sorrel, *Recollections of a Confederate Staff Officer,* 249.

12. Sorrel, *Recollections of a Confederate Staff Officer,* 249, 254; Gary W. Gallagher, ed., *Fighting for the Confederacy: The Personal Recollections of General Edward Porter Alexander* (Chapel Hill, N.C., 1989), 365.

13. Sorrel, *Recollections of a Confederate Staff Officer,* 249–50; Special Order, in *OR,* Vol. XXXVI, Pt. 2, p. 967.

14. Butt Hewson, "Battle of Spotsylvania Court House," in *Lee's Sharpshooters; or, The Forefront of Battle: A Story of Southern Valor That Never Has Been Told,* by William S. Dunlop (Little Rock, Ark., 1899), 433–35.

15. Samuel Finley Harper to father, May 7, 1864, in Samuel Finley Harper Collection, NCDAH; George S. Bernard Diary, May 7, 1864, in George S. Bernard Collection, UV; Carrie Ester Spencer, comp., *A Civil War Marriage in Virginia: Reminiscences and Letters* (Boyce, Va., 1956), 216; Walter H. Taylor, *Four Years with General Lee* (New York, 1877), 129.

16. The reporter Swinton claimed that Grant's purpose was to "plant himself between Lee's army and Richmond, by a movement upon Spotsylvania Court House" (Swinton, *Campaigns of the Army of the Potomac,* 440–41). A correspondent with the New York *Daily Tribune* reported Grant's goal as "either to reach Richmond before the enemy, or, if we should be unable to turn his flank and the enemy should succeed in presenting himself in force upon our front, that we might gain so complete a victory over him as to render the capture of Richmond a comparatively easy task" ("The Great Contest," New York *Daily Tribune,* May 12, 1864). Grant later explained that his "object in moving to Spotsylvania was two-fold: first, I did not want Lee to get back to Richmond in time to crush Butler before I could get there; second, I wanted to get between his army and Richmond if possible; and if not, draw him into the open field" (Ulysses S. Grant, *Personal Memoirs* [2 vols.; New York, 1885], II, 211).

17. Adam Badeau, *Military History of General Ulysses S. Grant, from April, 1861, to April, 1865* (3 vols.; New York, 1881), II, 131–32; Frank Wilkeson, *Recollections of a Private Soldier in the Army of the Potomac* (New York, 1887), 79.

18. Porter, *Campaigning with Grant,* 76.

19. Ulysses S. Grant to George G. Meade, May 7, 1864, in *OR,* Vol. XXXVI, Pt. 2, p. 481. Grant apparently labored under a misapprehension, shared by Meade, that Piney Branch Church Road continued south to Spotsylvania. It entered Brock Road a few miles below Todd's Tavern, which meant that the entire Union army would be funneled back onto one roadway. The erroneous positioning of Piney Branch Church Road on Union war maps is discussed by William D. Matter in *If It Takes All Summer: The Battle of Spotsylvania* (Chapel Hill, N.C., 1988), 23–24.

20. Grant to Meade, May 7, 1864, in *OR,* Vol. XXXVI, Pt. 2, p. 481; Meade's General Orders, *ibid.,* 483–84.

21. James H. Wilson, *Under the Old Flag* (2 vols.; New York, 1912), I, 389.

22. Philadelphia *Inquirer,* May 12, 1864; Badeau, *Military History of General Ulysses S. Grant,* II, 133.

23. Lyman to family, May 18, 1864, in *Meade's Headquarters,* ed. Agassiz, 101; Harold A. Small, ed., *The Road to Richmond: The Civil War Memoirs of Major Abner R. Small of the Sixteenth Maine Volunteers* (Berkeley, Calif., 1939), 134.

24. George W. Pearsoll to wife, May 7, 1864, in George W. Pearsoll Collection, NCDAH; Austin C. Dobbins, ed., *Grandfather's Journal: Company B, Sixteenth Mississippi Infantry Volunteers, Harris' Brigade, Mahone's Division, Hill's Corps, A.N.V.* (Dayton, 1988), 191; Porter Farley, "Reminiscences of the 140th Regiment New York Volunteer Infantry," *Rochester Historical Society Publication,* XXII (1944), 246; John O. Casler, *Four Years in the Stonewall Brigade* (Girard, Kans., 1906), 208; Terry L. Jones, ed., *The Civil War Memoirs of Captain William J. Seymour: Reminiscences of a Louisiana Tiger* (Baton Rouge, 1991), 116–18.

25. "Opening of Saturday's Work," New York *Daily Tribune,* May 10, 1864; Hyland C. Kirk, *Heavy Guns and Light: A History of the 4th New York Heavy Artillery* (New York, 1890), 180; Stephen D. Burger Diary, May 7, 1864, in FSNMP.

26. Morris Schaff, *The Battle of the Wilderness* (New York, 1910), 330–31.

27. James W. Latta Diary, May 7, 1864, in James W. Latta Collection, LC; Schaff, *The Battle of the Wilderness,* 330; Thomas W. Hyde, *Following the Greek Cross; or, Memories of the Sixth Army Corps* (Boston, 1894), 188.

28. Alfred M. Apted Diary, May 7, 1864, in Civil War Miscellaneous Collection, USAMHI; William Y. W. Ripley, *Vermont Riflemen in the War for the Union, 1861 to 1865: A History of Company F, First United States Sharpshooters* (Rutland, Vt., 1883), 154; Joseph J. Bartlett to Catharinus B. Mervine, May 7, 1864, in *OR,* Vol. XXXVI, Pt. 2, p. 503.

29. Eugene A. Nash, *A History of the Forty-Fourth Regiment New York Volunteer Infantry in the Civil War, 1861–1865* (Chicago, 1911), 186; Apted Diary, May 7, 1864; D. P. Marshall, *History of Company K, 155th Pennsylvania Volunteer Zouaves* (N.p., 1888), 157; John D. Vautier, *History of the 88th Pennsylvania Volunteers in the War for the Union, 1861–1865* (Philadelphia, 1894), 175; J. L. Smith, *History of the Corn Exchange Regiment: 118th Pennsylvania Volunteers, from Their First Engagement at Antietam to Appomattox* (Philadelphia, 1888), 404–405.

30. Gouverneur K. Warren to Andrew A. Humphreys, 7:00 A.M., 7:40 A.M., May 7, 1864, in *OR,* Vol. XXXVI, Pt. 2, p. 499.

31. Ambrose E. Burnside to Ulysses S. Grant, May 7, 1864, in *OR,* Vol. XXXVI, Pt. 2, p. 511; Frederick W. Swift Diary, May 7, 1864, in Gregory Coco Collection, USAMHI; Winfield S. Hancock to Andrew A. Humphreys, May 7, 1864, in *OR,* Vol. XXXVI, Pt. 2, p. 486.

32. Winfield S. Hancock to Andrew A. Humphreys, May 7, 1864, in *OR,* Vol. XXXVI, Pt. 2, p. 487.

33. George G. Meade to John Sedgwick, May 7, 1864, in *OR,* Vol. XXXVI, Pt. 2, p. 507; George G. Meade to Winfield S. Hancock, May 7, 1864, *ibid.,* 487.

34. John Sedgwick to Andrew A. Humphreys, May 7, 1864, in *OR,* Vol. XXXVI, Pt. 2, p. 507; John Sedgwick to Andrew A. Humphreys, May 7, 1864, *ibid.,* 508; Judson Knight, "How Scouts Worked," *National Tribune,* March 23, 1893. The two cavalry units belonged to the 9th Corps but were on loan to Sedgwick. A third regiment, the 3rd New

Jersey Cavalry, remained north of the Rapidan. Around 8 A.M., the cavalryman Wilson had explored the region between Sedgwick and the river and found "no sign of enemy" (Wilson, *Under the Old Flag,* I, 388).

35. Meade to Sedgwick, May 7, 1864, in *OR,* Vol. XXXVI, Pt. 2, p. 507; Charles E. Pease to John Sedgwick, May 7, 1864, *ibid.;* John Sedgwick to Seth Williams, May 7, 1864, *ibid.*

36. John Sedgwick to Andrew A. Humphreys, May 7, 1864, in *OR,* Vol. XXXVI, Pt. 2, 508.

37. Favill, *The Diary of a Young Officer,* 291; Charles N. Walker and Rosemary Walker, eds., "Diary of the War by Robert S. Robertson," *Old Fort News,* XXVIII (1965), 165; John Gibbon to Winfield S. Hancock, May 7, 1864, in *OR,* Vol. XXXVI, Pt. 2, p. 494; Nelson A. Miles's report, in *OR,* Vol. XXXVI, Pt. 1, p. 370. Captain William N. McDonald, of Rosser's brigade, referred to the incident in his memoirs, noting that "[Robert P.] Chew's battery was in the fight and came near being captured, our troops having been driven back and the Yanks near his battery" (William N. McDonald Manuscript, 105, in SHC). Colonel Elijah V. White's battalion arrived in time to save the guns.

38. Nathan Church's report, in *OR,* Vol. XXXVI, Pt. 1, p. 372.

39. Jeb Stuart to Robert E. Lee, May 7, 1864, in *OR,* Vol. XXXVI, Pt. 2, p. 969.

40. William N. Pendleton's report, in *OR,* Vol. XXXVI, Pt. 1, p. 1041.

41. Westwood A. Todd Reminiscences, in Westwood A. Todd Collection, SHC; Bird Willis Diary, May 7, 1864, in VSL; John Bratton, "Report of Operations of Bratton's Brigade from May 7th, 1864, to January, 1865," in *SHSP,* VIII, 547.

42. John S. Crocker Diary, May 7, 1864, in CU; Heinz K. Meier, ed., *Memoirs of a Swiss Officer in the American Civil War* (Bern, 1972), 151; "Addenda," in *OR,* Vol. XXXVI, Pt. 1, p. 355; Ruth L. Silliker, ed., *The Rebel Yell and the Yankee Hurrah: The Civil War Journal of a Maine Volunteer, Private John W. Haley, 17th Maine Regiment* (Camden, Maine, 1985), 147. Crocker's brigade had been led by the flamboyant Brigadier General Alexander Hays, who was killed on May 5 in the Wilderness. On the seventh, Hays's body was on its way to Boston.

43. C. A. Stevens, *Berdan's United States Sharpshooters in the Army of the Potomac, 1861–1865* (St. Paul, 1892), 409–10; Meier, ed., *Memoirs of a Swiss Officer,* 151.

44. Samuel McConihe's report, in *OR,* Vol. XXXVI, Pt. 1, p. 481; Meier, ed., *Memoirs of a Swiss Officer,* 151–52; Crocker Diary, May 7, 1864.

45. David B. Birney to Winfield S. Hancock, May 7, 1864, in *OR,* Vol. XXXVI, Pt. 2, p. 495.

46. Joseph J. Bartlett's report, in *OR,* Vol. XXXVI, Pt. 1, p. 572; Apted Diary, May 7, 1864; Ellis Spear's report, in *OR,* Vol. XXXVI, Pt. 1, p. 573; Charles Herring's report, in *OR,* Vol. XXXVI, Pt. 1, pp. 590–91; Guy W. Fuller's report, in *OR,* Vol. XXXVI, Pt. 1, p. 584; Smith, *History of the Corn Exchange Regiment,* 405; McHenry Howard, *Recollections of a Maryland Confederate Soldier and Staff Officer Under Johnston, Jackson, and Lee* (Baltimore, 1914), 280. The 20th Maine had thirteen soldiers killed or wounded in this action. See *Reunions of the Twentieth Maine Regiment Association at Portland* (Waldoboro, Maine, 1881), 22.

47. O. R. Howard Thomson and William H. Rauch, *History of the Bucktails: Kane Rifle Regiment of the Pennsylvania Reserve Corps* (Philadelphia, 1906), 297; Gouverneur K. Warren to Samuel W. Crawford, 10:00 A.M., May 7, 1864, in *OR,* Vol. XXXVI, Pt. 2, p. 504;

Samuel W. Crawford to Gouverneur K. Warren, 1:20 P.M., May 7, 1864, in *OR,* Vol. XXXVI, Pt. 2, pp. 504–505.

48. Lyman to family, May 18, 1864, in *Meade's Headquarters,* ed. Agassiz, 101–102; Lyman Journal, May 7, 1864; Comstock Diary, May 7, 1864; "Battles Following That of the Wilderness," New York *Daily Tribune,* May 12, 1864. A reporter at Grant's headquarters wrote that "towards noon, our skirmishers advanced and discovered that the enemy had retreated from their line of last night. It is believed at headquarters that they are withdrawing from our front" (Boston *Daily Advertiser,* May 10, 1864).

49. "Memoir of the 64th New York," 65, in IU; George Clark, *A Glance Backward; or, Some Events in the Past History of My Life* (Houston, 1914), 45.

50. Lyman Journal, May 7, 1864.

51. *Ibid.*; John B. McIntosh to John Sedgwick, May 7, 1864, in *OR,* Vol. XXXVI, Pt. 2, p. 508; George G. Meade to Samuel J. Crooks, May 7, 1864, *ibid.,* 509.

52. David S. Sparks, ed., *Inside Lincoln's Army: The Diary of Marsena Rudolph Patrick, Provost Marshal General, Army of the Potomac* (New York, 1964), 369; Knight, "How Scouts Worked"; "Saturday's Report," New York *Daily Tribune,* May 10, 1864; Henry C. Carr Diary, May 13, 1864, in Civil War Miscellaneous Collection, USAMHI; Lyman to family, May 18, 1864, in Lyman Collection, MHS; Jennings C. Wise, *The Long Arm of Lee; or, The History of the Artillery of the Army of Northern Virginia* (2 vols.; Lynchburg, Va., 1915), II, 775; Louis N. Beaudry, *Historic Records of the Fifth New York Cavalry, First Ira Harris Guard* (Albany, N.Y., 1874), 126–27; Robert Hunt Rhodes, ed., *All for the Union: The Civil War Diary and Letters of Elisha Hunt Rhodes* (New York, 1991), 147. Lyman thought that Crooks "ought to have been shot! The force the enemy sent along there is pretty known now to have been most trifling and nothing prevented us from driving them off" (Lyman Journal, May 7, 1864).

53. Armistead L. Long's report, in *OR,* Vol. XXXVI, Pt. 1, p. 1085; Armistead L. Long to Richard S. Ewell, May 7, 1864, *ibid.,* Pt. 2, p. 968.

54. Walker and Walker, eds., "Diary of the War by Robert S. Robertson," 165–66; Charles H. Morgan to Winfield S. Hancock, May 7, 1864, in *OR,* Vol. XXXVI, Pt. 2, p. 491.

55. Winfield S. Hancock to Andrew A. Humphreys, May 7, 1864, in *OR,* Vol. XXXVI, Pt. 2, p. 492; Kirk, *Heavy Guns and Light,* 180; Stevens, *Berdan's United States Sharpshooters,* 410.

56. Mark D. Howe, ed., *Touched with Fire: Civil War Letters and Diary of Oliver Wendell Holmes, Jr., 1861–1864* (New York, 1969), 108.

57. Walter H. Taylor to Jeb Stuart, May 7, 1864, in *OR,* Vol. XXXVI, Pt. 2, pp. 969–70; Jeb Stuart to Robert E. Lee, May 7, 1864, *ibid.,* Vol. LI, Pt. 2, Supplement, pp. 897–98; Bird Willis Diary, May 7, 1864, in VSL; R. L. T. Beale, *History of the Ninth Virginia Cavalry in the War Between the States* (Richmond, 1899), 117. Bird Willis, of the 9th Virginia Cavalry, of Chambliss' brigade, expressed astonishment at the "immense quantity" of abandoned Federal provisions, observing that the "quarters of the officers and the men were left with blankets and everything just as if they had gone out on a parade and would be back in an hour or two" (Willis Diary, May 7, 1864). Returning to Lee's army the next day, troopers from the 9th Virginia captured three Negro soldiers, "the first we had seen," according to Willis, who added, "They were taken out on the road side and shot and their bodies left there" (May 8, 1864).

58. George Q. Peyton, *A Civil War Record for 1864–1865,* ed. Robert A. Hodge (Fred-

ericksburg, Va., 1981), 23; William H. Palmer to William L. Royall, May 11, 1908, in *Some Reminiscences,* by William L. Royall (New York, 1909), 35. Brigadier General John B. Gordon placed Lee's visit in the morning. See his *Reminiscences of the Civil War* (New York, 1903), 267. But Taylor's dispatch to Stuart, issued after 1:30 P.M., noted that "the General is now starting to visit Ewell's lines" (*OR,* Vol. XXXVI, Pt. 2, p. 970). A soldier from the 39th Virginia Cavalry assigned to Lee's headquarters wrote in his diary, "In the afternoon rode with Gen. Lee along our line to the left. Found Gen. Ewell's headquarters on the [turnpike]. . . . Returned to headquarters about sundown" (Franklin Gardner Walter Diary, May 7, 1864, in FSNMP).

59. Richard H. Anderson's report, in Richard H. Anderson Collection, DU; Walter H. Taylor to Richard S. Ewell, in *OR,* Vol. XXXVI, Pt. 2, p. 968.

60. Anderson's account of his conversation with Lee is from his report, in Anderson Collection, DU. See also Richard H. Anderson to Edward R. Robins, May 11, 1874, in "The Operations of the Army of the Potomac, May 7–11, 1864," by Charles L. Peirson, in *PMHSM,* IV, 229; Joseph P. Fuller Diary, May 7, 1864, in Confederate Miscellaneous Collection, GDAH; Pendleton's report, in *OR,* Vol. XXXVI, Pt. 1, p. 1041; Diary of the First Army Corps, in *OR,* Vol. XXXVI, Pt. 1, p. 1056.

61. Anderson to Robins, May 11, 1874, in "The Operations of the Army of the Potomac," by Peirson, 229; Anderson's report, in Anderson Collection, DU; John Coxe, "Last Struggles and Successes of Lee," *Confederate Veteran,* XXII (1914), 356. Sorrel noted the starting time as 11 P.M. See G. Moxley Sorrel Diary, May 7, 1864, in MC. The reporter Butt Hewson wrote that Kershaw's division started first, led by the brigades of Brigadier Generals William T. Wofford and Goode Bryan. See his "Battle of Spotsylvania Court House," in *Lee's Sharpshooters,* by Dunlop, 437.

62. Frank M. Mixson, *Reminiscences of a Private* (Columbia, S.C., 1910), 73; Pearsoll to wife, May 7, 1864, in Pearsoll Collection, NCDAH; James Eldred Phillips Memoir, May 8, 1864, in VHS.

63. Jedediah Hotchkiss, "Report of the Camps, Marches, and Engagements of the Second Corps," in Jedediah Hotchkiss Collection, LC; S. D. Thruston, "Report of the Conduct of General George H. Steuart's Brigade from the 5th to the 12th of May, 1864, Inclusive," in *SHSP,* XIV, 150; Howard, *Recollections of a Maryland Confederate,* 282; Peyton, *A Civil War Record,* ed. Hodge, 23.

64. Dunlop, *Lee's Sharpshooters,* 43–44; Edward G. Longacre, "From the Wilderness to Cold Harbor in the Union Artillery," *Manuscripts,* XXXV (1983), 205; Susan W. Benson, ed., *Berry Benson's Civil War Book: Memoirs of a Confederate Scout and Sharpshooter* (Athens, Ga., 1991), 66.

65. Frank M. Myers, *The Comanches: A History of White's Battalion, Virginia Cavalry, Laurel Brigade, Hampton Division, A.N.V., C.S.A.* (Baltimore, 1871), 276; Wade Hampton's report, in Wade Hampton Collection, SCL.

66. James W. Forsyth to David McM. Gregg, May 7, 1864, in *OR,* Vol. XXXVI, Pt. 2, p. 516.

67. Thomas C. Devin's report, in *OR,* Vol. XXXVI, Pt. 1, p. 833.

68. *Ibid.*; George A. Custer's report, in *OR,* Vol. XXVI, Pt. 1, pp. 816–17.

69. Charles E. Pease to Philip H. Sheridan, May 7, 1864, in *OR,* Vol. XXXVI, Pt. 2, p. 513.

70. Philip H. Sheridan to Andrew A. Humphreys, May 7, 1864, in *OR,* Vol. XXXVI, Pt. 2, p. 514. Wilson's division was not involved in the engagement at Todd's Tavern. One

of his brigades—McIntosh's—had already departed for Germanna Ford, and his other brigade—Colonel George H. Chapman's—was actively employed guarding wagons.

71. Fitzhugh Lee's report, in MC; J. D. Ferguson, "Memoranda of the Itinerary and Operations of Major General Fitz. Lee's Cavalry Division of the Army of Northern Virginia, May 4th to October 5, 1864, Inclusive," in Thomas T. Munford Collection, DU; David McM. Gregg's report, in *OR,* Vol. XXXVI, Pt. 1, p. 853.

72. Myers, *The Comanches,* 277; William N. McDonald, *A History of the Laurel Brigade, Originally the Ashby Cavalry of the Army of Northern Virginia and Chew's Battery* (Baltimore, 1907), 237; "Itinerary of the Eighth Pennsylvania Cavalry, May 1–June 30," in *OR,* Vol. XXXVI, Pt. 1, p. 867. A section of Martin's battery was posted on a hill near Todd's Tavern, and a section of Lieutenant Rufus King, Jr.'s battery was placed farther left. See "Another Account," Philadelphia *Inquirer,* May 12, 1864.

73. "Barringer's North Carolina Brigade of Cavalry," Raleigh (N.C.) *Daily Confederate,* February 22, 1865; Edward P. Tobie, *History of the First Maine Cavalry, 1861–1865* (Boston, 1887), 253–54. For the participation of Young's brigade, see Joseph F. Waring Diary, May 7, 1864, in Joseph F. Waring Collection, SHC; Nobel J. Brooks Diary, May 7, 1864, in Nobel J. Brooks Collection, SHC; Robert J. Trout, ed., *Riding with Stuart: Reminiscences of an Aide-de-Camp, by Captain Theodore Stanford Garnett* (Shippensburg, Pa., 1994), 56–57.

74. Rufus H. Peck, *Reminiscences of a Confederate Soldier of Co. C, 2nd Va. Cavalry* (Fincastle, Va., 1913), 44–45; and Alexander Hunter, *Johnny Reb and Billy Yank* (New York, 1905), 543. Peck maintained that Wickham's brigade held the first line. See also "The Second Virginia Cavalry in the Late Fight," Richmond *Sentinel,* May 21, 1864. Other accounts— among them "The Fight Near Spotsylvania Court House Between Fitzhugh Lee and the Enemy," Richmond *Daily Examiner,* May 11, 1864—placed Lomax in front.

75. Richard J. Del Vecchio, ed., "With the First New York Dragoons" [Jared L. Ainsworth Letters], in Harrisburg Civil War Round Table Collection, USAMHI; J. R. Bowen, *Regimental History of the First New York Dragoons During Three Years of Active Service in the Great Civil War* (Lyons, Mich., 1900), 143.

76. Alfred Gibbs's report, in *OR,* Vol. XXXVI, Pt. 1, p. 846; Louis Boos, "My Experience as a Soldier," in William O. Bourne Collection, LC; New York *Herald,* May 17, 1864. Starr, commanding the 6th Pennsylvania, was shot in the face, "making him speechless, and forcing him to go to the rear" (Samuel L. Gracey, *Annals of the Sixth Pennsylvania Cavalry* [Philadelphia, 1868], 235–36). Captain Charles L. Leiper assumed the popular Starr's position.

77. Devin's report, in *OR,* Vol. XXXVI, Pt. 1, p. 833.

78. Peck, *Reminiscences of a Confederate Soldier,* 44–45; Hunter, *Johnny Reb and Billy Yank,* 543.

79. Isaac R. Christian to editor of Richmond *Dispatch,* June 8, 1897, Richmond *Dispatch,* June 20, 1897; "The Fight Near Spotsylvania Court House Between Fitzhugh Lee and the Enemy," Richmond *Daily Examiner,* May 11, 1864; St. George Tucker Brook Memoir, 36, in St. George Tucker Brook Collection, VHS.

80. Ferguson Memoranda, in Munford Collection, DU; Devin's report, in *OR,* Vol. XXXVI, Pt. 1, p. 833; George Perkins Memoir, in Michael T. Russert Private Collection; Well A. Bushnell Memoir, 264, in William P. Palmer Collection, WRHS; Hunter, *Johnny*

Reb and Billy Yank, 544. According to Ferguson, Lee's second line was where Brock Road and Piney Branch Church Road joined, approximately two miles below Todd's Tavern.

. 81. G. W. Goler to Thomas T. Munford, January 24, 1898, in Munford Collection, DU; William G. Hills Diary, May 7, 1864, in William G. Hills Collection, LC; Newel Cheney, *History of the Ninth Regiment New York Volunteer Cavalry* (Jamestown, N.Y., 1901), 158; Bowen, *Regimental History of the First New York Dragoons,* 143–45. The Richmond *Sentinel* of May 9, 1864, reported two Union captains and forty-eight privates captured, mostly from New York regiments. The 1st New York Dragoons suffered the "greatest loss of any Federal cavalry regiment in any one engagement during the entire war" (Del Vecchio, ed., "With the First New York Dragoons," 78).

82. Katherine Couse to unknown, May 4–22, 1864, in UV.

83. Peck, *Reminiscences of a Confederate Soldier,* 46; Couse to unknown, May 4–22, 1864, in UV.

84. Peck, *Reminiscences of a Confederate Soldier,* 46; B. J. Haden, *Reminiscences of J. E. B. Stuart's Cavalry* (Charlottesville, Va., n.d.), 30; "Cavalry Engagement Near Spotsylvania Court House," Richmond *Daily Dispatch,* May 9, 1864; "The Second Virginia in the Late Fight," Richmond *Sentinel,* May 21, 1864; Asa B. Isham, "Through the Wilderness to Richmond," in *Sketches of War History, 1861–1865: Papers Read Before the Ohio Commandery of the Military Order of the Loyal Legion of the United States* (3 vols.; Cincinnati, 1888), I, 204.

85. "The Cavalry Fight Near Spotsylvania CH," Richmond *Daily Dispatch,* May 10, 1864; Woodford B. Hackley, *The Little Fork Rangers: A Sketch of Company D Fourth Virginia Cavalry* (Richmond, 1927), 89. Fitzhugh Lee lost about 225 men, mostly from Wickham's brigade.

86. Alexander R. Boteler Diary, in William E. Brooks Collection, LC.

87. Philip H. Sheridan to Andrew A. Humphreys, May 7, 1864, in *OR,* Vol. XXXVI, Pt. 2, pp. 515–16; Luther W. Hopkins, *From Bull Run to Appomattox: A Boy's View* (Baltimore, 1908), 152–53. Fitzhugh Lee ordered some Maryland troopers to rescue Collins' body, but the Federals drove them back. See John Gill, *Reminiscences of Four Years as a Private Soldier in the Confederate Army* (Baltimore, 1904), 95.

88. James H. Kidd, *Personal Recollections of a Cavalryman with Custer's Michigan Cavalry Brigade in the Civil War* (Ionia, Mich., 1908), 280–81.

89. Washington A. Roebling's report, in Gouverneur K. Warren Collection, NYSLA; Howe, ed., *Touched With Fire,* 108.

90. Roebling's report, in Warren Collection, NYSLA; Robert G. Carter, *Four Brothers in Blue; or, Sunshine and Shadows of the War of the Rebellion* (Austin, Tex., 1978), 393; Vautier, *History of the 88th Pennsylvania Volunteers,* 175–76; Robert Tilney, *My Life in the Army: Three Years and a Half with the Fifth Army Corps, Army of the Potomac, 1862–1865* (Philadelphia, 1912), 70; Avery Harris Reminiscences, in USAMHI; Charles S. Wainwright's report, in *OR,* Vol. XXXVI, Pt. 1, p. 641; Allan Nevins, ed., *Diary of Battle: The Personal Journals of Colonel Charles S. Wainwright, 1861–1865* (New York, 1962), 355. Accounts variously describe the order in which Warren's divisions marched. I have followed Roebling's unpublished report. As Warren's chief aide, Roebling was well positioned to know Warren's deployments.

91. Gouverneur K. Warren's report, in *OR,* Vol. XXXVI, Pt. 1, p. 540; William B. Rawle *et al., History of the Third Pennsylvania Cavalry, Sixtieth Regiment Pennsylvania Volunteers in the American Civil War, 1861–1865* (Philadelphia, 1905), 421–22.

92. Charles E. Phelps, "Seventh Regiment Infantry," in *History and Roster of Maryland Volunteers, War of 1861–1865,* by Allison Wilmer *et al.* (2 vols.; Baltimore, Md., 1898), I, 269–70.

93. Free B. Bowley, "A Boy Lieutenant in a Black Regiment," *National Tribune,* May 4, 1899.

94. Tilney, *My Life in the Army,* 70.

95. Wilkeson, *Recollections of a Private,* 78–80.

96. Porter, *Campaigning with Grant,* 78–79; Gilbert Thompson, "My Journal, 1861–1865," in Gilbert Thompson Collection, LC.

97. John Day Smith, *The History of the Nineteenth Regiment of Maine Volunteer Infantry, 1862–1865* (Minneapolis, 1909), 147–48; Badeau, *Military History of General Ulysses S. Grant,* II, 134–35.

98. Lyman to family, May 18, 1864, in *Meade's Headquarters,* ed. Agassiz, 103; Andrew A. Humphreys, *The Virginia Campaign of '64 and '65* (New York, 1883), 58n2.

99. Robert S. Robertson's account appears, with slight variations, in "Diary of the War by Robert S. Robertson," ed. Walker and Walker, 166, and in *Personal Recollections of the War,* by Robert S. Robertson (Milwaukee, 1895), 94–95. Todd's Tavern was a long wooden structure one and a half stories high with a broad front porch and chimneys at each end. It occupied the west side of Brock Road, just above Catharpin Road. A passing artilleryman remarked that the tavern had "no merits, architectural or otherwise, to warrant its becoming a conspicuous landmark" (Noel G. Harrison, *Gazetteer of Historic Sites Related to the Fredericksburg and Spotsylvania National Military Park* [2 vols.; Fredericksburg, Va., 1986], II, 278–79).

100. Lyman to family, May 18, 1864, in *Meade's Headquarters,* ed. Agassiz, 103; Porter, *Campaigning with Grant,* 82.

101. George G. Meade to Wesley Merritt, in *OR,* Vol. XXXVI, Pt. 2, p. 552.

102. George G. Meade to Philip H. Sheridan, in *OR,* Vol. XXXVI, Pt. 2, 551; Humphreys, *The Virginia Campaign,* 58–59.

103. James W. Forsyth to David McM. Gregg, in *OR,* Vol. XXXVI, Pt. 2, p. 553.

104. Philip H. Sheridan's report, in *OR,* Vol. XXXVI, Pt. 1, pp. 788–89. The erroneous recital of events that originated in Sheridan's report was repeated and amplified by Grant's aide Badeau in *Military History of General Ulysses S. Grant,* II, 138–39; by Grant in *Personal Memoirs,* II, 212–13; and by Sheridan in *Personal Memoirs* (2 vols.; New York, 1888), I, 364–65. Humphreys offers his rejoinder in *The Virginia Campaign,* 67–70.

105. "Civil War Journal of Major John Chester White," in John Chester White Collection, LC; Luther E. Cowles, *History of the Fifth Massachusetts Battery* (Boston, 1902), 810; Charles E. Davis, Jr., *Three Years in the Army: The Story of the Thirteenth Massachusetts Volunteers from July 16, 1861, to August 1, 1864* (Boston, 1894), 332; Theodore Gerrish, *Army Life: A Private's Reminiscences of the Civil War* (Portland, Maine, 1882), 174; Roebling's report, in Warren Collection, NYSLA.

106. Gerrish, *Army Life,* 173; Fuller's report, in *OR,* Vol. XXXVI, Pt. 1, p. 584; Hancock's report, in *OR,* Vol. XXXVI, Pt. 1, p. 329; Stevens, *Berdan's United States Sharpshooters,* 411; Meier, ed., *Memoirs of a Swiss Officer,* 152.

107. S. F. Hildebrand, "Notes and Reminiscences of Service in the 139th Regiment," in Harold C. George Collection, LC; Medical director's report, in *OR,* Vol. XXXVI, Pt. 1, p. 220; Edward B. Dalton's report, in *OR,* Vol. XXXVI, Pt. 1, pp. 269–70; Byron M. Cutcheon Autobiography, 73–74, in Michigan Historical Collection, BL; John E. Irwin

Diary, May 7–8, 1864, in Book 47, FSNMP. About five hundred wounded Federals remained in temporary hospitals in the Wilderness. They were retrieved a week later under a flag of truce, according to Roebling's report, in Warren Collection, NYSLA.

108. Gordon, *Reminiscences of the Civil War,* 268–69; Walter H. Taylor, *General Lee: His Campaigns in Virginia, 1861–1865, with Personal Reminiscences* (Norfolk, Va., 1906), 238.

109. Walter H. Taylor to J. E. B. Stuart, May 7, 1864, in *OR,* Vol. XXXVI, Pt. 2, pp. 969–70; Robert E. Lee to secretary of war, May 8, 1864, *ibid.,* 974.

110. Sparks, ed., *Inside Lincoln's Army,* 370.

111. Hildebrand, "Notes and Reminiscences," in George Collection, LC; William T. Schoyer, ed., *The Road to Cold Harbor: Field Diary, January 1–June 12, 1864, of Samuel L. Schoyer, Captain, Company G, 139th Pennsylvania Volunteer Regiment* (Apollo, Pa., 1986), 76–77; Hyde, *Following the Greek Cross,* 189–90.

II MAY 8 *The Armies Meet at Laurel Hill*

1. Gouverneur K. Warren to Andrew A. Humphreys, May 8, 1864, in *OR,* Vol. XXXVI, Pt. 2, pp. 538–39; Washington A. Roebling's report, in Gouverneur K. Warren Collection, NYSLA; Isaac R. Dunkleberger Memoir, in Michael Winey Collection, USAMHI; William G. Hills Diary, May 8, 1864, in William G. Hills Collection, LC.

2. Roebling's report, in Warren Collection, NYSLA; Abner R. Small, *The Sixteenth Maine Regiment in the War of the Rebellion, 1861–1865* (Portland, Maine, 1896), 177; Davis, *Three Years in the Army,* 333.

3. Theodore Lyman Journal, May 8, 1864, in Theodore Lyman Collection, MHS; Warren to Humphreys, May 8, 1864, in *OR,* Vol. XXXVI, Pt. 2, pp. 538–39.

4. Nevins, ed., *Diary of Battle,* 356.

5. Robert P. Chew's report, in Lewis Leigh Collection, USAMHI; William R. Carter Diary, May 8, 1864, in William R. Carter Collection, Hampden-Sydney College Library; Haden, *Reminiscences of J. E. B. Stuart's Cavalry,* 30; "The Fight Near Spotsylvania Court House Between Fitzhugh Lee and the Enemy," Richmond *Daily Examiner,* May 11, 1864; Hunter, *Johnny Reb and Billy Yank,* 536. Breathed proposed to Fitzhugh Lee the unusual expedient of placing the rebel horse artillery directly on the battle line, and Lee consented. "I succeeded in getting one section in position," Breathed recounted, "and for a half hour sent charge after charge of canister and short range shell into the ranks of the enemy with great effect" (James Breathed's report, in SHC).

6. Theodore F. Rodenbough, "Sheridan's Richmond Raid," in *B&L,* IV, 189.

7. Benjamin F. Cook, *History of the Twelfth Massachusetts Volunteers (Webster Regiment)* (Boston, 1882), 129; Gouverneur K. Warren to Andrew A. Humphreys, May 8, 1864, in *OR,* Vol. XXXVI, Pt. 2, p. 539; Sheridan, *Personal Memoirs,* I, 367–68.

8. Peirson, "The Operations of the Army of the Potomac," in *PMHSM,* IV, 214; Arthur A. Kent, ed., *Three Years with Company K: Sergt. Austin C. Stearns, Company K, 13th Mass. Infantry* (Rutherford, N.J., 1976), 262; Phelps, "Seventh Regiment Infantry," in *History and Roster of Maryland Volunteers,* by Wilmer *et al.,* I, 270.

9. Vautier, *History of the 88th Pennsylvania Volunteers,* 12; Warren to Humphreys, May 8, 1864, in *OR,* Vol. XXXVI, Pt. 2, p. 539.

10. Roebling's report, in Warren Collection, NYSLA; "The Battle on Sunday," Boston *Evening Transcript,* May 11, 1864.

11. Henry B. McClellan, *The Life and Campaigns of Major-General J. E. B. Stuart, Commander of the Cavalry of the Army of Northern Virginia* (Boston, 1885), 407–408; Alfred S. Roe, *The Thirty-Ninth Regiment Massachusetts Volunteers, 1862–1865* (Worcester, Mass., 1914), 184–85; G. N. Saussy, "Tribute to Major Breathed," *Confederate Veteran,* XVII (1909), 414; Chew's report, in Leigh Collection, USAMHI. Although the location of Breathed's exploits is uncertain, the Alsop farm is the likeliest place. Warren's aide Roebling wrote that Robinson's troops "emerged from the woods into the open fields at Alsop's and made a dash at the section behind the house coming within an ace of capturing it" (Roebling's report, in Warren Collection, NYSLA).

12. Andrew R. Linscott to parents, May 19, 1864, in Andrew R. Linscott Collection, MHS; Davis, *Three Years in the Army,* 333; Roebling's report, in Warren Collection, NYSLA; Charles E. Phelps, "Personal Recollection of the Wilderness Campaign," in Maryland Historical Society, Baltimore.

13. Hackley, *The Little Fork Rangers,* 89. When Lyman visited the area a few years later, the people living there told him that Laurel Hill was a different ridge a short distance away. But to the soldiers who fought at Spotsylvania, Laurel Hill was the shallow ridge line south of the Spindle place.

14. James H. Wilson's report, in *OR,* Vol. XXXVI, Pt. 1, p. 878.

15. J. D. Ferguson Memoranda, in Thomas T. Munford Collection, DU; W. A. Croffut and John M. Morris, *The Military and Civil History of Connecticut During the War of 1861–1865* (New York, 1869), 572.

16. Wilson's report, in *OR,* Vol. XXXVI, Pt. 1, p. 878; Rodenbough, "Sheridan's Richmond Raid," in *B&L,* IV, 188.

17. Nobel J. Brooks Diary, May 8, 1864, in Nobel J. Brooks Collection, SHC; Richard H. Anderson's report, in Richard H. Anderson Collection, DU; Gallagher, ed., *Fighting for the Confederacy,* 366.

18. D. Augustus Dickert, *History of Kershaw's Brigade* (Newberry, S.C., 1899), 357; Gilbert E. Govan and James W. Livingood, eds., *The Haskell Memoirs: John Cheves Haskell* (New York, 1960), 67.

19. Dickert, *History of Kershaw's Brigade,* 357; Richard H. Anderson to Edward B. Robins, May 14, 1879, in *PMHSM,* IV, 227–30; Joseph B. Kershaw to Edward B. Robins, October 7, 1886, in *PMHSM,* IV, 231.

20. Dickert, *History of Kershaw's Brigade,* 357–58; Govan and Livingood, eds., *The Haskell Memoirs,* 67; Gallagher, ed., *Fighting for the Confederacy,* 367; John W. Wofford, "A Gallant Company: Company K, Third South Carolina Regiment," in *History of the Wofford Family,* by Jane Wofford Wait *et al.* (Spartanburg, S.C., 1928), 207; Haden, *Reminiscences of J. E. B. Stuart's Cavalry,* 30; Coxe, "Last Struggles and Successes of Lee," 357. Stuart, accompanied by a few aides, had passed Anderson early in the morning on Shady Grove Church Road and joined Lee near the Spindle place. See Trout, ed., *Riding with Stuart . . . by . . . Garnett,* 57–58.

21. Coxe, "Last Struggles and Successes of Lee," 357. John Wofford wrote, "Well do all remember the person of that cavalry officer, Stuart, as he sat his charger on that morning at the edge of the open field and encouraged us to run for the rail piles" ("A Gallant Company," in *History of the Wofford Family,* by Wait *et al.,* 207).

22. Coxe, "Last Struggles and Successes of Lee," 357. Humphreys noted that the

Federals were a hundred yards away when he reached the earthworks. See Benjamin G. Humphreys, "Sunflower Guards," in J. F. H. Claiborne Collection, SHC.

23. Small, ed., *The Road to Richmond,* 126.

24. Peirson, "The Operations of the Army of the Potomac," in *PMHSM,* IV, 214–15.

25. William H. Powell, *The Fifth Army Corps* (New York, 1896), 633; Roebling's report, in Warren Collection, NYSLA; Nash, *A History of the Forty-Fourth Regiment New York Volunteer Infantry,* 187.

26. Phelps, "Seventh Regiment Infantry," in *History and Roster of Maryland Volunteers,* by Wilmer *et al.,* I, 271. Colonel Charles E. Phelps, of the 7th Maryland, considered Warren's reference to rations a "very practical suggestion, and doubtless to the majority a more effective appeal than any address to abstract sentiments of loyalty or patriotism. This general very well understood that what the men wanted at that particular time was not the Constitution and the Union so much as bread and meat. They had started from Culpeper Court House with six days' rations in their haversacks. They were supposed to have yet one day's supply on hand. In point of fact there were very few who had so much as a cracker left" (Phelps, "Personal Recollection of the Wilderness," in Maryland Historical Society).

27. "The Battle on Sunday," Boston *Evening Transcript,* May 11, 1864; "Our Battle Field Dispatches," New York *Herald,* May 11, 1864; Amos M. Judson, *History of the Eighty-Third Regiment Pennsylvania Volunteers* (Erie, Pa., 1865), 196; Nash, *A History of the Forty-Fourth Regiment New York Volunteer Infantry,* 188.

28. Judson, *History of the Eighty-Third Regiment Pennsylvania Volunteers,* 197; Hopkins, *From Bull Run to Appomattox,* 153.

29. Roebling's report, in Warren Collection, NYSLA; Coxe, "Last Struggles and Successes of Lee," 357; Wofford, "A Gallant Company," in *History of the Wofford Family,* by Wait *et al.,* 207.

30. Peirson, "Operations of the Army of the Potomac," in *PMHSM,* IV, 215; Charles H. Porter to Charles L. Peirson, April 18, 1879, in Military Historical Society of Massachusetts Collection, BU.

31. Phelps, "Seventh Regiment Infantry," in *History and Roster of Maryland Volunteers,* by Wilmer *et al.,* I, 271–73; Davis, *Three Years in the Army,* 334–35. The 1st and 8th Maryland formed Denison's front line, with the larger 7th Maryland extending behind. The brigade's remaining regiment—the 4th Maryland—attacked east of the road with the 39th Massachusetts and 90th Pennsylvania, of Lyle's brigade. See Phelps, "Personal Recollection of the Wilderness," in Maryland Historical Society.

32. Humphreys, "Sunflower Guards," in Claiborne Collection, SHC; "Gen. Robinson's Division Roughly Handled," New York *Daily Tribune,* May 12, 1864.

33. Peirson, "The Operations of the Army of the Potomac," in *PMHSM,* IV, 215; Phelps, "Seventh Regiment Infantry," in *History and Roster of Maryland Volunteers,* by Wilmer *et al.,* I, 272–73. Phelps observed that the "front rank was goaded into a return fire; individual progress was as naturally retarded by the act of aiming and reloading; men from the rear pressed impatiently forward to repeat the process. In this way, ranks and regiments soon became intermingled, straggling was made easy, the time of exposure was fatally prolonged" (p. 272).

34. George G. Hopper Reminiscences, in MOLLUS Collection, BL; Nash, *A History of the Forty-Fourth Regiment New York Volunteer Infantry,* 188; Judson, *History of the Eighty-Third Regiment Pennsylvania Volunteers,* 197; Augustus Buell, *The Cannoneer:*

Recollections of Service in the Army of the Potomac (Washington, D.C., 1890), 178–79; Humphreys, "Sunflower Guards," in Claiborne Collection, SHC; J. B. Clifton Diary, May 8, 1864, in J. B. Clifton Collection, NCDAH. A Confederate chaplain saw rebels who had been stabbed in their backs while crouching behind the works. See William P. DuBose Reminiscences, in William P. DuBose Collection, SHC.

35. Judson, *History of the Eighty-Third Regiment Pennsylvania Volunteers,* 198; Nash, *A History of the Forty-Fourth Regiment New York Infantry,* 188.

36. Charles Thomas Bowen Diary, May 8, 1864, in FSNMP; "Civil War Journal of Major John Chester White," in John Chester White Collection, LC; Burgess E. Ingersoll Diary, May 8, 1864, in Civil War Miscellaneous Collection, USAMHI; Farley, "Reminiscences of the 140th Regiment New York Volunteer Infantry," 248–49; George W. Debeck, "Laurel Hill," *National Tribune,* October 31, 1895; Alfred Pearson's report, in *OR,* Vol. XXXVI, Pt. 1, p. 557; Brian A. Bennett, *Sons of Old Monroe: A Regimental History of Patrick O'Rorke's 140th New York Volunteer Infantry* (Dayton, 1993), 385–92.

37. Vautier, *History of the 88th Pennsylvania Volunteers,* 178; William H. Locke, *The Story of the Regiment* (Philadelphia, 1868), 332; Kent, ed., *Three Years with Company K,* 264.

38. William Wallace, "Operations of Second South Carolina Regiment in Campaigns of 1864–1865," in *SHSP,* VII, 129; Hopkins, *From Bull Run to Appomattox,* 155.

39. Roe, *Thirty-Ninth Regiment Massachusetts Volunteers,* 182–83; "Extract of Diary of Theodore Lyman," April 13, 1866, in *PMHSM,* IV, 239; Peirson, "The Operations of the Army of the Potomac," in *PMHSM,* IV, 216.

40. Coxe, "Last Struggles and Successes of Lee," 357.

41. New York *Times,* May 13, 1864; Davis, *Three Years in the Army,* 334; Small, *The Sixteenth Maine Regiment,* 177; Roe, *Thirty-Ninth Regiment Massachusetts Volunteers,* 188–89; Vautier, *History of the 88th Pennsylvania Volunteers,* 178.

42. George Bucknam Memoir, in William O. Bourne Collection, LC; William S. Tilton's report, in *OR,* Vol. XXXVI, Pt. 1, p. 560.

43. Charles S. Wainwright's report, in *OR,* Vol. XXXVI, Pt. 1, pp. 641–42; Carter, *Four Brothers in Blue,* 393; Bucknam Memoir.

44. Notes of Lieutenant Appleton, in *History of the Fifth Massachusetts Battery,* by Cowles, 816. Coulter's brigade was assigned to Crawford, and Lyle's to Cutler. Denison's Maryland brigade was not assigned to a division but reported directly to Warren. Thirty-one years later, Robinson received a medal of honor for his service at Laurel Hill.

45. Roebling's report, in Warren Collection, NYSLA; Farley, "Reminiscences of the 140th Regiment New York Volunteer Infantry," 249.

46. Nevins, ed., *Diary of Battle,* 356.

47. William M. Dame, *From the Rapidan to Richmond and the Spotsylvania Campaign* (Baltimore, 1920), 100; Charles S. Venable, "The Campaign from the Wilderness to Petersburg," in *SHSP,* XIV, 527.

48. Gouverneur K. Warren to Andrew A. Humphreys, May 8, 1864, in *OR,* Vol. XXXVI, Pt. 2, pp. 539–40.

49. Charles W. Field, "Campaign of 1864 and 1865," in *SHSP,* XIV, 547; William C. Oates, *The War Between the Union and the Confederacy and Its Lost Opportunities* (New York, 1905), 354; Richard Lewis, *Camp Life of a Confederate Boy, of Bratton's Brigade, Longstreet's Corps, C.S.A.* (Charleston, S.C., 1883), 95; Robert T. Coles, *From Huntsville to Appomattox,* ed. Jeffrey D. Stocker (Knoxville, Tenn., 1996), 167. Haskell arrayed his

batteries in echelon, each supporting the others. At one time the guns of Captain John R. Potts's North Carolina battery were firing in three directions. Potts was killed, along with nearly half his men, but officers and orderlies continued servicing the guns. See Govan and Livingood, eds., *The Haskell Memoirs,* 67–68; and William N. Pendleton's report, in *OR,* Vol. XXXVI, Pt. 1, p. 1042.

50. Coxe, "Last Struggles and Successes of Lee," 357; Harrison, *Gazetteer,* I, 283–84.

51. Roebling's report, in Warren Collection, NYSLA.

52. *Ibid.*

53. Lysander Cutler's report, in *OR,* Vol. XXXVI, Pt. 1, p. 611; Avery Harris Reminiscences, in Avery Harris Collection, USAMHI; Thomas Chamberlin, *History of the One Hundred and Fiftieth Regiment Pennsylvania Volunteers, Second Regiment, Bucktail Brigade* (Philadelphia, 1905), 225–26; Oates, *The War Between the Union and the Confederacy,* 354–55. There is a fine narrative of Bragg's action in Richard E. Matthews' *The 149th Pennsylvania Volunteer Infantry Unit in the Civil War* (Jefferson, N.C., 1994), 151–52.

54. Chamberlin, *History of the One Hundred and Fiftieth Regiment Pennsylvania Volunteers,* 225–26; John O. Johnson to unknown, July 2, 1864, in State Historical Society of Wisconsin, Madison; Rufus R. Dawes's report, in *OR,* Vol. XXXVI, Pt. 1, pp. 618–19; Rufus R. Dawes, *Service With the Sixth Wisconsin Volunteers* (Marietta, Ohio, 1890), 264–65; Oates, *The War Between the Union and the Confederacy,* 355.

55. A. P. Smith, *History of the Seventy-Sixth Regiment New York Volunteers* (Cortland, N.Y., 1867), 295; J. William Hofmann's report, in *OR,* Vol. XXXVI, Pt. 1, p. 625; Harris Reminiscences. One of Rice's soldiers claimed that the brigade held its own until the Pennsylvania Bucktails on its right gave way. See Thomas Kearney to brother, May 17, 1864, *Irish American,* June 21, 1864.

56. Thomson and Rauch, *History of the "Bucktails,"* 300; Edwin A. Glover, *Bucktailed Wildcats: A Regiment of Civil War Volunteers* (New York, 1960), 248; J. R. Sypher, *History of the Pennsylvania Reserve Corps* (Lancaster, Pa., 1865), 522; James W. Latta Diary, in James W. Latta Collection, LC.

57. Roebling's report, in Warren Collection, NYSLA; Frank B. Williams. Jr., ed., "From Sumter to the Wilderness: Letters of Sgt. James Butler Suddath, Co. E, 7th Regiment, S.C.V.," *South Carolina Historical Magazine,* LXIII (1962), 77.

58. Gouverneur K. Warren to Andrew A. Humphreys, May 8, 1864, in *OR,* Vol. XXXVI, Pt. 2, pp. 540–41. A reporter assigned to Warren's corps vividly described the day's toll: "Brigades have lost their commanders, and one regiment—the 4th Michigan—is commanded by a First Lieutenant. General Robinson was shot through the knee. Colonel Coulter now commands this division. Colonel Denison, commanding the 3rd brigade of the 4th division, is wounded in the arm. Captain Martin is slightly wounded in the neck. His battery lost two killed and seven wounded. Among the killed is Colonel Ryan of the 140th New York Regiment, and Major Stark of the same regiment was also killed. Several regiments have suffered heavily. The 1st Michigan, which went in with nearly 200 men, came out at the end of the closing fight with only 28 men left" ("The Battle on Sunday," Boston *Evening Transcript,* May 11, 1864).

59. Carter Diary, May 8, 1864; Ferguson Memoranda, in Munford Collection, DU; Erastus Blakeslee's report, in *Annual Report of the Adjutant-General of the State of Connecticut for the Year Ending March 31, 1865* (New Haven, 1865), 411.

60. "Wofford's Georgia Brigade: Its Conduct in the Recent Engagements," Atlanta *Southern Confederacy,* June 15, 1864; Field, "Campaign of 1864–1865," in *SHSP,* XIV, 547.

61. Edward P. Alexander to father, May 29, 1864, in Edward P. Alexander Collection, SHC; Wilson's report, in *OR,* Vol. XXXVI, Pt. 1, p. 878.

62. Wilson's report, in *OR,* Vol. XXXVI, Pt. 1, p. 878; "Extract of Diary of Theodore Lyman," April 13, 1866, in *PMHSM,* IV, 240.

63. Wilson, *Under the Old Flag,* I, 394. Wilson wrote that he "withdrew when menaced by infantry on front and right. Pity we had not been backed by a division of infantry" (James H. Wilson Diary, May 8, 1864, in LC).

64. For the timing of Burnside's march from the Wilderness to Chancellorsville, see Byron M. Cutcheon Autobiography, in Michigan Historical Collection, BL; Frederick W. Swift Diary, May 7–8, 1864, in Gregory Coco Collection, USAMHI; Paul Wirtz, ed., *John Parker Brest, Company E, 100th Pennsylvania Volunteer Regiment: Journal, 1861–1865* (Baltimore, 1991), 24–25; Charles D. Todd Diary, May 8, 1864, in Gregory Coco Collection, USAMHI.

65. Theodore Lyman to family, May 19, 1864, in *Meade's Headquarters,* ed. Agassiz, 104; Charles W. Reed Diary, May 8, 1864, in Charles W. Reed Collection, LC.

66. Porter, *Campaigning with Grant,* 82–83.

67. *Ibid.,* 83–84; Sheridan, *Personal Memoirs,* I, 368.

68. Sheridan, *Personal Memoirs,* I, 368–69; Lyman Journal, May 8, 1864; Rodenbough, "Sheridan's Richmond Raid," in *B&L,* IV, 189.

69. Porter, *Campaigning with Grant,* 83–84; Sheridan, *Personal Memoirs,* I, 368–69.

70. Sheridan, *Personal Memoirs,* I, 368–69.

71. Field, "Campaign of 1864 and 1865," in *SHSP,* XIV, 547; Dame, *From the Rapidan to Richmond,* 108–11. From west to east, Field's division consisted of Gregg's mixed Texas and Arkansas brigade, Tige Anderson's Georgians, Perry's Alabamians, Dudley M. DuBose's Georgians, and John Bratton's South Carolinians.

72. Dame, *From the Rapidan to Richmond,* 113–15.

73. *Ibid.,* 116–17. Porter Alexander, commanding Anderson's artillery, wrote that he had thirty-five guns in the works and nineteen in reserve. See Alexander to father, May 29, 1864, in Alexander Collection, SHC.

74. Nevins, ed., *Diary of Battle,* 357; Wainwright's report, in *OR,* Vol. XXXVI, Pt. 1, p. 642.

75. Bucknam Memoir.

76. Nevins, ed., *Diary of Battle,* 357.

77. Dame, *From the Rapidan to Richmond,* 118–19; Robert Stiles, *Four Years Under Marse Robert* (New York, 1903), 249–51; Nevins, ed., *Diary of Battle,* 357–59. Dame estimated the affair lasted three hours; Wainwright recorded it as half an hour.

78. Buell, *The Cannoneer,* 181–83.

79. George G. Meade to Gouverneur K. Warren, in *OR,* Vol. XXXVI, Pt. 2, p. 541.

80. Hyde, *Following the Greek Cross,* 191.

81. Howe, ed., *Touched with Fire,* 108–109; Joseph K. Newell, *Ours: Annals of Tenth Regiment Massachusetts Volunteers in the Rebellion* (Springfield, Mass., 1875), 261; George T. Stevens, *Three Years in the Sixth Corps* (Albany, N.Y., 1866), 325; Camille Baquet, *History of the First Brigade New Jersey Volunteers, from 1861 to 1865* (Trenton, 1910), 118–19.

82. George G. Meade to John Sedgwick, in *OR,* Vol. XXXVI, Pt. 2, p. 545; George W. Bicknell, *History of the Fifth Regiment Maine Volunteers* (Portland, Maine, 1871), 307; Dwight W. Blight, ed., *When This Cruel War Is Over: The Civil War Letters of Charles Harvey Brewster* (Amherst, Mass., 1992), 292; Elbert Corbin Diary, May 8, 1864, in Civil War Miscellaneous Collection, USAMHI.

83. Edmund D. Halsey Diary, May 8, 1864, in Edmund D. Halsey Collection, USAMHI; Alanson A. Haines, *History of the Fifteenth Regiment New Jersey Volunteers* (New York, 1883), 158.

84. Wilson, *Under the Old Flag,* I, 395–96.

85. Lyman Journal, May 8, 1864.

86. Lyman to family, May 19, 1864, in *Meade's Headquarters,* ed. Agassiz, 105–106. By afternoon, headquarters had moved to the Hart house, west of Brock Road. The house was surrounded by a wheat field and "commanded an extensive view towards the Po River and beyond" (Lyman Journal, May 8, 1864). A reporter placed Grant's and Meade's visits to the front at 5:30. See "The Battle on Sunday," Boston *Evening Transcript,* May 11, 1864.

87. William H. Morris' report, in *OR,* Vol. XXXVI, Pt. 1, pp. 723–24.

88. Henry J. Hunt, "Journal of Siege Operations," in Henry J. Hunt Collection, LC; Lyman to family, May 19, 1864, in *Meade's Headquarters,* ed. Agassiz, 104–105; Sparks, ed., *Inside Lincoln's Army,* 370; Cyrus B. Comstock Diary, May 8, 1864, in Cyrus B. Comstock Collection, LC. In several places, 5th and 6th Corps units were intermixed. Brigadier General David A. Russell's brigade, for example, was placed near Warren's western flank, on Cutler's right. The 5th Wisconsin found itself beside the Iron Brigade's three Wisconsin regiments. A soldier noted that "had we gone in the night all the Wisconsin regiments in the Army of the Potomac would have gone in together" (J. S. Anderson, "Through the Wilderness with Grant," in *Report of the Proceedings of the 5th Wisconsin Volunteer Infantry* [Chicago, 1902], 12).

89. Francis A. Walker, *History of the Second Army Corps* (New York, 1887), 444–45; Francis A. Walker, *General Hancock* (New York, 1895), 184; Second Corps Daily Memoranda, in *OR,* Vol. XXXVI, Pt. 1, p. 355; Winfield S. Hancock's report, in *OR,* Vol. XXXVI, Pt. 1, p. 329. Forced to wait until Warren's last units had cleared his southern flank, Hancock was unable to vacate his Wilderness trenches until after 6:30 A.M. on May 8.

90. Joseph F. Waring Diary, May 8, 1864, in Joseph F. Waring Collection, SHC; Winfield S. Hancock to Andrew A. Humphreys, May 8, 1864, in *OR,* Vol. XXXVI, Pt. 2, p. 531. The encounter is detailed from the Union perspective by Noble D. Preston in "Annals of the War: Sheridan's Ten Thousand," Philadelphia *Weekly Times,* February 3, 1883.

91. Hancock's report, in *OR,* Vol. XXXVI, Pt. 1, p. 329; Walker and Walker, eds., "Diary of the War by Robert S. Robertson," 167; Favill, *The Diary of a Young Officer,* 292; Wade Hampton's report, in Wade Hampton Collection, SCL; Lyman Journal, May 8, 1864.

92. Winfield S. Hancock to George G. Meade, May 8, 1864, in *OR,* Vol. XXXVI, Pt. 2, p. 532; Gouverneur K. Warren to Winfield S. Hancock, May 8, 1864, *ibid.,* 532; Winfield S. Hancock to Andrew A. Humphreys, May 8, 1864, *ibid.,* 533; Andrew A. Humphreys to Winfield S. Hancock, May 8, 1864, *ibid.,* 533.

93. John E. Holland to Peter A. Taylor, May 8, 1864, in *OR,* Vol. XXXVI, Pt. 2, p. 533; Nathaniel Michler to Andrew A. Humphreys, May 8, 1864, *ibid.*

94. Robert S. Robertson to parents, May 14, 1864, in FSNMP; Robert S. Robertson, "From the Wilderness to Spotsylvania," in *Sketches of War History, 1861–1865: Papers Read Before the Ohio Commandery of the Military Order of the Loyal Legion of the United States* (Cincinnati, 1883), I, 269–71. Donald Pfanz, of the National Park Service, presented an excellent summary of the fighting on Catharpin Road in a letter to William C. Sparks, March 23, 1994, included with Robertson's letters at FSNMP.

95. Butt Hewson, "The Battle of Spotsylvania Court House," in *Lee's Sharpshooters*, by Dunlop, 443; Robert E. Lee to Richard S. Ewell, May 8, 1864, in *OR*, Vol. LI, Pt. 2, Supplement, pp. 902–903.

96. Lee to Ewell, May 8, 1864, in *OR*, Vol. LI, Pt. 2, Supplement, pp. 902–903. After the reorganization, Gordon's division consisted of Gordon's former brigade, commanded by Colonel Clement A. Evans; Brigadier General John Pegram's brigade, commanded by Colonel John S. Hoffman; and Brigadier General Robert D. Johnston's brigade.

97. Dunlop, *Lee's Sharpshooters*, 44–46; George Clark, *A Glance Backward; or, Some Events in the Past History of My Life* (Houston, 1914), 49–50. I concur with Matter's identification of the horses as originally belonging to a detachment from the 22nd New York Cavalry. See Matter, *If It Takes All Summer*, 79–80. See also Winfield S. Hancock to Andrew A. Humphreys, May 8, 1864, in *OR*, Vol. XXXVI, Pt. 2, p. 535; and James A. Beaver to Francis A. Walker, May 8, 1864, in *OR*, Vol. XXXVI, Pt. 2, pp. 537–38.

98. Lee to Ewell, May 8, 1864, in *OR*, Vol. LI, Pt. 2, Supplement, p. 902; Robert E. Lee to secretary of war, May 8, 1864, *ibid.*, Vol. XXXVI, Pt. 2, p. 974.

99. Peyton, *A Civil War Record*, ed. Hodge, 23–24; Cullen A. Battle, "The Third Alabama Regiment," in Regimental Collection, ADAH; Thomas S. Doyle Memoir, in Jedediah Hotchkiss Collection, LC; James M. Thompson, "Reminiscences of the Autauga Rifles," in Regimental Collection, ADAH; Archie P. McDonald, ed. *Make Me a Map of the Valley: The Civil War Journal of Stonewall Jackson's Topographer* (Dallas, 1973), 202.

100. Oscar O. Mull Diary, May 8, 1864, in VHS; Cadmus M. Wilcox' report, in VHS.

101. James Eldred Phillips Memoir, in James Eldred Phillips Collection, VHS. Fragmentary Confederate accounts preclude a definitive statement concerning which of Mahone's brigades assaulted Miles. Weisiger's Virginians and some of Harris' Mississippians clearly bore the brunt of the combat. Perrin's Alabamians were slightly involved at Bradshaw's farm, probably acting in conjunction with Mahone's men, and Perry's Floridians were not engaged. See Hilary A. Herbert, "History of the Eighth Alabama Volunteer Regiment, C.S.A.," edited by Maurice S. Fortin, *Alabama Historical Quarterly*, XXXIX (1977), 138; Eugene M. Ott, Jr., ed., "The Civil War Diary of James J. Kirkpatrick, Sixteenth Mississippi Infantry, C.S.A." (M.A. thesis, Texas A & M University, 1984), 191; William H. Harris, comp., *Movements of the Confederate Army in Virginia and the Part Taken Therein by the Nineteenth Mississippi Brigade: From the Diary of General Nat H. Harris* (Duncansby, Miss., 1901), 26; and Captain C. Seton Fleming's Notes, May 8, 1864, in *Memoir of Captain C. Seton Fleming, of the Second Florida Infantry, C.S.A.*, ed. Francis P. Fleming (Alexandria, Va., 1985), Appendix.

102. Hampton's report, in Hampton Collection, SCL.

103. Robertson, "From the Wilderness to Spotsylvania," in *Sketches of War History*, I, 269–72; Second Corps Daily Memoranda, in *OR*, Vol. XXXVI, Pt. 1, pp. 355–56.

104. Robertson to parents, May 14, 1864, in FSNMP; Newton T. Kirk, "Civil War Reminiscences," in Archives and Historical Collection, Michigan State University Libraries; Robertson, "From the Wilderness to Spotsylvania," in *Sketches of War History*, I,

271–72; Hampton's report, in Hampton Collection, SCL; McDonald, *A History of the Laurel Brigade,* 238; William N. McDonald Manuscript, in SHC.

105. Robertson to parents, May 14, 1864, in FSNMP; "He Checked the Panic," in *Deeds of Valor: How America's Civil War Heroes Won the Congressional Medal of Honor,* ed. W. F. Beyer and O. F. Keydel (Stamford., Conn., 1992), 325–26; Walker and Walker, eds., "Diary of the War," 168; Robertson, "From the Wilderness to Spotsylvania," in *Sketches of War History,* I, 269–72; Second Corps Daily Memoranda, in *OR,* Vol. XXXVI, Pt. 1, pp. 355–56; George W. Scott's report, in *OR,* Vol. XXXVI, Pt. 1, p. 379; Thomas Henry's report, in *OR,* Vol. XXXVI, Pt. 1, p. 383.

106. Leroy S. Edwards to George S. Bernard, March 25, 1891, in George S. Bernard Collection, SHC; George S. Bernard Diary, May 9, 1864, in VHS.

107. St. Claire Augustine Mulholland, *The Story of the 116th Regiment Pennsylvania Infantry* (Philadelphia, 1899), 182–83.

108. Charles H. Weygant, *History of the One Hundred and Twenty-Fourth Regiment New York State Volunteers* (Newburgh, N.Y., 1877), 305–306; Brooks Diary, May 8, 1864; Joseph Mullen, Jr., Diary, May 8, 1864, in MC; Henry Clay Albright Diary, in Henry Clay Albright Collection, NCDAH; George Washington Hall Diary, in George Washington Hall Collection, LC; Early, *Autobiographical Sketch and Narrative,* 252; William H. Palmer to William L. Royall, May 11, 1908, in *Some Reminiscences,* by Royall, 35.

109. Hancock's report, in *OR,* Vol. XXXVI, Pt. 1, pp. 329–30; George A. Bruce, *The Twentieth Regiment of Massachusetts Volunteer Infantry, 1861–1865* (Boston, 1906), 362; Walker, *History of the Second Army Corps,* 445.

110. Swinton, *Campaigns of the Army of the Potomac,* 447n.

111. J. W. Bone Reminiscences, in Lowrey Shuford Collection, NCDAH; James W. Roberts, "The Wilderness and Spotsylvania, May 4–12, 1864: Narrative of a Private Soldier," *Quarterly Periodical of the Florida Historical Society,* XI (1932), 66; Phillip H. Powers to wife, May 9, 1864, in Leigh Collection, USAMHI; Laura Elizabeth Lee, *Forget-Me-Nots of the Civil War: A Romance Containing Reminiscences and Original Letters of Two Confederate Soldiers* (St. Louis, 1909), 114.

112. "Official Report of Movements of Fifteenth Regiment N.J. During Grant's Wilderness Campaign," in Edmund D. Halsey Collection, USAMHI; John Hoffman Diary, May 8, 1864, in Richmond National Battlefield Park Library; Unidentified federal diary, 15th New Jersey, May 8, 1864, in Book 37, FSNMP; Baquet, *History of the First Brigade New Jersey Volunteers,* 119; Haines, *History of the Fifteenth Regiment New Jersey Volunteers,* 158–59; Charles to father, May 15, 1864, in Leigh Collection, USAMHI; Lyman Journal, May 8, 1864. Charles tells how, after dark, soldiers from the 10th New Jersey huddling in front of the rebel works heard a voice sing out, "What regiment is this?" The northerners answered, "The 10th New Jersey." At that, Confederates climbed over their barricade and captured much of the regiment.

113. "The Great Contest," New York *Daily Tribune,* May 12, 1864; James M. Read Diary, May 8, 1864, in James B. Ricketts Collection, Manassas National Battlefield Park Library.

114. Thomson and Rauch, *History of the Bucktails,* 301. The 10th Massachusetts and 2nd Rhode Island formed Eustis' first line, the 7th and 37th Massachusetts his second.

115. Roberts, "The Wilderness and Spotsylvania," 66; Mixson, *Reminiscences of a Private,* 73–74; Thomson and Rauch, *History of the Bucktails,* 301.

116. Battle, "The Third Alabama Regiment," in Regimental Collection, ADAH; Roberts, "The Wilderness and Spotsylvania," 66.

117. Nelson V. Hutchinson, *History of the Seventh Massachusetts Volunteer Infantry in the War of the Rebellion of the Southern States Against Constitutional Authority, 1861–1865* (Taunton, Mass., 1890), 183; Cyrenus Pullen Stevens Diary, May 8, 1864, in Harrisburg Civil War Round Table Collection, USAMHI.

118. Francis A. Boyle Diary, May 8, 1864, in Francis A. Boyle Collection, SHC; "From a Special Correspondent," Raleigh (N.C.) *Daily Confederate,* May 25, 1864; Cyrus B. Watson, "Forty-Fifth Regiment," in *Histories of the Several Regiments and Battalions from North Carolina in the Great War, 1861–65,* ed. Walter Clark (5 vols.; Goldsboro, N.C., 1901), I, 255; E. A. Osborn, "Fourth Regiment," in *Histories of the Several Regiments and Battalions from North Carolina,* ed. Clark, III, 45–46; Henry W. Thomas, *History of the Doles-Cook Brigade, Army of Northern Virginia, C.S.A.* (Atlanta, 1903), 478; Stephen D. Ramseur's report, in *OR,* Vol. XXXVI, Pt. 1, p. 1081; Cullen A. Battle's report, in *OR,* Vol. XXXVI, Pt. 1, pp. 1083–84; Willie Walker Caldwell, *Stonewall Jim: A Biography of General James A. Walker, C.S.A.* (Elliston, Va., 1990), 100–101.

119. Lyman Journal, May 8, 1864; Albert M. Haywood to brother, May 17, 1864, in FSNMP.

120. Rhodes, ed., *All for the Union,* 150; Blight, ed., *When This Cruel War Is Over,* 293.

121. Smith, *History of the Corn Exchange Regiment,* 408–14; Gerrish, *Army Life,* 176–79; John J. Pullen, *The Twentieth Maine: A Volunteer Regiment in the Civil War* (Philadelphia, 1957), 198–200; Carter, *Four Brothers in Blue,* 394–95. Herring's detachment contained elements from the 20th Maine, 118th Pennsylvania, 16th Michigan, and 9th and 22nd Massachusetts.

122. Ulysses S. Grant to Henry W. Halleck, May 8, 1864, in *OR,* Vol. XXXVI, Pt. 2, p. 526; John A. Rawlins to Ambrose E. Burnside, May 8, 1864, *ibid.,* 546; Orders of 4:10, 11:05, *ibid.,* 529

123. Lyman Journal, May 8, 1864; Gouverneur K. Warren to George G. Meade, May 8, 1864, in *OR,* Vol. XXXVI, Pt. 2, p. 542.

124. Roebling's report, in Warren Collection, NYSLA; Tabular List of Casualties, Fifth Army Corps, RG94, Entry 729, Box 69, NA.

125. "Confidential Note," May 9, 1864, in Warren Collection, NYSLA; Charles H. Morgan to Gouverneur K. Warren, March 14, 1868, *ibid.*

126. Robert E. Lee to James A. Seddon, May 8, 1864, in *OR,* Vol. XXXVI, Pt. 2, p. 974. Alfred Young assisted me in estimating Henagan's and Humphreys' casualties.

127. William W. Old, "Personal Reminiscences," in *SHSP,* XXXIII, 20–21; Howard, *Recollections of a Maryland Confederate,* 284–85; Doyle Memoir.

128. James H. Stine, *History of the Army of the Potomac* (Philadelphia, 1892), 617.

129. Powers to wife, May 9, 1864, in Leigh Collection, USAMHI.

III   MAY 9 *Grant and Lee Shift for Position, and Sheridan Starts South*

1. Caldwell, *Stonewall Jim,* 101–102; Roberts, "The Wilderness and Spotsylvania," 68; J. F. J. Caldwell, *The History of a Brigade of South Carolinians, First Known as*

Gregg's, and Subsequently as McGowan's Brigade (Philadelphia, 1866), 139; Howard, *Recollections of a Maryland Confederate,* 285–87.

2. Butt Hewson, "Battle of Spotsylvania Court House," in *Lee's Sharpshooters,* by Dunlop, 444; Old, "Personal Reminiscences," in *SHSP,* XXXIII, 21, 23; Jones, ed., *The Civil War Memoirs of Captain William J. Seymour,* 119–20.

3. Crawford's 5th Corps division shifted toward the Po and formed Warren's extreme right wing. Cutler deployed on Crawford's left; then came Griffin, who entrenched immediately west of Brock Road. In Sedgwick's corps, Ricketts' division straddled Brock Road, Brigadier General Thomas H. Neill's division entrenched on Ricketts' left, and Wright's division formed the Federal left flank, across from the western face of Ewell's salient.

4. S. F. Hildebrand, "Notes and Reminiscences of Services in the 139th Regiment," in Harold C. George Collection, LC; Howard, *Recollections of a Maryland Confederate,* 285.

5. Humphreys, *The Virginia Campaign,* 75–76; Boston *Evening Transcript,* May 12, 1864.

6. James L. McCown Memoirs, May 9, 1864, in Handley Library, Winchester, Va.

7. Dame, *From the Rapidan to Richmond,* 132; Thomas S. Doyle Memoir, May 9, 1864, in Jedediah Hotchkiss Collection, LC.

8. F. W. Morse, *Personal Experiences in the War of the Great Rebellion, from December, 1862, to July, 1865* (Albany, N.Y., 1866), 87; Hyde, *Following the Greek Cross,* 197; Haines, *History of the Fifteenth Regiment New Jersey Volunteers,* 162; Alfred Thompson to mother, May 10, 1864, in FSNMP.

9. Gallagher, ed., *Fighting for the Confederacy,* 370–71; Williams, ed., "From Sumter to the Wilderness," 78.

10. Andrew A. Humphreys to John Sedgwick, May 9, 1864, in *OR,* Vol. XXXVI, Pt. 2, pp. 576–77; Theodore Lyman Journal, May 8, 1864, in Theodore Lyman Collection, MHS; Washington A. Roebling Memorandum, May 9, 1864, in *OR,* Vol. XXXVI, Pt. 2, p. 574. Roebling later wrote that "Sedgwick was placed in command of the line embracing his corps and the greater part of ours" (Washington A. Roebling's report, in Gouverneur K. Warren Collection, NYSLA).

11. Charles A. Whittier, "Reminiscences of the War," in Charles A. Whittier Collection, BPL.

12. H. R. Schell Narrative, in *The Cannoneer,* by Buell, 184; Edmund D. Halsey Diary, May 8, 1864, in USAMHI; Haines, *History of the Fifteenth Regiment New Jersey Volunteers,* 161. Morris was shot in the leg, which ended his active service in the war.

13. Martin T. McMahon, "The Death of General John Sedgwick," in *B&L,* IV, 175.

14. Martin T. McMahon to Horatio G. Wright, May 9, 1864, in *OR,* Vol. XXXVI, Pt. 2, p. 579.

15. Hyde, *Following the Greek Cross,* 192–93. The new guns belonged to Battery A, 1st Massachusetts Light Artillery. See A. J. Bennett, *The Story of the First Massachusetts Light Battery* (Boston, 1886), 152; and Charles H. Tompkins' report, in *OR,* Vol. XXXVI, Pt. 1, p. 755. But see also Charles E. Mink's report, in *OR,* Vol. XXXVI, Pt. 1, p. 655, which claims that Sedgwick was shot near Lieutenant David F. Ritchie's New York section. Stuart G. Vogt describes the competing accounts in "The Death of Major-General John Sedgwick, U.S.A., May 9, 1864," 8n14, in FSNMP. A map of where Sedgwick was shot

appears in James M. Read Diary, May 9, 1864, in James B. Ricketts Collection, Manassas National Battlefield Park Library.

16. Porter, *Campaigning with Grant,* 89.

17. Haines, *History of the Fifteenth Regiment New Jersey Volunteers,* 161; McMahon, "The Death of General John Sedgwick," in *B&L,* IV, 175.

18. Whittier, "Reminiscences of the War," in Whittier Collection, BPL; McMahon, "The Death of General John Sedgwick," in *B&L,* IV, 175; Schell Narrative, in *The Cannoneer,* by Buell, 184.

19. Theodore Lyman to family, May 20, 1864, in *Meade's Headquarters,* ed. Agassiz, 107–108; Porter, *Campaigning with Grant,* 90; New York *Herald,* May 11, 1864; Alexander R. Boteler Diary, May 9, 1864, in William E. Brooks Collection, LC.

20. Lyman to family, May 20, 1864, in *Meade's Headquarters,* ed. Agassiz, 108; Gouverneur K. Warren to George G. Meade, May 9, 1864, in Warren Collection, NYSLA.

21. D. R. Sanborn to Augustus Buell, n.d., in *The Cannoneer,* by Buell, 184–85; Dunlop, *Lee's Sharpshooters,* 49; Ben M. Powell to wife, November 21, 1907, in Book 200, FSNMP. A friend later observed that Burgess was "sensitive on the subject and could never divorce the thought from his mind that the occurrence was something akin to murder" (V. M. Fleming, "How General Sedgwick Was Killed," *Confederate Veteran,* XVI, [1908], 347). The identity of Sedgwick's killer is thoroughly canvassed by Vogt in "The Death of Major-General John Sedgwick," in FSNMP. Vogt questions Powell's claim, for Powell shot a mounted general, which fits Morris but not Sedgwick. Since rebel sharpshooters filled the area in front of Sedgwick, the marksman cannot be positively identified.

22. Dawes, *Service with the Sixth Wisconsin Volunteers,* 265; Chamberlin, *History of the One Hundred and Fiftieth Regiment Pennsylvania Volunteers,* 227; Farley, "Reminiscences of the 140th Regiment New York Volunteer Infantry," 250; Judson, *History of the Eighty-Third Regiment Pennsylvania Volunteers,* 98; William S. Tilton's report, in *OR,* Vol. XXXVI, Pt. 1, p. 561.

23. George G. Benedict, *Vermont in the Civil War: A History of the Part Taken by the Vermont Soldiers and Sailors in the War for the Union, 1861–65* (2 vols.; Burlington, Vt., 1886), I, 442. Colonel Oliver Edwards assumed command of what had been Eustis' brigade.

24. Sheridan, *Personal Memoirs,* I, 369–70.

25. *Ibid.,* 370–71.

26. Philip H. Sheridan's report, in *OR,* Vol. XXXVI, Pt. 1, 776–77, 789.

27. Samuel J. Marks to Carrie, May 8, 1864, in Civil War Miscellaneous Collection, USAMHI; Stanton P. Allen, *Down in Dixie: Life in a Cavalry Regiment in the War Days, from the Wilderness to Spotsylvania* (Boston, 1892), 271–72; Henry R. Pyne, *Ride to War: The History of the First New Jersey Cavalry* (New Brunswick, N.J., 1961), 195.

28. Stephen R. Smith *et al., Record of Service of Connecticut Men in the Army and Navy of the United States During the War of the Rebellion* (Hartford, 1889), 57.

29. Allen, *Down in Dixie,* 274–75; N. D. Preston, *History of the Tenth Regiment of Cavalry New York State Volunteers* (New York, 1892), 174; "The Great Cavalry Expedition Through the Rebel Lines," New York *Herald,* May 17, 1864.

30. Isham, "Through the Wilderness to Richmond," in *Sketches of War History,* I, 206–207; Allen, *Down in Dixie,* 275–79; Rodenbough, "Sheridan's Richmond Raid," in *B&L,* IV, 189.

31. Kidd, *Personal Recollections of a Cavalryman,* 291; Isham, "Through the Wilderness to Richmond," in *Sketches of War History,* I, 207; James D. Rowe Reminiscences,

May 9, 1864, in Michigan Historical Collection, BL; Well A. Bushnell Memoir, in William P. Palmer Collection, WRHS.

32. Kidd, *Personal Recollections of a Cavalryman,* 291; Sheridan, *Personal Memoirs,* I, 372–73.

33. Wilson, *Under the Old Flag,* I, 406; George Perkins Memoir, May 9, 1864, in Michael T. Russert Private Collection.

34. Badeau, *Military History of General Ulysses S. Grant,* II, 146.

35. New York *Times,* May 13, 1864.

36. Abram L. Lockwood to Winfield S. Hancock, May 9, 1864, in *OR,* Vol. XXXVI, Pt. 2, p. 564; Winfield S. Hancock to Andrew A. Humphreys, May 9, 1864, *ibid.,* 564–65; Stevens, *Berdan's United States Sharpshooters,* 416; Ripley, *Vermont Riflemen,* 157; Nobel J. Brooks Diary, May 9, 1864, in Nobel J. Brooks Collection, SHC; Joseph F. Waring Diary, May 9, 1864, in Joseph F. Waring Collection, SHC.

37. Andrew A. Humphreys to Winfield S. Hancock, May 9, 1864, in *OR,* Vol. XXXVI, Pt. 2, p. 565.

38. Ulysses S. Grant to Ambrose E. Burnside, May 8, 1864, in *OR,* Vol. XXXVI, Pt. 2, p. 548.

39. Byron M. Cutcheon Autobiography, in Michigan Historical Collection, BL; Isham, "Through the Wilderness to Richmond," in *Sketches of War History,* I, 206–207.

40. Orlando B. Willcox to Ambrose E. Burnside, May 9, 1864, in *OR,* Vol. XXXVI, Pt. 2, p. 581; Fitzhugh Lee's report, in MC.

41. Before the campaign, maps of the area were printed in bulk and distributed to the Union commanders to ensure uniformity regarding place names. The maps, however, contained erroneous information. Some roads that appeared did not exist, some distances were incorrect, and some landmarks, such as the "gate" on Fredericksburg Road, were not recognizable by the troop commanders. The confusion engendered by the 9th Corps officers' assumption that *gate* and *Gayle* were the same is explored by C. F. Atkinson in *Grant's Campaigns of 1864 and 1865: The Wilderness and Cold Harbor* (London, 1908), 251–52, and by Matter in *If It Take All Summer,* 99–100.

42. Cutcheon Autobiography; Orlando B. Willcox to Ambrose E. Burnside, May 9, 1864, in *OR,* Vol. XXXVI, Pt. 2, p. 581.

43. Cutcheon Autobiography; Byron M. Cutcheon's report, in *OR,* Vol. XXXVI, Pt. 1, p. 967; Orlando B. Willcox' report, in *OR,* Vol. XXXVI, Pt. 1, p. 943.

44. John A. Rawlins to Ambrose E. Burnside, May 9, 1864, in *OR,* Vol. XXXVI, Pt. 2, p. 581; Ambrose E. Burnside to Ulysses S. Grant, May 9, 1864, *ibid.,* 583.

45. Walter A. Montgomery, "Twelfth Regiment," in *Histories of the Several Regiments and Battalions from North Carolina,* ed. Clark, I, 641. A postwar account by a soldier from the 1st Virginia Cavalry confirms that Wickham's brigade and a brigade of infantry were sent "down some distance on our extreme right to engage [Burnside] and hold [him] in check as long as possible" (Haden, *Reminiscences of J. E. B. Stuart's Cavalry,* 30). A 9th Corps history published shortly after the war asserted that one of Anderson's brigades attacked Christ. See Augustus Woodbury, *Major General Ambrose E. Burnside and the Ninth Army Corps* (Providence, 1867), 376. Anderson's men, however, were at Laurel Hill, and no Confederate sources place them on Fredericksburg Road.

46. Martin P. Avery's report, in *OR,* Vol. XXXVI, Pt. 1, p. 979.

47. Cutcheon Autobiography; John E. Irwin Diary, May 9, 1864, in Book 47, FSNMP; Avery's report, in *OR,* Vol. XXXVI, Pt. 1, p. 979; William Todd, *The Seventy-Ninth High-*

landers New York Volunteers in the War of the Rebellion, 1861–1865 (Albany, N.Y., 1886), 462.

48. Cutcheon Autobiography; Charles V. De Land's report, in *OR,* Vol. XXXVI, Pt. 1, p. 973; Cutcheon's report, in *OR,* Vol. XXXVI, Pt. 1, pp. 967–68, 977; Charles D. Todd Diary, May 9, 1864, in Gregory Coco Collection, USAMHI; Todd, *The Seventy-Ninth Highlanders,* 462–63; Haden, *Reminiscences of J. E. B. Stuart's Cavalry,* 30.

49. Constant Luce's report, in *OR,* Vol. XXXVI, Pt. 1, p. 958; Cutcheon Autobiography; Wirtz, ed., *John Parker Brest . . . Journal,"* 25; V. E. Turner, "Twenty-Third Regiment," in *Histories of the Several Regiments and Battalions from North Carolina,* ed. Clark, II, 241. According to Young's tabulations, Johnston lost about 140 soldiers in the Fredericksburg Road action.

50. Orlando B. Willcox to Ambrose E. Burnside, May 9, 1864, in *OR,* Vol. XXXVI, Pt. 2, p. 584.

51. Gregory A. Coco, ed., *Through Blood and Fire: The Civil War Letters of Major Charles J. Mills, 1862–1865* (Lanham, Md., 1982), 81; Massachusetts Historical Society, comp., *War Diary and Letters of Stephen Minot Weld, 1861–1865* (Boston, 1979), 289.

52. Willcox to Burnside, May 9, 1864, in *OR,* Vol. XXXVI, Pt. 2, p. 584.

53. Willcox' report, in *OR,* Vol. XXXVI, Pt. 1, p. 943; Tabular Statement of Casualties in Ninth Army Corps, RG 94, Entry 729, Box 93, NA; Cutcheon Autobiography.

54. Charles F. Walcott, *History of the Twenty-First Regiment Massachusetts Volunteers in the War for the Preservation of the Union, 1861–1865* (Boston, 1882), 319–20; Alexander Newburger Daily Journal, May 9, 1864, in Alexander Newberger Collection, LC.

55. Trout, ed., *Riding with Stuart . . . by . . . Garnett,* 59. Brigadier General James H. Lane reported that his Confederate brigade reached Spotsylvania Court House around noon on May 12, passed through the hamlet, and entrenched on the north side of Fredericksburg Road. See his "Battle of Spotsylvania Court-House," in *SHSP,* IX, 145. His division commander Wilcox claimed that the corps was not all up until 3 P.M. See Cadmus M. Wilcox' report, in VHS. Wilcox also there described the Confederate 3rd Corps' deployment with such accuracy that the line can be followed by a determined walker to this day: "[My] division took position in line, immediately in front of the Court-House across the Fredericksburg Road and at right angles to it, two brigades on the left and two on the right, the field extended beyond my right 200 or 300 yards and then came woods in which Mahone's division subsequently formed, Heth on my left. To the left of the Fredericksburg Road, 400 or 500 yards, the line rose, and near a barn were several batteries, beyond the barn the line descended gently for several hundred yards, and then bent back to the rear forming a salient, from this to the left the line descended till it crossed a boggy little stream (200 yards from the salient), it then ascended 300 or 400 yards, crossed a ridge and again descended and crossed two little streams and connected with Ewell's right (Brigadier General George H. Steuart's Brigade). About 300 yards to the right of Ewell on a ridge, a line of pits had been made, but this did not connect with Steuart's right. General Lane made the connection by running his line down the slope across the little stream direct to Steuart's right, the line on the ridge being in his rear." In fact, Lane did not shift to the northern end of the 3rd Corps line and effect the junction with Steuart until the morning of May 10. See Lane, "Battle of Spotsylvania Court-House," 145.

56. Winfield S. Hancock to George G. Meade, May 9, 1864, in *OR,* Vol. XXXVI, Pt. 2, p. 566; Early, *Autobiographical Sketch and Narrative,* 353.

57. Charles E. Pease to Winfield S. Hancock, May 9, 1864, in *OR,* Vol. XXXVI, Pt.

2, p. 566; Ulysses S. Grant to George G. Meade, May 9, 1864, *ibid.,* 562; Ulysses S. Grant to Henry W. Halleck, May 9, 1864, *ibid.,* 561.

58. George G. Meade to Andrew A. Humphreys, May 9, 1864, in *OR,* Vol. XXXVI, Pt. 2, p. 562.

59. Grant to Meade, May 9, 1864, in *OR,* Vol. XXXVI, Pt. 2, p. 562; Atkinson, *Grant's Campaigns,* 253.

60. Ulysses S. Grant to Ambrose E. Burnside, May 9, 1864, in *OR,* Vol. XXXVI, Pt. 2, p. 582; Charles A. Dana to Edwin M. Stanton, May 9, 1864, *ibid.,* Pt. 1, p. 65.

61. Francis A. Walker to Gershom Mott, May 9, 1864, in *OR,* Vol. XXXVI, Pt. 2, p. 572; Stevens, *Berdan's United States Sharpshooters,* 417.

62. 2nd Corps Addenda, in *OR,* Vol. XXXVI, Pt. 1, p. 356; Robert S. Robertson to parents, May 14, 1864, in FSNMP.

63. Lyman Journal, May 9, 1864; Albert N. Ames Diary, May 9, 1864, in Albert N. Ames Collection, NYSLA; Schaff, *The Battle of the Wilderness,* 319.

64. Frederick M. Edgell's report, in *OR,* Vol. XXXVI, Pt. 1, p. 519; John H. Rhodes, *The History of Battery B, First Regiment Rhode Island Light Artillery, in the War to Preserve the Union, 1861–1865* (Providence, 1894), 278; Mulholland, *The Story of the 116th Regiment Pennsylvania Volunteers,* 185; T. Frederick Brown's report, in *OR,* Vol. XXXVI, Pt. 1, p. 533; J. W. Muffly, ed., *The Story of Our Regiment: A History of the 148th Pennsylvania Volunteers* (Des Moines, 1904), 852.

65. Robert P. Chew's report, in Lewis Leigh Collection, USAMHI; George N. Neese, *Three Years in the Confederate Horse Artillery* (New York, 1911), 265–66; Ames Diary, May 9, 1864; "Forty-Eighth Regiment Georgia Volunteers," in *Heroes and Martyrs of Georgia: Georgia's Record in the Revolution of 1861,* by James M. Folsom (Macon, Ga., 1864), 94; William Mahone to Edward B. Robins, May 9, 1879, in Military Historical Society of Massachusetts Collection, BU. According to Chew, the elements supporting Thomson's guns "retired without fight and the enemy continued to advance in the face of a severe fire of shell and canister" (Chew's report, in Leigh Collection, USAMHI). A gun was nearly captured when a caisson's tongue snapped.

66. Walker, *History of the Second Army Corps,* 447; David B. Birney to Winfield S. Hancock, May 9, 1864, in *OR,* Vol. XXXVI, Pt. 2, p. 570; Weygant, *History of the One Hundred and Twenty-Fourth Regiment New York State Volunteers,* 306–307; Warren L. Goss, *Recollections of a Private: A Story of the Army of the Potomac* (New York, 1890), 285; Wade Hampton's report, in Wade Hampton Collection, SCL.

67. "The Incomplete Civil War Memoir of Joseph S. Wicklein, Pvt., B Co., 53rd Pennsylvania Infantry," in FSNMP. Brooke relieved Colonel McMichael.

68. B. Y. Draper Diary, May 9, 1864, in FSNMP; Winfield S. Hancock to Andrew A. Humphreys, May 9, 1864, in *OR,* Vol. XXXVI, Pt. 2, p. 567; Walker, *History of the Second Army Corps,* 447; Francis A. Walker to David B. Birney, May 9, 1864, in *OR,* Vol. XXXVI, Pt. 2, p. 570.

69. Sypher, *History of the Pennsylvania Reserve Corps,* 524–25; Roebling's report, in Warren Collection, NYSLA. According to Roebling, the troops "fell back at nightfall contrary to General Warren's orders and those of General Crawford. They were under the impression that a long line of battle was advancing on them, and did not stop long enough to fire on them and find out for certain."

70. G. Moxley Sorrel Diary, May 9, 1864, in MC.

71. Hewson, "Battle of Spotsylvania Court House," in *Lee's Sharpshooters,* by Dunlop, 445.

72. Hancock to Humphreys, May 9, 1864, in *OR,* Vol. XXXVI, Pt. 2, p. 567.

73. Andrew A. Humphreys to Winfield S. Hancock, May 9, 1864, *ibid.,* 568.

74. John F. Sale Diary, May 10, 1864, in VSL; George S. Bernard Diary, May 10, 1864, in George S. Bernard Collection, UV; Seton Fleming Diary, May 9, 1864, in *Memoir of Captain C. Seton Fleming,* ed. Fleming, Appendix; Joseph Mullen, Jr., Diary, May 10, 1864, in MC; Gallagher, ed., *Fighting for the Confederacy,* 371. Only four days before, on May 6, Lee had sent Mahone on a similar maneuver against Hancock's flank on Orange Plank Road, and Mahone had succeeded brilliantly.

75. Jeb Stuart to Robert E. Lee, May 9, 1864, in *OR,* Vol. LI, Pt. 2, pp. 905–906; Fitzhugh Lee's report, in MC; J. D. Ferguson Memoranda, in Thomas T. Munford Collection, DU; William R. Carter Diary, May 9, 1864, in William R. Carter Collection, Hampden-Sydney College Library; Peck, *Reminiscences of a Confederate Soldier,* 46; McClellan, *The Life and Campaigns of Major-General J. E. B. Stuart,* 409.

76. Rodenbough, "Sheridan's Richmond Raid," in *B&L,* IV, 188; Allen, *Down in Dixie,* 279–80; Sheridan, *Personal Memoirs,* I, 374.

77. Bushnell Memoir; Allen Parker Diary, May 9, 1864, in Book 198, FSNMP; Allen, *Down in Dixie,* 279–80; Perkins Memoir, May 9, 1864.

78. "The Second Virginia Cavalry in the Late Fights," Richmond *Sentinel,* May 21, 1864; Allen, *Down in Dixie,* 280; Sheridan, *Personal Memoirs,* I, 374.

79. William P. Lloyd, *History of the First Regiment Pennsylvania Reserve Cavalry* (Philadelphia, 1864), 92; Allen, *Down in Dixie,* 281–82; "Fitz. Lee's Cavalry Division," Richmond *Daily Examiner,* May 21, 1864. Many accounts mix the fighting at Jerrell's Mill and Mitchell's Shop. The presentation here attempts to reconcile the conflicting accounts.

80. James J. Robinson Narrative, in "Papers Discovered Describing Actions of Cumberland Troop," *Cumberland County, Virginia, Historical Bulletin,* December, 1986, p. 25; Bushnell Memoir; Fitzhugh Lee's report, in MC; Allen, *Down in Dixie,* 281–85.

81. Robinson Narrative, in "Papers Discovered Describing Actions of Cumberland Troop," 25–26; Bushnell Memoir.

82. "T. M. Fowler's Experience in the Charge at Mitchell's Shop, May 9, 1864," in MC; Allen, *Down in Dixie,* 281–85; McClellan, *The Life and Campaigns of Major-General J. E. B. Stuart,* 409–10; Henry Davies' report, in *OR,* Vol. XXXVI, Pt. 1, p. 857; Bushnell Memoir; "The Great Cavalry Expedition Through the Rebel Lines," New York *Herald,* May 17, 1864.

83. John W. Kester's report, in *OR,* Vol. XXXVI, Pt. 1, p. 861; Return of Casualties in the Union Forces, *ibid.,* 184; Pyne, *Ride to War,* 197–98; "The Great Cavalry Expedition Through the Rebel Lines," New York *Herald,* May 17, 1864. Robbins detailed his splendid charge in *War Record and Experiences of Walter Raleigh Robbins, from April 22, 1861, to August 4, 1865,* ed. Lilian Rea (Chicago, 1913), 82–83.

84. Kidd, *Personal Recollections of a Cavalryman,* 292–93.

85. *Ibid.*; Alonzo Foster, *Reminiscences and Record of the 6th New York V. V. Cavalry* (Brooklyn, N.Y., 1892), 67–68; Preston, *History of the Tenth Regiment of Cavalry New York State Volunteers,* 175. A list of liberated officers appears in New York *Herald,* May 17, 1864.

86. Kidd, *Personal Recollections of a Cavalryman,* 293–94; Foster, *Reminiscences and Record of the 6th New York,* 68–69. James Wilson was "disgusted" when he learned that

the station and large quantities of stores had been destroyed by "unauthorized men before command could reap the benefit of them" (James H. Wilson Diary, May 9, 1864, in LC).

87. George W. Booth, *Personal Reminiscences of a Maryland Soldier in the War Between the States* (Baltimore, 1898), 107–108; W. W. Goldsborough, *The Maryland Line in the Confederate States Army* (Baltimore, 1869), 233–35; Samuel H. Miller, ed., "The Civil War Memoirs of the First Maryland Cavalry, C.S.A., by Henry Clay Mettam," *Maryland Historical Magazine,* LVIII (1963), 151–52. The Maryland battalion's commander, Colonel Bradley T. Johnson, was on a mission to Yorktown and had left Brown at Hanover Junction with about four companies. See Samuel H. Miller, "Yellow Tavern," *Civil War History,* II (1956), 63–64. Hanover Junction is now called Doswell.

88. Kidd, *Personal Recollections of a Cavalryman,* 293–94; Allen, *Down in Dixie,* 286; Pyne, *Ride to War,* 199; Matthew W. King, *To Horse: With the Cavalry of the Army of the Potomac, 1861–1865* (Cheboygan, Mich., 1926), unpaginated. A Confederate in charge of the prisoners delighted in calling them "hirelings, thieves, invaders, robbers, etc.," and habitually ended his fulminations by declaring that "one Confederate soldier was worth more than the whole damned Yankee army." On the ninth, the party forded the North Anna, and the Confederates let them wash and dry their clothing. "This halt proved our salvation," a prisoner reminisced, for it delayed the captives from reaching Beaver Dam station before Custer arrived (S. A. Chamberlain, "Plenty to Do in Old Virginia in the Spring of 1864," *National Tribune,* April 16, 1896).

89. Boteler Diary. Boteler mistakenly dated Stuart's departure as occurring on May 10.

90. Trout, ed., *Riding with Stuart . . . by . . . Garnett,* 62.

91. Fitzhugh Lee to John Esten Cooke, March 21, 1868, in John Esten Cooke Collection, DU; Trout, ed., *Riding with Stuart . . . by . . . Garnett,* 61.

92. Fitzhugh Lee reported that Stuart "joined me after dark but with no additional troops" (Fitzhugh Lee's report, in MC). Stuart's aide Henry McClellan, however, claimed that "Stuart and Fitz Lee joined Wickham, with Lomax's and Gordon's brigades" (McClellan, *The Life and Campaigns of Major-General J. E. B. Stuart,* 410).

93. Trout, ed., *Riding with Stuart . . . by . . Garnett,* 62–63; "Cavalry Fights Around Richmond," Charlotte (N.C.) *Western Democrat,* May 31, 1864. Gordon's brigade had started the campaign in "quite a reduced condition on account of the rigors of the winter, and the excessive outpost duty" ("Barringer's North Carolina Brigade of Cavalry," Raleigh [N.C.] *Daily Confederate,* February 22, 1865).

94. Ferguson Memoranda, in Munford Collection, DU; McClellan, *The Life and Campaigns of Major-General J. E. B. Stuart,* 410. Accounts disagree over where the rebels intended to cross the North Anna. All sources concur that Wickham was to cross at Anderson's. Lee, in his report, states that Lomax was to cross at Davenport but does not mention where Gordon was to go. McClellan states that Lee was to cross at Anderson's and that Gordon was to cross at Davenport. The aide Garnett states that Lee took the direct road to Beaver Dam, that is, over Anderson's Ford, while Stuart took Gordon's brigade *east* to cross. See Trout, ed., *Riding With Stuart . . . by . . . Garnett,* 63. Since Davenport is *west* of Anderson's Ford, either Garnett was confused concerning the direction of Gordon's march, or McClellan was wrong about where Gordon crossed. I have assumed that Lee took only Wickham's brigade, and that Stuart took Lomax' and Gordon's. That scenario best fits Lee's and Ferguson's accounts and is supported by a contemporaneous dispatch. At 8:45 A.M. on the tenth, Stuart wrote Robert E. Lee that Fitzhugh Lee was

crossing at Anderson's, and that "the other brigades, Gordon's and Lomax's, will cross above at Davenport's Bridge and will sweep down on south side" (Jeb Stuart to Robert E. Lee, May 10, 1864, in *OR,* Vol. XXXVI, Pt. 2, p. 913).

95. Humphreys, *The Virginia Campaign,* 83.

96. Orders, May 9, 1864, in *OR,* Vol. XXXVI, Pt. 2, p. 563; John A. Rawlins to Ambrose E. Burnside, May 10, 1864, *ibid.,* 610.

97. Mullen Diary, May 9, 1864; Lane, "Battle of Spotsylvania Court House," in *SHSP,* IX, 145; Caldwell, *The History of a Brigade of South Carolinians,* 139; "The Campaign of 1864; Cooke's North Carolina Brigade," New Bern (N.C.) *Our Living and Our Dead,* January 14, 1874; Benson, ed., *Berry Benson's Civil War Book,* 68–69.

IV MAY 10 *Grant Feels for Openings at the Po and Laurel Hill*

1. Washington A. Roebling's report, in Gouverneur K. Warren Collection, NYSLA.

2. Letter to friend Sam, May 19, 1864, in Samuel Bradbury Collection, DU; Mulholland, *The Story of the 116th Regiment Pennsylvania Infantry,* 186–87; Nathaniel H. Harris to William Mahone, August 2, 1866, in William Mahone Collection, VSL; Harris, comp., *Movements of the Confederate Army in Virginia and the Part Taken Therein by the Nineteenth Mississippi Brigade,* 26–27; Robertson, *Personal Recollections of the War,* 99; Thomas F. Galwey, *The Valiant Hours: An Irishman in the Civil War* (Harrisburg, Pa., 1961), 203.

3. William N. Pendleton's report, in *OR,* Vol. XXXVI, Pt. 1, p. 1043; Winfield S. Hancock's report, *ibid.,* 331.

4. Winfield S. Hancock to Andrew A. Humphreys, May 10, 1864, in *OR,* Vol. XXXVI, Pt. 2, p. 599.

5. "Historical Sketch," New Bern (N.C.) *Our Living and Our Dead,* April 15, 1874; Survivors Association of Lamar Rifles, *Lamar Rifles: A History of Company G, Eleventh Mississippi, C.S.A.* (Roanoke, Va., 1902), 63; Joseph F. Waring Diary, May 10, 1864, in Joseph F. Waring Collection, SHC; Nobel J. Brooks Diary, May 10, 1864, in Nobel J. Brooks Collection, SHC; Silliker, ed., *The Rebel Yell and the Yankee Hurrah,* 150–51.

6. David Craft, *History of the One Hundred Forty First Regiment Pennsylvania Volunteers,* 1862–1865 (Towanda, Pa., 1885), 189; Silliker, ed., *The Rebel Yell and the Yankee Hurrah,* 151–52; Survivors Association, *Lamar Rifles,* 63–64; Steven E. Stubbs, *11th Mississippi Infantry Regiment* (Galveston, Tex., n.d.), 375–76, in CRC; William H. Green, "From the Wilderness to Spotsylvania," in *War Papers Read Before the Commandery of the State of Maine, Military Order of the Loyal Legion of the United States* (3 vols.; Portland, Maine, 1902), II, 94–96. Young's brigade, of Hampton's division, and Brigadier General John R. Chambliss, Jr.'s brigade, of Rooney Lee's division, assisted the Lamar Rifles in driving Briscoe back across Glady Run. See Brooks Diary, May 10, 1864, and Waring Diary, May 10, 1864. Crocker, whose brigade contributed the Maine regiments, estimated that Briscoe lost about fifty men. See John S. Crocker Diary, May 10, 1864, in CU.

7. "Historical Sketch," New Bern (N.C.) *Our Living and Our Dead,* April 15, 1874.

8. Robertson, *Personal Recollections of the War,* 99; George W. Scott's report, in OR, Vol. XXXVI, Pt. 1, p. 379.

9. Muffly, ed., *The Story of Our Regiment,* 852–53; Simon Pincus' report, in *OR,* Vol.

XXXVI, Pt. 1, p. 421; Butt Hewson, "Battle of Spotsylvania Court House," in *Lee's Sharpshooters,* by Dunlop, 448–49; Walker, *History of the Second Army Corps,* 449–50. The 12th Virginia had been detached from Weisiger's brigade and lay entrenched on Wright's left.

10. James W. Latta Diary, May 10, 1864, in James W. Latta Collection, LC; Luther A. Rose Diary, May 10, 1864, in Luther A. Rose Collection, LC.

11. Pendleton's report, in *OR,* Vol. XXXVI, Pt. 1, pp. 1042–43; Robert K. Krick, *Parker's Virginia Battery, C.S.A.* (Berryville, Va., 1975), 236–37; Joseph A. Graves, *The History of the Bedford Light Artillery* (Bedford, Va., 1903), 43.

12. Mixson, *Reminiscences of a Private,* 76–77; Beyer and Keydel, eds., *Deeds of Valor,* 327–28.

13. Gallagher, ed., *Fighting for the Confederacy,* 372–73; Dame, *From the Rapidan to Richmond,* 145–48; J. Mark Smither to family, n.d., in CRC; Nicholas Pomeroy Memoir, in CRC; Joe Joskins, "A Sketch of Hood's Texas Brigade of the Virginia Army," in CRC.

14. Dame, *From the Rapidan to Richmond,* 149–50. Alexander wrote that the "guns in the trenches were subject to a terrible and continued fire of artillery and sharpshooters, the latter 60 yards off in front of my old battery, and three of its guns were hit in the muzzle by solid shot" (Edward P. Alexander to father, May 29, 1864, in Edward P. Alexander Collection, SHC).

15. Samuel W. Crawford to Gouverneur K. Warren, May 10, 1864, in *OR,* Vol. XXXVI, Pt. 2, p. 606.

16. "The Great Battle of Tuesday," Philadelphia *Inquirer,* May 13, 1864; Dame, *From the Rapidan to Richmond,* 151–53.

17. Gouverneur K. Warren to Samuel W. Crawford, May 10, 1864, in *OR,* Vol. XXXVI, Pt. 2, p. 607.

18. Avery Harris Reminiscences, in Avery Harris Collection, USAMHI; Coles, *From Huntsville to Appomattox,* 168; Alfred M. Apted Diary, May 10, 1864, in Civil War Miscellaneous Collection, USAMHI; Carter, *Four Brothers in Blue,* 395; Edwin C. Bennett, *Musket and Sword; or, The Camp, March, and Firing Line in the Army of the Potomac* (Boston, 1900), 227; William S. Tilton's report, in *OR,* Vol. XXXVI, Pt. 1, p. 561.

19. Dame, *From the Rapidan to Richmond,* 158.

20. Ulysses S. Grant to Henry W. Halleck, May 10, 1864, in *OR,* Vol. XXXVI, Pt. 2, p. 595.

21. George G. Meade to Ulysses S. Grant, May 10, 1864, in *OR,* Vol. XXXVI, Pt. 2, p. 596.

22. George G. Meade to Winfield S. Hancock, May 10, 1864, in *OR,* Vol. XXXVI, Pt. 2, p. 600; George G. Meade to Gouverneur K. Warren, May 10, 1864, *ibid.,* 604; George G. Meade to Horatio G. Wright, May 10, 1864, *ibid.,* 609; Ulysses S. Grant to Ambrose E. Burnside, May 10, 1864, *ibid.,* 610.

23. Theodore Lyman to family, May 20, 1864, in *Meade's Headquarters,* ed. Agassiz, 107; William Houghton, "A Staff Officer's Recollection of the Salient Angle," *National Tribune,* October 9, 1890; Favill, *The Diary of a Young Officer,* 284; Theodore Lyman, "Addenda," in *PMHSM,* IV, 169.

24. Silliker, ed., *The Rebel Yell and the Yankee Hurrah,* 152; Edward G. Longacre, *To Gettysburg and Beyond: The Twelfth New Jersey Volunteer Infantry, II Corps, Army of the Potomac, 1862–1865* (Hightstown, N.J., 1988), 196–97.

25. Hancock's report, in *OR,* Vol. XXXVI, Pt. 1, p. 331. Valuable in reconstructing

Barlow's position is a memorandum dated June 19, 1991, with maps, by Noel Harrison, of the Fredericksburg and Spotsylvania National Military Park, on file at FSNMP.

26. Winfield S. Hancock to Francis C. Barlow, May 10, 1864, in Francis C. Barlow Collection, MHS.

27. Unknown Confederate soldier to aunt, May 11, 1864, in Lewis Leigh Collection, USAMHI; David Gregg McIntosh, "A Ride on Horseback in the Summer of 1910, over Some of the Battlefields of the Great Civil War, with Some Notes on the Battles," in David Gregg McIntosh Collection, SHC.

28. Walker, *History of the Second Army Corps,* 450; Hancock's report, in *OR,* Vol. XXXVI, Pt. 1, p. 331.

29. Walker, *General Hancock,* 187–88.

30. Hancock's report, in *OR,* Vol. XXXVI, Pt. 1, p. 331.

31. "Letter from Kirkland's Brigade," Raleigh (N.C.) *Daily Confederate,* May 26, 1864; Joseph Mullen, Jr., Diary, May 10, 1864, in MC; "The Campaign of 1864: Cooke's North Carolina Brigade," New Bern (N.C.) *Our Living and Our Dead,* January 14, 1874; John A. Sloan, *Reminiscences of the Guilford Grays, Co. B, 27th N.C. Regiment* (Washington, D.C., 1883), 87; Kenneth Rayner Jones Diary, May 10, 1864, in SHC.

32. Hancock's report, in *OR,* Vol. XXXVI, Pt. 1, p. 332; John R. Brooke's report, *ibid.,* 408; Favill, *The Diary of a Young Officer,* 293; Charles Peabody, ed., *Memoirs of Alfred Horatio Belo* (Boston, 1904), 40; Goss, *Recollections of a Private,* 287; Mulholland, *The Story of the 116th Regiment Pennsylvania Infantry,* 189.

33. Pincus' report, in *OR,* Vol. XXXVI, Pt. 1, p. 421; Mulholland, *The Story of the 116th Regiment Pennsylvania Infantry,* 190; Muffly, ed., *The Story of Our Regiment,* 854.

34. Nelson Penfield's report, in *OR,* Vol. XXXVI, Pt.1, p. 404; Favill, *The Diary of a Young Officer,* 294; Norman M. Covert, ed., *Two Civil War Diaries: Sgt John L. Ryno and Bandmaster John Chadwick, Company C, 126th New York Regiment, 3rd Brigade, 2nd Division, II U.S. Corps* (N.p., n.d.), 20. Frank was replaced by the popular Colonel Hiram L. Brown, of the 145th Pennsylvania, renowned for his singing abilities and his dog Spot. "He is large, very stout, overflowing with good nature, and very gallant and capable," was Favill's assessment (*The Diary of a Young Officer,* 286).

35. Robertson, *Personal Recollections of the War,* 99–100; Hancock's report, in *OR,* Vol. XXXVI, Pt. 1, p. 332; Thomas M. Aldrich, *History of Battery A, 1st Rhode Island Light Artillery* (Providence, 1904), 306. Colonel Beaver, of the 148th Pennsylvania, detailed men to help save the gun, but they lacked sufficient axes. See Muffly, ed., *The Story of Our Regiment,* 122. The 44th North Carolina, of Kirkland's brigade, claimed the capture, as did Colonel Alfred H. Belo, of Davis' brigade. See "Letter from Kirkland's Brigade," Raleigh *Daily Confederate,* May 26, 1864; and Peabody, ed., *Memoirs of Alfred Horatio Belo,* 40.

36. Favill, *The Diary of a Young Officer,* 294–95; Peabody, ed., *Memoirs of Alfred Horatio Belo,* 40.

37. Stephen W. Coakley, "Count Von Haake: His Death in the Wilderness—Harrowing Experience in the Burning Woods," *National Tribune,* September 17, 1908.

38. Muffly, ed., *The Story of Our Regiment,* 120.

39. *Ibid.;* Brooke's report, in *OR,* Vol. XXXVI, Pt. 1, p. 409; Ezra D. Simons, *A Regimental History of the One Hundred and Twenty-Fifth New York State Volunteers* (New York, 1888), 204–205; E. A. Shiver, "Wright's Brigade at Spotsylvania Court House," Atlanta *Journal,* October 16, 1901; Hancock's report, in *OR,* Vol. XXXVI, Pt. 1, p. 332.

Shiver mistakenly describes events of May 10 as occurring on May 12. Frank and Brooke blamed each other for the precipitous retreat. According to a captain in the 125th New York, which constituted the right wing of Frank's formation, "We remained here after the line directly on our left had broke, partly rallied and again broke, and until the woods to our left took fire, which fire was sweeping rapidly toward us and until orders came for us to fall back" (Penfield's report, in *OR*, Vol. XXXVI, Pt. 1, p. 404). Colonel Beaver, of the 148th Pennsylvania, in Brooke's brigade, recorded that his men were "cut off from the balance of the army by a burning woods and were flanked on the right by reason of the retiring of [Frank's] brigade" (Beaver's Diary, May 10, 1864, in *The Story of Our Regiment,* ed. Muffly, 120).

40. Muffly, ed., *The Story of Our Regiment,* 120–21, 853–54; Memoir of the 64th New York, 66–67, in IU.

41. Mulholland, *The Story of the 116th Pennsylvania Infantry,* 190.

42. Hancock's report, in *OR,* Vol. XXXVI, Pt. 1, p. 333; Thomas J. Strayhorn to sister, May 17, 1864, in "Letters of Thomas Jackson Strayhorn," ed. Henry McG. Wagstaff, *North Carolina Historical Review,* XIII (1936), 313; Robert S. Robertson to parents, May 14, 1864, in FSNMP; Robertson, *Personal Recollections of the War,* 100–101.

43. John C. Tidball's report, in *OR,* Vol. XXXVI, Pt. 1, p. 509; John C. Tidball Narrative, in *Heavy Guns and Light,* by Kirk, 200–201; Henry J. Hunt, "Journal of Siege Operations," in Henry J. Hunt Collection, LC. Lieutenant Benjamin F. Rittenhouse's 5th Corps battery was already above the bridges. Brown's, Roder's, Lieutenant William B. Beck's, and a section of Gilliss' occupied the front line, with Captain Frederick M. Edgell's, Captain J. Henry Sleeper's, and Arnold's behind.

44. Pendleton's report, in *OR,* Vol. XXXVI, Pt. 1, p. 1043; Rhodes, *The History of Battery B,* 281; John D. Billings, *The History of the Tenth Massachusetts Battery of Light Artillery in the War of the Rebellion* (Boston, 1881), 170–71; Kirk, *Heavy Guns and Light,* 201; Favill, *The Diary of a Young Officer,* 295. The artillery exchange is described from the Federal perspective by L. Van Loan Naisawald in *Grape and Canister: The Story of the Field Artillery of the Army of the Potomac, 1861–1865* (Washington, D.C., 1960), 482–83.

45. Strayhorn to sister, May 17, 1864, in "Letters of Thomas Jackson Strayhorn," ed. Wagstaff, 313; Mullen Diary, May 10, 1864.

46. Hewson, "Battle of Spotsylvania Court House," in *Lee's Sharpshooters,* by Dunlop, 449–50. Mahone outlined his movements in a letter to Edward R. Robins, May 9, 1879, in Military Historical Society of Massachusetts Collection, BU.

47. Early, *Autobiographical Sketch and Narrative,* 353–54; H. C. Kearney, "Fifteenth Regiment," in *Histories of the Several Regiments and Battalions from North Carolina,* ed. Clark, I, 744; Charles M. Cooke, "Fifty-Fifth Regiment," in *Histories of the Several Regiments and Battalions from North Carolina,* ed. Clark, III, 305–306; Dunbar Rowland, *Military History of Mississippi, 1803–1898* (Jackson, Miss., 1908), 49, 57; Sloan, *Reminiscences of the Guilford Grays,* 87; Survivors Association, *Lamar Rifles,* 63; Gallagher, ed., *Fighting for the Confederacy,* 372; James L. Morrison, Jr., ed., *The Memoirs of Henry Heth* (Westport, Conn., 1974), 188. A Confederate in Kirkland's brigade termed Southern casualties "slight" (Henry Clay Albright Diary, in Henry Clay Albright Collection, NCDAH).

48. Walker, *History of the Second Army Corps,* 455; Hancock's report, in *OR,* Vol. XXXVI, Pt. 1, p. 333; Morrison, ed., *The Memoirs of Henry Heth,* 188. Walker's claim

that Barlow retreated only because Hancock ordered him to do so was incorrect. Hancock ordered Barlow back because he realized that the division was about to be overwhelmed.

49. Humphreys, *The Virginia Campaign,* 82; Swinton, *Campaigns of the Army of the Potomac,* 449. Swinton thought that the battle, "though illustrating the steady valor of the troops, was an unfortunate one in every respect." He considered Hancock's maneuver to have been "undertaken without any very well-defined military object, and abandoned under circumstances unfavorable to the spirit of the troops, and highly encouraging to the enemy." Swinton's critique was unfair. Hancock had a clearly defined objective and abandoned the movement for good cause.

50. Philadelphia *Inquirer,* May 12, 1864. It is also worth asking why Wright failed to probe the salient more insistently to determine whether Ewell was still there.

51. Andrew A. Humphreys to Winfield S. Hancock, May 10, 1864, in *OR,* Vol. XXXVI, Pt. 2, p. 600.

52. Smith, *History of the Corn Exchange Regiment,* 417; Judson, *History of the Eighty-Third Regiment Pennsylvania Volunteers,* 202–203; Coles, *From Huntsville to Appomattox,* 168.

53. John Gibbon, *Personal Recollections of the Civil War* (New York, 1928), 218–19.

54. "Life of Amos G. Bean as a Soldier," 18, in FSNMP.

55. Second Corps Daily Memoranda, in *OR,* Vol. XXXVI, Pt. 1, p. 357. At 3:45, Hancock wrote Meade offering to return Birney to Warren as soon as Barlow crossed the stream. Meade answered by directing Hancock to return Birney "as soon as possible, or to attack enemy with Barlow's and Birney's divisions" (p. 357). Hancock concluded that even with two divisions, it made no sense to renew battle below the Po. Around four o'clock, he ordered Birney back to Warren. The division was unable to retrace its steps in time to participate in the initial assault against Laurel Hill.

56. P. S. Potter. "Reminiscences of Spotsylvania," *National Tribune,* April 15, 1882.

57. Smith, *The History of the Nineteenth Regiment of Maine Volunteer Infantry,* 150; Galwey, *The Valiant Hours,* 205.

58. Alexander S. Webb's report, in *OR,* Vol. XXXVI, Pt. 1, p. 439; Samuel S. Carroll's report, *ibid.,* 447; Ernest L. Waitt, *History of the Nineteenth Regiment Massachusetts Volunteer Infantry, 1861–1865* (Salem, Mass., 1906), 307; Smith, *History of the Nineteenth Regiment of Maine Volunteer Infantry,* 150; Franklin Sawyer, *A Military History of the 8th Regiment Ohio Volunteer Infantry* (Cleveland, 1881), 166; Longacre, *To Gettysburg and Beyond,* 197; Charles D. Page, *History of the Fourteenth Regiment Connecticut Volunteer Infantry* (Meriden, Conn., 1906), 244; George A. Bowen Diary, May 10, 1864, in FSNMP; Gibbon, *Personal Recollections,* 219.

59. Vautier, *History of the 88th Pennsylvania Volunteers,* 179–80; Dame, *From the Rapidan to Richmond,* 158–59; Calvin L. Collier, *They'll Do to Tie To: Hood's Arkansas Toothpicks, Third Arkansas Infantry Regiment, C.S.A.* (Little Rock, Ark., 1988), 134–35.

60. Chamberlin, *History of the One Hundred and Fiftieth Regiment Pennsylvania Volunteers,* 230–32; Smith, *History of the Seventy-Sixth Regiment New York Volunteers,* 295–96; Thomas Kearney to brother, May 17, 1864, *Irish American,* June 21, 1864.

61. Harris Reminiscences; Philip Cheek and Mair Pointon, *History of the Sauk County Riflemen, Known As Company A, Sixth Wisconsin Veteran Volunteer Infantry, 1861–1865* (Madison, Wis., 1909), 95; "Operations of the Iron Brigade in the Spring Campaign of 1864," in Oshkosh (Wis.) Public Museum; Chamberlin, *History of the One Hundred and Fiftieth Regiment Pennsylvania Volunteers,* 231–32; O. B. Curtis, *History of the Twenty-*

Fourth Michigan of the Iron Brigade (Detroit, 1891), 240–41; Royall W. Figg, *Where Men Only Dare to Go! or, The Story of a Boy Company* (Richmond, 1885), 199.

62. Dawes, *Service with the Sixth Wisconsin Volunteers,* 265–66; Davis, *Three Years in the Army,* 338; Marshall, *History of Company K, 155th Pennsylvania Volunteer Zouaves,* 159; Roe, *The Thirty-Ninth Regiment Massachusetts Volunteers,* 192–94.

63. Charles H. Banes, *History of the Philadelphia Brigade* (Philadelphia, 1876), 242; New York *Daily Tribune,* May 13, 1864.

64. George Fairfield to R. G. Thwaite, June 21, 1889, with Fairfield's notes from back of manual, in State Historical Society of Wisconsin. Fairfield, who was with the 6th Wisconsin, took the manual from the knapsack of a soldier lying on the hill.

65. Lysander Cutler's report, in *OR,* Vol. XXXVI, Pt. 1, p. 611; Carter, *Four Brothers in Blue,* 395; Farley, "Reminiscences of the 140th Regiment New York Volunteer Infantry," 251; Andrew R. Linscott to parents, May 19, 1864, in Andrew R. Linscott Collection, MHS; Confederate Diary, author unknown, in Military Historical Society of Massachusetts Collection, BU; Philadelphia *Inquirer,* May 13, 1864.

66. Roebling's report, in Warren Collection, NYSLA.

67. Avery Harris Reminiscences.

68. Hancock's report, in *OR,* Vol. XXXVI, Pt. 1, p. 334; Humphreys, *The Virginia Campaign,* 82. At 6 P.M., Meade instructed Barlow, "If the enemy cross the river below you, you must attack them promptly and vigorously" (George G. Meade to Francis C. Barlow, May 10, 1864, in Barlow Collection, MHS).

69. Hancock's report, in *OR,* Vol. XXXVI, Pt. 1, p. 334; Second Corps Daily Memoranda, *ibid.,* 357; Philadelphia *Inquirer,* May 13, 1864. Sources disagree concerning whether the attack was rescheduled for 6:40 or 7:00.

V   MAY 10 *Grant Attacks Across Lee's Line*

1. Isaac O. Best, *History of the 121st New York State Infantry* (Chicago, 1921), 134–35; Hyde, *Following the Greek Cross,* 196–97.

2. Best, *History of the 121st New York State Infantry,* 135–36.

3. Emory Upton's report, in *OR,* Vol. XXXVI, Pt. 1, p. 667.

4. *Ibid.*; Nathaniel Michler's report, in *OR,* Vol. XXXVI, Pt. 1, p. 297.

5. Emory Upton to Edward B. Robins, April 26, 1879, in Military Historical Society of Massachusetts Collection, BU; Upton's report, in *OR,* Vol. XXXVI, Pt. 1, p. 667.

6. Unidentified soldier's diary, May 10, 1864, in Book 32, FSNMP; Emory Upton to Edward B. Robins, April 18, 1879, in Military Historical Society Collection, BU; Upton's report, in *OR,* Vol. XXXVI, Pt. 1, p. 667. Upton's four lines stood at ten-foot intervals. According to his report there were arrayed from right to left in the first line, the 121st New York, 96th Pennsylvania, and 5th Maine; in the second line the 49th Pennsylvania, 6th Maine, and 5th Wisconsin; in the third line the 43rd New York, 77th New York, and 119th Pennsylvania; and in the fourth line the 2nd Vermont, 5th Vermont, and 6th Vermont. The regiment on the right of each line marched along the right side of the road, and the left two regiments marched on the road's left. Robert S. Westbrook gives a slightly different regimental order in *History of the 49th Pennsylvania Volunteers* (Altoona, Pa., 1898), 190.

7. Upton's report, in *OR,* Vol. XXXVI, Pt. 1, p. 667; Best, *History of the 121st New York State Infantry,* 128–29.

8. Henry N. Blake, *Three Years in the Army of the Potomac* (Boston, 1865), 287; Upton to Robins, April 18, 1879, in Military Historical Society of Massachusetts Collection, BU; George G. Meade to Gershom Mott, May 10, 1864, in *OR*, Vol. XXXVI, Pt. 2, p. 602.

9. Andrew A. Humphreys to Gershom Mott, May 10, 1864, in *OR*, Vol. XXXVI, Pt. 2, p. 602; George G. Meade to Horatio G. Wright, May 10, 1864, *ibid.*, 609; Martin T. McMahon Orders, *ibid.*, 609; Howe, ed., *Touched with Fire*, 111; Best, *History of the 121st New York State Infantry*, 127–28. The straight-line distance from Mott to Burnside was about two miles. One of Upton's officers later reported the rumor that Mott was drunk. "But for whiskey drinking, I believe the war would have ended a year before it did and certainly the lives of thousands of brave men would have been saved," he added (Isaac O. Best, "Through the Wilderness with Grant," in James S. Schoff Collection, CL).

10. Howe, ed., *Touched with Fire*, 111; Jones, ed., *The Civil War Memoirs of Captain William J. Seymour*, 120.

11. George G. Meade to Gershom Mott, May 10, 1864, in *OR*, Vol. XXXVI, Pt. 2, pp. 602–603; Horatio G. Wright to Gershom Mott, May 10, 1864, *ibid.*, 603.

12. Gershom Mott to Horatio G. Wright, May 10, 1864, in *OR*, Vol. XXXVI, Pt. 2, p. 603; Horatio G. Wright to Gershom Mott, May 10, 1864, *ibid.*

13. Andrew A. Humphreys to Gouverneur K. Warren, May 10, 1864, in *OR*, Vol. XXXVI, Pt. 2, p. 604; Edmund D. Halsey Diary, May 10, 1864, in Edmund D. Halsey Collection, USAMHI; Official Report of Movements of Fifteenth Regiment New Jersey During Grant's Wilderness Campaign, in Halsey Collection, USAMHI. Accounts differ concerning when Mott attacked. Reports in *OR* indicate five o'clock, but an officer in the 11th Massachusetts placed the attack at 5:50. See Blake, *Three Years in the Army of the Potomac*, 288. Matter, in *If It Takes All Summer*, 161, accepts five o'clock as "likely." See also Frederick B. Arner, *The Mutiny At Brandy Station: the Last Battle of the Hooker Brigade* (Kensington, Md., 1993), which concludes as well that Mott had been repulsed well before Upton charged.

14. John E. Kittle Diary, May 10, 1864, in Book 32, FSNMP; Robert McAllister's report, in *OR*, Vol. XXXVI, Pt. 1, p. 490; James I. Robertson, Jr., ed., *The Civil War Letters of General Robert McAllister* (New Brunswick, N.J., 1965), 417; Edward Perkins Preble Diary, May 10, 1864, in FSNMP; Henry Harrison Stone Diary, May 10, 1864, in Harrisburg Civil War Round Table Collection, USAMHI; Thomas D. Marbaker, *History of the Eleventh New Jersey Volunteers from Its Organization to Appomattox* (Trenton, 1898), 168–69; John Schoonover's report, in *OR*, Vol. XXXVI, Pt. 1, p. 494; Thomas C. Thompson's report, in *OR*, Vol. XXXVI, Pt. 1, p. 499.

15. Upton's report, in *OR*, Vol. XXXVI, Pt. 1, pp. 667–68; Howe, ed., *Touched with Fire*, 112; Best, *History of the 121st New York State Infantry*, 128.

16. Howe, ed. *Touched With Fire*, 112; Best, *History of the 121st New York State Infantry*, 136–37; Richard S. Ewell's report, in *OR*, Vol. XXXVI, Pt. 1, p. 1072; James A. Walker, "The Bloody Angle," in *SHSP*, XXI, 234.

17. Westbrook, *History of the 49th Pennsylvania Volunteers*, 191; Best, *History of the 121st New York State Infantry*, 137; Howe, ed., *Touched with Fire*, 112; Morse, *Personal Experiences in the War of the Great Rebellion*, 86. Upton placed the assault at 6:10 (Upton's report, in *OR*, Vol. XXXVI, Pt. 1, pp. 667–68). Lewis Luckenbill, of the 96th Pennsylvania, recorded that "at about 6:30, the order [to advance] was given" (Lewis Luckenbill Diary, May 10, 1864, in Historical Society of Schuylkill County, Pottsville, Pa.).

18. William S. White, "A Diary of the War, or What I Saw of It," in *Contributions to a History of the Richmond Howitzer Battalion* (3 vols.; Richmond, 1883–86), II, 243–44.

19. Henry Keiser Diary, May 10, 1864, in Harrisburg Civil War Round Table Collection, USAMHI; Best, *History of the 121st New York State Infantry,* 129–30.

20. Doles's 44th Georgia was on the brigade's left, the 4th Georgia in the center, and the 12th Georgia on the right. The location of the single 21st Georgia company present for the battle is not known. See Irby G. Scott to family, June 8, 1864, in Irby G. Scott Collection, DU.

21. Thomas, *History of the Doles-Cook Brigade,* 478; William A. Wright, "Thomas J. Dingler, Color Bearer, Co. E, 44th Georgia Regiment," in United Daughters of the Confederacy Typescripts, Vol. XIII, GDAH; Scott to family, June 8, 1864, in Scott Collection, DU; J. B. Reese to William C. Davis, May 17, 1864, Putnam County (Ga.) *Countryman,* June 14, 1864; Westbrook, *History of the 49th Pennsylvania Volunteers,* 191. Wright noted of the color-bearer Dingler, "This hero with these precious fragments of the emblem of Southern heroism was buried in his old grey suit in Spotsylvania's bloody field."

22. Thomas, *History of the Doles-Cook Brigade,* 478; White, "A Diary of the War," in *Contributions to a History of the Richmond Howitzer Battalion,* II, 244.

23. Thomas, *History of the Doles-Cook Brigade,* 77; White, "A Diary of the War," in *Contributions to a History of the Richmond Howitzer Battalion,* II, 244–45; Westbrook, *History of the 49th Pennsylvania Volunteers,* 191; George Percy Hawes, "A Week with the Artillery, A.N.V.," *Confederate Veteran,* XXXI (1923), 370; Best, *History of the 121st New York State Infantry,* 130–31; Keiser Diary, May 10, 1864.

24. Upton's report, in *OR,* Vol. XXXVI, Pt. 1, p. 668.

25. Taylor, *General Lee,* 240.

26. Ewell's report, in *OR,* Vol. XXXVI, Pt. 1, p. 1072; Wharton J. Green, "Second Battalion," in *Histories of the Several Regiments and Battalions from North Carolina,* ed. Clark, IV, 259; Watson, "Forty-Fifth Regiment," in *Histories of the Several Regiments and Battalions from North Carolina,* ed. Clark, III, 47–48; Francis A. Boyle, "A Civil War Prison Diary," in Walter Ralph Steiner Collection, LC.

27. Roberts, "The Wilderness and Spotsylvania," 69.

28. Robert D. Johnston, "Brigadier General R. D. Johnston's Brigade on May 10th, 1864, at Spotsylvania," August 6, 1895, in John W. Daniel Collection, DU; Robert D. Johnston to John W. Daniel, June 30, 1905, in Daniel Collection, DU; Unknown Confederate soldier to family, May 11, 1864, in Lewis Leigh Collection, USAMHI.

29. Charles S. Venable, "General Lee in the Wilderness Campaign," in *B&L,* IV, 242; J.K.B. to *Journal,* June 7, 1864, Wilmington (N.C.) *Daily Journal,* June 17, 1864; Turner, "Twenty-Third Regiment," in *Histories of the Several Regiments and Battalions from North Carolina,* ed. Clark, II, 242; Watson, "Forty-Fifth Regiment," in *Histories of the Several Regiments and Battalions from North Carolina,* ed. Clark, III, 48. Johnston's version appears in his "Brigadier General R. D. Johnston's Brigade on May 10th," in Daniel Collection, DU, and in his "General Lee's Story, as Told on the Battlefield, and Recalled by General R. D. Johnston, of Alabama," in Stephen D. Ramseur Collection, SHC. Lee's letter to the secretary of war commending Johnston's brigade for capturing the flag is in "Twentieth Regiment," by Thomas F. Toon, in *Histories of the Several Regiments and Battalions from North Carolina,* ed. Clark, II, 120–21.

30. Thomas S. Doyle Memoir, in Jedediah Hotchkiss Collection, LC; Walker, "The Bloody Angle," in *SHSP,* XXI, 234; Abraham Schultz Miller to wife, May 11, 1864, in

FSNMP; James I. Robertson, Jr., *The Stonewall Brigade* (Baton Rouge, 1963), 222; Randolph Barton Memoir, in *Defend the Valley: A Shenandoah Family in the Civil War,* comp. Margaretta Barton Colt (New York, 1994), 311. Barton was understandably proud that he had "blundered into a good suggestion, not so bad for a youngster of twenty" (p. 311).

31. Howard, *Recollections of a Maryland Confederate,* 287–89; Thruston, "Report of the Conduct of General George H. Steuart's Brigade," in *SHSP,* XIV, 150–51; John Cowan, "Third Regiment," in *Histories of the Several Regiments and Battalions from North Carolina,* ed. Clark, I, 202–203; James Huffman, *Ups and Downs of a Confederate Soldier* (New York, 1940), 87.

32. John B. Gordon's report, in *OR,* Vol. XXXVI, Pt. 1, p. 1078; Gordon, *Reminiscences of the Civil War,* 273; I. G. Bradwell, "Spotsylvania, Va., May 8 and 9, 1864," *Confederate Veteran,* XXVIII (1920), 56–57; White, "A Diary of the War," in *Contributions to a History of the Richmond Howitzer Battalion,* II, 246.

33. Watson, "Forty-Fifth Regiment," in *Histories of the Several Regiments and Battalions from North Carolina,* ed. Clark, III, 48–49; Armistead L. Long's report, in *OR,* Vol. XXXVI, Pt. 1, p. 1086; Asbury H. Jackson to Luticia Jackson, May 11, 1864, in Edward Harden Collection, DU; Creed T. Davis Diary, May 10, 1864, in *Contributions to a History of the Richmond Howitzer Battalion,* III, 10; "Extract from the Diary of an Officer of Gen. Lee's Army," Richmond *Whig,* May 23, 1864. Hardaway's remaining batteries fired into Upton, and two of Major Wilfred E. Cutshaw's batteries rushed back from Spotsylvania Court House. Soldiers from Captain Asher W. Garber's battery, of Cutshaw's battalion, manned two of Smith's guns and turned them on the Federals. See William N. Pendleton's report, in *OR,* Vol. XXXVI, Pt. 1, pp. 1043–44; John Lipscomb Johnson, *The University Memorial Biographical Sketches* (Baltimore, 1871), 570; Wise, *The Long Arm of Lee,* II, 786–87.

34. Upton to Robins, April 26, 1879, in Military Historical Society of Massachusetts Collection, BU; Wilbur Fisk Retrospect, January 1, 1865, in *Hard Marching Every Day: The Civil War Letters of Wilbur Fisk, 1861–1865,* ed. Emil Rosenblatt and Ruth Rosenblatt (Lawrence, Kans., 1992), 296–97.

35. Mason Whiting Tyler, *Recollections of the Civil War* (New York, 1912), 168–69; Upton's report, in *OR,* Vol. XXXVI, Pt. 1, p. 668; Benedict, *Vermont in the Civil War,* I, 444–45. The 37th Massachusetts of Edwards' brigade tried to help but was inexplicably withdrawn.

36. Benedict, *Vermont in the Civil War,* I, 444–45; Samuel E. Pingree to Cousin Hunton, June 10, 1864, in Pingree Family Collection, Vermont Historical Society.

37. Morse, *Personal Experiences in the War of the Great Rebellion,* 87; Best, *History of the 121st New York State Infantry,* 132–33.

38. Upton's report, in *OR,* Vol. XXXVI, Pt. 1, p. 668; Keiser Diary, May 10, 1864; Tyler, *Recollections of the Civil War,* 169; Westbrook, *History of the 49th Pennsylvania Volunteers,* 196–97; Best, *History of the 121st New York State Infantry,* 138–39.

39. Upton to Robins, April 18, 1879, in Military Historical Society of Massachusetts Collection, BU; Unidentified soldier's diary, May 10, 1864, in Book 32, FSNMP; Keiser Diary, May 10, 1864.

40. Charles A. Dana to Edwin M. Stanton, May 11, 1864, in *OR,* Vol. XXXVI, Pt. 1, p. 67; Howe, ed., *Touched with Fire,* 113; Theodore Lyman to family, August 8, 1864, in *Meade's Headquarters,* ed. Agassiz, 208; Grant, *Personal Memoirs,* II, 224.

41. Pingree to Hunton, June 10, 1864, in Pingree Collection, Vermont Historical So-

ciety; Unidentified soldier's diary, May 10, 1864, in Book 32, FSNMP; J. S. Anderson, "Through the Wilderness with Grant," in *Report of the Proceedings of 5th Wisconsin Volunteer Infantry* (Chicago, 1902), 13.

42. Theodore Lyman to John C. Ropes, n.d., in *Recollections of a Maryland Confederate,* by Howard, 290n8. Hancock's aide Walker asserted that "support of Upton should not have been left to a single division. If the position he was ordered to attack was practicable, the assaulting columns should have been backed up by the divisions for the VI Corps, by Gibbon, and by the divisions of the V Corps uselessly engaged in assaulting the center" (Walker, *History of the Second Army Corps,* 463).

43. Jackson to Jackson, May 11, 1864, in Harden Collection, DU; Thomas, *History of the Doles-Cook Brigade,* 14; Boyle, "A Civil War Prison Diary," in Steiner Collection, LC; Taylor, *General Lee,* 240–41; Sparks, ed., *Inside Lincoln's Army,* 371. I am indebted to Alfred Young for assistance in calculating Ewell's losses.

44. Thomas, *History of the Doles-Cook Brigade,* 479.

45. Craft, *History of the One Hundred Forty First Regiment Pennsylvania Volunteers,* 190; Weygant, *History of the One Hundred and Twenty-Fourth Regiment New York State Volunteers,* 310. Warren recorded the time of the attack as 6:45. See Gouverneur K. Warren Diary, May 10, 1864, in Gouverneur K. Warren Collection, NYSLA. From west to east, Hancock's battle array was Ward's, Owen's, Webb's, and Carroll's 2nd Corps brigades, then Crawford's, Cutler's, and Griffin's 5th Corps divisions, the latter anchored on Brock Road. Across from them was Field's division, which consisted, from west to east, of Gregg's Texans and Arkansans, Tige Anderson's Georgians, DuBose's Georgians, Perry's Alabamians, and Bratton's South Carolinians.

46. Banes, *History of the Philadelphia Brigade,* 243; Chamberlin, *History of the One Hundred and Fiftieth Regiment Pennsylvania Volunteers,* 232–35.

47. Dana to Stanton, May 11, 1864, in *OR,* Vol. XXXVI, Pt. 1, p. 67; Judson, *History of the Eighty-Third Regiment Pennsylvania Volunteers,* 203; Porter Farley, "The 140th New York Volunteers," in RL; John O. Johnson to unknown, July 2, 1864, in State Historical Society of Wisconsin; Chamberlin, *History of the One Hundred and Fiftieth Regiment Pennsylvania Volunteers,* 235.

48. Warren Diary, May 10, 1864; Dana to Stanton, May 11, 1864, in *OR,* Vol. XXXVI, Pt. 1, p. 67; Vautier, *History of the 88th Pennsylvania Volunteers,* 181; Nevins, ed., *Diary of Battle,* 364.

49. Coles, *From Huntsville to Appomattox,* 169; Small, *The Road to Richmond,* 138; Andrew R. Linscott to parents, May 19, 1864, in Andrew R. Linscott Collection, MHS.

50. George A. Bowen Diary, May 10, 1864, in FSNMP; Banes, *History of the Philadelphia Brigade,* 242–44; Goss, *Recollections of a Private,* 290; Smith, *The History of the Nineteenth Regiment of Maine Volunteer Infantry,* 151; Alexander S. Webb's report, in *OR,* Vol. XXXVI, Pt. 1, p. 439; Alexander S. Webb, "Through the Wilderness," in *B&L,* IV, 168.

51. "Life of Amos G. Bean as a Soldier," 18, in FSNMP; Henry Roback, *The Veteran Volunteers of Herkimer and Otsego Counties in the War of the Rebellion, Being a History of the 152nd New York* (Little Falls, N.Y., 1888), 76. Details of Ward's conduct on May 6 are related by Gordon C. Rhea in *The Battle of the Wilderness, May 5–6, 1864* (Baton Rouge, 1994), 394n74.

52. Weygant, *History of the One Hundred and Twenty-Fourth Regiment New York State Volunteers,* 310; "Life of Amos G. Bean as a Soldier," 18, in FSNMP; J. Mark Smither

to family, n.d., in CRC; Miles V. Smith, *Reminiscences of the Civil War, Company D, Fourth Texas Regiment, Hood's Brigade, Longstreet's Corps, Army Northern Virginia, C.S.A.* (N.p., n.d.), 53; Dame, *From the Rapidan to Richmond,* 164–65. The order of Ward's attack, by regiment, was the 86th New York, 3rd Maine, 124th New York, 99th Pennsylvania, 141st Pennsylvania, 20th Indiana, 110th Pennsylvania, and 40th New York, according to P. Regis de Trobriand's report, in *OR,* Vol. XXXVI, Pt. 1, p. 470.

53. Nicholas Pomeroy Memoir, in CRC.

54. Weygant, *History of the One Hundred and Twenty-Fourth Regiment New York State Volunteers,* 310–11; Stiles, *Four Years Under Marse Robert,* 254; Dame, *From the Rapidan to Richmond,* 165; J. B. Minor, "Rallying with a Frying Pan," *Confederate Veteran,* XIII (1905), 72–73; Collier, *They'll Do to Tie To,* 185; O. T. Hanks, *History of Captain B. F. Benton's Company, Hood's Texas Brigade, 1861–1865* (Austin, Tex., 1984), 40; W. P. Johnson, "Third Arkansas and Richmond Howitzers," *Confederate Veteran,* XIII (1905), 210.

55. Dame, *From the Rapidan to Richmond,* 166–67, 169.

56. Weygant, *History of the One Hundred and Twenty-Fourth Regiment New York State Volunteers,* 311; Frederick F. Daniel, *Richmond Howitzers in the War: Four Years Campaigning with the Army of Northern Virginia* (Richmond, 1891), 117–18; Craft, *History of the One Hundred Forty First Regiment Pennsylvania Volunteers,* 190; Pomeroy Memoir; Dame, *From the Rapidan to Richmond,* 167–68; Stiles, *Four Years Under Marse Robert,* 254; A. J. McBride, "The Tenth Georgia at Spotsylvania," Atlanta *Journal,* July 20, 1901. A soldier recounted that until this incident, the Texans had refused to use bayonets. The next day, they all requisitioned bayonets "and were never without them afterwards" (Coles, *From Huntsville to Appomattox,* 169).

57. Trobriand's report, in *OR,* Vol. XXXVI, Pt. 1, p. 470; Winfield S. Hancock's report, *ibid.,* 334.

58. Dame, *From the Rapidan to Richmond,* 169; Hanks, *History of Captain B. F. Benton's Company,* 40; D. H. Hamilton, *History of Company M, First Texas Volunteer Infantry* (Waco, Tex., 1962), 58–59; James P. Coburn Memoir, Coburn Family Papers, USAMHI; Paul E. Wilson and Harriett Stephens Wilson, eds., *The Civil War Diary of Thomas White Stephens, Sergeant, Company K, 20th Indiana Regiment of Volunteers* (Lawrence, Kans., 1985), 178.

59. Stephen P. Chase Memoirs, in Civil War Times Illustrated Collection, USAMHI. According to Roebling, "Birney's men became scared and ran back a quarter of a mile behind some old breastworks" (Washington A. Roebling's report, in Warren Collection, NYSLA).

60. Zenas R. Bliss Memoirs, Vol. IV, unpaginated, in Zenas R. Bliss Collection, USAMHI.

61. Committee of the Regiment, *History of the Thirty-Sixth Regiment Massachusetts Volunteers, 1862–1865* (Boston, 1884), 161; Orlando B. Willcox to Ambrose E. Burnside, May 10, 1864, in *OR,* Vol. XXXVI, Pt. 2, p. 612.

62. Charles J. Mills to family, May 11, 1864, in *Through Blood and Fire,* ed. Coco, 81–82; Bliss Memoirs, Vol. IV, unpaginated; R. A. Smith, "How General Stevenson Died," *National Tribune,* January 20, 1898. Burnside wrote that Stevenson "has shown great courage and skill in action, and in organization and discipline has no superior" (Woodbury, *Major General Ambrose E. Burnside and the Ninth Army Corps,* 380).

63. Orlando B. Willcox to Ambrose E. Burnside, May 10, 1864, in *OR,* Vol. XXXVI, Pt. 2, p. 612; Ambrose E. Burnside to Orlando B. Willcox, May 10, 1864, *ibid.,* 613.

64. Ulysses S. Grant to Ambrose E. Burnside, May 10, 1864, in *OR,* Vol. XXXVI, Pt. 2, p. 610; Ambrose E. Burnside to Orlando B. Willcox, May 10, 1864, *ibid.,* 612; Ambrose E. Burnside to Ulysses S. Grant, May 10, 1864, *ibid.,* 611; Ulysses S. Grant to Ambrose E. Burnside, May 10, 1864, *ibid.,* 611; Porter, *Campaigning with Grant,* 93–95.

65. Daniel Reed Larned to Orlando B. Willcox, May 10, 1864, in *OR,* Vol. XXXVI, Pt. 2, pp. 613–14; John F. Hartranft's report, *ibid.,* Pt. 1, p. 949; Byron M. Cutcheon's report, *ibid.,* 968–69; Byron M. Cutcheon Autobiography, in Michigan Historical Collection, BL.

66. William P. Hopkins, *The Seventh Regiment Rhode Island Volunteers in the Civil War, 1862–1865* (Providence, 1903), 168; Committee of the Regiment, *History of the Thirty-Sixth Regiment Massachusetts Volunteers,* 162; Hartranft's report, in *OR,* Vol. XXXVI, Pt. 1, p. 949; Cutcheon's report, in *OR,* Vol. XXXVI, Pt. 1, pp. 968–69; Cutcheon Autobiography; John E. Irwin Diary, May 10, 1864, in Book 47, FSNMP.

67. Todd, *The Seventy-Ninth Highlanders,* 466–67; Ambrose E. Burnside's report, in *OR,* Vol. XXXVI, Pt. 1, p. 909; Porter, *Campaigning with Grant,* 95.

68. Massachusetts Historical Society, comp., *War Diary and Letters of Stephen Minot Weld,* 290.

69. Orlando B. Willcox to Ambrose E. Burnside, 6:30 P.M., May 10, 1864, in *OR,* Vol. XXXVI, Pt. 2, p. 615; Orlando B. Willcox to Ambrose E. Burnside, 7:15 P.M., May 10, 1864, *ibid.;* Orlando B. Willcox to Ambrose E. Burnside, May 10, 1864, *ibid.,* 614. Contrary to Willcox' assertion that all was quiet, a soldier in the 17th Michigan recorded that "heavy fighting continued all the time till ten o'clock" (Charles D. Todd Diary, May 10, 1864, in Gregory Coco Collection, USAMHI).

70. Grant, *Personal Memoirs,* II, 225; Porter, *Campaigning with Grant,* 95; Henry C. Houston, *The Thirty-Second Maine Regiment of Infantry Volunteers* (Portland, Maine, 1903), 118. According to one source, "The withdrawal was made against the remonstrance of General Burnside, and the mistake was afterwards seen—unfortunately not till it was too late to rectify it except by hard fighting" (Woodbury, *Major General Ambrose E. Burnside and the Ninth Army Corps,* 379).

71. Dana to Stanton, May 11, 1864, in *OR,* Vol. XXXVI, Pt. 1, p. 67; Hopkins, *The Seventh Regiment Rhode Island Volunteers,* 168–69.

72. Daniel Reed Larned to sister, May 10, 1864, in Daniel Reed Larned Collection, LC; Early, *Autobiographical Sketch and Narrative,* 554.

73. Luther A. Rose Diary, May 10, 1864, in Luther A. Rose Collection, LC; Humphreys, *The Virginia Campaign,* 89; Walker, *History of the Second Army Corps,* 464; Thomas L. Livermore, "Grant's Campaign Against Lee," in *PMHSM,* IV, 436–37; "From a Special Correspondent," Raleigh (N.C.) *Daily Confederate,* May 25, 1864.

74. Humphreys, *The Virginia Campaign,* 82–83.

75. Charles A. Dana to Edwin M. Stanton, May 10, 1864, in *OR,* Vol. XXXVI, Pt. 1, p. 66.

76. Walker, *General Hancock,* 192; John Gibbon's report, in *OR,* Vol. XXXVI, Pt. 1, p. 430; Banes, *History of the Philadelphia Brigade,* 243; Nevins, ed., *Diary of Battle,* 363; Walker, *History of the Second Army Corps,* 463; Charles A. Griffin Diary, May 10, 1864, in Civil War Miscellaneous Collection, USAMHI.

77. Robert D. Johnston, "Gen. Lee's Story," in FSNMP.

78. Robert E. Lee to Richard S. Ewell, May 10, 1864, in *OR,* Vol. XXXVI, Pt. 2, p. 983; Robert E. Lee to secretary of war, May 10, 1864, *ibid.,* 982–83. At 9 P.M., Anderson informed Lee that the Federals had launched five or six attacks against Field's division. "The last assault on the left was made just after sunset," he wrote, "and was the most obstinate of them all, some of the enemy running up to and leaping over the breast-works and bayoneting some of our men." The Federals were repulsed, he added, and Confederate casualties were "very small indeed" (*OR,* Vol. LI, Pt. 2, pp. 910–11). Lee must have written his evening missive to Richmond after receiving Anderson's report, since he borrowed Anderson's language.

79. Henry Heth's report, in MC; "Historical Sketch," New Bern (N.C.) *Our Living and Our Dead,* April 15, 1874; Mamie Yeary, comp., *Reminiscences of the Boys in Gray, 1861–1865* (Dayton, 1986), 147; John G. Webb to father, May 11, 1864, in Leigh Collection, USAMHI; George W. Pearsoll to wife, May 11, 1864, in George W. Pearsoll Collection, NCDAH; Bradwell, "Spotsylvania, Va., May 8 and 9, 1864," 56; Abram Schultz Miller to wife, May 11, 1864, in FSNMP.

VI MAY 11 *A Cavalryman Dies, and Grant Prepares to Attack Again*

1. Sheridan, *Personal Memoirs,* I, 375.
2. Abraham K. Arnold, "A War Reminiscence: The Fifth U.S. Regular Cavalry with General Sheridan on Raid Towards Richmond, Va., in 1864," *Journal of the United States Cavalry Association,* II (1889), 29; Bowen, *Regimental History of the First New York Dragoons,* 157–58.
3. McClellan, *The Life and Campaigns of Major-General J. E. B. Stuart,* 410.
4. Tobie, *History of the First Maine Cavalry,* 256; "Cavalry's Bold Move," *National Tribune,* April 15, 1897; Preston, *History of the Tenth Regiment of Cavalry New York State Volunteers,* 176; Rodenbough, "Sheridan's Richmond Raid," in *B&L,* IV, 190.
5. Wilson, *Under the Old Flag,* I, 406; Allen, *Down in Dixie,* 288–89; William B. Poindexter, "A Midnight Charge and the Death of General J. E. B. Stuart," in *SHSP,* XXXII, 117–19. The 1st Connecticut was the last Federal unit over the river, according to Erastus Blakeslee's report, in *Annual Report of the Adjutant General of the State of Connecticut for the Year Ending March 31, 1865,* 412.
6. Arnold, "A War Reminiscence," 30–31.
7. *Ibid.,* 31–32; "Cavalry Fights Around Richmond," Raleigh (N.C.) *Daily Confederate,* May 23, 1864; "The Second Virginia Cavalry in the Late Fights," Richmond *Sentinel,* May 21, 1864; J. D. Ferguson Memoranda, in Thomas T. Munford Collection, DU. Bowen, in *Regimental History of the First New York Dragoons,* 158–60, vividly details Arnold's escape.
8. Arnold, "A War Reminiscence," 32–33; Alfred Gibbs's report, in *OR,* Vol. XXXVI, Pt. 1, p. 846; Wesley Merritt's report, in *OR,* Vol. XXXVI, Pt. 1, pp. 812–13. Sergeant B. J. Haden, of the 1st Virginia Cavalry, escorted the prisoners to Taylorsville. Unaccustomed to walking, they grumbled all the way. When a Federal lieutenant offered to drive the men along if Haden gave him his horse, Haden complied, but he held his pistol to the lieutenant all the while. See Haden, *Reminiscences of J. E. B. Stuart's Cavalry,* 31–32.
9. Well A. Bushnell Memoir, 268–69, in William P. Palmer Collection, WRHS; Trout, ed., *Riding with Stuart . . . by . . . Garnett,* 63.

10. McClellan, *The Life and Campaigns of Major-General J. E. B. Stuart,* 410–11; Fitzhugh Lee's report, in MC; Jeb Stuart to Braxton Bragg, May 10, 1864, in *OR,* Vol. LI, Pt. 2, p. 910; Fitzhugh Lee to Braxton Bragg, May 10, 1864, in *OR,* Vol. XXXVI, Pt. 2, p. 984. A soldier in the 9th Virginia Cavalry assigned to Stuart's headquarters claimed that Stuart had "impressively" said "that his purpose was, if possible, to throw his force of cavalry between the small army commanded by General Sheridan and the fortifications surrounding Richmond" (J. A. M'Laughlin, "Last Days of Stuart," Richmond *Times Dispatch,* June 12, 1904).

11. McClellan, *The Life and Campaigns of Major-General J. E. B. Stuart,* 410. The Army of the Potomac's returns for April 30, 1864, placed Sheridan's cavalry corps at 12,424 men "present for duty equipped" (*OR,* Vol. XXXIII, p. 1036). Sheridan stated that he began the campaign with 10,000 soldiers. See *OR,* Vol. XXXVI, Pt. 1, p. 787. Subtracting approximately 700 casualties for the Wilderness and Todd's Tavern, and adjusting for the 5th New York Cavalry, which did not accompany Sheridan on the raid, it appears that Sheridan confronted Stuart with between 9,000 and 11,000 troopers. Wilson estimated in *Under the Old Flag,* I, 408, that Fitzhugh Lee had no more than 2,500 men. See Stephen Z. Starr, *The Union Cavalry in the Civil War* (3 vols.; Baton Rouge, 1981), II, 102. The number was probably closer to 3,000. By Albert Young's calculations, Fitzhugh Lee started the campaign with 3,500 men and lost about 500 between May 6 and May 9.

12. Tobie, *History of the First Maine Cavalry,* 257; Kidd, *Personal Recollections of a Cavalryman,* 294–95.

13. Wilson, *Under the Old Flag,* I, 406; J. K. Lowden, "Michigan's 5th Cavalry in the Latter Period of the War," *National Tribune,* July 23, 1896.

14. Charles H. Smith to Horatio S. Libby, n.d., in *History of the First Maine Cavalry,* by Tobie, 260; Goldsborough, *The Maryland Line,* 236–37.

15. Merritt's report, in *OR,* Vol. XXXVI, Pt. 1, p. 812; Isham, "Through the Wilderness to Richmond," in *Sketches of War History,* I, 209; Allen, *Down in Dixie,* 298–99; William L. Greenleaf, "From the Rapidan to Richmond," in *War Papers of Vermont, and Miscellaneous States' Papers and Addresses, Military Order of the Loyal Legion* (Wilmington, N.C., 1994), 11.

16. Chamberlain, "Plenty to Do in Old Virginia in the Spring of 1864"; Allen, *Down in Dixie,* 296, 300–302; Preston, *History of the Tenth Regiment of Cavalry New York State Volunteers,* 176–77.

17. James D. Rowe Reminiscences, May 10, 1864, in Michigan Historical Collection, BL.

18. Preston, *History of the Tenth Regiment of Cavalry New York State Volunteers,* 177; Tobie, *History of the First Maine Cavalry,* 260–61; Jeb Stuart to Braxton Bragg, May 10, 1864, in *OR,* Vol. LI, Pt. 2, p. 912.

19. Chamberlain, "Plenty to Do in Old Virginia in the Spring of 1864."

20. Jeb Stuart to Braxton Bragg, May 10, 1864, in *OR,* Vol. LI, Pt. 2, p. 912. Stuart's route took him through Trinity Church, across Little River, and then on through Fork Church to Taylorsville. See Ferguson Memoranda, in Munford Collection, DU; and Fitzhugh Lee's report, in MC.

21. McClellan, *The Life and Campaigns of Major-General J. E. B. Stuart,* 411.

22. *Ibid.;* Ferguson Memoranda, in Munford Collection, DU; Wise, *The Long Arm of Lee,* II, 740, 796; Miller, "Yellow Tavern," 68–69; Robert P. Chew's report, in Lewis Leigh Collection, USAMHI. Sheridan probably had thirty-six guns.

23. Jeb Stuart to Braxton Bragg, May 11, 1864, in *OR,* Vol. LI, Pt. 2, p. 916; M'Laughlin, "Last Days of Jeb Stuart," Richmond *Times Dispatch,* June 12, 1904. In a dispatch marked 4:15 A.M., Bradley Johnson notified Richmond that Stuart's rear had "just passed out of Taylorsville" (Bradley T. Johnson to Braxton Bragg, May 11, 1864, in *OR,* Vol. LI, Pt. 2, p. 917).

24. Tobie, *History of the First Maine Cavalry,* 260–61.

25. *Ibid.,* 261; Samuel H. Merrill, *The Campaigns of the First Maine and First District of Columbia Cavalry* (Portland, Maine, 1866), 194–95.

26. B.M.V., "In Memoriam: General James B. Gordon," Raleigh (N.C.) *Daily Confederate,* May 25, 1865; Paul B. Means, "Additional Sketch, Sixty-Third Regiment," in *Histories of the Several Regiments and Battalions from North Carolina,* ed. Clark, III, 596–97.

27. Means, "Additional Sketch, Sixty-Third Regiment," in *Histories of the Several Regiments and Battalions from North Carolina,* ed. Clark, III, 597; "Cavalry Fights Around Richmond," Charlotte (N.C.) *Western Democrat,* May 31, 1864; Preston, *History of the Tenth Regiment of Cavalry New York State Volunteers,* 177; William H. Cheek, "Additional Sketch, Ninth Regiment (First Cavalry)," in *Histories of the Several Regiments and Battalions from North Carolina,* ed. Clark, I, 465.

28. Cheek, "Additional Sketch, Ninth Regiment (First Cavalry)," in *Histories of the Several Regiments and Battalions from North Carolina,* ed. Clark, I, 465; Merrill, *The Campaigns of the First Maine and First District of Columbia Cavalry,* 195–98; Preston, *History of the Tenth Regiment of Cavalry New York State Volunteers,* 177–78; Smith to Libby, n.d., in *History of the First Maine Cavalry,* by Tobie, 263; John P. White Account, in *History of the Tenth Regiment of Cavalry New York State Volunteers,* by Preston, 178–79. The 16th Pennsylvania Cavalry was also actively engaged. See Itinerary of the Sixteenth Pennsylvania Cavalry, May 1–June 30, in *OR,* Vol. XXXVI, Pt. I, p. 870.

29. "Barringer's N.C. Brigade of Cavalry," Raleigh (N.C.) *Daily Confederate,* February 22, 1865. Gregg sustained seventy-nine casualties. See Return of Casualties in the Union Forces, in *OR,* Vol. XXXVI, Pt. 1, p. 184. Lieutenant Colonel William H. H. Cowles temporarily replaced Cheek. Shortly after the war, Cheek found himself at the Willard Hotel, in Washington, D.C., in the company of several Union officers. He introduced himself as the former colonel of the 1st North Carolina Cavalry. One of the Federals shook his hand cordially and remarked, "I have the honor of having met Colonel Cheek once before. It was on the eleventh of May last, at a little place called Goodall's Tavern, about eighteen miles from Richmond. On that occasion Colonel Cheek, with his regiment, the 1st North Carolina Cavalry, which was considered the best regiment of cavalry on his side, met the 1st Maine, which held a similar reputation on our side. I saw these two fine regiments come hand to hand, in open field, with drawn sabers. The clash was terrific, the fighting was furious and obstinate, but the 1st Maine was driven from the field. An officer of the 1st Maine, after the surrender, speaking of his regiment, made the proud boast that it was never driven from the field but once during the war. 'But,' he said, 'we consider that no disgrace or reflection, for it was done by the 1st North Carolina'" (Cheek, "Additional Sketch, Ninth Regiment," in *Histories of the Several Regiments and Battalions from North Carolina,* ed. Clark, I, 466).

30. Bushnell Memoir, 268–69, Lloyd, *History of the First Pennsylvania Reserve Cavalry,* 93; Allen, *Down in Dixie,* 308–309; Henry E. Davies, Jr.'s report, in *OR,* Vol. XXXVI, Pt. 1, p. 857; Pyne, *Ride to War,* 200; "The Great Cavalry Expedition Through the Rebel

Lines," New York *Herald,* May 17, 1864; Ferguson Memoranda, in Munford Collection, DU; Lyman Tremain, *Memorial of Frederick Lyman Tremain, Late Lieutenant Colonel of the 10th New York Cavalry* (Albany, N.Y., 1865), 27; Fitzhugh Lee's report, in MC; Trout, ed., *Riding with Stuart . . . by . . . Garnett,* 65. The 1st Massachusetts reported twenty-six casualties. See Return of Casualties in the Union Forces, in *OR,* Vol. XXXVI, Pt. 1, p. 184. Slaves buried Hopkins and other dead Federals in two trenches at Ashland. Hopkins' father attempted to identify his son's body in June, 1865, but the corpse was too decomposed. He returned with a surgeon who made the identification, and on December 31, he laid his son's remains to rest in Williamstown, Massachusetts. See Allen, *Down in Dixie,* 309–12.

31. Jeb Stuart to Braxton Bragg, May 11, 1864, in *Jeb Stuart,* by John W. Thomason (New York, 1930), 496.

32. Philip Sheridan's report, in *OR,* Vol. XXXVI, Pt. 1, p. 790; Samuel Gracey, *Annals of the Sixth Pennsylvania Cavalry* (Philadelphia, 1868), 243.

33. Isham, "Through the Wilderness to Richmond," in *Sketches of War History,* I, 210.

34. By 1864, Confederate soldiers had dismantled Yellow Tavern for firewood, and what remained had burned to the ground. See "Yellow Tavern," Richmond *Dispatch,* March 3, 1889.

35. Fitzhugh Lee's report, in MC; Trout, ed., *Riding with Stuart . . . by . . . Garnett,* 65.

36. Jeb Stuart to Braxton Bragg, May 11, 1864, in *OR,* Vol. LI, Pt. 2, p. 918; McClellan, *The Life and Campaigns of Major-General J. E. B. Stuart,* 412.

37. "Civil War Experiences of Leiper Moore Robinson," 12, in VHS.

38. Rowe Reminiscences, May 11, 1864; Louis H. Carpenter, "Sheridan's Expedition Around Richmond, May 9–25, 1864," *Journal of the United States Cavalry Association,* II (1889), 307; Isham, "Through the Wilderness to Richmond," in *Sketches of War History,* I, 210–11; Kidd, *Personal Recollections of a Cavalryman,* 296–97; Merritt's report, in *OR,* Vol. XXXVI, Pt. 1, p. 813. Sources are wildly inconsistent concerning position, terrain, and the sequence of events at Yellow Tavern, and few writers have seriously attempted to reconstruct the fighting. I am grateful to Robert E. L. Krick, of the Richmond National Battlefield Park, for examining the field with me and sharing his insights.

39. George A. Custer's report, in *OR,* Vol. XXXVI, Pt. 1, p. 817.

40. Kidd, *Personal Recollections of a Cavalryman,* 303; Trout, ed., *Riding with Stuart . . . by . . . Garnett,* 66.

41. Merritt's report, in *OR,* Vol. XXXVI, Pt. 1, p. 813; Thomas C. Devin's report, *ibid.,* 834; Foster, *Reminiscences and Record of the 6th New York,* 74; Trout, ed., *Riding With Stuart . . . by . . . Garnett,* 66; Samuel B. Rucker, "Recollections of My War Record During the Confederacy," in Jones Memorial Library, Lynchburg, Va.

42. J. R. Oliver, "J. E. B. Stuart's Fate at Yellow Tavern," *Confederate Veteran,* XIX (1911), 531. Johnson, in *The University Memorial Biographical Sketches,* 589, placed the swale east of Telegraph Road. Garnett described it as "in" the road (Trout, ed., *Riding with Stuart . . . by . . . Garnett,* 66). A soldier in the 6th Virginia Cavalry recounted that most of his regiment waited dismounted "in the cuts made by the road and in ditches that the farmers had made in connection with their fences" (Thomas D. Gold, *History of Clarke County and Its Connection with the War Between the States* [Berryville, Va., 1914], 282– 83).

43. Trout, ed., *Riding with Stuart . . . by . . . Garnett,* 67. Stuart and Pate were on bad

terms, and stories abounded that they had reconciled shortly before Pate's death. According to one dramatic version, Stuart was moved by Pate's vigorous defense and rode to him "amid the singing of bullets." The men clasped hands, and Stuart gushed, "Colonel Pate, you have done all that man can do. How long can you hold this position?" Pate answered, "Until I die." Stuart again clasped Pate's hands, then rode away. "Pate is a hero," he reputedly remarked to a staffer ("Colonel Henry Clay Pate," Lynchburg [Va.] *Republican,* May 20, 1864; Johnson, *The University Memorial Biographical Sketches,* 589–90).

44. William G. Hills Diary, May 11, 1864, in William G. Hills Collection, LC; Bowen, *Regimental History of the First New York Dragoons,* 156; Custer's report, in *OR,* Vol. XXXVI, Pt. 1, p. 818; Devin's report, in *OR,* Vol. XXXVI, Pt. 1, p. 835; P. J. White, "The Fifth Virginia Cavalry," *Confederate Veteran,* XVII (1909), 73; Kidd, *Personal Recollections of a Cavalryman,* 302–303; "Civil War Experiences of Leiper Moore Robinson," 11, in VHS.

45. Russell A. Alger's report, in *OR,* Vol. XXXVI, Pt. 1, p. 828; Hopkins, *From Bull Run to Appomattox,* 158–59.

46. Devin's report, in *OR,* XXXVI, Pt. 1, pp. 834–35; Chamberlain, "Plenty to Do in Old Virginia in the Spring of 1864."

47. Trout, ed., *Riding with Stuart . . . by . . . Garnett,* 68.

48. McClellan, *The Life and Campaigns of Major-General J. E. B. Stuart,* 412.

49. Jeb Stuart to Braxton Bragg, May 11, 1864, in *SHSP,* IX, 138–39.

50. Custer's report, in *OR,* Vol. XXXVI, Pt. 1, p. 818; James H. Wilson's report, *ibid.,* 879; George H. Chapman's report, *ibid.,* 898; Greenleaf, "From the Rapidan to Richmond," in *War Papers of Vermont, and Miscellaneous States' Papers and Addresses, Military Order of the Loyal Legion,* 14; Benedict, *Vermont in the Civil War,* II, 637*n.*

51. "The Great Cavalry Expedition Through the Rebel Lines," New York *Herald,* May 17, 1864.

52. Lowden, "Michigan's 5th Cavalry in the Latter Period of the War," *National Tribune,* July 23, 1896. Wilson wrote that he deployed two of Chapman's regiments "as skirmishers and the other, 1st Vermont, with sabres assisted Custer's brigade on the Brook Pike" (James H. Wilson Diary, May 11, 1864, in LC).

53. L. E. Tripp, "With Custer at Yellow Tavern and in the Raid Around Richmond," *National Tribune,* July 31, 1884; Isham, "Through the Wilderness to Richmond," in *Sketches of War History,* I, 211; Peck, *Reminiscences of a Confederate Soldier,* 46.

54. Poindexter, "A Midnight Charge and the Death of General J. E. B. Stuart," in *SHSP,* XXXIII, 119–21.

55. Custer's report, in *OR,* Vol. XXXVI, Pt. 1, p. 818; Isham, "Through the Wilderness to Richmond," in *Sketches of War History,* I, 213–15; Gold, *History of Clarke County,* 284–85.

56. Wilson, *Under the Old Flag,* I, 407; Chapman's report, in *OR,* Vol. XXXVI, Pt. 1, p. 898; Lowden, "Michigan's 5th Cavalry in the Latter Period"; Tripp, "With Custer at Yellow Tavern."

57. Frank Dorsey, "Fatal Wounding of General J. E. B. Stuart," in *SHSP,* XXX, 237. Gus Dorsey's eyewitness account, there reproduced, has been generally accepted as definitive and was corroborated by another member of Company K who claimed to have been next to Stuart when he was shot. See Oliver, "J. E. B. Stuart's Fate at Yellow Tavern," 531. But conflicting stories have multiplied. Lieutenant John R. McNulty, of the Baltimore Light Artillery, asserted that he and Major Breathed retreated before Sheridan's onslaught

and met Stuart on the ridge's back slope holding a flag. McNulty insisted that Stuart was injured in leading a charge to recapture the guns. Lieutenant Elijah Colner, of the 1st Virginia, corroborated McNulty's statements, maintaining that when Breathed suggested to Stuart that he could recapture the battery with two squadrons, Stuart ordered the 1st Virginia to charge by column of fours. "As the head of the column passed over the hill," Colner continued, "Captain Hammond [of the 1st Virginia] was shot and fell from his horse, when the column instantly halted. General Stuart waved his saber and shouted, 'Forward, men!' and rushed forward himself," to be mortally wounded. Colner affirmed, "Captain Dorsey's narrative, as far as known to me, is almost an entire misconception of the facts, for it conflicts essentially with Major McNulty's account and my own." These versions, and more, are in "General Stuart's Death: How the Chieftain Received His Mortal Wound," by A. K. Matthews, *National Tribune,* June 23, 1887. Robert E. L. Krick has documented over twenty different tellings of Stuart's death, most by purported eye-witnesses.

58. Alger's report, in *OR,* Vol. XXXVI, Pt. 1, pp. 828–29; McClellan, *The Life and Campaigns of Major-General J. E. B. Stuart,* 413–15; Dorsey, "Fatal Wounding of General J. E. B. Stuart," in *SHSP,* XXX, 237; Oliver, "J. E. B. Stuart's Fate at Yellow Tavern," 531.

59. Fitzhugh Lee to John Esten Cooke, March 21, 1868, in John Esten Cooke Collection, DU. Fitzhugh Lee considered Stuart's parting comments as his "most precious legacy" (Fitzhugh Lee, "Speech . . . at A.N.V. Banquet, October 28, 1875," in *SHSP,* I, 102). Huff had but a short time to live. He was mortally wounded at the battle of Haw's Shop on May 28, 1864, and died during the summer in Michigan. Bowen, in *Regimental History of the First New York Dragoons,* 161–62, held that Shedrick L. Pealer, of the Dragoons, fired the shot that killed Stuart. That was not possible unless Pealer was separated from his unit.

60. Wilson's report, in *OR,* Vol. XXXVI, Pt. 1, p. 879; Chapman's report, *ibid.,* 898; Lowden, "Michigan's 5th Cavalry in the Latter Period"; Tripp, "With Custer at Yellow Tavern"; Sheridan, *Personal Memoirs,* I, 378; Wilson, *Under the Old Flag,* I, 407.

61. Allen Parker Diary, May 11, 1864, in FSNMP; Preston, *History of the Tenth Regiment of Cavalry New York State Volunteers,* 180–81; Sheridan, *Personal Memoirs,* I, 379; Pyne, *Ride to War,* 200–201; Henry P. Turner Diary, May 11, 1864, in Civil War Miscellaneous Collection, USAMHI.

62. Trout, ed., *Riding with Stuart . . . by . . . Garnett,* 71.

63. Poindexter, "A Midnight Charge and the Death of General J. E. B. Stuart," in *SHSP,* XXXII, 121; Gill, *Reminiscences of Four Years,* 96–97.

64. Trout, ed., *Riding with Stuart . . . by . . . Garnett,* 71.

65. "The Death of Major-General J. E. B. Stuart," in *SHSP,* VII, 107–109.

66. Fitzhugh Lee, *General Lee: A Biography of Robert E. Lee* (New York, 1894), 337; Wilson's report, in *OR,* Vol. XXXVI, Pt. 1, p. 879; Henry E. Davies, *General Sheridan* (New York, 1895), 115; Sheridan, *Personal Memoirs,* I, 386–87. I am indebted to Alfred Young for his help in estimating Stuart's losses.

67. Bowen, *Regimental History of the First New York Dragoons,* 162n1; Wilson, *Under the Old Flag,* I, 407–408; Return of Casualties in the Union Forces, in *OR,* Vol. XXXVI, Pt. 1, p. 184.

68. Porter, *Campaigning with Grant,* 97–98.

69. Ulysses S. Grant to Henry W. Halleck, May 11, 1864, in *OR,* Vol. XXXVI, Pt. 2, p. 627.

70. Anderson, "Through the Wilderness with Grant," in *Report of the Proceedings of 5th Wisconsin Volunteer Infantry,* 13.

71. Smith, *The History of the Nineteenth Regiment of Maine Volunteer Infantry,* 153; Stevens, *Berdan's United States Sharpshooters,* 423; Fred Sanborn Memoir, May 11, 1864, in LC; Silliker, ed., *The Rebel Yell and the Yankee Hurrah,* 153.

72. Haines, *History of the Men of Company F, with Description of the Marches and Battles of the 12th New Jersey Volunteers* (Mickleton, N.J., 1897), 59; Kenneth H. Power Memoir, Book 45, FSNMP; Mulholland, *The Story of the 116th Regiment Pennsylvania Infantry,* 194.

73. James P. Coburn to family, May 18, 1864, in Coburn Family Collection, USAMHI.

74. George M. Barnard to father, May 11, 1864, in George M. Barnard Collection, MHS; Philemon H. Fowler, *Memorials of William Fowler* (New York, 1875), 82.

75. Humphreys, *The Virginia Campaign,* 90.

76. Robertson, *Personal Recollections of the War,* 101–102; Nelson A. Miles's report, in *OR,* Vol. XXXVI, Pt 1, pp. 370–71; Nathan Church's report, in *OR,* Vol. XXXVI, Pt. 1, p. 373; Francis C. Barlow to Winfield S. Hancock, May 11, 1864, in *OR,* Vol. XXXVI, Pt. 2, p. 636; Newton T. Kirk, "Civil War Reminiscences," in Archives and Historical Collection, Michigan State University Libraries.

77. Cyrus B. Comstock Diary, May 11, 1864, in Cyrus B. Comstock Collection, LC; "Itinerary," in *OR,* Vol. XXXVI, Pt. 1, p. 502; Michael W. Burns's report, in *OR,* Vol. XXXVI, Pt. 1, p. 504.

78. Second Corps Daily Memoranda, in *OR,* Vol. XXXVI, Pt. 1, pp. 357–58; Comstock Diary, May 11, 1864.

79. Second Corps Daily Memoranda, in *OR,* Vol. XXXVI, Pt. 1, p. 358.

80. Ambrose E. Burnside's report, in *OR,* Vol. XXXVI, Pt. 1, p. 909; Todd, *The Seventy-Ninth Highlanders,* 468; Irwin Field Diary, May 11, 1864, in Book 47, FSNMP; C. T. Jeffers, "What the Gallant Ninth Corps Did," *National Tribune,* July 9, 1896; Lyman Jackman and Amos Hadley, *History of the Sixth New Hampshire Regiment in the War for the Union* (Concord, N.H., 1891), 239; Hopkins, *The Seventh Regiment Rhode Island Volunteers,* 169; Committee of the Regiment, *History of the Thirty-Sixth Regiment Massachusetts Volunteers,* 163.

81. Comstock Diary, May 11, 1864; Burnside's report, in *OR,* Vol. XXXVI, Pt. 1, p. 909; Charles E. Wood Diary, May 11, 1864, in Civil War Miscellaneous Collection, USAMHI; Committee of the Regiment, *History of the Thirty-Sixth Regiment Massachusetts Volunteers,* 164; Nathaniel W. Bunker, "War Record," in James S. Schoff Collection, CL. "We marched back across the creek and pitched tents for the night at 7 o'clock P.M., which time was raining hard we were ordered to the front again," one of Hartranft's soldiers complained. "Marched about a mile then countermarched and halted at eleven o'clock" (Charles D. Todd Diary, May 11, 1864, in Gregory Coco Collection, USAMHI).

82. Zenas R. Bliss Memoirs, Vol. IV, unpaginated, in Zenas R. Bliss Collection, USAMHI.

83. *Ibid.;* Massachusetts Historical Society, comp., *War Diary and Letters of Stephen Minot Weld,* 291; Hopkins, *The Seventh Regiment Rhode Island Volunteers,* 169; Lyman to family, May 23, 1864, in *Meade's Headquarters,* ed. Agassiz, 116–17.

84. Jackman and Hadley, *History of the Sixth New Hampshire Regiment,* 241.

85. J. Moxley Sorrel Diary, May 11, 1864, in MC; Edward P. Alexander, *Military Memoirs of a Confederate* (New York, 1907), 517; Dunlop, *Lee's Sharpshooters,* 55; Peyton, *A Civil War Record,* 25; Jones, ed., *The Civil War Memoirs of Captain William J. Seymour,* 122; Yeary, comp., *Reminiscences of the Boys in Gray,* 147.

86. Alexander, *Military Memoirs of a Confederate,* 516; Gallagher, ed., *Fighting for the Confederacy,* 372.

87. At 9 A.M. on May 11, Hoffman's brigade of Gordon's division occupied the portion of works formerly held by Doles. These Virginians, however, were "soon relieved" and replaced by the Louisiana Brigade, formerly under Hays (Buckner McGill Randolph Diary, May 11, 1864, in VHS).

88. Howard, *Recollections of a Maryland Confederate,* 292–93; Randolph Barton, "Confederate Troops at Spotsylvania C.H.," *Confederate Veteran,* XIX (1911), 291; John W. Daniel, "Major-General Johnson at Spotsylvania," in *SHSP,* XXXIII, 336; Jones, ed., *The Civil War Memoirs of Captain William J. Seymour,* 121–22. On Johnson's strength on May 12, see Thomas H. W. McIntire to Fulton, May 14, 1864, in Wilmington (N.C.) *Daily Journal,* May 24, 1864. The 1st North Carolina's acting adjutant estimated that the division contained between three thousand and four thousand men. His estimate most likely failed to include Hays's brigade, which was added to the division on May 8.

89. Early, *Autobiographical Sketch and Narrative,* 355. A Confederate war correspondent reported that "information was received . . . that Grant was retiring in the direction of Fredericksburg and Germanna Ford; a report to this effect was noised abroad throughout the army" (P. W. Alexander's account, Richmond *Daily Dispatch,* May 18, 1864). The shift of Thomas and Scales to the Po left Wilcox with only two brigades, one under Brigadier General Samuel McGowan and the other under Lane. McGowan was posted on the far right of Heth's division, at Fredericksburg Road, and Lane remained on Heth's left, connecting with Ewell's corps. See Cadmus M. Wilcox' report, in VHS.

90. McDonald, ed., *Make Me a Map of the Valley,* 203; Early, *Autobiographical Sketch and Narrative,* 354; William H. F. Lee to Robert E. Lee, May 11, 1864, in *OR,* Vol. LI, Pt. 2, pp. 916–17; Wilcox' report, in VHS.

91. Campbell Brown Memoir, in Ewell-Brown Collection, TSLA; Taylor, *General Lee,* 242; Venable, "The Campaign from the Wilderness to Petersburg," in *SHSP,* XIV, 528–29. The 1st Corps aide Sorrel jotted in his diary, "Toward evening, indications are apparent of the intended withdrawal of the enemy and preparations are made to move after him" (Sorrel Diary, May 11, 1864). Brown recorded that Lee "directed Ewell to withdraw the troops from the trenches and General Long to do the same with the artillery along the division front so as to rest the men and horses. The evening had been very wet and General Ewell suggested that the men would be more comfortable in the trenches than if they moved, as they already had shelters there. Accordingly they were allowed to remain" (Brown Memoir).

92. Porter, *Campaigning with Grant,* 100; Ulysses S. Grant to George G. Meade, in *OR,* Vol. XXXVI, Pt. 2, p. 629. Mott informed his troops that they were "sacrificing the reputation of 'Hooker's old division'" and had "no excuse for such conduct." He admonished them to "show to the army and the world that our part has been fully and faithfully performed" (Thomas W. Earye to division, May 11, 1864, in *OR,* Vol. XXXVI, Pt. 2, p. 637).

93. Sparks, ed., *Inside Lincoln's Army,* 372; George G. Meade to Winfield S. Hancock, May 11, 1864, in *OR,* Vol. XXXVI, Pt. 2, p. 635; Andrew A. Humphreys to Gouver-

neur K. Warren, May 11, 1864, in *OR,* Vol. XXXVI, Pt. 2, pp. 637–38; 6th Corp Orders, May 11, 1864, in *OR,* Vol. XXXVI, Pt. 2, p. 642.

94. Ulysses S. Grant to Ambrose E. Burnside, May 11, 1864, in *OR,* Vol. XXXVI, Pt. 2, p. 643.

95. Humphreys, *The Virginia Campaign,* 90–91.

96. Charles H. Morgan's account, in *History of the Second Army Corps,* by Walker, 468; Humphreys, *The Virginia Campaign,* 90.

97. Francis C. Barlow, "Capture of the Salient, May 12, 1864," in *PMHSM,* IV, 245–46; Gibbon, *Personal Recollections,* 219.

98. Smith, *The History of the Nineteenth Regiment of Maine Volunteer Infantry,* 153; Robertson, *Personal Recollections of the War,* 102–103; Joseph E. Miner, "Spotsylvania: The Way in Which the Rebels Were Surprised," *National Tribune,* March 18, 1886; Weygant, *History of the One Hundred and Twenty-Fourth Regiment New York State Volunteers,* 312; Haines, *History of the Men of Company F,* 59; Galwey, *The Valiant Hours,* 208.

99. Power Memoir; Mulholland, *The Story of the 116th Regiment Pennsylvania Infantry,* 195.

100. Weygant, *History of the One Hundred and Twenty-Fourth Regiment New York State Volunteers,* 312–13; George A. Bruce, *The Twentieth Regiment of Massachusetts Volunteer Infantry, 1861–1865* (Boston, 1906), 370; Craft, *History of the One Hundred Forty First Regiment Pennsylvania Volunteers,* 192; Haines, *History of the Men of Company F,* 60; Smith, *The History of the Nineteenth Regiment of Maine Volunteer Infantry,* 153–54.

101. Barlow, "Capture of the Salient, May 12, 1864," in *PMHSM,* IV, 246–47.

102. *Ibid.;* Morgan's account, in *History of the Second Army Corps,* by Walker, 469.

103. Houghton, "A Staff Officer's Recollection of the Salient Angle," *National Tribune,* September 11, 1890.

104. Barlow, "Capture of the Salient, May 12, 1864," in *PMHSM,* IV, 248–49.

105. John D. Black, "Reminiscences of the Bloody Angle," in *Glimpses of the Nation's Struggle: Papers Read Before the Commandery of the State of Minnesota, Military Order of the Loyal Legion of the United States* (St. Paul, 1898), 4.

106. Muffly, ed., *The Story of Our Regiment,* 256–57.

107. Winfield S. Hancock's report, in *OR,* Vol. XXXVI, Pt. 1, pp. 334–35; Second Corps Daily Memoranda, *ibid.,* 358; John R. Brooke's report, *ibid.,* 409; Black, "Reminiscences of the Bloody Angle," in *Glimpses of the Nation's Struggle,* 5; Robertson, "From the Wilderness to Spotsylvania," in *Sketches of War History,* I, 280. Barlow's regiments deployed in double columns on the center. The 2nd Delaware advanced on Barlow's left to guard against a surprise attack from the Landrum house. One of Miles's officers wrote home that Barlow's division "formed in columns closed in mass so that each brigade was four lines deep" (Robert S. Robertson to parents, May 14, 1864, in FSNMP).

108. William N. Pendleton's report, in *OR,* Vol. XXXVI, Pt. 1, p. 1044; Gallagher, ed., *Fighting for the Confederacy,* 374.

109. Armistead L. Long's report, in *OR,* Vol. XXXVI, Pt. 1, p. 1086; Richard C. M. Page to S. V. Southall, September 15, 1879, in *SHSP,* VII, 535. According to Hardaway, when he learned that Long had ordered all the guns to leave the salient, he went to Lee's headquarters in search of Long. There Lee told him that "he did not intend for the guns to be brought out until the troops left" ("Extracts from the Diary of an Officer of Gen. Lee's Army," Richmond *Whig,* May 23, 1864). Hardaway notified Ramseur of Lee's in-

tention and informed his battery heads not to move until the troops moved. Long did not give comparable instructions to the heads of his other battalions.

110. Edward Johnson's report, in *OR,* Vol. XXXVI, Pt. 1, pp. 1079–80; Thomas H. Carter to editor of Richmond *Times,* n.d., in *SHSP,* XXI, 239; Howard, *Recollections of a Maryland Confederate,* 293.

111. Dobbins, ed., *Grandfather's Journal,* 192; David Holt, *A Mississippi Rebel in the Army of Northern Virginia,* ed. Thomas D. Cockrell and Michael B. Ballard (Baton Rouge, 1996), 252.

112. Morrison, ed., *The Memoirs of Henry Heth,* 186. Heth surmised that Pendleton misunderstood Lee's injunction against moving the 3rd Corps' artillery as an order to move Long's artillery. It is inconceivable that Pendleton could have so poorly understood Lee's intentions. More likely Lee, expecting a Federal move around his right flank, wanted the 1st and 2nd Corps guns repositioned but saw no need to reorient Heth's guns, which were already on the right of his line.

113. Howard, *Recollections of a Maryland Confederate,* 294; Carter to editor of Richmond *Times,* n.d., in *SHSP,* XXI, 240; Jones, ed., *The Civil War Memoirs of Captain William J. Seymour,* 123; Robert Hunter, "Major Hunter's Story," in *SHSP,* XXXIII, 337.

114. Hunter, "Major Hunter's Story," in *SHSP,* XXXIII, 337; Johnson's report, in *OR,* Vol. XXXVI, Pt. 1, p. 1080.

115. Howard, *Recollections of a Maryland Confederate,* 294–95n14.

116. Long's report, in *OR,* Vol. XXXVI, Pt. 1, p. 1086; Carter to editor of Richmond *Times,* n.d., in *SHSP,* XXI, 240.

117. Page to Southall, September 15, 1879, in *SHSP,* VII, 535–36.

118. Hunter, "Major Hunter's Story," in *SHSP,* XXXIII, 337–38.

119. Burnside's report, in *OR,* Vol. XXXVI, Pt. 1, p. 909; Henry S. Burrage, *History of the Thirty-Sixth Regiment Massachusetts Volunteers* (Boston, 1884), 164; Bunker, "War Record," in Schoff Collection, CL.

120. Bruce, *The Twentieth Regiment of Massachusetts Volunteer Infantry,* 374; Black, "Reminiscences of the Bloody Angle," in *Glimpses of the Nation's Struggle,* 5.

121. Houghton, "A Staff Officer's Recollection of the Salient Angle"; Bruce, *The Twentieth Regiment of Massachusetts Volunteer Infantry,* 371; Humphreys, *The Virginia Campaign,* 92; Robertson to parents, May 14, 1864, in FSNMP; Mulholland, *The Story of the 116th Regiment Pennsylvania Infantry,* 196.

122. Houghton, "A Staff Officer's Recollection of the Salient Angle."

123. Weygant, *History of the One Hundred and Twenty-Fourth Regiment New York State Volunteers,* 320.

124. Luther A. Rose Diary, May 12, 1864, in Luther A. Rose Collection, LC.

125. Porter, *Campaigning with Grant,* 100–101.

126. Venable, "The Campaign from the Wilderness to Petersburg," in *SHSP,* XIV, 529.

127. Weygant, *History of the One Hundred and Twenty-Fourth Regiment New York State Volunteers,* 320; Houghton, "A Staff Officer's Recollection of the Salient Angle."

128. Craft, *History of the One Hundred Forty First Regiment Pennsylvania Volunteers,* 192; Edwin B. Houghton, *The Campaigns of the Seventeenth Maine* (Portland, Maine, 1866), 177; Silliker, ed., *The Rebel Yell and the Yankee Hurrah,* 155; Weygant, *History of the One Hundred and Twenty-Fourth Regiment New York State Volunteers,* 322.

129. F. C. Jones, "The Second Corps: Their Gallant Charge at the Bloody Angle," *National Tribune,* October 9, 1890; Mulholland, *The Story of the 116th Regiment Penn-*

sylvania Infantry, 197; Barlow, "Capture of the Salient, May 12, 1864," in *PMHSM,* IV, 250; Black, "Reminiscences of the Bloody Angle," in *Glimpses of the Nation's Struggle,* 6; "Letter of Robert W. S. Archer," in *SHSP,* XXI, 243; John H. Worsham to R. C. Oakes, October 29, 1906, in Book 139, FSNMP; John H. Worsham, *One of Jackson's Foot Cavalry* (Jackson, Tenn., 1964), 134–35; Overton Steger to unknown, May 16, 1864, in Lewis Leigh Collection, USAMHI. The 48th Virginia had been dispatched to relieve the 42nd and was on the picket line when Hancock's juggernaut hit. See Savannah (Ga.) *Republican,* May 29, 1864.

130. Barlow, "Capture of the Salient, May 12, 1864," in *PMHSM,* IV, 250; Memoir of the 64th New York, 68, in IU; Muffly, ed., *The Story of Our Regiment,* 857; Black, "Reminiscences of the Bloody Angle," in *Glimpses of the Nation's Struggle,* 6. The 8th Ohio and 1st Delaware, jointly commanded by Franklin Sawyer, were diverted to the Landrum place, where they dispersed the Confederates "after a sharp volley or two" (Sawyer, *A Military History of the 8th Regiment Ohio Volunteer Infantry,* 167).

VII MAY 12 *Grant Captures the Salient*

1. Porter, *Campaigning with Grant,* 101–102; Theodore Lyman Journal, May 12, 1864, in Theodore Lyman Collection, MHS; Badeau, *Military History of General Ulysses S. Grant,* II, 174.

2. Jones, ed., *The Civil War Memoirs of Captain William J. Seymour,* 123–24.

3. Samuel Dunham, "Spotsylvania: A 63rd Pennsylvania Comrade Tells About the Fight," *National Tribune,* June 10, 1886; Robertson, *Personal Recollections of the War,* 104; Bruce, *The Twentieth Regiment of Massachusetts Volunteer Infantry,* 375; John H. Weeks, "152nd New York Volunteers Infantry at Spotsylvania," in South Portland (Maine) Public Library.

4. Caldwell, *Stonewall Jim,* 104.

5. "Albert Marsh, 64th New York Infantry," in James Otis Kaler Collection, South Portland (Maine) Public Library; Memoir of the 64th New York, in IU; Muffly, ed., *The Story of Our Regiment,* 259, 857; E.T.H. to O. G. Parker, May 13, 1864, Wilmington (N.C.) *Daily Journal,* May 24, 1864. Corporal Charles L. Russell, of the 93rd New York, Crocker's brigade, was credited with capturing the 42nd Virginia's flag. Since Crocker struck the salient west of Witcher, it is likely that Corporal Russell encountered the color-bearer fleeing with the remnants of Witcher's already shattered brigade. See Report of Flags Captured by the Second Army Corps, from May 4 to November 1, 1864, in *OR,* Vol. XXXVI, Pt. 1, p. 348.

6. Mulholland, *The Story of the 116th Regiment Pennsylvania Infantry,* 197; Haines, *History of the Men of Company F,* 60.

7. Hunter, "Major Hunter's Story," in *SHSP,* XXXIII, 338–39.

8. Muffly, ed., *The Story of Our Regiment,* 259; Kenneth H. Power Memoir, in Book 45, FSNMP; John R. King, *My Experience in the Confederate Army and in Northern Prisons* (Clarksburg, W.Va., 1917), 25–25; Mulholland, *The Story of the 116th Regiment Pennsylvania Infantry,* 197–98. Sergeant Marsh received a serious leg wound that required amputation. It is recorded that "when carried from the field he still held the bit of bunting, . . . and it was in his hands when the surgeons mutilated him that he might live yet a little longer" ("Albert Marsh, 64th New York Infantry," in Kaler Collection, South Portland

[Maine] Public Library). He was awarded the medal of honor and promoted to second lieutenant.

9. Robert W. Withers to friend, May 16, 1864, Lynchburg (Va.) *Daily Virginian,* May 23, 1864. Another soldier wrote, "There is but a very few of [Witcher's] brigade left with the exception of [the 21st Virginia] which has more men than all the remaining five regiments and we have only 173 left" (Overton Steger to unknown, May 16, 1864, in Lewis Leigh Collection, USAMHI).

10. Robert S. Robertson to parents, May 14, 1864, in FSNMP; Robertson, *Personal Recollections of the War,* 104; Nelson A. Miles to Francis C. Barlow, January 6, 1879, in *PMHSM,* IV, 260–61; Robert Laird Stewart, *History of the One Hundred and Fortieth Regiment Pennsylvania Volunteers* (Philadelphia, 1912), 196–97. Miles reported that the rebels had time to fire and load three times before his men took the works, and he estimated his losses at about six hundred out of twenty-two hundred (Miles to Barlow, January 6, 1879, in *PMHSM,* IV, 262).

11. Hamilton A. Brown, "First Regiment," in *Histories of the Several Regiments and Battalions from North Carolina,* ed. Clark, I, 153; Cowan, "Third Regiment," *ibid.,* I, 203–204; Henry Kyd Douglas, *I Rode With Stonewall* (Chapel Hill, N.C., 1968), 281; Simons, *A Regimental History of the One Hundred and Twenty-Fifth New York State Volunteers,* 206–207; Favill, *The Diary of a Young Officer,* 297.

12. G. B. Samuel to wife, May 13, 1864, in *A Civil War Marriage in Virginia,* comp. Spencer, 218. Only thirty soldiers from the 1st North Carolina escaped, and the entire 3rd North Carolina was captured. The reporter Hewson attributed Steuart's precipitate collapse to poorly sited earthworks. "They occupied the line of a low ridge," he wrote, "and, by what appears to me to be a grave error, lay somewhat down its reverse slope. An enemy approaching them could not be seen from some parts of the works until he had appeared over the rise, in their immediate front" (Butt Hewson, "The Battle of Spotsylvania," in *Lee's Sharpshooters,* by Dunlop, 455).

13. Howard, *Recollections of a Maryland Confederate,* 296–97.

14. Report of Flags Captured by the Second Army Corps, from May 4 to November 1, 1864, in *OR,* Vol. XXXVI, Pt. 1, p. 348; "An Incident of the Bloody Angle on the 12th of May, 1864, Worthy of History," Fredericksburg (Va.) *Free Lance,* April 29, 1887.

15. Muffly, ed., *The Story of Our Regiment,* 857–58; Thruston, "Report of the Conduct of General George H. Steuart's Brigade," in *SHSP,* XIV, 151; Second Corps Daily Memoranda, in *OR,* Vol. XXXVI, Pt. 1, p. 359.

16. Thomas H. Carter to editor of Richmond *Times,* n.d., in *SHSP,* XXI, 241; P. W. Alexander's account, in Richmond *Daily Dispatch,* May 18, 1864; Edward Johnson's report, in *OR,* Vol. XXXVI, Pt. 1, p. 1080; Howard, *Recollections of a Maryland Confederate,* 296n18.

17. Mulholland, *The Story of the 116th Regiment Pennsylvania Infantry,* 199; Almira R. Hancock, *Reminiscences of Winfield Scott Hancock* (New York, 1887), 104; Second Corps Daily Memoranda, in *OR,* Vol. XXXVI, Pt. 1, p. 359. According to Mrs. Hancock, General Hancock had met Mrs. Steuart in Washington shortly before the campaign opened. That accounted for Hancock's friendly reception of Steuart, and probably for his subsequent anger as well. Samuel Dunham, of the 63rd Pennsylvania, gave a less complimentary account of Johnson's capture. He maintained that Captain Daniel Dougherty, of Company H of his regiment, captured the general at his tent before he had a chance to buckle on his sword. Johnson reportedly protested that he would surrender only to an officer of suitable

rank, to which Dougherty answered, "To hell with your rank. Give us your sword," and Johnson acquiesced (Dunham, "Spotsylvania").

18. Weygant, *History of the One Hundred and Twenty-Fourth Regiment New York State Volunteers,* 322–23. Hancock reported that Birney's and Barlow's divisions hit Ewell's works at virtually the same time. See Winfield S. Hancock's report, in *OR,* Vol. XXXVI, Pt. 1, p. 335. Barlow contended that his division "must have arrived a little earlier," arguing that he made better time than Birney because his division was compact and advanced over open ground, whereas Birney moved through wooded and marshy terrain in two lines that constantly had to be dressed. "But one thing is perfectly clear," Barlow emphasized. "The 1st Division [Barlow's] struck the very angle of the enemy's works, and Birney the line of works to our right. The intrenchments were full of the men of my division when I reached them, and there were few, if any, of Birney's men at that precise point" (Barlow, "Capture of the Salient, May 12, 1864," in *PMHSM,* IV, 252–53).

19. William P. Snakenberg Memoir, in Book 187, FSNMP; R. D. Funkhouser, "General Lee About to Enter Battle," *Confederate Veteran,* II (1894), 36.

20. Edwin Emery to sister, n.d., in Edward Harden Collection, DU; Stephen P. Chase Memoirs, 107, in Civil War Times Illustrated Collection, USAMHI; Weygant, *History of the One Hundred and Twenty-Fourth Regiment New York State Volunteers,* 322–23, 332–33; Craft, *History of the One Hundred Forty First Regiment Pennsylvania Volunteers,* 193. Ward's 20th Indiana continued into the salient, where First Lieutenant C. Fraunberg captured the flag of the 37th Virginia, Steuart's brigade. See Report of Flags Captured by the Second Army Corps, from May 4 to November 1, 1864, in *OR,* Vol. XXXVI, Pt. 1, p. 348.

21. Thomas B. Reed, *Private in Gray* (Camden, Ark., 1905), 75; R. G. Cobb to A. J. Bachelor, in Albert A. Bachelor Collection, LSU; Snakenberg Memoir; Jones, ed., *The Civil War Memoirs of Captain William J. Seymour,* 124; George P. Ring to wife, May 15, 1864, in Army of Northern Virginia Collection, Part 1, Louisiana Historical Association Collection, Tulane University Libraries; Emery to sister, n.d., in Harden Collection, DU; Wilson and Wilson, eds., *The Civil War Diary of Thomas White Stephens,* 179.

22. Funkhouser, "General Lee About to Enter Battle," 36.

23. Walker, "The Bloody Angle," in *SHSP,* XXI, 235–36.

24. Silliker, ed., *The Rebel Yell and the Yankee Hurrah,* 155; Green, "From the Wilderness to Spotsylvania," in *War Papers,* II, 101; Houghton, *The Campaigns of the Seventeenth Maine,* 177–78; Meier, ed., *Memoirs of a Swiss Officer,* 157.

25. Thomas S. Doyle Memoir, in Jedediah Hotchkiss Collection, LC; Casler, *Four Years in the Stonewall Brigade,* 212.

26. Robert McAllister, "McAllister's Brigade at the Bloody Angle," in *B&L,* IV, 176; Robert McAllister to Gershom Mott, January 24, 1882, in *The Civil War Letters of General Robert McAllister,* ed. Robertson, 418; Robert McAllister's report, in *OR,* Vol. XXXVI, Pt. 1, p. 491; Warren H. Cudworth, *History of the First Regiment Massachusetts Infantry* (Boston, 1866), 469–70. Lieutenant Colonel Waldo Merriam, who had briefed Hancock on the attack route, was killed during the assault. See Edward Perkins Preble Diary, May 12, 1864, in FSNMP.

27. Randolph Barton Memoir, in *Defend the Valley,* comp. Colt, 314; Doyle Memoir; James L. McCown Memoirs, in Handley Library, Winchester, Va. The fighting is summarized in *The Stonewall Brigade,* by Robertson, 223–25.

28. I. G. Bradwell, "Spotsylvania, May 12, 13, 1864," *Confederate Veteran,* XXVIII

(1920), 102; Watson, "Forty-Fifth Regiment," in *Histories of the Several Regiments and Battalions from North Carolina,* ed. Clark, III, 50–51.

29. Winfield S. Hancock to George G. Meade, May 12, 1864, in *OR,* Vol. XXXVI, Pt. 2, p. 657. The times at which messages arrived at headquarters were variously reported. I have relied primarily on Lyman's journal entries.

30. Winfield S. Hancock to Andrew A. Humphreys, May 12, 1864, in *OR,* Vol. XXXVI, Pt. 2, p. 657; Hancock to Seth Williams, May 12, 1864, *ibid.;* Porter, *Campaigning with Grant,* 102–103; Theodore Lyman to family, May 20, 1864, in *Meade's Headquarters,* ed. Agassiz, 110; Lyman Journal, May 12, 1864.

31. Barlow, "Capture of the Salient, May 12, 1864," in *PMHSM,* IV, 253–54; Dunham, "Spotsylvania."

32. Gibbon, *Personal Recollections,* 220; Bruce, *The Twentieth Regiment of Massachusetts Volunteer Infantry,* 376.

33. Haines, *History of the Men of Company F,* 61; Longacre, *To Gettysburg and Beyond,* 202–204; Galwey, *The Valiant Hours,* 191, 209–10; B. Y. Draper Diary, May 12, 1864, in Book 47, FSNMP. The 14th Indiana's and 12th New Jersey's colonels were killed, and those of the 7th West Virginia and 8th Ohio were wounded. See Sawyer, *A Military History of the 8th Regiment Ohio Volunteer Infantry,* 168.

34. Joseph R. C. Ward, *History of the One Hundred and Sixth Regiment Pennsylvania Volunteers* (Philadelphia, 1883), 206; Weeks, "152nd New York Volunteer Infantry," in Kaler Collection, South Portland (Maine) Public Library; Roback, ed., *The Veteran Volunteers of Herkimer and Otsego Counties,* 78; Banes, *History of the Philadelphia Brigade,* 245–47; John G. B. Adams, *Reminiscences of the Nineteenth Massachusetts Regiment* (Boston, 1899), 90; Waitt, *History of the Nineteenth Regiment Massachusetts Volunteer Infantry,* 308; Smith, *The History of the Nineteenth Regiment of Maine Volunteer Infantry,* 155–56.

35. David B. Birney to Francis A. Walker, June 4, 1864, in Book 32, FSNMP; John Rawlins to Seth Williams, June 4, 1864, *ibid.*

36. Page, *History of the Fourteenth Regiment Connecticut Volunteer Infantry,* 247; "From a Special Correspondent," Raleigh (N.C.) *Daily Confederate,* May 25, 1864; Barlow, "Capture of the Salient, May 12, 1864," in *PMHSM,* IV, 253; Bruce, *The Twentieth Regiment of Massachusetts Volunteer Infantry,* 376–77; George A. Bowen Diary, May 12, 1864, in FSNMP.

37. Harvey B. Wells, "Hancock in Battle," Philadelphia *Weekly Times,* February 20, 1886.

38. Simon G. Griffin, "The 9th Army Corps at the Battle of Spotsylvania Court House, May 12, 1864," in MOLLUS Collection, HU; Jackman and Hadley, *History of the Sixth New Hampshire Regiment,* 242; Houston, *The Thirty-Second Maine Regiment,* 131.

39. L. O. Merriam, "Personal Recollections of the War for the Union," 31, in FSNMP; Massachusetts Historical Society, comp., *War Diary and Letters of Stephen Minot Weld,* 291.

40. Lane, "Battle of Spotsylvania Court-House," in *SHSP,* IX, 146.

41. Griffin, "The 9th Army Corps," in MOLLUS Collection, HU. About a third of the 18th North Carolina and half of the 28th North Carolina were captured.

42. William S. Speer's, John W. McGill's, Robert Cowan's, and James S. Harris' reports, all in James H. Lane Collection, AU; James S. Harris, "Seventh Regiment," in *Histories of the Several Regiments and Battalions from North Carolina,* ed. Clark, I, 383–

84; J. A. Weston, "Thirty-Third Regiment," in *Histories of the Several Regiments and Battalions from North Carolina*, ed. Clark, II, 571; William H. McLaurin, "Eighteenth Regiment," in *Histories of the Several Regiments and Battalions from North Carolina*, ed. Clark, II, 50. As Wilcox described the movement, Lane "promptly retired the left of his brigade to the line on the creek in rear, the Federals moved on in a dense and confused mass in rear of the rifle pits abandoned by Lane's left, and came under a close and destructive fire from the ridge in rear, and a raking fire from the right of Lane" (Cadmus Wilcox' report, in VHS). Lane wrote, "It is impossible for me to speak in too high terms of my command in repulsing this terrible attack of the enemy—men could not fight better, nor officers behave more gallantly—the latter regardless of danger, would frequently pass along the line and cheer the former in their glorious work. We justly claim for this brigade *alone* the honor of not only successfully stemming, but rolling back this 'tide of Federal victory which came surging furiously to our right'" (Lane, "Battle of Spotsylvania Court-House," in *SHSP*, IX, 146–47). Venable confirmed that the Federals "were checked by General Lane, who, throwing his left flank back from the trenches, confronted their advance" (Venable, "The Campaign from the Wilderness to Petersburg," in *SHSP*, XIV, 530).

43. John B. Gordon's report, in *OR*, Vol. XXXVI, Pt. 1, p. 1078. Hoffman moved into the second line of works about half an hour before daybreak. See William W. Smith's account, in *SHSP*, XXXII, 210–11.

44. Gordon, *Reminiscences of the Civil War*, 274–75.

45. *Ibid.*; Gordon's report, in *OR*, Vol. XXXVI, Pt. 1, pp. 1078–79; Robert D. Johnston, "Brigadier General R. D. Johnston's Brigade on May 10th, in John W. Daniel Collection, DU; John B. Gordon to Charles S. Venable, May 24, 1878, in Charles S. Venable Papers, VHS; J.K.B. to *Journal*, June 7, 1864, Wilmington (N.C.) *Daily Journal*, June 17, 1864; Toon, "Twentieth Regiment," in *Histories of the Several Regiments and Battalions from North Carolina*, ed. Clark, II, 121; Turner, "Twenty-Third Regiment," in *Histories of the Several Regiments and Battalions from North Carolina*, ed. Clark, II, 243–44.

46. Gordon, *Reminiscences of the Civil War*, 276; Venable, "The Campaign from the Wilderness to Petersburg," in *SHSP*, XIV, 529–30. Venable confirmed Gordon's description of this daring ploy, which was similar to tactics that Gordon had used a few days before in the Wilderness. See Rhea, *The Battle of the Wilderness, May 5–6, 1864*, 159–61.

47. Montgomery, "Twelfth Regiment," in *Histories of the Several Regiments and Battalions from North Carolina*, ed. Clark, I, 641–42; Gordon to Venable, May 24, 1878, in Venable Papers, VHS; Muffly, ed., *The Story of Our Regiment*, 858–59; Robertson, *Personal Recollections of the War*, 105. The 12th North Carolina's historian reported two-thirds of the regiment killed or wounded. A few weeks later, a soldier in the 20th North Carolina wrote that the regiment had been "reduced to a mere handful of men, living monuments of the terrible strife they have passed through" (J.K.B. to *Journal*, June 7, 1864, Wilmington (N.C.) *Daily Journal*, June 17, 1864).

48. Gordon, *Reminiscences of the Civil War*, 277; M.S. Stringfellow to the editor of the Richmond *Times*, February 20, 1893, in *SHSP*, XXI, 246.

49. Gordon, *Reminiscences of the Civil War*, 40–41.

50. J. Catlett Gibson, "The Battle of Spotsylvania Court House, May 12, 1864," in *SHSP*, XXXII, 200–201; Old, "Personal Reminiscences," in *SHSP*, XXXIII, 18; Clement A. Evans, "The Twelfth of May," in *Report of the Gordon Monument Commission* (N.p., 1907), 43.

51. Hunter, "Major Hunter's Story," in *SHSP,* XXXIII, 339.

52. "General Lee and Gordon's Charge," Richmond *Dispatch,* June 2, 1864; James Bumgardner, Jr., "Memorial Day Speech," in *SHSP,* VIII, 34; Stringfellow to editor of Richmond *Times,* February 20, 1893, in *SHSP,* XXI, 246.

53. Gordon, *Reminiscences of the Civil War,* 278–79; Gibson, "The Battle of Spotsylvania Court House," in *SHSP,* XXXII, 202. Near the site of the McCoull house, the National Park Service has placed a drawing of Lee being led to the rear. The incident must have taken place near the Harrison house, not the McCoull house.

54. Gordon, *Reminiscences of the Civil War,* 279; Gibson, "The Battle of Spotsylvania Court House," in *SHSP,* XXXII, 202–203. Varying pronouncements are attributed to Lee and Gordon. The text follows John B. Gordon to Charles S. Venable, November 24, 1878, in Venable Papers, VHS, and the accounts by Evans in "The Twelfth of May," in *Report of the Gordon Monument Commission,* 43, and by Venable in "General Lee in the Wilderness Campaign," in *B&L,* IV, 243. A compilation of firsthand accounts of this Lee-to-the-rear episode appears in Ralph Lowell Eckert's splendid biography, *John Brown Gordon—Soldier, Southerner, American* (Baton Rouge, 1989), 77n.27.

55. Gibson, "The Battle of Spotsylvania Court House," in *SHSP,* XXXII, 204; Stringfellow to editor of Richmond *Times,* February 20, 1893, in *SHSP,* XXI, 247; Smith's account, in *SHSP,* XXXII, 212.

56. Gibson, "The Battle of Spotsylvania Court House," in *SHSP,* XXXII, 204. Lee remained behind with Major Hunter, whom he instructed to collect the remaining men of Johnson's division and report to General Gordon. After rounding up some stray staffers—including Captain Virginius Dabney, of Johnson's staff, and Captain Harman, of the 2nd Virginia—Hunter went in search of survivors and found three or four hundred Louisianians, North Carolinians, and Virginians. Hunter assumed command of them and reported to Gordon. See Hunter, "Major Hunter's Story," in *SHSP,* XXXIII, 340–41.

57. Evans, "The Twelfth of May," in *Report of the Gordon Monument Commission,* 43; Venable, "The Campaign from the Wilderness to Petersburg," in *SHSP,* XIV, 530.

58. Peyton, *A Civil War Record,* 26; Smith's account, in *SHSP,* XXXII, 213; Stringfellow to editor of Richmond *Times,* February 20, 1893, in *SHSP,* XXI, 247; Walker, *History of the Second Army Corps,* 478–79; Gibson, "The Battle of Spotsylvania Court House," in *SHSP,* XXXII, 204. The old farm building must have been the Harrison house.

59. Gordon, *Reminiscences of the Civil War,* 280; Roback, *The Veteran Volunteers of Herkimer and Otsego Counties,* 79.

60. Gibson, "The Battle of Spotsylvania Court House, May 12, 1864," in *SHSP,* XXXII, 205–206.

61. Stringfellow to editor of Richmond *Times,* February 20, 1893, in *SHSP,* XXI, 248.

62. Peyton, *A Civil War Record,* 26–27; Gibson, "The Battle of Spotsylvania Court House, May 12, 1864," in *SHSP,* XXXII, 206; A. S. Coffan Diary, May 12, 1864, in *Augusta Historical Bulletin* (Augusta County [Va.] Historical Society), XXVIII (1992), 19.

63. Clement A. Evans, "Northern Boys in Southern Armies," *Confederate Veteran,* V (1897), 5; George W. Nichols, *A Soldier's Story of His Regiment and Incidentally of the Lawton, Gordon, Evans Brigade* (Jesup, Ga., 1898), 152–53.

64. Gibson, "The Battle of Spotsylvania Court House, May 12, 1864," in *SHSP,* XXXII, 206.

65. Griffin, "The 9th Army Corps," in MOLLUS Collection, HU; Otis F. R. Waite, *New Hampshire in the Great Rebellion* (Concord, N.H., 1873), 416–17.

66. Zenas R. Bliss Memoirs, Vol. IV, unpaginated, in Zenas R. Bliss Collection, USAMHI.

67. Burrage, *History of the Thirty-Sixth Regiment Massachusetts*, 165; Massachusetts Historical Society, comp., *War Diary and Letters of Stephen Minot Weld*, 292; Robert B. Potter's report, in *OR*, Vol. XXXVI, Pt. 1, p. 928; Nathaniel W. Bunker, "War Record," in James S. Schoff Collection, CL; Horatio S. Soule Diary, May 12, 1864, in Book 46, FSNMP.

68. Lane, "Battle of Spotsylvania Court-House," in *SHSP*, IX, 147; Wilcox' report, in VHS; George H. Mills, *History of the 16th North Carolina Regiment (Originally 6th North Carolina Regiment)* (Rutherfordton, N.C., 1901), 50; Early, *Autobiographical Sketch and Narrative*, 355. Doles had camped near the salient's western leg in Lee's reserve line on the morning of the twelfth. The brigade's historian recounted that when Hancock attacked, "we were hurried to the right about half a mile and soon became engaged" (Thomas, *History of the Doles-Cook Brigade*, 77). According to one postwar account, Thomas' brigade accompanied Gordon in his charge to repulse Hancock, then shifted south to assist Lane. See W. T. Irvine, "Old 35th Georgia," Atlanta *Sunny South*, May 2, 1891.

69. Burwell Thomas Cotton to sister, May 20, 1864, in *The Cry Is War, War, War: The Civil War Correspondence of Lts. Burwell Thomas Cotton and George Job Huntley, 34th Regiment North Carolina Troops, Pender-Scales Brigade of the Light Division, Stonewall Jackson's and A. P. Hill's Corps, Army of Northern Virginia, C.S.A.*, ed. Michael W. Taylor (Dayton, 1994), 11; George W. Hall Diary, May 12, 1864, in George W. Hall Collection, University of Georgia Libraries; William H. H. Bush to S. J. Gillespie, June 17, 1864, in Gillespie Family Papers, GDAH; Wise, *The Long Arm of Lee*, II, 791. According to Lee's artillery chief, the rebel guns so effectively sweeping Burnside belonged to Nelson's, Poague's, and Pegram's battalions. See William N. Pendleton's report, in *OR*, Vol. XXXVI, Pt. 1, p. 1045. Several soldiers from the 13th Georgia surrendered to the 48th Pennsylvania, of Bliss's brigade. See Joseph Gould, *The Story of the Forty-Eighth Pennsylvania* (Philadelphia, 1908), 179–80.

70. Howard M. Hanson Diary, May 12, 1864, in Howard M. Hanson Collection, University of New Hampshire Libraries; Burrage, *History of the Thirty-Sixth Regiment Massachusetts*, 166–68; Octavious A. Wiggins, "Thirty-Seventh Regiment," in *Histories of the Several Regiments and Battalions from North Carolina*, ed. Clark, II, 666; Bunker, "War Record," in Schoff Collection, CL. A fine retelling of the fighting on Lane's front appears in "Four Years of Arduous Service: The History of the Branch-Lane Brigade in the Civil War," by William K. McDaid (Ph.D. dissertation, Michigan State University, 1987), 269–73.

71. Griffin, "The 9th Army Corps," in MOLLUS Collection, HU; Bunker, "War Record," in Schoff Collection, CL. Potter explained, "The connection on our right with the Second Corps being broken, that right was turned at the time that corps lost some of the ground they had taken, and were forced out of the enemy's work with the loss of a few prisoners. The enemy's works were charged repeatedly with heavy loss, but without our being able to carry them. Most of our line, however, was within a few yards of the work, and we took several prisoners" (Potter's report, in *OR*, Vol. XXXVI, Pt. 1, p. 928).

72. Venable, "The Campaign from the Wilderness to Petersburg, in *SHSP*, XIV, 530; Gordon's report, in *OR*, Vol. XXXVI, Pt. 1, p. 1079.

73. Campbell Brown Memoir, in Ewell-Brown Collection, TSLA; "Ramseur's North Carolina Brigade," New Bern (N.C.) *Our Living and Our Dead,* February 4, 1874; James E. Green Diary, May 12, 1864, in SHC.

74. Brown Memoir.

75. Jones, ed., *The Civil War Memoirs of Captain William J. Seymour,* 125; Columbus (Ga.) *Daily Sun,* December 22, 1864; Walter A. Montgomery, *The Days of Old and the Years That Are Past* (N.p., n.d.), 28. I am grateful to Donald Pfanz for sharing with me portions of his superb manuscript biography of Ewell.

76. Battle, "The Third Alabama Regiment," 104–105, in ADAH; Roberts, "The Wilderness and Spotsylvania," 71–72; Robert E. Park, "The Twelfth Alabama Infantry, Confederate States Army," in *SHSP,* XXXIII, 294.

77. Stephen D. Ramseur's report, in *OR,* Vol. XXXVI, Pt. 1, p. 1082; "Ramseur's North Carolina Brigade," New Bern (N.C.) *Our Living and Our Dead,* February 4, 1874; J. T. Watkins Memoir, in Book 85, FSNMP; J. A. Stikeleather Reminiscences, in NCDAH; J. W. Bone Reminiscences, 30, in Lowry Shuford Collection, NCDAH.

78. Ramseur's report, in *OR,* Vol. XXXVI, Pt. 1, p. 1082; Ripley, *Vermont Riflemen,* 162; Green, "From the Wilderness to Spotsylvania," in *War Papers,* II, 101. An excellent account of Ramseur's advance appears in "From a Special Correspondent," Raleigh (N.C.) *Daily Confederate,* May 25, 1864. According to the Watkins Memoir, Ramseur announced that soldiers who did not want to make the charge could go to the rear. Only one man chose not to participate. A shell killed him later in the day.

79. Osborne, "Fourth Regiment," in *Histories of the Several Regiments and Battalions from North Carolina,* ed. Clark, I, 257; R. T. Bennett, "Fourteenth Regiment," *ibid.,* 723; Watson, "Forty-Fifth Regiment," *ibid.,* III, 51; Stikeleather Reminiscences. The London *Morning Herald* account appears in "Major General Stephen D. Ramseur: His Life and Character," by William R. Cox, in *SHSP,* XVIII, 241.

80. Stephen D. Ramseur to wife, May 19, 1864, in Stephen D. Ramseur Collection, SHC; Bennett, "Fourteenth Regiment," in *Histories of the Several Regiments and Battalions from North Carolina,* ed. Clark, I, 723; William E. Ardrey Diary, May 12, 1864, in NCDAH; Bone Reminiscences, 30; "Ramseur's North Carolina Brigade," New Bern (N.C.) *Our Living and Our Dead,"* February 4, 1874; Bryan Grimes to wife, May 14, 1864, in Bryan Grimes Collection, SHC; Stikeleather Reminiscences.

81. Bennett, "Fourteenth Regiment," in *Histories of the Several Regiments and Battalions from North Carolina,* ed. Clark, I, 723–24; Cox, "Major General Stephen D. Ramseur," in *SHSP,* XVIII, 240–41; Ardrey Diary, May 12, 1864. Ramseur praised the 14th North Carolina's commander, Colonel Risden T. Bennett, for his "bold and hazardous" operation (Ramseur's report, in *OR,* Vol. XXXVI, Pt. 1, p. 1082).

82. D. Lane, "Some Recollections of the Battle of Spotsylvania, May 12, 1864," in George Holland Collection, NCDAH; Osborne, "Fourth Regiment," in *Histories of the Several Regiments and Battalions from North Carolina,* ed. Clark, I, 257; London *Morning Herald,* in "Major-General Stephen D. Ramseur," by Cox, in *SHSP,* XVIII, 241; Walter Raleigh Battle to mother, May 17, 1864, in *The Civil War Letters of George Boardman Battle and of Walter Raleigh Battle, of Wilson, North Carolina,* ed. Hugh Buckner Johnston (Wilson, N.C., 1953); Walter to family, May 14, 1864, in *Forget-Me-Nots of the Civil War,* by Lee, 116.

83. Robert McAllister to Gershom Mott, January 24, 1882, in *The Civil War Letters of General Robert McAllister,* ed. Robertson, 418–19.

84. Winfield S. Hancock to Seth Williams, May 12, 1864, in *OR,* Vol. XXXVI, Pt. 2, p. 657; Winfield S. Hancock to Ambrose E. Burnside, *ibid.,* 677.

85. Richard S. Ewell's report, in *OR,* Vol. XXXVI, Pt. 1, p. 1072; Venable, "The Campaign from the Wilderness to Petersburg," in *SHSP,* XIV, 533; Grimes to wife, May 14, 1864, in Grimes Collection, SHC; Stephen D. Ramseur to wife, June 4, 1864, in Ramseur Collection, SHC.

86. George G. Meade to Winfield S. Hancock, in *OR,* Vol. XXXVI, Pt. 2, p. 656; George G. Meade to Gouverneur K. Warren, *ibid.,* 661; John A. Rawlins to Ambrose E. Burnside, *ibid.,* 677. A telegrapher noted that "General Hancock wired Meade that if the 6th Corps on the right of him did not attack at once, he could not hold the works he had captured. In two minutes after the dispatch was sent, the 6th Corps was thundering away and Hancock held his own" (Luther A. Rose Diary, May 12, 1864, in Luther A. Rose Collection, LC).

87. Sparks, ed., *Inside Lincoln's Army,* 372; Lyman to family, May 20, 1864, in *Meade's Headquarters,* ed. Agassiz, 111; Lyman Journal, May 12, 1864; Dana, *Recollections of the Civil War,* 195–96; Porter, *Campaigning with Grant,* 103–105; James C. Biddle to wife, May 16, 1864, in James C. Biddle Collection, HSP.

88. Badeau, *Military History of General Ulysses S. Grant,* II, 175; Porter, *Campaigning with Grant,* 105.

89. Oliver Edwards, "Spotsylvania, Va., May 12th, 1864," in Oliver Edwards Collection, ISHL; James L. Bowen, "General Edwards' Brigade at the Bloody Angle," in *B&L,* IV, 177; Rhodes, ed., *All for the Union,* 151. The brigade had been commanded by Brigadier General Henry L. Eustis until May 9. In the corps' reorganization following Sedgwick's death, Eustis was transferred to the brigade formerly under Russell and Edwards assumed command of Eustis' brigade. On May 12, Edwards' fourth regiment—the 7th Massachusetts—was on picket duty elsewhere. See Hutchinson, *History of the Seventh Massachusetts Volunteer Infantry,* 185–86.

90. Rhodes, ed., *All for the Union,* 151; Lyman Journal, May 12, 1864. According to Rhodes, the 6th Corps column encountered Johnson while he was being taken to Grant. "How are you, Johnson?" Wheaton called out. "How are you, Frank?" Johnson shouted back.

91. Bowen, "General Edwards' Brigade at the Bloody Angle," in *B&L,* IV, 177; Lyman Journal, May 12, 1864.

92. McAllister, "McAllister's Brigade at the Bloody Angle," in *B&L,* IV, 176; Weygant, *History of the One Hundred and Twenty-Fourth Regiment New York State Volunteers,* 324–25.

93. Edwards, "Spotsylvania, Va., May 12th, 1864," in Edwards Collection, ISHL; Oliver Edwards, "Battle of Spotsylvania: The Defense of the Angle," in *Camp-Fire Sketches and Battle-Field Echoes,* comp. William C. King and W. P. Derby (Springfield, Mass., 1888), 309; Bowen, "General Edwards' Brigade at the Bloody Angle," in *B&L,* IV, 177; Silliker, ed., *The Rebel Yell and the Yankee Hurrah,* 155; Newell, *Ours,* 268; Charles Harvey Brewster to Mary, May 13, 1864, in *When This Cruel War Is Over,* ed. Blight, 296. The location and arrangement of Edwards' regiments became the subject of heated postwar controversy. Articles and letters from participants bearing on the question appeared in the Philadelphia *Weekly Times* for January 8 and November 26, 1881, November 18, 1882, February 16, 1884, and February 20, 1886, and in the Philadelphia *Weekly*

Press for October 27, 1886, and August 10 and October 12, 1887. The weight of evidence supports Edwards' claim that his brigade was the initial 6th Corps unit at the west angle.

94. Tyler, *Recollections of the Civil War,* 179, 358–65; Daniel Bidwell's report, in *OR,* Vol. XXXVI, Pt. 1, p. 720; Edwin C. Mason, "Through the Wilderness to the Bloody Angle at Spotsylvania Court House," in *Glimpses of the Nation's Struggle,* 305.

95. Frank Wheaton's report, in *OR,* Vol. XXXVI, Pt. 1, p. 684; John R. Brooke's report, *ibid.,* 411; Jacob Seibert to father, May 14, 1864, in FSNMP; Schoyer, ed., *The Road to Cold Harbor,* 81–82; S. F. Hildebrand, "Notes and Reminiscences of Service," in Harold C. George Collection, LC. An ambitious attempt to reconstruct the positions of the 6th Corps brigades appears in *Recollections of the Civil War,* by Tyler, 358–65. Reports filed after the fighting were so inconsistent that a definitive placement of units is impossible.

96. Second Corps Daily Memoranda, in *OR,* Vol. XXXVI, Pt. 1, p. 359; Lyman Journal, May 12, 1864.

97. Mulholland, *The Story of the 116th Regiment Pennsylvania Infantry,* 201; R. P. King, "The Irish Brigade," *Irish American,* May 28, 1864.

98. Black, "Reminiscences of the Bloody Angle," in *Glimpses of the Nation's Struggle,* 9.

99. *Ibid.,* 10–11.

100. *Ibid.,* 11–12.

101. Ambrose E. Burnside to Ulysses S. Grant, May 12, 1864, in *OR,* Vol. XXXVI, Pt. 2, p. 677; Winfield S. Hancock to Ambrose E. Burnside, May 12, 1864, *ibid.;* Ulysses S. Grant to Ambrose E. Burnside, May 12, 1864, *ibid.;* Cyrus B. Comstock Diary, May 12, 1864, in Cyrus B. Comstock Collection, LC. The Confederate guns trained on Burnside were from William Nelson's 2nd Corps battalion and from the 3rd Corps battalions of Poague and Pegram. See Pendleton's report, in *OR,* Vol. XXXVI, Pt. 1, p. 1045.

102. Benedict, *Vermont in the Civil War,* I, 446–47; Lewis A. Grant's report, in *OR,* Vol. XXXVI, Pt. 1, p. 703; Barlow, "Capture of the Salient, May 12, 1864," in *PMHSM,* IV, 254–55; Lewis A. Grant, "Review of Major-General F. C. Barlow's Paper on the Capture of the Salient at Spotsylvania, May 12, 1864," in *PMHSM,* IV, 266–67.

103. E. W. B. Reminiscences, in *Recollections and Reminiscences, 1861–1865,* comp. United Daughters of the Confederacy, South Carolina Division (3 vols.; N.p., 1990), I, 27–28.

104. *Ibid.*

105. Katherine Couse to unknown, May 4–22, 1864, in UV.

106. Philip H. Powers to wife, May 12, 1864, in Lewis Leigh Collection, USAMHI.

VIII   MAY 12 *The Armies Reach Stalemate at the Bloody Angle*

1. A reporter described the situation: "The Confederate line had been re-established by Ramseur to the position held during the night by [Witcher's] left. It had been restored by Gordon to the point occupied during the same time by [Witcher's] right. The gap originally made remained, however, still in the possession of the enemy; and with it all the guns—with the exception of the four retaken by Gordon—that had been captured at the time of the rush into the salient" (Butt Hewson, "The Battle of Spotsylvania Court House," in *Lee's Sharpshooters,* by Dunlop, 466–67).

2. William S. Shockley to Eliza, May 16, 1864, in William S. Shockley Collection, DU; G. Moxley Sorrel Diary, May 12, 1864, in MC; "Wofford's Georgia Brigade," Atlanta *Southern Confederacy,* June 15, 1864; Stiles, *Four Years Under Marse Robert,* 261.

3. Early, *Autobiographical Sketch and Narrative,* 355; Thomas T. Roche, "The Bloody Angle," Philadelphia *Weekly Times,* September 3, 1881; Holt, *A Mississippi Rebel,* 253; David E. Holt, "The Death Angle: War at Its Worst," in Mississippi Department of History and Archives, Jackson. Weisiger's Virginians and Perry's tiny Florida brigade shifted early in the morning from the Po to the salient's eastern face.

4. George Clark, "From the Rapidan to Petersburg," *Confederate Veteran,* XVIII (1909), 381–82; Alfred L. Scott, "Memoirs of Service in the Confederate Army," VHS; Clark, *A Glance Backward,* 51; Ezra J. Warner, *Generals in Gray: Lives of the Confederate Commanders* (Baton Rouge, 1959), 235. It was later disputed whether Perrin or Harris first entered the fray. Wilcox asserted in a postwar letter that "Perrin's brigade—known as Wilcox' old brigade—was the first to reach or support Ewell" (Cadmus M. Wilcox to Andrew A. Humphreys, n.d., in Andrew A. Humphreys Collection, Book 30, HSP). See also Hewson, "The Battle of Spotsylvania," in *Lee's Sharpshooters,* by Dunlop, 467; and Saladay dispatch, Richmond *Daily Dispatch,* May 25, 1864. Roche, in "The Bloody Angle," Philadelphia *Weekly Times,* September 3, 1881, claimed that Harris initially occupied the salient.

5. Scott, "Memoirs of Service," VHS.

6. *Ibid.* A Confederate correspondent confused Battle's and Perrin's Alabamians, contending that "Battle's Alabama brigade, of Rodes's division, was thrown in on Ramseur's right, his center passing the McCoull house, and drove the enemy back some distance into the woods, gaining a foothold in the wood which they resolutely held" (Richmond *Daily Dispatch,* May 25, 1864). The description tracks Perrin's movements, not those of Battle, who helped Daniel regain the earthworks on Ramseur's left.

7. Scott, "Memoirs of Service," VHS. The Federals near the McCoull house were from Ward's brigade. See Craft, *History of the One Hundred Forty First Regiment Pennsylvania Volunteers,* 193.

8. George Clark, "From the Rapidan to Petersburg," 382; D. I. Hendrix, "That Bloody Angle Battle," *Confederate Veteran,* XVII (1909), 438; Caldwell, *The History of a Brigade of South Carolinians,* 142; Scott, "Memoirs of Service," VHS. One postwar source reported that the 9th Alabama remained behind to defend the works "before occupied by the whole brigade, from sunrise until sunset" (James Edmonds Saunders, *Early Settlers of Alabama* [New Orleans, 1899], 158). But a participant claimed that the 9th Alabama played a major role in the counterattack. See Henry Minor to editor of Decatur (Ala.) *News,* March 4, 1876, in FSNMP. A story circulated that Perrin had been shot by his own men. A soldier later protested, "This was a mistake, as his gallantry had led our men not only to respect him highly, but to love him" (Clark, *A Glance Backward,* 51).

9. Roche, "The Bloody Angle," Philadelphia *Weekly Times,* September 3, 1881; Clark, *A Glance Backward,* 52.

10. Hewson, "The Battle of Spotsylvania Court House," in *Lee's Sharpshooters,* by Dunlop, 467–68. The actions of Perrin's shattered brigade during the rest of the day are impossible to reconstruct. Alabamians were reported on Ramseur's right and, later in the day, near the east angle, intermingled with Gordon's soldiers. See, *e.g.,* Worsham, *One of Jackson's Foot Cavalry,* 137.

11. John Ritchey, "General Lee's Readiness to Lead His Men," *Confederate Veteran,*

XV (1907), 546; Venable, "The Campaign from the Wilderness to Petersburg," in *SHSP,* XIV, 531; Burton R. Conerly's account, in *Reminiscences of the Boys in Gray,* comp. Yeary, 147–48.

12. Nathaniel H. Harris' report, in *OR,* Vol. XXXVI, Pt. 1, pp. 1091–92; Nathaniel H. Harris to Charles S. Venable, August 24, 1871, in *SHSP,* VIII, 105–106; Charles S. Venable to Nathaniel H. Harris, November 24, 1871, in *SHSP,* VIII, 107; Dobbins, ed., *Grandfather's Journal,* 194; Ritchey, "General Lee's Readiness to Lead His Men," 546; E. Howard McCaleb, *Address Delivered by E. Howard McCaleb of New Orleans, at the Reunion of the Surviving Veterans of Harris' Mississippi Brigade, Army of Northern Virginia, Held at Port Gibson, . . . Claiborne Co., Mississippi, November 13, 1879* (New Orleans, n.d), 10–11; Venable, "The Campaign from the Wilderness to Petersburg," in *SHSP,* XIV, 531. Thomas T. Roche, of the 16th Mississippi, recounted that when Lee rode to the brigade's front, the men "became alarmed for the safety of the man whom they idolized. Some members of the Twelfth Mississippi, at whose side he was riding, stepped from the ranks and seized his horse's bridle, told him he must go back and not expose himself, at the same time assuring him that they would reoccupy the works or every man would fall in the attempt" (Roche, "The Bloody Angle," Philadelphia *Weekly Times,* September 3, 1881). Roche believed that Lee never intended to lead the charge.

13. Venable to Harris, November 24, 1871, in *SHSP,* VIII, 106–107; Harris to Venable, August 24, 1871, in *SHSP,* VIII, 105–106; Nathaniel H. Harris to William Mahone, August 2, 1866, in William Mahone Collection, VSL; Harris, comp., *Movements of the Confederate Army in Virginia and the Part Taken Therein by the Nineteenth Mississippi Brigade,* 27.

14. Conerly's account, in *Reminiscences of the Boys in Gray,* comp. Yeary, 148; Venable to Harris, November 24, 1871, in *SHSP,* VIII, 106–107; Nathaniel H. Harris to Charles J. Lewis, March 22, 1899, in Nathaniel H. Harris Collection, SHC; Harris, comp., *Movements of the Confederate Army in Virginia and the Part Taken Therein by the Nineteenth Mississippi Brigade,* 27–28; Roche, "The Bloody Angle," Philadelphia *Weekly Times,* September 3, 1881. The 16th Mississippi led, followed by the 12th, 19th, and 48th regiments. A soldier in the 16th Mississippi recollected that the brigade "advanced by flank, till at close distance, then filed at right angles, to the right, the brigade length, fronted and charged" (Mott, "The Civil War Diary of James J. Kirkpatrick," 193).

15. Roche, "The Bloody Angle," Philadelphia *Weekly Times,* September 3, 1881; Harris to Mahone, August 2, 1866, in Mahone Collection, VSL.

16. Harris, comp., *Movements of the Confederate Army in Virginia and the Part Taken Therein by the Nineteenth Mississippi Brigade,* 28; Conerly's account, in *Reminiscences of the Boys in Gray,* comp. Yeary, 148; One of the Quitman Guards, *A Historical Sketch of the Quitman Guards, Company E, Sixteenth Mississippi Regiment, Harris' Brigade* (New Orleans, 1866), 65–66; Dobbins, ed., *Grandfather's Journal,* 194; Holt, *A Mississippi Rebel,* 256–57.

17. Edwards, "Battle of Spotsylvania," in *Camp-Fire Sketches and Battle-Field Echoes,* comp. William C. King and W. P. Derby, 309–10.

18. Richard S. Ewell to Nathaniel H. Harris, December 27, 1864, in *A Historical Sketch of the Quitman Guards,* by One of the Quitman Guards, 67–68.

19. Second Corps Daily Memoranda, in *OR,* Vol. XXXVI, Pt. 1, p. 359; Winfield S. Hancock's report, *ibid.,* 336; Oliver Edwards, "Spotsylvania, Va., May 12, 1864," in Oliver Edwards Collection, ISHL.

20. Hancock's report, in *OR,* Vol. XXXVI, Pt. 1, p. 336; John R. Brooke's report, *ibid.,* 411.

21. Grant, "Review of Major-General F. C. Barlow's Paper," in *PMHSM,* IV, 267; Lewis A. Grant's report, in *OR,* Vol. XXXVI, Pt. 1, pp. 703–704; Benedict, *Vermont in the Civil War,* I, 447–48; Conerly's account, in *Reminiscences of the Boys in Gray,* comp. Yeary, 149; Muffly, ed., *The Story of Our Regiment,* 859–60; Ott, "The Civil War Diary of James J. Kirkpatrick," 193.

22. Joseph N. Brown, "The Battle of the 'Bloody Angle,' " in *A Colonel at Gettysburg and Spotsylvania,* by Varina D. Brown (Columbia, S.C., 1931), 93.

23. *Ibid.,* 94; Caldwell, *The History of a Brigade of South Carolinians,* 140–42. It is impossible to give the precise time of McGowan's arrival at the battlefront. As with most events on May 12, recollections varied dramatically. Wilcox placed the time between 8 and 9 A.M., Colonel Brown remembered receiving marching orders "shortly after" nine, Ewell reported the attack as occurring at ten, and Harris thought it was at eleven. See Cadmus M. Wilcox' report, in VHS; Joseph N. Brown, Address at Reunion of Orr's Regiment (McGowan's Brigade) at Belton, S.C., August, 1910, in *A Colonel at Gettysburg and Spotsylvania,* by Brown, 109; Richard S. Ewell's report, in *OR,* Vol. XXXVI, Pt. 1, p. 1073; and Harris to Lewis, March 22, 1899, in Harris Collection, SHC. Careful analysis of the sequence in which Union and Confederate forces reached the salient, and the times of the various attacks as reported by Union and Confederate officers, persuades this writer that McGowan's assault occurred near nine o'clock.

24. Caldwell, *The History of a Brigade of South Carolinians,* 143; Conerly's account, in *Reminiscences of the Boys in Gray,* comp. Yeary, 149; J. S. McMahon to family, May 14, 1864, Columbia (S.C.) *Daily Southern Guardian,* May 26, 1864; Harris to Mahone, August 2, 1866, in Mahone Collection, VSL. After the war, Harris claimed that he assumed command of McGowan's brigade when McGowan was wounded, as well as continuing to command his own. See Harris to Lewis, March 22, 1899, in Harris Collection, SHC. Harris was certainly in error, since Colonel Brown clearly exercised command over the South Carolinians. It is probable that units from both brigades became so intermixed that both Harris and Brown issued orders to the nearest troops.

25. James Armstrong, "Battle of the Bloody Bend," in *A Colonel at Gettysburg and Spotsylvania,* by Brown, 121–22; Isaac F. Hunt to Joseph N. Brown, December 10, 1894, *ibid.,* 126–28. Recollections varied concerning which part of the salient McGowan occupied. William H. Harris maintained that McGowan "gained no ground to the right of Harris' brigade, but occupied the ground already held by Ramseur and Harris" (Harris, comp., *Movements of the Confederate Army in Virginia and the Part Taken Therein by the Nineteenth Mississippi Brigade,* 28). Roche, in "The Bloody Angle," Philadelphia *Weekly Times,* September 3, 1881, contended that McGowan overlapped Harris' right wing and extended considerably to the right. See also Conerly's account in *Reminiscences of the Boys in Gray,* comp. Yeary, 149.

26. Joseph N. Brown, "Address to the R. E. Lee Chapter of the Daughters of the Confederacy, November, 1900," in *A Colonel at Gettysburg and Spotsylvania,* by Brown, 95–97; Caldwell, *The History of a Brigade of South Carolinians,* 142–43; One of the Quitman Guards, *A Historical Sketch of the Quitman Guards,* 66; Unknown to *Courier,* Charleston (S.C.) *Daily Courier,* May 28, 1864.

27. Caldwell, *The History of a Brigade of South Carolinians,* 144, 146; Dobbins, ed., *Grandfather's Journal,* 194.

28. Bowen, "General Edwards' Brigade at the Bloody Angle," in *B&L,* IV, 177; Oliver Edwards' report, in "The Bloody Angle: Was Upton's or Edwards' Brigade at the Apex at Spotsylvania?" by James L. Bowen, Philadelphia *Weekly Press,* October 12, 1887; Joseph B. Parson's address to Massachusetts Commandery of the Loyal Legion of the United States, in *The Tenth Regiment Massachusetts Volunteer Infantry, 1861–1864,* by Alfred S. Roe (Springfield, Mass., 1909), 276–77.

29. Emory Upton's report, in *OR,* Vol. XXXVI, Pt. 1, p. 669.

30. Best, *History of the 121st New York State Infantry,* 144; Emory Upton to Edward R. Robins, November 9, 1879, in Military Historical Society of Massachusetts Collection, BU. A 6th Corps soldier asserted that "someone must have made a big blunder in placing the corps where it was. To properly support Hancock in his charge, we should have been as close up in his rear as possible to be of much use to him. Instead of that, we must have been fully a mile distant" (S. F. Hildebrand, "Notes and Reminiscences of Service," in Harold C. George Collection, LC).

31. Upton to Robins, November 9, 1879, in Military Historical Society of Massachusetts Collection, BU.

32. Upton's report, in *OR,* Vol. XXXVI, Pt. 1, p. 669.

33. Roe, *The Tenth Regiment Massachusetts Volunteer Infantry,* 276–77; Emory Upton to G. Norton Galloway, August 31, 1878, in "The Bloody Angle: What Troops Did the Fiercest Fighting at Spotsylvania," by G. Norton Galloway, Philadelphia *Weekly Press,* August 10, 1887; Cyrenus Pullen Stevens Diary, May 12, 1864, in Book 36, FSNMP; Henry Keiser Diary, May 12, 1864, in Harrisburg Civil War Round Table Collection, USAMHI; B. F. Johns, "The Bloody Angle," *National Tribune,* July 14, 1887; Edwards, "Spotsylvania, Va., May 12, 1864," in Edwards Collection, ISHL.

34. Anderson, "Through the Wilderness with Grant," in *Report of the Proceedings of 5th Wisconsin Volunteer Infantry,* 14.

35. Edwards, "Spotsylvania, Va., May 12, 1864," in Edwards Collection, ISHL; Stevens Diary, May 12, 1864; Keiser Diary, May 12, 1864.

36. Fred Sanborn Memoir, May 12, 1864, in LC; Isaac O. Best, "Through the Wilderness with Grant," in James S. Schoff Collection, CL; William E. Lines' narrative, in "Hand-to-Hand Fighting at Spotsylvania," by Galloway, in *B&L,* IV, 171–72n; James Gilliss' report, in *OR,* Vol. XXXVI, Pt. 1, p. 537; Richard Metcalf's report, in *OR,* Vol. XXXVI, Pt. 1, p. 539. Metcalf's travails are detailed by Naisawald in *Grape and Canister,* 485–87.

37. Beyer and Keydel, eds., *Deeds of Valor,* 332.

38. Metcalf's report, in *OR,* Vol. XXXVI, Pt. 1, p. 539; J. S. Anderson to family, May 15, 1864, in *Proceedings at the Annual Meeting of the Association of Fifth Wisconsin Volunteer Infantry Held at Milwaukee, June 27th–28th, 1900,* in State Historical Society of Wisconsin, Madison.

39. John C. Tidball's report, in *OR,* Vol. XXXVI, Pt. 1, p. 509; John W. Roder's report, *ibid.,* 534; Edwin B. Dow's report, *ibid.,* 514; Albert N. Ames Diary, May 12, 1864, in Albert N. Ames Collection, NYSLA; Albert N. Ames to family, May 16, 1864, in Ames Collection, NYSLA; Neese, *Three Years in the Confederate Horse Artillery,* 266–67; Kirk, *Heavy Guns and Light,* 211.

40. Hyde, *Following the Greek Cross,* 200; Buell, *The Cannoneer,* 194; David B. Swinfen, *Ruggles' Regiment: The 122nd New York Volunteers in the American Civil War* (Hanover, N.H., 1982), 39.

41. Morse, *Personal Experiences in the War of the Great Rebellion,* 88–89; Galloway, "Hand-to-Hand Fighting at Spotsylvania," in *B&L,* IV, 172.

42. Keiser Diary, May 12, 1864; Joseph N. Brown, Address to R. E. Lee Chapter of the Daughters of the Confederacy, November, 1900, in *A Colonel at Gettysburg and Spotsylvania,* by Brown, 98; D. Lane, "Some Recollections of the Battle," in George Holland Collection, NCDAH; Conerly's account, in *Reminiscences of the Boys in Gray,* comp. Yeary, 149.

43. Conerly's account, in *Reminiscences of the Boys in Gray,* comp. Yeary, 149–50; Bennett, "Fourteenth Regiment," in *Histories of the Various Regiments and Battalions from North Carolina,* ed. Clark, I, 724–25; J. T. Watkins Memoir, in Book 85, FSNMP.

44. Edmund D. Halsey Diary, May 12, 1864, in Edmund D. Halsey Collection, USAMHI.

45. *Ibid.*; James Maguire Memorandum, in William O. Bourne Collection, LC; Haines, *History of the Fifteenth Regiment New Jersey Volunteers,* 174–75, Baquet, *History of the First Brigade New Jersey Volunteers,* 124. The 15th New Jersey's monument is located near the Bloody Angle. In fact, the Jersey men assaulted over one hundred yards to the Union right, probably striking Ramseur's brigade.

46. "Official Report of Movements of 15th N.J. During Grant's Wilderness Campaign," in Halsey Collection, USAMHI; Unknown 15th New Jersey Soldier Diary, in FSNMP; Haines, *History of the Fifteenth Regiment New Jersey Volunteers,* 175–76, 178.

47. The Confederate flag—allegedly that of the 14th Georgia, although the Georgians denied that it was theirs—was given to the regiment's chaplain, who displayed it at reunions for years thereafter. See John H. White, "He Got the Flag: The Desperate Charge of a Jerseyman at Spotsylvania," *National Tribune,* January 20, 1887.

48. Baquet, *History of the First Brigade New Jersey Volunteers,* 125; Haines, *History of the Fifteenth Regiment New Jersey Volunteers,* 178–79; Dayton E. Flint to father, May 17, 1864, Washington (N.J.) *Star,* February 9, 1911. At the beginning of the campaign, the 15th New Jersey numbered 487 muskets. After eight days of fighting, including its attack on May 12, 153 men remained.

49. Theodore Lyman Journal, May 12, 1864, in Theodore Lyman Collection, MHS.

50. Andrew A. Humphreys to Gouverneur K. Warren, May 11, 1864, in *OR,* Vol. XXXVI, Pt. 2, pp. 637–38; Gouverneur K. Warren to Charles Griffin, May 11, 1864, *ibid.,* 638; Gouverneur K. Warren to Samuel W. Crawford, May 11, 1864, *ibid.,* 640.

51. Gouverneur K. Warren to Samuel W. Crawford, May 12, 1864, in *OR,* Vol. XXXVI, Pt. 2, pp. 666–67; George G. Meade to Gouverneur K. Warren, May 12, 1864, *ibid.,* 661; 5th Corps Circular, May 12, 1864, *ibid.,* 667.

52. George G. Meade to Gouverneur K. Warren, May 12, 1864, in *OR,* Vol. XXXVI, Pt. 2, p. 662; Washington A. Roebling's report, in Gouverneur K. Warren Collection, NYSLA. The 1st Michigan and 118th Pennsylvania, of Bartlett's brigade, remained on Warren's right, where they skirmished with Confederates across the Po. See William A. Throop's report, in *OR,* Vol. XXXVI, Pt. 1, p. 581; and Charles P. Herring's report, *ibid.,* 591.

53. George G. Meade to Gouverneur K. Warren, May 12, 1864, in *OR,* Vol. XXXVI, Pt. 2, p. 662; Gouverneur K. Warren to Andrew A. Humphreys, May 12, 1864, *ibid.,* 663.

54. George G. Meade to Winfield S. Hancock, May 12, 1864, in *OR,* Vol. XXXVI, Pt. 2, p. 658.

55. Roebling's report, in Warren Collection, NYSLA. Warren recorded that he attacked

at "8:15 A.M. by my watch" (Gouverneur K. Warren Diary, May 12, 1864, in Warren Collection, NYSLA).

56. George L. Prescott to Sallie, May 13, 1864, in George L. Prescott Collection, MHS; John Bratton's report, in *SHSP*, VIII, 548; Francis J. Parker, *The Story of the Thirty-Second Regiment Massachusetts Infantry* (Boston, 1880), 214–15.

57. Rufus Dawes's report, in *OR*, Vol. XXXVI, Pt. 1, p. 620; Small, *The Road to Richmond*, 139.

58. Gouverneur K. Warren to Andrew A. Humphreys, May 12, 1864, in *OR*, Vol. XXXVI, Pt. 2, p. 663.

59. Andrew A. Humphreys to Gouverneur K. Warren, May 12, 1864, in *OR*, Vol. XXXVI, Pt. 1, p. 663; Badeau, *Military History of General Ulysses S. Grant*, II, 177; Howe, ed., *Touched with Fire*, 116.

60. Andrew A. Humphreys to Gouverneur K. Warren, May 12, 1864, in *OR*, Vol. XXXVI, Pt. 2, p. 663. Humphreys noted that although there were no objective signs that rebels had left Laurel Hill to reinforce the salient, "the manner in which the contest there was carried on and the reinforcements the enemy received, together with the fact that Burnside was attacking on the east side of the salient, led to the conclusion that the enemy could not be very strong in Warren's front" (Humphreys, *The Virginia Campaign*, 101).

61. Gouverneur K. Warren to Charles Griffin, May 12, 1864, in *OR*, Vol. XXXVI, Pt. 2, p. 668; Gouverneur K. Warren to Samuel W. Crawford, May 12, 1864, *ibid.*, 669 ("The orders are peremptory to charge the enemy's entrenchments at once with all your force. Do it. It is but a repetition of my orders."); Gouverneur K. Warren to Lysander Cutler, May 12, 1864, *ibid.*, 671 ("General Meade reiterates his order to move on the enemy regardless of consequences.").

62. Small, *The Sixteenth Maine Regiment*, 180; Charles Thomas Bowen Diary, May 12, 1864, in FSNMP.

63. Alfred M. Apted Diary, May 12, 1864, in Civil War Miscellaneous Collection, USAMHI; Bratton's report, in *SHSP*, VIII, 548; Burgess E. Ingersoll Diary, May 12, 1864, in Civil War Miscellaneous Collection, USAMHI; Porter Farley, "The 140th New York Volunteers," in RL. Bartlett's brigade did not return in time to participate in the charge, and the 140th and 146th New York regiments from Ayres's brigade remained in reserve.

64. Dawes's report, in *OR*, Vol. XXXVI, Pt. 1, p. 620; Dawes, *Service with the Sixth Wisconsin Volunteers*, 266–67; Chamberlin, *History of the One Hundred and Fiftieth Regiment Pennsylvania Volunteers*, 236–38. Fowler had assumed command of Rice's brigade after Rice's fatal wounding on May 10.

65. Small, *The Sixteenth Maine Regiment*, 180; Orville Thomson, *From Philippi to Appomattox: Narrative of the Services of the Seventh Indiana Infantry in the War for the Union* (N.p., n.d.), 187–88.

66. Small, *The Sixteenth Maine Regiment*, 180–81; Chamberlin, *History of the One Hundred and Fiftieth Regiment Pennsylvania Volunteers*, 238; Alexander B. Pattison Diary, May 12, 1864, in Indiana Historical Society, Indianapolis.

67. Dawes, *Service with the Sixth Wisconsin Volunteers*, 267; Lysander Cutler to Gouverneur K. Warren, May 12, 1864, in *OR*, Vol. XXXVI, Pt. 2, p. 671; Gouverneur K. Warren to Lysander Cutler, May 12, 1864, in *OR*, Vol. XXXVI, Pt. 2, p. 671.

68. Vautier, *History of the 88th Pennsylvania Volunteers*, 182–83; Locke, *The Story of the Regiment*, 337.

69. Field, "Campaign of 1864 and 1865," in *SHSP*, XIV, 547–48; Oates, *The War Be-*

tween the Union and the Confederacy, 359; Richard H. Anderson's report, in Richard H. Anderson Collection, DU; William N. Pendleton's report, in *OR,* Vol. XXXVI, Pt. 1, p. 1045; Silas Chandler to wife, May 18, 1864, in Book 5, FSNMP.

70. Dawes, *Service with the Sixth Wisconsin Volunteers,* 266–67; George W. Burchell to M and M, May 13, 1864, in Sullivan Dexter Green Papers, BL.

71. Humphreys, *The Virginia Campaign,* 101n3; George G. Meade to Ulysses S. Grant, May 12, 1864, in *OR,* Vol. XXXVI, Pt. 2, p. 654; Ulysses S. Grant to George G. Meade, May 12, 1864, in *OR,* Vol. XXXVI, Pt. 2, p. 654.

72. George G. Meade to Andrew A. Humphreys, May 12, 1864, in *OR,* Vol. XXXVI, Pt. 2, p. 655; Samuel W. Crawford to Gouverneur K. Warren, May 12, 1864, *ibid.,* 669–70; Gouverneur K. Warren to Lysander Cutler, May 12, 1864, *ibid.,* 671; George G. Meade to Andrew A. Humphreys, May 12, 1864, *ibid.,* 655; Andrew A. Humphreys to George G. Meade, May 12, 1864, *ibid.*

73. Gouverneur K. Warren to Emily, May 3, 1864, in Warren Collection, NYSLA; Grant, *Personal Memoirs,* II, 216; Porter, *Campaigning with Grant,* 108.

74. George G. Meade to John A. Rawlins, June 21, 1864, in George G. Meade Collection, HSP.

75. Lyman Journal, May 12, 1864.

76. *Ibid.;* Grayson M. Eichelberger Memoir, May 12, 1864, in Civil War Miscellaneous Collection, USAMHI.

77. John E. McPeck, "Spotsylvania: The Battle As Seen from the Ranks of the 126th Ohio," *National Tribune,* October 20, 1887; William S. Truex' report, in *OR,* Vol. XXXVI, Pt. 1, p. 725; J. Warren Keifer's report, in *OR,* Vol. XXXVI, Pt. 1, p. 733. A soldier in the 138th Pennsylvania reported that Ricketts' division was "held partially in reserve and but slightly engaged" (Osceola Lewis, *History of the One Hundred and Thirty-Eighth Regiment Pennsylvania Volunteer Infantry* [Norristown, Pa., 1866], 97).

78. Bennett, "Fourteenth Regiment," in *Histories of the Several Regiments and Battalions from North Carolina,* ed. Clark, I, 724; Baquet, *History of the First Brigade New Jersey Volunteers,* 125; Bicknell, *History of the Fifth Regiment Maine Volunteers,* 321; Holt, *A Mississippi Rebel,* 260; Naisawald, *Grape and Canister,* 477–78.

79. Haines, *History of the Fifteenth Regiment New Jersey Volunteers,* 177–78.

80. Walker, *History of the Second Army Corps,* 473; Mason, "Through the Wilderness to the Bloody Angle at Spotsylvania Court House," in *Glimpses of the Nation's Struggle,* 307; B. F. Brown to Joseph N. Brown, January 22, 1901, in *A Colonel at Gettysburg and Spotsylvania,* by Brown, 136. The oak tree, the stump of which is at present displayed at the Smithsonian Institution, in Washington, D.C., figures in most accounts of the battle. Its journey from the battlefield to the capital is detailed by Matter in *If It Takes All Summer,* 373. The 37th Massachusetts' historian noted that "every regiment that fought anywhere in that part of the field claims to have shot down this particular tree; but in truth no single organization is entitled to all the credit" (Bowen, "General Edwards' Brigade at the Bloody Angle," in *B&L,* IV, 177).

81. Richard Meade Bache, *Life of General George Gordon Meade, Commander of the Army of the Potomac* (Philadelphia, 1897), 429; Hyde, *Following the Greek Cross,* 200; Lewis A. Grant to G. Norton Galloway, n.d., in "Capture of the Salient," Philadelphia *Weekly Times,* November 18, 1882.

82. Galwey, *The Valiant Hours,* 210; Silliker, ed., *The Rebel Yell and the Yankee Hurrah,* 157; Robertson, *Personal Recollections of the War,* 105; Cudworth, *History of the*

First Regiment Massachusetts Infantry, 471; Bruce, *The Twentieth Regiment of Massachusetts Volunteer Infantry,* 378; Maurus Oestreich Diary, May 12, 1864, in Harrisburg Civil War Round Table Collection, USAMHI.

83. Wells, "Hancock in Battle," Philadelphia *Weekly Times,* February 20, 1886; Waitt, *History of the Nineteenth Regiment Massachusetts Volunteer Infantry,* 309; Holt, "The Death Angle: War at Its Worst," in Mississippi Department of History and Archives. Cudworth, *History of the First Regiment Massachusetts Infantry,* 472.

84. Hyde, *Following the Greek Cross,* 201.

85. Ulysses S. Grant to Ambrose E. Burnside, May 12, 1864, in *OR,* Vol. XXXVI, Pt. 2, p. 677; Ulysses S. Grant to Ambrose E. Burnside, May 12, 1864, *ibid.,* 678; Ambrose E. Burnside to Ulysses S. Grant, May 12, 1864, *ibid.*

86. Ulysses S. Grant to Cyrus B. Comstock, May 12, 1864, in *OR,* Vol. XXXVI, Pt. 2, p. 679; Ulysses S. Grant to Ambrose E. Burnside, *ibid.*

87. Cyrus B. Comstock Diary, May 12, 1864, in Cyrus B. Comstock Collection, LC. The episode is interpreted favorably to Burnside by William Marvel in *Burnside* (Chapel Hill, N.C., 1991), 364.

88. The marchings of Willcox' division are described in Orlando B. Willcox' report, in *OR,* Vol. XXXVI, Pt. 1, p. 941; John F. Hartranft's report, *ibid,* 949–50; and William Humphrey's report, *ibid.,* 954. Willcox' other brigade, nominally under Christ, was commanded on May 12 by the 2nd Michigan's Colonel William Humphrey. The artillery that massed on the ridge included Captain Joseph W. B. Wright's 14th Massachusetts Battery, two sections from Captain Adelbert B. Twitchell's 7th Maine Battery, and two sections from Captain Edward W. Rogers' 19th New York Battery. See *OR,* XXXVI, Pt. 1, pp. 939, 954, 982.

89. Henry Heth's report, in MC; Wilcox' report, in VHS; Early, *Autobiographical Sketch and Narrative,* 355; Lane, "Battle of Spotsylvania Court-House," in *SHSP,* IX, 147, 150; James Eldred Phillips Memoir, in James Eldred Phillips Collection, VHS. Kirkland's brigade was positioned above Fredericksburg Road and Cooke's below the road. According to one account, Perry's Floridians were "behind breastworks a little to right of courthouse" (Fleming, ed., *Memoir of Captain C. Seton Fleming,* Appendix, May 12). An excellent attempt at reconstructing the brigade alignments appears in *If It Takes All Summer,* by Matter, 235–36.

90. Edmund Flournoy Record of Services, in *6th Virginia Infantry,* by Michael A. Cavanaugh (Lynchburg, Va., 1988), 45; Mills, *History of the 16th North Carolina Regiment,* 50; Charles P. Young, "War's Bravest Deeds: The Heroism of Private Chew Coleman, of Crenshaw's Battery," in *SHSP,* XXI, 374–75.

91. William D. Alexander Memorandum, in William D. Alexander Collection, SHC; Charlotte (N.C.) *Observer,* August 20, 1893.

92. Alexander Memorandum, in Alexander Collection, SHC. Wilcox wrote that Nicholson "ascertained that the enemy were in line facing the left face of [Heth's] salient, the right resting in the woods in front of the former face. Lane's Brigade filed into this woods, parallel to the right face. This brought it at right angles to the enemy's line" (Wilcox' report, in VHS).

93. Lane, "Battle of Spotsylvania Court-House," in *SHSP,* IX, 147–48; James S. Harris, *Historical Sketches of the Seventh Regiment North Carolina Troops* (Mooresville, N.C., 1893), 47; Wiggins, "Thirty-Seventh Regiment," in *Histories of the Several Regiments*

and Battalions from North Carolina, ed. Clark, 666–67. Lane's regiments, from right to left, were the 7th, 33rd, 37th, 18th, and 28th North Carolina.

94. Weisiger's role remains in dispute. There is no doubt that Lane attacked the guns, and there is also no doubt that Weisiger was heavily engaged against Burnside's infantry, implying that he struck the Federals north of Lane. Both Lane and Weisiger claimed Union battle flags, but some of those flags may have been taken from Federals who had already surrendered to other units. I am grateful to John Horn for helping me reconcile the contradictory accounts and for sharing with me his excellent manuscript on the 12th Virginia.

95. Lane, "Battle of Spotsylvania Court-House," in *SHSP,* IX, 148; Wiggins, "Thirty-Seventh Regiment," in *Histories of the Several Regiments and Battalions from North Carolina,* ed. Clark, 667; E.J.H., Jr., to unknown, May 17, 1864, Fayetteville (N.C.) *Observer,* May 26, 1864.

96. Edward W. Rogers' report, in *OR,* Vol. XXXVI, Pt. 1, p. 939; Humphrey's report, *ibid.,* 954–55; Lane, "Battle of Spotsylvania Court-House," in *SHSP,* IX, 149; James H. Lane to Seddon Carrington, in William Patterson Smith Collection, DU.

97. Constant Luce's report, in *OR,* Vol. XXXVI, Pt. 1, p. 958; Charles D. Todd Diary, May 12, 1864, in Gregory Coco Collection, USAMHI; George S. Bernard Diary, May 12, 1864, in George S. Bernard Collection, UV; John F. Sale Diary, May 12, 1864, in VSL; Phillips Memoir. After the war, Lane asserted that Weisiger played no significant part in the attack. Mahone disagreed, and the debate became bitter, with Jubal Early supporting Lane. See Early, *Autobiographical Sketch and Narrative,* 356; Charles S. Venable to Cadmus M. Wilcox, May 13, 1864, in *SHSP,* IX, 155; and Jubal A. Early to William Mahone, in *SHSP,* XVIII, 73–74. Weisiger's casualties—a man in the 12th Virginia reported the regiment's loss as "very heavy," including twelve killed, forty-two wounded, and three missing (Bernard Diary, May 14, 1864)—leave no doubt that the brigade was briskly engaged.

98. Byron M. Cutcheon's report, in *OR,* Vol. XXXVI, Pt. 1, p. 970; Irwin Field Diary, May 12, 1864, in Book 47, FSNMP.

99. Charles V. De Land's report, in *OR,* Vol. XXXVI, Pt. 1, p. 974; Cutcheon's report, *ibid.,* 960–70.

100. For an excellent description of the fighting on Leasure's front, see William G. Gavin, *Campaigning with the Roundheads: The History of the Hundredth Pennsylvania Volunteer Infantry Regiment in the American Civil War, 1861–1865* (Dayton, 1989), 416–20. See also William G. Gavin, ed., *Infantryman Pettit: The Civil War Letters of Corporal Frederick Pettit, Late of Company C, 100th Pennsylvania Volunteer Infantry Regiment, "The Roundheads," 1862–1864* (Shippensburg, Pa., 1990), 147–49; and Peter S. Carmichael, *Lee's Young Artillerist, William R. J. Pegram* (Charlottesville, Va., 1995), 118–20. Leasure was effectively finished for the war.

101. Early, *Autobiographical Sketch and Narrative,* 356; Folsom, *Heroes and Martyrs of Georgia,* 12; J. H. Moore, "How Archer's Tennesseeans Gave Relief to the Hard Pressed Center," Philadelphia *Weekly Times,* November 26, 1881; William H. Randall Reminiscences, in BL; Lane, "Battle of Spotsylvania Court-House," in *SHSP,* IX, 148–49.

102. Randall Reminiscences, 150, 152; James H. Lane to Peter A. Parker, June 30, 1893, in *Lee County Bulletin,* November 8, 1896; James H. Lane, "Incident of Individual Gallantry," in Military Collection, NCDAH; George S. Bernard Diary, May 14, 1864, in George S. Bernard Collection, UV; Charles E. Denoon to parents, May 15, 1864, in *Charlie's Letters: The Civil War Correspondence of Charles E. Denoon, 41st Virginia Infantry,*

Mahone's Brigade, Army of Northern Virginia, ed. Richard T. Couture (Collingwood, N.J., 1989), 96; Sale Diary, May 12, 1864. Lane's brushes with capture and death are detailed by McDaid in "Four Years of Arduous Service," 278. A southern newspaper carried a more flamboyant recital of Lane's brush with death, claiming that the unarmed general had been surrounded by a score of Yankees and ordered to surrender. According to the story, when the Federals declined Lane's command to throw down their arms instead, he remarked quietly, "Very well, wait a moment, till my line comes up." They quickly dropped their weapons, and the general escaped. See Fayetteville (N.C.) *Observer,* May 23, 1864.

103. John W. McGill's report, in James H. Lane Collection, AU.

104. Harris, *Historical Sketches of the Seventh Regiment North Carolina Troops,* 47–48; Lane, "Battle of Spotsylvania Court-House," in SHSP, IX, 151–52. According to Colonel John D. Barry, of the 18th North Carolina, Private Savage, of the 41st Virginia, came upon Grimsley and other Carolinians escorting Union prisoners and mistakenly concluded that the Federals had captured Grimsley and his companions. Savage "rescued" them, along with the disputed flag. Barry considered Savage's deed an "act, the daring and gallantry of which, like those of the vainglorious Knight Don Quixote, existed in his imagination without ever a Sancho Panza to witness his rash performances" (John Barry to Joseph Englehard, June 10, 1864, in Lane Collection, AU). A soldier in the 61st Virginia reported that his regiment captured numerous Federals, "among them several color sergeants with regimental colors"; he was "positively certain that our regiment was entitled to the credit of capturing one flag that was credited to another" (William H. Stewart, *A Pair of Blankets: War-Time History in Letters to the Young People of the South* [New York, 1914], 130). The debate about the flags is rehashed by McDaid in, "Four Years of Arduous Service," 277–82. Lane insisted that his men had captured the 17th Michigan's flag, as well as a flag from the 51st Pennsylvania and an artillery guidon. On May 13, he received a receipt from Lee's headquarters acknowledging the captures. Mahone claimed to have seized a different flag from the 51st Pennsylvania—which was not disputed—as well as the same 17th Michigan flag attributed to Lane. See correspondence in OR, XXXVI, Pt. 3, pp. 802–803.

105. "General Lee Compliments the Sharpshooters of Lane's Brigade," in *SHSP,* IX, 156; Charlotte (N.C.) *Observer,* August 20, 1893.

106. Early, *Autobiographical Sketch and Narrative,* 356–57; Samuel H. Walkup to unknown, in Samuel H. Walkup Collection, SHC. As the enraged Walkup put it in his letter, "We were then sent on a fool's errand, Cooke's and Mahone's brigades to flank the Yankee batteries, by drunken General Early under protest of our officers Cooke and Mahone."

107. Early, *Autobiographical Sketch and Narrative,* 357; Sloan, *Reminiscences of the Guilford Grays,* 90; Stewart, *A Pair of Blankets,* 131–32; Bernard Diary, May 12, 1864; Ambrose E. Burnside's report, in *OR,* Vol. XXXVI, Pt. 1, p. 910; Joseph Mullen, Jr., Diary, May 12, 1864, in MC. According to Mahone's ordnance officer, Niemeyer "lost his life in attempting to capture a beautiful iron gray horse elegantly caparisoned which was walking about riderless between the lines." Niemeyer was one of the Confederate army's most promising young officers, and his fall was "greatly lamented" (Westwood A. Todd Reminiscences, in Westwood A. Todd Collection, SHC.)

108. Howe, ed., *Touched with Fire,* 116; Andrew A. Humphreys to Ambrose R. Wright,

May 12, 1864, in *OR,* Vol. XXXVI, Pt. 2, p. 673; Ambrose R. Wright to Andrew A. Humphreys, May 12, 1864, in *OR,* Vol. XXXVI, Pt. 2, p. 673.

109. George G. Meade to Ulysses S. Grant, May 12, 1864, in *OR,* Vol. XXXVI, Pt. 2, p. 656; Ulysses S. Grant to Ambrose E. Burnside, *ibid.,* 679.

110. Lysander Cutler's report, in *OR,* Vol. XXXVI, Pt. 1, p. 611–12; Roe, *The Thirty-Ninth Regiment Massachusetts Volunteers,* 198; "Operations of the Iron Brigade in the Spring Campaign of 1864," in Oshkosh (Wis.) Public Museum; Pattison Diary, May 12, 1864.

111. Howard Barwis, "What Was Done by Russell's Brigade, First Division, Sixth Corps," *National Tribune,* September 3, 1891; "Avenged by His Comrade's Death," in *Deeds of Valor,* ed. Beyer and Keydel, 334. For more white-flag episodes, see Bowen, "General Edwards' Brigade at the Bloody Angle," in *B&L,* IV, 177; "Concurrent Testimony About an Interesting Incident of the War," in Charles Edgeworth Jones Collection, DU; and Robert R. Hemphill, "Gallant Enemies Become Friends in After Years," in FSNMP.

112. Joseph N. Brown, Address to Lee Chapter, November, 1900, in *A Colonel at Gettysburg and Spotsylvania,* by Brown, 100–101, 104–105; Nathan Church's report, in *OR,* Vol. XXXVI, Pt. 1, p. 373; Caldwell, *The History of a Brigade of South Carolinians,* 143–44.

113. Lentz's report, in *OR,* Vol. XXXVI, Pt. 1, p. 555; James A. Cunningham's report, *ibid.,* 570; Horatio G. Wright to Andrew A. Humphreys, May 12, 1864, *ibid.,* Pt. 2, pp. 674–75.

114. Wright to Humphreys, May 12, 1864, in *OR,* Vol. XXXVI, Pt. 2, p. 675.

115. John A. Rawlins to Ambrose E. Burnside, May 12, 1864, in *OR,* Vol. XXXVI, Pt. 2, p. 680; Ulysses S. Grant to Ambrose E. Burnside, May 12, 1864, *ibid.,* 681; Andrew A. Humphreys to Winfield S. Hancock, May 12, 1864, *ibid.,* 660; Andrew A. Humphreys to Gouverneur K. Warren, May 12, 1864, *ibid.,* 666; Andrew A. Humphreys to Horatio G. Wright, May 12, 1864, *ibid.,* 676; Horatio G. Wright to Andrew A. Humphreys, May 12, 1864, *ibid.*

116. Bratton's report, in OR, Vol. XXXVI, Pt. 1, p. 1067; Robert H. Anderson's report, in Robert H. Anderson Collection, DU; Sorrel Diary, May 12, 1864.

117. Edwards, "Spotsylvania, Va., May 12, 1864," in Edwards Collection, ISHL.

118. Best, *History of the 121st New York State Infantry,* 147; Westbrook, *History of the 49th Pennsylvania Volunteers,* 198; Keiser Diary, May 12, 1864.

119. Edwards, "Spotsylvania, Va., May 12, 1864," in Oliver Edwards Collection, ISHL.

120. Benedict, *Vermont in the Civil War,* I, 450; Merrit C. Welch's report, in *OR,* Vol. XXXVI, Pt. 1, p. 617; John Lucas Harding to family, May 17, 1864, in IU; Dawes, *Service with the Sixth Wisconsin Volunteers,* 268; Unidentified 24th Michigan soldier to unknown, May 13, 1864, in Sullivan Dexter Green Collection, BL; Cheek and Pointon, *History of the Sauk County Riflemen,* 97; Curtis, *History of the 24th Michigan,* 243. Lewis Grant's brigade sustained 254 casualties on May 12.

121. Caldwell, *The History of a Brigade of South Carolinians,* 147; Casler, *Four Years in the Stonewall Brigade,* 213–14.

122. Harris to Mahone, August 2, 1866, in Mahone Collection, VSL; Clark, *A Glance Backward,* 53; Brown to Brown, January 22, 1901, in *A Colonel at Gettysburg and Spot-*

sylvania, by Brown, 136; Edwards, "Spotsylvania, Va., May 12, 1864," in Edwards Collection, ISHL.

123. Holt, *A Mississippi Rebel,* 261–62.

124. Walter Raleigh Battle to mother, May 14, 1864, in *The Civil War Letters of George Boardman Battle and Walter Raleigh Battle,* ed. Johnston, 28; J. S. McMahon to family, May 14, 1864, Columbia (S.C.) *Daily Southern Guardian,* May 26, 1864; Conerly's account, in *Reminiscences of the Boys in Gray,* comp. Yeary, 150.

Epilogue

1. Dawes, *Service with the Sixth Wisconsin Volunteers,* 269; Charles Harvey Brewster to Mary, May 13, 1864, in *When This Cruel War Is Over,* ed. Blight, 296; Hyde, *Following the Greek Cross,* 202.

2. Chamberlin, *History of the One Hundred and Fiftieth Regiment Pennsylvania Volunteers,* 238–39; Houghton, *The Campaigns of the Seventeenth Maine,* 180; Stephen P. Chase Memoirs, in Civil War Times Illustrated Collection, USAMHI; Craft, *History of the One Hundred Forty First Regiment Pennsylvania Volunteers,* 195; Grant, "Review of Major-General F. C. Barlow's Paper," in *PMHSM,* IV, 270.

3. Dana, *Recollections of the Civil War,* 197.

4. *OR,* Vol. XXXVI, Pt. 2, pp. 724, 702, 713–14.

5. Humphreys, *The Virginia Campaign,* 104; Samuel S. Carroll's report, in *OR,* Vol. XXXVI, Pt. 1, p. 448; Winfield S. Hancock to Andrew A. Humphreys, May 13, 1864, in *OR,* Vol. XXXVI, Pt. 2, p. 704.

6. Dana, *Recollections of the Civil War,* 197.

7. Porter, *Campaigning with Grant,* 111.

8. Galloway, "Hand-to-Hand Fighting At Spotsylvania," in *B&L,* IV, 174; Fred Sanborn Memoir, May 13, 1864, in LC; Tyler, *Recollections of the Civil War,* 195.

9. Uberto Burnham to parents, May 14, 1864, in Uberto Burnham Collection, NYSLA.

10. George G. Meade's report, in *OR,* Vol. XXXVI, Pt. 1, p. 196; Humphreys, *The Virginia Campaign,* 104–105; Livermore, "Grant's Campaign Against Lee," in *PMHSM,* IV, 438; Sparks, ed., *Inside Lincoln's Army,* 372; Tabular List of Casualties in the Second Corps, RG 94, Entry 729, Box 92, NA; Tabular Statement of Casualties in Ninth Army Corps, RG 94, Entry 729, Box 93, NA. Albert Young generously shared his research with respect to Lee's losses.

11. Francis B. Carpenter, *Six Months at the White House with Abraham Lincoln* (New York, 1866), 283.

12. Charles H. Morgan to Gouverneur K. Warren, March 14, 1868, in Gouverneur K. Warren Collection, NYSLA; John C. Ropes, "Grant's Campaign in Virginia in 1864," in *PMHSM,* IV, 404–405.

13. Barlow, "Capture of the Salient, May 12, 1864," in *PMHSM,* IV, 256–57.

14. Winfield S. Hancock to Francis A. Walker, January 25, 1886, in Maine Commandery Folder, Military Order of the Loyal Legion of the United States Library and Museum, Philadelphia. Hancock had experienced a similar situation on May 6, when he charged Hill's formation on Orange Plank Road. Hill collapsed, but Hancock's troops were so jumbled from their advance that Longstreet was able to repel them with only two divisions.

15. Wilson, *Under the Old Flag,* I, 400–401. Talented officers were available to replace Wright, Warren, and Burnside. The 6th Corps included the likes of Upton, Grant, and Russell, all fine combat officers with a flair for initiative. The 5th Corps boasted such men as Griffin and Cutler. The 9th Corps held a wealth of talent in Potter, Willcox, Griffin, and Hartranft. And some of Hancock's exceptional subordinates—Barlow, Birney, Gibbon, and Miles, to name but a few—were of corps-commander caliber.

16. Charles A. Whittier, "Reminiscences of the War," 15, in Boston Public Library.

17. Badeau, *Military History of General Ulysses S. Grant,* II, 184; Wilson, *Under the Old Flag,* I, 397; George G. Meade to John A. Rawlins, June 21, 1864, in George G. Meade Collection, HSP.

18. Edward P. Alexander, "Grant's Conduct of the Wilderness Campaign," in *Annual Report of the American Historical Association* (N.p., 1908), 225.

19. Porter, *Campaigning with Grant,* 115.

20. Ulysses S. Grant's report, in *OR,* Vol. XXXVI, Pt. 1, p. 18; George G. Meade to wife, May 19, 1864, in Meade Collection, HSP; James C. Biddle to wife, May 16, 1864, in James C. Biddle Collection, HSP; Hyde, *Following the Greek Cross,* 200.

21. Humphreys, *The Virginia Campaign,* 83n1; Badeau, *Military History of General Ulysses S. Grant,* II, 186–87.

22. Meade's report, in *OR,* Vol. XXXVI, Pt. 1, p. 195; Humphreys, *The Virginia Campaign,* 104–105; Livermore, "Grant's Campaign Against Lee," in *PMHSM,* IV, 438.

23. Walker, *History of the Second Army Corps,* 464, 476–81; Tabular List of Casualties in the Second Corps, RG 94, Entry 729, Box 92, NA.

24. Tabular List of Casualties in the Fifth Corps, RG 94, Entry 729, Box 69, NA; Tabular Statement of Casualties in Ninth Army Corps, RG 94, Entry 729, Box 93, NA. The aide Holmes reported 6th Corps casualties as of May 13 at 10,547. See Howe, ed., *Touched with Fire,* 117.

25. Walter H. Taylor to Bettie Saunders, May 15, 1864, in *Lee's Adjutant: The Wartime Letters of Colonel Walter Herron Taylor, 1862–1865,* ed. R. Lockwood Tower (Columbia, S.C., 1995), 160; Alfred M. Scales to wife, May 20, 1864, in Alfred M. Scales Collection, East Carolina University.

26. Charles M. Blackford to wife, May 19, 1864, in *Letters from Lee's Army; or, Memories of Life in and out of the Army in Virginia During the War Between the States,* comp. Susan Leigh Blackford (New York, 1947), 246; Louis Warlick to Corrie, May 19, 1864, in Cornelia McGimsey Collection, SHC.

27. Robert E. Lee to secretary of war, May 12, 1864, in *OR,* Vol. XXXVI, Pt. 2, p. 993; Robert E. Lee to secretary of war, May 13, 1864, *ibid.,* 998; Robert E. Lee to Jefferson Davis, in *The Wartime Papers of R. E. Lee,* ed. Clifford Dowdey (New York, 1961), 729.

28. F. H. C. to Pa, May 13, 1864, Salisbury (N.C.) *Daily Carolina Watchman,* May 13, 1864; William H. Runge, ed., *Four Years in the Confederate Artillery: The Diary of Private Henry Robinson Berkeley* (Chapel Hill, N.C., 1961), 75–76. During the height of Burnside's attack against Heth's salient, Lee galloped to the front along a road that was under heavy artillery fire. After conferring with Early over the management of his guns, Lee dispatched a courier, who started off along the same road Lee had taken. "Have that officer take a road nearer the rear of the line of guns," Lee admonished. "It is safer that way" (William W. Chamberlaine, *Memoirs of the Civil War Between the Northern and Southern Sections of the United States of America* [Washington, D.C., 1912], 100).

29. Old, "Personal Reminiscences," in *SHSP,* XXXIII, 24; Armistead L. Long's report,

in *OR*, Vol. XXXVI, Pt. 1, pp. 1086–87; Alexander, *Military Memoirs of a Confederate*, 520. The artillerist Carter considered the salient "absolutely impregnable against successful assault" so long as it had infantry and artillery support (Thomas H. Carter to editor of Richmond *Times*, n.d., in *SHSP*, XXI, 240). The aide McHenry Howard asserted that the "absence of the artillery was fatal" (Howard, *Recollections of a Maryland Confederate*, 298).

30. Howard reported that either Ewell or Ewell's assistant adjutant general told him that Lee received a dispatch alerting him that the enemy was massing to attack, and that Lee also "ordered the artillery to be back at daylight" (Howard, *Recollections of a Maryland Confederate*, 294–95n14). Long reported that he received word to return the guns at 3:30 A.M.; Carter said that the order reached him twenty minutes before daybreak, and Page reported receiving his instructions at 3:40. See Long's report, in *OR*, Vol. XXXVI, Pt. 1, p. 1086; Carter to editor of Richmond *Times*, n.d., in *SHSP*, XXI, 240; R. C. M. Page to S. V. Southall, September 15, 1879, in *SHSP*, VII, 535.

31. William Allen's notes of a conversation with Lee, March 3, 1868, in William Allen Collection, SHC.

32. Edward Johnson's report, in *OR*, Vol. XXXVI, Pt. 1, p. 1080; Richard S. Ewell's report, *ibid.*, 1072; Overton Steger to unknown, May 16, 1864, in Lewis Leigh Collection, USAMHI; George D. Bushnell Diary, May 12, 1864, in FSNMP; Jones, ed., *The Civil War Memoirs of Captain William J. Seymour*, 124; Mary C. Moffett, ed., *Letters of General James Conner, C.S.A.* (Columbia, S.C., 1933), 129; Robert E. Withers to friend, May 16, 1864, Lynchburg (Va.) *Daily Virginian*, May 23, 1864. Johnson's staff officer Old recounted that Lee and Ewell later "spoke in the kindest manner of General Johnson and commended him for his bravery and the faithful discharge of his duties, General Ewell saying that he never failed to carry out his orders, both without question and with intelligence, and they both exonerated him from any blame for the disaster" (Old, "Personal Reminiscences," in *SHSP*, XXXIII, 24).

33. Walker, "The Bloody Angle," in *SHSP*, XXI, 237; Ewell's report, in *OR*, Vol. XXXVI, Pt. 1, p. 1073; Page to Southall, September 15, 1879, in *SHSP*, VII, 535–37; Worsham, *One of Jackson's Foot Cavalry*, 135–36. Walker observed that the "famous Stonewall Brigade, which had won renown on so many battlefields, ceased to exist as a separate organization, and the few remaining members, not above two hundred in all, with the other fragments of Johnson's division, were incorporated into a single brigade, called Terry's brigade" (p. 237).

34. Lee's losses are discussed by J. Michael Miller in *The North Anna Campaign: Even to Hell Itself* (Lynchburg, Va., 1989), 7–8; by Livermore in "Grant's Campaign Against Lee," in *PMHSM*, IV, 438; and by Humphreys in *The Virginia Campaign*, 105–106. Alfred Young was helpful in calculating approximate Confederate losses.

35. W. Gordon McCabe, "Major Andrew Reid Venable, Jr.," in *SHSP*, XXXVII, 68; Alexander Boteler Diary, May 13, 1864, in William E. Brooks Collection, LC.

36. Porter, *Campaigning with Grant*, 113; Cyrus B. Comstock Diary, May 13, 1864, in Cyrus B. Comstock Collection, LC.

37. Ulysses S. Grant to Henry Halleck, May 12, 1864, in *OR*, Vol. XXXVI, Pt. 2, p. 652; Ulysses S. Grant to Julia D. Grant, May 13, 1864, in *The Papers of Ulysses S. Grant*, ed. John Y. Simon (20 vols.; Carbondale, Ill., 1967–95), X, 443–44.

38. George G. Meade to Margaret Meade, May 13, 1864, in Meade Collection, HSP; Circular, May 13, 1864, in *OR*, Vol. XXXVI, Pt. 1, p. 197.

39. James C. Biddle to wife, May 13, 1864, in Biddle Collection, HSP; Samuel E. Pingree to father, May 13, 1864, in Pingree Family Collection, Vermont Historical Society, Montpelier; John A. Willoughby to James R. Simpson, May 13, 1864, in Civil War Miscellaneous Collection, USAMHI; Thomas H. Capern to mother, May 15, 1864, in Leigh Collection, USAMHI; George L. Prescott to Sallie, May 13, 1864, in George L. Prescott Collection, MHS; George M. Barnard to father, May 11, May 13–14, 1864, both in George M. Barnard Collection, MHS.

40. Richard Elliott Winslow III, *General John Sedgwick: The Story of a Union Corps Commander* (Novato, Calif., 1982), 175–76.

41. Emory M. Thomas, *Bold Dragoon: The Life of J. E. B. Stuart* (New York, 1986), 296; Richmond *Examiner,* May 14, 1864; Trout, ed., *Riding with Stuart . . . by . . . Garnett,* 73.

42. Special Order, in *OR,* Vol. XXXVI, Pt. 2, p. 700; Ulysses S. Grant to Ambrose E. Burnside, May 13, 1864, *ibid.,* 732; Dana, *Recollections of the Civil War,* 198; Charles A. Dana to Edwin M. Stanton, May 13, 1864, in *OR,* Vol. XXXVI, Pt. 1, p. 69.

43. Humphreys, *The Virginia Campaign,* 107.

Bibliography

MANUSCRIPTS

Alabama Department of Archives and History, Montgomery

Battle, Cullen A. "The Third Alabama Regiment."
Thompson, James M. "Reminiscences of the Autauga Rifles."

Auburn University Libraries, Special Collections

James H. Lane Collection
    Barry, John. Letter.
    James H. Lane's Report.
    Report of 7th North Carolina.
    Report of 18th North Carolina.
    Report of 28th North Carolina.
    Report of 37th North Carolina.

Boston Public Library

Josiah F. Murphey Reminiscences.
Charles A. Whittier Reminiscences.

Boston University, Mugar Memorial Library

Military Historical Society of Massachusetts Collection
    Mahone, William. Letter.
    Upton, Emory. Letters.

Confederate Research Center, Hillsboro, Tex.

Joskins, Joe. "A Sketch of Hood's Texas Brigade of the Virginia Army."
Nicholas Pomeroy Memoir.
Smither, J. Mark. Letter.
Williams, Watson D. Letter.

Cornell University, John M. Olin Library

Crocker, John S. Letters and Diary.

Duke University, William R. Perkins Library

Richard H. Anderson's Report.
Bradbury, Samuel. Letter.
Cooke, John Esten. Letter.
John W. Daniel Collection.
  Robert D. Johnston Memorandum.
Dillard, John J. Letter.
Edward Harden Collection.
  Emery, Edwin. Letter.
  Jackson, Asbury H. Letter.
Charles Edgeworth Jones Collection.
  "Concurrent Testimony About an Interesting Incident of the War."
Thomas T. Munford Collection.
  J. D. Ferguson Memoranda.
  Goler, G. W. Letter.
Scott, Irby G. Letter.
Shockley, William S. Letter.
William Patterson Smith Collection.
  Lane, James H. Letter.

East Carolina University, J. Y. Joyner Library

Scales, Alfred M. Letter.

Fredericksburg and Spotsylvania National Military Park Library

Charles Thomas Bowen Diary.
George A. Bowen Diary.
Stephen D. Burger Diary.
George D. Bushnell Diary.
James A. Cadwallader Diary.
Chandler, Silas. Letter.
B. Y. Draper Diary.
Irwin Field Diary.
Haywood, Albert M. Letter.
Hemphill, Robert R. "Gallant Enemies Become Friends in After Years."
John E. Irwin Diary.
Johnston, Robert D. "Gen. Lee's Story."
John E. Kittle Diary.
L. O. Merriam Recollections.
"Life of Amos G. Bean as a Soldier."

Miller, Abram Schultz. Letter.
Minor, Henry. Letter.
Allen Parker Diary.
Powell, Ben M. Letter.
Kenneth H. Power Memoir.
Edward Perkins Preble Diary.
Robertson, Robert S. Letters.
Seibert, Jacob. Letter.
William P. Snakenberg Memoir.
Horatio S. Soule Diary.
Cyrenus Pullen Stevens Diary.
Thompson, Alfred. Letter.
Unknown 15th New Jersey Soldier Diary.
Vogt, Stuart G. "The Death of Major-General John
    Sedgwick, U.S.A., May 9, 1864."
Franklin Gardner Walter Diary.
J. T. Watkins Memoir.
Joseph S. Wicklein Memoir.
Worsham, John H. Letter.

Georgia Department of Archives and History, Atlanta

Joseph P. Fuller Diary.
Gillespie Family Papers.
    Bush, William H. H. Letter.
George W. Hopkins Memorandum.
United Daughters of the Confederacy Collection.
    Stilwell, W. R. Letter.
    William A. Wright Memorandum.

Hampden-Sydney College, Eggleston Library

William R. Carter Diary.

Handley Library, Winchester, Va.

James L. McCown Memoirs.

Harvard University, Houghton Library

Simon G. Griffin Memorandum.

Rutherford B. Hayes Presidential Center, Fremont, Ohio

Frederick W. Swift Diary.

Historical Society of Pennsylvania, Philadelphia

Biddle, James C. Letters.

E. C. Gardner Collection.
  Baird, Henry B. Letter.
Humphreys, Andrew A. Letters.
Meade, George G. Letters.

Historical Society of Schuylkill County, Pottsville, Pa.

Lewis Luckenbill Diary.

Illinois State Historical Library, Springfield

Edwards, Oliver. "Spotsylvania, Va., May 12th, 1864."

Indiana Historical Society, Indianapolis

Alexander B. Pattison Diary.

Indiana University, Lilly Library

64th New York Memoir.
Harding, John Lucas. Letter.

Jones Memorial Library, Lynchburg, Va.

Samuel B. Rucker Recollections.

Library of Congress, Manuscript Division

Arnold, John C. Letter.
William O. Bourne Collection.
  Boos, Louis. "My Experience as a Soldier."
  George Bucknam Memoir.
  James Maguire Memorandum.
Brinckle, John R. Letter.
William E. Brooks Collection.
  Alexander R. Boteler Diary.
Cyrus B. Comstock Diary.
Harold C. George Collection.
  S. F. Hildebrand Manuscript.
George W. Hall Diary.
William G. Hills Diary.
Jedediah Hotchkiss Collection.
  Thomas S. Doyle Memoir.
  Jedediah Hotchkiss' Report.
Henry J. Hunt Journal.
Larned, Daniel Reed. Letter.
James W. Latta Diary.
Alexander Newberger Daily Journal.
Maud Wood Park Collection.

James Wood Manuscript.
Charles W. Reed Diary.
Luther A. Rose Diary.
Fred Sanborn Memoir.
Walter Ralph Steiner Collection.
Francis A. Boyle Diary.
Gilbert Thompson Journal.
John Chester White Journal.
James H. Wilson Diary.

Louisiana State University Libraries, Special Collections

Albert A. Bachelor Collection.
Cobb, R. G. Letter.

Manassas National Battlefield Park Library

James B. Ricketts Collection.
James M. Read Diary.

Maryland Historical Society, Baltimore

Gibbon, John. Letters.
Phelps, Charles E. "Personal Recollection of the Wilderness Campaign."

Massachusetts Historical Society, Boston

Barlow, Francis C. Letters.
Barnard, George M. Letters.
Linscott, Andrew R. Letter.
Lyman, Theodore. Letters and Journal.
Prescott, George L. Letters.

Michigan State University Libraries

Newton T. Kirk Reminiscences.

Military Order of the Loyal Legion of the United States Library and Museum, Philadelphia

Maine Commandery Folder.
Hancock, Winfield S. Letter.

Mississippi Department of History and Archives, Jackson

Holt, David E. "The Death Angle: War at Its Worst."

Museum of the Confederacy, Eleanor S. Brockenbrough Library, Richmond

T. M. Fowler Memoir.
Henry Heth's Report.

Fitzhugh Lee's Report.
Joseph Mullen, Jr., Diary.
G. Moxley Sorrel Diary.

National Archives, Washington, D.C.

Record Group 94: The Adjutant General's Office.
2nd Corps Casualty Returns. Entry 729, Box 92.
5th Corps Casualty Returns. Entry 729, Box 69.
9th Corps Casualty Returns. Entry 729, Box 93.
Regimental Casualty Lists. Entry 652.

New York State Library and Archives, Albany

Albert N. Ames Diary and Letters.
Burnham, Uberto. Letters.
Gouverneur K. Warren Collection.
5th Corps Letterbooks.
Washington A. Roebling's Report.
Gouverneur K. Warren Diary and Letters.

North Carolina Department of Archives and History, Raleigh

Henry Clay Albright Diary.
William E. Ardrey Diary.
J. B. Clifton Diary.
Harper, Samuel Finley. Letter.
George Holland Collection.
D. Lane Recollections.
Lane, James H. "Incident of Individual Gallantry."
Pearsoll, George W. Letters.
Lowry Shuford Collection.
J. W. Bone Reminiscences.
J. A. Stikeleather Reminiscences.

Ontario County Historical Society, Canandaigua, N.Y.

Lee, Henry. Letter.

Oshkosh (Wis.) Public Museum

"Operations of the Iron Brigade in the Spring Campaign of 1864."

Richmond National Battlefield Park Library

John Hoffman Diary.

Rundel Library, Rochester, N.Y.

Farley, Porter. "The 140th New York Volunteers."

Michael T. Russert Private Collection, Cambridge, New York

Edgar O. Burts Diary.
George Perkins Memoir.

South Portland (Maine) Public Library

James Otis Kaler Collection.
"Albert Marsh, 64th New York Infantry."
John H. Weeks Memorandum.

State Historical Society of Wisconsin, Madison

5th Wisconsin Association Pamphlet.
Fairfield, George. Letter.
Johnson, John O. Letter.

Tennessee State Library and Archives, Nashville

Ewell-Brown Collection.
  Campbell Brown Memoir.

Tulane University Libraries, Louisiana Historical Association Collection

Ring, George P. Letter.

United States Army Military History Institute, Carlisle, Pa.

Zenas R. Bliss Memoirs.
Civil War Miscellaneous Collection.
  Alfred M. Apted Diary.
  Samuel A. Beddall Diary.
  Henry C. Carr Diary.
  Elbert Corbin Diary.
  Grayson M. Eichelberger Memoir.
  Charles A. Griffin Diary.
  Burgess E. Ingersoll Diary.
  Marks, Samuel J. Letter.
  Henry P. Turner Diary.
  Willoughby, John A. Letter.
  Charles E. Wood Diary.
Civil War Times Illustrated Collection.
  Stephen P. Chase Memoirs.
Coburn Family Papers.
  James P. Coburn Memoir.
Gregory Coco Collection.
  Frederick W. Swift Diary.
  Charles D. Todd Diary.

Halsey, Edmund D. "Official Report of Movements of 15th N.J. During Grant's
    Wilderness Campaign."
Edmund D. Halsey Diary.
Avery Harris Reminiscences.
Harrisburg Civil War Round Table Collection.
    Del Vecchio, Richard J. "With the First New York Dragoons."
    Henry Keiser Diary.
    Maurus Oestreich Diary.
    Cyrenus Pullen Stevens Diary.
    Henry Harrison Stone Diary.
Lewis Leigh Collection.
    Capern, Thomas H. Letter.
    Charles. Letter.
    Robert P. Chew's Report
    Powers, Philip H. Letters.
    Smith, William F. Letters.
    Steger, Overton. Letter.
    Unknown Confederate Soldier. Letter.
    Webb, John G. Letter.
Michael Winey Collection.
    Isaac R. Dunkleberger Memoir.

University of Georgia Libraries

George W. Hall Diary.

University of Michigan, Bentley Historical Library

Byron M. Cutcheon Autobiography.
Sullivan Dexter Green Papers.
    Burchell, George W. Letter.
George G. Hopper Reminiscences.
William H. Randall Reminiscences.
James D. Rowe Reminiscences.

University of Michigan, William L. Clements Library

James S. Schoff Collection.
    Best, Isaac O. "Through the Wilderness with Grant."
    Bunker, Nathaniel W. "War Record."

University of New Hampshire Libraries

Howard M. Hanson Diary.

University of North Carolina, Southern Historical Collection

Alexander, Edward P. Letter.
William D. Alexander Memorandum and Diary.

William Allen Notes.
Bernard, George. Letters.
Francis A. Boyle Diary.
James Breathed's Report.
Nobel J. Brooks Diary.
J. F. H. Claiborne Collection.
  Humphreys, Benjamin G. "Sunflower Guards."
William P. DuBose Reminiscences.
Joseph F. Fuller Diary.
James E. Green Diary.
Grimes, Bryan. Letters.
Harris, Nathaniel. Letter.
Kenneth Rayner Jones Diary.
William N. McDonald Manuscript.
Cornelia McGimsey Collection.
  Warlick, Louis. Letter.
David Gregg McIntosh Memoir.
Parsley, Eliza H. Letter.
Pendleton, William N. Letter.
Stephen D. Ramseur Collection.
  "General Lee's Story, As Told on the Battlefield, and Recalled by General
  R. D. Johnston, of Alabama."
Anne L. Snuggs Collection.
  Linebarger, James T. Letter.
Westwood A. Todd Reminiscences.
Walkup, Samuel H. Letter.
Joseph F. Waring Diary.
Warlick, Louis. Letter.

University of South Carolina, South Caroliniana Library

Wade Hampton's Report.

University of Virginia, Alderman Library

George S. Bernard Diary.
Couse, Katherine. Letter.

Vermont Historical Society, Montpelier

Pingree, Samuel E. Letters.

Virginia Historical Society, Richmond

St. George Tucker Brook Memoir.
Oscar O. Mull Diary.
James Eldred Phillips Memoir.

Buckner McGill Randolph Diary.
Leiper Moore Robinson Memoir.
Alfred L. Scott Memoir.
Charles S. Venable Collection.
  Gordon, John B. Letter.
Cadmus M. Wilcox' Report.

Virginia State Library, Richmond

William Mahone Collection.
  Harris, Nathaniel. Letter.
John F. Sale Diary.
Bird Willis Diary.

Western Reserve Historical Society, Cleveland

William P. Palmer Collection.
Well A. Bushnell Memoir.

NEWSPAPERS

Atlanta *Journal,* July 20, October 16, 1901.
Atlanta *Southern Confederacy,* April 15, June 15, 1864.
Atlanta *Sunny South,* May 2, 1891.
Augusta (Ga.) *Chronicle,* June 1, 1864.
Boston *Daily Advertiser,* May 10, 1864.
Boston *Evening Transcript,* May 12, 1864.
Charleston (S.C.) *Daily Courier,* May 28, 1864.
Charlotte (N.C.) *Observer,* August 20, 1893.
Charlotte (N.C.) *Western Democrat,* May 31, 1864.
Columbia (S.C.) *Daily Southern Guardian,* May 26, 1864.
Columbus (Ga.) *Daily Sun,* December 22, 1865.
Fayetteville (N.C.) *Observer,* May 23, 26, 1864.
Fredericksburg (Va.) *Free Lance,* April 29, 1887.
Irish American, June 21, 1864.
Lynchburg (Va.) *Daily Virginian,* May 23, 1864.
Lynchburg (Va.) *Republican,* May 20, 1864.
Macon (Ga.) *Telegraph,* June 4, 10, 1864.
New Bern (N.C.) *Our Living and Our Dead,* January 14, 15, 1874.
New York *Daily Tribune,* May 10, 12, 1864.
New York *Herald,* May 11, 17, 1864.
New York *Times,* May 13, 1864.
Philadelphia *Inquirer,* May 12, 1864.
Philadelphia *Weekly Press,* October 27, 1886, August 10, October 12, 1887.

Philadelphia *Weekly Times,* January 8, September 3, November 26, 1881, November 18, 1882, February 3, 1883, February 16, 1884, February 20, 1886.
Putnam County (Ga.) *Countryman,* June 14, 1864.
Raleigh (N.C.) *Daily Confederate,* May 23, 25, 26, 1864, February 22, 1865.
Richmond *Daily Dispatch,* May 9, 10, 18, 1864.
Richmond *Daily Examiner,* May 11, 14, 21, 1864.
Richmond *Dispatch,* June 2, 1864, June 20, 1897.
Richmond *Enquirer,* May 17, 1864.
Richmond *Sentinel,* May 9, 21, 1864.
Richmond *Whig,* May 23, 1864.
Rochester (N.Y.) *Union and Advertisers,* May 18, 1864.
Salisbury (N.C.) *Daily Carolina Watchman,* May 30, 1864.
Savannah (Ga.) *Republican,* May 29, 1864.
Washington (N.J.) *Star,* February 9, 1911.
Wilmington (N.C.) *Daily Journal,* May 24, June 17, 1864.

OFFICIAL COMPILATIONS

Annual Report of the Adjutant-General of the State of Connecticut for the Year Ending March 31, 1865. New Haven, 1865.
Harrison, Noel G. *Gazetteer of Historic Sites Related to the Fredericksburg and Spotsylvania National Military Park.* 2 vols. Fredericksburg, Va., 1986.
War of the Rebellion: A Compilation of the Official Records of the Union and Confederate Armies. 130 vols. Washington, D.C., 1880–1901.

BIOGRAPHIES, MEMOIRS, AND NARRATIVES

Agassiz, George R., ed., *Meade's Headquarters, 1863–1865: Letters of Colonel Theodore Lyman from the Wilderness to Appomattox.* Boston, 1922.
Alexander, Edward P. *Military Memoirs of a Confederate.* New York, 1907.
Allen, Stanton P. *Down in Dixie: Life in a Cavalry Regiment in the War Days, from the Wilderness to Spotsylvania.* Boston, 1892.
Ambrose, Stephen E. *Upton and the Army.* Baton Rouge, 1964.
Anderson, J. S. "Through the Wilderness with Grant." In *Report of the Proceedings of 5th Wisconsin Volunteer Infantry.* Chicago, 1902.
Arner, Frederick B. *The Mutiny at Brandy Station: The Last Battle of the Hooker Brigade.* Kensington, Md., 1993.
Arnold, Abraham K. "A War Reminiscence: The Fifth U.S. Regular Cavalry with General Sheridan on Raid Towards Richmond, Va., in 1864." *Journal of the United States Cavalry Association,* II (1889), 28–33.
Bache, Richard Meade. *Life of General George Gordon Meade, Commander of the Army of the Potomac.* Philadelphia, 1897.
Badeau, Adam. *Military History of General Ulysses S. Grant, from April, 1861, to April, 1865.* 3 vols. New York, 1881.

Barlow, Francis C. "Capture of the Salient, May 12, 1864." In *PMHSM*, IV, 245–62.

Barton, Randolph. "Confederate Troops at Spotsylvania C.H." *Confederate Veteran*, XIX (1911), 291.

Barwis, Howard. "What Was Done by Russell's Brigade, First Division, Sixth Corps." *National Tribune*, September 3, 1891.

Bennett, Edwin C. *Musket and Sword; or, The Camp, March, and Firing Line in the Army of the Potomac*. Boston, 1900.

Benson, Susan W., ed. *Berry Benson's Civil War Book: Memoirs of a Confederate Scout and Sharpshooter*. Athens, Ga., 1991.

Beyer, W. F., and O. F. Keydel, eds. *Deeds of Valor: How America's Civil War Heroes Won the Congressional Medal of Honor*. Stamford, Conn., 1992.

Black, John D. "Reminiscences of the Bloody Angle." In *Glimpses of the Nation's Struggle: Papers Read Before the Commandery of the State of Minnesota, Military Order of the Loyal Legion of the United States, 1892–1897*, 1–17. St. Paul, 1898.

Blackford, Susan Leigh, comp. *Letters From Lee's Army; or, Memories of Life in and out of the Army in Virginia During the War Between the States*. New York, 1947.

Blackford, William W. *War Years with Jeb Stuart*. New York, 1945.

Blake, Henry N. *Three Years in the Army of the Potomac*. Boston, 1865.

Blight, Dwight W., ed. *When This Cruel War Is Over: The Civil War Letters of Charles Harvey Brewster*. Amherst, Mass., 1992.

Booth, George W. *Personal Reminiscences of a Maryland Soldier in the War Between the States*. Baltimore, 1898.

Bowley, Free B. "A Boy Lieutenant in a Black Regiment." *National Tribune*, May 4, 1899.

Boyd, David French. *Reminiscences of the War in Virginia*. Edited by T. Michael Parrish. Austin, Tex., 1989.

Bradwell, I. G. "Spotsylvania, May 12, 13, 1864." *Confederate Veteran*, XXVIII (1920), 102–103.

———. "Spotsylvania, Va., May 8 and 9, 1864." *Confederate Veteran*, XXVIII (1920), 56–57.

Brown, Varina D. *A Colonel at Gettysburg and Spotsylvania*. Columbia, S.C., 1931.

Buck, Samuel D. *With the Old Confeds: Actual Experiences of a Captain in the Line*. Baltimore, 1925.

Buell, Augustus. *The Cannoneer: Recollections of Service in the Army of the Potomac*. Washington, D.C., 1890.

Bumgardner, James, Jr. "Memorial Day Speech." In *SHSP*, VIII, 34–35.

Caldwell, Willie Walker. *Stonewall Jim: A Biography of General James A. Walker, C.S.A.* Elliston, Va., 1990.

Carmichael, Peter S. *Lee's Young Artillerist, William R. J. Pegram.* Charlottesville, Va., 1995.

Carpenter, Francis B. *Six Months at the White House with Abraham Lincoln.* New York, 1866.

Carter, Robert G. *Four Brothers in Blue; or, Sunshine and Shadows of the War of the Rebellion.* Austin, Tex., 1978.

Casler, John O. *Four Years in the Stonewall Brigade.* Girard, Kans., 1906.

"Cavalry's Bold Move." *National Tribune,* April 15, 1897.

Chamberlain, S. A. "Plenty to Do in Old Virginia in the Spring of 1864." *National Tribune,* April 16, 1896.

Chamberlaine, William W. *Memoirs of the Civil War Between the Northern and Southern Sections of the United States of America.* Washington, D.C., 1912.

Clark, George. "From the Rapidan to Petersburg." *Confederate Veteran,* XVIII (1909), 381–82.

―――. *A Glance Backward; or, Some Events in the Past History of My Life.* Houston, 1914.

Coakley, Stephen W. "Count Van Haake: His Death in the Wilderness—Harrowing Experience in the Burning Woods." *National Tribune,* September 17, 1908.

Coco, Gregory A., ed. *Through Blood and Fire: The Civil War Letters of Major Charles J. Mills, 1862–1865.* Lanham, Md., 1982.

Coffman, A. S. "Diary, 1864." *Augusta Historical Bulletin,* XXVIII (1992), 17–28.

Coles, Robert T. *From Huntsville to Appomattox.* Edited by Jeffrey D. Stocker. Knoxville, Tenn., 1996.

Colt, Margaretta Barton, comp. *Defend the Valley: A Shenandoah Family in the Civil War.* New York, 1994.

Couture, Richard T. *Charlie's Letters: The Civil War Correspondence of Charles E. Denoon, 41st Virginia Infantry, Mahone's Brigade, Army of Northern Virginia.* Collingwood, N.J., 1989.

Covert, Norman M., ed. *Two Civil War Diaries: Sgt. John L. Ryno and Bandmaster John Chadwick, Company C, 126th New York Regiment, 3rd Brigade, 2nd Division, II U.S. Corps.* N.p., n.d.

Cox, William R. "Major General Stephen D. Ramseur: His Life and Character." In *SHSP,* XVIII, 217–60.

Coxe, John. "Last Struggles and Successes of Lee." *Confederate Veteran,* XXII (1914), 356–59.

Dame, William M. *From the Rapidan to Richmond and the Spotsylvania Campaign.* Baltimore, 1920.

Dana, Charles A. *Recollections of the Civil War.* New York, 1899.

Daniel, John W. "Major-General Johnson at Spotsylvania." In *SHSP,* XXXIII, 335–36.

Davies, Henry E. *General Sheridan.* New York, 1895.

"The Death of Major-General J. E. B. Stuart." In *SHSP,* VII, 107–109.

Debeck, George W. "Laurel Hill." *National Tribune,* October 31, 1895.

Dobbins, Austin C., ed. *Grandfather's Journal: Company B, Sixteenth Mississippi Infantry Volunteers, Harris' Brigade, Mahone's Division, Hill's Corps, A.N.V.* Dayton, 1988.

Dorsey, Frank. "Fatal Wounding of General J. E. B. Stuart." In *SHSP,* XXX, 236–38.

Douglas, Henry Kyd. *I Rode with Stonewall.* Chapel Hill, N.C., 1968.

Dowdey, Clifford, ed. *The Wartime Papers of R. E. Lee.* New York, 1961.

Dunham, Samuel. "Spotsylvania: A 63rd Pennsylvania Comrade Tells About the Fight." *National Tribune,* June 10, 1886.

Durkin, Joseph, ed. *Confederate Chaplin: A War Journal of Rev. James B. Sheeran, C.S.S.R., 14th Louisiana, C.S.A.* Milwaukee, 1960.

Early, Jubal A. *Autobiographical Sketch and Narrative of the War Between the States.* Bloomington, Ind., 1960.

Eckert, Ralph Lowell. *John Brown Gordon—Soldier, Southerner, American.* Baton Rouge, 1989.

Edwards, Oliver. "Battle of Spotsylvania: The Defense of the Angle." In *Camp-Fire Sketches and Battle-Field Echoes,* comp. William C. King and W. P. Derby, 308–10. Springfield, Mass., 1888.

Evans, Clement A. "Northern Boys in Southern Armies." *Confederate Veteran,* V (1897), 5–6.

———. "The Twelfth of May." In *Report of the Gordon Monument Commission,* 42–45. N.p., 1907.

Farley, Porter. "Reminiscences of the 140th Regiment New York Volunteer Infantry." *Rochester Historical Society Publication,* XXII (1944), 199–253.

Favill, Josiah M. *The Diary of a Young Officer Serving with the Armies of the United States During the War of the Rebellion.* Chicago, 1909.

Field, Charles W. "Campaign of 1864 and 1865." In *SHSP,* XIV, 542–63.

Fleming, Francis P., ed. *Memoir of Captain C. Seton Fleming, of the Second Florida Infantry, C.S.A.* Alexandria, Va., 1985.

Fleming, V. M. "How General Sedgwick Was Killed." *Confederate Veteran,* XVI (1908), 347.

Fowler, Philemon H. *Memorials of William Fowler.* New York, 1875.

Freeman, Douglas Southall. *Lee's Lieutenants.* 3 vols. New York, 1949–51.

———. *R. E. Lee: A Biography.* 4 vols. New York, 1934–35.

———. ed. *Lee's Dispatches to Jefferson Davis.* New York, 1957.

Funkhouser, R. D. "General Lee About to Enter Battle." *Confederate Veteran,* II (1894), 36–37.

Gallagher, Gary W., *Stephen Dodson Ramseur: Lee's Gallant General.* Chapel Hill, N.C., 1985.

———, ed. *Fighting for the Confederacy: The Personal Recollections of General Edward Porter Alexander.* Chapel Hill, N.C., 1989.

Galloway, G. Norton. "Hand-to-Hand Fighting at Spotsylvania." In *B&L*, IV, 170–74.

Galwey, Thomas F. *The Valiant Hours: An Irishman in the Civil War.* Harrisburg, Pa., 1961.

Gavin, William G., ed. *Infantryman Pettit: The Civil War Letters of Corporal Frederick Pettit, Late of Company C, 100th Pennsylvania Veteran Volunteer Infantry Regiment, "The Roundheads," 1862–1864.* Shippensburg, Pa., 1990.

"General Lee Compliments the Sharpshooters of Lane's Brigade." In *SHSP*, IX, 156.

Gerrish, Theodore. *Army Life: A Private's Reminiscences of the Civil War.* Portland, Maine, 1882.

Gibbon, John. *Personal Recollections of the Civil War.* New York, 1928.

Gibson, J. Catlett. "The Battle of Spotsylvania Court House, May 12, 1864." In *SHSP*, XXXII, 200–210.

Gill, John. *Reminiscences of Four Years as a Private Soldier in the Confederate Army.* Baltimore, 1904.

Gordon, John B. *Reminiscences of the Civil War.* New York, 1903.

Goss, Warren L. *Recollections of a Private: A Story of the Army of the Potomac.* New York, 1890.

Govan, Gilbert E., and James W. Livingood, eds. *The Haskell Memoirs: John Cheves Haskell.* New York, 1960.

Grant, Lewis A. "Review of Major-General F. C. Barlow's Paper on the Capture of the Salient at Spotsylvania, May 12, 1864." In *PMHSM*, IV, 263–71.

Grant, Ulysses S. *Personal Memoirs.* 2 vols. New York, 1885.

Green, William H. "From the Wilderness to Spotsylvania." In *War Papers Read Before the Commandery of the State of Maine, Military Order of the Loyal Legion of the United States,* II, 91–104. Portland, Maine, 1902.

Greenleaf, William L. "From the Rapidan to Richmond." In *War Papers of Vermont, and Miscellaneous States Papers and Addresses, Military Order of the Loyal Legion,* 1–24. Wilmington, N.C., 1994.

Haden, B. J. *Reminiscences of J. E. B. Stuart's Cavalry.* Charlottesville, Va., n.d.

———. "Stuart's Death Wound." *Confederate Veteran,* XXII (1914), 352–53.

Hancock, Almira R. *Reminiscences of Winfield Scott Hancock.* New York, 1887.

Hawes, George Percy. "A Week with the Artillery, A.N.V." *Confederate Veteran,* XXXI (1923), 370–71.

Hendrix, D. I. "That Bloody Angle Battle." *Confederate Veteran,* XVII (1909), 438.

Holt, David. *A Mississippi Rebel in the Army of Northern Virginia.* Edited by Thomas D. Cockrell and Michael B. Ballard. Baton Rouge, 1996.

Hopkins, Luther W. *From Bull Run to Appomattox: A Boy's View.* Baltimore, 1908.

Houghton, William. "A Staff Officer's Recollection of the Salient Angle." *National Tribune,* September 11, 1890.

Howard, McHenry. *Recollections of a Maryland Confederate Soldier and Staff Officer Under Johnston, Jackson, and Lee.* Baltimore, 1914.

Howe, Mark D., ed. *Touched with Fire: Civil War Letters and Diary of Oliver Wendell Holmes, Jr., 1861–1864.* New York, 1969.

Huffman, James. *Ups and Downs of a Confederate Soldier.* New York, 1940.

Hunter, Alexander. *Johnny Reb and Billy Yank.* New York, 1905.

Hunter, Robert. "Major Hunter's Story." In *SHSP,* XXXIII, 337–39.

Hyde, Thomas W. *Following the Greek Cross; or, Memories of the Sixth Army Corps.* Boston, 1894.

Isham, Asa B. "Through the Wilderness to Richmond." In *Sketches of War History, 1861–1865: Papers Read Before the Ohio Commandery of the Military Order of the Loyal Legion of the United States,* I, 199–217. Cincinnati, 1888.

Johns, B. F. "The Bloody Angle." *National Tribune,* July 14, 1887.

Johnson, John Lipscomb. *The University Memorial Biographical Sketches.* Baltimore, 1871.

Johnston, Hugh Buckner, ed. *The Civil War Letters of George Boardman Battle and of Walter Raleigh Battle, of Wilson, North Carolina.* Wilson, N.C., 1953.

Jones, F. C. "The Second Corps: Their Gallant Charge at the Bloody Angle." *National Tribune,* October 9, 1890.

Jones, Terry L., ed. *The Civil War Memoirs of Captain William J. Seymour: Reminiscences of a Louisiana Tiger.* Baton Rouge, 1991.

Jordan, David M. *Winfield Scott Hancock: A Soldier's Life.* Bloomington, Ind., 1988.

Kent, Arthur A., ed. *Three Years with Company K: Sergt. Austin C. Stearns, Company K, 13th Mass. Infantry.* Rutherford, N.J., 1976.

Kidd, James H. *Personal Recollections of a Cavalryman with Custer's Michigan Cavalry Brigade in the Civil War.* Ionia, Mich., 1908.

King, John R. *My Experience in the Confederate Army and in Northern Prisons.* Clarksburg, W.Va., 1917.

King, Matthew W. *To Horse: With the Cavalry of the Army of the Potomac, 1861–1865.* Cheboygan, Mich., 1926.

Knight, Judson. "How Scouts Worked." *National Tribune,* March 23, 1893.

Krick, Robert K. *Lee's Colonels: A Biographical Register of the Field Officers of the Army of Northern Virginia.* Dayton, 1992.

Lane, James H. "Battle of Spotsylvania Court-House." In *SHSP,* IX, 145–56.

Lee, Fitzhugh. *General Lee: A Biography of Robert E. Lee.* New York, 1894.

———. "Speech . . . at A.N.V. Banquet, October 28th, 1875." In *SHSP,* I, 99–103.

Lee, Laura Elizabeth. *Forget-Me-Nots of the Civil War: A Romance Containing Reminiscences and Original Letters of Two Confederate Soldiers.* St. Louis, 1909.

Lewis, Richard. *Camp Life of a Confederate Boy, of Bratton's Brigade, Longstreet's Corps, C.S.A.* Charleston, S.C., 1883.

Longacre, Edward G. "From the Wilderness to Cold Harbor in the Union Artillery." *Manuscripts,* XXXV (1983), 202–13.

McAllister, Robert. "McAllister's Brigade at the Bloody Angle." In *B&L,* IV, 176.

McCabe, W. Gordon. "Major Andrew Reid Venable, Jr." In *SHSP,* XXXVII, 65–70.

McCaleb, E. Howard. *Address Delivered by E. Howard McCaleb of New Orleans, at the Reunion of the Surviving Veterans of Harris' Mississippi Brigade, Army of Northern Virginia, Held at Port Gibson, . . . Claiborne Co., Mississippi, November 13th, 1879.* New Orleans, n.d.

McClellan, Henry B. *The Life and Campaigns of Major-General J. E. B. Stuart, Commander of the Cavalry of the Army of Northern Virginia.* Boston, 1885.

McDonald, Archie P., ed. *Make Me a Map of the Valley: The Civil War Journal of Stonewall Jackson's Topographer.* Dallas, 1973.

McMahon, Martin T. "The Death of General John Sedgwick." In *B&L,* IV, 175.

McPeck, John E. "Spotsylvania: The Battle As Seen from the Ranks of the 126th Ohio." *National Tribune,* October 20, 1887.

Marvel, William. *Burnside.* Chapel Hill, N.C., 1991.

Mason, Edwin C. "Through the Wilderness to the Bloody Angle at Spotsylvania Court House." In *Glimpses of the Nation's Struggle: Papers Read Before the Commandery of the State of Minnesota, Military Order of the Loyal Legion of the United States, 1892–1897,* 281–312. St. Paul, 1898.

Massachusetts Historical Society, comp. *War Diary and Letters of Stephen Minot Weld, 1861–1865.* Boston, 1979.

Matthews, A. K. "General Stuart's Death: How the Chieftain Received His Mortal Wound." *National Tribune,* June 23, 1887.

Meade, George, ed. *The Life and Letters of George Gordon Meade, Major General, United States Army.* 2 vols. New York, 1913.

Meier, Heinz K., ed. *Memoirs of a Swiss Officer in the American Civil War.* Bern, 1972.

Miller, Richard F., and Robert F. Mooney. *The Civil War: The Nantucket Experience, Including the Memoirs of Josiah Fitch Murphey.* Nantucket, Mass., 1994.

Miller, Samuel H., ed. "The Civil War Memoirs of the First Maryland Cavalry, C.S.A., by Henry Clay Mettam." *Maryland Historical Magazine,* LVIII (1963), 137–69.

Miner, Joseph E. "Spotsylvania: The Way in Which the Rebels Were Surprised." *National Tribune,* March 18, 1886.

Minor, J. B. "Rallying with a Frying Pan." *Confederate Veteran,* XIII (1905), 72–73.

Mixson, Frank M. *Reminiscences of a Private.* Columbia, S.C., 1910.

Moffett, Mary C., ed. *Letters of General James Conner, C.S.A.* Columbia, S.C., 1933.

Montgomery, Walter A. *The Days of Old and the Years That Are Past.* N.p., n.d.

Morrison, James L., Jr., ed. *The Memoirs of Henry Heth.* Westport, Conn., 1974.

Morse, F. W. *Personal Experiences in the War of the Great Rebellion, from December, 1862, to July, 1865.* Albany, N.Y., 1866.

Neese, George N. *Three Years in the Confederate Horse Artillery.* New York, 1911.

Nevins, Allan, ed. *Diary of Battle: The Personal Journals of Colonel Charles S. Wainwright, 1861–1865.* New York, 1962.

Nichols, George W. *A Soldier's Story of His Regiment and Incidentally of the Lawton, Gordon, Evans Brigade.* Jesup, Ga., 1898.

Oates, William C. *The War Between the Union and the Confederacy and Its Lost Opportunities.* New York, 1905.

Old, William W. "Personal Reminiscences." In *SHSP,* XXXIII, 16–24.

Oliver, J. R. "J. E. B. Stuart's Fate at Yellow Tavern." *Confederate Veteran,* XIX (1911), 531.

Page, Charles A. *Letters of a War Correspondent.* Boston, 1899.

"Papers Discovered Describing Actions of Cumberland Troops." *Cumberland County, Virginia, Historical Bulletin,* III (December, 1986), 21–30.

Peabody, Charles, ed. *Memoirs of Alfred Horatio Belo.* Boston, 1904.

Peck, Rufus H. *Reminiscences of a Confederate Soldier of Co. C, 2nd Va. Cavalry.* Fincastle, Va., 1913.

Peyton, George Q. *A Civil War Record for 1864–1865.* Edited by Robert A. Hodge. Fredericksburg, Va., 1981.

Poindexter, William B. "A Midnight Charge and the Death of General J. E. B. Stuart." In *SHSP,* XXXII, 117–21.

Porter, Horace. *Campaigning with Grant.* New York, 1897.

Potter, P. S. "Reminiscences of Spotsylvania." *National Tribune,* April 15, 1882.

Rea, Lilian, ed. *War Record and Experiences of Walter Raleigh Robbins, from April 22, 1861, to August 4, 1865.* Chicago, 1913.

Reed, Thomas B. *Private in Gray.* Camden, Ark., 1905.

Rhodes, Robert Hunt, ed. *All for the Union: The Civil War Diary and Letters of Elisha Hunt Rhodes.* New York, 1991.

Ritchey, John. "General Lee's Readiness to Lead His Men." *Confederate Veteran,* XV (1907), 546.

Roberts, James W. "The Wilderness and Spotsylvania, May 4–12, 1864: Narrative of a Private Soldier." *Quarterly Periodical of the Florida Historical Society,* XI (October, 1932), 58–76.

Robertson, James I., Jr., ed. *The Civil War Letters of General Robert McAllister.* New Brunswick, N.J., 1965.

Robertson, Robert S. "From the Wilderness to Spotsylvania." In *Sketches of War History, 1861–1865: Papers Read Before the Ohio Commandery of the Military Order of the Loyal Legion of the United States,* I, 252–92. Cincinnati, 1883.

————. *Personal Recollections of the War.* Milwaukee, 1895.

Rodenbough, Theodore F. "Sheridan's Richmond Raid." In *B&L,* IV, 188–94.

Rosenblatt, Emil, and Ruth Rosenblatt, eds. *Hard Marching Every Day: The Civil War Letters of Wilbur Fisk, 1861–1865.* Lawrence, Kans., 1992.

Royall, William L. *Some Reminiscences.* New York, 1909.

Runge, William H., ed. *Four Years in the Confederate Artillery: The Diary of Private Henry Robinson Berkeley.* Chapel Hill, N.C., 1961.

Saunders, James Edmonds. *Early Settlers of Alabama.* New Orleans, 1899.

Saussy, G. N. "Tribute to Major Breathed." *Confederate Veteran,* XVII (1909), 414.

Schoyer, William T., ed. *The Road to Cold Harbor: Field Diary, January 1–June 12, 1864, of Samuel L. Schoyer, Captain, Company G, 139th Pennsylvania Volunteer Regiment.* Apollo, Pa., 1986.

Sheridan, Philip H. *Personal Memoirs.* 2 vols. New York, 1888.

Silliker, Ruth L., ed. *The Rebel Yell and the Yankee Hurrah: The Civil War Journal of a Maine Volunteer, Private John W. Haley, 17th Maine Regiment.* Camden, Maine, 1985.

Simon, John Y., ed. *The Papers of Ulysses S. Grant.* 20 vols. Carbondale, Ill., 1967–95.

Slade, A. D. *That Sterling Soldier: The Life of David A. Russell.* Dayton, 1995.

Small, Harold A. *The Road to Richmond: The Civil War Memoirs of Major Abner R. Small of the Sixteenth Maine Volunteers.* Berkeley, Calif., 1939.

Smith, Miles V. *Reminiscences of the Civil War, Company D, Fourth Texas Regiment, Hood's Brigade, Longstreet's Corps, Army Northern Virginia, C.S.A.* N.p., n.d.

Smith, R. A. "How General Stevenson Died." *National Tribune,* January 20, 1898.

Smith, William W. "Account." In *SHSP,* XXXII, 210–15.

Sorrel, G. Moxley. *Recollections of a Confederate Staff Officer.* New York, 1917.

Sparks, David S., ed. *Inside Lincoln's Army: The Diary of Marsena Rudolph Patrick, Provost Marshal General, Army of the Potomac.* New York, 1964.

Spencer, Carrie Ester, comp. *A Civil War Marriage in Virginia: Reminiscences and Letters.* Boyce, Va., 1956.

Starr, Louis M. *Reporting the Civil War: The Bohemian Brigade in Action, 1861–65.* New York, 1962.

Stewart, William H. *A Pair of Blankets: War-Time History in Letters to the Young People of the South.* New York, 1914.

Stiles, Robert. *Four Years Under Marse Robert.* New York, 1903.

Stringfellow, M. S. "Letter to Editor of Richmond Times." In *SHSP,* XXI, 244–51.

Tarbell, Ida. *A Reporter for Lincoln.* New York, 1927.

Taylor, Emerson. *Gouverneur Kemble Warren: Life and Letters of an American Soldier.* New York, 1932.

Taylor, Michael W., ed. *The Cry Is War, War, War: The Civil War Correspondence of Lts. Burwell Thomas Cotton and George Job Huntley, 34th Regiment North Carolina Troops, Pender-Scales Brigade of the Light Division, Stonewall Jackson's and A. P. Hill's Corps, Army of Northern Virginia, C.S.A.* Dayton, 1994.

Taylor, Walter H. *Four Years with General Lee.* New York, 1877.

————. *General Lee: His Campaigns in Virginia, 1861–1865, with Personal Reminiscences.* Norfolk, Va., 1906.

Thomas, Emory M. *Bold Dragoon: The Life of J. E. B. Stuart.* New York, 1986.

Thomason, John W. *Jeb Stuart.* New York, 1930.

Tilney, Robert. *My Life in the Army: Three Years and a Half with the Fifth Army Corps, Army of the Potomac, 1862–1865.* Philadelphia, 1912.

Tower, R. Lockwood, ed. *Lee's Adjutant: The Wartime Letters of Colonel Walter Herron Taylor, 1862–1865.* Columbia, S.C., 1995.

Tremain, Lyman. *Memorial of Frederick Lyman Tremain, Late Lieutenant Colonel of the 10th New York Cavalry.* Albany, N.Y., 1865.

Tripp, L. E. "With Custer at Yellow Tavern and in the Raid Around Richmond." *National Tribune,* July 31, 1884.

Trout, Robert J., ed. *Riding with Stuart: Reminiscences of an Aide-de-Camp, by Captain Theodore Stanford Garnett.* Shippensburg, Pa., 1994.

Tyler, Mason Whiting. *Recollections of the Civil War.* New York, 1912.

United Daughters of the Confederacy, South Carolina Division, comp. *Recollections and Reminiscences, 1861–1865.* 3 vols. N.p., 1990.

Venable, Charles S. "General Lee in the Wilderness Campaign." In *B&L,* IV, 240–46.

Wagstaff, Henry McG. "Letters of Thomas Jackson Strayhorn." *North Carolina Historical Review,* XIII (1936), 311–34.

Wait, Jane Wofford, *et al. History of the Wofford Family.* Spartanburg, S.C., 1928.

Walker, C. Irvin. *The Life of Lieutenant General Richard Heron Anderson, of the Confederate States Army.* Charleston, S.C. 1917.

Walker, Charles N., and Rosemary Walker, eds. "Diary of the War by Robert S. Robertson." *Old Fort News,* XXVIII (1965), 160–67.

Walker, Francis A. *General Hancock.* New York, 1895.

Walker, James A. "The Bloody Angle." In *SHSP,* XXI, 228–38.

Warner, Ezra J. *Generals in Blue: Lives of the Union Commanders.* Baton Rouge, 1964.

————. *Generals in Gray: Lives of the Confederate Commanders.* Baton Rouge, 1959.

Webb, Alexander S. "Through the Wilderness." In *B&L,* IV, 152–69.

Welch, Spencer Glasgow. *A Confederate Surgeon's Letters to His Wife.* New York, 1911.

White, John H. "He Got the Flag: The Desperate Charge of a Jerseyman at Spotsylvania." *National Tribune,* January 20, 1887.

White, William S. "A Diary of the War, or What I Saw of It." In *Contributions to a History of the Richmond Howitzer Battalion,* II, 89–286. Richmond, 1883.

Wilkeson, Frank. *Recollections of a Private Soldier in the Army of the Potomac.* New York, 1887.

Williams, Frank B., Jr. "From Sumter to the Wilderness: Letters of Sgt. James Butler Suddath, Co. E., 7th Regiment, S.C.V." *South Carolina Historical Magazine,* LXIII (1962), 93–104.

Wilson, James H. *Under the Old Flag.* 2 vols. New York, 1912.

Wilson, Paul E., and Harriett Stephens Wilson, eds. *The Civil War Diary of Thomas White Stephens, Sergeant, Company K, 20th Indiana Regiment of Volunteers.* Lawrence, Kans., 1985.

Wing, Henry E. *When Lincoln Kissed Me: A Story of the Wilderness Campaign.* New York, 1913.

Winslow, Richard Elliott, III. *General John Sedgwick: The Story of a Union Corps Commander.* Novato, Calif., 1982.

Wirtz, Paul, ed. *John Parker Brest, Company E, 100th Pennsylvania Volunteer Regiment: Journal, 1861–1865.* Baltimore, 1991.

Woodbury, Augustus. *Major General Ambrose E. Burnside and the Ninth Army Corps.* Providence, 1867.

Worsham, John H. *One of Jackson's Foot Cavalry.* Jackson, Tenn., 1964.

Yeary, Mamie, comp. *Reminiscences of the Boys in Gray, 1861–1865.* Dayton, 1986.

Young, Charles P. "War's Bravest Deeds: The Heroism of Private Chew Coleman, of Crenshaw's Battery." In *SHSP,* XXI, 374–75.

UNIT HISTORIES

Adams, John G. B. *Reminiscences of the Nineteenth Massachusetts Regiment.* Boston, 1899.

Aldrich, Thomas M. *History of Battery A, 1st Rhode Island Light Artillery.* Providence, 1904.

Banes, Charles H. *History of the Philadelphia Brigade.* Philadelphia, 1876.

Baquet, Camille. *History of the First Brigade New Jersey Volunteers, from 1861 to 1865.* Trenton, 1910.

Beale, R. L. T. *History of the Ninth Virginia Cavalry in the War Between the States.* Richmond, 1899.

Bean, William G. *The Liberty Hall Volunteers: Stonewall's College Boys.* Charlottesville, Va., 1964.

Beaudry, Louis N. *Historic Records of the Fifth New York Cavalry, First Ira Harris Guard.* Albany, N.Y., 1874.

Benedict, George G. *Vermont in the Civil War: A History of the Part Taken by the Vermont Soldiers and Sailors in the War for the Union, 1861–65.* 2 vols. Burlington, Vt., 1886.

Bennett, A. J. *The Story of the First Massachusetts Light Battery.* Boston, 1886.

Bennett, Brian A. *Sons of Old Monroe: A Regimental History of Patrick O'Rorke's 140th New York Volunteer Infantry.* Dayton, 1993.

Bennett, R. T. "Fourteenth Regiment." In *Histories of the Several Regiments and Battalions from North Carolina in the Great War, 1861–65,* ed. Clark, I, 705–32.

Best, Isaac O. *History of the 121st New York State Infantry.* Chicago, 1921.

Bicknell, George W. *History of the Fifth Regiment Maine Volunteers.* Portland, Maine, 1871.

Billings, John D. *The History of the Tenth Massachusetts Battery of Light Artillery in the War of the Rebellion.* Boston, 1881.

Bowen, J. R. *Regimental History of the First New York Dragoons During Three Years of Active Service in the Great Civil War.* Lyons, Mich., 1900.

Bowen, James L. "General Edwards' Brigade at the Bloody Angle." In *B&L,* IV, 177.

Bowley, Free B. "A Boy Lieutenant in a Black Regiment." *National Tribune,* May 4, 1899.

Brainard, Mary G. *Campaigns of the One Hundred and Forty-Sixth Regiment New York State Volunteers.* New York, 1915.

Bratton, John. "Report of Operations of Bratton's Brigade from May 7th, 1864, to January, 1865." In *SHSP,* VIII, 547–59.

Brown, Hamilton A. "First Regiment." In *Histories of the Several Regiments and Battalions from North Carolina in the Great War, 1861–65,* ed. Clark, I, 134–56.

Bruce, George A. *The Twentieth Regiment of Massachusetts Volunteer Infantry 1861–1865.* Boston, 1906.

Burrage, Henry S. *History of the Thirty-Sixth Regiment Massachusetts Volunteers.* Boston, 1884.

Caldwell, J. F. J. *The History of a Brigade of South Carolinians, First Known As Gregg's, and Subsequently as McGowan's Brigade.* Philadelphia, 1866.

Cavanaugh, Michael A. *6th Virginia Infantry.* Lynchburg, Va., 1988.

Chamberlin, Thomas. *History of the One Hundred and Fiftieth Regiment Pennsylvania Volunteers, Second Regiment, Bucktail Brigade.* Philadelphia, 1905.

Cheek, Philip, and Mair Pointon. *History of the Sauk County Riflemen, Known As Company A, Sixth Wisconsin Veteran Volunteer Infantry, 1861–1865.* Madison, Wis., 1909.

Cheek, William H. "Additional Sketch, Ninth Regiment (First Cavalry)." In *Histories of the Several Regiments and Battalions from North Carolina in the Great War, 1861–65,* ed. Clark, I, 445–84.

Cheney, Newel. *History of the Ninth Regiment New York Volunteer Cavalry.* Jamestown, N.Y., 1901.

Clark, Walter, ed. *Histories of the Several Regiments and Battalions from North Carolina in the Great War, 1861–65.* 5 vols. Goldsboro, N.C., 1901.

Coker, James Lide. *History of Company G, Ninth South Carolina Infantry, S.C. Army, and of Company E, Sixth S.C. Regiment, Infantry, S.C. Army.* Greenwood, S.C., n.d.

Collier, Calvin L. *They'll Do to Tie To: Hood's Arkansas Toothpicks, Third Arkansas Infantry Regiment, C.S.A.* Little Rock, Ark., 1988.

Committee of the Regiment. *History of the Thirty-Sixth Regiment Massachusetts Volunteers, 1862–1865.* Boston, 1884.

Contributions to a History of the Richmond Howitzer Battalion. 3 vols. Richmond, 1883–86.

Cook, Benjamin F. *History of the Twelfth Massachusetts Volunteers (Webster Regiment).* Boston, 1882.

Cooke, Charles M. "Fifty-Fifth Regiment." In *Histories of the Several Regiments and Battalions from North Carolina in the Great War, 1861–65,* ed. Clark, III, 287–312.

Cowan, John. "Third Regiment." In *Histories of the Several Regiments and Battalions from North Carolina in the Great War, 1861–65,* ed. Clark, I, 177–214.

Cowles, Luther E. *History of the Fifth Massachusetts Battery.* Boston, 1902.

Craft, David. *History of the One Hundred Forty First Regiment Pennsylvania Volunteers, 1862–1865.* Towanda, Pa., 1885.

Croffut, W. A., and John M. Morris. *The Military and Civil History of Connecticut During the War of 1861–1865.* New York, 1869.

Cudworth, Warren H. *History of the First Regiment Massachusetts Infantry.* Boston, 1866.

Curtis, O. B. *History of the Twenty-Fourth Michigan of the Iron Brigade.* Detroit, 1891.

Daniel, Frederick S. *Richmond Howitzers in the War: Four Years Campaigning with the Army of Northern Virginia.* Richmond, 1891.

Davis, Charles E., Jr. *Three Years in the Army: The Story of the Thirteenth Massachusetts Volunteers from July 16, 1861, to August 1, 1864.* Boston, 1894.

Dawes, Rufus R. *Service with the Sixth Wisconsin Volunteers.* Marietta, Ohio, 1890.

Dickert, D. Augustus. *History of Kershaw's Brigade.* Newberry, S.C., 1899.

Dunlop, William S. *Lee's Sharpshooters; or, The Forefront of Battle: A Story of Southern Valor That Never Has Been Told.* Little Rock, Ark., 1899.

Figg, Royall W. *Where Men Only Dare Go! or, The Story of a Boy Company.* Richmond, 1885.

Folsom, James M. *Heroes and Martyrs of Georgia: Georgia's Record in the Revolution of 1861.* Macon, Ga., 1864.

Foster, Alonzo. *Reminiscences and Record of the 6th New York V. V. Cavalry.* Brooklyn, N.Y., 1892.

Gavin, William G. *Campaigning with the Roundheads: The History of the Hun-*

dredth *Pennsylvania Volunteer Infantry Regiment in the American Civil War, 1861–1865.* Dayton, 1989.

Glover, Edwin A. *Bucktailed Wildcats: A Regiment of Civil War Volunteers.* New York, 1960.

Gold, Thomas D. *History of Clarke County and Its Connection with the War Between the States.* Berryville, Va., 1914.

Goldsborough, W. W. *The Maryland Line in the Confederate States Army.* Baltimore, 1869.

Gould, Joseph. *The Story of the Forty-Eighth: A Record of the Campaigns of the Forty-Eighth Regiment Pennsylvania Veteran Volunteer Infantry.* Philadelphia, 1908.

Gracey, Samuel L. *Annals of the Sixth Pennsylvania Cavalry.* Philadelphia, 1868.

Graves, Joseph A. *The History of the Bedford Light Artillery.* Bedford, Va., 1903.

Green, Wharton J. "Second Battalion." In *Histories of the Several Regiments and Battalions from North Carolina in the Great War, 1861–65,* ed. Clark, IV, 243–60.

Hackley, Woodford B. *The Little Fork Rangers: A Sketch of Company D Fourth Virginia Cavalry.* Richmond, 1927.

Haines, Alanson A. *History of the Fifteenth Regiment New Jersey Volunteers.* New York, 1883.

Haines, William P. *History of the Men of Company F, with Description of the Marches and Battles of the 12th New Jersey Volunteers.* Mickleton, N.J., 1897.

Hamilton, D. H. *History of Company M First Texas Volunteer Infantry.* Waco, Tex., 1962.

Hanks, O. T. *History of Captain B. F. Benton's Company, Hood's Texas Brigade, 1861–1865.* Austin, Tex., 1984.

Harris, James S. *Historical Sketches of the Seventh Regiment North Carolina Troops.* Mooresville, N.C., 1893.

———. "Seventh Regiment." In *Histories of the Several Regiments and Battalions from North Carolina in the Great War, 1861–65,* ed. Clark, I, 361–86.

Harris, William H., comp. *Movements of the Confederate Army in Virginia and the Part Taken Therein by the Nineteenth Mississippi Brigade: From the Diary of Gen. Nat H. Harris.* Duncansby, Miss., 1901.

Herbert, Hilary A. "History of the Eighth Alabama Volunteer Regiment, C.S.A." Edited by Maurice S. Fortin. *Alabama Historical Quarterly,* XXXIX (1977), 5–160.

Hopkins, William P. *The Seventh Regiment Rhode Island Volunteers in the Civil War, 1862–1865.* Providence, 1903.

Houghton, Edwin B. *The Campaigns of the Seventeenth Maine.* Portland, Maine, 1866.

Houston, Henry C. *The Thirty-Second Maine Regiment of Infantry Volunteers.* Portland, Maine, 1903.

Hutchinson, Nelson V. *History of the Seventh Massachusetts Volunteer Infantry in the War of the Rebellion of the Southern States Against Constitutional Authority, 1861–1865.* Taunton, Mass., 1890.

Jackman, Lyman, and Amos Hadley. *History of the Sixth New Hampshire Regiment in the War for the Union.* Concord, N.H., 1891.

Jeffers, C. T. "What the Gallant Ninth Corps Did." *National Tribune,* July 9, 1896.

Johnson, W. P. "Third Arkansas and Richmond Howitzers." *Confederate Veteran,* XIII (1905), 210.

Jones, Terry L. *Lee's Tigers: The Louisiana Infantry in the Army of Northern Virginia.* Baton Rouge, 1987.

Judson, Amos M. *History of the Eighty-Third Regiment Pennsylvania Volunteers.* Erie, Pa., 1865.

Kearney, H. C. "Fifteenth Regiment." In *Histories of the Several Regiments and Battalions from North Carolina in the Great War, 1861–65,* ed. Clark, I, 733–49.

Kirk, Hyland C. *Heavy Guns and Light: A History of the 4th New York Heavy Artillery.* New York, 1890.

Krick, Robert K. *Parker's Virginia Battery, C.S.A.* Berryville, Va., 1975.

LaRocca, Charles J., comp. *This Regiment of Heroes: A Compilation of Primary Materials Pertaining to the 124th New York State Volunteers in the American Civil War.* N.p., 1991.

Lewis, Osceola. *History of the One Hundred and Thirty-Eighth Regiment Pennsylvania Volunteer Infantry.* Norristown, Pa., 1866.

Lloyd, William P. *History of the First Regiment Pennsylvania Reserve Cavalry.* Philadelphia, 1864.

Locke, William H. *The Story of the Regiment.* Philadelphia, 1868.

Longacre, Edward G. *To Gettysburg and Beyond: The Twelfth New Jersey Volunteer Infantry, II Corps, Army of the Potomac, 1862–1865.* Hightstown, N.J., 1988.

Lowden, J. K. "Michigan's 5th Cavalry in the Latter Period of the War." *National Tribune,* July 23, 1896.

McDonald, William N. *A History of the Laurel Brigade, Originally the Ashby Cavalry of the Army of Northern Virginia and Chew's Battery.* Baltimore, 1907.

McLaurin, William H. "Eighteenth Regiment." In *Histories of the Several Regiments and Battalions from North Carolina in the Great War, 1861–65,* ed. Clark, II, 15–78.

Marbaker, Thomas D. *History of the Eleventh New Jersey Volunteers from Its Organization to Appomattox.* Trenton, 1898.

Marshall, D. P. *History of Company K, 155th Pennsylvania Volunteer Zouaves.* N.p., 1888.

Matthews, Richard E. *The 149th Pennsylvania Volunteer Infantry Unit in the Civil War.* Jefferson, N.C., 1994.

Means, Paul B. "Additional Sketch, Sixty-Third Regiment." In *Histories of the*

Several Regiments and Battalions from North Carolina in the Great War, 1861–65, ed. Clark, III, 546–657.

Merrill, Samuel H. *The Campaigns of the First Maine and First District of Columbia Cavalry.* Portland, Maine, 1866.

Mills, George H. *History of the 16th North Carolina Regiment (Originally 6th North Carolina Regiment).* Rutherfordton, N.C., 1901.

Montgomery, Walter A. "Twelfth Regiment." In *Histories of the Several Regiments and Battalions from North Carolina in the Great War, 1861–65,* ed. Clark, I, 605–52.

Moore, J. H. "Archer's Tennesseeans at Spotsylvania." In *Camp-Fire Sketches and Battle-Field Echoes,* comp. William C. King and W. P. Derby, 311–13. Springfield, Mass. 1888.

Muffly, J. W., ed. *The Story of Our Regiment: A History of the 148th Pennsylvania Volunteers.* Des Moines, 1904.

Mulholland, St. Claire Augustine. *The Story of the 116th Regiment Pennsylvania Volunteers in the War of the Rebellion: The Record of a Gallant Command.* Philadelphia, 1899.

Myers, Frank M. *The Comanches: A History of White's Battalion, Virginia Cavalry, Laurel Brigade, Hampton Division, A.N.V., C.S.A.* Baltimore, 1871.

Naisawald, L. Van Loan. *Grape and Canister: The Story of the Field Artillery of the Army of the Potomac, 1861–1865.* Washington, D.C., 1960.

Nash, Eugene A. *A History of the Forty-Fourth Regiment New York Volunteer Infantry in the Civil War, 1861–1865.* Chicago, 1911.

Newell, Joseph K. *Ours: Annals of Tenth Regiment Massachusetts Volunteers in the Rebellion.* Springfield, Mass., 1875.

One of the Quitman Guards. *A Historical Sketch of the Quitman Guards, Company E, Sixteenth Mississippi Regiment, Harris' Brigade.* New Orleans, 1866.

Osborne, E. A. "Fourth Regiment." In *Histories of the Several Regiments and Battalions from North Carolina in the Great War, 1861–65,* ed. Clark, I, 229–80.

Page, Charles D. *History of the Fourteenth Regiment Connecticut Volunteer Infantry.* Meriden, Conn., 1906.

Park, Robert E. "The Twelfth Alabama Infantry, Confederate States Army." In *SHSP,* XXXIII, 193–296.

Parker, Francis J. *The Story of the Thirty-Second Regiment Massachusetts Infantry.* Boston, 1880.

Phelps, Charles E. "Seventh Regiment Infantry." In *History and Roster of Maryland Volunteers, War of 1861–1865,* by Allison Wilmer *et al.,* I, 261–77. Baltimore, 1898.

Polley, Joseph B. *Hood's Texas Brigade: Its Marches, Its Battles, Its Achievements.* New York, 1910.

Powell, William H. *The Fifth Army Corps.* New York, 1896.

Preston, N. D. *History of the Tenth Regiment of Cavalry New York State Volunteers.* New York, 1892.

Pullen, John J. *The Twentieth Maine: A Volunteer Regiment in the Civil War.* Philadelphia, 1957.

Pyne, Henry R. *Ride to War: The History of the First New Jersey Cavalry.* New Brunswick, N.J., 1961.

Rawle, William B., *et al. History of the Third Pennsylvania Cavalry, Sixtieth Regiment Pennsylvania Volunteers in the American Civil War, 1861–1865.* Philadelphia, 1905.

Reunions of the Twentieth Maine Regiment Association at Portland. Waldoboro, Maine, 1881.

Rhodes, John H. *The History of Battery B, First Regiment Rhode Island Light Artillery, in the War to Preserve the Union, 1861–1865.* Providence, 1894.

Ripley, William Y. W. *Vermont Riflemen in the War for the Union, 1861–1865: A History of Company F, First United States Sharpshooters.* Rutland, Vt., 1883.

Roback, Henry. *The Veteran Volunteers of Herkimer and Otsego Counties in the War of the Rebellion, Being a History of the 152nd New York.* Little Falls, N.Y., 1888.

Robertson, James I., Jr. *The Stonewall Brigade.* Baton Rouge, 1963.

Roe, Alfred S. *The Tenth Regiment Massachusetts Volunteer Infantry, 1861–1864.* Springfield, Mass., 1909.

———. *The Thirty-Ninth Regiment Massachusetts Volunteers, 1862–1865.* Worcester, Mass., 1914.

Rowland, Dunbar. *Military History of Mississippi, 1803–1898.* Jackson, Miss., 1908.

Sawyer, Franklin. *A Military History of the 8th Regiment Ohio Volunteer Infantry.* Cleveland, 1881.

Seville, William P. *History of the First Regiment Delaware Volunteers, from the Commencement of the "Three Months' Service" to the Final Muster Out at the Close of the Rebellion.* Wilmington, Del., 1884.

Simons, Ezra D. *A Regimental History of the One Hundred and Twenty-Fifth New York State Volunteers.* New York, 1888.

Sloan, John A. *Reminiscences of the Guilford Grays, Co. B, 27th N.C. Regiment.* Washington, D.C., 1883.

Small, Abner R. *The Sixteenth Maine Regiment in the War of the Rebellion, 1861–1865.* Portland, Maine, 1896.

Smith, A. P. *History of the Seventy-Sixth Regiment New York Volunteers.* Cortland, N.Y., 1867.

Smith, J. L. *History of the Corn Exchange Regiment: 118th Pennsylvania Volunteers, from their First Engagement at Antietam to Appomattox.* Philadelphia, 1888.

Smith, John Day. *The History of the Nineteenth Regiment of Maine Volunteer Infantry, 1862–1865.* Minneapolis, 1909.

Smith, Stephen R., *et al. Record of Service of Connecticut Men in the Army and Navy of the United States During the War of the Rebellion.* Hartford, 1889.

Smith, W. A. *The Anson Guards: Company C, Fourteenth Regiment North Carolina Volunteers, 1861–1865.* Charlotte, N.C., 1914.

Starr, Stephen Z. *The Union Cavalry in the Civil War.* 3 vols. Baton Rouge, 1981.

Stevens, C. A. *Berdan's United States Sharpshooters in the Army of the Potomac, 1861–1865.* St. Paul, 1892.

Stevens, George T. *Three Years in the Sixth Corps.* Albany, N.Y., 1866.

Stewart, Robert Laird. *History of the One Hundred and Fortieth Regiment Pennsylvania Volunteers.* Philadelphia, 1912.

Stubbs, Steven E. *11th Mississippi Infantry Regiment.* Galveston, Tex., n.d.

Survivors Association of Lamar Rifles. *Lamar Rifles: A History of Company G, Eleventh Mississippi, C.S.A.* Roanoke, Va., 1902.

Swinfen, David B. *Ruggles' Regiment: The 122nd New York Volunteers in the American Civil War.* Hanover, N.H., 1982.

Sypher, J. R. *History of the Pennsylvania Reserve Corps.* Lancaster, Pa., 1865.

Thomas, Henry W. *History of the Doles-Cook Brigade, Army of Northern Virginia, C.S.A.* Atlanta, 1903.

Thomson, O. R. Howard, and William H. Rauch. *History of the Bucktails: Kane Rifle Regiment of the Pennsylvania Reserve Corps.* Philadelphia, 1906.

Thomson, Orville. *From Philippi to Appomattox: Narrative of the Services of the Seventh Indiana Infantry in the War for the Union.* N.p., n.d.

Thruston, S. D. "Report of the Conduct of General George H. Steuart's Brigade from the 5th to the 12th of May, 1864, Inclusive." In *SHSP,* XIV, 146–53.

Tobie, Edward P. *History of the First Maine Cavalry, 1861–1865.* Boston, 1887.

Todd, William. *The Seventy-Ninth Highlanders New York Volunteers in the War of Rebellion, 1861–1865.* Albany, N.Y., 1886.

Toon, Thomas F. "Twentieth Regiment." In *Histories of the Several Regiments and Battalions from North Carolina in the Great War, 1861–65,* ed. Clark, II, 111–27.

Turner, V. E. "Twenty-Third Regiment." In *Histories of the Several Regiments and Battalions from North Carolina in the Great War, 1861–65,* ed. Clark, II, 181–268.

Vautier, John D. *History of the 88th Pennsylvania Volunteers in the War for the Union, 1861–1865.* Philadelphia, 1894.

Waite, Otis F. R. *New Hampshire in the Great Rebellion.* Concord, N.H., 1873.

Waitt, Ernest L. *History of the Nineteenth Regiment Massachusetts Volunteer Infantry, 1861–1865.* Salem, Mass., 1906.

Walcott, Charles F. *History of the Twenty-First Regiment Massachusetts Volunteers in the War for the Preservation of the Union, 1861–1865.* Boston, 1882.

Walker, Francis A. *History of the Second Army Corps in the Army of the Potomac.* New York, 1887.

Wallace, William. "Operations of Second South Carolina Regiment in Campaigns of 1864–1865." In *SHSP,* VII, 128–31.

Ward, Joseph R. C. *History of the One Hundred and Sixth Regiment Pennsylvania Volunteers.* Philadelphia, 1883.

Watson, Cyrus B. "Forty-Fifth Regiment." In *Histories of the Several Regiments and Battalions from North Carolina in the Great War, 1861–65,* ed. Clark, I, 35–61.

Westbrook, Robert S. *History of the 49th Pennsylvania Volunteers.* Altoona, Pa., 1898.

Weston, J. A. "Thirty-Third Regiment." In *Histories of the Several Regiments and Battalions from North Carolina in the Great War, 1861–65,* ed. Clark, II, 537–80.

Weygant, Charles H. *History of the One Hundred and Twenty-Fourth Regiment New York State Volunteers.* Newburgh, N.Y., 1877.

White, P. J. "The Fifth Virginia Cavalry." *Confederate Veteran,* XVII (1909), 72–75.

Wiggins, Octavious A. "Thirty-Seventh Regiment." In *Histories of the Several Regiments and Battalions from North Carolina in the Great War, 1861–65,* ed. Clark, II, 653–74.

Wilkinson, Warren. *Mother, May You Never See The Sights I Have Seen: The Fifty-Seventh Massachusetts Veteran Volunteers in the Last Year of the Civil War.* New York, 1990.

Wilmer, L. Allison, *et al. History and Roster of Maryland Volunteers, War of 1861–5.* Baltimore, 1898.

Wise, Jennings C. *The Long Arm of Lee; or, The History of the Artillery of the Army of Northern Virginia.* 2 vols. Lynchburg, Va., 1915.

Wyckoff, Mac. *A History of the 2nd South Carolina Infantry, 1861–65.* Fredericksburg, Va., 1994.

CAMPAIGN STUDIES

Alexander, Edward P. "Grant's Conduct of the Wilderness Campaign." In *Annual Report of the American Historical Association.* N.p., 1908.

Atkinson, C. F. *Grant's Campaigns of 1864 and 1865: The Wilderness and Cold Harbor.* London, 1908.

Carpenter, Louis H. "Sheridan's Expedition Around Richmond, May 9–25, 1864." *Journal of the United States Cavalry Association,* II (1889), 300–23.

Dowdey, Clifford. *Lee's Last Campaign: The Story of Lee and His Men Against Grant, 1864.* New York, 1960.

Humphreys, Andrew A. *The Virginia Campaign of '64 and '65.* New York, 1883.

Livermore, Thomas C. "Grant's Campaign Against Lee." In *PMHSM,* IV, 409–59.

Longacre, Edward G. *Mounted Raids of the Civil War.* South Brunswick, N.J., 1975.

Matter, William D. *If It Takes All Summer: The Battle of Spotsylvania.* Chapel Hill, N.C., 1988.

Miller, J. Michael. *The North Anna Campaign: Even to Hell Itself.* Lynchburg, Va., 1989.

Miller, Samuel H. "Yellow Tavern." *Civil War History,* II (March, 1956), 57–80.

Peirson, Charles L. "The Operations of the Army of the Potomac, May 7–11, 1864." In *PMHSM,* IV, 207–41.

Rhea, Gordon C. *The Battle of the Wilderness, May 5–6, 1864.* Baton Rouge, 1994.

Ropes, John C. "Grant's Campaign in Virginia in 1864." In *PMHSM,* IV, 372–407.

Schaff, Morris. *The Battle of the Wilderness.* New York, 1910.

Stine, James H. *History of the Army of the Potomac.* Philadelphia, 1892.

Swinton, William. *Campaigns of the Army of the Potomac.* New York, 1866.

Venable, Charles S. "The Campaign from the Wilderness to Petersburg." In *SHSP,* XIV, 522–42.

THESES AND DISSERTATIONS

McDaid, William K. " Four Years of Arduous Service: The History of the Branch-Lane Brigade in the Civil War." Ph.D. dissertation, Michigan State University, 1987.

Ott, Eugene M., Jr., ed. "The Civil War Diary of James J. Kirkpatrick, Sixteenth Mississippi Infantry, C.S.A." M.A. thesis, Texas A & M University, 1984.

Index

nication with, 183; and Grant's May
12 plan of attack, 215, 217, 218–19,
221–22, 228, 294–95, 302–304; May
11 position and maneuvers of, 217–
22, 392n81; and leadership changes in
9th Corps, 218; May 12 early morning
position of, 230, 232; and May 12
morning attack and fighting, 233,
244–46, 252–55, 258–59, 263–64,
401n69, 404n101; Lane's fighting
against, on May 12 morning, 252–55;
Grant's May 12 communications with,
294–95, 302–304; and May 12 assault on Heth's Salient, 295–302,
417n28; May 12 afternoon plans for,
302–303; May 12 attack against entrenchments of, above Fredericksburg
Road, 302, 414n106; on May 13 early
morning, 304
Burt, Maj. Mason W., 130
Butler, Maj. Gen. Benjamin, 1–3, 17, 85,
97, 142, 214

Cabell, Col. Henry C., 62, 128, 140
Campbell, Maj., 288
Carroll, Col. Samuel S., 134, 144–47,
179, 243, 310, 382n45
Carter, Col. Thomas H., 226, 227, 235,
418n29
Carter, Capt. William P., 23, 227, 238
Casualties: Confederate, 10, 12, 17, 23,
30, 35, 42, 72, 84, 87, 106, 117, 128–
29, 141, 170, 173–76, 188, 211, 213,
236, 239, 248, 268–71, 274, 277, 279,
291–94, 296, 298, 300, 302, 304,
307–12, 324–25, 326, 354n85,
359n34, 360n49; Union, 17, 27, 29,
34–36, 42, 44, 56–59, 62, 72, 85, 86,
92, 93, 96, 99, 107, 111, 112, 117,
119, 120, 130, 139, 140, 147–49,
174–75, 180, 185–86, 192, 195, 199,
200, 212, 213, 219, 239, 243, 254,
263, 275–81, 284, 286, 291–94, 298,

299, 304, 307–12, 319, 326, 350nn42,
46, 354n81, 356n107, 360n58, 373n6,
376n47, 385n78, 386n11, 387n29,
388n30, 396nn9, 10, 12, 398nn26, 33,
399n47, 409n48, 413n97, 415n107
Catharpin Road: Grant's plan for movement to Spotsylvania Court House
along, 15, 27, 67; and May 7 skirmishes, 22; Lee's plan for movement
to Spotsylvania Court House along,
23, 28, 36, 77, 78; intersection of, with
Orange Plank Road, 30, 49; and
Todd's Tavern expedition, 30, 32–33,
35, 36; May 7 night march along, 41;
May 8 movement along, 71, 72, 75,
77, 81; Miles's regiments along, 76,
78; May 9 reconnaissance along,
101–102; and May 11 maneuvers,
215; Todd's Tavern located above,
355n99
Cavalry. See Confederate Cavalry; Union
Cavalry
Chambliss, Brig. Gen. John R., 23, 27,
351n57, 373n6
Chancellorsville, 15, 30, 37, 38, 42–43,
49, 66, 67, 71, 72
Chapman, Col. George H., 49, 50, 206,
212, 353n70, 389n52
Chattanooga, battle of, 7
Cheek, William H., 198–99, 387–88n29
Chew, Robert Preston, 350n37, 370n65
Chewning house and farm, 28, 77
Chickahominy River, 209, 210
Chickamauga, 64
Chilesburg, 85, 103, 114–15, 117, 120
Christ, Col. Benjamin C., 104–107, 182,
183, 298–99, 368n45, 412n88
Church, Maj. Nathan, 303–304
City Point, 3, 17
Cobb's Legion, 80
Cold Harbor, 312
Coleman, Pvt. Chew, 296
Collins, Col. Charles R., 36, 354n87

along, 41; May 8 maneuvers along, 49, 66; May 9 maneuvers along, 90, 104–105, 107, 114; gate on, misconstrued on map, 103–104, 359*n*41; Wilcox' division along, 112, 121, 181, 183–84, 217, 228, 392*n*89; May 10 position of Burnside along, 123, 142, 183–84, 228; Lee's thinning of defenses along, 186, 187; Heth's troops along, 226; May 12 maneuvers along, 301–302, 412*n*89; on May 13 morning, 310
Freeman, Archibald, 239
Frey, Sgt. Charles A., 177, 178
Fry, Capt. Charles W., 227
Furnace Road, 30, 36

Garber, Capt. Asher W., 254, 381*n*33
Garett, Col. Thomas M., 248
Garnett, Theodore S., 108, 120, 204, 205, 210, 327, 372*n*94, 389*n*42
Gayle house, 103–105, 107, 122, 181, 183, 217, 368*n*41
Georgia units: *2nd* battalion, 111; *4th,* 380*n*20; *9th,* 180; *12th,* 380*n*20; *13th,* 401*n*69; *14th,* 409*n*47; *21st,* 380*n*20; *44th,* 170, 380*n*20; *45th,* 254; *48th,* 111; *61st,* 241, 250
Germanna Ford, 15, 22, 25, 353*n*70, 392*n*89
Germanna Plank Road, 14, 21–23, 26
Getty, Brig. Gen. George W., 294
Gettysburg, battle of, 1, 8, 9, 12, 29, 64, 73, 87, 132, 212, 230, 291, 318
Gibbon, Brig. Gen. John: Lyman's view of, 40; May 8 position of, 75, 81; and May 9 maneuvers, 103, 110, 111; May 10 position of, 125, 149; and withdrawal of troops from Po River on May 10 morning, 132, 134, 135; and Laurel Hill attack on May 10 afternoon, 142; and Warren's attack against Field on May 10 afternoon,

143–49; and Hancock's attack against Laurel Hill on May 10 evening, 179; May 11 position and maneuvers of, 221–25; May 12 early morning attack by, 232, 242–44, 248, 266; and battle of Bloody Angle, 272; and Upton's attack on May 10 evening, 382*n*42; assessment of, 417*n*15
Gibbs, Col. Alfred: and Todd's Tavern expedition, 30, 32–34, 36; May 8 early morning movement of, 45; May 10 maneuvers of, 192; May 11 maneuvers of, 200, 203–205, 207–208, 212; and Yellow Tavern fighting, 203–205, 207–208, 212
Gibson, Col. J. Catlett, 250–51
Gilliss, Lt. James, 277, 278, 376*n*43
Glady Run, 126, 127, 373*n*6
Goodall's Tavern, 198, 387*n*29
Gordon, Brig. Gen. James B.: and Todd's Tavern expedition, 33; May 9 maneuvers of, 120, 372*n*92; and Stuart's plan to catch Sheridan, 120, 372–73*n*94; May 10 maneuvers of, 191–94; May 11 maneuvers of, 198–99, 205, 206, 209; physical appearance of, 198
Gordon, Brig. Gen. John B.: on Lee's foresight, 43; in Battle of the Wilderness, 76; in charge of 2nd Corps division, 76, 173, 363*n*96; May 9 position and maneuvers of, 90, 105; May 9 reduced condition of, 120, 372*n*93; May 12 morning fighting and counteroffensive by, 239, 246–52, 255, 258, 259, 263, 264, 266, 268, 399*n*46, 400*n*56, 401*n*68, 405*n*1; on May 11 afternoon, 246–47; personality of, 246; assessment of, 323; casualties of troops under, 324; and Lee's inspection of Ewell's line, 352*n*58; and battle of Bloody Angle, 406*n*10
Gordonsville, 97
Graham, Capt. Archibald, 241

Gen. Philip H.; Wilson, Brig. Gen. James H.
Union Infantry: 11th United States Infantry, 57; 12th United States Infantry, 57; 17th Regulars, 57
Union Mills, 4
Upton, Col. Emory: and May 8 fighting, 84; and May 10 plans, 132, 149; and lightning forays as style of attack, 161, 163; May 10 evening attack by, 161–77, 184, 187, 215, 225, 248, 315, 378n6, 379–80n17, 380nn20, 21, 381n33, 382n42; personality of, 163; assessment of, 175, 181, 417n15; and May 11 maneuvers, 213; in battle of Bloody Angle, 275–77, 281, 283, 290, 305

Valley Pike, 3
Venable, Lt. Col. Charles S., 60, 250, 255, 259, 399nn42, 45
Vermont units: 1st Cavalry, 206–209, 389n52; 2nd, 164–65, 174, 303, 378n6; 4th, 273; 5th, 164–65, 174, 378n6; 6th, 95–96, 164–65, 174, 273, 378n6; 7th, 208; Vermont Brigade, 23
Vicksburg, battle of, 7, 188
Virginia Central Railroad, 97, 118, 192, 196, 210, 326
Virginia units: 1st Cavalry, 207–209, 368n45, 386n8, 390n57; 2nd, 172, 400n56; 2nd Cavalry, 34, 36, 115, 192, 199–200, 204; 3rd, 65, 69; 3rd Cavalry, 47, 50, 52, 116–17, 192, 204; 4th, 226, 240; 4th Cavalry, 35, 36, 49, 192, 204; 5th, 241; 5th Cavalry, 201, 203, 204; 6th, 203, 204; 6th Cavalry, 201, 208, 389n42; 9th Cavalry, 351n57, 386n10; 10th, 172, 296, 298, 300, 302, 374n9, 413nn94, 97; 15th Cavalry, 35, 36, 201, 203, 204; 21st, 231, 396n9; 23rd, 237; 25th, 172, 236; 33rd, 172, 240, 243;

37th, 397n20; 39th Cavalry, 352n58; 41st, 301, 414n104; 42nd, 231, 236, 324, 395nn129, 5; 44th, 236; 48th, 231, 395n129; 49th, 250–52; 52nd, 249–52; 61st, 302, 414n104; Richmond Howitzers, 69–71, 128–29, 146, 147, 169–70, 173, 180

Wadsworth, Brig. Gen. James S., 62
Wainwright, Col. Charles S.: and movement to Spotsylvania Court House, 38, 42, 45–47, 59; and May 8 late morning fighting, 70–71, 85, 361n77; and Hancock's attack against Laurel Hill on May 10 evening, 178; on May 10 attacks against Laurel Hill, 186
Waite's Shop, 125–26, 134, 136
Wakefield, Miles, 170
Walcott, Lt. Aaron F., 58, 70
Walker, Maj., 207
Walker, Francis A., 80–81, 111, 135, 141, 187, 292, 376–77n48, 382n42
Walker, Brig. Gen. Henry H. "Mud," 136, 141, 295, 324, 325
Walker, Brig. Gen. James A.: and Meade's attack on May 8 evening, 84; conflict of, with Ewell on May 8 night, 88; and Upton's attack on May 10 evening, 169, 172, 173; leadership of, 220; and May 12 morning fighting, 235, 238, 240–41, 258; on May 11 afternoon, 247; wounding of, 268, 324; on demise of Stonewall Brigade, 418n33
Walkup, Samuel H., 414n106
Walters, Tom, 209
Ward, Brig. Gen. J. H. Hobart, 177, 179–81, 238–40, 243–44, 382n45, 383n52, 397n20
Warren, Maj. Gen. Gouverneur K.: in Battle of the Wilderness, 9, 60, 65; at Gettysburg, 9, 73; May 6–7 position of, 14; and movement to Spotsylvania